INSTRUCTIONAL DESIGN

PATRICIA L. SMITH

TILLMAN J. RAGAN
The University of Oklahoma

WILEY John Wiley & Sons, Inc.

Acquisitions Editor	Brad Hanson
Production Assistant	Mary Savel
Marketing Manager	Laura McKenna
Senior Designer	Kevin Murphy
Production Services	Pine Tree Composition
Cover Illustration	©Curtis Parker/Stock Illustration Source/Images.com

This book was set in 10/12 Meridien by Pine Tree Composition and printed and bound by Courier Companies (Westford). The cover was printed by Phoenix Color

This book is printed on acid free paper. ∞

Library of Congress Cataloging in Publication Data:
Smith, Patricia L. (Patricia Lucille)
  Instructional design / Patricia L. Smith, Tillman J. Ragan.—3rd ed.
    p. cm.
  Includes bibliographical references and index.
  ISBN 978-0-471-39353-5 (pbk.)
  1. Instructional systems—Design.   I. Ragan, Tillman J.   II. Title.

LB1028.38.S65 2005
371.3—dc22

2004048818

ISBN 978-0-471-39353-5

Printed in the United States of America

10 9 8 7 6

To our daughters, Bessie and Patty,
from whom we have learned
more than we have taught

ABOUT THE AUTHORS

Patricia L. Smith is Professor Emeritus in the Instructional Psychology and Technology program at the University of Oklahoma. She received her Ph.D. in Instructional Systems from Florida State University in 1982. Dr. Smith is author of two books and numerous journal articles, technical reports, and chapters on computer-based instruction and instructional design. She has served as president of the Research and Theory Division and as a member of the board of directors of that division as well as the Division of Instructional Development (now "Design and Development") of the Association for Educational Communications and Technology. She has also served as co-chair of the Professors of Instructional Design and Technology conference and as president of the Instructional Technology Special Interest Group of the American Educational Research Association. Her primary areas of interest are instructional design, particularly the design of organizational strategies, design of print-based instruction, instructional feedback, and program evaluation.

Tillman J. Ragan is Professor Emeritus in the Instructional Psychology and Technology program at the University of Oklahoma. He received his Ph.D. in Instructional Technology from Syracuse University in 1970. Dr. Ragan is author of five books and numerous articles, technical reports, and chapters on instructional technology, and he has been a columnist for *Educational Technology* magazine. He has served on many committees and has been president of the Research and Theory Division and of the Division of Instructional Development (now "Design and Development") of the Association for Educational Communications and Technology, vice-president of the International Visual Literacy Association, and co-chair of the Professors of Instructional Design Technology conference. His area of interest is instructional technology, with particular interest in learner characteristics, visual literacy, and applications of computer technology to the facilitation of learning.

PREFACE

This book is intended to be of assistance to anyone who is interested in facilitating learning.

We hope that this text is helpful to people who are both interested in learning what has become known as "mainstream" instructional design, as well as alternatives, innovations, and enrichments. In addition to a number of truly valuable contributions from recent work, we find that not all that is characterized as "new" in our field is in fact so new, and hope to provide a thorough-enough background to allow the reader to decide. This text is predicated upon the belief that designers need both skill in using procedures from accepted practice as well as the ability to engage in problem solving from the standpoint of underlying concepts and principles. Thus, although we offer extensive procedural assistance, we emphasize the foundations and first principles upon which most of the models and procedures in our field are built. The text provides a foundation upon which users can adapt the design process to fit their unique contexts.

Despite the youth of the instructional design specialty, it has developed a rich mainstream. In recent years, theory and practice involved in designing instruction have been enriched by ideas and approaches from many perspectives. However, too many people from both within the specialty and outside it have begun to speak of the design of instruction as if it were uninfluenced by new ideas, or that it is an atheoretic, procedure-bound practice with little or no research, or that it gets new ideas in the facilitation of learning only from outside the specialty. Our experience with instructional design is that it is a rapidly changing, theory rich, challenging and rewarding field of research and practice.

Organization of the Text

The text is organized into five main sections.

The first section, *Introduction*, provides an introduction to instructional design itself and a discussion of philosophical and theoretical foundations.

The second section, *Analysis and Assessment*, includes chapters on analysis of context (including needs assess-

ment), learners, and learning tasks. The section also contains the chapter on assessment of learning.

The third section, *Instructional Strategies*, is concerned primarily with micro-level strategies to facilitate learning. A separate chapter is provided for strategies leading to the learning of eight distinct categories of learning: declarative knowledge, concepts, principles, procedures, domain-specific problem solving, cognitive strategies, attitude change and motivation, and psychomotor skills. The approach to design of instructional strategies is tied closely to cognitive learning theory and related research, in which the cognitive requirements of particular learning tasks, along with context and learner characteristics, are used to inform instructional strategy decisions. The final chapter in this section is devoted to macro-level strategies and integration of learning in larger units of study.

The fourth section, *Implementation, Management, and Evaluation* is comprised of a chapter on implementation of instruction, a chapter on management of instruction, and a chapter on formative and summative evaluation of instruction.

The fifth section, *Conclusion*, has one chapter which supplies concluding comments and recommendations such as "fast track" design approaches and the principle of appropriate technology. The chapter also includes an effort at pulling the material of the whole book together into a summary. The chapter concludes with observations on future directions of interest to the field.

Changes in the 3rd Edition

Two chapters, Chapter 17, Implementation, and Chapter 18, Management of Instruction, are new additions. We are pleased to be able to offer what we believe is a helpful treatment of these two areas of critical importance to most instructional designers. The new chapter on implementation provides recommendations that can substantially increase the likelihood that instructional design efforts will be successful. The chapter contains practical implementation suggestions. These suggestions draw heavily upon information about context, learners, and learning tasks, and we think readers will find that this underscores and clarifies the relevance of instructional analysis. The new chapter on management emphasizes project management concepts and tools of relevance to instructional designers and also discusses instructional management, the overarching strategies that guide the scheduling of instructional events and the mechanisms for delivering these events.

Users of earlier editions may notice the absence of two chapters from the Table of Contents: Production and Delivery Strategies. These chapters were particularly difficult to maintain currency, but rather than eliminate them completely, they have been updated and moved to our Learning Resources Web Site.

The Learning Resources Web Site, http:www.wiley.com/college/smith, a helpful supplement in the past, has increased in its role and importance. Beyond the addition of two chapters, the site also contains an updated and revised Extended Example. The Extended Example in the 1st and 2nd editions gave an example of application of each of the major design activities applied to one course. Continuing in the 3rd edition, the Extended Example is provided in addition to those provided in each chapter which draw from many subject areas and task domains. The Extended Example gives the reader not only an illustration of application in addition to those which appear in chapters, but it also has the unique function of providing the continuity of relating to a single subject area and course. Most chapters in the text have an example in the Extended Example. We selected a course in Digital Photography as our vehicle, and we hope you find it to be interesting and helpful as an illustration of application of instructional design concepts and techniques. Each chapter for which there is an Extended Example contribution contains a pointer to the example and recommendation to examine it.

The Learning Resources Web Site contains materials that we hope are useful to learners and faculty alike. The site contains:

- Feedback for all chapter exercises
- Example course syllabi and schedules for courses which use the text in a variety of contexts
- Learning activities for classroom use
- Figures and illustrations, in the text, as a file that instructor (or students) can use and modify
- Presentations in PowerPoint[TM] form related to many of the chapters
- Job aids which may be either printed out or used within your computer as forms to facilitate application
- Example objectives for each type of learning, along with a summary of events of instruction from each of the strategies chapters (Chapters 8-16)

- Online Chapter W-1: Production of Media
- Online Chapter W-2: Delivery Strategies
- Extended Example: Design of one course through each of the phases of the instructional design process, using a course. in digital photography, with illustration of:
  - Context analysis
  - Learner Analysis
  - Learning Task Analysis
  - Assessment
- Instructional Strategy Design for lessons leading to
  - Declarative knowledge learning
  - Concept learning
  - Procedure learning
  - Principle learning
  - Problem-solving learning
  - Cognitive strategy learning
  - Attitude learning
  - Psychomotor skill learning
  - Macro-Level Design (Course Structure)
  - Example Instructor-led Instruction Lesson Plan
  - Formative and Summative Evaluation Plans

Features of the Third Edition

The text includes features found to be of most utility in the first and second editions, expands the use of those of most importance, and eliminates those which were not of particular value.

1. **Performance objectives** begin each chapter. In addition to providing a preview and expectation-setting function, the objectives in an instructional design text serve an additional function. Chapter objectives provide examples of ways of expressing intention for learning in addition to other examples in the text. Many chapter objectives reflect higher order learnings such as principles, procedures, and problem solving.

2. **Examples** from a variety of settings, including business and industry as well as K–12 education. Examples of the application of tools and principles place design in a context that helps learners better understand relevance and application than by reading explanations alone. We have made an effort to make the text rich with examples of application in a variety of settings and content domains.

3. **The Extended Example** for the design of components in an instructional photography course is provided in the book's Learning Resources Web Site.

The Extended Example, described earlier, exemplifies the major principles presented in each chapter. It has been our experience that while learners benefit from the diversity of short examples within each chapter, they also greatly benefit from seeing the instructional design for one content unfold across the entire instructional design process.

4. **Exercises** are embedded within the chapters to assist learners in active interaction with the material as well as providing the opportunity for students to monitor their learning as they progress through the chapter. Exercises often include practice of procedures and application of principles being discussed. In our own teaching uses of this book as a text, we base the exams that we give our students on the item specifications from which these exercises were derived. (Model answers to these Exercises are provided in the Learning Resources Web Site described earlier.)

5. **Graphic summaries** are included at the end of each chapter. Although some are more "graphic" than others, each can assist in summarizing through a table or graphically enhanced representation.

6. **Reading and reference** information is extensive. In addition to thorough citation of sources used throughout the text, a few useful references not cited are included. The references sections are wide-ranging in scope, including research reports, literature reviews, technical reports, and books in both theoretical and application domains.

7. **Access structures** such as author and subject indexes, extensive illustrations, careful use of explicit typographic structures such as heading use, bolding, and italics, and extensive cross-referencing are employed to help users navigate and use this book as not only a text but a reference for practitioners.

Acknowledgements

We wish to thank our colleagues. We are especially indebted to colleagues in the Instructional Technology and Psychology program at the University of Oklahoma, the Professors of Instructional Design Technology group (PIDT), the Association for Educational Communications and Technology (AECT), the American Educational Research Association (AERA), and the International Visual Literacy Association (IVLA). In particular we would thank Barbara Greene, Ray Miller, and Terri DeBacker, who have listened to our ideas, provided books for our education, and critiqued portions of this text. Also to Amy Bradshaw, Barry Brown, Beth Butts, John Cochenour, L.K. & Steve Curda, Gayle Davidson-Shriver, Scott DeClue, Phil Doughty, Jim Ellsworth, Marsha Ferguson, Paul Kleine, Sandy Quesada, Rita Richey, Willi Savenye, Rick Schwier, Annette Sherry, Jennifer Summerville, and Patty White for their help and friendship. And special acknowledgement and thanks to Patricia Hardre, who in addition wrote the new chapter on management (Chapter 18), a significant contribution to this edition.

We are also indebted to our esteemed former professors and colleagues for their ground-breaking scholarship, especially L. J. Briggs, W. Dick, R. M. Gagné, J. Keller, and W. Wager. After writing this text, we more fully realize that we "stand on the shoulders" of our predecessors!

We are grateful for the contributions which our students have made to our learning. We appreciate the thoughtful questions of our students from all of the institutions at which we have taught. We are also indebted to the students from many classes for their formative feedback on the various versions of the text over the years. We must specifically mention Tom Bergman and Mary Beth Smith, who provided us with detailed written feedback over an entire semester. One student, not ours, but a student in Syracuse University's Instructional Design, Development and Evaluation program, contributed to revisions of the example problem-solving lesson to bring it into the 21st century with sample instruction on beginning Java programming. Thank you, Patty (so many Patricias—this one is Patricia T. Ragan).

We gratefully acknowledge the insightful and scholarly comments of our reviewers: T. C. Bassoppo-Moyo, Illinois State University; Don E. Descy, Minnesota State University; Patricia L. Hardre, University of Oklahoma; Badrul Khan, George Washington University; Tiffany A. Koszalka, Syracuse University; Victor Nolet, Western Washington University; Pam Northup, University of West Florida; Francine Shuchat Shaw, New York University; and Michael E. Wiggins, Embry-Riddle Aeronautical University

Finally, we acknowledge the guidance and careful attention to our manuscript provided by our editors and production team at Wiley: Brad Hanson, Alec Borenstein, Mary Savel, and Patty Donovan of Pine Tree Composition.

Patricia L. Smith
Tillman J. Ragan
Professors Emeriti
The University of Oklahoma
Norman, Oklahoma
April, 2004

BRIEF CONTENTS

CONTENTS

C H A P T E R   1 6

MACRO STRATEGIES: INTEGRATION OF TYPES OF LEARNING   285

IV   IMPLEMENTATION, MANAGEMENT, AND EVALUATION   301

C H A P T E R   1 7

IMPLEMENTATION   303

C H A P T E R   1 8

MANAGEMENT OF INSTRUCTION   312

C H A P T E R   1 9

FORMATIVE AND SUMMATIVE EVALUATION   326

V   CONCLUSION   353

C H A P T E R   2 0

CONCLUSIONS AND FUTURE DIRECTIONS   355

SECTION

I

INTRODUCTION

In this section, we introduce and provide foundation for your study of instructional design.

In Chapter 1, "Introduction to Instructional Design," the idea of instructional design is presented. The concept of instruction is compared with related concepts such as education, training, and teaching. We also will look at the major activities of instructional designers and who performs them in what settings. This review of activities also provides a preview of the variety of settings to which this book is addressed: corporate, K–12, and other. Also discussed are advantages and limitations of the instructional design approach.

In Chapter 2, "Foundations of Instructional Design," a review of philosophical and theoretical foundations is provided. The philosophical perspectives of constructivism, empiricism, and pragmatism are explored, as well as the major assumptions held by authors of this text. Theories that are also foundational to instructional design are discussed, including the learning theories of behaviorism, cognitive learning theory, and developmental theories. Finally, the use of instructional theories throughout the text will be overviewed, along with a relatively simple example of an instructional theory, which is provided for orientation.

INTRODUCTION TO INSTRUCTIONAL DESIGN

CHAPTER OBJECTIVES

At the conclusion of this chapter, you should be able to do the following:

- Explain what is meant by instructional design.

- Define instruction, distinguish it from related terms (such as education, training, and teaching), and when given descriptions of educational activities, determine which of these are instruction.

- Identify and describe the three major activities of the instructional design process, and when given descriptions and instructional design activities, identify which activity is being employed.

- Describe advantages of using instructional design: for school curriculum developers, for teachers, for training designers and trainers.

- Discuss the types of contexts in which instructional designers work and how their activities may differ in these different contexts.

INTRODUCTION

Fourth-grade teacher Dora Brady is sitting at her desk after school, looking at the scores that her class made on the long-division quiz she gave today. She is reviewing the students' performance in her mind and recalling how she taught the students. She is working on new ways to teach the kids next week and next year. She is drawing upon her knowledge of something called *instructional design* in her thinking.

Dick Montiville is in conference with three coworkers at Amalgamated Airlines. Mr. Montiville and his team are figuring out the exact nature of the learning that aircrew members need in order to improve the safety of the company's flights. The areas of required learning have already been established, and now the team is breaking those learning tasks down into the components and prerequisites. Montiville and his team are using some techniques from instructional design to guide their work.

Faye Hartman and William Burke are in charge of evaluating a new textbook series in organic chemistry being developed by MacBurdick Publishers. The series is intended to capture the market in its subject area, and principles of instructional design were used in many phases of the project, including the evaluation work of Hartman and Burke.

WHAT DOES INSTRUCTIONAL DESIGN MEAN?

The term **instructional design** refers to the systematic and reflective process of translating principles of learning and instruction into plans for instructional materials, activities, information resources, and evaluation. An instructional designer is somewhat like an engineer. Both plan their work based upon principles that have been successful in the past—the engineer on the laws of physics, and the designer on basic principles of instruction and learning. Both try to design solutions that are not only functional but also attractive or appealing to the end-user. Both the engineer and instructional designer have established problem-solving procedures that they use to guide them in making decisions about their designs.

Through this systematic process, both the engineer and the instructional designer plan what the solution—often a finished product—will be like. Both write specifications (plans) for the solutions, but they do not necessarily translate their specifications into an actual product. They often hand their plans to someone who specializes in production (in the case of an engineer, a building contractor; in the case of the instructional designer, a software development or media production

specialist). This holds true for many instructional designers. However, some designers, such as those with production skills (computer programming, video production, or development of print materials), may themselves translate their specifications into the final instructional material. Classroom teachers often implement their own plans. In any event, the designer typically begins the production or implementation once the specifications are completed.

Perfection is neither a goal nor an option in design. It is attractive and easy to assume that with sufficient sophistication, designers will develop flawless designs that have no drawbacks. Petroski (2003) has made it clear that all design involves trade-offs, even the most elegant and widely admired designs. Instructional designers, no less than civil engineers or industrial designers, seek to analyze, plan, implement, and evaluate in such a way that their work will do the most good with the least harm, and to learn from mistakes to improve.

Careful, systematic planning is important no matter what media of instruction are used in implementation. When the medium of instruction is something other than a teacher, and when it is possible that a teacher may not be available or prepared to compensate for poorly planned instructional materials, careful instructional design is critical. When the instructional medium is not immediately adaptable (as with printed materials, video materials, and computer-based instruction), having a design that is based upon principles of instruction is very important. Any oversights that were made in the design of these instructional materials cannot be easily remedied because the instruction is being delivered via instructional media. When the primary medium of instruction is a teacher/trainer or when a teacher/trainer has a major role as coordinator of instruction, then high-quality instructional design is also highly beneficial. The systematic planning needed prior to implementation and the reflection that should occur afterward are well informed, guided, and organized by instructional design principles and processes. Teachers'/trainers' careful planning allows them to allocate their mental resources during instruction to adaptations that are necessary because of the differing prior experiences of the learners; motivation, behavior, or administrative problems; or serendipitous events that require instructional planning on the spot.

To understand the term *instructional design* more clearly, we will review the meanings of the words *instruction* and *design*.

What Is Instruction?

Instruction is the intentional facilitation of learning toward identified learning goals. Driscoll (2000) defines **instruction** from a similar perspective: "the deliberate arrangement of learning conditions to promote the attainment of some intended goal" (p. 345). In both definitions, instruction is the intentional arrangement of experiences, leading to learners acquiring particular capabilities. These capabilities can vary qualitatively in form, from simple recall of knowledge to cognitive strategies that allow a learner to find new problems within a field of study. For example, a teacher or trainer may wish to help learners use a particular kind of computer software to solve a certain set of problems. The instructional designer will develop materials and activities that are intended to prepare the learners to use the software effectively. Every experience that is developed is focused toward one or more goals for learning. In addition to effective instruction, designers also wish to create instruction that is efficient (requiring the least time and cost necessary) and appealing.

Terms such as *education, training,* and *teaching* are often used interchangeably with *instruction.* However, in this text we will make some distinctions among these terms. Certainly, these distinctions may not be made in the same way among all individuals in the field of education, or even in the field of instructional design. However, we have found these definitions helpful in laying the framework for this text. Figure 1.1 illustrates the relationships among these terms.

We will use the term **education** very broadly to describe all experiences in which people learn. Many of these experiences are unplanned, incidental, and informal. For example, many people learn to drive a car in city traffic through a trial-and-error process involving many harried morning trips. The driver learns, so these experiences can be considered part of her general education; however, no one has specifically arranged this learning experience so that she can learn well, quickly, and with a minimum of danger and frustration. It would be possible to create a series of particular experiences (perhaps using a simulator or videotapes and city maps) that would be specifically focused on preparing one to navigate city traffic easily. We would call the delivery of these focused educational experiences **instruction.**

So, all instruction is part of education because all instruction consists of experiences leading to learning. But not all education is instruction because many experiences that lead to learning are not specifically developed and implemented to ensure effective, efficient, and appealing experiences leading toward particular learning goals. A common misapprehension of instruction relates instruction to particular strategies—such as expository or didactic ones—and avoids the term when referring to learning environments that employ a more student-centered approach. The tools and principles of instructional design that you will see described in this book are applicable to all forms of experience, as long as the experience in question has facilitation of particular goals for learning as its purpose. However, learning environments that are truly "goal free"—if such exist— would not be examples of instruction.

We generally use the term **training** to refer to those instructional experiences that are focused upon individuals acquiring very specific skills that they will normally apply almost immediately. For example, many instructional experiences in vocational education classes can be considered training. The students learn skills, specifically focused toward job competencies, that they will use almost immediately. Much instruction in business, military, and government settings can be termed *training* because the experiences are directed toward preparing learners with specific on-the-job skills. In addition, the instruction in certain special education classes is "training" because the learning experiences have been developed to provide students with life skills, such as counting change, which we anticipate they will use almost immediately.

Not all instruction can be considered *training,* however. For instance, in military education programs, learners may be provided with some general instruction in math and reading. These learning experiences can be termed *instruction* because the lessons were developed with some specific goals in mind, such as a certain level of proficiency in reading and mathematics. However, these goals are often not directed toward a specific job task, nor is there anticipation of immediate impact upon a specific job task. The influence on job performance is anticipated to be more diffuse throughout job responsibilities and outside job tasks. Therefore, in our terminology, these learning experiences would not be termed *training.* Similar to the misapprehension of the meaning of instruction, training is sometimes mistakenly identified with a particular style or strategy of teaching. Training is conducted using all of the varieties of method and approach seen in any other form of education: Training is distinguished from other forms by *immediacy* of application.

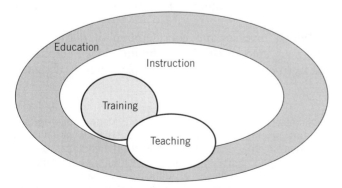

Figure 1.1 Relationships Among Terms Associated with Instruction

Of all the terms just discussed, *teaching* and *instruction* may be most often used interchangeably. In this text, we will use the term **teaching** to refer to those learning experiences that are facilitated by a human being—not a DVD, textbook, or educational Web site, but a live teacher. Instruction, on the other hand, includes *all* learning experiences in which facilitation and support for learning are conveyed by teaching and other forms of mediation. As you will discover later, one of the primary tenets of instructional design is that a live teacher is not essential to all instruction.

As Figure 1.1 shows, not all teaching is considered to be instruction. There are occasions in an educational environment in which a teacher does not focus learning experiences toward any particular learning goal. On these occasions, teachers may provide many learning activities, and during these activities learning goals may emerge, often from the learners themselves as they encounter the activities. For example, some preschool education falls within this category, such as instances in which learners are provided with a variety of manipulative materials that they can use to pursue many problems. These pursuits might lead to various learning outcomes, many of which have not been specifically anticipated by the teacher.

In summary, this text focuses on the facilitation of learning: instruction. Here, we will consider *instruction* to be a subset of *education*. The term *training* will be considered a subset of *instruction*. In some cases, teaching will be considered instruction, and in others it will fit the more general category of education but will not have the focus that characterizes instruction. We will concentrate on the design and development of activities that are directed toward identified learning goals.

WHAT IS DESIGN?

Design is an activity or process that people engage in that improves the quality of their subsequent creations. Design is related to *planning,* the difference being that once the expertise and care with which planning is conducted reaches a certain point, we begin to refer to the activity as "design." When projects become complex, at some point the term "planning" no longer fits and "design" becomes a better descriptor. Thus, before an earth orbit laboratory is built, it must be designed. To say that the space station will be planned would not make sense if we were referring to the development of actual specifications for its construction and operation. Likewise, a teacher may engage in planning for a class or semester, but if the term "design" is well-applied to the activity, a high level of care and sophistication is implied. The term design comes with an implication that a good amount of specialized knowledge and skill

is being brought to bear, regardless of the size of the project. Schön (1987, 1991), a student of effective professional practice, described design as a process of "reflective conversation with the materials of a given situation."

Many fields use the term *design* as part of their title; examples include interior design, architectural design, and industrial design. The term *design* implies a systematic or intensive planning and ideation process prior to the development of something or the execution of some plan in order to solve a problem. Fundamentally, design is a type of problem solving and has much in common with problem solving in other professions. In this text, we classify the capability that designers apply as "domain-specific problem solving," which involves the solution of "ill-structured" or "ill-defined" problems. Such problems cannot be solved by following an algorithm, nor will all designers reach the same solution to a particular learning problem. (Readers might wish to refer to Chapter 12, Strategies for Problem-solving Lessons, to clarify what is meant by "domain-specific problem solving.")

Design is distinguished from other forms of instructional planning by the level of precision, care, and expertise that is employed in the planning, development, and evaluation process. Designers employ a high level of precision, care, and expertise in the systematic development of instruction because they perceive that poor planning can result in serious consequences, such as misuse of time and other resources and even in loss of life. Specifically, instructional designers fear that poor instructional design can result in ineffective encounters, inefficient* activities, and unmotivated learners—a consequence that can have serious long-term effects. Indeed, experienced instructional designers intensify the degree of precision, care, and expertise expended on a design project relative to the impact of the potential consequences of ineffective, inefficient, or unmotivated learning that can result from less carefully designed instruction. (For more detail on the subject of adjusting design intensity to the learning situation, refer to Chapter 20, Conclusions and Future Directions.)

Design involves the consideration of many factors that may affect or be affected by the implementation of an instructional plan. For example, interior designers

---

*Efficiency is a controversial concept. Many educators and learning scientists are appropriately suspicious of concerns with instructional efficiency. Although efficiency can be worshiped at the expense of meaningful learning, we use the term to reflect the avoidance of unnecessary and unproductive waste, and when meaningful learning is implicit in learning goals, as it often is, the criterion of effectiveness takes it quite seriously.

must consider the purpose and level of use of a facility, the anticipated traffic patterns, and the needs of the people who will be using the facility. Interior designers must consider the engineer's plans, such as the location and strength of walls. They must follow laws and regulations with regard to accessibility and safety. If they do not consider all these factors and how they interrelate, the designers risk creating a work or living space that is unusable or even dangerous. Just as interior designers have critical factors that they must consider to make their solutions usable and effective, instructional designers have a vast number of factors, which often interact, that they must consider as they create instruction. The rest of this text details factors that instructional designers must consider in designing instruction.

Creativity also has a role in design. Novice designers sometimes have the impression that doing design work is a "cut-and-dried" activity. This is not the case. For example, if one were to give several architects the same conditions—site, materials, and purpose—the plans for the structures that they would create would vary radically. Some would be highly imaginative and innovative, while some might be more mundane and standard. All of the designs may "work" in the sense that, when executed, the buildings would remain standing and serve their purposes. However, some imaginative and ingenious structures may inspire awe, while more mundane structures may be totally forgettable.

Just as the design of the architect benefits from creativity and imagination, so do the designs of the instructional designer. A critical need exists for imagination and ingenuity in all instructional design activities. For example, during context analysis designers may have to exert considerable ingenuity in creating ways to ascertain the true nature of the "problem." Sometimes this involves restructuring the problem to redefine it into one that can be solved (Akin, 1994). In addition, designers must make instruction inspiring and memorable. Certainly, evaluation of instruction requires inventiveness. Frequently, assessing the actual goals of an instructional activity seems a practical impossibility. Some designers are ingenious in devising ways of simulating targeted situations, so that learners get to demonstrate activities and cognitive processing that are very near the actual goal behavior.

How can instructional designers become more creative in their work? We have noticed some common characteristics of particularly ingenious design students and practitioners in the field. First, highly creative designers are voracious consumers of examples of learning environments and instructional materials, both those from the instructional design tradition and those from other traditions. Second, although they have conducted a thorough analysis of the component learning requirements (objectives) of the design project, the best designers clearly maintain a sense of the major goal and generalized perception of the content of the materials: They can still see the forest, despite the trees. Third, excellent designers use message design conventions and techniques, such as metaphors, narratives, or visual images to lend a sense of continuity, interest, and wholeness to the instruction.

Another key aspect of instructional design is its extensive and demanding nature. Experienced designers (not to mention novices) frequently express concern about the time and effort that they expend applying what is currently known about designing effective, efficient, and appealing instruction. Clearly, there is enough of a "technology" undergirding the design process that a casual approach to either learning or application of skills in instructional design will not do it justice. However, those who are beginning their study of instructional design should know that once the concepts and principles of instructional design are learned, they can be appropriately applied with a wide range of effort, precision, and formality.

Even classroom teachers in public schools (who by virtue of their teaching loads do not generally have time to engage in instructional design in a full-blown fashion) can significantly improve the effectiveness of their teaching by informally applying instructional design principles (Wiggins, McTighe, & McTighe, 1998). They may choose to apply these principles mentally and document little, if any, of their thinking on paper. Of course, in instructional design classes, learners are asked to document their thought processes so that the instructor can evaluate them and provide remediation where necessary. And, in many contexts—particularly those situations in which teams work together on a design project in which legal liability for the quality of the instruction is an issue—a hard-copy documentation of the design process may be essential.

Recent developments in the field are specifically directed at reducing the time and effort required by the instructional design process. We review a number of these "fast-track" approaches to instructional design in the final chapter of this text.

Rowland (1992, 1993, 1994) has studied the process of design across a number of professions and has examined instructional design specifically. Several of his observations of design in general are particularly salient to the design of instruction (1993):

- Design is a goal-directed process in which the goal is to conceive and realize some new thing.
- The new thing that results from designing has practical utility.
- A basic task of designing is to convert information in the form of requirements into information in the form of specifications.

- Design requires social interaction.
- Designing involves problem solving, but not all problem solving is designing.
- In designing, problem understanding and problem solving may be simultaneous or sequential processes.
- Design may be a science, or a combination of science and art, or neither science nor art.
- Designing involves technical skills and creativity and rational and intuitive thought processes.
- A design process is a learning process. (pp. 80–85)

THE INSTRUCTIONAL DESIGN PROCESS

Another way to define *instructional design* is to describe the process involved in the systematic planning of instruction. At the most basic level, the instructional designer's job is to answer three major questions (Mager, 1984):

1. Where are we going? (What are the goals of the instruction?)
2. How will we get there? (What is the instructional strategy and the instructional medium?)
3. How will we know when we have arrived? (What should our tests look like? How will we evaluate and revise the instructional materials?)

These three questions can be stated as major activities that an instructional designer completes during the design and development process:

1. Perform an *instructional analysis* to determine "where we're going."
2. Develop an *instructional strategy* to determine "how we'll get there."
3. Develop and conduct an *evaluation* to determine "how we'll know when we're there."

These three activities form the foundation of the approach to instructional design* that this book describes. We will expand on these three problem-solving activities throughout the text.

*We use the term *instructional design* to refer to the entire process of design, development, implementation, and revision of instruction. The term *instructional development* is a related term, and if it were not so awkward, we might refer to the process as *instructional design and development*. Some aspects, particularly production, would seem to fit more easily under a term such as *development* rather than *design*. Since the term *instructional design* is currently the most widely used of the choices available, we will use it in this text.

An Overview of the Design Process: Designing Training for Digital-Magic Repair Persons

The following section provides an overview of the entire process of designing instruction. We will describe how designers might prepare a system of instructional materials to train individuals to repair the fictitious Digital-Magic 3-D/HD Hyperspheroid Plasma video system that will soon be marketed throughout the world.

ANALYSIS. During the activity the designers will learn as much as they can about the environment in which the learners (repair persons) will be trained, about the learners themselves, and about the repair tasks for which the learners must be prepared. The designer will ask many questions of the managers and supervisors in the Digital-Magic company, the developers of the new television system, those who have provided training for repair persons in the past, and of the learners themselves. They will analyze the learning task itself, asking what learners must know or be able to do to learn to make repairs. The designers will want the answers to questions such as:

1. Will the learners be brought together in a central location, or will they be trained in their own work environments?
2. How much time is available for training?
3. Will it be possible for the learners to have access to the new television systems to work with as they learn about them?
4. How do learners feel about the training? What sorts of incentives to learn will they be given?
5. What kinds of people are the prospective learners? What interests them? What kinds of educational backgrounds do they have?
6. Do all of the learners have to reach the same goals?
7. What do the learners already know that will help them learn the new information or skills?
8. What are the skills and knowledge that the learners must acquire in order to make the repairs on the new system? Do they need to know only the technical procedures of repair, or do they also need to know the conceptual or theoretical *whys* of the procedures?
9. How should the learners' achievement of the goals be assessed? Is a pencil-and-paper test adequate? Should learners be assessed on actually repairing a Digital-Magic 3-D/HD video system? Can this performance be simulated?

SELECTING THE INSTRUCTIONAL STRATEGY. During this activity, the designers determine the way that instructional material relating to repair of the television sets should be presented. They also decide which learning activities the learners can experience. In addition, the designers determine what sequence of instruction should follow. They choose the medium (a single medium) or media (a combination of multiple media) that will support the instruction. This is the stage at which the designers will determine exactly how instruction will take place.

Some of the questions that Digital-Magic's instructional designers would answer in this activity are the following:

1. What kinds of content must be learned by the students? In what size segments should the content be presented? Should information be presented, or should the content be embedded within an activity?

2. In what activities should the learners engage? What role will learners' activities have? Will activities or projects supplement informational presentations, or will they be the primary means of learning? Should activities include learners answering written questions? Should learners practice troubleshooting problems on the actual equipment? For what topics (if any) will reading be an appropriate learning activity? What topics will require viewing demonstrations and visual examples? Are discussions needed?

3. In what sequence should instruction proceed? Should a "discovery" sequence be followed, or should an "expository" approach be used? If expository, what sequence of presentation should be employed?

4. What media are most appropriate for the support of instruction? Should learners see a live demonstration of repair procedures, a videotaped presentation, or an interactive video presentation? Should they read about it in a text or workbook, or should they use both? Should the students have a job performance aid (such as a manual) available to them for reference?

5. What groupings should learners be placed in for learning? Should they study independently, in a small group, or in a large group?

Notice that instructional design in no way implies that the instructional strategy must be "direct instruction" or something "done to" the learner. Instructional strategy decisions are based on many factors that may influence what will best facilitate learning. (We will discuss this particular issue further in Chapter 7, A Framework for Instructional Strategy Design.)

EVALUATION. When designing evaluation, the designers plan an approach for evaluating the instructional materials to determine what kinds of changes need to be made in them. At Digital-Magic some of the questions that may be asked include the following:

1. Is the content accurate? Have there been design changes in the Digital-Magic 3-D/HD video systems since the instruction was originally developed?

2. What learners should use the materials in order to get information to guide revisions? How should we conduct these tryouts? Should the sample be large or small? Should students be observed one at a time or in groups?

3. What questions should be answered in order to determine problems in the instruction?

4. What revisions should be made in the instruction?

When we use the term *evaluation,* it will often be in reference to the broad topic including both assessment of learners and evaluation of the instruction. When we are talking about evaluation of students' learning, we will generally use the term *assessment* instead of the more familiar but often misleading term *tests* (see Chapter 6), and we will generally use the term *evaluation* in the context of evaluating the instruction itself; the terms *formative evaluation* and *summative evaluation* will be used in this fashion (see Chapter 18).

THE DIGITAL-MAGIC STORY: A POSTMORTEM. The instructional designers at Digital-Magic did a good job of instructional design. The training system for repair persons was highly effective and efficient. Not only did the student technicians learn what they needed to learn, but they also enjoyed the process and developed a good attitude about their work. It was a good thing, too, because the new television set was very popular in the market, and the first 10,000 Digital-Magic televisions that were manufactured had a mysterious tendency to fade after six months of use. The well-trained service technicians fixed the problems, and as time passed they acquired the reputation of being excellent repair persons and the video system eventually became a success in the marketplace.

Congruence Among the Activities of Instructional Design

Instructional designers insist on creating instruction in which the goals, the instructional strategy, and the evaluation all match. By "match," we mean that the strategy (instructional method) that is used is appropriate for the learning task (goals) and that the tests measure how well the learners have achieved the learning task (assessment).

For example, let's say you are an instructional designer now and that you are working on designing instruction in which students will learn to classify objects as either transparent, translucent, or opaque. **Learning tasks** are the things students are to learn, so being able to classify objects as either transparent, translucent, or opaque is the learning task, and this particular learning task involves *concept learning*. The idea of "matching" learning tasks and instructional strategy means that you would select an instructional strategy that is appropriate for learning concepts; you would ensure that students were given several examples and nonexamples of the concepts to be learned. To match evaluation with the learning task and instructional strategy, you would devise your test to determine whether students have learned the concepts by asking them to classify objects as either transparent, translucent, or opaque. In this instruction, the objective, the learning activities, and the assessment are congruent with one another. In other words, they match.

This consistency between intent and action is seen in other approaches to the improvement of education. For example, in the specialties of curriculum development and teaching methods, the idea of "curriculum alignment" is another reflection of congruence between objectives, instruction, and assessment. Examples of faulty congruence are regrettably commonplace. Most of us have had at least one sad experience with a course in which goals, class work, and tests were unrelated to one another, resulting in poor learning and attitude on students' parts.

Instructional Design Models

To answer the questions "Where are we going?" "How will we get there?" and "How will we know when we've arrived?" the designer engages in three major activities: analysis, strategy development, and evaluation. These three activities are the essence of most *instructional design models.** Andrews and Goodson (1980) have described forty such models for systematic design of instruction. Gustafson and Branch (1997) provide a more extensive analysis of fourteen models. In this text, we will recommend a simple model of design (see Figure 1.2). It is similar to the design models suggested by Dick and Carey (1985, 2001) and Davis, Alexander, and Yelon (1974).

We lay no claim of uniqueness to this model. It could be accurately termed "A Common Model of

*Instructional design models may be defined as visualized depictions of instructional design process, emphasizing main elements and their relationships.

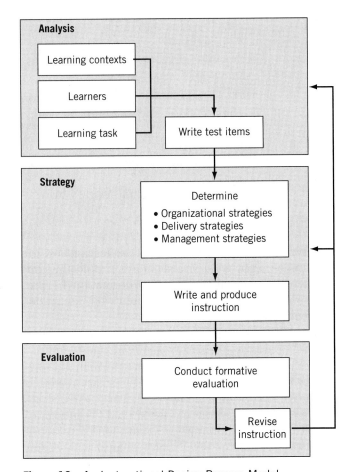

Figure 1.2 An Instructional Design Process Model

Instructional Design." There are some attributes of it, however, which, though not unique, are not universally seen. These attributes are inclusion of context analysis as a function in the design process, sequencing of test development, and the placement of revision within the formative evaluation phase.

One attribute of the model that is more apparent than we intend is sequentiality. Notice in Figure 1.2 that we have listed some more specific activities of design within each major activity in a particular sequence. We have presented the model in what appears to be a linear sequence in order to *simplify* a discussion of the activities of instructional design and to preview the sequence of that discussion. Both inexperienced and experienced designers may occasionally follow this sequence; however, particular circumstances may cause a designer to modify the sequence of design activities. Many times the steps within a particular phase may occur concurrently. Indeed, we might depict the activities of practicing instructional designers—especially their mental activities—to resemble more nearly the representation in Figure 1.3.

Figure 1.3 portrays the interwoven, nonlinear nature of actual design activity. Analysis, strategy development, and evaluation activities may, in some cases,

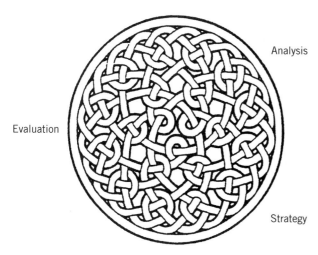

Analysis

Evaluation

Strategy

Figure 1.3 A More Realistic Representation of Instructional Design Practice

occur concurrently, especially if one is following a rapid prototyping technique (described in Chapter 20 of this text). During strategy development, new issues may emerge that send the designer back to more analysis of the learners, task, or context. During analysis, designers are often developing plans for evaluation of the instruction. Inevitably, working on one design activity leads to implications or solutions for other design activities. Unlike foundational models of design, such as Gagné-Briggs (see Gagné, Briggs, & Wager, 1992; Dick & Carey, 1985), which might have implied that instructional design is a linearly sequenced process and that the designer should not even entertain thoughts of a subsequent phase until a previous phase is complete, current models, such as the "ball of worms" model in Figure 1.3 acknowledge the interrelatedness and concurrency of all activities of design. Tessmer & Wedman (1995) provide a model that embodies simultaneity within a systematic, reflective approach (we will revisit this model in Chapter 20).

Although representing design in a fundamentally nonlinear manner more accurately reflects relationships among processes in which instructional designers engage and has the potential to promote "fast tracking" of instructional design (see Chapter 20), there are dangers in the concurrency model. For example, moving to strategy development before one has sufficient information regarding the nature of the learners or the characteristics of the learning task may increase the probability that a designer or client fixates on a particular strategy that is inadequate and becomes clearly so when more information about the learners and task becomes available. The concurrency model demands greater flexibility of designer and client so that they do not become dedicated to a solution that is later found to be inappropriate.

A POSITION STATEMENT ON MODELS.   For far too long the instructional design literature has placed an inordinate focus on models, particularly their physical attributes. In fact, instructional design models tend only to be modifications and elaborations of a basic problem-solving model tailored to the needs of the instructional design specialty. We do not advocate any particular model but recommend that you select and modify elements based on demands of the situation. This process of building your own model is enabled by a thorough knowledge of the *principles* that guide design. A model, as exemplified by instructional design models, is no more than a way to begin thinking and learning about important principles in a relationship that assists their initial comprehension. The model presented in Figure 1.2 will assist you in building a mental framework, a scaffold, which should help your learning of critical principles, your mastery of which will make the outlines of the original scaffold unnecessary and open to your modification and change as situations require.

Advantages of Using Systematic Instructional Design

For those involved in developing instruction, there are a number of advantages to using a systematic process. Following is a list of some of the advantages of systematic instructional design:

1. *Encourages advocacy of the learner.* To a very large degree, the learner is the focus of instruction. Designers spend a great deal of effort during the beginning stages of a design project trying to find out about the learner. Information about learners should take precedence over other factors that might drive design decisions, including the content itself. Often the designer is not a content expert. In their constant querying of a subject matter expert for clarification, designers are standing in the place of the learner, trying to obtain information to make the content clearer to the learner.

2. *Supports effective, efficient, and appealing instruction.* All of these factors are considered indicators for success. The process of design itself focuses on effective instruction. Efficiency is particularly facilitated by the process of instructional analysis in which inappropriate content is eliminated. The consideration of the learner and the concentration on designing appropriate strategies promotes the appeal of instruction. The process of formative evaluation provides the opportunity to revise instruction to make it more effective, efficient, and appealing.

3. *Supports coordination among designers, developers, and those who will implement the instruction.* The systematic process and resulting written documentation allow for communication and coordination among individuals involved in designing, producing, and delivering instruction. It allows for common language and general procedure. The written plans (goals, description of target audience, and analysis of task) and the written products that are results of instructional design efforts assist the process of review and revision of work in progress in a coordinated team effort.

4. *Facilitates diffusion/dissemination/adoption.* Because the products of systematic instructional design are in fact physical "products," they may be duplicated, distributed, and used in the field. In addition, because design and development have employed information about the learners and setting, products will have a high likelihood of being practical, workable, and acceptable solutions to the instructional problems that they are designed to solve.

5. *Supports development for alternate embodiments or delivery systems.* Much of the work that goes into an instructional design project is independent of the specific form that the finished product takes (such as print, Web. computer, or video). The front-end analysis and consideration of instructional strategies will be valid beginning points for projects that result in embodiments other than those used by the original project.

6. *Facilitates congruence among objectives, activities, and assessment.* The systematic approach to instructional design helps ensure that what is taught is what is needed for learners to achieve stated goals for learning and that evaluation will be accurate and appropriate.

7. *Provides a systematic framework for dealing with learning problems.* Frequently, creative individuals not trained in systematic instructional design will develop ingenious approaches to instruction that are rather like "solutions looking for a problem." Although these approaches may add to the repertoire of possible approaches, they seldom appeal to high-level management in government or business, to school system administrators, or to other funding agencies. The innovations that are generally appealing are those that have clarified the problem into a learning goal, have developed an instructional approach that gives reason to believe that the problem can be solved and the learning goals will be met, and has a well-constructed plan for gathering evidence to determine whether the approach has solved the initial problem and what undesirable effects it might have.

Limitations of Systematic Instructional Design

Instructional design does have limits of applicability; it is not the solution to all the ills and problems of education and training, nor is it the only method for creating education. In particular, instructional design has limited applicability to educational experiences in which (a) learning goals cannot be identified in advance, or (b) no

particular goals are ever identified (i.e., non-instructional education). In such cases, because there is no "lead time" to the education, and since reflection and planning are central to instructional design, there is limited opportunity to apply many of its principles and procedures. An example of such a situation might be an advanced graduate class or other educational environment in which the learners have exceptional prior knowledge of the content; these students would have well-developed cognitive strategies and be required to identify the goals of the course, devise the educational strategies, and assess their learning themselves. If a teacher is available in this situation, a skilled instructor might be able to process information rapidly enough so that as learners identify goals and devise strategies, the instructor could make suggestions for better or alternative strategies. In such a case, the teacher's knowledge of instructional design may be very helpful in his consultant role; however, he may not have time to employ much of the instructional design process and principles. In a situation without prespecified learning goals, if a teacher is not available, then the responsibility for structuring the learning experience rests totally on the learners, and their success depends on their own cognitive strategies, prior knowledge, and motivation. The educational process in such an environment rests on an almost completely generative strategy (see Chapter 7 for a discussion of instructional strategies).

In addition to goal-free learning environments, many other problems and situations are not amenable to instructional design. (In Chapter 3, we will discuss solutions, such as management, policy, and incentives, that are not instructional solutions). Finally, instructional design is not intended to take the place of expertise in particular teaching methods for individual subject areas (although instructional design can be a helpful undergirding for such methods).

People Who Do Instructional Design

As you may (or may not) recall from the Preface, the treatment of instructional design in this text is intended for everyone who may benefit from it. Consequently, you will see more or less equal attention given to examples from corporate contexts as from K–12 or higher-education settings. With the variety of application settings in mind, who are the people in those settings who do instructional design?

TRAINING DESIGNERS. Probably the most identifiable group of individuals who practice instructional design are trainers of adults in business, industry, government, and private agencies. Trainers may be part of a human resources department or they may have their own separate department. They may work in a centralized location, consulting with any of the divisions of the organization that may request their assistance, or they may be permanently attached to a particular division, providing all of the training that division requires.

Not all trainers are instructional designers. Some trainers are experts in their skill or subject area, who are either permanently or temporarily assigned to conduct training in that area. Other trainers are technical writers, videographers, or other production specialists and have high-skill levels in communication within their medium. Many trainers come from an adult education background that emphasizes adult development. Human resource development (HRD) programs also prepare trainers for employment in this area.

Many instructional designers who are involved in training design have developed additional competencies in a more inclusive specialty that is termed "performance technology." These individuals are prepared to develop interventions that address contributors to poor employee performance (other than not knowing how to do the job). These other causes are discussed in Chapter 3 in the section on "needs assessment." The trend toward preparing instructional designers as performance technologists is discussed in Chapter 20.

TEACHERS AS DESIGNERS.   Some individuals employed as teachers are directly involved in the design of new instruction (or new "curricula," as is more commonly described in public and private K–12 and postsecondary education). These teachers may be involved in ongoing and long-term projects. Certainly, instructional design procedures and principles can be employed effectively in their curriculum design and development activities. These instructional design practices may be as formal, precise, and well documented as any other instructional design project because of the need for group communication and the development of a record that codifies the decisions that they have made and why they have made them.

Do teachers not involved in curriculum design projects use instructional design principles and procedures? Indeed, they do. Although they may receive goal statements based on statewide initiatives, they do consider these goals and may add goals or identify subgoals (objectives) that will lead to these goals with aid from curriculum guides, textbooks, or their own task analysis reflection. Teachers select or develop activities and information sources that will assist learners in reaching these goals. The development of engaging activities seems to be a particular strength of practicing teachers. Teachers also select or develop ways to assess learners' progress toward reaching goals. These assessment approaches may include written tests, performance tests, observation, oral questioning, and a variety of other techniques for assessing learning. Teachers use informa-

tion from their testing to revise their instruction, especially for remediation. These design activities are completed both planfully in advance of implementation and spontaneously as circumstances suggest their use.

Both teachers who have taken courses in instructional design and teachers who have not engage in these types of instructional design activities (Martin, 1990). However, those trained in systematic instructional design tend to engage in these activities more consistently, thoroughly, and reflectively than their untrained colleagues (Reiser & Mory, 1991). Most often, these instructional design activities are conducted mentally with little documentation of the decisions made.

OTHER DESIGNERS.   Instructional designers are also engaged in developing instruction that is embodied in textbooks, multimedia, instructional software, and videos used in K–12 and postsecondary settings. Such individuals are often employed in settings such as publishing houses and regional educational laboratories. We also see instructional designers as members of development teams of educational videos, such as "Sesame Street" and "Reading Rainbow" and of many Web-based education projects both publicly and privately funded.

Instructional designers are sometimes called upon to make contributions in the visual realm. Not only is the form and content of illustrations a critical part of much instruction, but also visualizations and visual metaphors which may underlie a simulation, microworld, virtual reality, or exploratory learning environment may benefit from the contributions of an instructional designer who possesses a high proficiency in visual literacy skills in addition to core instructional design competencies.

Competencies, Standards, and Ethics of Instructional Designers

COMPETENCIES.   Various agencies have compiled sets of competencies for instructional designers. Although your work with this text in a single course will not prepare you for all of the competencies in any set, a substantial proportion of these desired skills is reflected in the learning goals and content of this text. Your review of these competencies can assist you in orienting to the specialty as well as a self-check in the future.

One of the more widely used set of competencies for instructional designers is that developed by IBSTPI (International Board of Standards for Training, Performance, and Instruction). The IBSTPI instructional designer competencies can be found in the organization's website: http://www.ibstpi.org.

Another useful set of competencies is that developed by the American Society for Training and Development

(ASTD). The ASTD competencies are directed toward human resource development and performance improvement in corporate contexts. The ASTD competencies may be found at http://www.astd.org. In addition, Analysis & Technology, Inc. has developed a set of competencies, which is available at http://www.coedu.usf.edu/IT/resources/competen.html

STANDARDS. Fields and his associates (Fields, Foxton, & Richey, 2001) elaborated the IBSTPI competencies with training standards as well as providing a description of common specializations and uses of standards by various subgroups. In addition, the Association for Educational Communications and Technology (AECT) has developed the standards used by the National Council for Accreditation of Teacher Education (NCATE) to support for accrediting of both the technology component of undergraduate teacher education programs, as well as graduate programs in instructional design and technology; more information on the AECT/NCATE standards may be found at http://www.aect.org/standards/index.html.

ETHICS. Like competencies and standards, professional codes of ethics provide guidance for good practice. Ethics provide a different insight from that provided by performance standards: a moral compass. Although ethicists are quick to point out that morals and ethics are not the same thing, it is a sense of right that ethics provide that other codes are missing. Elsewhere in this text, your authors describe themselves, philosophically, as striving to be "pragmatists with a moral compass." To identify what merely works well or what is effective is not always sufficient to recommend what should (or should not) be done. For the broader profession of education, focusing more on K–12 school professionals, the National Education Association (NEA) has developed a short but useful statement of ethics for educators which focuses on commitments to students and to the profession of education (http://www.nea.org/code.html). Closer to our specialty, Welliver (2001) has edited a volume for AECT on ethics for educational communications and technology professionals. Welliver's statement includes relationships to individuals, to society, and to the profession. The Welliver ethics volume is available online at http://www.aect.org and is available in full text online without charge to AECT members.

E X E R C I S E S

1. What activities other than those of an engineer are similar to the role of an instructional designer? Describe these similarities in your own words.

2. Following is a description of the design procedures that an instructional designer is conducting. Identify by writing on the line beside the description which phase—analysis (A), strategy development (SD), or evaluation (E)—the designer is completing.

_____ **a.** The designer determines that the prospective learners are able to read (on the average) at the ninth-grade reading level.

_____ **b.** The designer decides to use a simulation method as part of training a department store's customer service representatives.

_____ **c.** The designer determines what the learners need to know in order to learn to balance chemical equations.

_____ **d.** After a tryout of the prototype of a computer-based instruction (CBI) lesson on writing instructional objectives, the designer adds additional practice items on identifying the "conditions" of an objective.

_____ **e.** The designer writes test items to assess whether learners have achieved the objectives of a CBI lesson.

3. Which of the following activities would be education, instruction, training, and/ or teaching? Circle the term or terms that apply.

a. The teacher presents a lesson in which she hopes that the learners will learn the difference between polygons and non-polygons. She has carefully planned activities in which she will present examples and nonexamples of polygons and will help students determine the differences. She will test the students at the end of instruction to confirm that they have learned to identify those geometric figures that are polygons.

education   instruction   teaching   training

b. The instructional designer for a large corporation has developed a print-based instructional package for managers who are involved in hiring to prepare them to follow legal practices during the hiring process. The learning materials inform them of the rules and show them examples and nonexamples of the rules' application. The tests provide a copy of an interview dialog between a manager and a potential employee. The learners must indicate whether all laws were followed. If they were not followed, learners must identify which laws were broken and what should have been said to avoid breaking the law.

education   instruction   teaching   training

c. A television documentary presents information on types of whales, where whales live, what whales do, what whales eat, and the history of whales. Viewers tend to remember and learn different things from the program depending on what they already knew and their interests.

education   instruction   teaching   training

SUMMARY

One of the reasons that the quality of much instructional material is poor is because it is not carefully planned. Instructional design activities offer a process for the systematic planning of instruction that may improve the effectiveness of the materials. The design process includes the activities of analysis, strategy development, evaluation, and revision. Although the instructional design process may often be portrayed as linear, in practice it is frequently iterative, moving back and forth between activities as the project develops. Some implementations of instructional design include rapid prototyping in which a trial version of the completed instructional plans and materials are produced early during the process and are revised and elaborated upon as new information becomes available. The components of instruction—goals, learning activities, and information resources—and assessment tools, which are the products of the design process, should be congruent with each other. Before you begin actually designing and producing your own materials, you will learn in the following chapters a few of the fundamen-

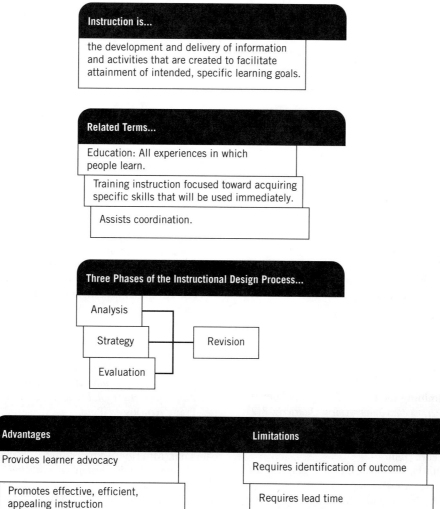

Instruction is...

the development and delivery of information and activities that are created to facilitate attainment of intended, specific learning goals.

Related Terms...

Education: All experiences in which people learn.

Training instruction focused toward acquiring specific skills that will be used immediately.

Assists coordination.

Three Phases of the Instructional Design Process...

Analysis

Strategy

Evaluation

Revision

Advantages

Provides learner advocacy

Promotes effective, efficient, appealing instruction

Assists coordination

Facilitates dissemination

Supports development of alternative delivery

Has congruence among objectives, activities, and assessment

Limitations

Requires identification of outcome

Requires lead time

Is not applicable to noninstructional problems

Figure 1.4 Summary Diagram for Chapter 1

tal principles and procedures of instructional design. Figure 1.4 summarizes the major points in this chapter thus far.

EXTENDED EXAMPLE: A PREVIEW

You can see the design process described in this text applied to a single course in the Extended Example, on a chapter-by-chapter basis. If you wish you can overview the Extended Example now at: http://www.wiley.com/college/smith.

Later on, as you read each chapter, you can study application of it in the Extended Example. The Extended Example uses one course, a course in beginning photography, to provide continuity of application. In addition to the Extended Example, examples using a variety of topics and contexts are provided in each chapter.

READINGS AND REFERENCES

Akin, O. (1994). Creativity in design. *Performance Improvement Quarterly, 7*(3), 9–21.

Andrews, D. H., & Goodson, L. A. (1980). A comparative analysis of models of instructional design. *Journal of Instructional Development, 3,* 2–16.

Braden, R. (1996). The case for linear instructional design and development: A commentary on models, challenges, and myths. *Educational Technology, 36*(2), 5–23.

Bratton, B. (1995). Professional competencies and certification in the instructional technology field. *Instructional Technology Past, Present and Future.* Englewood, CO: Libraries Unlimited, Inc.

Briggs, L. J. (Ed.). (1977). *Instructional design: Principles and applications.* Englewood Cliffs, NJ: Educational Technology Publications.

Davis, R. H., Alexander, L. T., & Yelon, S. L. (1974). *Learning system design.* New York: McGraw-Hill.

Dean, P. J. (1995). Examining the practice of human performance technology. *Performance Improvement Quarterly, 8*(2), 68–94.

Dick, W., & Carey, L. (1985). *The systematic design of instruction.* Glenview, IL: Scott, Foresman.

Dick, W., & Carey, L. (2001). *The systematic design of instruction,* (5th ed.). New York: Addison-Wesley.

Driscoll, M. P. (2000). *Psychology of learning for instruction,* 2nd ed. Needham Heights, MA: Allyn & Bacon.

Edmonds, G. S., Branch, R. C., & Mukherjee, P. (1994). A conceptual framework for comparing instructional design models. *Educational Technology Research and Development, 42*(2), 55–72.

Fields, D. C., Foxton, M., & Richey, R. (2001). *Instructional Design Competencies: The Standards,* third edition. ERIC Document Reproduction Service #ED453803.

Gagné, R. M. (1974). *Essentials of learning for instruction.* New York: Dryden Press.

Gagné, R. M. (1985). *The conditions of learning* (4th ed.). New York: Holt, Rinehart, & Winston.

Gagné, R. M., Briggs, L. J., & Wager, W. W. (1992). *Principles of instructional design* (4th ed.). Orlando, FL: Harcourt Brace Jovanovich.

Gagné, R. M., & Dick, W. (1983). Instructional psychology. *Annual Review of Psychology, 34,* 261–295.

Gustafson, K. L., & Branch, R. M. (1997). *Survey of instructional development models* (3rd ed.) Syracuse: ERIC Clearinghouse on Information & Technology. IR-103.

Heinich, R., Molenda, M., Russell, J. D., & Smaldino, S. E. (1996). *Instructional media and the new technologies of instruction.* New York: Macmillan.

Mager, R. F. (1984). *Preparing instructional objectives* (2nd ed.). Belmont, CA: Fearon-Pittman.

Martin, B. L. (1990). Teachers' planning processes: Does ISD make a difference? *Performance Improvement Quarterly, 3*(4), 53–73.

Nelson, H. (1994). The necessity of being "un-disciplined and out-of-control": Design actions and systems thinking. *Performance Improvement Quarterly, 7*(3), 22–29.

Petroski, H (2003) *Small things considered: Why there is no perfect design.* New York: Knopf.

Reiser, R. A. (1994, March). Examining the planning practices of teachers: Reflections on three years of research. *Educational Technology 34*(3), 11–16.

Reiser, R. A. & Mory, E. H. (1991). An examination of the planning practices of two experienced teachers. *Educational Technology Research and Development, 39*(3), 71–82.

Rossett, A. (1996). Training and organizational development: Siblings separated at birth? *Training 33*(4), 53–59.

Rossett, A., & Czech, C. (1995). The really wanna, but . . . the aftermath of professional preparation in performance technology. *Performance Improvement Quarterly, 8*(4), 115–132.

Rowland, G. (1992). What do instructional designers actually do? An initial investigation of expert practice. *Performance Improvement Quarterly, 5*(2), 65–86.

Rowland, G. (1993). Designing and instructional design. *Educational Technology Research and Development, 41*(1), 79–91.

Rowland, G., & Wilson, G. (1994). Liminal states in designing. *Performance Improvement Quarterly, 7*(3), 30–45.

Schön, D. (1987). *Educating the reflective practitioner.* San Francisco: Jossey-Bass.

Schön, D. (Ed.) (1991). *The reflective turn: Case studies in and on educational practice.* New York: Teachers College.

Tessmer, M. (1990). Environment analysis: A neglected stage of instructional design. *Educational Technology Research & Development, 38*(1), 55–64.

Tessmer, M., & Wedman, J. (1995). Context-sensitive instructional design models: A response to design research, studies, and criticism. *Performance Improvement Quarterly, 8*(3), 37–53

Welliver, P. (2001). *A code of professional ethics: A guide to professional conduct in the field of educational communications and technology.* Bloomington, IN: Association for Educational Communications and Technology.

Wiggins, G. L., McTighe, J., & McTighe, J. (1998). *Understanding by design.* Alexandria, VA: Association for Supervision and Curriculum Development.

FOUNDATIONS OF INSTRUCTIONAL DESIGN

CHAPTER OBJECTIVES

At the conclusion of this chapter, you should be able to do the following:

- Discuss how some philosophical perspectives, particularly *constructivism, empiricism,* and *pragmatism,* have influenced the assumptions, beliefs, and values of instructional designers.

- Describe at least four major assumptions of the authors of this text regarding instructional design and discuss how these assumptions relate to your own philosophy of education.

- Discuss why it is important that instructional designers know the philosophical perspectives and theory bases associated with their field.

- Recognize whether a description of learning or instruction constitutes a *theory* and discuss the purpose of *theory.*

- Describe each of the major theory bases and the ways in which they have contributed to instructional design practices.

- Given a description of a learning situation, describe how learning occurs according to information processing theory.

WHY DISCUSS PHILOSOPHY AND THEORY IN AN INSTRUCTIONAL DESIGN TEXT?

Instructional design is an applied, decision-oriented field. So why include information on philosophy and theory, particularly so early in the text? We have three major reasons for including this material. First, theories are the source of principles from which many of the prescriptions for design arise, and your understanding of the bases will help both your learning from this text and your ability to engage in excellent application in the field. We will be referring to these theory bases throughout the book, particularly in the chapters on instructional strategies. We suggest prescriptions and techniques for doing design work that are based upon conditions (learners and context) and learning goals (tasks). In the field, you will face situations that have particular conditions or goals not covered by this (or any) text. Or you may try our suggestions and find that they don't work. In such situations, you must reflect on what you know to develop your own prescriptions for instruction. If you know relevant theory bases, you can make intelligent and reasoned decisions in such situations.

The second reason for treating philosophy and theory involves the relationships of specialists and scholars to their field of study and practice along with *your* relationship to that field. We feel that it is imperative that writers in our field acknowledge the bases of their conclusions and recommendations. Some of our bases are the beliefs and values that represent our own educational philosophy. In other cases, the statements are not just our studied opinions, nor are they just based upon experiences with "what works." They are based upon theories that have been substantiated and modified upon the basis of empirical research. Of course, to a degree, the theories and research that we deem most valuable are colored by our philosophy. However, the theories that we present in this chapter are also the theories that have definitely shaped the directions of instructional design. Your awareness of these theories may give you the historical insight to understand why certain areas have been emphasized in this field. Theory bases are the common ground that we share with other professionals in the field. The third reason for studying philosophy and theory is because these theories allow designers to explain *why* they make the decisions they do. Sometimes designers must justify or even defend their decisions to clients or students. Theory, as well as educational philosophy, can provide a rationale for many of our decisions.

This chapter briefly describes philosophies and theories that have formed the basis of instructional design. It is an introductory treatment and is not intended to represent a sufficient background of theory or philoso-

phy for professional instructional designers. We recommend that the education of instructional designers include as much preparation in learning theory and instructional theory as possible. In addition, it should also include as much reading as possible about philosophy as it relates to learning and instruction. In particular, references by Anderson (2000); Driscoll (1994); E. Gagné, C. Yekovich, and F. Yekovich (1993); R. Gagné (1985); and Jonassen (2004) will supply critical learning theory background for instructional designers. These and other references at the end of the chapter should provide a good starting point.

THE PHILOSOPHICAL PERSPECTIVES OF INSTRUCTIONAL DESIGNERS

In the first edition of this text, we did not include a section on philosophy related to instructional design. We did, however, include a few assumptions that we held. These assumptions did not formally represent any traditional classification of philosophies, but they *did* represent potential differences in beliefs from some individuals in the areas of education and training. We wished to make these assumptions public for readers' consideration. We have expanded this section briefly because in recent years one particular philosophical position, "constructivism," has been strongly debated by individuals within the field of education—both those working in training and those working in public education. This philosophy (some describe it as a theory, but we feel it does not have the explanatory power of a learning theory) and its implications for instructional design have been much discussed among practitioners, as well as scholars in the field. The philosophy also has had a strong impact on many educators in our learning communities, so some readers will be aware of its current popularity and may wonder how such a philosophy may relate to this text.*

Fields of study, such as instructional design, do not have educational philosophies; people who study in these fields do. This personal nature of educational philosophy makes it very difficult to make general statements about a particular philosophical perspective.

---

*Some readers may find the discussion of constructivism irrelevant, uninteresting, or difficult to follow. If you do find it difficult to "connect" with, we urge you to skim it briefly and come back to it at some time in the future, particularly after reading the section on "generative instructional strategies" in Chapter 7 or after reading Chapter 12's discussion of strategies for instruction in problem solving. However, we do hope that you will read and reflect on this section at some point, as it examines some Really Big questions regarding the nature of knowledge and how we come to acquire it (epistemology).

However, we will briefly describe three educational philosophies that seem to have a strong influence on instructional designers. We will begin with constructivism, as it is the most recently popular position within many educational communities. After discussing constructivism, a much shorter treatment of two other commonly held philosophical perspectives, empiricism and pragmatism, will be presented. Space does not permit a full discussion of philosophical systems, but the treatment here of a few particularly relevant philosophies should assist in providing perspective on differing fundamental orientations.

Constructivism

Constructivism is an educational philosophy within a larger category of philosophies that are described as "rationalism." A rationalist philosophy is characterized by the belief that reason is the primary source of knowledge and that reality is constructed rather than discovered. Most rationalists would propose that there is not a single reality to be discovered, but that each individual has constructed a personal reality.

We included a fairly extensive discussion of constructivism because it is a current incarnation of a rationalist philosophy. In the past, other movements have represented similar rationalist orientations, and no doubt in the future these issues will be raised under a different label. Although the labels may change, the tension between rationalism and empiricism appears to be long-standing and therefore worthy of consideration.

Many educators trace the roots of constructivism to Jean Piaget. A foundational tenet of constructivism is the assumption that "Knowledge is not transmitted: it is constructed." We would be surprised to find any educational scholars who do not espouse this fundamental position. Indeed, most educators with whom we have worked and whom we have observed even *behave* as if this is their belief. Aside from this fundamental tenet, educators who describe themselves as constructivists have quite a wide range of beliefs about knowledge and how it can be acquired. Most of the controversy is not in disagreement with the major tenet of personal construction of knowledge, but with what the *implications* of this tenet should be. Another contributor to diversity is the division of constructivists into "individual constructivist" and "social constructivist" groupings. Also, many constructivists include a contemporary world view, "contextualism," as a component of their philosophy. Given such a diversity, we have chosen to represent the major assumptions as they were induced by Merrill (1992) and reproduced by Wilson, Teslow, & Osman-Jouchoux (1995) as a foundation for our brief description of constructivism.

INDIVIDUAL CONSTRUCTIVISM. The key assumptions of individual constructivism are the following:

- Knowledge is constructed from experience.
- Learning results from a personal interpretation of knowledge.
- Learning is an active process in which meaning is developed on the basis of experience.

These assumptions can be derived from a branch of constructivism that can be called "individual constructivism." Background in cognitive psychology and human development suggests that these precepts are credible. Certainly, it appears to us that most knowledge is constructed in an active, effortful way by learners who are engaged in experiences that promote an opportunity for reflection and assimilation/accommodation to existing knowledge (see the section on Development Theories later in this chapter).

Interpretations regarding the nature of this "construction" vary greatly among educators. For example, some constructivist writings suggest that in constructing knowledge, learners must "recreate" knowledge that may be recorded from noted and enduring experts in a field of study in order for this learning to be properly experienced and interpreted. Others view construction of knowledge to be the unique combination of new knowledge and a learner's individual prior knowledge, which includes values, experiences, and beliefs. This more conservative perspective proposes that such construction is inevitable and is the essence of learning. However, individuals from this perspective may feel that, depending upon the nature of the learners, the learning task, and the learning context, this construction may be also supported through abstract and vicarious experiences as well as direct "recreation."

Radical constructivists propose that since learners' particular combination of prior experiences are unique, it is inappropriate to propose goals for these learners because educators do not know what the learners' need or want to learn, and designers should not develop particular sequences of instruction, provide specific aids to learning, or restrict the content presented on the learning topic. More moderate constructivists suggest that the active and personal construction of meaning does not necessarily require that all of the responsibility for developing a learning environment be demanded of the learner. Some constructivist designers would propose that the amount of responsibility for arranging the situation for learning should be variable depending upon a number of learner, task, and context factors. (For more on this position, see our discussion of generative and supplantive learning strategies in Chapter 7.) Indeed, some designers who ascribe to the general tenets of individual constructivism would point out that to assume that individuals who neither possess an expert's knowledge in either a subject matter or in instructional design would have great difficulty in determining what they need to know in order to devise a satisfactory approach to acquire this knowledge. Delegating all of the load of information processing associated with instruction onto learners may place an unrealistic burden on most learners for the vast majority of learning goals. Of course, many contexts, both public education and training environments, have long-term goals that learners become competent as self-regulated, lifelong learners. However, many educators suggest that this capability is acquired over time and is not an inherent ability of learners.

SOCIAL CONSTRUCTIVISM.   One key assumption follows:

- Learning is collaborative with meaning negotiated from multiple perspectives.

Some constructivists do not ascribe to this more social interpretation of constructivism. Others find it absolutely central to their philosophy. Some radical constructivists suggest that on all subjects all perspectives are equally viable and should take equal weight in the negotiation of meaning. More moderate constructivists would propose that the universality of the nature of "truth" varies by topic and subject matter. They would suggest that for some topics there is a general "truth for now" that has been negotiated and agreed upon by experts in the field (e.g., the Earth revolves around the sun, not the sun around the Earth). Although this "truth" may be amended or replaced when more knowledge is acquired, it is not legitimately "multiperspectived" now. Such constructivists would agree that there are topics (e.g., Was the engagement of the North Vietnamese in war an appropriate response by the United States?) in which "rules of evidence" (that is, how can we judge what is "true") (DeVaney, 1990) are quite varied depending upon the perspective, culture, or context and that it would be inappropriate to suggest that one "truth" is more viable than another.

Some educators interpret this assumption to mean that all learning should occur in collaborative work groups. An alternate perspective of the social constructivism tenet might be that whether learning occurs in work groups, in a group discussion, or in an individual interaction with a text, there is some sense of collaboration in that the individuals involved are working toward agreement, or at least understanding. Such constructivists might suggest that there is collaboration in negotiating meaning as learners interact individually with the text of a book or video because the learner is wholeheartedly engaged in trying to interpret the author's perspective and compare it to his own. As well, the author's efforts, although displaced in time, are equally a struggle to find a common ground with readers.

Certainly, many instructional designers would propose that collaborative learning groups are part of a powerful instructional strategy. Many designers would also concur that learning to apply the standards of viability for ideas, how these standards have changed over time, and what issues can and cannot be subjected to these standards within a particular field are excellent learning goals in many contexts.

CONTEXTUALISM.   The key assumptions of contextualism are the following:

- Learning should occur (or be "situated") in realistic settings.
- Testing should be integrated into the task, not a separate activity.

Not all constructivists would include contextualism as part of their basic philosophy. However, many constructivists do endorse the above tenets. Contextualists propose that thinking is inextricably tied to the real-life contexts to which it is applied. Educators frequently refer to the learning that is related to a context as "situated cognition" (Brown, Collins, & Duguid, 1989; Henning, 2004). Contextualists recommend presenting problems in situations that are realistic to learners and common to everyday applications of knowledge. This type of learning is termed "authentic learning," and the instruction related to the learning situation as "anchored instruction" (that is, instruction "anchored" in a realistic problem situation) (Cognition and Technology Group, 1990; Streibel, 1995). Some contextualists suggest that certain types of problems should not be simplified for novice learners but should be presented in their full complexity early in the learning process so as to not give learners the false impression that such problems are simple and easily solved (Spiro, Feltovich, Jacobson, & Coulson, 1992). Numerous scholars in the field of instructional design have suggested how the concepts of situated cognition may apply to the design of mediated instruction, resulting in applications such as learning environment, microworlds, phenomenaria, and construction sets (e.g., Choi & Hannafin, 1995; Rieber, 1992, 2004; Wilson, 1996).

The second constructivist assumption that can be attributed to contextualism is that assessment should be "authentic." Swanson, Norman, and Linn (1995) proposed that authentic assessment is synonymous with "performance assessment," defining performance assessment as "testing complex, 'higher order' knowledge and skills in the real-world context in which they are actually used, generally with open-ended tasks that require substantial examinee time to complete" (p. 5). Authentic assessment is generally integrated in a seamless manner with learning activities, not as a separate event. Some constructivists would caution that although it is important that learners perceive assessment to be part of the process of learning, initial activities, or initial tries at solving a type of problem, should be considered "practice," which along with feedback would take place during the initial phases of learning. They would propose that all assessments are indicators of learning at some point in the learning process, but a more accurate reflection of what learners have learned can be obtained *after* some initial opportunities to process both practice and feedback. A sample of additional resources on these and other aspects of contextualism and ecological psychology may be found in Allen, Otto, and Hoffman (2004); Barab, Evans, and Baek (2004); and Young, (2004).

CONTRIBUTIONS AND LIMITATIONS OF CONSTRUCTIVISM.
Constructivists both within and outside of the field of instructional design have made what we consider to be substantial contributions to instructional psychology and instructional design. Tenets of constructivism encourage instructional designers to increase the care of their consideration of the intentionality of the learners. Constructivists also point out the perspectives that learners bring to the learning situation that may extend beyond what designers typically consider to be "specific prior knowledge." Constructivism suggests to educators new goals to consider: recognition of the tentative nature of knowledge, of understanding the importance of considering multiple perspectives on issues, and of the rules within a subject matter for determining what represents a viable interpretation in a field and what does not. In addition, designers in the spirit of constructivism have developed creative strategies that utilize technology in significant ways, expanding the instructional strategy options that designers might consider. We tend to agree with Cobb's (1996) conclusions regarding three major instructional implications of constructivism:

> (a) Priority should be given to the development of meaning and understanding rather than the training of behavior, (b) researchers and teachers should assume that students' actions are rational given the way that they currently make sense of things, and (c) students' errors and unanticipated responses should be viewed as occasions to learn about students' understanding. (p. 56)

Constructivism as it is currently and generally conceptualized is far from providing an adequate single basis from which instructional designers can operate. Indeed, there are educational scholars who suggest that constructivism has no implications at all for instruction (e.g., Gruender, 1996). Constructivism is frequently presented as a theory, but we concur with a number of scholars that it is an educational philosophy that particularly addresses epistemology. Indeed, constructivism has very little to offer as a theory that explains the processes that occur in the cognition that accompanies

learning. Many constructivists reject the explanations of learning cognitions offered by information processing theory, but as yet, they have not proposed a substitute theory. Some constructivists' concentration on the relationship of perception, action, and the environment might put them closer to behaviorism than would make them comfortable (Anderson, 2000).

One potential danger of the misinterpretation of constructivism is a reinforcement of a perennial problem in education, slipping into the "activity for activity's sake" mode. This problem is represented by the belief that if learners are engaged and enthusiastic, then they must be learning. There are, of course, occasions when engagement and enthusiasm are accompanied by only trivial learning. For example, we observed a class in which the learners in a high school Latin class had been enthusiastically engaged for two weeks in building a salt sculpture of Pompeii. Unmistakably, the teacher expected that learners would learn about the Pompeii culture. When I queried a learner about what he had learned during the two weeks, he replied that he had learned that the salt will crack if you don't put enough water in it. (This anecdote is reminiscent of the research findings regarding some "instructional" computer games in which all the learners learned were the rules of the game.)

Research suggests that too often teachers think first of designing activities during instructional planning (Bullough, 1987; Clark & Peterson, 1986; McCutcheon, 1980). Although many teachers simultaneously consider goals, it is also not uncommon for the goal to become lost from the activity (Brophy & Alleman, 1991). Dewey, who can be considered a forefather of constructivism, recognized this potential for interpretation of his own philosophy (Prawat & Floden, 1994). With radical constructivists' reluctance to identify goals and the activity-oriented perspective of constructivism, there is clearly the potential for educators to erroneously claim constructivism as providing theoretical support for activities that have questionable value.

By far the greatest danger that we perceive regarding constructivism is that practitioners in our own field will be persuaded by extreme positions to eliminate from their practice some of the most singular and beneficial tools of instructional design. For example, some constructivists would recommend the elimination of statements of goals and objectives. Of course, untold harm has been done by educators writing goals and objectives to describe relatively trivial learning and failing to express the difficult-to-portray goals and objectives that reflect higher-order thinking, such as problem solving. However, goals and objectives do not lead to trivial and low-level learning; low-level goals do. With effort, learning goals can represent the high-level goals that constructivists advocate. Some constructivists advocate the elimination of task analysis and the identification of prerequisite learning, suggesting that they lead to piecemeal and inert knowledge. Of course, it is how these task and prerequisite analyses are used that can lead to disconnected learning, not the tools themselves. Certainly there are occasions that the degree of precision with which these tools are used may be less or more (Wedman & Tessmer, 1990); however, this does not suggest that the tools should not be in an instructional designer's repertoire. Dunn (1994) suggested that the tools of objectives, learning analysis, and evaluation are instructional design tools that would allow constructivist designers to meet their goals of higher-order learning more effectively.

Empiricism

A second philosophical tradition is empiricism, sometimes termed *objectivism,* and it postulates that knowledge is acquired through experience. Most empiricists would propose that this experience allows an individual to come to know a reality that is objective and singular. That is, most experience is defined as sensory experience, as opposed to any "experience" that one might obtain through a "mental life" of reconceptualization and interpretation. Empiricism is also often typified by "reductionism," efforts to reduce complex entities to their more simple components, and "associationism," a tendency to relate ideas if they are experienced contiguously in either space or time. John Locke (1690) is often identified as a major empiricist philosopher. Locke is well-known for his belief that little, if any, knowledge or ability comes "wired" in an individual. Not all empiricists would agree with this perspective.

Some scholars would label any educational approach that employs experimentation and seeks to draw generalizations based upon data as empiricist. However, empiricists may also subscribe to other tenets, such as a belief in a singular and objective reality, the devaluing of mental experience, and the *tabula rasa* (blank slate) perspective of Locke (e.g., Driscoll, 1994). We would agree that a valuing of experimentation and generalization are clearly qualities of empiricists, but various scholars in the empiricist tradition reflect a wide range of beliefs about reality, the mind, and inherent qualities.

Pragmatism

Pragmatism might be considered a "middle ground" between rationalism (constructivism) and empiricism (Driscoll, 1994). Although pragmatists, like empiricists, believe that knowledge is acquired through experience, they believe that this knowledge is interpreted through reason and is temporary and tentative. Most pragmatists are not too concerned with whether there is a common reality, such as general principles of learning that are "out there" to be discovered. Pragmatists propose that the question of whether there is a "real" reality is an unproductive question, since, if there is a reality, it can never be totally known. When faced with the issue of reality, pragmatists "would simply like to change the subject" (Rorty, 1982, p. xiv). Pragmatists suggest that knowledge in a particular field is negotiated based upon an agreement of experts as to a common interpretation of experience. They would describe knowledge in terms of "truth for now." Pragmatists propose that knowledge is built up by testing this "truth for now" hypothesis and revising or discarding this "truth" as common experience and interpretation implies it should be modified.

The noted educational philosopher John Dewey (1924) was a pragmatist. Leahey and Harris (1989) state that the majority of psychologists are pragmatists. It is our belief that most instructional designers are pragmatists. We would categorize ourselves, personally, as pragmatists, with beliefs that are also consistent with moderate constructivism. We also share with empiricists a valuing of testing knowledge through the accumulation of data, and a belief that there are some generalizable principles of learning that can be "discovered."

Assumptions Underlying Instructional Design

A number of assumptions underlie the process of instructional design. Novice designers should encounter these assumptions in an explicitly stated form. Although they may not totally agree with the assumptions (and often design excellent instruction without this agreement), novice designers can find the design process more meaningful when these assumptions are made explicit. Following are some of the most critical assumptions:

1. To design instruction, the designer must have a clear idea of what the learner should learn as a result of the instruction.
2. The "best" instruction is that which is effective (facilitates learners' acquisition of the identified knowledge and skills), efficient (requires the least possible amount of time necessary for learners to achieve the goals), and appealing (motivates and interests learners, encouraging them to persevere in the learning task).
3. Students may learn from many different media; a "live teacher" is not always essential for instruction.
4. There are principles of instruction that apply across all age groups and all content areas. For example, students must participate actively, interacting mentally as well as physically with material to be learned.

5. Evaluation should include the evaluation of the instruction as well as the evaluation of the learner's performance. Information from the evaluation of instruction should be used to revise the instruction in order to make it more efficient, effective, and appealing.

6. When the purpose of assessment is to determine whether learners have achieved learning goals, the learners should be evaluated in terms of how nearly they achieve those instructional goals rather than how they "stack up" against their fellow students.

7. There should be a congruence among goals, learning activities, and assessment. Along with learners' characteristics and learning context, learning goals should be the driving force behind decisions about activities and assessment.

These assumptions will be alluded to and further explained throughout this text.

WHAT IS A THEORY?

A theory is an organized set of statements that allow us to explain, predict, or control events. The theories from which instructional design draws are of two kinds: descriptive theory and prescriptive theory. **Descriptive theory** describes phenomena as they are hypothesized to exist. Many learning theories are descriptive: They describe how learning occurs. **Prescriptive theories** prescribe actions to take that will lead to certain results. Instructional theories are basically prescriptive in nature: They suggest that if instruction includes certain features, it will lead to certain types and amounts of learning.

The term "theory" is often misused in popular culture. Characters on television detective thriller programs are quite prone to say that they have a "theory" about who committed the crime when they mean to say that they have a "hypothesis" or "supposition." This frequent misuse of the term, as well as some unfortunate arguments on the theory of evolution from a certain religious perspective, contributes to the widespread impression that theories are made up of casual conjectures, when the very opposite is the case.

MAJOR THEORY BASES CONTRIBUTING TO INSTRUCTIONAL DESIGN

Instructional design has drawn from many theory bases. However, the major contributions have been communication theory, systems theory, theories of learning, and theories of instruction. Although general systems theory and communication theory have had a substantial impact on the development of the procedures of instructional design and development, it is learning and instructional theory that continue to have the most substantial influence on the principles of instructional design. Therefore, we will limit our review of communication and systems theories to a brief discussion and deal in greater detail with learning and instructional theories. We recommend that instructional designers become familiar with their historical roots in systems theory and communication theories, and we recommend Richey's (1986) review of the contribution of these two theory bases on instructional design models.

Communication Theory

Two groundbreaking works by communication theorists have a deep foundational relationship to instructional design, both developed in the 1940s. One was Shannon and Weaver's *A Mathematical Theory of Communication* (1949), which was the first successful approach to the quantification and hence measurement of information, including a model which is so familiar now that it seems part of our cultural heritage (see Figure 2.1); the other was Norbert Weiner's work on feedback control, popularly published in *The Human Use of Human Beings* (1969). Weiner coined the term "cybernetics" (the science of feedback control). These two books were intended for nonspecialist audiences and are English-language translations of primarily mathematical work. Both are mechanistic and transmission-centered, but from these two lines of work

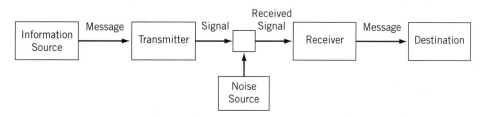

Figure 2.1 Shannon & Weaver General Model of Communication

have come concepts that it would be hard to do without, such as entropy, feedback, and noise.

Approaches to the study of communication from process-centered and meaning-based standpoints can be illustrated by work by Wilbur Schramm and others in interpersonal communication, mass communication, and the orientations of general semantics and semiotics.

The study of interpersonal and mass communication has provided concepts and models that have a foundational influence on instructional design thinking. For example, Schramm's (1956) model of interpersonal communication emphasizes a dialogic process, in which what is feedback and what is the "message" is more or less arbitrary. Looking at the illustration provided in Figure 2.2, hold your book upside-down and notice that the "receiver" and the "sender" are nominal. Either person is a sender, depending on how you view it. In the model, we have added the term "Construct Meaning" to "Interpret" in congruence with current popular views without changing the original meaning of the model substantially.

General semantics is the study of how language impacts our thinking, especially how language habits support irrational, neurotic, or imprecise thinking (Lee, 1941; Hayakawa, 1953) This interdisciplinary body of thought was originated by Alfred Korzybski, the seminal work being *Science and Sanity: An Introduction to Non-Aristotelian Systems and General Semantics* in 1933 (Korzybski, 1973), available online at http://www.esgs.org/uk/art/sands.htm.

The fundamental concepts of general semantics rest on a general principle: that even though our language use makes it appear otherwise, no two events over time are the same. Techniques such as dating are recommended to lend precision to thinking as well as language. Tim[1973] helps underscore the idea that Tim[2004] is not the same as he once was. In addition to the dating technique, common general semantics concepts are: The map is not the same as the territory; words do not contain their definitions but have meaning only by social agreement; habitual use of "etc." as a reminder that what is said is not all there is to something; and mental indexing as a reminder of multiple values and the multidimensional nature of reality (ID_1, ID_2, ID_3, ID_4, etc.).

Although the pursuit of objectivity inherent in general semantics may smack of 1950s modernism in a world of postmodern thought, a great deal of what is currently revered in educational theory has unacknowledged roots in general semantics.

Systems Theory

Systems thinking and general systems theory have had an often misunderstood influence on instructional design. The origins of the interdisciplinary body of thought called "general systems theory" can be traced to Ludwig von Bertalanffy, whose work in the 1930s on unifying separate disciplines in the study of biology led to a general theory of the interrelated and dynamic qualities of open systems. Although the term "systems" is often associated with the idea of being systematic and the use of systems tools such as PERT, Gantt, and flowcharts, the heart of systems thinking is an urge to see the big picture. Chaos theory is often characterized as a polar opposite to the somewhat older systems theory, but the two differ not so much in kind as degree, with chaos theory emphasizing and illustrating the complex depths to which relatedness can go.

A system is often defined as a "set of interrelated and interacting parts that work together toward some common goal." Systems exist naturally, such as the human body, the solar system, and the atom. Systems are also contrived, as in human-made systems, such as a business organization, the heating–cooling unit of a house, and a school system. Systems are thought of as existing within systems. The larger system of which the system under study is a part is called the "supra-system." The elements of the system under study, which themselves are systems, are called "subsystems." Each subsystem serves a purpose and is viewed as interdependent upon each other subsystem. Therefore, a change in one component will cause a change in its interdependent components.

Most instructional design approaches have a "systematic" quality to one degree or another. The care and attention which is associated with instructional design, as well as the general form of most models, suggest a systematic approach. Attention to context and appropriate evaluation (see Chapters 3 and 19) lend a systemic quality as well. In Andrews and Goodson's (1980) article reviewing models of instructional design, 70 percent of the models employed some elements of systems theory. Gustsafson and Branch (1997) have performed a wider analysis from an instructional development standpoint. Their survey is extremely helpful in gaining a grasp of the nature of the major approaches to instructional development.

Although any form of instruction may be viewed from a systems perspective, we are convinced that distance education is one which needs a systems view in

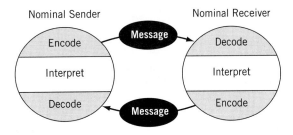

Figure 2.2   An Adaptation of Schramm's Communication Process Model

order to operate successfully. In that context, we highly recommend Moore and Kearsley's, (1996) discussion of distance education from a systems perspective. Banathy (1992, 2004) and Kaufman (2000) are a sample of additional resources in systems thinking applied to education.

Learning Theories

Promoting cognitive processes that lead to learning is what instructional design is all about. Therefore, instructional designers are very interested in learning theories, those theories that attempt to describe, explain, and predict learning. It is probably helpful at this point to define what is commonly meant by **learning:** R. Gagné defined learning as a "change in human disposition or capability that persists over a period of time and is not simply ascribable to processes of growth" (1985, p. 2). Mayer (1982) elaborated on this concept in his definition of learning:

> "Learning" is the relatively permanent change in a person's knowledge or behavior due to experience. This definition has three components: (1) the duration of the change is long-term rather than short-term; (2) the locus of the change is the content and structure of knowledge in memory or the behavior of the learner; (3) the cause of the change is the learner's experience in the environment rather than fatigue, motivation, drugs, physical condition, or physiological intervention. (p. 1040)

According to this definition, has a person who has successfully followed the directions for assembling a backyard swing set learned something? Not necessarily. The individual may have simply performed each step without trying to remember or understand any aspects of the process. There may be no lasting change in the individual's memory, nor change in ability to assemble objects in the future. In such a case, we would say that learning has *not* occurred. Conversely, the individual may have acquired a new understanding of how certain types of pieces fit together, new knowledge in selecting an appropriate tool for a particular task, or new ability to manipulate a tool. In such a case, we would say that learning *has* occurred. We may see evidence of this learning in the individual's ability to perform future assembly tasks more rapidly or with more aptitude.

As you recall from a previous discussion in this chapter, learning theories are chiefly descriptive. They describe how learning takes place. They are not necessarily prescriptive (i.e., they do not directly suggest what kinds of instructional intervention should support learning). Two major categories of learning theory that have influenced instructional design procedures and decisions are behavioral learning theories and cognitive learning theories.

BEHAVIORISM.   The predominant school of thought in learning theory for the first half of the twentieth century has been labeled *behaviorism.* Behaviorists usually subscribed to an educational philosophy of extreme empiricism. The behaviorist view of psychology had its beginnings in the late nineteenth century and in the first decade of this century with Ivan Pavlov's (1927) "classical conditioning." Other important research includes E. L. Thorndike's (1913) work that culminated in his "laws of learning" and J. B. Watson's (1913) articulation and formation of the behaviorist movement. B. F. Skinner's work on "operant conditioning" in the 1940s and 50s marked the maturation of the movement. Although some research on learning was being pursued from perspectives other than behaviorism during this time, the dominance of the behaviorist view, particularly in the United States, was almost complete during the first half of this century.

The behaviorist view held that the only things about human learning worth studying are those that can be observed. Although most behaviorists did not deny the existence of mental activity, they did not conjecture about these thinking processes, mental states, and other unobservable phenomena. Rather, they concentrated on the observable *behavior* of organisms. At first, it may appear that a behaviorist view would be so limiting as to make it absurd. However, even though our current interests go beyond the strict limitations of the behaviorists, the behaviorist view has spawned the research and theory of many important phenomena of learning.

Behavioral theory emphasized the influence of the environment on learning. According to behaviorism, learning has occurred when learners evidence the appropriate response to a particular stimulus. How this connection or association between stimulus and response is developed is the major explanation that characterizes behavioral theory. Later behavioral theories, particularly that of Skinner's operant conditioning, explained the development of this association as the result of learners receiving the appropriate reinforcement when the appropriate response is given to a particular stimulus.

The principles of behaviorism in terms of classical and operant conditioning, specifically the influence of reinforcers in building stimulus-response associations, have relatively no influence on instructional design practice today. (This assertion is also supported by Case and Bereiter, 1984.) However, some of the applications of behaviorism, such as programmed instruction, have had a lasting impact. Although programmed instruction did not revolutionize education as many thought it would, its legacy has been significant. Innovations that were a part of programmed instruction include recognition that effective nonhuman mediated instruction could be developed and that evaluation and revision of the materials through an empirical test of their effects could improve the effectiveness of instruction. As you can see from the key assumptions of instructional design listed earlier in this chapter, these two ideas are major building blocks in the principles of instructional design. They have had an enormous impact on the design of quality instruction for education and training contexts.

Often, instructional designers and other educators point to behaviorism as the source for the practice of writing explicit objectives. This attribution seems to be inaccurate. The origin of instructional objectives appears to be Herbert Spencer, a curriculum developer who lived in the middle of the nineteenth century. Davies (1976) traced the idea of specific objectives to well before the rise of behaviorism. The term "behavioral objectives" has less link to behaviorism than it does to relatively atheoretical curriculum development. Objectives and some goals developed by instructional designers may continue to have forms that are reminiscent of behaviorism. However, the rationale for current instructional designers writing objectives that reflect action is not on the same basis as the behaviorists (disinterest in cognitive activities or processes such as understanding) but is from an attempt to gain "best evidence" of cognitive processes and states that cannot be directly perceived or recorded. (For all of that, we have expunged the term "behavioral objective" from our vocabulary, to the extent possible, and have substituted such terms as "learning objective" wherever possible, and more importantly, recommend in following chapters that you approach the writing of learning goals and objectives from a standpoint that is considerably less rule-bound in format than the behavioral objectives tradition has emphasized.)

COGNITIVE LEARNING THEORIES. Currently, cognitive learning theories are the dominant theoretical influence on instructional design practice. Cognitive learning theory has generally corresponded to a rationalist philosophy and frequently appears compatible with the central tenets of constructivism. Cognitive learning theory places much more emphasis on factors within the learner and less emphasis on factors within the environment than behavioral theories. Schuell (1986) credits five major ways that cognitive psychology has influenced learning theory:

(a) the view of learning as an active, constructive process; (b) the presence of high-level processes in learning; (c) the cumulative nature of learning and the corresponding role

played by prior knowledge; (d) concern for the way knowledge is represented and organized in memory; and (e) concern for analyzing learning tasks and performance in terms of the cognitive processes that are involved. (p. 415)

Clearly, cognitive learning theory focuses on explaining the development of cognitive structures, processes, and representations that mediate between instruction and learning. In attending to these structures and processes, the role of the learner as an active participant in the learning process takes on great importance. The learner is viewed as constructing meaning from instruction, rather than being a recipient of meaning residing alone within instruction (a perspective that is very compatible with a constructivist philosophy). Therefore, cognitive learning theories attempt to explain learning in terms of cognitive processes, structures, and representations that are hypothesized to operate within the learner. Anderson (2000), Greeno, Colllins, and Resnick (1996), Haberlandt (1997), and Winn (2004) are samples of additional resources in cognitive psychology, with Winn's work written specifically for instructional design and technology audiences.

INFORMATION-PROCESSING THEORY. One of the most influential contributions from cognitive learning theory to instructional design practice is information-processing theory. Most current cognitive learning theorists advocate a theory (actually a set of theories) called *information processing.* **Information-processing theories,** in strong contrast to behavioral theories, describe learning as a series of transformations of information (i.e., processing) through a series of postulated structures within the brain. These structures currently are merely hypothesized and utilized to explain learning processes. To date, brain research has not identified specific locations of these particular structures, nor have information-processing theorists ever considered them in a physical sense. One of the most influential information processing theories is the conceptualization of "Multi-Store Models." These models explain learning as a series of transformations of information through several types of storage or memory. Atkinson and Shiffrin (1968) were the first to model a Multi-Store Model. R. Gagné's (1974) elaboration of this model illustrates the structures and processes of information processing (see Figure 2.3).

Two other influential information-processing theories, Schema theory (Rummelhart, 1980) and Level of Processing theory (Craik & Lockhart, 1972) were originally posited as alternatives to Multi-Store theory. However, in recent years they have been viewed more as theories that are compatible with Multi-Store theory and capable of explaining subprocesses or structures

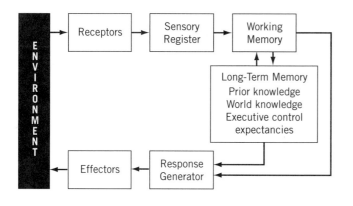

Figure 2.3 An Information Processing Model of Learning and Memory

within it. In the following section, we will briefly summarize these theories, but we encourage you to read more complete descriptions, such as those texts suggested earlier in this chapter.

Sensory Register and Selective Perception.   We receive information from our environment through our sensory receptors, our senses. The sensations are converted to electrochemical messages and sent to the brain where these impulses are stored very briefly (approximately one quarter of a second for visual images [Sperling, 1960], slightly longer for auditory information) in a structure, or a cluster of structures, labeled the **sensory register.** Perceptions of many environmental stimuli enter this register, but very few receive the attention, sometimes termed **selective perception,** to be further processed within the brain. The unattended stimuli receive no further consideration. Without such a process, we would be overwhelmed by the multitude of environmental stimuli we encounter in every instant. Our prior experience, including our expectancies, values, and beliefs, influence the stimuli to which we attend. For example, you may have noticed how easily you overhear your own name in a conversation at a party, or how easily you can find your name in an extensive list.

Working Memory.   Information to which attention has been paid passes into a structure called **working memory,** sometimes equated with an older concept called *short-term memory.* Working memory has been likened to a desktop or workbench, which is where everything actually happens but which can only hold a finite amount on its surface. Working memory is also similar to the RAM memory of a computer, which is certainly limited in size, but within which everything must at least momentarily reside to be processed.

Working memory and other structures hypothesized by information theory are increasingly seen as dynamic and flexible entities, the qualities of which are seen in interaction with factors such as development and expertise (Case, 1993; Kantowitz, 1987).

Under traditional information-processing theory, working memory is characterized by its limited capacity, in terms of amount of information that it can retain (seven plus or minus two units of information [Miller, 1956]), and its short duration, in terms of the limited amount of time that information can be retained there (10 seconds [Murdock, 1961] to 20 seconds [R. Gagné, 1985]). As you can see from the bidirectional arrows in Figure 2.3, there is continuous transfer of information between long-term and working memory. Information is brought out of long-term memory into working memory (retrieval) in order to make sense out of new, incoming information. This activity is controlled by executive control processes. Not all information that enters working memory is transferred to long-term memory. We have all experienced such a dropout of information when we have retained a phone number only long enough to be able to redial it. We can keep that information in working memory longer than 10 to 20 seconds by rehearsing or repeating it. However, such a process would be an impossible method to retain all the information we need. Therefore, information that we remember for more than a short period of time is transferred, or encoded, into long-term memory.

Encoding and Long-Term Memory.   Transfer of information into **long-term memory,** memory that provides long-term storage of information transferred from working memory, is the most critical process of all the information processing to those who are interested in learning. A critical characteristic of information that is stored in long-term memory is that it must be meaningful. It is very difficult to store nonmeaningful information in long-term memory. In order for information to be meaningful, it must be integrated with related prior knowledge (i.e., information that is already stored in long-term memory). We can store fairly nonsensical information in long-term memory if we artificially make it meaningful. For example, we can remember a phone number by making it meaningful. A number like 799-2779 can be remembered by noticing the relationship of the numbers 7, 2, and 9, with the repetition of the nines in the first set of numbers and the sevens in the second set. Likewise, we may try to "learn" (store in long-term memory, or LTM) someone's name by connecting it with the interests or physical appearance of the person.

The more effortful this meaning-making is (that is, the more "elaboration" we make of the contents of LTM), the more likely it is that this information will be remembered. Craik and Lockhart (1972) suggested that the more "deeply" information is processed, the more likely it is to be remembered. Deep processing involves considering information at the meaningful or "semantic" level, whereas shallow processing involves considering only the surface features or stimulus features of the information. They suggested that deep processing strengthens the memory trace in long-term memory (much as exercise strengthens a muscle). The effects of semantic elaboration are often explained in a different manner by theorists who suggest that it leads to more connections to more information in long-term memory, thus creating more possible paths to the stored information.

Organization is also a critical characteristic of long-term memory. Most theorists suggest that information is stored in nonrandom patterns. They generally conjecture that information is represented within memory in networks of propositions, ideas, or concepts that are connected with relationships (Anderson & Bower, 1973; Kintsch, 1974). The richness of these relationships and the adequacy of the organization will influence how available the stored information is for retrieval and use. In addition, some theorists believe that images may be stored as images in long-term memory (Paivio, 1971). There are many other theories that propose how knowledge is represented in long-term memory.

In addition to network-based representations, some scholars suggest a specific type of propositional networks termed *schemata* (the singular is *schema*). **Schemata** are data structures that represent the generic concepts, such as "face," "restaurant," and "burglary," that are stored in memory and have "slots" that are filled with information related to a specific situation (Rummelhart, 1980). Other scholars propose another type of memory representation termed *mental model.* **Mental models** are similar to schemata but in addition to the concepts and their relationships that are stored in schema, mental models contain information about task demands and task performances that are used for problem solving. Theorists suggest that learners use a mental model representation to store information regarding how machines work or how situations are organized. Cognitive theorists, such as Anderson (2000), suggest that a different type of knowledge (i.e., procedural knowledge) is stored and represented in a form quite different from propositions. They theorize that procedural knowledge is stored in a *production,* an IF-THEN statement that connects conditions (in the IF part of the production) with actions (in the THEN part of the production). (We will provide a lot of examples of these productions in Chapter 5 and later chapters that discuss intellectual skills.)

In recent years, **connectionism** has attempted to describe how thinking might occur at the neuron level without permanent memory representations. According to Parallel Distributed Processing theory (McClelland & Rummelhart, 1988), information is represented in patterns of activation among neural elements. These basic elements are nodes that are subsymbolic; that is, they alone do not constitute a concept or rule. It is the pattern of activation among neurons that creates meaningful constructs, such as concepts and principles. Input from the environment activates the connections among nodes, making some links stronger and others weaker. So some links have stronger weights than others. (This concept of "weight of memory link" is reminiscent of the "strength of a memory trace" described earlier in the discussion of Levels of Processing.) Bereiter (1991) pointed out that according to theory, all knowledge resides in weights themselves.

A third characteristic of long-term memory is its relatively unlimited capacity and permanency. Unlike working memory, long-term memory's capacity is theoretically open-ended, and its duration may last a lifetime. While in learning we may experience a feeling of being "overloaded," this is caused by the overloading of working memory or a difficulty in retrieving relevant prior knowledge with which to integrate it, rather than a saturation of long-term memory. While we may be unable to retrieve information stored in long-term memory, it may not be lost from memory, but rather the cues or strategies we are using are inappropriate. We have all experienced the inability to retrieve a person's name on one occasion, only to find that we could retrieve it on a later occasion.

Information related to particular subject matter or experiences is stored in long-term memory. In addition, executive control strategies, which are cognitive or learning strategies that influence how we manipulate information, are stored in long-term memory. Also, affective memories, including expectancies regarding learning experiences, are stored there. All of these memories influence the stages of information processing. For example, our prior knowledge of a particular content, our expectancies regarding the goal and relevance of a lesson, and the strategies that we have learned to use in approaching a particular content all influence that which we choose to "selectively attend to" in a lesson on that particular content.

Retrieval and Response Generator. As we described earlier, memories of relevant information are retrieved from long-term memory into working memory to allow us to understand incoming information and in order to integrate the new information with the old. In some cases, this information is simply re-coded in its enriched form and restored in long-term memory. In other cases, in addition to this re-coding and storage, people may act upon the information by speaking or writing an answer, manipulating objects, or any of a number of other physical responses. The form, organization, and sequence of the response is determined by the response generator. This information is sent to the effectors, muscles, nerves, and glands, which in turn act and affect the environment.

A number of theorists have elaborated and expanded upon the processes and structures in information processing, particularly as they apply to learning. In contrast to the gestalt psychologists who primarily concerned themselves with the initial stages of information processing, recent cognitive learning theorists have concentrated primarily upon the later stages of information processing. Specifically, they have conjectured upon the structures and processes surrounding encoding information into long-term memory from working memory and retrieval of information from long-term memory into working memory.

INFLUENCE OF COGNITIVE PSYCHOLOGY ON INSTRUCTIONAL DESIGN.   We will now briefly review how each of the phases of design (analysis, strategy development, and evaluation) is affected by cognitive psychology.

The analysis phase involves analysis of the learner, the task, and the context. What is included in the analysis of the learner and the task has been influenced by cognitive psychology. The analysis of the context is much more strongly influenced by systems theory and by sociological theories, such as principles regarding the dissemination and diffusion of innovations.

As you might expect, with the shift from behavioral to cognitive theory bases, the attention given to the analysis of the learner has grown. The learner plays a constructive role according to cognitive theory. Therefore, in order to provide learners with instruction from which they can build, designers must acquire knowledge about the learners' prior knowledge and the organization of that knowledge. In addition, knowledge of the learners' general aptitudes in terms of processing skills is becoming increasingly sought by designers. As you will see in Chapter 4, designers also draw from cognitive and social development theories for other learner characteristics, such as attitudes, motivations, attributions, and interests that should be analyzed because of their strong influence on learning.

One of the points at which cognitive psychology has had its strongest influence is in the way that a learning task is analyzed. In the past, a task was analyzed by noting the observable behaviors that had to be completed to do a particular task. This procedure has been greatly enriched and supplemented by attention to the mental tasks required in order to perform the observable tasks. This type of analysis is called an *information-processing analysis* or a *cognitive task analysis*. Some designers may even analyze the difference between the

ways novices and various levels of experts complete mental and physical tasks in order to understand the levels of expertise that can be learned. This emphasis on the cognitive, as well as the performance aspects of the task is reflected in the types of goals and objectives that are developed. Attention is given within objectives to tapping the "understanding" underlying a performance.* For example, it is not uncommon to find objectives that ask learners to explain the reasoning processes behind their performance.

Development of instructional strategy is the area in which cognitive psychology, including gestalt psychology and cognitive load theory, has its greatest influence. Instructional designers draw upon the conclusions of cognitive psychologists' research to infer principles for design. Cognitive load theory has provided a research basis for the identification of "bottlenecks" which can interfere with the effectiveness of learning environments along with ways of reducing cognitive load when needed (e.g., Mayer & Moreno, 2003; Renkl & Atkinson, 2003). In addition, designers draw upon theories themselves to infer instructional treatments that may support particular learning outcomes. Gestalt psychology influences in this fashion the techniques used in instructional message display (the way information is arranged on a page or screen). The chapters on strategy development in this text contain many references to these influential bodies of research and theory.

The two aspects of evaluation—evaluation of the learners' performance and evaluation of the instruction—are both influenced by cognitive psychology. For example, evaluation may include test forms that solicit information on the learners' reasoning, in congruence with objectives that reflect an interest in the learners' acquiring understanding. Evaluation of instruction, particularly of instruction that includes materials, may include the use of techniques such as "read-think-aloud" protocols (Smith & Wedman, 1988) in formative evaluation. This procedure allows the designer to obtain information about the internal processing of learners as they interact with the instruction.

We have merely described a few of the influences that cognitive psychology has had and continues to have on instructional design practice. For a more comprehensive review, we suggest that you review articles by Bonner (1988), Di Vesta and Rieber (1987), Low (1981), Richey (2000), and Wildman (1981).

---

*A forceful argument on the importance of "understanding" is provided by Bereiter (2002). His discussion of declarative knowledge (pp. 133–138) and of concepts (pp. 306–318) provides examples of learning goals that are typically misapprehended by failure to appreciate and describe the understanding which underlies significant learning that is too frequently trivialized in educational practice.

Developmental Theories

Until recent years, many instructional designers have made little use of theories of cognitive development. With the popularization of such theories by constructivists, instructional designers may reconsider whether principles within these theories have application to our field.

PIAGET.   One of the most influential development theories is Piaget's theory (Piaget & Inhelder, 1969) of cognitive development. Many educators are familiar with his stage theory of development, which proposes four distinct stages through which all humans proceed in a fixed order. Each stage is identified with the emergence of new cognitive abilities. These cognitive abilities require a reorganization of a learner's cognitive structure. (These stages of cognitive development are described in Chapter 4, Analyzing the Learner.)

Piaget proposed that (a) the sequence of stages is invariant and nonreversible; (b) learners cannot be taught key cognitive tasks until they reach a particular stage of development; (c) stages represent qualitative changes in cognition; (d) children exhibit the characteristics of each stage; and (e) global restructuring characterizes the shift from stage to stage, cutting across all domains of learning. Research (reported in Berk, 1994; Driscoll, 1994; Slavin, 1994) suggests that these stages are not invariant, that instruction can assist learners to achieve cognitive tasks beyond their current stage, that learners do revert to earlier stages of cognition, and that stages are not global across domains (i.e., learners may operate at different stages, perhaps because of the varying prior knowledge that learners have in different domains of knowledge).

Although Piaget's stage theory is the most familiar aspect of his theory, perhaps his more long-lasting and relevant contribution is his description of the processes that lead to shifts from one cognitive stage to another. Educators today generally view these processes as an explanation of cognitive learning processes, not just those that lead to major shifts in cognitive ability. Many of these terms are common to schema theory that we discussed earlier in this chapter. The major processes suggested by Piaget are:

- *Assimilation.* Cognitive processes that can fit new learning into existing cognitive structures.
- *Accommodation.* Cognitive processes that modify existing cognitive structures based upon new information that will not "fit" into existing structures.
- *Disequilibrium.* A cognitive state of confusion, dissonance, or discomfort when new information cannot be integrated within existing structures.
- *Equilibration.* Cognitive processes that create major restructuring of knowledge to accommodate or assimilate information that caused disequilibrium.

Piaget clearly perceived that development preceded learning. In other words, learners must be cognitively "ready" before they can achieve certain kinds of tasks.

VYGOTSKY.   In contrast to Piaget, Vygotsky (1978) proposed that learning precedes development. He coined the term "zone of proximal development" to describe the type of problem-solving cognitions that are not possible for a learner independently but can be generated with the assistance ("scaffolding") of a teacher or more knowledgeable peer. Such a representation of learning and development are consistent with Vygotsky's belief in the social origins of cognitive processes.

Vygotsky's theory of development is termed a *sociocultural theory,* as he proposed that learners and their sociocultural contexts interact, assisting learners to develop cognitions that will enable them to adapt to their environments. Vygotsky also proposed that language, which is a social action, is critical to the development of higher cognitive processes. Not surprisingly, social constructivists and contextualists find Vygotsky's theory to be very compatible with their beliefs.

There is a difference in orientation between learning theory and developmental theory, a difference that is sometimes subtle and potentially confusing when one is trying to understand both perspectives. With some risk at doing injustice to the developmental perspective, it seems to us that developmentalists want to attribute all major changes in cognition to development, whereas a learning theory perspective tends to attribute major cognitive changes to cumulative learning effect, with development relating more to physical and emotional capacity factors. It may be helpful to think of these differences in perspective as illuminating, just as looking at a physical object from different standpoints can help better discern its actual shape. To think of these differences as a contest between right and wrong is less helpful. Various perspectives can be true at once; the difference may lie in which ones are the most helpful.

INFORMATION-PROCESSING DEVELOPMENTAL THEORIES. Theorists in this tradition have attempted to explain cognitive development in terms of changes to the human information-processing system. For example, Case (1993), explained Piaget's stage theory in information-processing terms. He proposed that "mental space," a concept similar to working memory, increases during development. He suggested that this increase occurs because of three processes: brain maturation and its resulting myelinization increases processing speed; cognitive strategies become automatic; and prior knowledge becomes more extensive and better organized. He suggested that Piaget's stages represented increasing demands on working memory and that transition from one Piagetian stage to another results from increased working memory rather than conceptual re-organization. A contrasting interpretation might be that instead of working memory capacity increasing, less working memory is required as this cognitive development occurs.

In contrast to Case, Siegler (1986) proposed that it is the process of encoding that distinguishes cognitive development. He observed children attempting a Piagetian-like task that involved the consideration of two variables and four principles. During his investigations, he observed that learners at a "lower" stage of development than an assigned task (requiring the manipulation of two variables and four rules that related them) tended to concentrate on only one of the task's variables and the rules related to this variable. He found that with coaching they could be encouraged to consider both variables and all four rules. He concluded that it was the learners' limited prior knowledge that inhibited their ability to use all of the features and rules necessary to solve the problem.

Contrary to Piaget, who perceived development as preceding learning, and Vygotsky, who perceived development as following learning, Case and Siegler appear to perceive learning and development as almost concurrent.

To this point, our discussion of theories of cognitive development has described cognitive development regardless of age, although some educators would view these theories as more relevant to the cognitive development of children than adults. We could locate no theories of cognitive development that were specifically targeted at adults. This may be because the primary development in adults is social and personal, as opposed to cognitive (Rice, 1995). Therefore, the major theories dealing with adult development relate to social and personal maturation, as opposed to cognitive development. These social and personal issues strongly influence adult learners' motivation and should be seriously considered by instructional designers. However, we will not discuss them in depth here.

Of course, designers who are designing for older adults should keep in mind that both sensory receptors and cognitive processes change for this audience. Sight, hearing, and tactile responses tend to show decrements in adults past the age of fifty. These senses, in addition to taste and smell, tend to decrease in acuity even more seriously for many adults in their seventies, eighties, and beyond. Although sensory and working memory do not appear to diminish with increasing age, long-term memory may be affected more seriously. Cognitive tasks that are difficult for all ages, such as remembering meaningless information and information for which one has little related prior knowledge, appear to become even more difficult for older adults (Hess & Flanagan, 1992).

CONTRIBUTIONS OF DEVELOPMENTAL THEORIES TO INSTRUCTIONAL DESIGN. Although theories of development have not had as much impact on instructional design as other cognitive theories, specific implications may affect decisions made during at least two instructional design activities. During the analysis of the learner, considering the learner's level of cognitive development may be beneficial. (We discuss this further in Chapter 4.). Also, during the development of instructional activities, designers might consider both the implications of Piagetian stages of development and the processes of cognitive development in selecting ways of organizing information and designing learning activities. In addition, designers may consider what might be described as the "zone of proximal development" of learners and the role of teachers and peers in supporting learning as they extend their ability to the level of independent performance. Finally, in keeping with Vygotsky's belief in the social nature of learning, many designers may wish to consider strategies that support the formation of a learning community.

We must now acknowledge a fundamental question that often arises in instructional design classes that include both teachers of children and trainers of adults: Are the cognitive processes of children and adults qualitatively different, or are the differences that we often see between how adults learn and how children learn more an artifact of prior learning (strategic, domain-specific, and world knowledge)? This question has not yet been answered definitely, and there are persuasive anecdotes on both sides. Our experiences suggest that a novice adult and a novice child have many similarities in processing and in instructional needs, taking into account other factors considered during learner analysis. To a degree, the research investigating the theories presented in this section tend to support this position. A factor that may play the most distinguishing role between adult and child learners is motivation. (We will discuss this issue further in Chapter 14, Strategies for Attitude Change, Motivation, and Interest.)

The next section discusses instructional theories, which have developed primarily from cognitive learning theory.

Instructional Theories

Of all theory bases, instructional theories are those that instructional designers draw from most directly. Bruner (1966) is usually credited with being the first to describe the characteristics of instructional theory. More recently, Gagné and Dick (1983) described instructional theories as follows:

> Theories of instruction attempt to relate specified events comprising instruction to learning processes and learning outcomes, drawing upon knowledge generated by learn-

ing research and theory. Often instructional theories are prescriptive in the sense that they attempt to identify conditions of instruction which will optimize learning, retention, and learning transfer. To be classified as theories, these formulations may be expected, at a minimum, to provide a rational description of causal relationships between procedures used to teach and their behavioral consequences in enhanced human performance. (p. 264)

Although none of the theories is complete for all types of learning and all kinds of learners, many of the theories do attempt to prescribe the characteristics of instruction that will support learning. These theories are quite different from learning theories that describe how learning occurs, without attention to what the learner or others might do to foster this learning. In contrast, instructional theories explicitly address which and how features of the learning environment may be developed to intentionally promote learning.

Many instructional theories will be described and used throughout the text, including Conditions Theories of Instruction—notably Gagné's Theory on Conditions of Learning, Reigeluth's Elaboration Model, Collins's Theory of Inquiry Teaching, Keller's ARCs Model of Motivation, Mayers and others Cognitive Load Theory, and a variety of theories and models labeled as the New Paradigms of Instructional Theory. However to provide an example of instructional theory, we will describe one general instruction theory—Bloom's Model of Mastery Learning.

Bloom's (1968) most influential contribution to the field of instructional design is the proposition that the "normal curve" should not be the expected model of outcomes of instruction. According to Bloom, the normal curve, with a few students learning very well, some learning well, many learning medially, some learning less well, some learning poorly, and a few learning very poorly, is what we might expect to occur *without* the intervention of instruction. It is what we would expect if students were to learn totally on their own, with aptitude (and, perhaps, perseverance) being the only factors influencing learning. However, instruction should foster learning. Its very purpose should be to support (or "scaffold") learners at points where their own native aptitudes or attitudes might infringe on learning. Hence, Bloom contends the following: "Most students (perhaps more than 90 percent) can master what we have to teach them, and it is the task of instruction to find the means which will enable them to master the subject under consideration" (p. 51).

Through the years, Bloom has proceeded to investigate variables within learners and instruction that can be altered to promote "mastery learning" for almost all learners. He has identified two learner characteristics—cognitive entry behaviors and affective entry behaviors—and quality of instruction as factors that can be altered to promote mastery (Bloom, 1976). In his discussion of cognitive entry behaviors, he supported the identification of specific task prerequisites within instruction. If entry skills are missing, he suggested a number of ways to ameliorate the situation. With regard to affective entry behaviors, Bloom asserted that learners "vary in what they are emotionally prepared to learn as expressed in their interests, attitudes, and self-views" (p. 74). While he felt that these affective characteristics may be difficult to change, he asserted that quality instruction that promotes successful learning experiences and ensures that the learner finds reward in successful experiences will aid in promoting a positive affect toward learning.

Finally, Bloom discussed features of quality instruction that can promote mastery among most learners. He described four features of quality instruction: cues, participation, reinforcement, and feedback/correctives. Cues are communications to the learner as to the requirements of the learning task and how to go about meeting these requirements. Participation involves covert or overt active practice with the learning task. Bloom suggested that reinforcement, whether positive or negative, should be given to learners by teachers, peers, or other adults to indicate approval of positive learning performance and disapproval of poor performance. Feedback and corrective procedures follow participation or interaction by the learner. They may include "alternative cues or additional time and practice" (p. 125).

Bloom's model of mastery learning has had a strong impact upon instructional design practice, indeed upon its fundamental philosophy. The goal of instructional design is to develop instruction from which the majority of students can learn very well. For instance, it is very common to have a designer trying to design and revise instruction to an 80/80 criterion (at least 80 percent of the learners achieve at least 80 percent of the objectives). Although mastery learning models generally incorporate instructional design practices, the reverse is not always true. *Not all instructional programs created with instructional design principles and procedures are predicated on a mastery model.* An instructional system that adheres to a mastery model sets a minimum level of competence for all, or most, students. The system is developed to provide the remediation and reevaluation necessary to bring learners to this level of competence and has developed a scheme for grading that accommodates the mastery model. Instructional systems may use instructional design principles and procedures, but because of unfeasibility or alternate philosophies, their designers choose not to employ a mastery model.

The instructional theories included in this text are not exhaustive. A number of other theories might be included. We attempted to select those theories that have had or that we expect to have the greatest impact

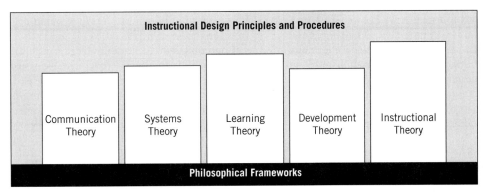

Figure 2.4 Summary Diagram

in the field. Refer to Reigeluth's texts on instructional design theories (1983, 1999) and Jonassen's *Educational Technology Research Handbook* (2004) for additional information in this area.

E X E R C I S E S

1. In your own words, explain why it is important for instructional designers to be able to describe and explain the philosophical foundations and theory bases of their field.

2. Discuss how the major educational philosophies of constructivism/rationalism, empiricism, and pragmatism relate to behaviorism and cognitive learning theories.

3. Describe the major differences between behaviorism and cognitive learning theories.

4. Ted is sitting in class listening to his teacher explain the difference between the concepts "liberal" and "conservative." Using the model of information processing described in this chapter, explain how this information flows through Ted's cognitive processes and structures. Give particular attention to the processes of selective perception, encoding, and retrieval.

S U M M A R Y

Both philosophy and theory provide foundations for instructional designers. In the first section of this chapter, we attempted to portray how educational philosophies may influence educators' beliefs about what knowledge is and how it is acquired. In the subsequent section, we discussed another way of viewing these same questions via the development and testing of learning theories. While this chapter does not exhaustively cover the philosophies and theories that have contributed to instructional design, it is our goal that as you read subse-

quent chapters, you will be able to relate assertions and principles that are stated to their particular philosophy and theory base. We also hope that we have pointed you toward additional sources of information to which you may refer throughout your career. Figure 2.4 summarizes key points in this chapter.

R E A D I N G S A N D R E F E R E N C E S

Allen, B. S., Otto, R. G., & Hoffman, B. (2004). Media as lived environments: The ecological psychology of educational technology. In D. H. Jonassen (Ed.), *Handbook of research for educational communications and technology* (pp. 215–241). Mahwah, NJ: Erlbaum.

Anderson, J. R. (2000). *Cognitive psychology and its implications* (5th ed.). New York: Worth.

Anderson, J. R., & Bower, G. H. (1973). *Human associative memory*. Washington, DC: V. H. Winston.

Andrews, D. H., & Goodson, L. A. (1980). A comparative analysis of models of instructional design. *Journal of Instructional Development, 11*(3), 2–16.

Arter, J. A., & Spandel, V. (1992, Spring). Using portfolios of student work in instruction and assessment. *Educational Measurement: Issues and Practices,* 36–43.

Atkinson, R. C., & Shiffrin, R. M. (1968). Human memory: A proposed system and its control processes. In K. W. Spence & J. T. Spence (Eds.), *The psychology of learning and motivation,* Vol. 2 (pp. 89–193). New York: Academic Press.

Banathy, B. H. (1992). *A systems view of education: Concepts and principles for effective practice*. Englewood Cliffs, NJ: Educational Technology.

Banathy, B. H. (2004). Systems inquiry and its application in education. In D. H. Jonassen (Ed.), *Handbook of research on educational communications and technology* (pp. 37–57). Mahwah, NJ: Erlbaum.

Barab, S. A., Evans, M. A., & Baek, E-O. (2004). Activity theory as a lens for characterizing the participatory unit. In D. H. Jonassen (Ed.), *Handbook of research for educational communications and technology* (pp. 199–214). Mahwah, NJ: Erlbaum.

Bednar, A. K., Cunningham, D. J., Duffy, T. M., & Perry, J. D. (1992). Theory into practice: How do we link? In T. M. Duffy & D. H. Jonassen (Eds.), *Constructivism and the technology of instruction.* (pp. 17–34). Hillsdale, NJ: Erlbaum.

Bereiter, C. (1991). Implications of connectionism for thinking about rules. *Educational Researcher, 20*(3), 10–16.

Bereiter, C. (2002). *Education and mind in the knowledge age.* Mahwah, NJ: Erlbaum.

Berk, L. (1994). *Child development* (3rd ed.). Boston: Allyn and Bacon.

Bloom, B. S. (1968). Learning for mastery. *Evaluation Comment 1* (2). Los Angeles: University of California.

Bloom, B. S. (1976). *Human characteristics and school learning.* New York: McGraw-Hill.

Bonner, J. (1988). Implications of cognitive theory for instructional design: Revisited. *Educational Communication and Technology Journal, 36,* 3–14.

Boud, D., & Feletti, G. (1991). *The challenge of problem-based learning.* New York: St. Martin's Press.

Bredo, E. (1994). Reconstructing educational psychology: situated cognition and Deweyian pragmatism. *Educational Psychologist, 29*(1), 23–35.

Briggs, L. J. (Ed.). (1977). *Instructional design: Principles and applications.* Englewood Cliffs, NJ: Educational Technology Publications.

Britton, B. K., Westbrook, R. D., & Holdredge, T. S. (1978). Reading and cognitive capacity usage: Effects of text difficulty. *Journal of Experimental Psychology: Human Learning and Memory, 4,* 582–591.

Brophy, J., & Alleman, J. (1991). Activities as instructional tools: a framework for analysis and evaluation. *Educational Researcher, 20*(4), 9–23.

Brown, D. (1988). Twelve middle-school teachers' planning. *The Elementary School Journal, 89,* 69–87.

Brown, J. S., Collins, A., & Duguid, P. (1989). Situated cognition and the culture of learning. *Educational Researcher, 18*(1), 32–42.

Bruner, J. S. (1966). *Toward a theory of instruction.* Cambridge, MA: Harvard University Press.

Bullough, R. (1987). Planning the first year of teaching. *Journal of Education for Teaching, 13,* 231–250.

Case, R. (1993). Theories of learning and theories of development. *Educational Psychologist, 23*(3), 219–233.

Case, R., & Bereiter, C. (1984). From behaviourism to cognitive behaviourism to cognitive development: Steps in the evolution of instructional design. *Instructional Science, 13,* 141–158.

Choi, J., & Hannafin, M. (1995). Situated cognition and learning environments: Roles, structures, and implications for design. *Educational Technology Research and Development, 43*(2), 53–70.

Clark, R. E. (1982). Antagonism between achievement and enjoyment in ATI studies. *Educational Psychologist, 17,* 92–101.

Clark, C., & Peterson, P. (1986). Teacher's thought process. In M. C. Wittrock (Ed.), *Handbook of research on teaching* (pp. 255–296). New York: Macmillan.

Cobb, P. (1996). Constructivism and learning. In T. Plomp and D. P. Ely (Eds.), *International encyclopedia of educational technology* (2nd ed.) (pp. 56–59). Tarrytown, NY: Elsevier Science.

Cognition and Technology Group. (1990). Anchored instruction and its relationship to situated cognition. *Educational Researcher, 19*(8), 2–10.

Cognition and Technology Group. (1992). An anchored instruction approach to cognitive skills acquisition and intelligent tutoring. In J. W. Regian and V. Shute (Eds.), *Cognitive approaches to automated instruction* (pp. 135–170). Hillsdale, NJ.: Erlbaum.

Cognition and Technology Group. (1992). The Jasper experiment: An exploration of issues in learning and instructional design. *Educational Technology Research and Development, 40*(1), 65–80.

Craik, F. I. M., & Lockhart, R. S. (1972). Levels of processing: A framework for memory research. *Journal of Verbal Learning and Verbal Behavior, 11,* 671–684.

Davies, I. K. (1976). *Objectives in curriculum design.* London: McGraw-Hill.

Davis, R. H., Alexander, L. T., & Yelon, S. L. (1974). *Learning system design.* New York: McGraw-Hill.

DeVaney, A. (1990). Rules of evidence. *Journal of Thought, 25*(1 & 2), 6–18.

Dewey, J. (1924). *Democracy and education.* New York: Macmillan.

Di Vesta, F. J., & Rieber, L. P. (1987). Characteristics of cognitive engineering: The next generation of instructional systems. *Educational Communications and Technology Journal, 35,* 213–230.

Dick, W. (1992). An instructional designer's view of constructivism. In T. M. Duffy & D. H. Jonassen (Eds.), *Constructivism and the technology of instruction* (pp. 91–98). Hillsdale, NJ: Erlbaum.

Dick, W., & Carey, L. (1985). *The systematic design of instruction.* Glenview, IL: Scott, Foresman.

Driscoll, M. P. (1994). *Psychology of learning for instruction.* Boston: Allyn and Bacon.

Duffy, T. M., & Jonassen, D. H. (Eds.). (1992). *Constructivism and the technology of instruction.* Hillsdale, NJ: Erlbaum.

Dunn, T. G. (1994). If we can't contextualize it, should we teach it? *Educational Technology Research and Development, 42*(3), 83–92.

Dwyer, F. M. (1972). *A guide for improving visualized instruction.* State College, PA: Learning Services.

Gagné, E. D., Yekovich, C. W., and Yekovich, F. R. (1993). *The cognitive psychology of school learning* (2nd ed.). New York: HarperCollins.

Gagné, R. M. (1974). *Essentials of learning for instruction.* New York: Dryden Press.

Gagné, R. M. (1985). *The conditions of learning* (4th ed.). New York: Holt, Rinehart, & Winston.

Gagné, R. M., & Dick, W. (1983). Instructional psychology. *Annual Review of Psychology, 34,* 261–295.

Gagné, R. M., & Driscoll, M. P. (1988). *Essentials of Learning for instruction* (2nd ed.). Upper Saddle River, NJ: Prentice-Hall.

Gergen, K. J. (1995). Social construction and the educational process. In L. P. Steffe & J. Gale (Eds.), *Constructivism in education* (pp. 17–40). Hillsdale, NJ: Erlbaum.

Goldman, S. R., Pellegrino, J. W., & Bransford, J. (1994). Assessing programs that invite thinking. In E. L. Baker & H. F. O'Neil (Eds.), *Technology assessment in education and training* (pp. 199–230). Hillsdale, NJ: Erlbaum.

Greeno, J. G., Collins, A. M., & Resnick, L. (1996). Cognition and learning. In D. C. Berliner & R. C. Calfee (Eds.), *Handbook of educational psychology* (pp. 15–46). New York: Macmillan.

Gruender, C. D. (1996, June). Constructivism and learning: A philosophical appraisal. *Educational Technology, 36*(3), 21–29.

Gustafson, K. L., & Branch, R. M. (1997). Survey of instructional development models (3rd ed.) Syracuse, NY: ERIC Clearinghouse on Information and Technology. Publication IR-103.

Haberlandt, K. (1997). *Cognitive psychology.* Needham Heights, MA: Allyn & Bacon.

Hamm, R. L. (1981). *Philosophy and education: Alternatives in theory and practice* (2nd ed.). Danville, IL: Interstate Publishers.

Hayakawa, S. I. (1953). *Symbol, status, and personality.* New York: Harcourt, Brace, & World.

Heinich, R., Molenda, M., Russell, J. D., & Smaldino, S. E. (1996). *Instructional media and the new technologies of instruction.* New York: Macmillan.

Henning, P. H. (2004). Everyday cognition and situated learning. In D. H. Jonassen (Ed.), *Handbook of research for educational communications and technology* (pp. 143–168). Mahwah, NJ: Erlbaum.

Hess, T. M., & Flanagan, D. A. (1992). Schema-based retrieval processes in young and older adults. *The Journals of Gerontology, 47,* 52–58.

Honebein, P. C. (1996). Seven goals for the design of constructivist learning environments. *Constructivist learning environments* (pp. 11–24). Englewood Cliffs, NJ: Educational Technology Publications.

Jonassen, D. H. (1992). Evaluating constructivistic learning. In T. M. Duffy & D. H. Jonassen (Eds.), *Constructivism and the technology of instruction* (pp. 137–148). Hillsdale, NJ: Erlbaum.

Jonassen, D. H. (Ed.). (2004). Handbook of research on educational communications and technology (2nd ed.) Mahwah, NJ: Erlbaum.

Kantowitz, B. H. (1987). Mental workload. In P. A. Hancock (Ed.), *Human factors of psychology* (pp. 81–121). North-Holland: Elsevier.

Kaufman, R. (2000). *Mega planning: Practical tools for organizational success.* Thousand Oaks, CA: Sage.

Kerr, S. T. (1983). Inside the black box: Making design decisions for instruction. *British Journal of Educational Technology, 14,* 45–58.

Kintsch, W. (1972). Notes on the structure of semantic memory. In E. Tulving & W. Donaldson (Eds.), *Organization of memory* (pp. 247–308). New York: Academic Press.

Kintsch, W. (1974). *The representation of meaning in memory.* Hillsdale, NJ: Erlbaum.

Kirst, M. W. (1991). Interview on assessment issues with Lorrie Shepard. *Educational Researcher, 20*(2), 21–23.

Kirst, M. W. (1991). Interview on assessment issues with James Popham. *Educational Researcher, 20*(2), 24–27.

Korzybski, A. (1973) *Science and sanity: An introduction to non-Aristotelian systems and general semantics* (5th ed.) Englewood, NJ: International Non-Aristotelian Library.

Language Development and HyperMedia Research Group. (1992). Bubble dialogue: A new tool for instructional and assessment. *Educational Technology Research and Development, 40*(2), 59–68.

Leahey, T. H., & Harris, R. (1989). *Human learning* (2nd ed.). Upper Saddle River, NJ: Prentice-Hall.

Lebow, D. (1995). Constructivist values for instructional systems design: Five principles toward a new mindset. In B. B. Seels (Ed.), *Instructional design: A reconsideration* (pp. 175–187). Upper Saddle River, NJ: Educational Technology Publications.

Lee, I. (1941). *Language habits in human affairs.* New York: Harper.

Lesgold, A., Eggan, G., Katz, S., & Rao, G. (1992). Possibilities for assessment using computer-based apprenticeship environments. In J. W. Regian & V. J. Shute (Eds.), *Cognitive approaches to automated instruction* (pp. 49–80). Hillsdale, NJ: Erlbaum.

Linn, R. L. (1994). Performance assessment: Policy promises and technical measurement standards. *Educational Researcher, 23*(9), 4–14.

Linn, R. L., Baker, E. L., & Dunbar, S. B. (1991). Complex, performance-based assessment: Expectations and validation criteria. *Educational Researcher, 20*(8), 15–21.

Locke, J. (1690/1995). *Essay concerning human understanding.* Amherst, NY: Prometheus Books.

Low, W. C. (1981). Changes in instructional development: The aftermath of an information processing takeover in psychology. *Journal of Instructional Development, 4,* 10–18.

Mager, R. F. (1984). *Preparing instructional objectives* (2nd ed.). Belmont, CA: Fearon-Pitman.

Mayer, R. E. (1982). Learning. In H. E. Mitzel (Ed.), *Encyclopedia of educational research* (pp. 1040–1058). New York: The Free Press.

Mayer, R. E., & Moreno, R. (2003). Nine ways to reduce cognitive load in multimedia learning. *Educational Psychologist, 38,* 1, 43–52.

McClelland, J. L., & Rummelhart, D. E. (1988). *Explorations in parallel distributed processing: A handbook of models, programs, and exercises.* Cambridge, MA: MIT Press/ Bradford Books.

McCutcheon, G. (1980). How do elementary school teachers plan? The nature of planning and influences on it. *The Elementary School Journal, 81,* 4–23.

Merrill, M. D. (1992). Constructivism and instructional design. In T. M. Duffy & D. H. Jonassen (Eds.), *Constructivism and the technology of instruction* (pp. 99–114). Hillsdale, NJ: Erlbaum.

Miller, G. A. (1956). The magical number seven, plus or minus two: Some limits on our capacity for processing information. *Psychological Review, 63,* 81–97.

Moore, M. G., & Kearsley, G. (1996). *Distance education: A systems view.* Belmont, CA: Wadsworth.

Morris, V. C., & Pai, Y. (1976). *Philosophy and the American school* (2nd ed.). Boston: Houghton Mifflin.

Murdock, B. B. (1961). The retention of individual items. *Journal of Experimental Psychology, 62,* 618–625.

Paivio, A. U. (1971). *Imagery and verbal processes.* New York: Holt, Rinehart, & Winston.

Pavlov, I. P. (1927). *Conditioned reflexes.* (G. V. Anrep, Trans.) London: Oxford University Press.

Perkins, D. N. (1992). What constructivism demands of the learner. In T. M. Duffy & D. H. Jonassen (Eds.), *Constructivism and the technology of instruction* (pp. 161–166). Hillsdale, NJ: Erlbaum.

Perkins, D. N., & Salomon, G. (1989). Are cognitive skills context-bound? *Educational Researcher, 18*(1), 16–25.

Phillips, D. C. (1995). The good, the bad, and the ugly: The many faces of constructivism. *Educational Researcher, 24*(7), 5–12.

Piaget, J., & Inhelder, B. (1969). *The psychology of the child.* New York: Basic Books.

Prawat, R. S., & Floden, R. E. (1994). Philosophical perspectives on constructivist views of learning. *Educational Psychology, 29*(1), 37–48.

Reigeluth, C. M. (Ed.). (1983). *Instructional design theories and models.* Hillsdale, NJ: Erlbaum.

Reigeluth, C. M. (Ed.). (1987). *Instructional theories in action.* Hillsdale, NJ: Erlbaum.

Reigeluth, C. M. (1992). Reflections on the implications of constructivism for educational technology. In T. M. Duffy & D. H. Jonassen (Eds.), *Constructivism and the technology of instruction* (pp. 149–156). Hillsdale, NJ: Erlbaum.

Reigeluth, C. M. (Ed.). (1999). *Instructional-design theories and models: New paradigms on instructional theory.* Mahwah, NJ: Erlbaum.

Renkl, A. & Atkinson, R. K. (2003). Structuring the transition from example study to problem solving in cognitive skill acquisition: A cognitive load perspective. *Educational Psychologist, 38,* 1, 15–22.

Rice, F. P. (1995). *Human development: A lifespan approach* (2nd ed.). Upper Saddle River, NJ: Prentice-Hall.

Richey, R. (1986). *The theoretical and conceptual bases of instructional design.* London: Kogan Page.

Richey, R. (Ed.). (2000) *The legacy of Robert M. Gagné.* Syracuse, NY: ERIC Clearinghouse on Information and Technology. Publication IR-108.

Rieber, L. P. (1992). Computer-based microworlds: A bridge between constructivism and direct instruction. *Educational Technology Research and Development, 40*(1), 93–106.

Rieber, L. P. (2004). Microworlds. In D. H. Jonassen (Ed.), *Handbook of research for educational communications and technology.* Mahwah, NJ: Erlbaum.

Rorty, R. (1982). *Consequences of pragmatism.* Minneapolis: University of Minnesota.

Rousseau, J. (1950). *Emile.* (B. Foxley, Trans.) New York: E. P. Dutton.

Rummelhart, D. E. (1980). Schemata: The building blocks of cognition. In R. J. Spiro, B. C. Bruce, & W. F. Brewer (Eds.), *Theoretical issues in reading comprehension* (pp. 33–58). Hillsdale, NJ: Erlbaum.

Schneider, W., & Braham, D. J. (1992). Introduction to connectionist modeling in education. *Educational Psychologist, 27*(4), 513–542.

Schott, F. (1992). The contributions of cognitive science and educational technology for the advancement of instructional design theory. *Educational Technology Research and Development, 40*(2), 55–58.

Schramm, W. (1956). Procedures and effects of mass communication. In N. B. Henry (Ed.), *Mass media and education, NSSE Yearbook 53* (pp. 113–138). Chicago: The University of Chicago Press.

Schuell, T. J. (1986). Cognitive conceptions of learning. *Review of Educational Research, 56,* 411–436.

Seels, B. B. (Ed.). (1995). *Instructional design: a reconsideration.* Englewood Cliffs, NJ: Educational Technology Publications.

Shannon, C., & Weaver, W. (1949). *The mathematical theory of communication.* Urbana, IL: University of Illinois Press.

Siegler, R. S. (1986). *Children's thinking.* Upper Saddle River, NJ: Prentice-Hall.

Slavin, R. E. (1994). *Educational psychology: Theory and practice.* (4th ed.). Needham Heights, MA: Allyn and Bacon.

Smith, P. L., & Wedman, J. F. (1988). Read-think-aloud protocols: A new data-source for formative evaluation. *Performance Improvement Quarterly, 1,* 13–22.

Sperling, G. A. (1960). The information available in brief visual presentation. *Psychological Monographs, 74,* Whole No. 498.

Spiro, R. J., Feltovich, P. J., Jacobson, M. J., & Coulson, R. L. (1992). Knowledge representation, content specification, and the development of skill in situation specific knowledge assembly: Some constructivist issues as they relate to cognitive flexibility theory and hypertext. In T. M. Duffy & D. H. Jonassen (Eds.), *Constructivism and the technology of instruction* (pp. 57–76). Hillsdale, NJ: Erlbaum.

Steffe, L. P., & Gale, J. (Eds.). (1995). *Constructivism in education.* Hillsdale, NJ: Erlbaum.

Streibel, M. J. (1995). Instructional plans and situated learning: The challenge of Suchman's theory of situated action for instructional designers and instructional systems. In G. Anglin (Ed.), *Instructional technology: Past present and future* (2nd ed.) (pp. 145–160). Englewood, CO: Libraries Unlimited.

Swanson, D. B., Norman, G. R., & Linn, R. L. (1995). Performance-based assessment: Lessons from the health professions. *Educational Researcher, 24*(5), 5–11, 35.

Thorndike, E. L. (1913). *Educational psychology: Vol. II. The psychology of learning.* New York: Teachers College, Columbia University.

Tripp, S. D. (1993). Theories, traditions, and situated learning. *Educational Technology, 33*(3), 71–77.

von Glasersfeld, E. (1995). A constructivist approach to teaching. In L. P. Steffe and J. Gale (Eds.), *Constructivism in education* (pp. 3–16). Hillsdale, NJ: Erlbaum.

Vygotsky, L. S. (1978). *Mind and society: Development of higher psychological processes.* Cambridge, MA: Harvard University Press.

Watson, J. B. (1913). Psychology as the behaviorist views it. *Psychological Review, 20,* 158–177.

Wedman, J., and Tessmer, M. (1990). A layers of necessity instructional development model. *Educational Technology Research and Development, 38* (2), 77–85.

Weiner, N. (1969). *The human use of human beings: Cybernetics in society.* New York: Avon (original publication date: 1954).

Wildman, T. M. (1981, July). Cognitive theory and the design of instruction. *Educational Technology, 23,* 14–20.

Wilson, B., Teslow, J., & Osman-Jouchoux, R. (1995). The impact of constructivism (and postmodernism) on ID fundamentals. In B. B. Seels (Ed.), *Instructional design: A reconsideration* (pp. 137–157). Englewood Cliffs, NJ: Educational Technology Publications.

Wilson, B. G. (1996). Introduction: What is a constructivist learning environment? In B. G. Wilson (Ed.), *Constructivist learning environments* (pp. 3–10). Englewood Cliffs, NJ: Educational Technology Publications.

Wilson, B. G. (Ed.). (1996). *Constructivist learning environments.* Englewood Cliffs, NJ: Educational Technology Publications.

Winn, W. (1995). Instructional design and situated cognition: Paradox or partnership. In B. B. Seels (Ed.). *Instructional design: A reconsideration* (pp. 159–169). Englewood Cliffs, NJ: Educational Technology Publications.

Winn, W. (2004). Cognitive perspectives in psychology. In D. H. Jonassen (Ed.), *Handbook of Research for Educational Communications and Technology* (pp. 79–112). Mahwah, NJ: Erlbaum.

Young, M. F. (1993). Instructional design for situated learning. *Educational Technology Research and Development, 41(*1*),* 1042–1629.

Young, M. (2004). An ecological psychology of instructional design: Learning and thinking by perceiving-acting systems. In D. H. Jonassen (Ed.), *Handbook of research for educational communications and technology* (pp. 169–177). Mahwah, NJ: Erlbaum

ANALYSIS AND ASSESSMENT

In this section, the idea of instructional analysis is explored, and the three primary domains of analysis are discussed: Context, Learner, and Task. In addition, this section contains the chapter on assessment, as we consider designing assessment to be best thought of within the context of the analysis phase of instructional design.

Chapter 3, "Analyzing the Learning Context" treats two dimensions of context: needs and the learning environment. Three primary approaches to needs assessment are described and synthesized into a helpful model for instructional designers. Factors of critical importance in the learning environment are explored along with ways to analyze and describe them that will be helpful to subsequent design work. Since it is a task often encountered in all phases of instructional analysis, a short but helpful discussion is included of ways of working with an expert to get the information you need.

Chapter 4, "Analyzing the Learner" looks at the characteristics of learners that are relevant to instructional designers. The majority of the chapter treats the topic from the standpoint of the status of scientific knowledge, using a framework that can help you conceptualize that body of knowledge. In addition, ways in which knowledge of learners can be put to use in instructional design are described.

Chapter 5, "Analyzing the Learning Task" focuses on techniques for gaining knowledge of what learning goals are involved and what those goals imply for cognitive processing and learning. Techniques for learning goal description, information processing analysis, prerequisite analysis, and determination of type of learning are presented.

Chapter 6, "Assessing Learning from Instruction," has to do with the design of tests and other forms of assessment of learning. It concentrates on the characteristics of assessment instruments, techniques for designing criterion referenced assessment including guidance in selecting forms of assessment and consideration of trade-offs in assessment design alternatives. Two techniques that contribute to high-quality criterion referenced assesssment are described: developing item specifications and instrument blueprints.

INSTRUCTIONAL ANALYSIS: ANALYZING THE LEARNING CONTEXT

CHAPTER OBJECTIVES

At the conclusion of this chapter, you should be able to do the following:

- Describe the purposes of analysis activities of the design process, and list the three components that are analyzed in this phase.

- Describe the purpose of an analysis of the instructional context.

- Describe the purpose of a needs assessment, the conditions that might require a needs assessment, and the steps in a needs assessment procedure.

- Describe factors that should be analyzed in the learning environment, and discuss why these factors should be considered.

- When given an instructional situation, describe the procedures you would follow and questions you would ask in conducting an analysis of the instructional context.

- Distinguish an instructional need from a noninstructional need. Explain.

- Determine information needs for a given instructional problem, and suggest from whom to gather information for learner and context analysis.

OVERVIEW OF ANALYSIS

Consider this episode involving a fictitious e-learning company, *EduSpider, L.L.C.* The five founders of *EduSpider* sank their savings into the company. In their first e-learning development effort, they decided to produce a Web-based learning management system to market to K–12 school systems throughout the country. The system's name was *WeeLearn.* The company founders spent thousands of hours in developing a front-end and tools to support teachers' development of precisely controlled reward-based learning environments in all areas of the curriculum. *WeeLearn* employed a sophisticated streaming multimedia system called *Instantaneous+* to support real-time sound and motion, 5.1 audio, virtual reality, and expert system enhancements. The *EduSpider* developers made drivers to support use of clever input formats, such as a light pen and a game pad. They paid a team of programmers a great deal of money to develop "virtual school" curriculum activities using the sophisticated authoring tools built into *WeeLearn.* They invested the remainder of their resources in slick packaging and lots of advertising.

Much to the developers' surprise and disappointment, *WeeLearn* didn't sell. A few months later they attended a regional computer conference and spoke to some school administrators teachers to whom they loaned the package in return for the teachers' evaluation and reports about the system, as well as a few that had bought the system based on the compelling and attractive advertising.

What information did they gain from the teachers' comments?

The reward-based approach that the system used to structure learning activities was contrary to the popular educational theory of the day.

Teachers especially enjoyed teaching with a hands-on approach, and they felt that this approach was successful.

Many of the content areas of *WeeLearn* were areas in which previously available materials, with which teachers were already comfortable, were considered excellent.

Few schools had the server software required to support the *Instantaneous+*-based Web materials. Some of the school found that when they employed proxy servers or the most common Internet security firewalls, the *Instantaneous+* software locked up the server.

The version of *Instantaneous+* used by *WeeLearn,* version 14, was a newer version than any of the schools had on their servers. A server upgrade to the latest version of *Instantaneous+* cost \$5,000, and new versions appear at three-month intervals.

In schools where *WeeLearn* could be used, teachers reported that the students learned a lot about navigating within the system and the rules of the games in the software but very little about the content being studied.

Many content errors and inaccuracies plagued much of the virtual school materials because of the lack of content expertise of the programmers and absence of any field testing of the materials before they were released.

Although the arithmetic modules were remarkably free of content errors, many students were unable to use them because the developers had assumed that they were skilled in determining the least common denominator, and many students were not competent in this skill.

Some students reported that the games were too cute and that the characters and rewards used in the games were insulting.

EduSpider had learned a painful lesson about instructional design: Instructional designers must become clever investigators, examining the characteristics of the potential users, the learning environments, the perceived need for the instruction, and the instructional task before investing time and resources in the costly production of instructional systems, materials, or learning environments.

Of course, few education or training enterprises make all of the mistakes that *EduSpider* made, but many developers, trainers, and teachers, to their sorrow, have failed to "do their homework" in analyzing the learning environment, learners, and tasks, with sufficient detail. This chapter and the two that follow will discuss some factors that developers of instruction, whether they are developing materials for their own classrooms or for national distribution, should consider. This stage of development is sometimes called *front-end analysis.* During front-end analysis, designers analyze three basic components: the instructional context, the prospective learners, and the learning task.

Although many people develop instruction without front-end analysis and begrudge the time investment that such an analysis takes, we have found that investing time and thought early in the design process saves time, cost, and frustration in the end. This investment allows one to design and develop instructional materials that support learning what is truly critical, in a way that the materials can actually be used by the intended learners in their learning environment.

Front-end analysis may seem like wasted effort to instructional materials developers who are in a hurry to get their products out as soon as possible. In training environments, there is always a rush to make training available to employees because time delays often mean loss of revenue. Developers of commercial educational materials may be fearful that other developers will "scoop" their ideas and put a competing product on the market before their product is out. So they take shortcuts where they can, and that often happens to be at the analysis stage. Teachers may give little attention to front-end analysis because they must prepare so much instruction with little time for planning. There are, however, sufficient instances (like the *EduSpider* scenario) in which a great deal of time and money has been invested in preparing instruction without front-end analysis, and the resulting product was (1) unacceptable to the teachers/trainers; (2) not suitable for the available equipment; or (3) not capable of meeting a real instructional need. In these situations, the instruction is not implemented.

Although *EduSpider* corporation and the *WeeLearn* materials are fictitious, mistakes and problems on the order of those depicted in our scenario are commonplace. A good sampling of actual problems, many of which are attributable to weaknesses in analysis, can be seen in *The ID Casebook* (Ertmer & Quinn, 2003).

ANALYZING THE LEARNING CONTEXT

Before we embark upon learning particulars of context analysis, it seems appropriate to reflect briefly on the broader conception of context. All learning environments come with a context, whether the context is a school, a place of business, a home, or elsewhere. But context is not just a place. Context includes not only the physical realities within which learning takes place but also the temporal and social environment that is a part of the learning process itself (Richey & Tessmer, 1995). Many scholars in the study of instruction and learning consider contextual matters absolutely central, focusing their attention upon "the mind in real-world contexts." (Duffy, 2004, p. 13).

In addition, the context of the design process itself has been studied, and techniques have been described by which the context within which a designer finds oneself can be taken into consideration to guide the design process itself. Throughout this text, we will provide suggestions and examples of ways in which the design process can be altered to suit the situation. We summarize these suggestions, as well as provide some additional excellent approaches to modifying the design process in Chapter 20. This chapter will treat context from an analytic standpoint: generally accepted instructional design principles and practices associated with context analysis.

The analysis of the learning context involves two major components: (1) the substantiation of a need for instruction to help learners reach learning goals and (2) a description of the learning environment in which the instruction will be used.

DETERMINING INSTRUCTIONAL NEEDS

Designers often conduct a *needs assessment* to find out whether instruction should be designed. The purpose of a needs assessment is to determine that there actually is a need for new instruction to be developed. In a broad way, we could say that this step arises out of developers' desire to adhere to the adage, "If it ain't broke, don't fix it." Violations of this principle are common in the development of instructional materials: The instruction that is already available in a subject matter for a particular group of students and in a particular setting is effective, efficient, and appealing. It is generally a mistake to invest in the development of new instructional materials for topics that students are learning well with existing cost-effective instruction.

In other cases, if there seems to be no compelling argument that students learn a particular skill or information (e.g., there is no subsequent learning goal or future job task that seems to require the acquisition of skill or knowledge now), it may be a waste of precious resources designing instruction to reach these goals. In both cases, there is no clear indication that more instruction needs to be designed.

For teachers or trainers who are designing instruction for their own classrooms, a needs assessment can be rather informal but is nonetheless important. At the most basic level, such needs assessment can be directed at determining what portions of the curriculum involve learning goals with which, year after year, a large number of students experience difficulty in learning and for which no readily available instructional solution exists. For designers who are creating instruction to be used in a more extended environment, such as designing software to be used by fourth-graders across the state or employees in offices across the country, a more formal needs assessment is in order.

In most cases, needs assessment and summative evaluation plans should be constructed simultaneously. Although the relationship between needs assessment and evaluation is often viewed as chronologically linear, in well-designed systems the relationship is cyclical, as indicated in Figure 3.1. At the conclusion of a needs assessment, the reasons for developing instruction are very clear. At this point, describing the indicators that one would expect to see if the problem is solved and learning goals are met is relatively straightforward.

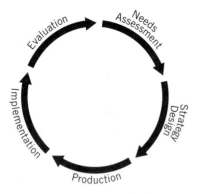

Figure 3.1 Relationship Between Needs Assessment and Evaluation

When Should a Needs Assessment Be Conducted?

Needs assessment processes vary somewhat in terms of the precipitating event(s) that sets the needs assessment activities in motion. Although, as we identified above, numerous factors may instigate a needs assessment, we divide them into three major types:

Condition A: There is a problem: Clients are not satisfied; students are dropping out in unexpected numbers; parents are complaining; products are defective; test scores are down; and so on.

Condition B: There is or may be something new that learners need to learn: New guidelines from the state Department of Education suggest that all learners be proficient in computer-mediated communica-

tion; new equipment is being added that employees need to operate; new employees require remediation in order to do their jobs; and so on.

Condition C: No big problem is apparent, but the organization wishes to or is required to engage in evaluation of its learning/training program to see if goals and reality are congruent. An NCATE accreditation review is coming next year; the inspector general is visiting next week; line operations training needs review to see if it is of the quality wanted; and so on.

Not all of these precipitating conditions fit equally well with the traditional "discrepancy" model of needs assessment (Kaufman & English, 1979; Rossett, 1988). Under the discrepancy model, the designer determines whether there is a gap between "what ought to be" (what learners should know or be able to do) and "what is" (what learners are currently able to do) and then to determine which of these gaps should be addressed with the design and development of new instruction. Indeed, the discrepancy model appears to work best with Condition C. The other conditions may involve some of the same activities but in different order and are combined with additional questions, as indicated in Figure 3.2. In the next three sections, we will propose approaches for addressing each of the three types of needs assessment conditions.

A. HOW TO CONDUCT A NEEDS ASSESSMENT USING THE PROBLEM MODEL. This model might also be described as the "crisis" model. Someone in management or administration; some member of the constituency, such

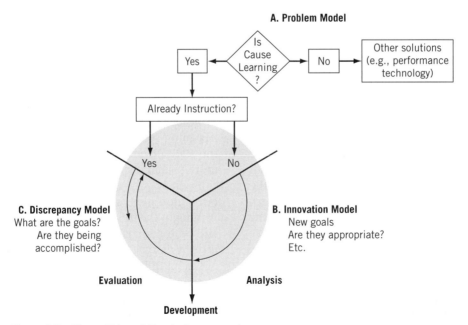

Figure 3.2 Three Sides of Needs Assessment

as parents, clients, or community leaders; or some employees or students have identified that a problem exists in the organization's achieving its mission.

1. *Determine whether there really is a problem.* Of course, achieving this part of the process can be awfully tricky. The procedures here are very similar to some of those in learning environment analysis discussed in the second part of this chapter. The keys to success of this activity are to ask the right questions of the right people and to get complete and non-evasive answers. Following are some of the questions that might be asked at this point:

- Who says there is a problem?
- Why do they say there is a problem?
- Do others perceive it to be a problem?
- Who does not agree that there is a problem? Why?
- When was the problem first noticed?
- Who is affected by the problem?
- How pervasive is the problem?
- In what way and how seriously does the problem affect the mission of the organization?

The goal of this investigation is to clarify the problem and determine how serious it is.

2. *Determine whether the cause of the problem is related to employees' performance in training environments or to learners' achievement in educational environments.* Employee performance may not be the cause of a problem, but malfunctioning equipment or other work conditions may be. In schools, parallel situations exist when student scores appear to go down on standardized achievement tests, but the score change is caused by differences in measurement or in different learner populations being included in the group being tested. Asking some of the following, or related, questions may lead to information on this question.

- How does employees' performance (or learners' achievement) relate to the problem identified in step 1?
- Is this relationship correlational? That is, when performance or achievement improves, does the problem get better and vice versa?
- Does performance (or achievement) appear to be impacted by another factor that causes both the problem and the performance or achievement deficits?
- What evidence is there that suggests that performance or achievement deficits cause the problem or affect it?

If the problem appears to be caused partially or totally by employees' performance (or learner achievement), the designer can move on to step 3.

3. *Determine whether the solution to the achievement/performance problem is learning.* Again, designers can ask a series of questions that can be answered with a variety of data sources, which we will address later in this section on needs assessment.

- "Could they demonstrate that they have achieved the learning reflected by this goal, if their lives depended on it?" (Rothwell & Kazanas, 1992, p. 35).
- Is there evidence that achievement/performance problems may be caused by motivation, incentives, facilities' design, tools design, the climate of the agency, the interaction with peers, policy decisions, or other nonlearning factors?

Instructional designers should not immediately assume that poor performance on learning tasks implies a need to correct or revise instruction. Often this is the case, and instruction *is* required. However, as you can see, there are additional reasons why learners may not perform well. The designer must become a detective who delays determination that instruction is the solution to achievement/performance problems until the problem has been thoroughly investigated. This investigation is often conducted in tandem with the needs assessment through the development of a thorough description of the instructional environment, and, as will be described in the following chapters, an analysis of the learners and the instructional task.

Frequently, poor achievement or performance has more than one cause. In such a case, designers must work with organizational development specialists and other noninstructional personnel in order to coordinate interventions that may together improve learners' achievement or employees' performance.

4. *Determine whether instruction for these learning goals is currently offered.* If the answer is "no," proceed to the Innovation model (described in the following section). If the answer is "yes," then proceed to the Discrepancy model (described in the subsequent section).

B. HOW TO CONDUCT A NEEDS ASSESSMENT USING THE INNOVATION MODEL The innovation model examines changes or innovations in the educational system or organization or in the environment outside the organization and determines whether new learning goals should be added to the curriculum to accommodate these changes or innovations. As this process may add or change goals in an organization, stakeholders, such as students, teachers/trainers, managers/administrators, parents, and clients, should be carefully involved in this process.

1. *Determine the nature of the innovation or change.*

- Has there been a change in the composition of the learner population? Often a change in the composition of the learner population signals that new learning goals are needed. For example, the addition of many Vietnamese students into some school populations during the 1970s stimulated needs assessments to determine what goals needed to be added to the public school systems' curricula. A change in the composition of the personnel entering the armed services with the inception of all-volunteer induction policies may have instigated a needs assessment to determine what changes in basic skills instruction might be required with the new population of service personnel.

- Has there been a significant change in the tools, policies, or organization?
- Has there been a significant change in the educational/ training philosophy of the organization?
- How will the innovation affect the mission of the organization?

2. *Determine the learning goals that accompany this innovation.*

- How will the innovation or change affect what is expected in learners' achievement or employees' performance?
- Does this effect significantly change what learners or employees must understand, know, or do?
- Can these new understandings, knowledge, or actions be taught?

3. *If there is a choice, determine whether these goals are appropriate and high priority in the learning system.*

- Are the resources available to support this new instruction? Are they adequate to design and develop this instruction?
- Do these goals conflict with existing goals?
- How will these goals be interpreted by affected groups (e.g., students, teachers/trainers, managers/administrators, parents, clients)?
- Do these goals represent partisan positions or vested interest groups?
- Are there groups that may object to these new goals?

If, after due reflection, the new learning goals are judged important and feasible, then the designer may advance to step 4.

4. *Begin learning environment analysis design activities;* in other words, proceed with the next phase of instructional design.

C. HOW TO CONDUCT A NEEDS ASSESSMENT USING THE DISCREPANCY MODEL.

The discrepancy-based needs assessment, as we will present it, is actually a summative evaluation model. Designers using this model presume that learning goals are already identified and that instruction is currently offered related to these goals. Key ideas from the discrepancy model can be seen in examination of a five-phase approach to performing a needs assessment.

1. *List the goals of the instructional system.* In other words, one should first determine "what ought to be" (what must learners be able to do or know at the end of their instruction). These goals can be for a lesson, unit, course, semester, year, or several years. These descriptions of "what ought to be" are called *learning* goals. In public schools, quite often committees of community members, educators, and students have been involved in determining these goals. Some states have involved individuals statewide in prescribing goals for students in specific contents for particular grade levels. These individuals may refer to other documents, such as other states' goal statements, national goal statements, and goals identified by professional organizations, such as the National Council of Teachers of Mathematics. A number of Web sites have been established to provide information to educators regarding goals or standards for content areas and grade levels. Examples are PASSport, a tool for using the learning standards developed by the Oklahoma State Department of Education at http://www.sde.state.ok.us/passport or a site sponsored by the U.S. Office of Educational Research and Improvement at http://www.ncrel.org/standards-benchmarks/.

In businesses and other environments, the identification of learning goals generally involves interviewing and observing persons who are expert in performing skills that learners must learn. Key management personnel may have been involved in describing the type of knowledge or skill that they wish their employees to possess. Employees may be involved in describing the skills and knowledge they feel they must possess to perform their jobs adequately. Goals may be also identified from certification or licensing requirements for vocational or professional schools.

It is not unusual to find operating training/educational agencies that do not have statements of goals. In such a case, designers may proceed in two different ways. In one approach, designers may initiate a goal definition activity in which stakeholders go through the process of formalizing the learning goals for their agency. Then the designer can proceed with the subsequent activities listed below. Or, using another approach, designers may engage in a modified "goal-free" analysis (Scriven, 1972), in which, after observations, interviews, examination of learning artifacts, and examination of instructional materials, they attempt to infer the goals of the agency. (We call this a modified "goal-free" evaluation because Scriven did not intend that evaluations should be undertaken with learning systems that do not have goals. He merely meant that, using this method, evaluators would not be informed of the goals in advance of their evaluation, so that they would not be biased by them. "Goal-free" evaluation is discussed further in Chapter 19.) Designers would then present these inferred goals to stakeholders in the agency as a beginning point for making formal statements of goals. This second approach is high risk in that designers may spend a lot of time attempting to infer goals that may not be at all what the agency wishes to achieve.

2. *Determine how well the identified goals are already being achieved.* With goal statements located and in hand, the next step is to determine how well the learners in the system are already reaching these goals. The reason for this step is obvious: If learners are learning well with the instruction that they are receiving, there is no need to design and develop new instruction. Of course, very rarely do we find this ideal state of affairs. Most often we find that there are certain goals that are not adequately being achieved by at least a portion of the learning population. The current level of achievement of learning goals can be determined through the use of paper-and-pencil tests, observations of individuals completing tasks on the job or in simulated situations, learners' self-assessments, or evaluation of products of learners, such as error rates and reports from quality-control sections. Of course, combinations of several of these assessment techniques would probably render the most reliable estimate of the current level of performance of learning goals. An additional question that might also be investigated at this time is "Is existing instruction being delivered efficiently?" There are occasions in educational and training environments when learning goals are being reached by an acceptable percentage of the learners but only with a Herculean effort on the part of teachers/trainers and/or learners. For example, in an educational setting, teachers may spend many hours outside of class tutoring individual learners who have fallen behind or who are ahead of the pace of most learners. In training environments, learners may spend an exorbitant number of hours outside of class studying to compensate for inadequate or inappropriate instruction. Instruction that requires the expending of effort, time, and other resources beyond that needed by alternate or revised instruction can be considered inefficient. Inefficient instruction often indicates that an alternate form of instructional delivery is appropriate, such as computers, video, or another alternative medium. The same type of examination might be instigated to examine the appeal of the current instruction: "Is existing effective instruction appealing?"

3. *Determine the gaps between "what is" and "what should be."* Identify the gap between what learners should be able to do and what they are currently able to do for each of the identified goals. This gap may be precisely stated in percentages, such as: "All of the students should be able to make correct change when given a bill of ten dollars or less and the cost of the purchase. Only 67 percent of the students were able to do this. Thirty-three percent of the students are unable to reach this goal." The gap may be less formally stated: "Fewer than half of our secretaries can compose letters that clearly communicate the intention of the letter and whose work is free of grammatical or spelling errors. We want to do better."

For some goals, this gap is easily seen. For instance, if a business has added a new learning goal to its curriculum for its employees, such as being able to correctly apply a new business policy, one might assume that the gap is 100 percent; that is, none of the employees currently know how to apply the policy. Or when new employees enter the business or when students enter a new grade, one can assume that there are considerable gaps between what they must know and what they do know. Be cautious when making assumptions of this nature; when learners haven't had instruction on something, assuming they do not know it can be dangerous. As you will recall from the discussion in Chapter 1, people learn from many different situations, only some of which are formal education. You would want to confirm your assumption of prior knowledge with some of the same techniques used in step 2; otherwise, you might find yourself spending much energy designing instruction for goals that learners have already attained.

4. *Prioritize gaps according to agreed-upon criteria.* Quite often, especially when working with many goals, such as an entire curriculum for a grade level or level of employees, there will be many gaps between what learners should be able to do and what they are currently able to do. Often it is impossible to attend to all of these gaps immediately. A teacher, school system, or business organization must determine which of the gaps are most critical and attend to those gaps first. Decision makers can use several criteria to determine which gaps to attend to first. These criteria might include the following:

- The size of the gap, attending to the biggest gaps first.
- The importance of the goal, working on the goals that are most critical first.
- The number of students affected, choosing those gaps that affect the largest number of students first.

- The consequences of not meeting the goal, selecting those gaps that have the most serious consequences if the gaps are not closed first.

- The probability of reducing the gap, attending to the gaps that have the greatest probability of being closed with the available resources first.

5. *Determine which gaps are instructional needs and which are most appropriate for design and development of instruction.* One of the biggest mistakes that designers, teachers, and educators make is assuming that instruction is the solution to all performance problems. In other words, they are determining a solution (instruction) before completely analyzing the problem (that learners are not performing well on some task). This leap can lead to investing both instructional and learners' resources and time into instruction that may not be required. Learners may not perform well for many reasons, only one of which is that they do not know how to do something.

For example, a school system may find that first-graders in a certain school (or perhaps a group of schools) are performing very poorly on standardized tests in reading. Without investigating the problem carefully, the school district might assume that the reading instruction is poor and requires revision, either in approach or in delivery. However, if the members of the needs assessment team investigated a little further, they might discover that the students in question have an extremely high absenteeism rate—27 percent. Therefore, it may not be that reading instruction is poor; it may be that students are simply not present in the classroom often enough to learn. The absenteeism problem must be attended to before instigating any changes in the instruction.

Similar performance problems that are not caused by poor instruction can be observed in the business world. An employer might observe that employees are completing work tasks very slowly. She might assume that this slow rate of completion is because employees do not know how to complete the job quickly, and she might begin developing a training program. Further investigation might reveal, however, that this is not a training problem. It could be that employees are not motivated to work quickly or well. Perhaps there are hidden rewards for working slowly, such as the approval of other employees, or punishments for completing work quickly, such as being given more or distasteful tasks when work is completed. Thiagarajan (1984) listed eight solutions other than training that might solve performance problems in business: job redesign, recruitment (selection), job reassignment, organizational development, selling (motivation), incentive and feedback systems, facilities design, and tools design.

Certain performance problems may be better solved by support rather than training. Performance support systems, particularly Electronic Performance Support Systems (EPSSs), can provide information, advice, and tools to guide a person through a task within the job, *in situ*, rather than teaching the person new skills. Typically, EPSSs are less expensive than training, and if an EPSS will solve the problem, it will often be the better choice than instruction. Some of these other-than-instruction solutions might translate to K–12 and post-secondary education as well. There is more on performance support systems in Chapter 7, A Framework for Instructional Strategy Design.

Techniques for Data Gathering

Many sources should be considered to obtain an adequate picture of the issues identified in the three models just presented. Rossett (1988) suggested that these data can be acquired through a variety of techniques: analysis of extant data, analysis of subject matter, interviewing, observing, focus groups, and questionnaires and surveys. Each of these techniques has its own advantages and limitations. For example, questionnaires and surveys can gather a lot of information from a lot of people. However, the information reported on these instruments can be highly influenced by what participants think is the desirable response. Responses may reveal information that is provocative but uninterpretable without probing follow-up questions. Hopefully, the designer can obtain information on the same issues from multiple sources to gain as full a picture as possible of the perspectives on the questions asked.

We have described models and techniques in this section on needs assessment that are most often employed in large-scale needs assessments. As with other instructional design activities, the precision, depth, formality, and amount of documentation required in this activity may vary depending upon the impact of the decisions resulting from it. For example, trainers and teachers may assess the gaps between desired and current achievement very informally with only a mental review of the questions posited in the Discrepancy model. A teacher might think to himself at the end of a week, "What goals for learning in my class are not being well met?" He recalls some, and then thinks: "What are the most important learning gaps I need to work on next week?"

Although the Problem-Based and Innovation-Based models expand upon the traditional Discrepancy model to better meet the requirements of specific types of information needs, they are not exhaustive. You may find that in particular situations you have to combine models or construct additional steps to answer the specific types of questions presented to determine which learning goals require instructional attention.

DESCRIBING THE LEARNING ENVIRONMENT

The second major component of learning context analysis is a description of the current learning environment. As in the case of the needs assessment described previously, if you are designing instruction for your own class, this description can be rather informal but is nevertheless important. If you are designing instruction for a more distant or larger environment, it is more difficult to describe the learning system, but of even greater importance. The primary task at this point is to think about the "system" in which the instruction will be implemented. This "learning system" is composed of all factors that affect and are affected by the learning that takes place: learners (which we will discuss in the next section), instructional materials, the teacher/trainer, instructional equipment (such as computers, displays, projectors, video, and so forth), the instructional facilities, and the community or organization.

A designer is often wise to consider, beyond the immediate learning system, the larger learning system into which the classroom environment belongs, such as the local or state school system or the business organization in which training is to be conducted. An in-depth investigation into what the environment is like where instruction will be implemented helps to ensure that the instruction will, indeed, be used in that environment. For example, if you are designing computer-based instruction to be used as training material in a business, it is important that you know how many and what kind of computers are available for instructional purposes and where the computers are located, as well as how the trainer feels about computer-based instruction.

Here are some of the questions that you may wish to ask about the learning environment when contemplating developing instructional materials:

1. What are the characteristics of the teachers/trainers who will be using these materials?

- What are the interests and preferences of the teachers/trainers? How do they see their roles in the classroom?
- How do the teachers/trainers in the learning environments feel about having instruction delivered via media or other nontraditional methods?

Some teachers and trainers may find certain forms of instruction, such as computer tutorials, unacceptable because they take over the role of disseminator of information that teachers particularly enjoy or view as their main function. Teachers in specific content areas may feel that a particular medium is an inappropriate form of instruction for their content area. In these cases, even the best instructional material may not be adopted because it conflicts with what the potential adopters view as the appropriate role of instructional materials.

- Do teachers/trainers like to use technology-based instruction for the central portion of instruction in a particular content area? Or do they plan to use technology-based instruction for remediation, enrichment, or review? What experience have teachers/trainers had with the Web, computer-based learning environments, integrated learning systems, and so forth?

Whether it is from limited hardware availability or from teachers' perceptions of their roles, media that are designed to be the primary instructional support may not be adoptable in some learning environments. In other environments, problems with availability of teachers with the necessary expertise or the variability of learners' backgrounds may mean that the mediated materials have to be the primary source of instruction, at least for particular units of instruction. Whatever the case, developers must have some idea of how the software can and will be used in the learning environment. Teachers and trainers who have positive experiences with technology-based instruction will probably feel more comfortable using alternative forms of instruction as the primary instructional delivery system.

- What is the level of experience of the teachers/trainers with the content, learners, and teaching in general?

The more inexperienced teachers and trainers are with the content, the learners, or teaching in general, the more they may benefit from structure and organization within the materials. In addition, the school system and organization must have this information to plan the training that instructors and teachers will require in order to use new instructional materials effectively.

2. Are there existing curricula into which this piece of instruction must fit? If so, what is the philosophy, strategy, or theory used in these materials? If a particular approach is used to teach a specific content, such as reading, then in order to be compatible and integratable into the curriculum, material should be developed that utilizes this theory or philosophy. There may be occasions when instruction that portrays an alternate philosophy or theory may be appropriate, but developers should be aware that this is what they are doing.

3. What hardware is commonly available in the potential learning environments? Are there video playback machines, and what are their formats (VHS, DVD, MiniDV, etc.)? Are computer workstations available? If so, what kind, how many, and in what configurations and networks? What about slide or overhead projectors? What software and other materials are available? One of the biggest impediments to utilization of mediated instruction seems to be hardware availability. To assure that instruction is usable by the projected learning environments, developers should conduct surveys that indicate what hardware is available. In the EduSpider example presented at the beginning of this chapter, the developers required server software that was incompatible with target school computers. If the EduSpider employees had investigated the learning environment, they might have chosen different supporting software. Designers sometimes assume that the computer software they are accustomed to using is available everywhere. Even the most commonplace productivity software, such as a particular word processing package or database, may not be available at another site.

4. *What are the characteristics of the classes and facilities that will use the new instruction?* The size and location of facilities and classes can affect the way instructional materials should be developed and what they should include. Obviously, a designer planning instruction in high school chemistry must consider the lab facilities, equipment, and materials that are generally available in high schools. When designing a course to prepare workers to interview anxious potential clients, the designer must consider whether room and facilities are available to spread out into role-playing and discussion groups. A more subtle factor to consider is class climate. Are learners more accustomed to being information receivers or active learners? Are they accustomed to working cooperatively in groups or individually? These factors may have a substantial effect on what instructional techniques a designer may choose or how much preparation or training the designer must build into the instruction to prepare learners to use an unfamiliar technique.

5. *What are the characteristics of the school system or organization in which the new instruction will take place?* Here again, the designer becomes something of a detective, investigating the beliefs of the organization in terms of the roles and expectations of the learners, the teachers/trainers, and the management. What does the school system or the organization see as its primary mission? How does the proposed instruction relate to the mission of the organization? Who are the primary decision makers in the organization? The risk in not considering these factors is designing instruction that runs contrary to organizational beliefs. There is also the risk of not considering the input of critical individuals in the organization. The ultimate effect of this is designing instruction that cannot be implemented into the existing system.

6. *What is the philosophy and what are the taboos of the larger community in which the organization or school system exists?* Often, this is not a critical issue. However, due to the serious consequences of *not* considering these is-

sues in certain circumstances, it is worth the time to consider the larger system into which the instruction will be placed. For instance, developers of science curricula have learned to consider the established beliefs of the community when designing instruction that touches on Darwinism. Business organizations must consider reigning political and economic attitudes when designing instruction on labor relations.

We have barely touched on some of the factors within the learning environment that should be considered when designing instruction. You will probably be able to generate some additional factors that influence the design of instruction for your particular circumstances. Tessmer (1990) and Tessmer and Harris (1992) provide an extensive discussion of "environment analysis." What is critical is that you consider instruction as a system in which many factors are interrelated, and changing one factor will affect other factors. To create instruction that can be used in the learning system, it is important that you consider these effects as you design the instruction. This will save you from rude surprises like those EduSpider received. Following is an example of how a state educational system examined instructional needs and the learning environment as it considered the design of a physics curriculum.

An Example of Validation of Need and Analysis of Learning Environment

The mythical state of Corona has many small rural school districts. A problem identified among these small districts, as well as in many of the larger ones, is a lack of teachers who are qualified to teach advanced high school science courses, particularly physics. The Corona State Education Agency is investigating the possibility of delivering this instruction via a series of DVDs. A task force has been created to investigate the learning environments into which this instruction might be implemented to help determine the feasibility of video as a delivery system. Following are some of the questions they asked and the answers they found.

1. *Are there learning goals in advanced high school physics not currently being met in school districts in the state?* Surveys of high school math teachers, administrators, current and graduated students, and parents of current and graduated students indicate a dissatisfaction with advanced science instruction in high schools in 80 percent of smaller school districts and 45 percent of larger school districts. Standardized test scores on advanced placement tests in science indicate that only 20 percent of the state's students who take these exams receive advanced placement credit. In other words, the instruction is inadequate to prepare students to pass advanced placement exams.

2. *Is instruction already offered in this area or is it a new learning goal?* A survey of school districts found that 90 percent of the larger school districts and 50 percent of the smaller districts offer courses in physics. In the larger districts, 65 percent of the high schools in the district offer the advanced courses. In the smaller districts, 35 percent of the high schools in the district offer these courses. The schools that do not offer the courses list lack of teacher expertise and small numbers of students interested in the courses as reasons for not offering them. In general, acquisition of skills and knowledge in physics seems to be a learning goal that is espoused by most school districts and for which many school districts offer instruction. However, this instruction is by no means available in all high schools.

3. *Is existing instruction delivered efficiently?* In many of the smaller school districts offering physics courses, classes contain ten or fewer students. Teachers in these courses report that they spend much time in remedial instruction because students often enter the class with insufficient math or science background to learn successfully from available instructional materials on physics. Therefore, instruction seems to be inefficient in terms of teachers' resources.

4. *Does the learning context seem to require the particular capabilities of a particular medium?* This question will be answered in more detail later, but it does seem initially that the diversity of the student population and the lack of qualified teachers suggest video as a partial solution to the instructional problem. Many of the topics of advanced physics cannot be studied in laboratory experiments in high schools and must be simulated. Video can simulate reality but is rather limited in providing opportunities for feedback or other learner interaction with the material. Additional materials such as lab supplies, print-based instruction, and computer software could be developed and integrated with the video lessons to provide demonstrations of principles, active student practice and exploration in microworlds, and other opportunities for application and feedback.

5. *What is the existing philosophy, strategy, or theory behind the current physics curriculum?* Surveys of existing physics curriculum materials, physics teachers, and physics education specialists indicate that there seem to be two divergent philosophies with regard to physics education. One school of thought holds that the goals of physics education should be that learners are able to remember and apply the concepts and principles of physics. The other school of thought thinks that the goal of physics education should be that learners acquire the skills of a scientist: to identify and define researchable problems and to conduct experimentation. Some physics educators believe that both sets of goals may be achieved in the same curriculum. The majority of physics teachers in Corona agree that the primary goal of physics education

should be that learners can remember and apply the concepts and principles of physics. The ability to conduct experimentation is a secondary goal. However, most teachers support the hands-on experimentation available in a physics lab in which learners directly experience and "prove" established physics principles. This finding suggests that either (1) the instructional program be designed to achieve the current goals of physics instruction, or (2) strategies be planned to convince teachers of the importance of alternate goals.

6. *What types and quantities of hardware are available in Corona school districts?* Surveys of school districts in Corona indicate that 95 percent of the larger school districts and 80 percent of the smaller school districts have an adequate number of video playback machines in their high schools. Of these, 65 percent are VHS machines, 30 percent are DVD players, and 5 percent are DV, 8mm, and others. In addition, 98 percent of the larger school districts and 94 percent of the smaller districts have some personal computer workstations available for supplemental instructional uses (50 percent Windows®, 40 percent Macintosh®, and 10 percent Linux and other).

The results of this survey suggest that although the school districts are, in general, limited in the availability of hardware, both video and computer hardware is available in most schools. In addition, the survey suggests that there is a diversity of hardware available in the districts. This finding suggests that the instructional materials must be developed in forms that will accommodate this diversity. (Duplication of videotapes in required formats is not much of a problem, but provision of computer software for the major brands of computers may be somewhat difficult.)

7. *Do teachers/administrators plan to use mediated instruction as the central portion of instruction? What experiences have the teachers had with media-based systems?* Some of the physics instructors have had experience teaching with some of the media-based learning systems that were originally developed during the 1960s. When questioned, many of the teachers liked the idea of media-based systems but found the management of such systems, particularly individualized systems, onerous. A survey indicated that many teachers feel that the primary source of instruction must be the teacher and that instructional materials can only serve supplemental functions. The survey revealed that some teachers supported the use of mediated instruction, but they did not see how this might be feasible with the hardware limitations that they have in their schools.

The implications of such findings are threefold. First of all, teachers may be open to a video/computer combination as a way to deliver mediated instruction, particularly if the system makes evaluation of student products, prescription of future lessons, and management and reporting of student records easy. Second, some teachers may feel that using video as the primary delivery system is antithetical to the role of a teacher. In this case, either programs must be developed that support the role of the teacher, or teachers must be educated to accept a different role and to perceive instruction as something that can be delivered via a variety of media. Last, if the instructional video/computer products are developed to be the primary sources of instruction, then developers must identify what constitutes an adequate amount of hardware in a classroom and suggest management techniques for teachers to employ with assignment of students.

WORKING WITH AN EXPERT

How do you find out all of the information that you must know about the context, learner, and instructional task? In each case you will locate individuals who have experience, knowledge, and expertise in one or more of these areas. An expert may be very well informed about the learning environment, its organization, the curriculum, and so on. An expert may have taught or worked with learners who are similar to the target audience. An individual may be expert in completing the task(s) represented by the learning goal, or the person may be expert in all of these areas. Instructional designers must form a relationship with such experts and interview them in a way that provides complete and accurate information. Often, experts have not been in such a role before, and it is the designers' responsibility to get the information they need. At the end of this chapter are several references that are invaluable when planning to work with an expert. We will describe some rudimentary suggestions for a first meeting with an expert.

Before the First Meeting

1. Learn about the expert. Determine the expert's area of expertise. Does the expert know the content? The learners? The context? All three? What is the length and degree of the expert's experience? What common experiences do the designer and expert have?

2. Do your "homework" on background information. Read as much documentation as possible about the organization, the learners, and the content. Are there documents available from recent self-studies? Is there a written profile of the learners? What is written about the content?

3. Develop a written project description for the expert. In terms as simple as possible, write down your understanding of the project. What are the deliverables? What is the time line? Who is the audience and what is the scope of the context?

4. Find sample products to use as examples. Show example deliverables that are similar to your project. Explain what the differences will be for your project.

5. Develop a written set of questions. Determine what specific information you need to obtain from the expert. How should you organize your questions? What is a logical sequence? What language will convey your needs most clearly? Which are the priority questions?

6. Plan how to take notes. Decide how you can obtain the most complete record of the expert's responses. Can you record them with videotape or audiotape? What is the best form for your written notes?

During the First Meeting

1. Establish a rapport. Ask some general questions about the expert. Listen to the replies. Respond positively to information given. Try to identify common experiences. Be professional but warm.

2. Share expectations. Determine why the expert believes he is there. Explain why you think the expert is there and in general what kinds of information you require. Communicate how much of the expert's time is required. Discuss any terminology that you will consistently use and explain your meaning. Determine discrepancies in use of terms and negotiate their meanings for the project.

3. Develop a communication plan. Provide a way that you can be reached via phone, fax, or electronic mail. Identify the times when it is easiest to contact you directly. Solicit the same information from the expert. Preview when communications or other meetings may be necessary. Obtain a general overview of the expert's schedule in coming months.

4. Gather information. Use questions to guide your interview. Be sensitive to cues in responses that lead to new questions. Be open to volunteered information. On any sensitive issues provide as much anonymity as possible. Obtain written information that answers any questions.

After the First Meeting

1. Consolidate notes. Integrate information obtained in written materials, notes, and tapes.

2. Determine gaps and inconsistencies. Once information is integrated, ascertain what information is incomplete. Locate information that appears to be contradictory.

3. Arrange to gather missing information. Determine whether gaps and inconsistencies must be addressed in face-to-face, written, or oral form. Gather missing information.

4. Plan the next meeting. Decide whether an additional meeting is required and identify what the direction and scope of this meeting will be. Begin a list of questions for this meeting.

E X E R C I S E S

1. In your own words, describe the purposes of the analysis phase of the design process, and list the three components that are analyzed in this phase.

2. In your own words, describe the purpose of an analysis of the learning environment.

3. In your own words, describe the following: (1) the purpose of a needs assessment, (2) the conditions that might require a needs assessment, and (3) the steps in a needs assessment procedure.

4. For each of the following situations, decide which model of needs assessment (Problem Solution, Innovation, or Discrepancy) best fits the circumstances. Explain your answer.

a. The teacher preparation program at the University of Corona has learned that it will undergo an accreditation review in two years. The University implemented a new, improved program two years ago, including a fifth year, extensive mentoring, and other innovations, but enrollments are down and a great deal of unrest is expressed by both faculty and students.

b. The Commandant of the Corona Merchant Marine Academy's "Navigation in Open Seas" course has learned of the existence of the Global Positioning Satellite (GPS) and availability of highly accurate and inexpensive location devices.

c. The state's largest newspaper, *The Corona Flare*, has been losing advertisers and is in financial trouble, apparently due to insertion errors for ads in their timing, placement, and content. Affected departments appear to be advertising, graphic arts, copy-editing, and production scheduling.

5. In your own words, describe factors that should be analyzed in the learning environment, and discuss why these factors should be considered.

6. Suppose you were on an instructional development team that was developing materials to be used in adult basic education classes. The course that you are considering delivering via mediated instruction would cover financial issues. The goal is that students will learn about managing checking and savings accounts, paying bills, and managing credit accounts. What would you want to know about the instructional need and the learning environment before you begin actually designing instruction? How would you go about answering these questions relating to need and learning environment?

7. **Your Role:** You are faculty in the Electronics Technology Department of High Mountain Plains Area Vocational-Technical School (HMPAVTS).

The Situation: Ms. Sara Burnheart is the director of personnel at Electro-Tronics Corporation (ETC), a major employer of your program's graduates. At a reception of the Corona Chapter of the Association for Computing Machinery (ACM), Ms. Burnheart collars you near the hors d'oeuvres and regales you with the following: "I just can't believe you are still teaching C++ at HMPAVTS. Nobody uses C++ anymore, don't you know that? Good heavens," she shrieked, "you people are wasting your time and our tax dollars with that obsolete language. Tactile BASIC is what you should be teaching!" Then Mr. Ruddertail, the current president of the VoTech State Board, joins you, giving Ms. Burnheart a hearty greeting and discussing with her their last week's golf game.

Two days later, you get a call from the state Department of Vocational-Technical Education, asking why you are still teaching C++. Your school decides that this might be as good a time as any to evaluate all of the offerings in your Electronic Technology program.

The Problem: Develop a needs assessment procedure that will allow you to respond to the state's request. Include the types of people you would involve in each step, the types of questions you would ask, and the techniques that you would use.

SUMMARY

This chapter was the first of three that address instructional analysis, this chapter describing the analysis of the learning context. In subsequent chapters we will take a look at analysis of learners and analysis of learning tasks. Analysis of instructional context involves needs assessment and a description of the environment in which instruction will take place. Figure 3.3 summarizes key points in this chapter.

Needs assessments can be initiated for any of a number of reasons, including learning goals not being met

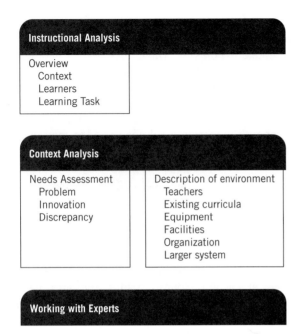

Figure 3.3 Summary Diagram for Chapter 3.

given current instruction, current instruction being inefficient, current instruction being unappealing, lack of instruction in a given area, new goals being added to the curriculum, and changes in the learner population. Three primary models of needs assessment fit different initiating conditions: Problem-Based, Innovation-Based, and Discrepancy-Based,

Problem-Based needs assessments begin with problem determination, which leads to determination of relationship between problem(s) and employees' (or learners') knowledge, and correlating with determination if problem is learning-related and therefore amenable to a solution through instructional interventions.

Innovation-Based needs assessments look at the nature of innovations and determine learning goals that may be associated with them. Analysis of the learning environment involves looking at existing conditions that surround and support instruction, including teachers, existing curricula, instructional media equipment available, school or training organization, and factors in the larger community.

Discrepancy-Based needs assessments can be accomplished through a five-step process: (1) Describe the learning goals of the current instructional system, (2) evaluate achievement of goals in the current system, (3) describe the gaps between what is desired and what is accomplished, (4) set priorities for action, and (5) determine what needs are instructional needs, and of those needs that are instructional, determine which ones are appropriate for resolution through design and development of instruction.

Description of the learning environment entails learning about teachers and trainers, existing instruction, orientations, equipment, facilities, organization and system characteristics, and larger system concerns.

Recommendations for working with an expert include pre-meeting, meeting, and post-meeting tasks. Suggestions provided can help designers get the most information in the least time when working with experts who may be needed in all phases of analysis: context, learner, and task. Figure 3.3 summarizes key points in this chapter.

EXTENDED EXAMPLE

For this and the remaining chapters of this text, we will follow the design and development of one course through each of the phases of the instructional design process in an online Extended Example. The course being developed is titled "Instructional Photography Basics," an introductory course for graduate students in the instructional technology programs at a fictitious (but plausible) university. Go to the Instructional Design Learning Resources Web site to begin review of the Extended Example. In this chapter's installment of the Extended Example, we present a needs assessment and a learning environment analysis for our photography course.

READINGS AND REFERENCES

Becker, J. M., & Hahn, C. L. (1977). *Wingspread workbook for educational change.* Boulder, CO: Social Science Educational Consortium.

Bratton, B. (1979–80). The instructional development specialist as consultant. *Journal of Instructional Development, 3*(2), 2–8.

Briggs, L. J. (Ed.). (1977). *Instructional design: Principles and applications.* Englewood Cliffs, NJ: Educational Technology Publications.

Briggs, L. J., & Wager, W. W. (1981). *Handbook of procedures for the design of instruction* (2nd ed.). Englewood Cliffs, NJ: Educational Technology Publications.

Coscarelli, B. (1988). Performance Improvement Quarterly and human performance technology. *Performance Improvement Quarterly, 1*(1), 2–5.

Davis, R. H., Alexander, L. T., & Yelon, S. L. (1974). *Learning system design.* New York: McGraw-Hill.

Dick, W., & Carey, L. (1985). *The systematic design of instruction* (2nd ed.). Glenview, IL: Scott, Foresman.

Duffy, T. (2004). Theory and the design of learning environments: Reflections on differences in disciplinary focus. *Educational Technology. xx, 44*(3), 13–15.

Ertmer, P. A. & Quinn, J. (2003). *The ID casebook: Case studies in instructional design.* Upper Saddle River, NJ: Merrill.

Gery, G. J. (1989). Training vs. performance support: Inadequate training is now insufficient. *Performance Improvement Quarterly, 2*(3), 51–71.

Greer, M. (1992). *ID project management.* Englewood Cliffs, NJ: Educational Technology Publications.

Havelock, R. J. (1973). *The change agent's guide to innovation in education.* Englewood Cliffs, NJ: Educational Technology Publications.

Hutchison, C. (1989, October). Moving from instructional technologist to performance technologist. *Performance and Instruction, 28,* 5–8.

Kaufman, R., & English, F. W. (1979). *Needs assessment: Concept and application.* Englewood Cliffs, NJ: Educational Technology Publications.

Leitzman, D. F., Walter, S., Earle, R. S., & Myers, C. (1979). Contracting for instructional development. *Journal of Instructional Development, 3*(2), 23–28.

Lewis, T., & Bjorkquist, D. C. (1992). Needs assessment—A critical reappraisal. *Performance Improvement Quarterly, 5*(4), 33–54.

Richey, R. C., & Tessmer, M. (1995). Enhancing instructional systems design through contextual analysis. In B. B. Seels (Ed.), *Instructional design fundamentals: A Reconsideration* (pp. 189–199). Englewood Cliffs, NJ: Educational Technology Publications.

Rossett, A. (1988). *Training needs assessment.* Englewood Cliffs, NJ: Educational Technology Publications.

Rothwell, W. M., & Kazanas, H. C. (1992). *Mastering the instructional design process: A systematic approach.* San Francisco: Jossey-Bass Publishers.

Scriven, M. (1972). Pros and cons about goal-free evaluation. *Evaluation Comment, 3*(4), 1–4.

Sleezer, C. M. (1992). Needs assessment: Perspectives from the literature. *Performance Improvement Quarterly, 5*(2), 34–46.

Tessmer, M. (1990). Environment analysis: A neglected stage of instructional design. *Educational Technology Research & Development, 38*(1), 55–64.

Tessmer, M. (1993). *Front-end and formative multimedia evaluation: Sharpening "cutting edge" technology.* Paper presented at the annual convention of the American Educational Research Association, Atlanta, GA.

Tessmer, M., & Harris, D. (1992). *Planning and conducting the instructional setting:* Environmental analysis. London: Kogan Page.

Tessmer, M., & Wedman, J. (1995). Context-sensitive instructional design models: A response to design research, studies, and criticism. *Performance Improvement Quarterly, 8*(3), 37–53.

Thiagarajan, S. (1984). How to avoid instruction. *Performance and Instruction, 23,* 10.

Tobin, K., & Dawson, G. (1992). Constraints to curriculum reform: Teachers and the myths of schooling. *Educational Technology Research and Development, 40*(1), 81–92.

INSTRUCTIONAL ANALYSIS: ANALYZING THE LEARNERS

CHAPTER OBJECTIVES

At the conclusion of this chapter, you should be able to do the following:

- Describe the stable and changing similarities and differences among learners.

- Describe the categories of cognitive characteristics that should be considered in designing instruction.

- Describe the difference between general characteristics and specific prior knowledge of a learner population.

- Describe some instructional strategy variables that may be influenced by learner characteristics and explain how different learner characteristics may influence how the variables are implemented.

- Describe sources of information about learner characteristics of a particular audience.

- When given a description of a situation, list questions regarding learner characteristics that you would wish to know before designing instruction, as well as techniques and procedures you would use to find the answers to these questions.

- Determine whether a particular learner characteristic should be relevant to a particular learning task.

AN OVERVIEW OF LEARNER ANALYSIS

You will remember in our sad story of the EduSpider Company (see Chapter 3) that its Web-based learning management system and instructional software was unsuccessful for many reasons. Two of these reasons had to do with the knowledge and perceptions of the learners that the instructional designers had not anticipated: (1) Many students were unable to use the software because the developers had assumed that they were skilled in determining least common denominator, and many students were not competent in this skill; and (2) some students reported that the games were too cute and that the characters and rewards used in the games were insulting.

The designers had not done their homework in analyzing the characteristics of the learners that they anticipated using the instruction, usually termed the **target audience** or **target population.** It is critical that designers consider their target audiences, as this knowledge will be important in designing instruction that is effective and interesting to learners. As in earlier analyses, if you are designing instruction for your own students, this stage will be relatively easy but is nonetheless critical and should not be overlooked. Analyzing learners who are remote, such as the merchandise managers in a nationwide department store chain, can be quite a challenging task. Sometimes designers must ask a lot of questions before they have an adequate profile of their audience.

A common error resulting from failure to analyze the characteristics of an audience is assuming that all learners are alike. An even more common error is assuming that the learners are like the designers. This means that we tend to explain things the way we will understand them, use examples that are familiar to us, and use instructional techniques that work well for us. This hidden form of ethnocentrism can play havoc with the design of instruction. For one thing, we are generally familiar with, or quickly become familiar with, the content for which we are designing instruction. Thus, we are tempted to inadequately explain some things and overexplain others. In addition, this ethnocentrism may limit the effectiveness of the examples we select. In one example, a designer was creating instruction on heart-healthy menus to be used in a part of the United States with a large Hispanic population. She was embarrassed during evaluation of her materials to find that there were no references to foods that Hispanic populations commonly include in their daily menus. We need to consciously examine the diversity and commonalties of the target audience so that we can design appropriate and effective instruction for those learners.

It is critical that you create instruction with a particular audience in mind, rather than centering design around the content and then searching for an audience for which it is appropriate. In the latter case, you could find that you have created instruction that is appropriate for *no one.*

There are occasions when you may find yourself developing instruction that is appropriate for more than one audience. In such a case, it is valuable to identify the **primary audience** and the **secondary audience,** describing each as completely as possible. Later in the design process, you may have to make decisions that focus on the primary audience.

A caution is needed here. Novice instructional designers often find themselves describing the characteristics that they *hope* their learners have, rather than the actual characteristics of their target audience. Carrying this approach to its extreme, you could find yourself designing instruction for an audience that doesn't exist! You can detect this faulty thinking in your written descriptions: "Learners ought to be motivated to learn this skill" or "Learners should have a reading level of at least sixth grade." In the next chapter, you will learn to identify the skill and knowledge that learners must obtain in order to reach an instructional goal; however, during learner analysis you should not be thinking of what learners should be like or what they need to know, but what they *are* like and what they *do* know.

Beyond the specifics of learner analysis, all designers can be informed by models of what learners are. Bruner (1985) spoke eloquently of the various models of learners that may be held by educators, including the learner as a blank slate, or *tabula rasa,* upon which to write; the learner as a more active hypothesis generator; nativist views of the learner that emphasize presence of inherent categories or known representations that organize experience; constructivist views in which the world is not learned or discovered but is created by the learner; and the highly analytic novice-to-expert model. (These models can be related to the educational philosophies described in Chapter 2.) Knowledge of the varieties of ways in which learning and learners have been and are being studied is useful in providing perspective to the design enterprise. In this text, we tend to employ the novice-to-expert model most frequently, with references to learner as hypothesis generator and knowledge creator at certain points.

While this chapter provides an overview of learner characteristics for instructional designers, we would highly recommend Jonassen and Grabowski's (1993) more complete review of individual differences as they apply to learning and instruction.

SIMILARITIES AND DIFFERENCES BETWEEN LEARNERS

What things are important to know about the people for whom we will be designing instruction? Although each learner is a unique individual, possessing a complexity that defies complete description, there is a finite and manageable array of human characteristics that are useful to instructional designers. The importance of understanding these characteristics is demonstrated by the requirements for courses such as Human Learning and Human Development (in training programs for instructional designers). As the knowledge that psychologists have amassed about the characteristics of humans is formidable indeed, we can only provide an overview of this area. To simplify this overview, we will organize relevant learner characteristics into four major classes. On the following pages, we will look at this classification scheme, the characteristics that are contained within it, and implications of these characteristics for instructional designers. This classification scheme will help gain a perspective of how learners' characteristics have been studied. The four major classes are *not* of equal importance to designers. In a later section, we will reformulate knowledge about learners into an outline form that is more useful for practitioners in day-to-day application.

Taking a look at human characteristics from within a framework such as the following can be helpful in organizing the knowledge about learners that has been developed over the years. Although some information about a particular target group of learners and about the individuals within that group can be gained by casual or unsupported observation, a great deal of information about learners that we can consider in the design of instruction does not come directly from studying learners in a particular target audience. Rather, it comes from the instructional designer's knowledge about human characteristics applied to a specific target audience of learners.

To begin, we can consider two broad types of human characteristics: individual differences among people and similarities among people. Some schools of thought in education have emphasized individual differences, ignoring the important ways in which people are alike. Others, particularly in psychology, have studied only the ways in which people are the same. In fact, both similarities and differences are important in the design of instruction. Individual differences are aspects of human form, function, and experience about which people are more characterized by their variation than by their sameness. The study of individual differences has been well integrated within instructional psychology (Corno & Snow, 1986; Snow & Swanson,

1992; Kyllonen & Lajoi, 2003) and makes important contributions to instructional design. Widely studied individual difference factors include aptitudes, styles, developmental states or stages, and prior learning. Similarities, on the other hand, are aspects that are characterized by a relative sameness among people rather than differences. These similarities include sensory capacities, information-processing capabilities and limits, human cognition, and developmental processes (not states but the dynamics and process aspects of development), including intellectual, physical, psychosocial, and language development processes. Mainstream learning theory is built upon the study of likenesses among people as learners, and this knowledge is fundamental to instructional psychology and, consequently, to instructional design. The critical thing to remember at this point is that we have knowledge of both differences and similarities among learners, and that both of these kinds of knowledge are helpful to designers. We will return to this point later on in the chapter to describe exactly what sort of value these different perspectives provide.

In addition to similarities and differences, we can consider whether a characteristic exhibits change over time or remains relatively stable over time. Some human characteristics, such as information-processing limits and intelligence, are more or less stable over time. People from childhood through mature adulthood may change very little in some ways and, even though some small change can be observed, stability is a defining feature of the learner characteristic. Other characteristics are notable for their quality of change. The most notable of these characteristics are development (both the process of development and the developmental states or stages themselves) and learning. Both development and learning are constantly changing for all people. Bloom (1964) provided an excellent review of the varieties of changing and stable characteristics.

The result of considering similarities and differences among people, along with changing and stable characteristics, is a matrix of four categories of human characteristics (see Figure 4.1):

1. Stable similarities: similarities among people that are relatively unchanging over time.
2. Stable differences: differences among people that are relatively unchanging over time.
3. Changing similarities: similarities among people that change over time.
4. Changing differences: differences among people that change over time.

It is worth noting that most major conceptualizations of learner characteristics tend to involve only one

	Similarities	Differences
Stable	• Sensory Capacities • Information Processing • Types and Conditions of Learning	• Aptitudes • Cognitive Styles • Psychosocial Traits • Gender, Ethnicity, & Racial Group
Changing	Development Processes • Intellectual • Language • Psychosocial • Moral • Other	Development State • Intellectual • Other Prior Learning • General • Specific

Figure 4.1 Four Categories of Learner Characteristics

or another of these four major categories, generally neglecting to place the characteristic being discussed within the context of others that are qualitatively different. There is a widespread tendency among Educators to adopt a single orientation to learners as being the only one of any relevance (with a most popular orientation emerging once every ten to 20 years on the average). One of the benefits to the study of learner characteristics in the fashion that is presented here, we believe, will be your ability to evaluate the nature and significance of knowledge of learners. We hope you will become "immunized" against whatever may be the latest fad and retain a broadly based, comprehensive view of learners.

STABLE SIMILARITIES

There are many obvious stable similarities among learners that have very little to do with most instructional design decisions, such as where the lungs and ears are located. Another stable similarity may be seen in response to classical conditioning. As is widely known, classical or Pavlovian conditioning consists of a stimulus substitution (Hilgard & Bower, 1965). For instructional designers, knowledge of the characteristics of this sort of learning and conditions for its attainment is not particularly important, since this knowledge represents learning only in a narrow, technical sense—Pavlov's dogs did not learn to do anything *new*, only to produce a preexisting involuntary response (salivation) in the presence of a substitute stimulus (the sound of a bell ringing).

One stable similarity among people that is more useful to instructional design is that of **sensory capacities,** the capabilities and limitations of our sensory organs. Although people vary in their eyesight, hearing,

tactile sensitivity, and so forth, human sensory capacities and perceptual responses are more alike than they are different. The human sense of hearing, for example, is amazingly sensitive, but it is terribly limited compared to that of a dog. And, although eagles or hawks could do it if they knew how, no person is able to read typewritten material with unaided vision from 200 feet away. There are capabilities and limitations for all of our senses. In addition, the perceptual mechanisms, as illustrated by common optical illusions, are well known and shared by us all.

For instructional designers, knowledge of sensory and perceptual characteristics becomes important when attempting to fully involve the senses in learning. The success of an audiovisual presentation, interactive educational game, activity package, or simulation trainer will often rely upon appropriate visual detail, use of color, auditory characteristics, and so forth. The more ambitious one becomes in such treatments, the more critical a knowledge of perception and the characteristics of sense modalities becomes. But even in more mundane situations, knowledge of sensory and perceptual characteristics is helpful. All of us have had enough experience with presentations with inadequate light, low contrast, and microscopic image size to know that decisions about such matters are easy to misjudge. Common characteristics of sensory capabilities contribute to general principles of instructional message design. (For example, see Fleming & Levie, 1993.)

In addition to sensory characteristics, characteristics associated with human **information processing** are also stable similarities that can be helpful to instructional designers (see Chapter 2 for a description of information processing). Whether one is discussing the capacity to make discrete judgments about a single stimulus (Miller, 1956), capacity for temporary storage of isolated, nonmeaningful units of information (Miller, 1956), processing multisensory simultaneous inputs as studied by Broadbent (1958), or Paivio's (1971) work in encoding and memory of visual and verbal information, capabilities and limits in the processing of information that are part of being human are found that do not vary with intelligence, college major, or even much with age.

The limits imposed by information-processing characteristics are real, and they are a commonplace source of learning problems in schools and training settings. Information overload, confusion, and inability to keep up with material being presented are typical student learning problems caused by ignoring human information-processing characteristics.

Knowledge of information-processing characteristics can not only help the designer avoid problems caused by limits in processing capability, but can also help the designer find solutions to processing-based problems. For example, remembering isolated, nonmeaningful bits of information can be made easier by chunking individual units into groups, with each group of bits becoming a single set of information.

Although it is not typical to think of the **types of learning** as a human characteristic, it is a fundamental fact that people are more or less alike in how they acquire different sorts of learnings (types of learning such as declarative knowledge, concepts, rules, and problem solving, which we will discuss further in Chapter 5). Robert Gagné (1985) developed a synthesis of the various psychologically distinguishable products of learning. Gagné pointed out that once we know that a person is going to learn, for example, a concept, we know that certain conditions must exist both within the learner and outside of the learner for that learning to take place. These **conditions of learning,** which are themselves a similarity among people, do not vary between people, or even between subject areas. In many important respects, the psychological conditions for learning a concept in mathematics are identical to the conditions for learning a concept in grammar. The similarity in the conditions for attainment of different types of learning is a fundamental building block for instructional design (Ragan & Smith, 2003; Smith & Ragan, 2000). (For more information on types of learning, see Chapter 5. For more information on conditions of learning, see Chapters 8 through 16, which present instructional strategy recommendations for different types of learning.)

The principles on which instructional design is based, particularly instructional strategy, are largely drawn from a knowledge of the similarities among learners—not only Gagné's work but also human information-processing and sensory characteristics. It is upon these principles that much of this text is based.

A number of factors that are relatively stable over time vary among individual learners. Aptitudes, styles, traits, and group membership factors such as gender and ethnicity are all areas in which individuals differ from one another in ways that change little with the years.

Aptitudes

Among the most widely studied stable differences are aptitudes. An aptitude is an ability related to readiness or facility to learn or achieve. A major division in theory and practice involves general aptitude, a single, general (or "G") factor, which might be possessed by an individual, versus specific aptitudes, of which an individual person possesses many.

Single Factor. The most common single-factor aptitude construct is that of intelligence along with measurement attempts typically reflected in a score called an intelligence quotient, or "IQ." Although there is some disagreement among the experts in this area, all would agree that IQ is *not* a measure of some global, qualitative factor such as "good brains." A good general definition of IQ is "aptitude for school learning." An excellent overview of issues in the study of intelligence is provided by Sternberg's multivolume series (Sternberg, 1982, 1984, 1986).

Intelligence testing has acquired some vigorous critics, and the accusations made are not entirely groundless. The worst abuses resulting from uses of IQ information have come from making inappropriate use of individual students' IQ test scores, and the harm done has generally rested upon the "good brains" conception of IQ and blanket judgments made and communicated to students based on IQ test scores.

Most designers make little if any use of IQ scores. Although not supported by research, we can speculate that IQ scores can help a designer make inferences about a number of factors that are related to learning from instruction, including cognitive strategies available and amount of general prior knowledge available to build upon. IQ indices may also help predict which students will (1) need more/fewer examples, (2) be able to interpret analogies, (3) require more/less learning time, (4) need more/less practice, (5) have positive/negative attitudes toward learning, or 6) persevere in learning for short/long periods of time.

Multiple Factor. Rather than approach the question of ability or aptitude in a global, single-factor fashion, many people have viewed aptitude from the standpoint of multiple, specialized aptitudes and clusters of them. Time-honored tests of vocational aptitude, such as the Armed Services Vocational Aptitude Battery (ASVAB) as well as tests for particular academic aptitudes, such as the Scholastic Aptitude Test (SAT), Graduate Record Exam (GRE) or the Miller Analogies Test (MAT) have been used for many years to assist in placement and student selection in careers, military specialties, college, and graduate school. Although these widely used tests of academic and job-related aptitudes are more well-known, other aptitude factors have been developed and studied. Two such approaches to the study and use of multiple aptitudes are Gardner's Multiple Intelligences and Snow's study of aptitude complexes.

Multiple Intelligences. A popular typological categorization of aptitudes is Howard Gardner's conception of "multiple intelligences" (Gardner, 1993). Using the term "intelligence" rather than "aptitude" may have had an influence on the popularity of this construct with teachers. Seven areas human functioning are represented as intelligences: verbal, logical/mathematical, visual/spatial, musical, interpersonal, intrapersonal, and bodily/kinesthetic. Gardner noted that these seven areas of functioning are a property of all human beings and are dimensions in which human beings differ, but are unlike learning styles (Gardner, 2003).

Aptitudes and Aptitude Complexes. Rather than develop a typology as Gardner did, Richard Snow led the study of interactions of aptitudes and sets of traits, in conjunction with the study of instructional strategies or "treatments" (Cronbach & Snow, 1977). Various complexes of aptitudes and treatments have emerged from this line of research, including a social trait complex, a clerical/conventional trait complex, a science/math complex, and an intellectual/cultural trait complex (Ackerman, 2003). A large body of research has been conducted over the years called "aptitude-treatment interaction" (ATI) studies. By combining different instructional methods with learner groups with different apti-

tudes, ATI studies have sought to find particular approaches which best meet the needs of students with particular characteristics. For example, a study by Shute & Towle (2003) found an interaction between learning environment (exploratory and structured) and learner exploratory traits (high and low). The researchers found a disordinal interaction between these factors: Students who had a high aptitude for exploration performed better in an exploratory learning environment, and students who exhibited less aptitude for exploration performed better with structured instruction.

Cognitive Styles

Another type of stable individual difference can be seen in the ways that people receive and process information. These differences are variously called cognitive styles, cognitive controls, cognitive tempo, and perceptual styles. We will refer to them collectively here as cognitive styles. Terms that are also frequently used interchangeably with *cognitive styles* and bear important distinctions are factors called *learning styles*. We will discuss learning styles separately from cognitive styles due to important differences between them.

A good deal is known about a variety of processing-style differences. In an extensive review, Ragan et al. (1979) found 11 style dimensions that have potential usefulness to the design of technical training. Of these, four styles—field independent/dependent cognitive style (Witkin et al., 1977), leveling/sharpening cognitive controls (Klein, 1970; Santostephano, 1978), impulsive/reflective cognitive tempo (Kagan, 1966), and visual/haptic perceptual style (Lowenfeld & Brittain, 1970)—seem to have the most potential utility to instructional design. Key points about each of these four style dimensions are presented in summary form in Figure 4.2.

Cognitive styles are useful to instructional designers because they provide information about individual differences from a cognitive and information-processing standpoint. Information about a learner's cognitive

Style Dimension	Key Investigator(s)	Primary Measures
Field Independent/ Dependent Cognitive Style	Witkin et al.	Rod & Frame Group-Embedded Figures
Leveling/Sharpening Cognitive Controls	Klein Santostephano	L/S Wagon Test (child) L/S Wagon Test (adult)
Impulsive/Reflective Cognitive Tempo	Kagan	Matching familiar Figures
Visual/Haptic Perceptual Style	Lowenfeld & Brittain	Successive Perception Test —1

Figure 4.2   Some Cognitive Styles and Their Measures

style can provide insight into not only whether an individual is likely to be able to learn to complete a particular learning task but also why. Information from cognitive style measures is relevant only when considered with regard to particular learning tasks.

For example, if an individual is "field dependent," it does not mean that the individual learns all things well or poorly, or even that the individual learns all things in a particular way that is different from other people. It does mean, however, that if the learning task involves isolating and manipulating a detail from within a complex visual field, it is likely that field-dependent people would need more help from instruction to perform the task successfully than would field-independent people. Such tasks would include the following: learning to find particular elements in complex electronic circuit diagrams; learning to determine from a printed diagram or pattern where different fabric layers are supposed to go in complex junctions found in sewing a suit; or learning to quickly find and extract information from an instrument in a complicated instrument panel in a cockpit.

Performance of these same tasks would also be influenced by differences in the leveling/sharpening and visual/ haptic dimensions, with people who are relative "sharpeners" and "visual" being much like the field-independent people, and those who are relative "levelers" and "haptic" responding similarly to field-dependent people (Ausburn, Ausburn, & Ragan, 1980). The impulsive/reflective cognitive tempo most specifically affects tasks requiring learners to select choices from among multiple alternatives. Thus, if the learning task presented multiple options, such as being able to match a logic diagram to given Boolean expressions (AND, OR, NOT, NAND, NOR), the impulsive learner may quickly select an incorrect match, as contrasted with a reflective learner who considers all alternatives before making a choice. Figure 4.3 presents an example analysis of a training objective from a cognitive-style standpoint.

Cognitive styles can be differentiated from other constructs with which they are frequently confused by the specificity with which cognitive styles may be applied. In the case of **learning styles** and so-called "educational cognitive styles," applicability of information about learners is presumed to be of equal utility regardless of learning task. In such schemes, an individual may be diagnosed as being, for example, a "visual learner," an "auditory learner," or a "horizontal learner." The "horizontal learner," for example, is said to learn best when lying down (rather than sitting or standing, presumably), and the superiority of the prone position for learning is assumed regardless of the skill or topic being learned. Another characteristic of learning-style constructs is that they are frequently measured by

Objective: Given an AN/PSM-6 multimeter and a resistor, measure the resistance to the nearest graduation.

(1) AN/PSM-6 ohmmeter function
(2) Resistance measurements

Analysis: This objective requires knowledge of the current use of the AN/PSM-6 multimeter. Learning to use this piece of equipment could be related to cognitive style because the equipment is complex in terms of the visual field of stimuli it presents. Since the multimeter comprises a complex visual array, discrimination and analysis of its components might be made easier for field-dependent, haptic, constricted field control, and impulsive students through the use of visual and verbal attention-focusing and cueing techniques as each component is discussed. One alternative might be to begin instruction with a progressive series of illustrations of the multimeter, gradually building up to it's elements in an increasingly complex visual field, explaining the function and operation of elements as they are added. Then instruction could proceed with the real item.

Figure 4.3 Example Analysis of a Training Objective from United States Air Force Course, Weapons Mechanic, from Ausburn, Ausburn, & Ragan (1980), page 37.

self-report of preference rather than measured by tasks that differentiate abilities. Some efforts at learning-style measurement appear to be relatively robust, even if they are measures of preference (e.g., Kirby, Moore, & Schofield, 1988). However, the difficulty in substantiating the validity of the styles, as well as the apparent free-wheeling generation and application of these styles to any and all situations, leads us to recommend viewing learning styles with extreme caution. While information about an individual's learning style may be helpful to that individual in regulating his own learning within a learning situation, typically this information is not sufficiently prescriptive to aid instructional designers in making design decisions. More powerful self-regulatory approaches relate to goals, self-efficacy, and learning strategy use have been studied (Dillon & Greene, 2003), which we will discuss further in Chapter 13, Strategies for Cognitive Strategy Instruction.

Locus of control is a personality variable associated with an individual's perception of the source of major life influences and is frequently associated with "style" variables (Lefcourt, 1976). The primary measure used for locus of control is the Rotter I/E Scale, a paper-and-pencil instrument that yields a score reflecting the extent to which an individual reflects "internal" or "external" locus of control. An individual with a predominantly internal locus of control would attribute the major influences on life to factors within the person—perseverance, effort, one's own actions, and so forth. An individual with a relatively external locus of control, on the other hand, attributes major influences to come from outside one's self—luck, what the other person does, the boss, and so forth. Of all the "styles" discussed here, locus of control presents the greatest amount of change (in the "change versus stable" classification). Individuals can experience major changes in their locus of control depending upon life circumstances or contexts, and they can experience small changes from morning to evening.

Determining what has been conscientiously developed and what has not been so developed is particularly important in the cognitive-style and learning-style areas. The line is not always easy to see between worthwhile and pointless schemes. In making your own investigations, look for information about the theoretic construct behind the style, validity, and reliability of instruments used to measure, evidence of the independence of styles from one another, independence of the style from general measures of aptitude and intelligence, and the breadth of application claimed. Even the most conservatively developed and heavily researched style dimensions may not be what they appear. An illustrative critical review of cognitive styles, particularly their posited bipolar nature, may be found in Tiedemann (1989).

Psychosocial Traits

Three personality characteristics can also be viewed as stable differences among learners: trait anxiety, trait locus of control, and academic self-concept. These personality characteristics are not the only personality constructs that we could consider; however, all three are particularly helpful for the instructional designer to utilize. A "trait" characteristic is a characteristic that tends to be stable over time in contrast with a related characteristic that is changing. For example, an individual would be described as high on trait anxiety if that individual has a tendency to be generally anxious, regardless of the circumstances. Spielberger (1972) has developed an instrument, the Manifest Anxiety Scale (MAS), to determine an individual's level of trait anxiety (as well as the changing characteristic of "state" anxiety). Although anxiety at or above a certain level can inhibit learning, various instructional accommodations, such as frequent feedback, clear specification of expectations, and overlearning, can minimize the negative influence of anxiety on learning.

Locus of control, described earlier as a style, can also be considered a psychosocial trait. Locus of control is expressed as varying tendencies to be "internal" or "external" in one's perceptions of the primary source of influence in life events. For example, to attribute a recent promotion on the job to hard work and persistence would be consistent with internal locus of control, whereas attribution of the event to good fortune or the influence of other people would be consistent with ex-

ternal locus of control. A failure to achieve a goal would be likely to be associated with lack of sufficient effort or ability from an internal locus of control perspective, whereas the external perspective would tend to attribute the failure to something like bad luck, "the system," or some other cause external to one's self. As noted above, locus of control can change in an individual. In addition, many people tend to attribute a persistent leaning toward "internal-ness" or "external-ness" over time as a personality trait. For these individuals, some adaptation can be made to instruction to promote greater learning. One instructional manipulation that can accommodate differences in locus of control is the amount of structure built into a lesson. Whereas extreme "internals" appear to learn best in a relatively unstructured learning environment, extreme "externals" appear to require more structure.

A third, similar characteristic is academic self-concept. Although a person's assessment of academic ability may vary by circumstance, it is often the case that after a surprisingly short time in schooling, learners have developed a generalized image of themselves as learners. If this image is positive, it will promote a positive attitude toward learning and perseverance in learning tasks. If academic self-image is negative, it can seriously impede learning. Instructional adaptation to poor academic self-concepts is similar to strategies to assist highly anxious learners.

You may be thinking that in addition to being stable characteristics, anxiety, locus of control, and academic self-concept may vary depending upon the circumstance. This is true. We will discuss these characteristics as "state" characteristics in the section on changing differences.

Gender, Ethnicity, and Racial Group

Three additional stable differences may be considered when designing instruction: gender, ethnicity, and racial group identification. One must be cautious in reflecting upon why these three factors might be considered when analyzing the learner population. We consider these differences not because members of one gender or racial group process information differently, but because members of a gender, ethnic, or racial group tend to have common experiences because of their group membership that may be quite different from those had by members of other groups. Designers should consider these group memberships in their learner analyses to ensure that they include contexts and examples that are relevant and comprehensible to members of all groups represented in the target audience. Regardless of particular ethnic considerations, all learners will come from a culture. Cultural factors are important, whether it is a multicultural situation or not.

Implications for Designers of Stable Differences

Designers of instruction can accommodate stable differences by either (1) making sure that a single instructional treatment or approach can accommodate learners across the range of differences or (2) creating several instructional treatments, each of which is adjusted to a narrowed range of characteristics (e.g., "tracks" for high-, average-, and low-ability learners; different instructional strategies for learners with different backgrounds or aptitudes; and so forth). The approach of designing multiple treatments is reflected the aptitude-treatment interaction (ATI) research tradition described earlier in the chapter. Conclusions we might draw from this research include on the one hand some startling individual differences between people, some interesting and helpful adaptations, and some unique insights into learning from instruction. On the other hand, although ATI research has produced some positive, helpful results, it has been a surprisingly difficult area in which to find those positive results. The difficulties which ATI research has encountered can help remind designers of the utility of approaches which are not based on stable individual differences but which are based on ways in which learners are alike or similar (such as information processing and developmental processes) and of approaches based on individual differences that are not stable ones (such as prior learning).

CHANGING SIMILARITIES

A number of physiological similarities exist that change over time but are not of any particular significance to instructional design. The "startle response" in infants is an example of this sort of characteristic. All neurologically normal newborn infants wave their arms in a particular way when they are quickly lowered. The particulars of this reflex go away in a short period of time and probably form the neurological basis for a more localized response that soon develops: facial manifestations of surprise. The startle response serves to illustrate the category of characteristic that we are considering here—a characteristic that changes over time but that we share as a similarity among us.

More relevant characteristics in the changing similarity category can be seen in **development processes.** People are continuously changing in their development, but the process or dynamics of development is more or less the same for everyone. In other words, if a particular developmental theory is valid, it will produce some degree of predictability in the changes to which it addresses itself. The dynamics of various processes of development are similarities among us. (The stages or states of development at which individuals find themselves may be different; therefore, the idea of stages of development is discussed separately in a section called "Changing Differences" later in this chapter.)

Two **intellectual development** theorists, Piaget and Vygotsky, provide insights into the shared mechanisms possessed by all people which enable and govern the process of increasing capacity to reason and think. Both Piaget and Vygotsky posit particular development processes. The work of Piaget and his followers has aided educators in understanding what kinds of cognitive operations are involved in outcomes that involve abstract thinking. Piaget (Piaget & Inhelder, 1969) saw intellectual development as a process as being the same for everyone. As you will recall from Chapter 2, he described development as an essentially adaptive process involving the interplay of two processes: assimilation and accommodation. Piaget's ideas about how people come to acquire capabilities for certain kinds of abstract thought have been used to suggest generative, inquiry-oriented instructional strategies for helping people achieve these capabilities. (We will have more to say about implications of intellectual development in the section called "Changing Differences" later in this chapter.) Vygotsky's view of intellectual development (Vygotsky, 1978), which was presented in Chapter 2, emphasizes interactions with the sociocultural environment and the role of language as a primary tool of intellectual adaptation. The emphasis on social facilitation and context makes Vygotsky's theory particularly attractive and useful for constructivists in thinking about the design of learner-centered and context-sensitive learning environments. Although different in specific elements addressed, both Piaget's and Vygotsky's theories provide insights into the processes which underlie intellectual development

Like intellectual development, the dynamics of **language development** reflect a process of change that is, in many respects, the same for all people, no matter what person or language is in question, with the exception of major language dysfunctions or disabilities. One view of language development that underscores the similarity dimension is that of Chomsky (1965). In general, Chomsky's theory holds that a propensity or talent for the structure of language is in a sense "wired in" to human brains. His theory was in part stimulated by the observation of children learning to speak. Chomsky found that you would think a child would make many kinds of errors when learning to speak. However, there are syntactical-logical errors of various sorts that are simply never made, regardless of the language being learned. Apparently, changes that occur over time in the facility and use of language are enabled and governed by common attributes that all persons possess.

Other developmental theories are similarly illustrative of changing similarities. The dynamics of **psychosocial** and **personality development** have been treated by Freud, Maslow, Erikson, and others. If we look at the dynamics or change processes that major personality theories propose, we see ways in which people change that lend some degree of predictability to their behavior. Perhaps the most commonly applied of these theories in training settings is Maslow's "hierarchy of needs" (Maslow, 1954). In its simplest form, the Maslow needs hierarchy describes types of human needs: (1) physiological needs, (2) safety needs, (3) love and belonging needs, (4) esteem needs, and (5) the self-actualization need. These needs are proposed to operate in a sequential, hierarchical fashion. If a person is extremely hungry (a physiological need), considerations for safety will be secondary. If you expect truly creative behavior (an aspect of human functioning that resides at the self-actualization level), it will not be likely to occur if there are major frustrations at the lower levels of need. Although Maslow's is the most familiar, other approaches that lend insight into individual growth provide insights into changing similarities that instructional designers can take into consideration. Certainly designers should be aware of how these basic needs, if not considered, can lead to the failure of the most carefully designed instruction that fails to consider whether these needs are met or how these needs may be threatened in an instructional context.

Changing similarities are those learner characteristics that relate to phenomena of developmental processes, processes that govern and enable development in a predictable pattern over time. Knowledge of these processes is useful to a designer when designing instruction for a target population, for whom, regardless of their levels development, share a common process which governs their changing developmental states—cognitive, language, psychosocial, and moral. It is useful for the designer to analyze the population along these dimensions because it will provide some sense of the similarities among the population and therefore some sense of how learning activities, examples, and content may be cast. The dynamics of development often provide theoretic support to major movements in educational thought, such as the contribution of Piaget and Vygotsky to constructivist ideas. Finally, and perhaps most importantly, knowledge of the dynamics of development can assist designers in understanding learners' cognitive structures and, consequently, can assist designers in developing ways in which learners can be assisted to make desired changes.

As described in Chapter 2, these stages are flexible, permeable, and open to advancement through instruction. It is not uncommon to find educators who adhere to developmental theories so rigidly that they believe learners to be impervious to change as a result of instruction. Such individuals oppose teaching certain concepts and principles because they perceive the learners of a particular stage to be developmentally "not ready." This position is particularly true of those who strictly adhere to theories of intellectual development. Instructional designers tend to believe that developmental states are mutable; that is, they are changed "naturally" through the cumulative effect of incidental learning, and therefore can be advanced intentionally through instruction of the right sort. This instruction involves determining learners' current state of knowledge and identifying prerequisite knowledge that must be acquired for a learner to move on to the next stage of "development." Case (1972) has successfully employed these tactics in advancing learners through stages of intellectual development. (We will discuss the process of prerequisite analysis in the next chapter.)

CHANGING DIFFERENCES

The many differences of people that change over time include physical features such as weight, strength, stamina, and details of appearance. These particular changing differences are so obvious that they are among the least useful to an instructional designer. However, there are several areas of changing differences for which a target audience should be analyzed: values and beliefs, personality states, developmental stages, and levels of prior knowledge.

Although some **values, beliefs, motivations,** and **interests** may devolve from the psychosocial and moral stages of development (of which several stages may be represented in a population), many of these affective dimensions may vary among individuals because of their own unique experiences. If the designer is creating instruction for a national or international population, it is clear that these affective characteristics may vary greatly based on cultural mores. In order to make learning relevant and meaningful, it is important that the designer obtain information on these values, beliefs, and interests. It may be impossible to accommodate this variety in instruction, but at least the knowledgeable designer can actively avoid offending those who hold these values and beliefs.

Remember the three trait characteristics: anxiety, locus of control, and academic self-concept. These factors can also be "states" that change among individuals depending upon the circumstance. For example, an individual who has a low trait anxiety and a high academic self-concept may have a high state anxiety and a low academic self-concept when encountering highly unfamiliar or complex content. A person who is normally very internal in terms of locus of control may become very external in an unfamiliar or threatening learning environment. Measurement instruments to assess anxiety, locus of control, and academic self-concept have been revised so that they can be used to determine learners' states at a particular point in time. Designers may consider using these instruments to assess the target audience if they suspect that the context or the content (learning task) may negatively affect these states. If these states are found to be sufficiently extreme, so as to negatively affect learning performance, then, as mentioned in the section on stable differences, certain instructional strategy techniques can be used to accommodate them.

Developmental theories, the dynamics of which were noted earlier as examples of similarities among people, also tend to contain descriptions of people at various states or stages that they may achieve. These **developmental states** or **stages,** which are described within developmental theories, are examples of changing differences. Although individuals in a target audience, particularly if they are of similar age, will tend to be at a similar developmental stage, it is quite possible that learners may fall into two or even more stages. And, as the year goes by, a teacher will be able to observe many children changing in this regard, moving from one stage to another. Typically, developmental states or stages are seen to be age-related but not age-bound; therefore, there is a tendency to move upward in a developmental sequence, but the change itself varies with the individual and is not inevitable. Indeed, as mentioned in Chapter 2, an individual's stage of development may vary across content areas.

An example of a developmental theory offering a perspective on a changing difference that is useful to instructional designers may be seen in the **stages of intellectual development** as identified by Piaget, which reflect an increasing capacity to engage in certain kinds of abstract thought. These stages of development are sensorimotor, preoperational, concrete operations, and formal operations (Inhelder & Piaget, 1958). Briefly, the sensorimotor period extends from birth to approximately eighteen months. During this period, senses and motor abilities develop rapidly; however, development of language and other cognitive maturation is less apparent. During the preoperational period (approximately ages eighteen months to seven years), children learn to reason and problem solve. However, children at this age are not bothered by inconsistencies in their reasoning, nor are they able to view a problem from another person's perspective. During the stage of concrete operations (approximately ages seven to twelve), learners acquire such skills as classification, seriation (ordering), reversal of operations, reciprocity, and identity. Learners at this stage of development can

think logically but require concrete objects to support this thought process. The stage of formal operations was thought to commonly extend from approximately twelve years of age and on. Learners at this stage can think abstractly and mentally manipulate symbols without requiring concrete supports, and learners can isolate and deal with the variables contained in abstract problems in which multiple propositions are present and interacting. Research in intellectual development has demonstrated fairly clearly that a large proportion of adults, including college students, has not achieved formal operations across all content areas. The ability to achieve formal operations reasoning is believed to be within the potential of practically everyone (Phillips, 1969). An instructional designer who neglects to consider state of intellectual development can make fundamental errors in assuming that learners will be able to benefit from instruction that is impossible for some of them to comprehend or in assuming that learners possess a level of development beneath their actual attainment and subsequently fail to sufficiently challenge them or promote cognitive growth.

Many of the psychosocial and personality development theories described earlier include descriptions of stages of development. **Stages of psychosocial development,** like intellectual development stages, represent changing differences among people. For example, Erikson (1968) described an eight-stage model of psychosocial development. He described each stage in terms of the psychosocial crisis that must be dealt with during this period:

1. *Trust versus Mistrust.* During infancy, the attentions and comfort provided by the infant's mother are the focus of the infant's life. Being an infant under the care of a loving parent generates a capacity for trust, but the times that the parent cannot or will not satisfy needs (Mommy can't always be there) produce frustration and mistrust.

2. *Autonomy versus Shame.* As a toddler, the child first acquires mobility, producing a sense of being able to do something. At the same age, learning the existence and control of elimination of waste and other bodily functions generally involves a degree of shame.

3. *Initiative versus Guilt.* During early childhood, with development of language and improved thinking and motor skills, the child begins to be able to take the initiative (let's do this; I want to wear that shirt; and so forth). First experiences with guilt come from knowledge of having done wrong things.

4. *Competence versus Inferiority.* During middle childhood, roughly corresponding to Piaget's period of concrete operations, the child acquires many important skills—not only the fundamentals of school learning such as reading, writing, and arithmetic, but also fine-motor and athletic skills that give the child a new sense of competence. Yet, when the child looks at adults, she or he sees a fundamental inferiority to them in skills, size, and authority.

5. *Identity versus Identity Confusion.* During adolescence, the sense of one's self as an adult begins to form, but the new identity is a confusing one.

6. *Intimacy versus Isolation.* During young adulthood, a typical pattern is to experience intimate relationships and learn how to handle intimacy, while at the same time experiencing isolation as a product of being out on one's own for the first time.

7. *Generativity versus Stagnation.* During adulthood, people have mature powers to be creative contributors and can learn to channel and direct their capabilities to productive ends, while at the same time feeling the pull toward complacency and self-satisfaction.

8. *Integrity versus Despair.* As an aging adult, the individual has the potential to achieve an ego integrity impossible at a younger age (because of a rich life of learning and experience), while dealing with the knowledge that death is unavoidable and near.

Another facet of personality development is **moral development.** Kohlberg (1969) has suggested that people generally develop in their morality through stages. The preconventional morality stage includes an egocentric period, in which people suppress their own desires only because of the fear of punishment, and a reciprocity period, in which members do kindnesses only out of an agreement to get something in return.

The conventional morality stage is the next stage, characterized by an initial phase of behaving morally in order to please an authority figure or in a sense of doing one's duty. This phase involves a legalistic and rote adherence to laws (in the extreme) to maintain order. Most intermediate elementary and middle school students and some high school students fall within the conventional morality stage.

Kohlberg's final stage of moral development is postconventional, or principled, morality. The initial phase in this stage is characterized by viewing laws as means to ends, a set of social contracts, and the view that certain social values may take precedence over the law. The final phase describes individuals whose behavior is guided by universal principles such as human dignity and fairness. Kohlberg tends to describe this phase by "best examples" such as Gandhi and Martin Luther King, Jr. (see Chapter 12 for a discussion of the best example technique for teaching concepts). These individuals characterized the values they possessed. (For more information on characterization of values, see Chapter 16.) During high school and young adulthood, many learners move into the stage of principled morality, although many adults do not develop into this stage. An understanding of the **stages of moral development** can be quite helpful to designers, particularly as they design for attitude objectives, design instructional management strategies, or design instruction in psychosocial content areas.

A number of characteristics of interest to the designer are associated with learners' level of psychosocial growth. In general, individuals in the same cohort tend to have similar interests, motivations, relationships to peers, feelings toward authority, and role models. Of course, the characteristics will vary within an age group, but there are more similarities than differences. Designers should consider these characteristics when selecting examples, creating relevancy statements, and making grouping decisions. These characteristics are particularly important when designing attitude lessons and when designing the motivational aspects of a lesson. The review of a good text on human development for the age of your target audience will aid you in learning these general characteristics.

Another view holds that an individual's evolving capabilities are the results of **prior learning** rather than development. Although people who work from the prior learning perspective do not deny the validity of the developmental view, they believe that the instructional designer might be better served by looking at major capabilities not as representatives of stages of development but rather as reflections of accumulated learning. As instructional designers, if we view a major capability that we wish to teach (such as the ability to solve a particular type of problem) as the reflection of accumulated learning, then we are led to ask the question, "What learnings are accumulated to reach this capability?" We call these learnings *prior learning*—specific, lower-level learnings that are prerequisite to achieving a capability of a higher order, such as an intellectual skill. (Specific prior learning is discussed in the following section.) Another result of prior learning is general world knowledge. Every person has a storehouse of knowledge, which varies with age, culture, and many other factors, and can be called **general world knowledge.** Although general world knowledge is not used in the same way as specific prior learning, it is an essential element upon which meaningfulness of instruction depends.

One type of prior knowledge that is relevant to instructional designers is learners' levels of "visual literacy." Dondis (1973) has defined **visual literacy** as "the ability to manipulate symbols in visual format for thinking and communicating" (p. 22). Learner factors that have been postulated to influence ability to decode visuals are age, experience, culture, and training. Learners' ability to decode visual messages increases with age. For example, Saiet (1978) found that children develop the ability to decode visual elements that convey motion over time. Individuals who have not had much experience with visuals, such as learners in nonliterate cultures, may have difficulty interpreting commonly used visual conventions. For example, learners who have not experienced many visuals may be confused by an elephant in the background of a visual being smaller than a human in the foreground (Hudson, 1960). Culture also influences learners' ability to decode visual messages. Bagby (1957) found that learners do not even "see" (notice) visuals that do not have meaning in their culture. There is evidence that visual decoding skills can be taught (Dondis, 1973). One method used is to provide opportunities for learners to develop their own visuals, utilizing the conventions they find in visuals around them.

SIGNIFICANCE OF TYPES OF LEARNER CHARACTERISTICS

As noted earlier, the four categories of learner characteristics that we have discussed are not of equal significance to designers, nor will their usefulness to you be the same in all design projects. Changing differences, particularly prior learning, provide the most specific guidance to the designer on organizational strategy decisions. Stable differences provide information that can help designers generate different strategies for different groups or individuals. Similarities, both changing and stable, provide more general perspective, which can translate into powerful approaches such as those we will see in the use of types and conditions of learning in Chapters 7 through 15.

Specific Prior Learning

The most important factor for a designer to consider about the audience is specific prior learning. What do the learners already know in the area they will be learning? Thus, instructional designers must ask many questions about the target audience members: Do they have some background knowledge or skills that will help them learn the current task? Will the instructor have to fill in this background knowledge for some of the students? Is there a wide variation in background knowledge among prospective learners? Do some of the prospective learners already have some of the skills and knowledge that the instructor plans to teach?

For example, if the designer is creating materials on operating a digital still camera, he will need to obtain as much information as possible on what the targeted learners already know about cameras, capacity and sensitivity characteristics, the effect of light on an exposure medium such as an imaging chip, the composition of a good photograph, image editing, and so on. It is also important to consider prior knowledge not directly related to photography that may be critical to students' learning the new information. For example, do they have prior experience and knowledge of art that will serve as important background information on which they can build?

Sometimes designers acquire this information from actually testing representative students from the target audience. Sometimes they question the trainers/teachers that work with the target audience. Sometimes they cautiously base their assumptions about prior knowledge on information about the instruction that the learners have had in the past. Remember, these assumptions should be made with caution. The fact that a learner has taken a course in Algebra I does not necessarily mean that she has all the knowledge she needs to begin Algebra II. Just because something has been taught does not mean that it has been learned. In addition, some of the student's knowledge and skill may have been forgotten, or some of the information that the designer assumes was included in Algebra I might not have been included. In any case, the more designers know about the relevant knowledge and skills that the learners already have, the more effective and efficient they can make the instruction.

An Outline of Learner Characteristics

The following list contains the major characteristics that should be used in a target audience description. We have re-categorized learner characteristics from the changing/stable, similarities/differences system because we have found that while it is easier to conceptualize scholarly knowledge about learners using that system, it is easier to embark upon learner analysis with the following outline. Depending upon the instructional task, some characteristics may be more critical than others. For an individual design project, it is unlikely that all factors will be included in the learner analysis.

1. Cognitive Characteristics
   a. General characteristics
      - General aptitudes
      - Specific aptitudes
      - Developmental level, such as Piaget's levels of cognitive development
      - Language development level
      - Reading level
      - Level of visual literacy; ability to gain information from graphic
      - Cognitive processing styles—preferred and most effective
      - Cognitive and learning strategies
      - General world knowledge
   b. Specific prior knowledge

2. Physiological Characteristics
   a. Sensory perception
   b. General health
   c. Age
3. Affective Characteristics
   a. Interests
   b. Motivation
   c. Motivations to learn
   d. Attitude toward subject matter
   e. Attitude toward learning
   f. Perceptions of and experience with specific forms of mediation
   g. Academic self-concept
   h. Anxiety level
   i. Beliefs
   j. Attribution of success (i.e., locus of control)
4. Social Characteristics
   a. Relationships to peers
   b. Feelings toward authority
   c. Tendencies toward cooperation or competition
   d. Moral development, such as Kohlberg's stages of moral development
   e. Socioeconomic background
   f. Racial/ethnic background, affiliations
   g. Role models

The designer may not consider all of these characteristics for all learning tasks and all audiences. For example, physiological characteristics may be very important for geriatric audiences but of little importance for general public school audiences. In general, the designer should collect a great deal of information, because often when one is conducting a learner analysis, one is not aware of information that will be critical later in the design process.

Information on learner characteristics may help the designer create effective, efficient, and interesting instructional materials. For instance, knowledge about the learners' socioeconomic and ethnic background and regional location may help the designer determine their interests and, consequently, select examples and contexts that make the instruction relevant and interesting. The designer may also wish to obtain information on students' interest in the content area and their interest in learning in general.

Assessing Learner Characteristics

How do designers find out about the general characteristics of the target audience? If the designers are developing for their own classrooms, they can observe, talk to, and assess their learners to determine their characteristics. Even then they may wish to conduct some additional investigation to find out more about the learners. However, suppose a designer is developing instruction to be used by learners whom he has never met. How can he obtain information about this audience? Here are some of the things that he can do:

Interview teachers, trainers, and other educators who work with the target audience.

Interview and/or observe members of the target audience.

Have members of the target audience complete surveys that provide information about their backgrounds and interests.

Have members of the target audience complete assessment instruments that provide information about cognitive strategies, processing styles, and preferred instructional delivery modes.

Examine job descriptions and personnel profiles of organization.

Read texts and articles about particular age groups and developmental levels that provide information on their interests, social development, and physical characteristics.

Read texts and articles that discuss the interests and motivations of individuals with particular socioeconomic, ethnic, or racial backgrounds.

To avoid stereotyping members of a particular target audience, the designer should use several of these sources of information to describe the diversity as well as the similarities of the members.

Implications of Learner Characteristics for Design

A careful consideration of the general characteristics of the target audience may be what elevates a mundane segment of instruction into compelling, imaginative, and memorable instruction. These factors are considered when the designer determines what information and instructional techniques, which we call *strategies*, to use in the instruction. Following is a beginning list of instructional strategy factors that are directly related to learner characteristics. These information and instructional techniques, which are illustrative but by no means exhaustive, may be varied according to learner characteristics:

Speed of presentation (pace)

Number of successful experiences learners should have in practice

Types of statements to convince students of the relevancy of the instruction

Techniques for gaining and focusing attention and the frequency of use of these techniques

Context of examples and practice items

Amount of structure and organization

Medium/media of instruction

Level of concreteness/abstraction

Grouping of students

Size of instructional chunks

Response mode (written, oral, etc.)

Number and difficulty of examples and practice

Type of feedback given after practice items

Level of learner control

Reading level

Vocabulary and terminology used

Amount and types of reinforcement

Amount of time allowed for instruction

Amount and type of learning guidance, cues, and prompts provided

When designers conduct the learner analysis and begin writing a description of the learners, it is important that they include some of the implications that these characteristics have for the design of the instruction. Learner characteristics can influence instruction at the most fundamental levels. As Case (1991) pointed out, knowledge of the limits of learners' existing cognitive structures is required to extend them. Occasionally these implications are very apparent; occasionally they require a great deal of thought and research to determine how to adjust the instruction to learner characteristics. The following example describes the characteristics of a target audience and discusses some of the implications of these characteristics for the design of instruction.

AN EXAMPLE OF A LEARNER ANALYSIS

In this example, the target audience is computer hardware service professionals who are to be trained to repair the HSG-7, a new high speed graphics workstation from MetaCom Corporation (a fictitious computer manufacturer), and to train customers to operate the computer.

The Target Audience

The approximately four hundred service professionals (SPs) who must be trained to repair the MetaCom HSG-7 range in age from twenty-three to fifty-two. Seventy percent of the SPs are male, and 30 percent are female. Forty percent of the SPs have been repairing systems for ten years or more (30 percent for five to ten years, and 20 percent for two to five years). Consequently, the majority of SPs have had considerable experience in repairing high-speed computers. Sixty percent of the SPs have two or more years of college education, the majority in electrical engineering

and mathematics programs. Thirty percent of the SPs attended technical schools and received training in electronics. On the average, these employees have received 150 hours of on-the-job and classroom training while working with MetaCom. This instruction has centered on repair of workstations and peripherals (printers, storage systems, input tablets, and so on), electronic circuit analysis and fault-trace procedures, time management, and customer training.

When tested, the reading levels of these SPs ranged from tenth grade to higher than a twelfth-grade level. The SPs scored exceptionally well on exam questions requiring them to interpret complex diagrams and charts. This skill is perhaps a result of their on-the-job requirements to use schematics.

The SPs have received, on the average, forty hours of Web-based-training (WBT) in their regional offices. All SPs have received some training via the Web. They are somewhat ambivalent about this instruction. They like it because it allows them to remain at home or near home during training, rather than having to go to a central location for instruction. However, many of the SPs find this WBT boring. Many SPs say they would prefer hands-on training on the new systems rather than WBT. On WBT lessons that allow learners to control the selection of content and the pace of instruction, evaluation indicates that the majority of learners tend to speed through the learning modules without interacting with sufficient examples and practice exercises before testing. Hence, test performance on this type of instruction tends to be low when using WBT that allows a high level of learner control. SPs generally prefer instruction from a lecturer, followed with hands-on practice on a real workstation. The credibility of the lecturer is extremely important in obtaining the SP's attention and motivation.

Interest assessments indicate that the learners are unusually analytical and skilled at quantitative skills. In addition, aptitude assessments, surveys, and on-the-job observations indicate the SPs have a greater-than-average difficulty in establishing interpersonal relationships. This is of some concern as the SP's job entails an element of sales and a large amount of customer training.

The majority of the SPs report a higher-than-average level of job satisfaction. The factors that the learners identify as contributing most to this level of satisfaction are job security, the challenge of troubleshooting malfunctioning equipment, and relationships with long-term customers.

Implications for Design

The characteristics of the MetaCom service professionals have implications for the design of WBT training for their use. The SPs possess a considerable level of background knowledge and expertise upon which the designers can build. Instruction on the new system can center around how this system differs from previous, similar systems. A WBT delivery system may be appropriate as the learners are able to learn from textual and graphic information. The WBT system will be more popular with learners if designers incorporate strategies that simulate hands-on, on-the-job activities (perhaps with embedded interactive video). The designers will probably wish to restrict the level of learner control over content and pace of instruction. This can be achieved by using pretests or responses to practice exercises embedded in the instruction.

The designers may want to provide for some small group instruction so that SPs can practice, perhaps through role-playing, the human interactions required in training a customer to use the new system. The designers could use experienced and credible lecturers for some of the content. They may wish to reserve this costly medium for skills that are particularly difficult for these learners to acquire, such as the interpersonal skills.

E X E R C I S E S

1. Describe the four categories of characteristics that should be considered in designing instruction. List four particular characteristics that might be described under each of these major categories.

2. In your own words, describe the difference between general characteristics and specific prior knowledge of a learner population.

3. List and describe at least seven instructional strategy variables that may be influenced by learner characteristics.

4. Suppose you were a member of the task force that is investigating the possibility of a mediated physics program in Corona (review this scenario in Chapter 3, Context Analysis). What information would you wish to know about the high school students who will receive this mediated physics program? List the questions that you would ask. Tell how you would go about finding the answers to your questions.

S U M M A R Y

Learner characteristics are an important aspect of instructional design. The four major categories of learner characteristics are cognitive (general and specific), physiological, affective, and social. Cognitive characteristics have these dimensions: similarities/differences and changing/stable. The four dimensions of cognitive characteristics each possess different qualities and implications for instructional designers.

Specific prior knowledge is generally the most important single learner characteristic to consider. Figure 4.4 summarizes key points in this chapter.

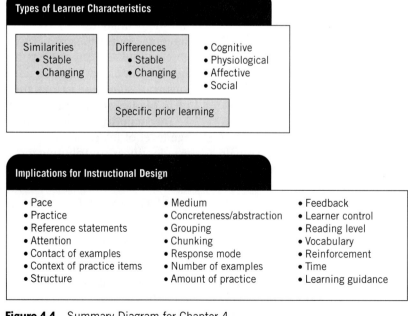

Figure 4.4 Summary Diagram for Chapter 4

EXTENDED EXAMPLE

See the Instructional Design Learning Resources Web site for this chapter's contribution to the Extended Example. In it, you will see an analysis of the cognitive characteristics and the general characteristics of the anticipated learner population for our instructional photography course.

READINGS AND REFERENCES

Ackerman, P. L. (2003). Aptitude complexes and trait complexes. *Educational Psychologist, 38,* 2, 85–94.

Ausburn, F. B., Ausburn, L. J., & Ragan, T. J. (1980). *Task analysis schema based on cognitive style and supplantational instructional design with application to an Air Force training course.* AFHRL TR 79-59. Brooks AFB, Texas: Air Force Human Resources Laboratory.

Bagby, J. W. (1957). A cross-cultural study of perceptual predominance in binocular rivalry. *Journal of Abnormal and Social Psychology, 54,* 331–334.

Bloom, B . (1964). *Stability and change in human characteristics.* New York: Wiley.

Broadbent, D. E. (1958). *Perception and communication.* New York: Pergamon.

Bruner, J. S. (1966). *Toward a theory of instruction.* Cambridge, MA: Harvard University Press.

Bruner, J. (1985). Models of the learner. *Educational Researcher, 14*(6), 5–8.

Case, R. (1972). Validation of a neo-Piagetian mental capacity construct. *Journal of Experimental Child Psychology, 14,* 287–302.

Case, R. (1978). A developmentally based theory and technology of instruction. *Review of Educational Research, 48,* 439–463.

Case, R. (1985). *Intellectual development: Birth to adulthood.* Orlando, FL: Academic Press.

Case, R. (1991). Potential contributions of research in the Piagetian tradition to the planning of curriculum and instruction. In M. Carretero, M. Pope, R. Simons, & J. I. Pozo (Eds.), *Learning and Instruction, Vol. 3* (pp. 1–25). Oxford, England: Pergamon.

Chomsky, N. (1965). *Aspects of the theory of syntax.* Cambridge, MA: The M.I.T. Press.

Corno, L., & Snow, R. E. (1986). Adapting teaching to individual differences among learners. In M. C. Wittrock (Ed.), *Handbook of research on teaching* (3rd. ed.) (pp. 605–629). New York: Macmillan.

Cronbach, L. J., & Snow, R. E. (1977). *Aptitudes and instructional methods: A handbook for research on interactions.* New York: Irvington.

Dillon, C., & Greene, B. (2003). Learner differences in distance learning: Finding differences that matter. In M. G. Moore and W. G. Anderson (Eds.), *Handbook of distance education* (pp. 235–244). Mahwah, NJ: Erlbaum.

Dondis, D. A. (1973). *A primer of visual literacy.* Cambridge, MA: The M.I.T. Press.

Erikson, E. (1968). *Identity: Youth in crises.* New York: W. W. Norton.

Fleming, M., & Levie, W. H. (1993). *Instructional message design* (2nd ed.). Englewood Cliffs, NJ: Educational Technology Publications.

Gagné, R. M. (1985). *The conditions of learning* (4th ed.). New York: Holt, Rinehart, & Winston.

Gardner, H. (1993). *Frames of mind: the theory of multiple intelligences.* New York: Basic Books.

Gardner, H. (2003). Multiple intelligences after twenty years. Paper presented at the American Educational Research Association, Chicago, IL, April 21.

Hilgard, E. R., & Bower, G. H. (1965). *Theories of learning* (3rd ed.). New York: Appleton-Century-Crofts.

Hudson, W. (1960). Pictorial depth perception in sub-cultural groups in Africa. *Journal of Social Psychology, 52,* 183–208.

Inhelder, B., & Piaget, J. (1958). *The growth of logical thinking.* New York: Basic Books.

Jonassen, D. H. & Grabowski, B. L. (1993). *Handbook of individual differences.* Hillsdale, NJ: Erlbaum.

Kagan, J. (1966). Reflection-impulsivity: The generality and dynamics of conceptual tempo. *Journal of Abnormal Psychology, 71,* 17–24.

Kirby, J. R., Moore, P. J., & Schofield, N. J. (1988). Visual and verbal learning styles. *Contemporary Educational Psychology, 13,* 169–184.

Klein, G. S. (1970). *Perception, motives and personality.* New York: Knopf.

Kohlberg, L. (1969). Stage and sequence: The cognitive-developmental approach to socialization. In D. Goslin (Ed.), *Handbook of socialization theory and research* (pp. 347–480). Chicago: Rand McNally.

Kyllonen, P. C., & Lajoi, S. P. (2003). Reassessing aptitude: introduction to a special issue in honor of Richard E. Snow. *Educational Psychologist, 38,* 2, 79–84.

Lefcourt, H. M. (1976). *Locus of control: Current trends in theory and research.* Hillsdale, NJ: Erlbaum.

Lowenfeld, V., & Brittain, W. L. (1970). *Creative and mental growth.* New York: Macmillan.

Maslow, A. H. (1954). *Motivation and personality.* New York: Harper & Row.

Miller, G. A. (1956). The magical number 7, plus or minus two: Some limits on our capacity for processing information. *Psychological Review, 63,* 81–97.

Newell, A., & Simon, H. A. (1972). *Human problem solving.* Upper Saddle River, NJ: Prentice-Hall.

Paivio, A. (1971). *Imagery and verbal processes.* New York: Holt, Rinehart & Winston.

Phillips, J. L., Jr. (1969). *The origins of the intellect: Piaget's theory.* San Francisco: W. H. Freeman.

Piaget, J., & Inhelder, B. (1969). *The psychology of the child.* New York: Basic Books.

Ragan, T. J., Back, K. T., Stansell, V., Ausburn, L. J., Ausburn, F. B., Butler, P. A., & Burkett, J. R. (1979). *Cognitive styles: A review of the literature.* AFHRL-TR-78-90-I. Brooks AFB, Texas: Air Force Human Resources Laboratory.

Ragan, T. J., & Smith, P. L. (2003). Conditions theory and models for designing instruction. In D. H. Jonassen (Ed.), *Handbook of research for educational communications and technology* (2nd ed.) (pp. 623–649). Mahwah, NJ: Erlbaum.

Saiet, R. A. (1978). *Children's understanding of implied motion cues*. (Doctoral dissertation, Indiana University, 1978). *Dissertation Abstracts International*, 39, 09A.

Santostephano, S. G. (1978). *A biodevelopmental approach to clinical child psychology*. New York: Wiley.

Shute, V., & Towle, B. (2003). Adaptive E-learning. *Educational Psychologist, 38*(2), 105–114.

Smith, P. L., & Ragan, T. J. (2000).The impact of R.M. Gagné's work on instructional theory, in R. Richey (Ed.), *The Legacy of Robert M. Gagné* (pp. 147–181) Syracuse, NY: ERIC Clearinghouse on Information and Technology.

Snow, R. E. (1977). Individual differences and instructional theory. *Educational Researcher, 6*(10), 11–15.

Snow, R. E., & Lohman, D. F. (1984). Toward a theory of cognitive aptitude for learning from instruction. *Journal of Educational Psychology, 76*(3), 347–376.

Snow, R. E., & Swanson, J. (1992). Instructional psychology: Aptitude, adaptation, and assessment. *Annual Reviews of Psychology, 43*, 583–626.

Spielberger, C. D. (Ed.) (1972). *Anxiety: Current trends in theory and research*. New York: Academic Press.

Sternberg, R. J. (1980, September). Factor theories of intelligence are all right, almost. *Educational Researcher, 9*, 6–18.

Sternberg, R. J. (Ed.) (1982). *Advances in the psychology of human intelligence, Volume 1*. Hillsdale, NJ: Erlbaum.

Sternberg, R. J. (Ed.) (1984). *Advances in the psychology of human intelligence, Volume 2*. Hillsdale, NJ: Erlbaum.

Sternberg, R. J. (Ed.) (1986). *Advances in the psychology of human intelligence, Volume 3*. Hillsdale, NJ: Erlbaum.

Tiedemann, J. (1989). Measures of cognitive styles: A critical review. *Educational Psychologist, 24*(3), 261–275.

Vernon, M. D. (1971). *The psychology of perception* (2nd ed.). Baltimore, MD: Penguin.

Vygotsky, L. S. (1978). *Mind in society: Development of higher psychological processes*. Cambridge, MA: Harvard University Press.

Witkin, H. A., Moore, C. A., Goodenough, D. R., & Cox, P. W. (1977). Field-dependent and field-independent cognitive styles and their educational implications. *Review of Educational Research, 47*, 1–64.

INSTRUCTIONAL ANALYSIS: ANALYZING THE LEARNING TASK

CHAPTER OBJECTIVES

At the conclusion of this chapter, you should be able to do the following:

- Recognize and write an appropriate learning goal.
- Conduct an information-processing analysis of a learning goal.
- Conduct a prerequisite analysis of an information-processing analysis.
- Define, give examples of, recognize examples of, and describe the differences between different types of learning.
- Recognize and write appropriate learning objectives.
- When given a learning goal, conduct a complete learning task analysis.

AN OVERVIEW OF ANALYSIS OF THE LEARNING TASK

At the completion of a needs assessment (described in Chapter 3), the designer has a list of "goals," which reflect what learners currently are unable to do. These are generally not in a form upon which one can begin designing instruction. The process of task analysis transforms goal statements into a form that can be used to guide subsequent design. Designers expend a great deal of effort in obtaining as clear a description and as thorough an analysis as possible of the learning task.

There are many approaches to learning task analysis available to the instructional designer (Jonassen, Tessmer, & Hannum, 1999). Some are highly specialized with regard to application setting, and each has its own strengths and weaknesses. The approach which follows is a somewhat eclectic one, involving both information processing and prerequisite analysis.

The primary steps in performing a learning task analysis are as follows:

1. Write a learning goal.
2. Determine the types of learning of the goal.
3. Conduct an information-processing analysis of that goal.
4. Conduct a prerequisite analysis and determine the type of learning of the prerequisites.
5. Write learning objectives for the learning goal and each of the prerequisites.
6. Write test specifications.

The final product of the learning task analysis is a list of goals, amplified with test specifications, that describe what the learners should know or be able to do at the completion of instruction and the prerequisite skills and knowledge that learners will need in order to achieve those goals. These steps will form the primary organization of this chapter, except for the last step, writing test specifications which will be treated in the next chapter, Assessing Learning from Instruction.

Why should one complete such an analysis? Recall that in the EduSpider fiasco, one of the problems that the designers found out too late was that many students were unable to use the software because the developers had assumed that they were able to determine least common denominator, and many students were not competent in this procedure. As we noted in Chapter 4, the EduSpider designers did not complete a learner analysis to determine what the learners were like and what specific prior knowledge they possessed. They may have also failed to analyze the learning task—calculating with fractions—to determine what learners actually need to know in order to solve such problems. Apparently, they failed to include instruction on determining the least common denominator or to write any notice in the instructor's manual accompanying the software that this skill was a prerequisite. Had they conducted a learning task analysis, they would have identified the prerequisites for the learning task.

In conducting a learning task analysis, we determine what content needs to be included in a segment of instruction for learners to achieve the learning goal. Traditionally, this content has been determined by the following: (1) including what has always been taught on the subject in the past (what is included in texts or reference materials on the subject); (2) trial-and-error (teaching learners a certain amount and then adding more information as confusions arise); and (3) following the structure of the content (for example, organizing and including information in science topics according to "systems"). These traditional approaches may provide some good information about the content to be included in a lesson. However, designers do not start at this point because the traditional approach to determining content has two pitfalls. The designer may include deadwood, and she may fail to consider prerequisite information.

Deadwood is information that is not essential or especially supportive in attaining a learning goal. Deadwood is often included in instruction when a content expert writes the instruction. The expert may include information that is nice to know or especially interesting to him, but may not be essential to the learning task. Deadwood is a problem because it detracts from the central learning task; it may even confuse a learner who is encountering a particular learning goal for the first time. Deadwood is also a problem because including it in instruction may waste precious instructional time that could be better spent in studying information or practice that is focused toward the learning goal. If efficiency of instruction is not a clear priority in a particular context and if learners are judged to be capable of utilizing this additional information to pursue important goals, then "nice to know" information may be included. Of course, what might be considered deadwood for one goal might be essential for another. For example, if we were trying to teach learners to recognize multiple thematic interpretations of a film based on various sociological perspectives, an extensive store of information might be needed to provide learners with sufficient background so they could understand how the context of a perspective affects interpretation. However, learning to recognize a video graphic device called "Dutch tilt" and explain how it affects mood in a film might require considerably less information.

The second problem with the traditional approach is that it may fail to identify critical **prerequisite information and skills.** Prerequisites are things a person needs to know or be able to do before a person is in a position to learn something else. The content-centered approach typically does not look at the content from the novice's perspective but from the expert's perspective. Experts may not be able to remember all the things that they needed to learn or know to attain the learning goal. They may, therefore, fail to include critical prerequisite information in the instruction.

It is important to note here that analyzing for prerequisites does not specify a particular strategy for instruction. Some educators assume that if one analyzes for prerequisites, then on principle one will use a bottom-up, highly structured instructional strategy. Nothing could be further from the truth! An analysis for prerequisites will be just as useful for a top-down, problem-based learning environment. Constructing a model of the knowledge that goes into being able to achieve a goal makes for good instruction, no matter the strategy. (Later we will discuss how a designer might use this information to develop widely varying instructional strategies.)

WRITING LEARNING GOALS

After conducting a needs assessment, the designer has a list of learning goals, such as "Learners need to be able to read at the fifth-grade level" or "Learners need to be able to repair a broken VCR." To put these statements in a form so that we can continue with their analysis, we write them as learning goals. **Learning goals** are statements of purpose or intention, what learners should be able to do at the conclusion of instruction. These can be lesson goals, unit goals, or course goals. Objectives, as we will discuss later, are subparts of goals (see Writing Learning Objectives). At this point, we are not making decisions as to which of our goals are at the lesson, unit, or course level. We are intent on developing clear descriptions of what capabilities learners will come to possess, what they should know or be able to do, after instruction.

The degree to which the goal statement is intended to be taken literally as reflecting exactly what should be learned should match the problem or issue established in the needs assessment. On many occasions, there is a clear problem and gap that requires a very direct goal that all learners in the target audience must achieve. On other occasions, an array of possible goals may be identified, along with instruction suitable for achieving any or all of them. This array of goals might vary in terms of sophistication or level of expertise or in context of application. Fundamental to the issue of whether a single goal or an array of possible goals is desirable is whether the needs assessment indicated that all students must reach a certain level of compe-

tency or different knowledge in an area, or whether different competency levels will be acceptable in the instructional and application context. Our experience has suggested that the more focused the goal, the easier the design and development of the instructional strategy and assessment will be.

Another aspect of specificity that the designer may consider, in addition to whether there should be a single, or multiple goals, is the nature of the goal statement itself. Traditionally in instructional design practice, goals have been stated in observable terms. We say goals are stated in *observable terms* when they describe what we would accept as evidence that the learners have acquired the cognitive capabilities suggested by the goal. We use such descriptive terms because we often need statements in this form to clearly communicate what learners are to learn so that we can continue with the design process. Without these clear statements, completion of the other activities of instructional task analysis and other design work can be more difficult. The following statements (EX 1 and EX 2) are examples of learning goals that are sufficiently unambiguous and specific to clearly guide further design efforts:

- EX 1: When given a broken VCR with one of four possible malfunctions, the learner will be able to locate the malfunction and repair it.
- EX 2: When given relevant information and the purpose of a business letter, the learner will be able to write an appropriate business letter.

The following two statements are somewhat ambiguous and might lead to some wasted effort if design efforts continue before achieving more clarity:

- EX 3: Given a malfunctioning VCR, the learners will understand how to repair it.
- EX 4: When given a videotape lesson, the learner will watch a demonstration of VCR repair.

EX 3 is an example of an ambiguous and, therefore, preliminary learning goal because it does not tell what the learners would do to demonstrate that they "understand." Do they need to be able to explain how to repair a VCR? Do they need to be able to recognize the parts and functions of a VCR? Do they need to be able to actually fix a VCR? Depending upon what is meant by *understand,* the instruction would be designed in quite different ways. The designer must have a more precise knowledge of the intent of the goal. If you are creating instruction based upon a needs assessment conducted by someone other than yourself, you may have to discuss the intent of the goal statements with those individuals who contributed to the needs assessment.

EX 4 does not describe what learners should be able to do *after* instruction. It describes a learning activity that the learner will complete while learning. At this point, the designer is not ready to make decisions yet about *how* to teach; she is still trying to determine *what* to teach. Remember, a goal describes what learners should be able to do after instruction. In general, the effort of being specific cannot be avoided: If it is not made during goal specification, it must be made at later stages of the design process, such as when designing assessment instruments or narrowing the content to be included.

Many educators are opposed to writing specific statements of learning outcome because they believe it leads to lower levels of learning. This inference may have developed because of the common practice of writing objectives that describe declarative knowledge that in no way represents the real goal of the instruction, which is often a problem-solving goal. This trivialization of objectives is not a fault of the process of writing goals, but of the expertise, creativity, and perseverance of the designer. It is *more difficult* to write good goals for high-level cognitive and affective outcomes, but not impossible. This text explains and exemplifies how good, high-level goals may be developed.

In recent years some educators have declared that they do not use goals to guide instruction or, more dogmatically, that it is inappropriate to use goals to guide instruction. (You will remember from Chapter 2 that this latter position has been proposed by radical constructivists.) It has been our observation that most individuals who make instructional decisions about the activities in which learners will engage, what content will be included in a lesson, or how learning will be assessed do have learning goals: They are simply unexpressed. For example, we once worked with a kindergarten teacher who claimed that she did not use learning goals. As we walked around the room, we encountered an activity in which children were to trace around cookie cutter shapes and then cut out the shapes. We asked why the children were doing this activity. The teacher said, "The children need to learn to use scissors, and they need to practice their fine-motor skills." These statements are goals. Perhaps, until questioned, the goals were unconscious, but clearly they were there guiding the decisions that she made. In most cases, we feel it is to the designer's benefit, whether he is a classroom teacher, trainer, or materials' developer, to consciously consider goals in the design of instruction.

Those readers who are familiar with outcome statements may wonder how learning goals differ from learning objectives. Both are written in terms that describe what learners should be able to do after a segment of instruction. However, learning goals are generally more inclusive and less precise than learning objectives. We generally do not write a learning goal for a segment smaller than a lesson. However, a lesson may contain many objectives that must be learned to achieve the lesson goal. We may convert a learning goal, which describes the outcome of a lesson, into a more precise form: a lesson objective. (We will return to this distinction between goals and objectives later in this chapter.)

E   X   E   R   C   I   S   E   S   A

Which of the following goals are stated unambiguously so that they can clearly guide further design activities? Rewrite the ambiguous statements so that they give a clearer description of exactly what the learners should be able to do or know at the conclusion of instruction. Explain the decisions that you make.

1. Students will hear lectures and attend discussions on future trends in technology, philosophy, and business.

2. The student can select examples of the concept *conservative* (in the political dichotomy of liberal versus conservative) from a list of examples and nonexamples.

3. The student will understand the procedure for applying for welfare.

4. The student will administer an allergy injection following sterile technique.

5. The student can compute the mean, range, and standard deviation of a series of ten numbers.

6. The student has acquired the ability to deal with angry parents.

7. Each student will be able to view clear, precise, and correctly demonstrated examples of the A-4 technique as presented in the video, "The A-4 Technique in Action."

DETERMINING TYPES OF LEARNING

After you have written a learning goal for a course, unit, or lesson, it is valuable to identify the type of learning outcome the goal represents. Identifying the type of learning helps the designer to determine how to analyze the learning goal into its component parts. Later this will provide clues as to how to teach and assess student learning of the goal.

Some learning tasks are substantially different from others in terms of the amount and kind of cognitive effort required in learning, in the kinds of learning conditions that support their learning, and in the ways to test for their achievement. For instance, learning to recite the Prologue to Chaucer's *Canterbury Tales* seems to be a qualitatively different task from learning to prove a geometric theorem.

The learning task of memorization requires attention and perseverance, as well as a particular type of mental effort, rehearsal. The conditions that support this kind of learning are explaining the meaning and context of the prologue, breaking the task up into smaller pieces, memorizing one piece at a time, putting all the pieces together, and then practicing recital of the entire poem. Prompting from a friend or teacher may help. Practice and repetition over a period of time improve the chances that the poem will be remembered.

In contrast, learning to prove geometric theorems requires a different kind of mental effort. A student must keep many principles or laws (relational rules) in mind at one time, select from the available principles those that appear most appropriate in a particular proof, and decide in which sequence these principles should be applied. Unlike the memorizing task, which is always the same (there is one way to recite the poem correctly), with each different proof the appropriate principles and sequences will vary. You may guide students in their learning by reminding them of appropriate principles, by asking what the goals and subgoals might be, and by giving them many practice exercises with feedback as to whether their answers are correct or incorrect. This learning outcome is not tested by having students prove a theorem they have already proved, but by having them prove previously unencountered problems.

Bloom's work (Bloom et al., 1956) described these differences among types of learning with a taxonomy of objectives in the cognitive domain: recall, comprehension, application, analysis, synthesis, and evaluation. This categorization is often useful in lesson planning, especially in encouraging teachers to aim their objectives, when appropriate, toward higher-order, more mentally demanding outcomes. Another excellent task analysis system was developed by M. David Merrill (Merrill, 1983), who described tasks in terms of the intersection of two dimensions—content and performance level. Merrill identified types of content as facts, concepts, procedures, and principles (these outcomes are similar to four of Robert M. Gagné's categories). Merrill then crossed each of these content outcomes with three levels of performance that he suggests learners may demonstrate within each content category: remember, use, and find. Merrill's system is in wide use by instructional designers. However, we find the categorization system developed by Gagné to be the most fundamental, most widely used, and most useful in designing instructional materials. We will use Gagné's system throughout this text as our foundation for learning task analysis. Once you have learned the Gagné system, it is not difficult to transfer to other systems. Discussion of research and theory related to categories of learning and their implications for the design of instruction can be found in Ragan & Smith (2003).

R. Gagné (1985) divided possible learning outcomes into five large categories or "domains": verbal information (or declarative knowledge), intellectual skills, cognitive strategies, attitudes, and psychomotor skills. Most learning objectives can be classified into these categories. Gagné conjectured that the type of mental processing required for achieving outcomes in each category is qualitatively different from the mental activities required in other categories. Hence, the types of instructional support (the instructional strategy) needed in each category will be substantially different also. The bulk of Gagné's *The Conditions of Learning* (1985) described these categories of human learning outcomes and the instructional "conditions" that support learning in each of these categories. We will outline each of these categories and the types of goals or objectives that fit in each category because we believe that thinking of learning goals in such a way can be most profitable in aiding the identification of prerequisite objectives, designing effective instructional strategies, and designing appropriate tests.

Gagné's Types of Learning Outcomes

DECLARATIVE KNOWLEDGE. The learning task mentioned earlier—memorizing the Prologue to Chaucer's *Canterbury Tales*—can be classified as a declarative knowledge learning task. Declarative knowledge objectives require a learner to recall in verbatim, paraphrased, or summarized form facts, lists, names, or organized information. Learners are not required to apply the knowledge that they have acquired but merely to recall, recognize, or state it in their own words. **Declarative knowledge** is sometimes described as "knowing that" something is the case (E. Gagné, 1985). It is also comparable to Bloom's (1956) levels of *recall* and *understanding*. Examples of verbal information objectives include the following:

- Write the names of at least three types of synthetic fabric.
- Recite the multiplication table for the number 7.
- In your own words, summarize the three steps that you must follow in converting a BASIC file into a DOS 3.3 text file.

Instructional materials that allow students to practice their multiplication facts most likely have a declarative knowledge objective. So does instruction that helps children to practice their spelling words.

Declarative knowledge objectives have received a lot of bad press in recent years. We agree that the majority of learning objectives in a lesson or unit should not be in this category. Schooling or training that starts and stops at recall of facts and memorization of lists falls far short of students' needs.* However, knowing declarative knowledge helps students learn higher-order, more complex objectives. For instance, the ability to recall multiplication facts aids students in solving quadratic equations, and the ability to spell correctly aids students in composing essays. In other words, recall of declarative knowledge can be a suitable objective if it leads to more complex learning outcomes, such as intellectual skills.

INTELLECTUAL SKILLS. Intellectual skill outcomes are the predominant objectives of instruction in both school and training settings. Intellectual skills are typified by the application of rules to previously unencountered examples. This type of learning outcome differs from declarative knowledge objectives because students learn how to not only recall, but also to apply knowledge to instances not encountered during instruction. Anderson (1976) described this type of learning as *procedural knowledge.* E. Gagné (1985) distinguished it from declarative knowledge: Procedural knowledge is "knowing how," and declarative knowledge is "knowing that." Intellectual skills are analogous to Bloom et al.'s (1956) levels of application, analysis, synthesis, and evaluation.

The objective of proving a geometric theorem is an intellectual skill objective because students learn how to respond to a *class* of problems, not just individual problems that they have been taught to solve. There are a number of subcategories of intellectual skills that we will discuss briefly here.

When learners learn to differentiate between two stimuli—whether the stimuli are visual, auditory, tactile, olfactory, or gustatory—they have learned to make **discriminations.** A discrimination skill is the ability to perceive that something either matches or differs from other things. A lot of the learning of very young children falls into this category. They learn to discriminate between Mother's and all others' faces. They learn that a square block will fit into a square hole and not a round hole. People learn to make discriminations in later life, too. When learning a foreign language, we learn to distinguish the differences between sounds that we have not had to distinguish before. While cooking, we learn to discriminate when there is too much or not enough spice in the food. Some early childhood instructional materials teach discriminations, asking children to tell whether two things are alike or different. For instance, a workbook may ask a student to mark a figure that is the same as another figure that is given. Discriminations are fundamental to learning; however, we rarely teach them by themselves in school or training environments because discriminations are simply the ability to tell whether things are alike or different, not the ability to recognize these things as members of a large class of entities with a particular name. That ability is what the next level, concepts, is all about.

The acquisition of **concepts** helps the learner to simplify the world. For now, think of a concept as a container. Rather than having to respond to each thing in the world as different, the learner can respond to things as members of groups. For instance, when encountering a large metal object with glass windows and four rubber tires, we can think "Oh, yes, this is a car. I can expect it to move fast, cost a lot, and need fuel." We do not have to figure out for ourselves that each individual car goes fast, costs a lot, and needs fuel. We need never have seen a particular kind of car before to know that it is a car. Grouping things into categories makes us more efficient thinkers.

Two different kinds of concepts have been described: concrete concepts and defined concepts (R. Gagné, 1985). The ability to classify things into categories by their physical characteristics—whether visual, auditory, tactile, olfactory, or gustatory—is the ability to identify **concrete concepts.** Concrete concept learning differs from discrimination learning in that if learners have acquired a concrete concept, they can identify examples of that concept. For example, if a child could match one oak leaf with another oak leaf when they were placed alongside a maple leaf, the child would be exhibiting the ability to make discriminations. However, you could teach a child this discrimination and the child might still be unable to tell you what kind of leaf you are pointing to when you point to an oak leaf out in the woods. If the child said, "That's an oak leaf" when you point to an oak leaf (one the child has not seen before), you can be fairly certain that she has learned the concept "oak leaf." In addition, "trapezoid" (to recognize a previously unobserved object or illustration as being a trapezoid), hydrogen sulfide (by smell), or major/minor chord (by sound) are examples of concrete concepts.

Concepts that are classified by whether they match a definition or a list of characteristics are known as **defined concepts.** The terms *democracy, Marxism,* and *anarchy* are defined concepts, as are the terms *acid* and *base* to a chemist (who defines *acid* and *base* in terms of pH level).

Students must be able to do more than simply state the definition of a concept for us to be able to say that they have learned a defined concept. Learners who

---

*Some cognitive psychologists would divide learning into information and problem solving, others would divide into information, concepts, and problem solving. The scheme we will use involves more categories. However, practically all cognitive psychologists agree on the existence of a type of learning that is informational, most often referred to as declarative knowledge, and that such learning is qualitatively different from the rest.

have acquired defined concepts are able to classify previously unencountered examples and nonexamples of the concepts. An instructional package that teaches students to determine whether a teacher's reaction to a student's actions can be described as "negative reinforcement," "positive reinforcement," or "punishment" is providing instruction on defined concepts. Every content area has its own set of concepts that a learner must be able to use to go on to more complex learning tasks, such as rule using.

Much of our lives are "rule-governed": We avoid touching hot things because we know they will burn us; we follow certain prescribed steps when planting a vegetable garden; we look both ways before crossing a street because we know that failure to do so can lead to accidents. Much of learning is composed of learning rules, both principles and procedures. These are learned capabilities that involve multiple concepts working together. Instruction in math science, and social sciences is filled with principles and procedure outcomes.

Principles (also known as **relational rules**) can typically be expressed in the form of "if-then" statements:

- If gas is heated, then it expands.
- If demand goes up, then supply goes up.
- If the subject is plural, then the plural verb form is used.

These examples are all relational rules. Relational rules help us to predict, explain, or control circumstances in our environment by describing either natural or volitional responses to those circumstances. For instance, we might say that learners have acquired the rule "If gas is heated, then it expands" if they can (1) predict what will happen to a filled balloon that is left in a hot car all afternoon, (2) explain why a filled balloon shrinks when left in the freezer, or (3) tell how to fix a balloon of a certain size so that it will fit through a ring that it currently will not fit through.

Procedures, on the other hand, tell us in what order certain steps should be taken. Much math instruction is directed at the learning of procedural rules. For example, the process for calculating an average is a procedure: First, you find the sum of the individual numbers, and then you divide by the number of individual numbers. Training in vocational, business, military, and industrial settings often includes outcomes that are procedures, teaching learners how to do certain portions of their jobs.

Problem solving, the last type of intellectual skill, refers to a learned capability involving selection and application of multiple rules. Many times, as in the case of students' proving geometric theorems, learners must select from a number of possible rules, whether relational or procedural, and apply those rules in a unique sequence and combination to solve a previously unencountered problem. We call this kind of learning "domain-specific problem solving." Once learners have acquired the ability to solve problems in a specific domain, they may apply that ability to similar types of problems. Nursing students acquire problem-solving ability when they learn to write nursing-care plans for patients who have a unique set of physical problems, medications, and other treatments. Graduate students learn domain-specific problem-solving skill when they determine a methodology to utilize to research a specific question. Students of marketing who plan an advertising campaign for a particular product are acquiring domain-specific problem-solving abilities. Developing the design plans for a new restaurant is the application of domain-specific problem-solving skill for an interior design student.

Finally, notice that intellectual skills build on each other; that is, they are hierarchical. Learners must be able to make discriminations among objects before they can identify concrete concepts. They must have acquired the concepts that are used in rules, and they must have acquired the rules they will combine in unique ways to create domain-specific problem solving. This hierarchical arrangement of learning tasks is a great help to us when we are analyzing a learning task. For example, if our terminal objective is a rule (principle), then we must examine that rule for concepts that the learners must know in order to learn the rule.

COGNITIVE STRATEGIES. Students use cognitive strategies to manage their own learning. Sometimes these are referred to as **learning strategies** (Weinstein & Mayer, 1986) or "learning how to learn." For instance, most of us have learned particular strategies that we use to study a textbook. We may, for example, skim through the chapter, read the headings and the summary, and then closely read the text. Cognitive strategies support learning in other domains. They are particularly evident when students are completing problem-solving tasks. Some cognitive strategies are effective across content and across domains. Students often "discover" these strategies; until recently they were rarely directly taught in public schools.

Weinstein and Mayer (1986) organized these strategies into five major categories: (1) Rehearsal strategies are used for basic learning tasks and complex learning tasks that aid in selection of information to be recalled and enhance retention of that information; (2) elaboration strategies are used for basic learning tasks and complex learning tasks that tie new information to prior knowledge; (3) organizational strategies are used for basic learning tasks and complex tasks that select information to be retained and define the relationships among this information so that it may be integrated into memory; (4) comprehension monitoring strategies are sometimes referred to as *metacognition*, or "students' knowledge about their own cognitive processes and their ability to control these processes by organizing, monitoring, and modifying them as a function of learning outcomes" (p. 323); and (5) affective strategies are those strategies that learners use to "focus attention, maintain concentration, manage performance anxiety, establish and maintain motivation, and manage time effectively" (p. 324).

ATTITUDES. Like cognitive strategies, attitudes influence learning across content and domains. An **attitude** is a mental state that predisposes a learner to choose to behave in a certain way (R. Gagné, 1985). Gagné describes attitudes as having cognitive, affective, and behavioral components that interact. Attitudes influence the choices that learners make. For instance, an individual's dislike of math may cause him to choose to avoid all courses that contain a math component. A child who loves animals may choose to purchase a pet. Certainly attitudes play a strong role in learners' motivation to initiate and persevere in learning.

Instruction in attitudes in schools and training settings is often subtle and indirect. As a matter of fact, we are often hard-pressed to intentionally design components into our instruction that can influence attitudes. Very few instructional materials attempt intentional instruction in attitude change or attitude formation. However, materials used by agencies such as the American Heart Association, American Cancer Association, and many other health and welfare groups have strong attitude components.

This is not to say that instruction cannot be designed for attitudes and other learning outcomes in the affective domain. Simulation games in which a learner is actually playing a role are powerful tools for influencing learners' attitudes. Films or videos, especially when used with discussion, can be used to influence deeply held beliefs and attitudes, as demonstrated by research on the "Why We Fight" film series produced during World War II by noted director Frank Capra.

Finally, the way in which instruction is conducted inevitably generates attitudes about the material being learned, whether there are affective objectives in the content or not. For example, the constant feedback, reinforcement, and instruction adapted to an individual's level of proficiency that is possible in a well-developed individualized system of learning may positively influence learners both toward the content being taught and toward learning in general.

PSYCHOMOTOR SKILLS. Coordinated muscular movements that are typified by smoothness and precise timing are called **psychomotor skills** (R. Gagné, 1985).

We learn a lot of motor skills in our early lives: grasping, crawling, walking, and drawing. These early skills become automatic with enough practice. In later years, we may choose to acquire other psychomotor skills, such as typing on a keyboard, playing tennis, or waterskiing. Although psychomotor skills have a visible muscular component, they also depend on a cognitive component, usually a procedural rule that organizes the kind and sequence of actions. When we are learning a psychomotor skill, this procedure is very much in evidence. For instance, a novice tennis player, when confronted with an approaching ball, may be heard repeating to herself, "Side to net, eye on ball, racket back, step into the ball, follow through." Eventually, with sufficient practice, this procedure becomes automatic, and the player stops verbalizing the steps. Instruction may be designed to teach the procedures related to motor skills; however, psychomotor skills must be physically practiced to be learned.

LEARNING ENTERPRISES. In an effort to develop a type of learning which reflected capabilities that combine types of learning into more general expertise, Gagné and Merrill (1990) developed the idea of "learning enterprises." A learning enterprise may be defined as "a purposive activity that may depend for its execution on some combination of declarative knowledge, intellectual skills, and cognitive strategies, all related by their involvement in the common goal" (p. 25). (We will briefly treat learning enterprises in Chapter 16, along with other approaches to the concern for integration of multiple goals that generated the idea of learning enterprises.)

A note of reassurance and caution: Classifying learning goals into categories is a tool for instructional designers. Completing this activity should make completing later design activities more productive. These categories are not straight-jackets. There are goals that "fall through the cracks." Sometimes it is important to consider what learners already know to determine what a particular goal will demand of them. Sometimes what category a goal falls into depends upon how you choose to teach toward the goal. When you are unable to classify a particular goal, we suggest that you move on to other design activities, continuing to reflect from time to time about the nature of the cognitive requirements of the goal.

E X E R C I S E S   B

Following are some learning goal statements. Decide which category the goals represent: declarative knowledge, discrimination, concept, rule (principle or procedure), domain-specific problem solving, cognitive strategy, psychomotor skill, or attitude.

1. The student must be able to select the beakers from a set of laboratory equipment.

2. The learner must be able to type sixty words per minute.

3. The student teacher must choose to utilize positive reinforcement rather than punishment.

4. The student must select the appropriate pronoun so that the noun (referent) and pronoun agree in number.

5. The student must select curtains that exactly match the color of the carpet.

6. The student must list all fifty states and their capital cities.

7. When given a series of poems, the learner must tell which ones are examples of haiku.

8. The student must tell the date of the Norman invasion of Britain.

9. The learner must locate the source of the problem in a malfunctioning printer.

10. The student must invent a way to remember people's names.

11. The learner must convert a number from standard notation (16,301) to scientific notation (1.6301×10^4).

CONDUCTING AN INFORMATION-PROCESSING ANALYSIS

Whether you are designing a course, unit, or lesson, once you have identified the learning goal and determined what type of learning outcome it is, you will find an analysis of the goal a useful tool in determining the needed content of that instruction. This goal analysis involves two stages: (1) an information-processing analysis of the goal and (2) a prerequisite analysis of the steps identified in the information-processing analysis. Although this is not the only approach to "decomposing" the task (sometimes called *task analysis*), it seems to be the easiest, most straightforward approach to take.

Why is it necessary to analyze the goal? For effective instruction, you want to ensure that students are provided with the opportunity to learn everything they must learn to achieve that goal (the superordinate objective of the lesson). In other words, there are some prerequisite skills and knowledge that students must acquire. At the same time, for efficient instruction, you do not want students to learn things that are irrelevant to the learning goal. How can you determine what should be included in the instruction and what can be left out? Conducting an *information-processing analysis* (Briggs, 1977; Dick & Carey, 1996) is the first step in

"decomposing" or breaking down the goal into its constituent parts, identifying what the students need to learn to attain the goal.

In conducting an information-processing analysis, one asks, "What are the mental and/or physical steps that someone must go through in order to complete this learning task?" Suppose our lesson goal was the following:

> Given a topic in the area of "instruction" and the resources of a college or university library, the learner will be able to locate journal articles relevant to that topic.

We might identify the following eleven steps for someone who knew how to complete the goal (an expert):

1. Locate the ERIC thesaurus (a book containing the key words used to classify materials that are held in the Educational Resources Information Clearinghouse).

2. Determine a related descriptor from the thesaurus.

3. Locate the most recent cumulative *CIJE (Current Index of Journals in Education)*.

4. Find the descriptor in the *CIJE* (under which will be listed journal article titles that relate to the descriptor).

5. Read through the journal titles and select possible articles.

6. Locate and read the abstracts of the possible articles.

7. Select the most appropriate articles and write down the citations.

8. Locate the journal names in the library holdings index, and write down the call numbers of the journals.

9. Locate the journal volumes.

10. Locate the articles, read them, and determine if they are appropriate.

11. Photocopy the articles.

Of course, depending upon the library, its resources, its holdings, and the preferences of the learners, these steps might vary. However, if we've done a good job of performing the learning environment and learner analyses, we will have clues as to what these resources and preferences might be.

How can we determine what the information-processing steps are for a particular goal? One of the simplest and most often-used techniques is to simply mentally review the steps that we might go through in completing the task. Often that is exactly what we do if time is short or the task is simple. However, as we discussed in Chapter 4, it is not a good idea to assume that all individuals will go about things the same way we do. Following is a procedure you might follow to determine these information-processing steps.

1. *Read and gather as much information as possible about the task and content implied by the goal.* This will allow you to familiarize yourself with common terminology and help you begin to understand what is involved in the skill. You may begin to develop a list of questions about this knowledge or skill, such as "How does someone know when to do that?" or "What does this term mean?" For example, if our task is learning how to solder, we might read all that we could about soldering. We might even begin a rudimentary information-processing analysis on what we think a person does and thinks as she completes a soldering task. Then we could create a list of questions, things we would like to ask subject matter experts.

2. *Convert the goal into a representative "test" question.* For example, for our library problem, we might write the question, "If you were asked to use the university library to find three articles on 'feedback in instruction,' what would you do?" Or, for the soldering task, we might ask, "What do you do when you solder two things together?" For declarative knowledge goals, the question might be to explain the declarative knowledge to the designers: "Explain the periods of art history."

3. *Give the problem to several individuals who know how to complete the task and do one or several of the following activities:*

- Observe them completing the task, and ask them to talk aloud about their thought processes as they complete the task. Ask them to describe how and why they are making the decisions they make.
- Observe them completing the task, and write down or videotape the steps.
- Have the individuals complete the task, and ask them to write down the steps they went through.
- Ask the individuals to write down the steps they would go through if they were asked to complete the task.

The first two techniques will give you the most information because people who are experts often forget how they do things. Many actions and thoughts become automatic. However, it may not be feasible to actually observe individuals in action. In this case, the other approaches listed will also provide you with information that you can use in writing the information-processing analysis. The first technique (which asks experts to think aloud as they complete a task) has much promise because it allows us insights into information and cognitive processes that the expert is utilizing that may not be observable. It is helpful to complete this process with more than one expert, as people can develop some idiosyncratic ways of addressing a problem.

4. *Review the written steps or replay a videotape of the expert completing the task and ask questions about the process.* During this process you can ask for clarification or elaboration. Many of your questions will be aimed at trying to find out the unobservable cognitive knowledge that underlies the expert's behavior. You should ask, "What? When? Where? How? Why? Why? Why?" Some of the questions we might ask our soldering expert include the following:

- How do you know that you need to solder? When? Why?
- When wouldn't you use solder?
- Can you solder all metals?
- Do you always solder the same way? Why not? What other ways can you do it? When would you use other techniques?
- How do you know how much insulation to strip off the wire?
- Why did you twist the wires together like that?
- How do you know if it's a good solder joint? What might you have done if it hadn't been a good joint?
- Does everyone do this the same way you do?

5. *If more than one expert is used in steps 3 and 4, identify common steps and decision points used by the experts in steps 3 and 4.* In other words, locate the commonalities in the process that the experts followed. It may be advantageous if you do this with the group as a whole, because you may find the group together arriving at a consensus of the process that is best. Indeed, at this point you are trying to get a "fix" on what is "true for now," through a process in which experts negotiate the desirable approach to a cognitive task. (Using the philosophical bases discussed in Chapter 2, we might observe that this activity is congruent with aspects of both the constructivist and pragmatist philosophies.) If you complete this step with a group of experts, you will often find that there is individual disagreement as to how a task is performed. Noting the disagreements will help you find decision points in the cognitive procedure (points at which experts assess the characteristics of the particular task and, based upon these characteristics, take alternative routes in completing the task). Note these decision points and alternative routes.

6. *Identify the shortest, least complex path for completing the task, noting factors that require this simpler path.* For example, the shortest, least complex path for completing the library task is listed in the eleven steps on the previous page. It assumes that a descriptor for the topic could be found easily, that the descriptor was included in the most recent *CIJE,* that some of the abstracts appeared to be appropriate for the topic, and so on. Circumstances in which these assumptions are incorrect would require additional steps to deal with the complexity of the situation. If you find disagreements among experts in step 5, you may find that some are describing very complex paths with many decision points. Often you may find, upon inquiry, that these very complex paths are used only under rare circumstances. There may be another, more commonly used information-processing path that occurs in the majority of occasions. This information-processing path should be described first, as it is probably the one you will design for first. (See Scandura, 1983, for more information on path analysis.) In noting these alternative scenarios that make a task more or less complex, you may find that you are able to refine your learning goal, gaining a clearer idea of your intentions. Such a procedure may allow you to identify the abilities of intermediate level learners, those learners who fall on the continuum somewhere between novice and expert.

7. *Note factors that may require a more complex path or more steps (these may indicate decision points).* As described above, the more complex path for the library example would include some situations in which information could not be found. The complex path would indicate an "if-then" plan. Here is an example: "If you cannot find a descriptor for the topic, then locate by hand one article about the topic and work backwards through the article and the *CIJE,* finding the descriptors that *CIJE* used for that particular article." Note the factors that make a more difficult or simpler path, and try to obtain some information about the frequency of occurrence of the more complex solutions. You may wish to analyze and describe a number of these paths, or only the most simple ones, depending upon the level of proficiency that the learner must have in order to apply that learning.

8. *Select the circumstances, and the simpler or more complex paths, that best match the intentions of your goal(s).* Often we wish to teach learners to complete the simpler path. Later we may return to the learning task and explain circumstances that might require a more complex procedure and teach learners to complete that more complex procedure. (See a discussion of this technique in Chapter 11.)

9. *List the steps and decision points appropriate to your goal(s).* Whether it is the steps determined in the less complex path identified in step 4 or the more complex paths identified in step 5, list those steps in sequential order. The information-processing analysis should contain three to twelve steps. This may be accomplished by making sure the steps are comparable in size and that a similar amount of mental effort seems to be required for each step; consolidating some steps and breaking up

others can help you achieve a reasonable step size and number of steps.

10. *Confirm the analysis with other experts.* If time permits, it is a good practice to give the original question (step 1) and the steps from the information-processing analysis to another group of experts and ask the experts to review, confirm, or revise the analysis.

A note of caution is in order: Occasionally, novice designers make the error of writing an analysis of how one might *teach* toward the goal. Remember, we are not yet making any decisions about how we will teach or instruct. We are still working on obtaining a clear description of *what* the learner must learn to do. We are describing how someone who already knows how to do the learning task goes about doing that task. We are breaking it into its component parts so that we can identify what the learner must learn. A key aspect of instructional design is that we separate making decisions about *how* to instruct from conceptions of *what* it is we are going to teach.

The development of an information-processing analysis is iterative. In other words, you will find yourself revising the analysis several times as you gain a better perspective of the learning goal itself. Often the information-processing analysis is revised even at the point of writing objectives and test items. Rather than being a source of frustration, the analysis should be an encouragement. You will be gaining a clearer and clearer picture of the actual cognitive requirements of the task and, hence, you will be able to create much more effective and efficient instruction. Another encouraging fact is that there are many "correct" ways to represent an information-processing analysis. This process is not like solving a math problem in which there is only one answer. There is not just one "right" answer because generally there are many ways that experts address a learning task. Remember, you are trying to identify one, workable information-processing procedure.

Nelson (1989), Ryder and Redding (1993), and Schlager, Means, and Roth (1988) describe additional techniques for "getting at" the cognitive processes of experts. Although space limitations preclude our complete discussion of these techniques, those who wish to learn more will find these references clear and useful.

Information-processing analysis can also be used to assess prior knowledge of learners. Case (1993) used such a technique to determine how children approached Piagetian tasks that were supposedly beyond their cognitive abilities. Case then diagnosed these processes to determine what rudimentary processes he could build on and how these novices "went wrong." Although such an approach to entry-level testing may be too time-consuming in many situations, it is a technique that would certainly avoid "piecemeal" consideration of entry-level knowledge.

EXAMPLE ANALYSES

We have found that information-processing analyses for particular categories of learning outcomes tend to have some similar characteristics. Therefore, we have included examples of information-processing analyses for the major types of learning outcomes. We will begin with learning outcomes in the intellectual skills domain. (Since discriminations are so seldom taught in schools and training environments—and their analyses look quite similar to concepts—we have omitted that analysis from the examples.)

Declarative Knowledge

Information-processing analyses for declarative knowledge are in some ways quite different from intellectual skills analyses. The sequence of application of information is often not so critical in declarative knowledge analyses as with intellectual skills. More important is how an expert organizes the declarative knowledge into meaningful, memorable segments. These relationships may be represented graphically in many ways, such as webs, networks, or maps. (You may wish to review declarative knowledge and the varieties of graphic representation in Chapter 8.) An example of such an analysis might be developed for a learning goal in which the learner would learn to summarize the characteristics, composers, and a chronology of the major periods of music history. Of course, as the goal involves knowledge of chronology, sequence does somewhat enter into the information-processing analysis of this goal. An instructional analysis for this goal might have the following pattern:

1. Recall major periods in music.
2. Describe Renaissance music characteristics.
3. Describe Baroque music characteristics.
4. Describe Classical music characteristics.
5. Describe Romantic music characteristics.
6. Describe Contemporary music characteristics.

A graphic representation of the analysis is provided in Figure 5.1. You may wish to review declarative knowledge learning in Chapter 8.

Concept Learning

Applying a concept typically involves determining whether a particular instance is an example of that concept. This involves comparing the characteristics of the instance with the defining attributes of the concept. (If this idea is unclear to you, see the first two sections of Chapter 9.) Concept learning involves (1) recalling the critical attributes of a concept and

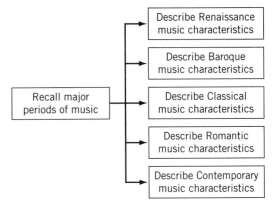

Figure 5.1   Information-Processing Analysis for Declarative Knowledge

(2) sequentially or simultaneously comparing attributes of an instance to attributes of the concept. (If the instance does not have the required attributes, it is not an example of the concept.)

Suppose the learning goal were that the learner could identify which of a number of figures is a rhombus (see Figure 5.2). We might find through interviews or observation that "experts" use the following information-processing procedure:

1. Recall the characteristics of a rhombus. (Many experts do this unconsciously.)
2. Determine if the figure is a polygon. If yes, continue on to step 3. If no, go to step 5.
3. Determine if the figure is a parallelogram. If yes, continue on to step 4. If no, go to step 5.
4. Determine if the figure's sides are equal in length (the figure is equilateral). If yes, continue on to step 5. If no, go to step 5.
6. The figure is not a rhombus.

Note that the defining attributes of the concept "rhombus" are that (1) it is a polygon, (2) it is a parallelo-

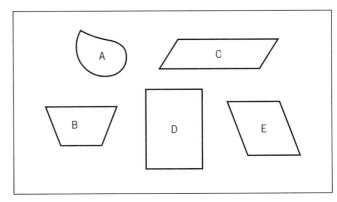

Figure 5.2   Concept Example

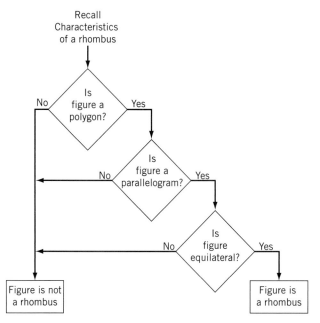

Figure 5.3   Information-Processing Analysis for a Concept

gram, and (3) it has equilateral sides. Experts might vary as to the order in which they checked the attributes against the characteristics of the figure; however, they would probably agree on the most efficient order to follow. Here, considering the most inclusive attribute first (i.e., polygon) would be most efficient. We could also show this information-processing analysis in graphic form (see Figure 5.3).

If you are still not clear about what concepts are, you may wish to look at the first sections of Chapter 9 for further discussion.

Procedures

Learning goals that are procedures are the easiest goals upon which to conduct an instructional analysis. Generally, application of procedures involves these steps:

1. Determine whether a particular procedure is applicable.
2. Recall the steps of the procedure.
3. Apply the steps in order, with decision steps if required.
4. Confirm that the end result is reasonable.

If you are still not clear about what a "procedure" is, you may wish to refer to the first sections of Chapter 10 for further discussion.

For example, a procedural learning goal might be that learners are able to apply the Fry Readability Graph to determine the reading level of some printed material. The information-processing analysis for such a goal might follow this pattern:

1. Determine if application of the Fry Readability Graph is appropriate to the reading material.
2. Recall the steps in the procedure.
3. Select representative passages.
4. Calculate the number of sentences for each hundred-word passage.
5. Determine the number of syllables in each passage.
6. Determine the average number of sentences and average number of syllables.
7. The intersection of average number of sentences and average number of syllables on the graph.
8. Read grade level from graph.
9. Confirm that value is reasonable (check answer).

This information-processing analysis is graphically represented in Figure 5.4.

More complex procedures may have sub-procedures based upon decision steps. These decision steps would involve determining which set of conditions exist. Such an information-processing analysis would have yes/no decision points with branches of different operations following each side of the decision.

Principles

Applying a principle involves doing the following:

1. Determine which concepts or variables are involved.
2. Determine the principle that relates those concepts or principles.
3. Recall the principle.
4. Determine which concept or variable has varied and the direction or magnitude of its variation.
5. Determine which concept or variable has been affected.
6. Then determine the magnitude and direction of the effect on the affected concept or variable.
7. Confirm that the value is reasonable.

If you are still not clear about what a "principle" is, you may wish to refer to the first sections of Chapter 11 for further explanation.

For example, a learning goal in which a learner could apply Boyle's law (when the temperature remains constant, the volume of a confined gas varies inversely as its pressure) might be represented in the following question:

A piston is placed in a cylinder that has a volume of 150 cubic inches and is pushed into the cylinder until the en-

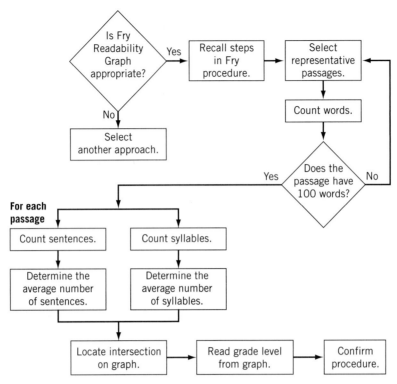

Figure 5.4   Information-Processing Analysis for a Procedure

closed air is compressed to 50 cubic inches. If the pressure of the air at the beginning was 15 pounds per square inch, what is the pressure of the trapped air?

We might find through interviews or observation that "experts" use the following information-processing procedure:

1. Determine the variables in the problem (air pressure and volume of gas).
2. Determine the relational rule that states the relationship of these variables (Boyle's law).
3. Recall Boyle's law.
4. Determine which variable (pressure or volume) has varied.
5. Determine the direction and magnitude of the variation (how much greater or less).
6. Determine which variable (pressure or volume) will be affected.
7. Determine the direction and magnitude of the effect (by placing values into the equation stating the relationship).
8. Confirm that the value is reasonable.

We can also present this information-processing analysis graphically (see Figure 5.5).

Domain-Specific Problem Solving

Information-processing analyses for domain-specific problem solving generally include the following major procedural steps:

1. Determine the knowns, the givens.
2. Determine the unknowns, the problem.
3. Determine the class of problems to which this problem belongs.
4. Determine the relational rules that relate the knowns and unknowns in the situation.
5. Determine the procedural rules that determine the application of the relational rules.
6. Apply the procedural rules and the "nested" relational rules.
7. Confirm that the problem is solved; unknowns are determined.

If you are still unclear about problem solving, you might want to review the first two sections of Chapter 12.

An example of the application of domain-specific problem solving would be the development of a nursing-care plan for a patient. The nurse would be given a history of the patient, the patient's current symptoms, and the doctor's diagnosis and prescrip-

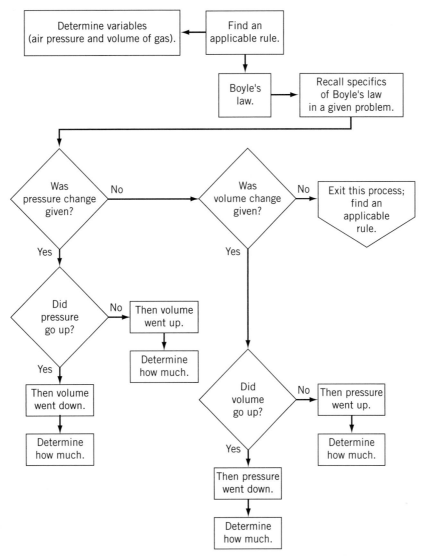

Figure 5.5 Information-Processing Analysis for a Principle

tion. This information-processing analysis is described as follows:

1. Assess patient's status.
2. Analyze data collected.
3. Determine nursing diagnosis.
4. Develop plan of care.
5. Implement care.
6. Evaluate care.

This analysis can also be represented graphically (see Figure 5.6).

Generally, course and unit learning goals are domain-specific problem solving. Lesson goals, on the other hand, more often involve concept and rule learning that are required to acquire domain-specific problem-solving ability.

Cognitive Strategies

The information-processing analysis of a cognitive strategy outcome resembles that of a problem-solving analysis. Typically, the steps in applying a cognitive strategy involve the following:

1. Determine the characteristics and requirements of the learning task.
2. Select or invent strategies appropriate for the task.
3. Select the optimum strategy.
4. Apply strategy.

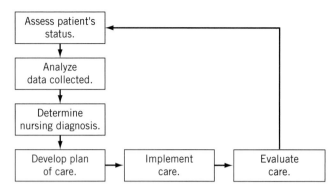

Figure 5.6 Information-Processing Analysis for Application of Domain-Specific Problem Solving

5. Evaluate effectiveness of strategy.

6. If effective, continue using strategy; if ineffective, return to first step.

You may wish to review cognitive strategies in Chapter 13.

An example of a cognitive strategy is the use of a text structure application strategy that can be used to aid the selection, encoding, and retrieval of pertinent information from a selection of expository prose. One way to represent application of this strategy would be with the following steps:

1. Is this a reading task? If yes, continue; if no, select another strategy.

2. Is the selection continuous prose? If yes, continue; if no, select another strategy.

3. Is the selection expository prose? If yes, continue; if no, select another strategy.

4. Is the purpose to recall main ideas and details? If yes, continue; if no, select another strategy.

5. Examine main overviews, summaries, and topic sentences for statements of structural organization or cue words for structure.

6. Determine overarching structure for entire selection. (Note: These structures are typically cause-effect, time-order, problem-solution, comparison/contrast, or description.)

7. Predict main ideas and supporting details based upon prior knowledge and structure.

8. Read selection.

9. Examine secondary overviews, summaries, and topic sentences for statements of structural organization or cue words for structure.

10. Determine secondary structures.

11. Review and take notes utilizing overarching structures and substructures.

12. Assess whether comprehension is adequate for the situation. If yes, end; if no, return to step 1.

A graphic representation of this analysis is provided in Figure 5.7.

Attitudes

Although attitudes are seldom a major learning goal, they frequently play an important role in courses, units, and lessons. Information-processing analysis of attitude objectives has not been researched a great deal. We suggest that such an analysis include the following:

1. Evaluate the situation, and consider possible courses of action.

2. Determine which course of action is valued.

3. Choose that course of action.

4. Perform that course of action.

The analysis is represented graphically in Figure 5.8. You may wish to review attitude learning in Chapter 14.

An example for this type of analysis might be the attitude goal "the learner will choose to solve class disputes in a nonviolent way." Here are the steps:

1. Evaluate the dispute, and consider possible courses of action.

2. Determine that nonviolent solution is valued.

3. Choose nonviolent behavior.

4. Behave in a nonviolent manner.

The steps are graphically represented in Figure 5.9.

Psychomotor Learning

An information-processing analysis for a psychomotor task is very similar to an analysis for a procedural rule. It usually involves the following steps:

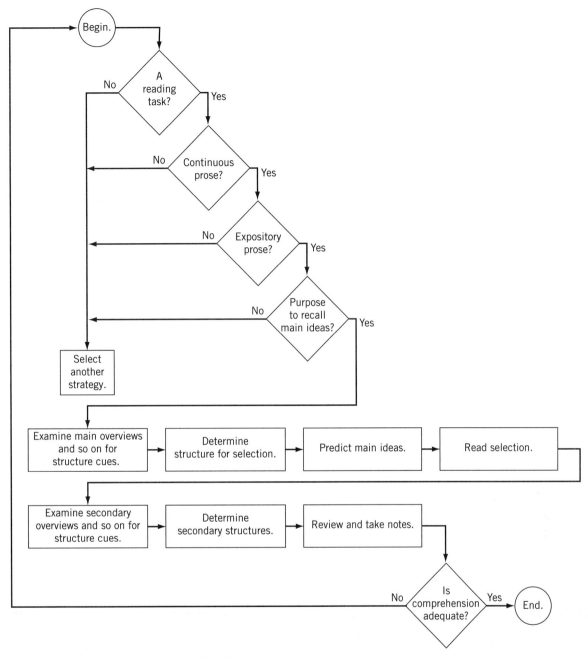

Figure 5.7   Cognitive Strategy Information-Processing Analysis

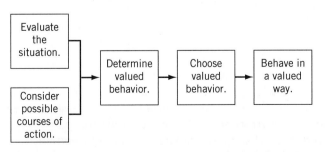

Figure 5.8   General Information Processing Analysis for Attitudes

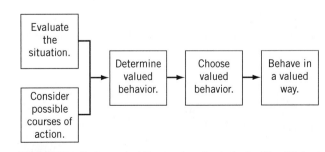

Figure 5.9   Information Processing Analysis for Non-Violent Dispute Resolution

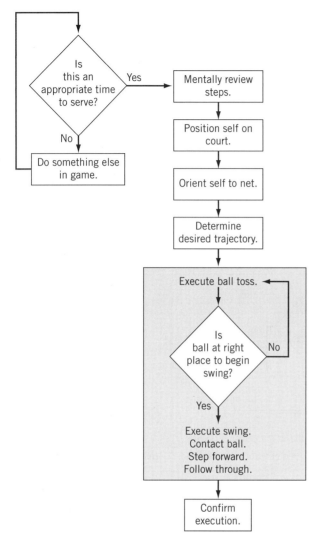

Figure 5.10 Psychomotor Skill Information-Processing Analysis

1. Determine whether a particular psychomotor action is required (although this may be automatic).

2. Recall the steps of the procedure (although this may be unconscious).

3. Execute the steps of the psychomotor procedure in order, with decision steps and consequent actions, if required.

4. Confirm that the steps have been correctly applied.

You may wish to review psychomotor learning in Chapter 15.

An example of a psychomotor information-processing analysis for the learning goal of completing a tennis serve could look like this:

1. Determine that this is an appropriate moment for a serve.

2. Mentally review the steps in executing a serve.

3. Position self in appropriate court and location on court.

4. Orient self to net.

5. Determine desirable trajectory of ball.

6. Execute ball toss.

7. Execute racquet swing.

8. Contact ball.

9. Step forward.

10. Follow through.

11. Confirm correct execution of serve.

Figure 5.10 presents a graphic representation of psychomotor skill information-processing analysis.

Notice that this analysis resembles the analysis of a procedural rule. Indeed, the procedural rule is the "psycho-" portion of the psychomotor skill. The precision and timing of the execution of these steps is the "-motor" part of the psychomotor skill. As with procedural rules, the information-processing analysis for psychomotor skills may be more complex if alternative subprocedures are invoked, depending upon which set of conditions exists. For example, when returning a tennis serve, different procedures are followed depending upon whether the serve comes to the left, to the right, or straight-on to the player.

Later, when we discuss instructional strategies, we will point out that the sequence of instruction for complex psychomotor skills that involve multiple sub-skills should not always be bottom-up or simple-to-complex (see Chapter 7, "A Framework for Instructional Strategy Design," and Chapter 15, "Designing for Psychomotor Skill Lessons"). Remember, when we do a task analysis, we are not yet determining the instructional strategy.

E X E R C I S E S   C

Complete an instructional analysis on one of the following learning goals:

1. Look for a book on a certain topic in the library.

2. Change the oil in a car.

3. Find the average of five numbers.

CONDUCTING A PREREQUISITE ANALYSIS

Once you have decomposed the learning goal into its information-processing tasks, you have made much progress in determining what the content of the instruction must be. You have already determined much of what learners will need to know how to do in order to complete the goal. The next step in decomposing the task is called **prerequisite analysis.** Performing this function will convert the goal and tasks into a hierarchy. To determine prerequisites you will reflect on each one of the steps in the information-processing analysis and ask, "What must the learner know or be able to do to achieve this step?" You will continue to ask this question until each step has been broken down into everything the students must know to achieve the learning goal. You cease analysis when it can be assumed that all of the students have the described knowledge and skills. This process is often called top-down analysis, as you are starting at the top of analysis with the most superordinate task, which will be broken down into smaller prerequisite tasks and knowledge.

For example, to determine the content for this book, we started with the goal that you learn to systematically produce simple instruction. We decomposed that goal into the steps identified in the model for design that we presented in the first chapter (a procedural rule). Then we examined each step in the model and asked, "What must the learner know or be able to do to complete this step of the process?"

Remember, decomposing goals into their prerequisites does not mean that these prerequisites have to be taught in a piecemeal fashion. In fact, we suggest that you seriously consider strategies that integrate the instruction of these prerequisites in meaningful ways. The analysis of goals for prerequisites is conducted solely to identify what cognitions make up the higher-order goal. This information will be used to design instruction that in some way considers these prerequisites so that learners will not be challenged beyond their "zone of proximal development."

Example Prerequisite Analysis: Locating Journal Articles on a Topic

Let's trace the process of prerequisite analysis by using the first step of information processing from the previous library example. For the task of locating journal articles on the topic "instruction" given the resources of a college or university library, we determined the first step to be as follows:

1. *Locate the ERIC thesaurus.* If we were to conduct a prerequisite analysis on this first step, we would find that to locate the ERIC thesaurus, the learner must do the following:
   a. Know what ERIC means and its purpose.
   b. Know what a thesaurus is and its purpose.
   c. Know what an ERIC thesaurus looks like and where to locate it.
   d. Know what the term *reference* means with regard to library usage.
   e. Be able to locate reference books in the library.

We might break down any of these prerequisites into its prerequisites. For example, the step "know what a thesaurus is and its purpose" requires that the learner understand the concept "synonym." We would examine other prerequisites for step 1 to see if we could identify any additional prerequisites. When finished, step 1 might look like this:

1. *Locate the ERIC thesaurus.* The learner must do the following:
   a. Know what ERIC means and its purpose.
   b. Know what a thesaurus is and its purpose (understand concept of "synonym").
   c. Know what an ERIC thesaurus looks like and where to locate it.
   d. Know what the term *reference* means with regard to library usage.
   e. Be able to locate reference books in the library (know the layout of the library).

Further developed, the prerequisite analysis of the library example would look like this:

1. *Locate the ERIC thesaurus.*
   a. Know what ERIC means and its purpose.
   b. Know what a thesaurus is and its purpose (understand concept of "synonym").
   c. Know what an ERIC thesaurus looks like and where to locate it.
   d. Know what the term *reference* means with regard to library usage.
   e. Be able to locate reference books in the library (know the layout of the library).
2. Determine a related descriptor from the thesaurus.
3. Locate the most recent cumulative *CIJE.*
4. Find the descriptor in the *CIJE.*
5. Read through the article titles and select possible articles.
6. Locate and read the abstracts of the possible articles.
7. Select the most appropriate articles and write down the citations.
8. Locate the journal names in the library holdings index, and write down the call numbers of the journals.
9. Locate the journal volumes.
10. Locate the articles, read them, and determine if they are appropriate.
11. Photocopy the articles.

A graphic representation of this prerequisite analysis is shown in Figure 5.11. Space limitations entail that we have presented only a portion of this graphic analysis. Because a prerequisite analysis is rather complex, we'll provide you with one more example.

Example Prerequisite Analysis for the Concept "Rhombus"

1. Recall the characteristics of a rhombus. (Many experts do this unconsciously.)
   a. List the four major attributes of a rhombus (polygon, parallelogram, equilateral sides, and oblique angles).

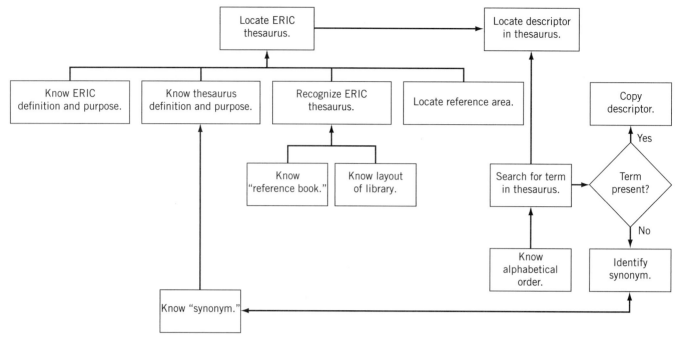

Figure 5.11 Prerequisite Analysis: Finding a Journal Article Using ERIC

2. Determine whether figure is a polygon. If yes, continue on to step 3; if no, go to step 5.
    a. Recognize examples of a polygon.
    b. Define a polygon (although the ability to define this and the following definitions may not be absolutely prerequisite).
    c. Recognize examples of geometric figures.
    d. Define geometric figures.
    e. Recognize examples of plane figures.
    f. Define plane figures.
    g. Recognize examples of closed figures.
    h. Define closed figures.
    i. Recognize straight-sided figures.
    j. Define straight-sided figures.
    k. Recognize examples of figures.
    l. Define *figure.*

(The relative subordination of prerequisites to other prerequisites is indicated by indentions.)

3. Determine if the figure is a parallelogram. If yes, continue on to step 4; if no, go to step 5. Be able to recognize examples of a parallelogram.
    a. Define a parallelogram.
    b. Recognize examples of a quadrilateral.
    c. Define the concept "quadrilateral."
    d. Recognize examples of "side."
    e. Recognize examples of "angle."
    f. Determine if sides in a figure are parallel.
    g. Identify sides of a figure.
    h. Define the concept of "parallel."

4. Determine if the figure's sides are equilateral. If yes, *it is a rhombus;* if no, go to step 5. Be able to recognize examples of figures with equilateral sides.
    a. Define equilateral.
    b. Recognize examples of the concept "side."
    c. Recognize examples of the concept "equal sides."
    d. Define *equal* in the geometric sense.

5. The figure is not a rhombus.

This prerequisite analysis is represented graphically in Figures 5.12 and 5.13.

The boxes containing skills in Figure 5.13 are the prerequisites that must be acquired before the learner can acquire the concept diagrammed in Figure 5.12. A skill that is listed below a second skill is prerequisite to it. Where physically possible, we have listed declarative knowledge (e.g., "List the characteristics of polygon") to the side of a skill to which it contributes, rather than below it. This is because often (technically speaking) declarative knowledge may not be prerequisite to intellectual skills (R. Gagné, 1985). (This position is somewhat contradicted by Anderson's "ACT*" Theory, 1995.)

After a review of the characteristics of the learners, the designer may determine that the learners already possess some of the skills and knowledge listed, particularly those listed at the bottom of the hierarchy (at the bottom of the graph). As you can see, these are the skills and knowledge that are the simplest (e.g., recog-

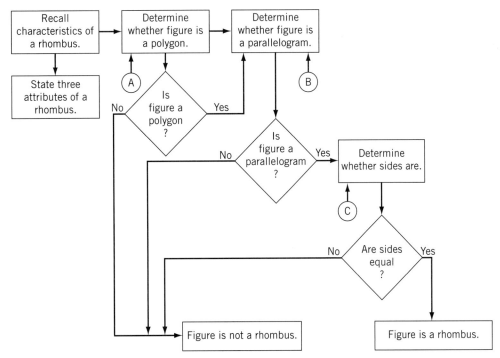

Figure 5.12   Part 1 of a Prerequisite Analysis of the Concept "Rhombus"

nizing sides of a figure). If the designer has a strong reason to assume that the learners already possess some of these simple skills and knowledge, he may indicate this by labeling it as an entry skill on the prose list or drawing it below a dotted line, marked "entry level skills," on the graphic.

Once the prerequisites (including both the information-processing steps and the prerequisites for these steps) of a learning goal have been identified, these outcomes can be converted into learning objectives. Before we discuss the development of learning objectives, it would be a good idea to look at the terms we will use when talking about objectives.

Some terms that we will use in the context of objectives are *terminal objective, enabling objective, prerequisites,* and *entry skills. Terminal objectives* are the more precise statements of learning goals. Whereas the intent for learning of a lesson or module of instruction may be expressed by one learning goal, there may be more than one terminal objective for the module or lesson. Terminal objectives are the skills and knowledge we expect learners to achieve as a result of instruction. *Enabling objectives* are the sub-objectives, the knowledge or skills that enable the learner to learn to do the terminal objective. The elements that your information-processing and prerequisite analyses reveal are the material out of which you will develop enabling objectives. *Prerequisites,* a term that we have already used, are the building blocks of a learning task. So enabling

objectives are also prerequisites. *Entry skills* are another kind of prerequisite, specifically referring to skills and knowledge that the learner brings to instruction. Entry skills are "prerequisites" in the everyday usage of the term: things you must know before you are qualified to begin a class or other form of instruction.

1. The following is an information-processing analysis of the learning goal "the learner will be able to divide two fractions."

a. Determine whether the situation requires the use of this procedure—dividing fractions.

b. Recall the steps in the procedure.

c. Write the problem horizontally.

d. Convert whole numbers or mixed fractions to fractions.

e. Invert second fraction.

f. Multiply two fractions.

g. Reduce resulting term to lowest terms.

h. Confirm that process was applied correctly.

Conduct a prerequisite analysis of each of these steps. If you do not know the proper mathematical terms, provide examples for what you mean.

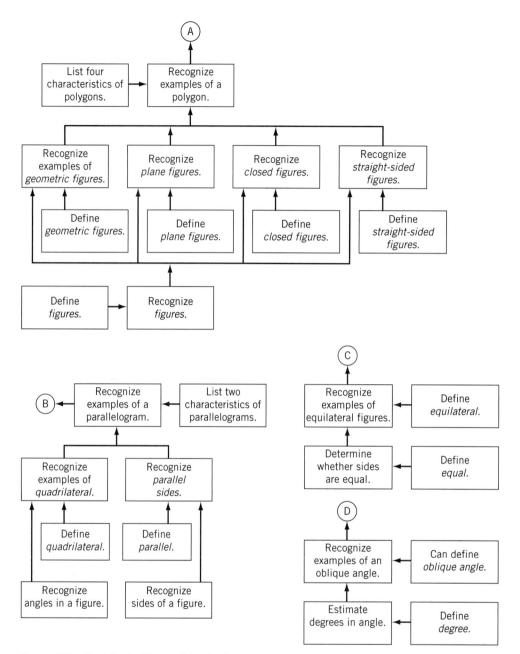

Figure 5.13   Part 2 of a Prerequisite Analysis of the Concept "Rhombus"

2. Conduct an instructional analysis (both information-processing and prerequisite analysis) to determine the prerequisite skills that learners must acquire in order to subtract one three-digit number from another.

WRITING LEARNING OBJECTIVES

Now that you have identified the prerequisites for a learning goal and have begun to think about what type of learning each prerequisite represents, you are ready to convert each of these prerequisite statements and the goal statement into more precise, concrete, and specific terms. You will be converting prerequisite statements and the goal statement into learning objectives. As we stated earlier, the precision and concreteness of this type of objective allows us to have a complete perspective of "where we are going." Also, as we have stated earlier, the degree of specificity required in these objectives may vary from situation to situation.

A **learning objective** is a statement that tells what learners should be able to do when they have completed a segment of instruction. Learning is a cognitive process that leads to a capability that the learner did not possess prior to instruction. Unfortunately, there is no way (at present) to directly study or measure changes in cognitive representations. So, at this point, in order to ascertain what learners have learned, we must determine what kind of evidence of learning we will accept as an indication that learning has occurred. The most explicit learning objectives describe what learners can do to demonstrate that they have learned. What learners "do" must be observable so that the learners know that they have learned and what they have learned. In addition, it is important for both teachers and instructional designers to know what learning is intended. Whether it is to write down that an object is translucent, transparent, or opaque when given a series of objects or whether it is to become able to design and develop effective instruction, it is critical that objectives be specified. (Some learners will note that this description of learning objectives seems to be synonymous with "performance" or "behavioral" objectives. That is true. We have abandoned those terms because they have acquired disagreeable connotations of behaviorist assumptions to which we do not ascribe.)

Nebulous objectives such as "the learners will be aware of metric measurements" or "the learner will understand the importance of the three branches of the U.S. government" do not give much guidance to the designer as to what the learners should actually know about converting to the metric system or about the three branches of government. They are not "wrong"; they are a good beginning point for further reflection on what is meant by "understand" or "be aware of." Learning objectives give much more direction as to what learners actually need to learn to do:

- Given a series of English measurements of length, weight, or volume, the learners can convert these measurements to their metric equivalents.
- The learners will be able to summarize the functions of each of the branches of the U.S. government and explain the "checks and balances" among the branches.

A second common problem in stating objectives (as with writing learning goals) is that designers sometimes write the objective to describe the learning activities in which the students will be involved, rather than what the students should be able to do when they finish these activities. For example, in a unit on ecology, a designer might inappropriately state the objective as a learning activity: "The learners will play a simulation game in which they experience the interactions of variables in the ecosystem." The designer should instead state the terminal objective of the lesson: "When given a description of an ecosystem, the learner will be able to identify potential sources of pollution and suggest methods to control or eliminate the pollution."

Objectives are valuable to all members of the learning system. They aid the designer since they provide a focus of the instruction, guiding the designer in making decisions about what content should be included, what strategy should be used, and how students should be evaluated. The specification of clear objectives is especially critical when a number of individuals—such as designers, content experts, graphic artists, and programmers—are working together to produce instruction. In these situations, learning objectives serve as a concrete focus of communication.

Objectives stated in explicit terms are also beneficial when stated in the documentation of instructional guides. They aid the potential adopters of the system—teachers or trainers and school administrators or training directors—in making decisions as to whether the material is suitable for helping the learners achieve the learning goals of the particular learning system. When expressed to students during instruction, objectives help them focus their efforts and conduct periodic assessments of their own learning.

One common problem with instructional material is designers' failure to utilize learning objectives. Often it is impossible to determine the purpose of the instruction even after going through the complete instructional materials. If the objectives are not listed in the instruction, are not listed in the documentation that accompanies the instruction, or, at the very least, are not inferable from the instruction itself, the potential user has a very good reason to seek better-designed instruction. Certainly you will want to have a clear idea of what you wish the learners to learn from your instruction before you begin writing.

How to Write Learning Objectives

Objectives can be written at the lesson level, the course level, or various intermediate levels such as units, blocks, or chapters. There are many different forms of objectives that can give equally precise and concrete descriptions of learning outcomes. We will demonstrate how to write the simplest form: three-component objectives, as first described by Robert Mager (1962).

Three-component objectives are verbal statements of learning outcomes that include three parts:

- A description of the terminal behavior or actions that will demonstrate learning.
- A description of the conditions of demonstration of that action.
- A description of the standard or criterion.

The most critical part of a learning objective is the description of the observable action. The statement of the **terminal behavior** includes a description of the actions that the learner can show that will demonstrate that he has learned. The action statement includes action verbs such as *select, identify, list, solve, repair,* and *write.* (We repeat this because this issue is so often confused by educators: All of these objectives are cognitive. They all represent changes in cognitive capability. In describing actions in objectives, designers are merely clarifying what evidence they will accept to indicate learning. The actions merely represent cognitive abilities.)

As with learning goals, avoid using terms that fail to communicate the intent of the objective. Some of these ambiguous terms are *understand, be aware of, appreciate,* and *become familiar with.*

Here are some examples of the terminal action description:

- Circle the polygons.
- Underline the verbs.
- List the steps in the instructional design process.
- Locate and repair the problem.
- Write a performance objective.

The description of the **conditions of demonstration** is the second most critical part of a learning objective. This component of the objective describes the tools or information that the learners will be given when they demonstrate their learning. Often this component is at the beginning of the objective statement. It usually begins with the word *given:*

- Given ten drawings of geometric figures, circle the polygons.
- Given a paragraph, underline the verbs.
- List the steps in the instructional design process.
- Given a malfunctioning VCR, locate and repair the problem.
- Given a learning goal, write a performance objective (for it).

As you can see, we took the terminal behaviors from earlier in this section and added appropriate conditions statements that describe what stimulus, or material, will be presented to the learners when they demonstrate their learning. You will notice that the third objective does not contain a conditions statement. There are occasions—particularly with declarative knowledge objectives—when no conditions are necessary: Learners will be given no tools or information when asked to demonstrate their learning. Novice instructional designers sometimes include the phrase "after instruction" in the statement of conditions of demonstration. This is an unnecessary statement within a learning objective, and it should be avoided.

The final component of a three-component objective is a description of the **standards** or **criteria.** This statement describes how well the learner must do for you to say the learner has achieved the objective. These standards (Mager, 1962) may refer to the following:

- Accuracy (e.g., "student's answer must be within ± 3 degrees").
- Number of errors (e.g., "with three mistakes or fewer").
- Number of correct responses (e.g., "with at least 80 percent correct").
- Time (e.g., "in twelve minutes or less").
- Consistent with an established standard (e.g., "in the order listed in the text").
- Consistent with a stated standard (e.g., "that includes the following three descriptors: plane, closed, and straight-line figure").
- Consequences (e.g., "so that the customer walks away satisfied").

The following examples complete the objectives that we have been developing in this section:

- Given ten drawings of geometric figures, circle *all* of the polygons.
- Given a paragraph, underline *at least 90 percent* of the verbs.
- Given a malfunctioning VCR, locate and repair the problem *so that the VCR functions correctly.*
- Given a learning goal, write a learning objective (for it) that includes a description of terminal behavior, conditions, and the standard.

An alternate approach to writing the criterion (especially in cases in which the criterion will be stated in terms of how many items must be correct out of a total number of items) is to delay writing the criterion until you write the assessment item specifications related to that objective. We actually prefer this approach as the idea of a standard or criterion fits more neatly into the concept of assessment than in a statement of purpose. You may find that you, too, prefer to write the conditions and action statement in the objective and place the criterion in your assessment item specifications (see Chapter 6).

Different design situations require different levels of specificity for their objectives. We must admit that we have become less and less rigorous in our standards for explicitness in objectives. We believe that the point of the greatest rigor is in developing assessment item specifications. We do not feel that objectives must be so explicit that they describe the assessment situation.

EXAMPLES OF LEARNING OBJECTIVES FOR VARIOUS LEARNING OUTCOMES

In the following section we have included a discussion and examples of objectives for each of the major categories of learning outcomes. The examples are provided in the form that we would accept as adequate (not including a criterion statement).

Declarative Knowledge

Declarative knowledge objectives need to reflect whether learning will be recognition (choosing from options) or recall, verbatim or paraphrased, and listed or summarized. Examples of declarative knowledge objectives follow:

- Learners can match chemical elements' symbols to their names.
- Learners can summarize the principal protections to individual liberties provided under the Bill of Rights.
- Learners can define instructional technology in their own words.
- Learners can list and describe instructional delivery systems in their own words.

Concepts

Concept objectives should reflect the learners' ability to classify and label ideas, objects, and events as examples/nonexamples of a concept. They may require that the learner state how/why such classification was made. Examples of concept objectives follow:

- Learners can identify design/development activities.
- Learners can identify polygons and explain their answers.
- Learners can give examples of transparent objects.

Principles

Principle objectives should reflect the intention that the learner can use the principle to predict, explain, or control something, The objectives may require that learners explain their application of the principle. Occasionally, objectives may ask students to recognize whether a rule was correctly or incorrectly applied and tell why or why not. Examples of principle objectives follow:

- Learners can identify diffusion/dissemination problems and explain how to avoid them.
- By manipulating aperture and shutter speeds, learners can create equivalent settings.

Procedures

Procedure objectives describe what learners can do to demonstrate that they can successfully complete a procedure defined by a procedural rule.

- Given a 1960 Studebaker Lark, the student can adjust the ignition timing.
- Learners can solve these kinds of problems: 123×16, 140×257, 367×6.

Domain-Specific Problem Solving

Problem-solving objectives should reflect the requirement that the learner do the following:

1. Assess the problem situation.
2. Determine which rules are applicable.
3. Synthesize these rules to solve a particular problem.

Examples of problem-solving objectives follow:

- Learners can write computer programs that use the following: conditional statements, print statements, loops, and assignment of value.
- Learners can use a word processor to write a paper.
- Learners can determine equivalent exposures using aperture size, shutter speed, and film type.

Cognitive Strategies

Cognitive strategy objectives require that the learner do the following:

1. Assess the learning task.
2. Select (or invent) a strategy appropriate to the task.
3. Apply the strategy.
4. Assess the success of the strategy.
5. Modify the strategy if it is not effective.

Examples of cognitive strategy objectives follow:

- Learners can use a text structure strategy.
- Learner applies a mnemonic to learn resistor color codes.

Attitudes

Attitude objectives must reflect what the learner must do to demonstrate acquisition of an attitude. They may also require that the learner tell why the performance is important. Lesser "levels of directness" may be used, which require the learner to simulate (either in writing or in role-playing) demonstration of the desired attitude. Examples of attitude objectives follow:

- Learner will choose to solve problems non-violently.
- Learner will decide to attend opera rehearsals regularly.

Psychomotor Skills

Psychomotor objectives should reflect what "new" muscular activities are required. The standards often reflect time or speed or consequences or number of times the learner must correctly execute the motions. Examples of psychomotor skill objectives follow:

- Learner can parallel park a manual transmission car.
- Learner can type forty words per minute.

E X E R C I S E S E

1. In the following objectives, underline the words that give a description of the conditions, circle the statement of the terminal behavior, and draw a box around the part of the sentence that gives the performance standards.

- Given a level parallel parking spot along a curb with two poles fifteen feet apart and a manual transmission car, the learner can parallel park the car between the two poles within three minutes without bumping either pole.
- Given a list of computers in education references and a word-processing program, the learner can generate a word-processed, three- to five-page paper on educational applications of computers in her subject area. The product should achieve at least seventy points when assessed with the checklist that is attached.
- Given fifteen multiplication problems in which the multiplier is a decimal with one, two, or three decimal places, the learner can solve at least twelve of them correctly.
- Given pictures of twelve geometric figures, some of which are polygons, the learner should be able to circle those that are polygons. He should correctly identify at least ten of these. In addition, the learner must state why he made the distinction that he did. This explanation should be couched in an explanation of how this figure does/does not represent the three key attributes of polygons. At least eight of these explanations must be correct.

2. Following are statements of learning goals. Rewrite them as learning objectives in a three-part Mager form.

- The student can select examples of the concept "conservative" (in the political dichotomy of liberal versus conservative) from a list of examples and nonexamples.
- The student will administer an allergy injection following sterile technique.
- The student can compute the mean, range, and standard deviation of a series of ten numbers.

3. For the learning goal that follows, conduct a complete instructional analysis (information-processing analysis and prerequisite analysis) including steps in the information- processing analysis as learning objectives. The goal is "The learner will be able to subtract one two-digit number from a second two-digit number."

S U M M A R Y

The result of the front-end analysis stage of design is a clear description of the learning environment, the learners, and the learning task. The learning task has been clearly specified in terms of both terminal objectives and, through an instructional analysis, enabling objectives. These objectives have been classified according to the types of learning outcomes required, which in our case is according to Gagné's learning outcomes taxonomy. This clear delineation of environment, learner, and task will enable the designer to design instruction that can and will be implemented in the targeted learning environment. The instructional analysis, specification of learning objectives, and categorization of the learning outcomes assist the designer in selecting the appropriate instructional strategy and appropriate evaluation items and procedures. Figure 5.14 summarizes key points in this chapter.

EXTENDED EXAMPLE

Go to the Learning Resources Web Site for a continuation the instructional design of the Photography Basics course. A learning task analysis for the course is provided.

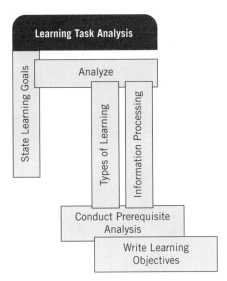

Figure 5.14 Summary Diagram for Chapter 5

READINGS AND REFERENCES

Anderson, J. R. (1995). *Cognitive psychology and its implications* (4th ed.). New York: W. H. Freeman.

Anderson, J. R. (1976). *Language, memory, and thought.* Hillsdale, NJ: Lawrence Erlbaum Associates.

Bloom, B. S., Englehart, M. D., Furst, E. J., Hill, W. H., & Krathwohl, D. R. (1956). *Taxonomy of educational objectives: Handbook I, cognitive domain.* New York: McKay.

Brien, R., & Duchastel, P. (1986). Cognitive task analysis underlying the specification of instructional objectives. *Programmed Learning and Educational Technology, 23* (4), 363–370.

Brien, R., & Eastmond, N. (1994). *Cognitive science and instruction.* Englewood Cliffs, NJ: Educational Technology Publications.

Briggs, L. J. (Ed.). (1977). *Instruction design: Principles and applications.* Englewood Cliffs, NJ: Educational Technology Publications.

Carlisle, K. E. (1986). *Analyzing jobs and tasks.* Englewood Cliffs, NJ: Educational Technology Publications.

Case, R. (1993). Theories of learning and theories of development. *Educational Psychologist, 23*(3), 219–233.

de Jong, T., & Ferguson-Hessler, M. G. M. (1996). Types and qualities of knowledge. *Educational Psychologist, 31*(2), 105–113.

Dick, W., & Carey, L. (1996). *The systematic design of instruction* (4th ed.). New York: HarperCollins.

Dunn, T. G., & Taylor, C. A. (1990). Hierarchical structures in expert performance. *Educational Technology Research & Development, 38* (2), 5–18.

Dunn, T. G., & Taylor, C. A. (April, 1994).*Learning analysis in ill-structured knowledge domains of professional practice.* Paper presented at American Educational Research Association, New Orleans.

Furst, E. J. (1981). Bloom's taxonomy of educational objectives for the cognitive domain: Philosophical and educational issues. *Review of Educational Research, 51* (5), 441–454.

Gagné, E. D. (1985). *The cognitive psychology of school learning.* Boston: Little, Brown.

Gagné, R. M. (1984). Learning outcomes and their effects: Useful categories of human performance. *American Psychologist, 39,* 377–385.

Gagné, R. M. (1985). *The conditions of learning* (4th ed.). New York: Holt, Rinehart & Winston.

Gagné, R. M., & Glaser, R. (1987). Foundations in learning research. In R. M. Gagné (Ed.), *Instructional technology foundations* (pp. 49–83). Hillsdale, NJ: Erlbaum.

Gagné, R. M., & Merrill, M. D. (1990). Integrative goals for instructional design. *Educational Technology Research & Development, 38* (1), 23–30.

Gardner, M. J. (1985). Cognitive psychological approaches to instructional task analysis. In E. Gordon (Ed.), *Review of Research in Education, 12,* 157–196. Washington, DC: American Educational Research Association.

Greeno, J. G. (1980). Some examples of cognitive task analysis with instructional implications. In R. Snow, P. Federico, & W. Montague (Eds.), *Aptitude, Learning, and Instruction, Vol. 2: Cognitive Process Analysis of Learning and Problem Solving* (pp. 1–21). Hillsdale, NJ: Erlbaum.

Jonassen, D. H., & Hannum, W. H. (1986). Analysis of task analysis procedures. *Journal of Instructional Development, 9,* 2–12.

Jonassen, D. H., Hannum, W. H., & Tessmer, M. (1989). *Handbook of task analysis procedures.* New York: Praeger.

Jonassen, D. H., Tessmer, M., & Hannum, W. H. (1999). *Task analysis methods for instructional design.* Mahwah: Erlbaum.

Kyllonen, P. C., & Shute, V. J. (1989). A taxonomy of learning skills. In P. L. Ackerman, R. J. Sternberg, & R. Glaser (Eds.), *Learning and individual differences: Advances in theory and research* (pp. 117–163). New York: W. H. Freeman.

Mager, R. F. (1962). *Preparing instructional objectives.* Palo Alto, CA: Fearon.

Melton, A. W. (Ed.) (1964). *Categories of human learning.* New York: Academic Press.

Merrill, M. D. (1983). Component display theory. In C. M. Reigeluth (Ed.), *Instructional design theories and models.* (pp. 279–333). Hillsdale, NJ: Erlbaum.

Merrill, P. F. (1987). Job and task analysis. In R. M. Gagné (Ed.), *Instructional technology: Foundations* (pp. 143–174). Hillsdale, NJ: Erlbaum.

Nelson, W. (1989). Artificial intelligence knowledge acquisition techniques for instructional development. *Educational Technology Research and Development, 37*(3), 81–94.

Ragan, T. J., & Smith, P. L. (2003). Conditions theory and models for designing instruction. In D. H. Jonassen (Ed.), *Handbook of research for educational communications and technology* (2nd ed.) (pp. 623–649). Mahwah, NJ: Erlbaum.

Rossett, A. (1988). *Training needs assessment.* Englewood Cliffs, NJ: Educational Technology Publications.

Ryder, J. M., & Redding, R. E. (1993). Integrating cognitive task analysis in instructional systems development. *Educational Technology Research and Development, 41* (2), 75–96.

Scandura, J. M. (1983). Instructional strategies based on the structural learning theory. In C. M. Reigeluth (ed.), *Instructional design theories and models* (pp. 213–246). Hillsdale, NJ: Erlbaum.

Schlager, M., Means, B., & Roth, C. (April, 1988). *Cognitive analysis of expert knowledge: Input into design of training.* Paper presented at the annual meeting of the American Educational Research Association, New Orleans.

Smith, P. L., & Ragan, T. J. (2000).The impact of R.M. Gagné's work on instructional theory. In R. Richey (Ed.), *The Legacy of Robert M. Gagné* (pp. 147–181) Syracuse, NY: ERIC Clearinghouse on Information and Technology.

Tolman, E. C. (1949). There is more than one kind of learning. *Psychological Review, 56,* 144–155.

Weinstein, C. F., & Mayer, R. F. (1986). The teaching of learning strategies. In M. C. Wittrock (Ed.), *Handbook of research on teaching* (3rd ed.) (pp. 315–329). New York: Macmillan.

ASSESSING LEARNING FROM INSTRUCTION

CHAPTER OBJECTIVES

At the conclusion of this chapter, you should be able to do the following:

- Determine the appropriate model—norm referenced or criterion referenced—to guide the development of assessments.

- Given a completed learning task analysis, identify which objectives would appear on entry skills assessment, preassessment, and postassessment.

- Given descriptions of types of assessment—simulation, observation, or written test—describe trade-offs among validity, reliability, and practicality.

- Write production and recognition items for objectives of different types of learning.

- Identify which of several possible assessment items are valid assessments of objectives for various types of learning.

- Given an objective, write appropriate item specifications, and write five assessment items (if appropriate) that are congruent with the item specs.

- Write an appropriate assessment instrument blueprint that includes test length, description of content domain, proportionality, directions and administration procedures, type and number of measures, scoring methods, weighting of items, and criterion level/cut-off score.

- Evaluate sample assessment items according to the characteristics of "good" assessment instruments and guidelines for that type of item, suggesting revisions where appropriate.

AN OVERVIEW OF ASSESSMENT OF LEARNING FROM INSTRUCTION

Jim Evans just finished teaching a workshop for trainers in state agencies on creating effective visuals. He had some admirable objectives for his workshop, such as the following:

- Given a description of the audience characteristics, purposes of the presentation, and source materials, the learner will be able to develop a transparency master that incorporates the principles of visual design and good lettering.

- Given a description of the audience characteristics, purposes of the presentation, and a handout developed for a presentation, the learner will be able to evaluate the handout based upon the principles of visual design, effective lettering, and appropriate use of the medium, and to suggest revisions.

Jim conducted only one assessment in the class, a fifty-item test at the conclusion of the workshop. The test included items such as

Which of the following is not a characteristic of the design element "surface"?

  a. texture

  b. color

  c. value

  d. form

Another test item was

"List and discuss the eight principles of visual design."

Some of the learners performed unexpectedly poorly on the test, and the mandated instructor evaluation forms at the end of the class contained statements such as "I don't think the test was fair." "I knew most of the stuff that the instructor taught. It wasn't very challenging." "There were a lot of times that I was lost. The instructor assumed that I already knew some things that I didn't know." However, despite these negative comments, Jim was pleased to see that when he plotted the learners' scores, they formed a normal, or "bell," curve. Despite his reaching this distribution of scores, Jim has problems with his own instruction. Specifically, his evaluation procedures and assumptions may have been inappropriate considering his objectives and the purposes for his evaluation. What problems do you notice with his procedures and approach? In this chapter we will address many of the issues related to assessment within an instructional design context.

PURPOSES OF EVALUATION

As Mager (1962) stated, the question that instructional designers must ask in addition to "Where are we going?" and "How will we get there?" is "How do we know when we're there?" Planning for evaluation allows us to determine "how we know when we're there." Evaluation serves two purposes in instructional design: to assess individual students' performances and to provide information about what kinds of revisions are needed in the instructional materials. Actually, then, there are two kinds of "getting there" that we must determine during evaluation. The first question is that of assessing whether individual learners are "getting there" (i.e., after instruction they can demonstrate the learning described in the objectives). That is the focus of this chapter. The second aspect of evaluation is determining how well the instruction "works": Is the instruction effective, efficient, and appealing? And if it is not working well, what changes need to be made? (This type of evaluation is the focus of Chapter 19.)

Sequencing Assessment Design Activity

In our instructional design model and in the text, we have chosen to sequence designing assessment items immediately after writing learning objectives, considering the design of assessments to be part of the analysis phase of design, specifically, as part of task anaysis. A good designer generally begins to think about assessment instruments* as she develops the learning objectives. This is done to help ensure that not only does the assessment match the objectives but appropriately amplifies and clarifies the objectives themselves. For example, the conditions and actions specified in the objectives are considered in the writing of each assessment item. This is why the stage for writing test items appears where it does in the design model.

In this way, we create what are called *criterion-referenced assessment items*. Imagine how easy it is for someone to create an item immediately after writing the following objective: "Given a list of objects, some of which are transparent, the learner should be able to circle those objects that are transparent." If the designer has been this specific in the description of the

---

*We have intentionally used the terms assessment, assessment instrument, and assessment item rather than testing, test, and test item to avoid connotations and preconceptions that interfere with learning techniques suggested in this text. For example, many novice designers assume that when the *term* test is used, we are referring to a pencil-and-paper assessment. As you will find, there are many formats for assessing learner achievement, only one of which is a written test format.

learning objective, all she must do at this point is fulfill the conditions of the objective; that is, list a number of objects for the learner, some of which are transparent and, through the directions (which are part of the assessment instrument), tell the learner to circle the transparent objects. If the designer chose to be less specific in describing the learning objectives, writing assessment items may be more demanding, because this is where she must determine what will constitute evidence that the learners have learned.

There is a definite benefit to writing assessment items immediately after writing objectives. First, the intentions of the objectives will be fresh in your mind. Second, if you cannot write an item for the objective, then you will know that you may have to reexamine your objective. Thus, a good time to write test items is immediately after writing objectives. The work you do in designing good assessments will provide information on the level of performance which you expect learners to achieve.

The success of developing good assessment instruments heavily depends on the quality of the objectives written. If these do not really reflect the intentions of the instruction, then the assessment that is based upon them certainly will be inadequate.

When designing assessment items for a lesson, you should do the following:

1. Identify the purpose of the assessment instrument and the type of model that will be followed in its development.
2. Determine what kinds of assessments are necessary and where they should occur in the instructional strategy.
3. Determine what forms the items should take (performance test, essay, multiple choice, portfolio, and so on) to adequately assess the type of learning that is represented by the objective.
4. Write test items and directions that are clear to the learner, originally in the form of item specifications.
5. Determine how many items are needed to assess learners' learning of an objective and what constitutes an adequate performance to reflect that learning.
6. Determine how to select among objectives or what proportion of objectives should appear on the assessment instrument by writing an instrument blueprint.

We will discuss each of these issues in the following sections. Good test writing is a skill that is not quickly or easily learned. There are many texts on test writing, and most universities have entire courses on the subject. However, as you will see later in the chapter, there are specific approaches to developing assessment items in the context of instructional design that may differ considerably from traditional techniques for test design.

PURPOSES AND MODELS OF ASSESSMENT OF LEARNERS' ACHIEVEMENT

In educational and training environments, there typically are two rather diverse reasons for assessing learners' achievement: (1) to determine level of competence, and (2) to compare or rank learners' abilities. The results of these assessments allow teachers, trainers, administrators, and learners to make two rather different kinds of decisions.

One example of an assessment of competence is a performance assessment designed to determine whether a physical therapist can correctly adjust the height of crutches. The scores from this assessment might enable the instructor to determine which learners are ready for further study and which learners need more instruction on the topic. The information provided by this assessment might also be used by licensing or accrediting agencies to determine whether an individual has the skills and/or knowledge to be licensed or accredited. Instruments designed to assess competence or identify gaps in learning are termed **criterion-referenced assessment instruments.** (They are also called *objective-referenced* or *domain-referenced* instruments.) Although criterion-referenced assessments are effective for determining who is "competent" and where individuals' weaknesses are, they are not very effective in enabling decision makers to compare or rank learners.

The Graduate Record Exam (GRE) is an example of an assessment designed to enable comparison or ranking of individuals. The GRE is designed to provide scores that assist admissions officers in selecting individuals for admission to graduate school. The goal of the test is to obtain a spread of scores that gives the admissions officers a clear picture of ranking and maximizes the ability to compare students. Instruments of this type are termed **norm-referenced tests.** Although instruments designed with this purpose in mind do aid selection decisions, they are much less helpful in determining whether an individual is competent in a particular skill or possesses particular knowledge. They are even less helpful in helping an instructor (or learner) determine where the learning gaps are and where remediation is needed.

While an assessment instrument might be designed with both purposes in mind, ordinarily one purpose or the other is predominant. It is important that assessment designers have a clear purpose in mind for their tests because the methods used to design instruments for these two purposes are somewhat different. In most cases, an instrument that is designed to rank or compare learners is designed using a norm-referenced model, and tests developed to determine competence are designed using a criterion-referenced model. As a rule, instructional designers are involved in designing tests to assess competence and to determine areas needing remediation; consequently, instructional designers typically use criterion-referenced models and instrument development procedures.

The two models of assessment design differ in the manner in which they define the content that is to be assessed and in the manner in which they choose items to include on an instrument. Typically, norm-referenced test designers define the scope of the material for the assessment instrument more broadly and with less precision than do criterion-referenced test designers. In contrast, when developing criterion-referenced instruments, designers use the precise objectives that they developed in the learning task description phase (as discussed in Chapter 5) to specifically guide their selection of skills and knowledge to be assessed. Therefore, the domain or scope of the type of items that are appropriate for assessment is carefully defined.

When determining which items will be included on an instrument, norm-referenced designers administer a trial form of the exam to a sample of individuals who represent the target audience of the test. After the administration of the test, the designers look at the difficulty level of each item (the ratio of the number of people who answered the item correctly to the total number of individuals taking the exam). They then eliminate items that were extremely easy (answered correctly by most individuals) or extremely difficult (answered correctly by only a few individuals).

This procedure for selecting items in norm-referenced instruments helps obtain a spread or variation of scores, leading to what is often described as *normal distribution* or a *bell curve* of scores. This promotes the ability to discriminate between the performance of individuals and rank them. Once this form of the test has been developed, it is again administered to a large group of individuals who represent the population for whom the test is being developed. Using the scores from this administration, performance "norms" are obtained. That is, information is collected so that in later administrations, once a score is obtained, the teacher and learner can be provided with information as to how the learner's score compares to others of his age or experience level. Often these scores are reported as percentiles; that is, what percent of scores rank below an individual's score. The theoretical basis for designing assessments in this fashion is often referred to as "classical" assessment theory. (Crocker & Algina, 1986)

In contrast, the criterion-referenced test designer writes items that match a goal or objective in terms of conditions presented and performance required. If the goal or objective has a range of possible difficulty levels, the writer will write several items to sample across the difficulty levels. In looking at test scores on items after trials of the test, the instructional designer will certainly not routinely discard items that are answered correctly by the majority of learners, as this is a desirable outcome. It may indicate instruction was effective. He will examine the item to ensure that nothing in the item "gives away" the answer, but if this is not a problem and the item truly requires the cognitive processes reflected in the objective, he will retain the item. Then he will examine the instruction to determine whether the coverage of that particular objective is adequate.

The criterion-referenced assessment designer is much less concerned with obtaining a wide spread of scores on an instrument than the norm-referenced designer. Quite often, scores from criterion-referenced instruments do not represent a normal distribution. They are often skewed by many individuals performing well: Many instructional designers argue that if instruction is effective, test results will not form a normal distribution on a well-designed test. There are multiple theoretical foundations that underlie the design of criterion-referenced assessments, but central among them is item response theory (Crocker & Algina, 1986).

So Jim Evans, whose workshop experience was described earlier in this chapter, should not be satisfied with his test results simply because he obtained a normal distribution. His workshop goals were to develop a high level of competence for developing good visuals in *all* of the participants, not to compare or rank them. Therefore, he should actually be disturbed by his test results. (You might like to refer back to Bloom's Model of Mastery Learning in Chapter 2, where the inappropriateness of normal distribution of scores on tests after instruction is discussed.)

E X E R C I S E S A

1. Following are descriptions of some assessment situations. Beside each situation, write whether a criterion-referenced model (C) or a norm-referenced model (N) is most appropriate for guiding assessment development.

a. Determine which students should be licensed as physical therapists.

b. Determine which applicants to admit to a graduate program with limited positions.

c. Determine whether a learner is ready to begin the next unit of study.

d. Determine which students should receive a scholarship when requests for scholarships exceed resources.

e. Determine how the reading abilities of one state's students compare to those in another state.

f. Determine in which areas a learner needs remediation.

2. In your own words, describe the differences in development of a norm-referenced and a criterion-referenced assessment.

TYPES OF ASSESSMENTS

There are three types of tests that may be given during instruction: entry skills assessments, preassessments, and postassessments.

Entry Skills Assessments

As discussed in Chapter 5, there are often skills and knowledge that students must have to begin instruction on a particular topic. For instance, we want learners to know how to add, subtract, multiply, and divide before they begin instruction in statistics. We can avoid a lot of grief by checking to make sure that learners have the prerequisite skills before they begin instruction on a current lesson. One should not assume that because students have had a course that included treatment of a particular topic that they ever learned, or have retained, the necessary skills and knowledge in that topic needed as prerequisites for a lesson. A good way to determine whether learners have these skills and knowledge is through an entry skills test. This test can be given prior to the instructional lesson, in combination with the pretest, or as a way of reviewing the prerequisite skills.

During the actual implementation of instruction, you may choose to omit an entry skills assessment if learners have just completed a valid and reliable postassessment of the skills that would be included in the entry test. For example, if learners have just completed a prerequisite course to a course that is currently being designed, and the completed course has a valid and reliable assessment of the skills and knowledge that would be included in the entry assessment, you might omit the entry skills assessment for the latter course. However, we recommend that you retain the entry assessment in the formative evaluation phase of design, so as to confirm that you indeed have made a valid assumption regarding the learners' skill level upon entering the course.

Preassessments

We often wish to know what learners already know about the topic that they are to learn about through instruction. For example, the learners in the target audience may already know some of the enabling objectives, or some of them may have already achieved the terminal objective. A teacher can give a pretest to determine what learners already know with regard to the objective(s) at hand. The teacher can administer this preassessment before a lesson begins or may use it as a way to gain students' attention and to inform them of the objective(s) of the lesson. Through a preassessment, the instructor can determine what the students need to learn. Then the instructor can help the learners focus on that portion of the instruction that has not been previously learned.

A designer may design preassessment so that the supervising instructor (or the computer program) can terminate the assessment if learners have evidenced that they cannot answer the items related to the new information to be learned. In this way, you may avoid possible frustration and negative feelings on the part of the learners. During formative evaluation, the instructor can monitor learners' performance on the preassessment and the advent of negative emotions as learners begin to encounter items that they cannot answer.

Postassessments

Generally, toward the end of a lesson, learners are ready for the "assess learning" event, which usually takes the form of a postassessment. Ideally a postassessment will assess whether the learner can achieve both the enabling objectives and the terminal objective of a lesson. Although tests that assess both enabling and terminal objectives can be time-consuming to write (and to take), they provide a great deal of useful information. If we were to test only for the terminal objective of a lesson, and the students were unable to perform well on those items, we would have no information as to where further instruction may be needed. If, however, we have tested the enabling objectives, we have some information as to where learning has "gone wrong." The teacher or instructional materials can then send the learners to appropriate remedial instruction. With the exception of items to test achievement of declarative knowledge objectives, the items that are included on the postassessment should be different from those included on the preassessment and on practice items within the instruction.

Occasionally, to deal practically with the limitations of time in assessment development, the preassessment and the postassessment may include only the most critical subordinate objectives, such as the objectives that reflect the major information-processing steps in the task and the terminal objective.

As should become increasingly clear, the type of assessments that we prescribe here could be characterized as "authentic." Many authors have recommended more "authentic" assessment (e.g., Jonassen, 1992; Wiggins, 1998), recommending that assessment not be separated conceptually from the remainder of the learning process. One of the implications of this authenticity is timing of assessments. The recommendation for authentic or "dynamic" assessment is often interpreted as suggesting that assessment should evaluate learners' activity throughout the initial phases of learning, as well as later learning toward a goal. Of course, all assessments are at a point in the learning process; none of them is a "true" measure. However, we suggest that activity during initial stages of learning be conceptualized as practice and in later parts in the learning process as more summative indications of learning.

E X E R C I S E S   B

1. Figure 6.1 shows the results of a prerequisite analysis. Indicate which objectives (identified by the letters A–Q) should appear on each of the following assessments.

    a. Entry skills assessment:

    b. Preassessment:

    c. Postassessment:

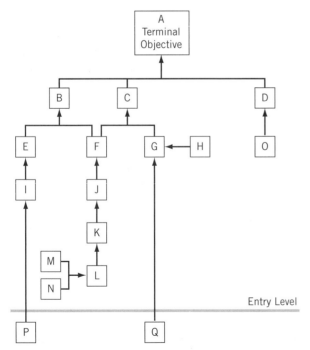

Figure 6.1 Results of a Prerequisite Analysis

2. In the situation just described, suppose "testing" time is severely limited for the postassessment. Which objectives would you assess? Why? What risks do you run in using this type of assessment?

CHARACTERISTICS OF GOOD ASSESSMENT INSTRUMENTS

"Good" criterion-referenced assessment instruments have several necessary qualities: validity, reliability, and practicality. We will discuss each of these characteristics below. We often describe these characteristics with a mnemonic, The Five C's: congruence, completeness, consistency, confidence, and cost. Figure 6.2 summarizes the Five C's of criterion referenced assessment instruments.

Validity

An assessment instrument is valid if it actually assesses or measures what it claims to assess or measure. For objective-based assessment instruments, an instrument is valid if: (1) its individual items are consistent with the goals or objectives they claim to assess (*congruence*), and (2) the items for each objective represent the range of items that are possible to develop for that objective (*completeness*), and (3) objectives upon which the instrument is based are adequately sampled (also completeness).

An individual item is congruent with its goal if the conditions and performance specified in the objective are represented in the item. Consider the objective that Jim Evans gave for his workshop:

> Given a description of the audience characteristics, purposes of the presentation, and source materials, the learner will be able to develop a transparency master that incorporates the principles of visual design and good lettering.

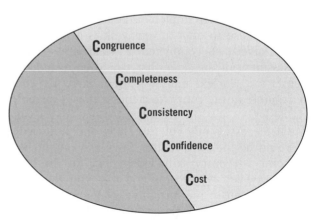

Figure 6.2 The Five C's of Criterion-Referenced Assessment Instruments

Now consider one of the items that he developed for the test that concluded the workshop:

Which of the following is not a characteristic of the design element surface?

    a. texture

    b. color

    c. value

    d. form

Although the item does possibly represent prerequisite knowledge that the learners might need to know to be able to demonstrate the learning represented by the objective, it certainly does not match the conditions of the objective, "Given a description of the audience characteristics, purposes of the presentation, and source materials," nor does it match the performance specified, "the learner will be able to develop a transparency master that incorporates the principles of visual design and good lettering." This is a typical error for designers to make. To achieve a more objective or easier-to-administer test, designers often create items that step back from the level of realism or directness that is specified in the objective. In the terminology of the day, this makes the assessment less "authentic." Designers such as Jim Evans develop items over more easily tested declarative knowledge or verbal information that may support the actual objective but certainly do not adequately assess it. A much more valid item would, of course, provide a scenario that describes an audience, the purpose of a presentation, and key resource information related to the topic. Then it would direct the learner to create a transparency master to convey the critical information.

Often, when attempting to write a valid item for an objective, a designer may find that it is impossible to create a way to assess the objective as written. This may be because the objective is too nebulous or because the designer has described a situation that is not practical to assess, such as performance of the targeted skill or knowledge on the job. If you find you are unable to devise a way to assess an objective, you should retain the original objective as a reference point and write a revised objective that reflects your closest intent that *can* be assessed. This could involve reducing the level of directness or realism, such as employing a simulation or pencil-and-paper test rather than an observation, or it might involve some disciplined clarification of the goal's intentions.

The exercise of trying to write an assessment instrument can often help you clarify the actual purpose of your instruction, which will certainly simplify the process of designing an instructional strategy. Revising objectives at this stage does not mean that you should reduce your intent to something that is easy to assess,

such as reducing intellectual skills to declarative knowledge. This is a common error that we see often in both training and public school environments. Reducing instruction to declarative knowledge levels simply to make writing objectives and test items easier makes a mockery of the process of instructional design and simply should not be done. You *must* develop objectives and related test items that reflect as closely as possible the original intent represented by the goal or objective.

There are procedures that will support the development of a valid instrument, such as writing item specifications and test blueprints, which we will discuss later in this chapter. A review of these item specifications and blueprints by a subject matter expert and an instructional designer during early formative evaluation can validate the parameters of the assessment instruments. These reviewers should be given copies of the objectives with their matched item specifications and the blueprint of the entire assessment instrument. They should also be asked to validate that (1) individual items are consistent with the objectives they purport to assess, (2) the items for each objective are representative of the range of items that are possible to develop for that objective, and (3) objectives upon which the instrument is based are adequately sampled.

The characteristic of validity is critical to all assessments. If a test does not measure what it purports to measure, the test is worthless, or perhaps worse, misleading. Developing valid criterion-referenced instruments is based on procedures described in this chapter.

Reliability

An assessment instrument is reliable if it *consistently* measures what it claims to measure and if we have a high degree of *confidence* in the scores that it produces. We would like to be able to say with confidence that (within a modest amount of inevitable error) learners who achieve a high score on an assessment are competent and learners who score poorly are not competent. We would like to believe that if we gave the same or a carefully matched assessment tomorrow or next week (without any intervening learning) learners would achieve basically equivalent scores on both assessments. What instrument characteristics would interfere with our being able to draw these conclusions? What makes an instrument unreliable?

Anything that causes unpredictable error in an instrument makes it unreliable. A number of factors can lead to this error. The lack of objectivity of an instrument can cause it to be unreliable. For example, an instrument that cannot be objectively graded can lead to errors in grading that make its measure unreliable. An instructor might grade an essay question quite differently today versus a day next week. The instrument would not yield a consistent score. "Objective" assessment formats, such as multiple choice, true-false, and matching, are easier to evaluate objectively than "constructed" responses, such as short answer, essay, simulation, or observed performance. Often, however, to assess an objective as realistically as possible, we utilize the constructed response format. The use of checklists, model responses, and other criteria, such as looking for key words or phrases in an essay response, can help to ensure more objective evaluation.

One of the goals of a criterion-referenced assessment may be to differentiate between individuals who are competent or incompetent with regard to a particular goal or set of goals. This is the purpose of a licensing assessment such as those used to certify barbers, nurses, physical therapists, physicians, and pilots. A test that does not differentiate between a skilled and unskilled learner is not a reliable test. The assessment designer attempts to eliminate or reduce factors that would allow incompetent learners to appear competent or would cause competent learners to appear to be incompetent.

An incompetent learner may appear to be competent if he arrives at a correct answer by guessing. Objective test formats such as multiple choice or matching are more vulnerable to the effects of guessing than constructed response items. Any time learners can select from possible answers, there is a chance that with no or incomplete knowledge, they can guess and correctly answer some items. For this reason, we recommend that you do not use true-false items in assessment. There is a fifty-fifty chance that learners can get a true-false item correct. It is also preferable that multiple-choice items have as many options, sometimes called *foils*, as possible. Each additional foil reduces the possibility of correctly answering by guessing.

Other factors that can contribute to the error in an instrument are the length of an instrument, the clarity of the items, the quality of the directions, or other problems in the administration of the assessment. With regard to test length, fewer items assessing an objective means the greater the possibility that a learner's knowledge may be inaccurately reflected in the responses. An instrument that uses too few items to evaluate an objective may not achieve a reliable measure. For example, if we used only one item to assess whether a learner can balance a chemical equation, a simple arithmetic error may interfere with a learner's getting that item correct. Or a lucky guess may allow some learners to get the item correct even though they have not actually acquired the procedural rules to solve the problem. This is why we typically try to create several items to assess each objective. As we stated earlier, it can be difficult to write more than one item

for a declarative knowledge objective; it is difficult to think of very many ways to ask for the capitol of Texas. However, intellectual skills, cognitive strategies, motor skills, and attitude objectives generally can have multiple items. We usually suggest that you use an odd number of items to assess an objective. The odd number simply allows you to make a decision about the achievement of an objective without "ties." This way, the learner can, for example, achieve two out of three or five out of seven of the items. Beyond this guideline, the number of items per each objective ultimately is affected by practicality and efficiency issues.

The reliability of an instrument is also affected by the clarity of the items and their directions. The instrument should be so designed that if a learner has actually acquired the ability associated with an objective, there is nothing that will interfere with the learner's demonstrating this ability. Ambiguity in the statement of an item, incomplete directions, unfamiliar vocabulary, or unfamiliar context of items can cause a skilled learner to fail to demonstrate this ability. For example, learners who were skilled in locating the main idea of prose performed poorly when they were asked to "Circle the statement that gives the gist of the preceding paragraph." Subsequent questioning of the learners indicated that the fourth-grade learners were not clear on the meanings of both *gist* and *preceding*. Formative evaluation of items with representative members of a target audience can help eliminate some of these problems.

It is also possible that conditions surrounding the administration of the assessment can cause learners to perform at a less-than-optimal level. For example, unfamiliar assessment formats, such as administering a computer-delivered exam to learners who have never experienced this format, can lead to unreliable test results. Classroom conditions, such as excess heat or cold or other unpleasant physical conditions, can also lead to unreliability. In addition, unpleasant emotional conditions, such as excessive anxiety, can lead to unreliable group performance. Planning for the administration of the assessment can usually eliminate these threats.

For those assessments that require constructed responses (written or physically performed), we often need to do things to ensure reliability, such as use a checklist or rating form, as well as grading all of one question for the entire class set, to encourage a more consistent measure. If it is desirable that the grader report an index of reliability, the grader may choose to have several graders rate a sample of the performances or written tests based on the scale used. Then an index of "inter-rater reliability" can be obtained by correlating the scores that each of the graders assigned. (See Shrock & Coscarelli, 1989, Chapter 10, for a more detailed description of this procedure.)

The reliability index of criterion-referenced assessments is generally obtained in a somewhat different manner than norm-referenced assessments. Test developers have traditionally used a measure of "internal consistency," such as the Kuder Richardson 20 (KR 20), Kuder Richardson 21 (KR 21), or Cronbach's *alpha*, to report the reliability of written tests. Although such measures work well with tests built on a norm-referenced model, they can be problematic for tests based on a criterion-referenced model. An index of internal consistency basically measures the consistency of responses from test respondents. It answers these questions: Do test respondents who make a high score tend to score high across all items? Do respondents who make a poor score tend to score poorly across all items? (For more information on determining the reliability of norm-referenced tests, refer to a traditional educational measurement text, such as Mehrens and Lehman, 1991.) The problem with this approach to estimating reliability is that criterion-referenced tests tend to assess several objectives at one time, and it would be entirely feasible that a test respondent would perform well on items testing one objective but not well on items for another objective. Norm-referenced assessments relate not to specific objectives but to underlying abilities possessed by test takers, as those abilities might relate to achievement in some subject area. Thus, whereas the norm-referenced test should possess internal consistency, there is no reason that a criterion-referenced test must. In addition, the statistics in calculating KR 20, KR 21, or Cronbach's *alpha* depend on the high variance of scores that tests constructed with norm-referenced techniques obtain. As you recall, it is quite common to obtain many high scores with little variation on criterion-referenced assessments because items that many students answer correctly are not eliminated from the test, as they are in norm-referenced tests.

So how is an index of reliability obtained for criterion-referenced tests? The most common procedure is to report the consistency of measurement across two administrations of a test (test-retest reliability). However, instead of correlating scores, the test-retest looks at the consistency of assignment to the master and nonmaster categories. Essentially, the test developer determines a criterion score for the test; those who score above it are considered "masters" or competent in the content, and those who score below the criterion are considered nonmasters. (We will discuss setting a mastery criterion later in this chapter.) The test (or a parallel form of the test) is administered twice to a group of individuals, some of whom are considered already knowledgeable in the content, some of whom are not. The tests are administered within a few days of each other with the admonishment to the test-takers

that they do not study the content in the interim. Then the consistency of assignments of the master/nonmaster groups is measured using correlation statistics. (For a more detailed review of these procedures, see Shrock & Coscarelli, 1989, Chapter 11.)

Practicality

Given the previously discussed recommendations to develop a valid and reliable test, you might conclude that the optimal assessment might be a many-itemed constructed response or performance (observational) exam that is as close as possible to the real-life situation in which the learners will apply their knowledge, for all objectives, with a carefully developed set of criteria for evaluating the responses. This is occasionally possible. However, generally there is a trade-off between our desire to create a valid and reliable test and the realities of the assessment situation (*costs*). Assessment resources are generally limited: We do not have many student hours for assessment, the instructor does not have unlimited grading time, we do not have many skilled evaluators available to help the instructor with evaluating learning, and the lag time between when assessment is administered and when scores must be reported is limited. For example, a course goal in instructional design might be "Given a subject matter expert, materials resources, and a target population, the learner will be able to design, develop, produce, evaluate, and revise instructional materials to meet an instructional need." An ideal assessment for this objective would be the complete design of several courses for varying situations to ensure a valid and reliable measure of competence. However, it is unrealistic to expect that in the course of a semester, learners could develop several complete designs, nor is it feasible that one instructor could evaluate them. Therefore, design courses often have learners complete designs for one situation for some degree of validity and use printed scenarios in written assessments in an attempt to obtain some degree of reliability.

Trade-Offs in Assessment Design

As you can see, we must make carefully considered decisions as to which factors are most important for the particular assessment situation and then make trade-offs among the factors of validity, reliability, and practicality. All design work involves consideration of trade-offs (Petroski, 2003), and assessment design is no exception. One of the bases upon which these trade-offs may be made is the consequences of the wrong decisions that might be made with a less-than-ideal assessment.

In the instructional design class previously described, the assessment is not ideally reliable because it really has an insufficient number of "items" to allow the instructor to conclude that the learners will be able to design for a variety of situations. In an attempt to compensate for this lack of items, the instructor might create printed scenarios in which the learners complete one part of the design process, or the instructor might develop situations in which the learners must evaluate and revise faulty, already created portions of a design project. This reduces the validity of the assessment as it does not match the conditions of the stated objective. Let us explore the implications of such a compromise.

It is possible that on the basis of the information provided from these assessments—given the compromises made among reliability, validity, and practicality—the instructor might mistakenly certify an instructional design student as competent who is actually unable to achieve the stated course goal. It is less likely that a learner who was unable to perform on these assessments would actually be able to perform the terminal goal as stated. The consequences of mistakenly certifying the student as competent would certainly be regrettable from the learner's standpoint, a future employer's standpoint, and the certifying institution's perspective, because the mistake could result in frustration on the student's part, loss of time and money on the employer's part, and loss of professional image on the institution's part. However, these consequences are not life-threatening. In life-and-death situations, such as training learners in CPR, training parachute packers, or training employees in safety practices, we should be less willing to make compromises in validity and reliability to bow to issues of practicality. Resources should be made available to ensure the most reliable and valid instruments possible in such circumstances. In contrast, in cases of informal education, such as a community center course on embroidery, the consequences of incorrect assessment of competence may not have severe consequences for anyone, in which case more radical compromises might be made for the sake of practicality.

E X E R C I S E S   C

1. Revisit the discussion of Jim Evans's workshop earlier in this chapter, and describe the ideal type of assessment.

2. Supposing that Jim's resources and time are limited, what might be a compromise form of assessment?

3. With this alternate assessment, what are the threats to validity and reliability?

4. Describe the possible consequences of these threats to validity and reliability.

FORMATS FOR ASSESSMENT

There are two major formats of tests: performance assessments and pencil-and-paper tests.

Performance Assessments

Swanson, Norman, and Linn (1995) proposed that "authentic assessment" is synonymous with performance assessment. They defined performance assessment as "testing complex, 'higher order' knowledge and skills in the real-world context in which they are actually used, generally with open-ended tasks that require substantial examinee time to complete" (p. 5). The types of assessments that have been included in this category are observation, open-ended problems, microworlds, essays, simulations, projects, and portfolios. We will describe four of the most common performance assessment forms—on-the-job observation, simulations, essays, and portfolios—in this section.

Observation of On-the-Job Performance

Probably the best way to see if students have learned what we want them to learn at the necessary level is to take them into the real world and have them perform what they have been instructed to do. For instance, we could take an electronics technician to a TV repair store, hand her a malfunctioning VCR, and tell her to locate the problem and repair it. Then we could confirm that the learner can actually find the problem and fix it and that she goes about it in a proper way. In this case, our test instrument might be a checklist containing all of the things the learner should do in order to adequately repair the VCR. Of course, to provide a *reliable* measure, we would probably want to see whether she could repair several malfunctioning VCRs with several problems before we were sure she could deal with the variety of problems we had taught her to repair. However, it is unlikely that we she could find a sufficient number of VCRs with all of the appropriate problems and in sufficient quantities to assess all learners. Even if we could find enough VCRs with the right problems, it is unlikely that many customers would like to have their VCRs repaired by novices.

Learners are occasionally assessed in on-the-job situations. In this case, the teacher or evaluator usually uses a rating scale or a checklist as the assessment instrument. Rating scales and checklists can be used to assess the quality of the process as the learner performs a particular skill (or skills), or they can be used to evaluate the product or outcome of this performance. For example, if we were assessing learners' skill in making bread, we could assess the learners' actions while making the bread: Do they wash their hands before beginning? Do they knead the bread properly and for the correct length of time? We could also evaluate the end product of the endeavor: Is the bread the proper consistency? Is it browned to the correct color? We could choose to evaluate both the process and the product and combine these two assessments into one grade or score according to some predetermined formula.

Checklists generally list behaviors that should be observed or characteristics that should be observed in the product. Checklists may be appropriate for on-the-job assessments if all critical cognitions in the newly acquired learning are manifested in observable behavior. You ascertain these behaviors or characteristics from an examination of the task analysis for the particular skills being assessed. These behaviors or characteristics are then judged dichotomously: present/absent, yes/no, appropriate/inappropriate, acceptable/unacceptable, correct/ incorrect. Sometimes we need a more refined evaluation of a process or product than just whether it is correct or incorrect, so we use a rating scale that indicates degrees or levels of quality for a performance or quality. Figure 6.3 is an example of a checklist and a rating scale that could be expanded and used to assess the quality of work performed by an intern instructional designer.

Simulations

Since it is often impractical or undesirable to assess a student's performance in real-life circumstances, we may wish to simulate those circumstances. We would not want learners to experience an actual house fire to assess whether they can apply principles they had learned about getting out of a house safely, but we may use a simulation that creates a real-world–like environment in critical aspects, such as blocked entrances, so learners must show that they can apply the principles of evacuating a burning house.

In addition to being excellent instructional strategies, simulations are excellent assessment forms, particularly for assessment of higher-order rule learning and attitude change. Simulations can be delivered with print, video, group interactions, computers, or interactive multimedia. An example of a print-based simulation is the "in basket" assessment. For example, an assessment in an instructional management class might portray an instructional designer as having been hired to replace a project manager of a design project who left suddenly three months ago. The learner would be provided with all of the memos and correspondence that had collected in the past three months (what would be in the managers "in basket") and be asked to provide written responses to all the correspondence. This would be one way to assess whether the learner

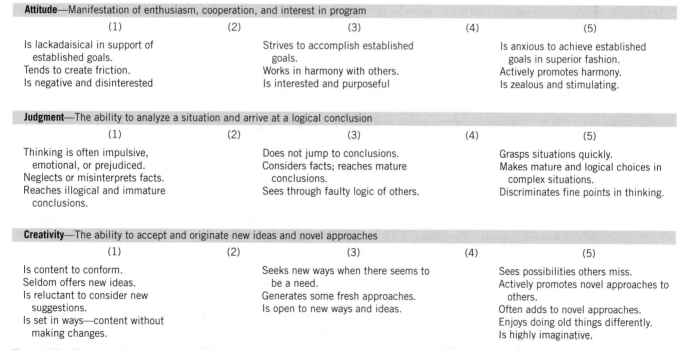

Attitude—Manifestation of enthusiasm, cooperation, and interest in program

(1)	(2)	(3)	(4)	(5)
Is lackadaisical in support of established goals. Tends to create friction. Is negative and disinterested		Strives to accomplish established goals. Works in harmony with others. Is interested and purposeful		Is anxious to achieve established goals in superior fashion. Actively promotes harmony. Is zealous and stimulating.

Judgment—The ability to analyze a situation and arrive at a logical conclusion

(1)	(2)	(3)	(4)	(5)
Thinking is often impulsive, emotional, or prejudiced. Neglects or misinterprets facts. Reaches illogical and immature conclusions.		Does not jump to conclusions. Considers facts; reaches mature conclusions. Sees through faulty logic of others.		Grasps situations quickly. Makes mature and logical choices in complex situations. Discriminates fine points in thinking.

Creativity—The ability to accept and originate new ideas and novel approaches

(1)	(2)	(3)	(4)	(5)
Is content to conform. Seldom offers new ideas. Is reluctant to consider new suggestions. Is set in ways—content without making changes.		Seeks new ways when there seems to be a need. Generates some fresh approaches. Is open to new ways and ideas.		Sees possibilities others miss. Actively promotes novel approaches to others. Often adds to novel approaches. Enjoys doing old things differently. Is highly imaginative.

Figure 6.3 Example Performance Rating Scale (portion) for Use with Intern Instructional Designers

could apply the principles that were to be learned during the course. Another example of a print-based simulation is a case study. Case studies are widely used for both instruction as well as assessment in such fields as management, law, and medicine.

With the interfacing of personal computers with videotape or videodisc, individuals may interact with realistic simulated environments. Simulations may be administered to a group, as in a role-playing situation, though it may be difficult to assess individual performance within a group simulation.

Checklists and rating scales may be utilized to determine that learners go through an appropriate process to solve the simulated problem. Some of this evaluation may be automated via a micro- or mainframe computer. Elaborate simulators used in pilot and astronaut training are probably the most sophisticated examples of this form of testing.

Essays

A correct response to an essay question may vary considerably in terms of sequence, language, and specificity, not to mention correctness of style and grammar. This can make it difficult to evaluate essay items objectively. Often designers develop checklists, rating scales, model answers, or multiple graders to evaluate essay exams to help eliminate some of the subjectivity in the assessment of essay questions.

Portfolios

Arter and Spandel (1992) define the portfolio as "a purposeful collection of student work that tells the story of the student's efforts, progress, or achievement in (a) given area(s). This collection must include student participation in selection of portfolio content; the guidelines for selection; the criteria for judging merit; and evidence of student self-reflection" (p. 36). Portfolios appear to be most useful to assess broad learning goals. Depending upon the subject matter being evaluated, portfolios may include writing samples, audio- or videotape recordings, art works, traditional assessment instruments, and a whole variety of work samples. Depending upon the samples collected, portfolios may be used to indirectly assess cognitive processes. For example, drafts of work may suggest criteria that learners are using to assess their own progress. Many advocates of portfolios recommend that learners are responsible for selecting the work samples to include in their portfolios and that they write a cover letter that explains their rationale for the products that they included. Such activities may be an indicator of how students are progressing on metacognitive goals. Arter and Spandel recommend that portfolios be carefully linked to the classroom curriculum by reflecting the same goals, using the same criteria, and implying the same values as everyday classroom activities.

The Web can provide helpful support for development of portfolios, their storage, distribution, management, and assessment. Helpful information on Web-based portfolios can be found with a simple search. One site we found to be informative and useful is Kathy Schrock's Guide for Educators at: http://school.discovery.com/schrockguide/assess.html#portfolios. In addition, Royer (2003) provides an excellent example of portfolio use in a higher-education setting. In addition to the reference cited, this paper is also available on the Web at: http://www.aace.org/dl/index.cfm/fuseaction/ViewPaper/id/11634/toc/yes

Evaluation of Performance Assessments

Linn (1994) recommended stringent criteria to evaluate the adequacy of performance assessments. These include standards of validity, consequences of assessments on instructional practice, directness, transparency, fairness, transfer and generalizability, adequate cognitive complexity of the tasks, content quality, content coverage, meaningfulness, cost, and efficiency. Obviously, these criteria include the same standards for "good" tests that we presented at the beginning of the chapter. There are critical trade-offs among these criteria when designing performance assessments. The acceptability of these trade-offs is directly related to the consequences of the decisions that will be made as a result of these assessments. The more critically these decisions affect the futures of learners and those whom their competency will influence, the more designers must sacrifice practicality for the sake of validity *and* reliability. The exercises at the end of this section will allow you to consider the nature of some of these trade-offs.

Pencil-and-Paper Assessment Forms

A second major category of assessment form is the pencil-and-paper test. This is what we usually think of as a "test." Since such tests may now be computer-delivered, the term *pencil-and-paper test* may be misleading. There are numerous types of items that fall into this category: multiple choice, true-false, matching, completion (fill in the blank), and short answer.

Generally, all of the test item forms can have a finite and relatively small number of correct responses. With imagination and ingenuity, multiple-choice, matching, completion, and short answer items may be used to assess declarative knowledge, intellectual skills, attitudes (to some extent), cognitive strategies, and portions of motor skills.

Pencil-and-paper tests can be designed in three different forms: recall, recognition, and constructed answer.

RECALL ITEMS.   We generally use recall items to assess declarative knowledge objectives, or the declarative knowledge component of another learning outcome, such as the declarative knowledge routine that supports motor skills. Recall items ask learners to simply reproduce the knowledge that they have been presented in instruction, in verbatim, paraphrased, or summarized form. These items place a high demand on memory but less demand on higher-reasoning processes. They generally take the form of written items, such as short answer, fill-in-the-blank, or completion items.

RECOGNITION ITEMS.   Recognition items require the learner to recognize or identify the correct answer from a group of alternatives. This type of item may be used to assess declarative knowledge that has been memorized, such as the following item:

1. Which of the following is the first step in loading a camera?
  a. Set the film speed dial.
  b. Raise the rewind hatch.
  c. Open the back of the camera.
  d. Place the film cartridge in the left slot.

Recognition items may require the use of the higher cognitive skills involved in intellectual skills. They may require that learners apply the principles or concepts that they have acquired to recognize a correct answer.

2. Which of the following will result in an equivalent exposure to a setting of f/8 at 1/125 sec?
  a. f/11 at 1/125 sec
  b. f/4 at 1/60 sec
  c. f/8 at 1/250 sec
  d. f/11 at 1/60 sec

In the preceding example, answer *d* is correct. Even if the learner had memorized shutter speeds and aperture sizes, the learner must apply the principle that relates shutter speeds and aperture sizes to exposure, rather than respond from rote memory.

Although multiple choice is the most commonly used type of recognition item, matching and true-false items also can be used as recognition items. Haladyna (1999) provides helpful assistance in the design, development, and validation of multiple choice items.

CONSTRUCTED ANSWER ITEMS.   Constructed answer items require that learners actually produce or construct a response. These responses may be actions that we described earlier in performance assessments, such

as on-the-job situations, written responses during a simulation, or written responses in a pencil-and-paper (or computer-based) assessment. The difference between constructed answer items and recall items is that the constructed answer items require more than memorized responses: They require the higher reasoning of intellectual skills. These items differ from recognition items in that they place a higher demand on memory and cognitive strategies. They are also less cued, and the options are less limited than in a recognition item. For example, the second photography question example could be converted to a production item:

3. What combination of shutter speed and aperture setting would lead to the same exposure as f/8 at 1/125 sec?

In this item, respondents not only must apply the rule that describes the relationship of shutter speeds to amount of light, they must also recall the shutter speeds and aperture settings that are available on a camera. As a recognition item, the possibilities were restricted to four, and the options available were cued because they were listed. This support was not available when the question was converted to a constructed answer item. Generally, constructed answer items are more cognitively demanding than recognition items. They take more time to answer; therefore, the test designer can include fewer items per objective. However, constructed answer items are often more congruent with the real-life situation that may be described by the objectives, and, therefore, they may be a more valid assessment. A thorough discussion of both theoretic and applied issues in selection and design of constructed versus selected assessment forms is provided by Bennett and Ward (1993).

E X E R C I S E S   D

1. Ann is developing a lesson to teach students how to use a photographic copy stand to make slides of graphics and other flat art. She plans to use a performance simulation in which the students will use the copy stand to make slides of art that will be supplied. There are 220 students per year in the classes that will use this instruction. Has Ann made a good selection of the format of her assessment? Why or why not?

2. What other ways might Ann assess the skills included in this unit? What trade-offs will she have to make? Use the terms *reliability*, *validity*, and *practicality* in your response.

3. The situation: Willi has just completed writing the objectives for a lesson she is writing on behavior modification techniques that can be used by pet owners to encourage desirable behavior in their dogs. Her class will include thirty pet owners each six weeks. Sometimes she will teach the class, and sometimes it will be taught by other workers at the Humane Society. She has determined that her terminal objective is "Given the portrayal of a desirable or undesirable behavior by her dog, the pet owner will appropriately respond based upon the principles of behavior modification." Willi has determined three different types of assessment forms:

a. An observational rating form to be used while observing the pet owner and her pet over a period of ten minutes.

b. A videotape of several scenes, five in which the dog behaves in a desirable manner, five in which the dog performs an undesirable behavior. After each scene, the videotape narrator asks, "What should the dog owner do now?" The participants must write their answers on a printed form.

c. A paper-and-pencil instrument in which the learners are given descriptions of situations in which dogs behave desirably or undesirably. The description explains the subsequent behavior of the dog owner. The learners are asked to rate the owner's behavior as "appropriate" or "inappropriate" and explain their answers.

The question: Evaluate the adequacy of the a, b, and c assessment methods to assess the objective by comparing their relative validity, reliability, and practicality.

4. Identify the following assessment items for an exam in an educational media course as constructed answer, recall, or recognition.

a. You are a middle school librarian working with a social studies teacher. The teacher is developing a unit on the life of Native Americans in the years 1850 to 1900. Based upon Dale's Cone of Experience, what would be a concrete medium/activity in learning about Native Americans? Why?

b. Match the instructional technologist to his contribution.

1. Teaching machines	**a. Crowder**
2. "Branching" instruction	**b. Skinner**
3. Programmed instruction	**c. Pressey**
	d. Dale

c. What does the number 500 on the shutter speed knob of a camera mean?

1. The film speed of the film is 500.

2. The shutter opens and shuts 500 times per minute.

3. The shutter stays open for 500 seconds.

4. The shutter stays open for 1/500 of a second.

d. Name a professional organization for educational technologists.

5. Write a constructed response and a recognition item for each of the following objectives. Explain which (recognition or constructed response) is the most valid measurement of the objective and how the objective might need to be revised to reflect the measurement item.

a. The learner can locate a word in a dictionary.

b. The learner can determine a train's rate of speed when given distance and time.

c. The learner can score a tennis match.

d. The learner can label the parts of a car engine.

e. The learner can touch-type on a keyboard.

ASSESSMENT ITEM SPECIFICATIONS

Once you have a clear idea of the type of learning outcomes described by the objectives you will be assessing and the forms of items that are available to you for those objectives, you can begin to write items. All too often, designers begin by simply writing items that reflect the objective. For one objective they may write items that will be included in the preassessment and postassessment, and they may even construct items that can be used during practice in the lesson. It is difficult to adequately cover the range of difficulty and scope of content covered by an objective by haphazardly constructing items in this manner. The hapless designer may end up constructing very easy items for all of one assessment and making all items difficult for a later form; or he might include only items that assess the ability to apply knowledge from a small portion of the possible content to which the knowledge may apply.

For these reasons, it is most helpful to use a test design device suggested by Popham (1978) called *item specifications*. This concept has evolved from Hively's (1974) concept of test item shells for developing domain-referenced tests. In writing item specifications, the designer describes the characteristics of the items and the forms that responses will take. Although development of item specifications can be a bit tedious at first, designers report their use to be invaluable in on-the-job situations. On design projects in which time and resources are fairly adequate, these specifications are formally written, reviewed, and revised as part of early formative evaluation. This formal statement of item specifications is especially necessary when design and development are a team effort, perhaps with some members writing objectives and others writing the assessment items. It is not unusual on large assessment development contracts for the writing of assessment items to be subcontracted to another group. In such a case, the item specifications must be precisely written because they serve as a clear statement of intention. Under other conditions, designers may use item specifications as a mental tool in the development of assessment items.

Designers ideally develop assessment item specifications for each objective to be assessed on an instrument.* According to Popham (1978), item specifications include the following components:

1. Objective
2. Description of test form
3. Sample item
4. Question characteristics
5. Response characteristics
6. Number of items and mastery criterion

Part 1, the statement of the objective, will guide the rest of the development of the item specifications. The objectives should be composed of the components described in Chapter 5: conditions, performance, and perhaps a standard or criterion. If conditions were not prescribed in the objective earlier, these conditions should be specified at this point in the design process. You may wish to elaborate on the objective if you feel the simple statement leaves some of the objective's intention unclear.

Part 2, the description of the test form, is a statement of the form that the assessment item will take. This statement may be as simple as "multiple-choice form" or as complex as "a computer-based simulation that presents graphic situations with a malfunctioning VCR, presents options for diagnostic procedures, provides output from these diagnostic procedures, and presents options to select from as solutions to the problem." The more clarity and detail that is provided in this step, the easier the following steps will be.

Part 3, the sample item, should assess the ability to perform the behavior described in the objective under the conditions described in the objective's conditions. The sample item should include the directions that will accompany all items of this type. The prepara-

tion of this sample item helps to clarify the intentions stated in the objective. It also may make later sections of the specifications more clear, as one example is often worth a hundred words.

Part 4, the question characteristics, defines the qualities of the questions, pencil-and-paper assessments, scenarios in simulations, or situations that will be observed during on-the-job assessments. This section is the most critical in the entire assessment specification. In this section, you specify the domain of content and range of difficulty of items to which the learner will respond. This section defines those features that must be included and those features that should not be included in the items. In all items there are factors that can be varied in the question as we generate items. It is the purpose of this section to identify those factors and the range of each factor's variation.

Let's look at an example of test item specifications from a topic that is fairly easy to define—mathematics. We will begin with the following rule-using objective:

When given a division problem with a two-, three-, four-, or five-digit dividend and a two-digit divisor, the learner can determine the quotient, including any remainder.

Given this objective, we have a number of options as to item form: matching, multiple choice, short answer, and even true-false. In this case, we specify the test form as the following:

The test form will be short answer, in which the learner will write in the value of the quotient.

Our sample item will have directions, and we have included three ways that the problem itself can be presented:

Directions: Write in the quotient of the following problems. Show your work on each problem.

$$1475/25 = \_\_\_\_\_$$
$$25) \_\_\_\_\_ \quad 1475 = \_\_\_\_\_$$
$$1475 \div 25 = \_\_\_\_\_$$

A considerable amount is already pointed out in this objective and the sample item. We can determine that there are three factors that may vary in the presentation of the problem: the value of the dividend, the value of the divisor, and the format of the presentation of the item (i.e., which of the three possible forms shown in the sample item will be used). Not so obvious, but apparent to all who have written such items, is the relationship between the dividend and the divisor. Will the problems have a remainder, or will the dividend and divisor be selected so that their quotient will be an integer? Will the problems be so devised that the quotient can contain a zero?

---

*It is possible to engage in extended debate on the question of whether *every* objective must be represented in item specifications. There are circumstances in which certain objectives of sets of them may not need specifications. For example, some declarative knowledge objectives, depending on their knowledge domain, may be limited in terms of how many ways you can ask the question and once one objective of fifty like it has been provided specification, repetition may not be needed. In this and many other questions, the final arbiter often comes down to context and the criticality of the learning tasks. What is appropriate in one context may be seriously deficient or ludicrous overkill in another. A critical thing to remember about item specifications is that they are written and applied objective-by-objective. As you may recall from Chapter Five, "Learning Task Analysis," developing item specifications is integral to the task analysis itself. In the approach we have taken to task analysis, objectives are not fully complete without associated specifications for their assessment.

The question characteristics will vary for this example objective, depending on the answers to the questions. They might read as follows:

1. Division problems will follow the form *x/y,* where *x* is the dividend and *y* is the divisor. Space will be provided above the problem for a one-, two-, or three-digit quotient. Space will be provided below the question for the partial solutions associated with long division.

2. The dividend may be a two-, three-, four-, or five-digit numeral. It may contain zeros in all of the place values, except in the leftmost place.

3. The divisor must be a two-digit number. It may contain a zero (i.e., be a multiple of ten), except it should not contain a zero in the tens' place.

4. The problems will be constructed so that they do not have remainders in their quotients. The problems should not result in zeros or fractions in the quotients.

5. Approximately 10 percent of the problems should have two-digit dividends, 40 percent three digits, 40 percent four digits, and 10 percent five digits.

Notice that the question characteristics give both the breadth and the limitations of the type of questions that are appropriate for this objective. Our question characteristics have also described, without specifying a fixed number of problems, the proportion of problems that should represent each type of possible problem that can be constructed using this specification. In this case, these proportions are based upon difficulty—simple (10 percent), medial (80 percent), and difficult (10 percent)—with the number of digits in the dividend determining the difficulty. Also note that in this particular case, it has been determined that items with remainders and zeros in the dividend are not appropriate.

Part 5, response characteristics, differs in form of description depending on whether the item is a recognition item, in which the learners select an answer, or whether the item is a recall or production item, in which they enter their own constructed answers.

Response Characteristics of Recognition Items

In describing responses to recognition items, the designer must outline the characteristics of the correct answer to be selected, which is relatively easy, and the incorrect answers, which is much more difficult. In describing the correct answers, it is often possible to actually list the entire pool of possible correct answers that could be assessed, such as on an instrument evaluating learners' ability to select a correct aperture size for a certain exposure. (There are a finite number of f-stops on common 35-mm cameras.) On other occasions, it

may be fairly easy to describe the correct answer option. For example, in mathematics questions you can simply state that the correct answer, perhaps in a specific form, will serve as the correct answer option.

It is more difficult to describe the incorrect options to be used in a multiple-choice, true-false, or matching question. The designer should identify common misconceptions that learners may mistakenly acquire during learning and transform these misconceptions into the incorrect options to be selected. These plausible options not only create an assessment that can discriminate between skilled and unskilled performance, they also provide data for remediation by indicating the learners' faulty/incomplete cognitions. In many content areas, the common "bugs" have been identified in the literature of the field. In other areas, instructors with experience in teaching the content may be able to provide these common errors. If these sources are unavailable, the designer may choose to use a recall or constructed response format in the instrument and use this constructed format during early formative evaluation to obtain a number of responses. It is quite likely that among these responses will be some incorrect responses, and among these incorrect responses will be some clusters of incorrect responses that will be suitable for plausible foils (called *distractors*) in a selected response item. For our math example on division, if we used a selected format, rather than the open response that we have identified, our response characteristics could look like this:

1. Learners will be asked to circle the letter of the correct answer. Each item will include four options—the correct answer and three distractors.

2. The correct answer will be the quotient of the problem—a one-, two-, three-, or four-digit number with no remainder. The quotient should not contain a zero.

3. One distractor should represent misplacing the "place value" of the quotient (e.g., 280 instead of 28).

4. One distractor should represent a subtraction error in the partial products.

5. One distractor should represent a failure to correctly "bring down" values from the dividend while calculating partial problems during the solution.

Response Characteristics of Production Items

The response characteristics for a recall or constructed answer have a different set of problems. It is fairly easy to specify the form that the answer should take. It may be difficult, however, to specify the characteristics of a correct response. The math example is fairly simple:

There is only one correct answer—most of us would agree on the answer—so the response specifications could be as follows:

1. Answers should be written in the area above the dividend. They should be mathematically correct as confirmed by a calculator and should include no remainder, including no $R = 0$.
2. Partial products and related subtraction should be shown and should be precisely calculated.

Suppose the question asked, "Give an example of an object that is translucent. Do not use an example from those given in the instruction." The number of possibilities for a correct answer is almost infinite, so we must define the characteristics of a correct response. We might use this type of definition of response characteristics:

1. Response must be a single, concrete object that has the following property: It must be an object that will allow light to pass through it, but other objects must not be clearly visible through it.
2. Examples of correct responses are a frosted mug, a frosted light bulb, a pink umbrella, and sheer lingerie.
3. Correct response should not include an object that was described as translucent in the instruction, either information presentation or practice.
4. Correct spelling should not be considered a criterion for correctness.

To determine the characteristics of a correct response, we must often construct a number of correct responses and attempt to analyze those features that make each a correct answer. This may also involve referring back to the instruction to review the critical characteristics of the skill that is being assessed, as we did when we referred back to the definition of the concept "translucent." In describing the response characteristics for problem solving, psychomotor skills, and cognitive strategies, we may wish to develop a checklist that should be used to evaluate the learner's constructed response. A checklist will include a list of features that should be present in the response and, perhaps, features that should not be present.

Part 6, number of items and mastery criteria specification comprises the final segment of the item specifications. As you will recall from our discussion of objectives in Chapter 5, we believe the decision as to number of assessment items and the criterion or standard for mastery is a decision that is more logically made while devising test items than when writing the objectives. At this point in development of item specifications, we have clearly described the form of the items that will be used to assess the objective, and we have a sense of the time and mental demands on both the learner and the grader. Therefore, we can make a more realistic esti-

mate of how many items should be included for this particular objective and how many of these items should be correct for one to confidently certify the performance as "competent" or "skilled" or "mastery."

In systematically designed instruction, we are typically more concerned with whether a student can demonstrate a certain skill or knowledge than we are with whether the student performs better or worse than his peers. In such cases, we use the term **mastery** to refer to adequate or passing performance. We identify for each objective the percentage of items learners must get correct for us to say they have achieved, or "mastered," that objective. In determining the number of items that we will ask on a particular objective, we weigh the considerations that we discussed earlier concerning reliability and practicality. Then we determine what percentage of those items students must answer correctly for us to say that they have achieved the objective.

How do we determine this percentage? This decision is typically based upon the experience of the instructor, and is often, therefore, left for the instructor to determine. Designers, in consultation with instructors, may set this level of mastery. They should determine a figure, generally between 70 and 100 percent, depending on the nature of the learning involved and the potential consequences of learners not learning to 100 percent mastery. Most of us would prefer that our dentists, surgeons, airline pilots, and parachute packers have learned their skills to 100 percent mastery. In this light, it is not so important that children learn their multiplication facts to the same level of proficiency.

We may not only describe how many of the items the learner must get correct, but we may also describe how many of each type or level of difficulty the learner must answer correctly. This is because it might be possible for a learner to reach a certain proficiency level over all items but still miss all of one particular type. For example, in the division example, we might describe the number and criterion section as follows:

1. Number of items may range from a minimum of 10 to a maximum of 30.
2. Mastery level is 70 percent. However, in addition, learners must get at least one correct out of each of the easy, medial, and difficult categories.

These descriptions are for an intellectual skill objective that involves application, so evaluation must assess the learner's ability to apply knowledge across several instances. Hence, in this example more than one item would be necessary. For our long division test specification earlier in this section, the percentages ascribed to the easy, medial, and difficult levels in the question specifications are 10 percent, 80 percent, and 10 percent, so a minimum of ten problems is necessary. Thirty problems is optimal, as this would allow at least three items for each

Objective:	additional space as needed
Description of Test Form:	additional space as needed
Sample Item:	additional space as needed
Question Characteristics:	additional space as needed
Response Characteristics:	additional space as needed
Number of Items:	additional space as needed
Mastery Criteria:	additional space as needed

Figure 6.4 A Simple Item Specifications Form

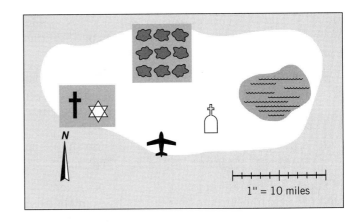

type of question. Production items for problem solving, psychomotor skills, and cognitive strategies may be of such length that only one item may be practically possible. Even if this is the case, the previous descriptions of questions and responses should be developed completely. For a question that requires a checklist for evaluation, the criterion of mastery may include what percentage of the criteria must be included or what average rating must be achieved. The checklist may also include features that must be present or undesirable features that must be absent for the performance to be rated as "mastery."

Figure 6.4 illustrates a format for recording item specifications. In addition, a simple job aid (worksheet) for developing item specifications is provided in the Learning Resources Web site for this book. See Preface for directions to the Learning Resources.

In the following example, one more complete item specification is provided, this one for a map-reading skill to be learned by upper-elementary-level students.

EXAMPLE

Objective

Given a line-drawing map that includes at least five landmarks and a scale, the learner can identify the landmark that is a certain direction and distance from a designated landmark.

Sample Item

Directions: Look at the map that comes with each question. Read the question carefully. Circle the name of the landmark that answers the question.

Which landmark is five miles northeast of the airport?

  1. A park
  2. A church
  3. A cemetery
  4. A lake

Question Form

Multiple choice with four foils.

Question Characteristics

  1. Five symbols should appear on each map—the designated symbol and four other symbols at various locations (see response characteristics for specific locations).

  2. Question format will be "Which landmark is _____X_____ miles _____Y_____ of the _____Z_____?

  3. X (distance) may be any value between two and forty miles.

  4. Y (direction) may be north, south, east, west, northeast, northwest, southeast, or southwest.

  5. Z (designated landmark) may be symbols for any of the following:

temple	bridge
woods	cemetery
railroad station	airport
lake	factory
campground	school
hills	church
cloverleaf	shopping center
park	mountains

  6. Scale should be included with one inch equal to an even number of miles up to ten (e.g., 1" = 8 miles). Increments for each mile should be marked on the scale.

Response Characteristics

  1. Correct answer will be randomly assigned to any foil position: a, b, c, or d.

  2. Distractors can be any of the names for the symbols included under Z in question characteristics.

  3. One distractor will be the name of the symbol that is located in the correct direction from the designated symbol but at an incorrect distance.

4. A second distractor will be the name of the symbol that is located a correct distance from the designated symbol but in an incorrect direction.

5. A third and fourth distractor may be (a) the name of a symbol randomly placed on the map and (b) the name of a symbol not included on the map but easily confused with the correct symbol.

Number of Items and Mastery Criteria

1. Objective should have a minimum of eight items with one each from the eight possible directions. A maximum number of items is 24, with three items from each direction.

2. Mastery is 75 percent of the items correct.

E X E R C I S E S E

Write test item specifications for the following objectives.

1. Given values of initial velocity, final velocity, and time, the learner will be able to calculate acceleration. (Hint: acceleration = change in velocity ÷ time.)

2. Given a list of the symbols for chemical elements and a list of names of the elements, the learner can match the symbol to the name. (Some of these elements and symbols are provided below.)

Aluminum	Al	Lithium	Li
Barium	Ba	Mercury	Hg
Boron	B	Nickel	Ni
Bromine	Br	Nitrogen	N
Calcium	Ca	Oxygen	O
Carbon	C	Phosphorus	P
Chlorine	Cl	Platinum	Pt
Copper	Cu	Radium	Ra
Fluorine	F	Silicon	Si
Helium	He	Sodium	Na
Hydrogen	H	Sulfur	S
Iodine	I	Uranium	U
Iron	Fe	Zinc	Zn

3. Given a list of scenarios, the learner can recognize those that represent the concept "ethnocentrism." (Definition of *ethnocentrism:* Tendency of a group's members to their own culture as superior and to regard other cultural groups as inferior.)

ASSESSMENT INSTRUMENT BLUEPRINTS

You have created item specifications that outline the characteristics of items to assess individual objectives, but an assessment instrument typically evaluates learners'

performance on more than one objective. Therefore, the assessment designer must consider all the item specifications together and define the entire instrument. This plan is sometimes called an *instrument blueprint.* A blueprint includes the following components:

1. Objectives.
2. Forms of items.
3. Total number of items in instrument.
4. Proportionality of items.
5. Directions for administration.
6. Scoring methods.
7. Weighing of items.
8. Passing or cut-off level.

If you have completed item specifications for each of your objectives, then you have completed parts 1 and 2 of the assessment blueprint. The next six components consider the item specifications together.

Number of Items

The first factor to consider is the total number of items for the instrument. You may need to determine the number of written items, the number of simulation experiences, the number of on-the-job observations, or the total of items combined. You have already identified the number of items that you have determined to adequately assess each individual objective. At this point, when you have considered all the objectives that must be assessed with an individual instrument, you may decide that it is practically impossible, either because of limited assessment time or grading time, to assess each objective, even with a minimum number of items. You must then determine the optimal trade-off. If you must have information for each prerequisite objective in a unit or course—for instance, if you are conducting formative evaluation or your primary purpose in assessment is diagnostic—then you may choose to break up the instrument into several assessment periods. If this is not feasible, you may decide to reduce the number of items for the more subordinate objectives and give ample number of items to the superordinate objectives, such as the terminal objective(s).

Beginning instructional designers often point out that it is unnecessary to assess subordinate objectives because if you have the task analysis correct, and students perform well on the superordinate objectives, then you can assume that they can perform the subordinate objectives; and this is so. However, suppose students are unable to correctly complete items for the superordinate objectives. If you have not adequately assessed the lower objectives, you have no information as to where learning broke down. There is no simple solution to this problem. In each individual design project, you must determine which is more important—efficiency of assessment or completeness of information. The purpose of your assessment can guide your decisions regarding this trade-off.

Proportionality of Items

The percentage of items that come from each objective is closely related to the total number of items. Assigning a greater proportion of items to specific objectives is one way to give attention to the more critical objectives in a unit or course. As you look at your task analysis, which is related to a particular goal, note that there are certain key objectives within that analysis. These are often the terminal objectives and the next level of subordination within the task analysis. You will generally wish to assign a greater proportion of items to these objectives. You will also quite naturally develop more items for intellectual skills objectives than for declarative knowledge objectives, because valid measurement of concept and rule learning requires that the learner demonstrate proficiency in multiple instances.

Some test designers suggest that in situations in which you cannot include all of the items you would desire, you should randomly sample across the possible objectives and items. We do not recommend this practice because sampling across objectives implies that all objectives are of equal importance. As we have pointed out earlier, this is generally not true. If you must sample, purposefully sample from possible items within a single objective, or purposefully sample from the objectives themselves.

Directions

As you wrote your item specifications, you determined the directions that are necessary for each type of item. You will also need to write directions for the entire instrument for the students and directions to administrators of the instrument. Directions to students may include the length and time limit of the instrument. Directions may also include cautions to notice particular instructions within the instrument and explanations as to how responses should be reported (e.g., "Completely fill in the bubble with a no. 2 lead pencil"). Directions to administrators may provide information as to how to respond to students' questions, how to set up the assessment area, what materials are needed during the assessment, time length, or other pertinent information that may be necessary to ensure the reliability, validity, or practicality of the assessment.

Scoring Methods

You have already provided general information concerning the form responses should follow as you prepared your item specifications. At this point, however, you have fulfilled those specifications and have actual sample items for your objectives. This is the point at which you can cre-

ate your scoring key. This key may be a simple template for items such as multiple-choice and true-false items, or it may need to be as complete and detailed as possible to alleviate errors in scoring other forms of items such as on-the-job observation, simulations, and essay items.

Weighting of Items

Since all objectives that are being assessed may not be of equal importance, you may give weight to those important objectives by including more items for those objectives. Another way to give weight to items for the more critical objectives is to value those individual items more in scoring than some other items. This is often done by making certain items "worth" more than others on the assessment. This is a legitimate practice, but if it is followed, it is important that the values for all items on the instrument be identified for the students as they take the test.

Passing or Cut-Off Score

You have already identified mastery levels for the items assessing individual objectives. At this point, you may wish to assign or suggest a "passing" or "mastery" criterion for the entire test. Instructional designers have been known to use the 80/80 criterion (i.e., in order to "pass," learners must achieve at least 80 percent of the items on at least 80 percent of the objectives). While this standard may be appropriate in some contexts, it is often inappropriate. For example, using this criterion, it might be possible to pass a learner who could have correctly answered many items relating to subordinate or enabling objectives but did not correctly answer any items that assess the terminal objectives. In setting your criterion, use a general performance level, such as 80 percent, but include a minimum performance level on critical objectives such as the terminal objective. This statement might be as simple as "To pass, learners must also correctly answer (or perform) 80 percent of the items representing the terminal objective."

Many times designers must use the combined expertise and judgment of instructors and subject matter experts, as well as their own judgment in setting cut-off scores. However, in some situations it is possible to gather information over a period of time to validate and even suggest and change mastery cut-off scores. Consider, for example, courses designed for the military service for which information about student performance on tests is available, after the students leave the course, for a prescribed number of years. Test designers with access to this sort of data from large numbers of students can follow the progress of students who made scores of 60 percent, 70 percent, 80 percent, and so on. They can obtain such information as superiors' evaluation of the performance of trained personnel

	Form	Number of Items	Criterion Level	Proportion
Objective 1	MC	15	80%	.25
Objective 2	Essay	1	70%	.15
Objective 3	Perf.	1	80%	.35
Objective 4	Short Ans.	10	80%.	.25

Figure 6.5 A Simple Instrument Blueprint Chart Format

on jobs related to the skills taught in the course. They can obtain other data, such as the trained personnel's own opinions about their preparedness to perform their jobs, accident rates, and other quality control data. Based upon this information, test designers can, over time, empirically ascertain a minimum criterion level that predicts an acceptable performance after leaving the course, and they may find it necessary to adjust the criterion level. Further guidance on setting and using cut-off scores is provided by Cizek (2001).

The careful planning that is required to create an assessment blueprint ensures that assessment designers consider the factors that may threaten the validity, reliability, or practicality of the instrument. Often you must make compromises among these factors, but in creating your blueprints, you will have the opportunity to seriously consider these factors and make conscious, informed decisions.

Figure 6.5 presents an example of an instrument blueprint. In addition, the Learning Resources for this text (see Preface) uses the same format as Figure 6.5 in providing a simple instrument blueprint worksheet (Job Aid).

Constructing Assessment Items

A substantial amount of guidance for item construction is provided in the previous sections. In addition, numerous lists of guidelines for developing different types of test items have been published (e.g., Sax, 1990), so it is unnecessary for us to list them here. It is possible that you already have material on this topic. If not, refer to *A List of Guidelines for Test Item Construction* in the Learning Resources that accompany this text (see the Preface). Also, guidelines and sample items for each type of learning are provided in Chapters 8 to 15.

SUMMARY

In this chapter, we looked at the assessment of student learning, or in common language, "testing." We began by noting that evaluation activities can be put toward two purposes: (1) assessing the learner's learning, and (2) evaluating the quality of the instruction. This chap-

ter deals with the first purpose, and Chapter 19, "Formative and Summative Evaluation," addresses the second purpose.

After contrasting norm-referenced and criterion-referenced assessment models, we found that the criterion-referenced approach generally fits the needs for assessments of products of systematic instructional design efforts.

Three types of assessments were discussed: entry skills (to see if learners are ready for the instruction), preassessments (to see what learners already know of the material to be taught), and postassessments (to see what learners learned from instruction). Next, we looked at the characteristics of assessment instruments: validity, reliability, and practicality. We found that trade-offs must frequently be made among these qualities in designing assessments. Next we discussed the three major formats for assessments: performance assessments and pencil-and-paper tests. We looked at typical pencil- and-paper assessment item forms: recall, recognition, and constructed answer.

We pointed out that the concept of "authentic assessment" includes use of performance assessments and the nature of the timing of assessment so that it is viewed as a part of the learning process. A third aspect of authentic assessment, which is not included in this chapter, is the evaluation of the strategic processes used in learning. We will discuss the assessment of such cognitive strategies in Chapter 13.

Purposes of Evaluation Are...
to assess learners' achievement of objectives and to evaluate effectiveness of instruction.

Assessment Models
Norm referenced-Developed to rank-order learners
Criterion referenced-Developed to determine learners competence on particular objectives.

Characteristics of Assessment Instruments
Validity-Does it measure what it purports to measure?
  –Does it sample the possible domain of items adequately?
Reliability– Is the measure objective and consistent?
  –Can one have confidence that scores represent learners' true abilities?
Practically- Are development and use of the instrument feasible?

Item Specifications

Objective	Question characteristics
Sample item	Response characteristics
Question form	Number of items and mastery criteria

Instrument Blueprints

Number of items	Scoring methods
Proportionality of items	Weighting items
Directions	Passing of cut-off score

Figure 6.6 Summary Diagram for Chapter 6

We described a procedure for constructing tests, beginning with development of assessment item specifications and assessment instrument blueprints. The item specifications are targeted to particular objectives and ensure that items are of an appropriate form and content for the objectives to which they relate. Item specifications help improve the quality of assessment items. We looked at how to develop instrument blueprints for the purpose of improving the quality of an entire test or other instrument. The blueprint builds upon item specifications and adds consideration of such things as proportional coverage of the content domain(s), number of items, weighting, and the minimum passing or cut-off level. Finally, we presented a few item construction tips for different forms of assessment items. Figure 6.6 summarizes key points in this chapter.

EXTENDED EXAMPLE

Go to the Learning Resources Web site for a continuation the instructional design of the Photography Basics course. For this chapter's contribution, an assessment plant for our photography course is provided, including sample item specifications and instrument blueprint.

READINGS AND REFERENCES

American Educational Research Association, American Psychological Association, & National Council for Measurement in Education. (1985). *Standards for educational and psychological testing.* Washington, DC: American Psychological Association.

Arter, J. A., & Spandel, V. (1992, Spring). Using portfolios of student work in instruction and assessment. *Educational Measurement: Issues and Practices,* 36–43.

Baker, E. L., & O'Neil, H. F. (1987). Assessing instructional outcomes. In R. M. Gagné (Ed.), *Instructional technology: Foundations, 11*(1) (pp. 337–343). Hillsdale, NJ: Erlbaum.

Bennett, R. E., & Ward, W. C. (Eds.). (1993). *Construction versus choice in cognitive measurement.* Hillsdale , NJ: Erlbaum.

Carlson, R. D. (1993–94). Computer adaptive testing: A shift in the evaluation paradigm. *Journal of Educational Technology Systems, 22*(3), 213–224.

Cizek, G. J. (2001). *Setting performance standards: Concepts, methods, and perspectives.* Mahwah, NJ: Erlbaum.

Clauser, B. E., Subhiyah, R. G., Nungester, R. J., Ripkey, D. R., Clyman, S. G., & McKinley, D. (1995). Scoring a performance-based assessment by modeling the judgments of experts. *Journal of Educational Measurement, 32*(4), 397–415.

Crocker, L., & Algina, J. (1986). *Introduction to classical and modern test theory.* New York: Holt, Rinehart and Winston.

Delandshere, G., & Petrosky, A. R. (1994). Capturing teachers' knowledge: Performance assessment. *Educational Researcher, 23*(5), 11–18.

Frederiksen, N., Glaser, R., Lesgold, A., & Shafto, M. G. (Eds.). (1990). *Diagnostic monitoring of skill and knowledge acquisition.* Hillsdale, NJ: Erlbaum.

Frederiksen, N., Mislevy, R. J., & Bejar, I. I. (Eds.). (1993). *Test theory for a new generation of tests.* Hillsdale, NJ: Erlbaum.

Gronlund, N. E. (1985). *Measurement and evaluation in teaching* (5th ed.). New York: Macmillan.

Haladyna, T. M. (1999). *Developing and validating multiple-choice test items* (2nd ed.). Mahwah, NJ: Erlbaum.

Hively, W. (1974). *Domain referenced testing.* Englewood Cliffs, NJ: Educational Technology Publications.

Jonassen, D. H. (1992). Evaluating constructivist learning. In T. H. Duffy & D. H. Jonassen (Eds.), *Constructivism and the technology of instruction* (pp. 137–148). Hillsdale, NJ: Erlbaum.

Kirst, M. W. (1991a). Interview on assessment issues with Lorrie Shepard. *Educational Researcher, 20*(2), 21–23.

Kirst, M. W. (1991b). Interview on assessment issues with James Popham. *Educational Researcher, 20*(2), 24–27.

Linn, R. L. (1994). Performance assessment: Policy promises and technical measurement standards. *Educational Researcher, 23*(9), 4–14.

Linn, R. L., Baker, E. L., & Dunbar, S. B. (1991). Complex, performance-based assessment: Expectations and validation criteria. *Educational Researcher, 20*(8), 15–21.

Mager, R. M. (1962). *Preparing instructional objectives.* Palo Alto, CA: Fearon.

Mehrens, W. A., & Lehman, I. J. (1991). *Measurement and evaluation in education and psychology* (4th ed.). Fort Worth: Holt, Rinehart, and Winston.

Morris, L. L., & Fitz-Gibbon, C. T. (1978). *How to measure achievement.* Beverly Hills, CA: Sage Publications.

Morris, L. L., & Fitz-Gibbon, C. T. (1978). *How to measure attitudes.* Beverly Hills, CA: Sage Publications.

Petroski, H. (2003). *Small things considered: Why there is no perfect design.* New York: Knopf.

Popham, W. J. (1978). *Criterion-referenced assessment.* Upper Saddle River, NJ: Prentice-Hall.

Priestley, M. (1982). *Performance assessment in education and training.* Englewood Cliffs, NJ: Educational Technology Publications.

Rink, J. E. (1985). *Teaching physical education for learning.* St. Louis: Times Mirror/Mosby.

Royer, R. (2003). Web-based portfolio assessment in a graduate instructional technology program. *Society for Information Technology and Teacher Education International Conference 2003*(1), 169–174.

Sadler, D. R. (1989). Formative assessment and the design of instructional systems. *Instructional Science, 18,* 119–144.

Sax, G. (1990). *Principles of educational and psychological measurement and evaluation* (3rd ed.). Belmont, CA: Wadsworth.

Shrock, S. A., & Coscarelli, W. C. C. (1989). *Criterion-referenced test development.* Reading, MA: Addison-Wesley.

Swanson, D. B., Norman, G. R., & Linn, R. L. (1995). Performance-based assessment: Lessons from the health professions. *Educational Researcher, 24*(5), 5–11, 35.

Wiggins, G. (1998). *Educative assessment.* San Francisco, CA: Jossey-Bass.

SECTION

III

INSTRUCTIONAL STRATEGIES

The largest section of this book, a prescriptive and heavily documented approach to designing instructional strategies, includes an introductory framework and chapters for facilitating the learning of each of eight distinct types of learning: declarative knowledge, concepts, procedures, principles, problem solving, cognitive strategies, attitudes, and psychomotor skills.

Chapter 7, "A Framework for Instructional Strategy Design" summarizes major concerns in designing strategies and develops an approach to viewing and engaging in design of environments that facilitate learning using both "generative" and "supplantive" approaches.

Chapters 8 through 15, review salient cognitive processing activities associated with each of the eight types of learning addressed, followed with alternatives for supporting learning from both the generative and supplantive standpoints. Each chapter provides an example lesson discussed in terms of the cognitive events involved.

Chapter 16, "Macro Strategies: Integration of Types of Learning," shifts our point of view from the "micro" level on which Chapters 8 to 15 concentrate to a broader, multitopic, longer-term, curriculum level. Alternative curriculum structures are presented, and the primary concerns of curriculum such as articulation and integration are discussed as well as the learning objects concept. Alternate forms of curriculum organization and views on curriculum design are discussed, and the chapter concludes with prescriptions for macro-level design which complement the prescriptions made previously at the micro level.

A FRAMEWORK FOR INSTRUCTIONAL STRATEGY DESIGN

CHAPTER OBJECTIVES

At the conclusion of this chapter, you should be able to do the following:

- Describe the function of the instructional strategy stage in the instructional design process.
- Recognize and explain examples of the three categories of instructional strategies: organizational, delivery, and management strategies.
- List, describe, and identify examples of the expanded instructional events.
- Describe how a typical lesson proceeds from the standpoint of instructional events.
- Explain the differences between supplantive and generative organizational strategies and the advantages and disadvantages of each.
- Given a description of a strategy, identify it as more supplantive or more generative.
- Given a description of context, task, and learners, specify whether you would choose a more supplantive or more generative strategy, and justify your answer.

AN OVERVIEW OF INSTRUCTIONAL STRATEGY CONCERNS IN INSTRUCTIONAL DESIGN

Try to imagine this lesson: It is in the form of a printed booklet, and it begins with a graphic of a cartoon character puzzling over a sentence with nonparallel sentence construction:

To grow to the correct size, swallow the contents of the bottle marked "Smell Me," dancing in a circle, and write your name in the air three times.

The next paragraph tells students that the lesson is on the parallel construction of sentences and paragraphs and that nonparallel structure is one of the most common problems for adult writers. This paragraph also states that nonparallel structure greatly confuses readers. Next, the lesson reviews the concepts of "verb," "participle," "verb tense," "infinitive," "noun," and "adverb." The following page displays the principle that parallel construction requires that each element of information presented in a series should be in a parallel form of a clause or phrase. Subsequent pages contain examples of the correct application of the principle with textual information explaining why the principle is correctly applied. In addition, violations of the principle are shown with textual and graphic information explaining why the writing sample is incorrect and showing how to correct it. Then learners are presented with sentences and paragraphs and asked to tell whether they are parallel or nonparallel. When learners correctly identify nonparallel structure, they are asked to edit the sentence so that it is parallel. Feedback follows, which tells learners several correct methods of editing.

This description outlines the instructional strategy of a lesson with a relational rule (a principle) objective. Notice that the lesson is carefully organized to provide a high level of support for learners' cognitive processes of attention, encoding, and retrieval of information. Other lessons might be designed to provide much less instructional support, requiring learners to engage their own cognitive strategies in structuring information so that they can learn from it. Both lessons are the products of carefully designed instruction based upon context, task, and learner analysis. Both lessons could be effective. Both lessons could be designed within the constructivist philosophy. Instructional support may legitimately be (1) supplied by the instruction, (2) supplied by the learner, or (3) shared between the learner and the instruction. In this chapter we will present information and practice on designing the organizational elements of an instructional strategy. Then, we will present a model and principles for making decisions regarding optimal instructional support in a learning situation.

According to Reigeluth (1983) instructional strategies are composed of three different aspects: organizational strategy characteristics, delivery strategy characteristics, and management strategy characteristics. **Organizational strategy characteristics** refer to how instruction will be sequenced, what particular content will be presented, and how this content will be presented. **Delivery strategy characteristics** deal with what instructional medium will be used and how learners will be grouped. **Management strategy** characteristics include the scheduling and allocation of resources to implement the instruction that is organized and delivered as planned within the previous two strategy aspects. These strategies can be planned at the course or unit (macro) level or at the lesson (micro) level. By *lesson* we generally mean the amount of instruction that can typically be completed in one meeting (although *lessons* may also extend across two or three days, if little time is spent each day).

In this chapter we will concentrate on *organizational strategy* concerns that apply at the lesson level. Chapters 8 to 15 will focus on how to design an organizational strategy for each of the major types of learning outcomes: declarative knowledge, concepts, procedures, principles, problem solving, cognitive strategies, psychomotor skills, and attitudes. Although we have sequenced the chapters that present these strategies beginning with less complex tasks moving to more complex ones, a good approach to reading can be to begin with problem solving (Chapter 12) as it is the "highest" order or most complex form of learning, since that is the ultimate goal to which much instruction leads. Chapter 16 discusses macro-level design—design issues at larger levels, such as entire courses. Media and learner groupings, what Reigeluth called "delivery strategies" are treated in an online chapter in the Web-based Learning Resources for this text. Chapter 18 discusses management strategies as well as other management-related concerns of interest to instructional designers.

E X E R C I S E S A

Following are descriptions of designers' activities. Identify the activity that the designer is preparing: organizational strategy (O), delivery strategy (D), or management strategy (M).

_____ **1.** Designer determines that practice questions will be completed in groups of five students.

_____ **2.** Designer plans the clustering and sequence of the objectives for the lesson.

_____ **3.** Designer writes an instructor's guide that suggests the scheduling of the unit across six weeks.

_____ **4.** Designer determines that a lesson will be mediated with an instructor and print-based materials.

_____ **5.** Designer lists in the teacher's manual the materials, supplies, and equipment that will be required for the course.

_____ **6.** Designer decides that the lesson will follow an inquiry strategy.

_____ **7.** Designer determines what will occur during each of the events of instruction.

LESSON-LEVEL ORGANIZATIONAL STRATEGIES

The predominant decisions that must be made at the lesson level are organizational strategy decisions: What content should be presented? How should this content be presented? What sequence should the instruction follow?

To introduce these aspects of instructional strategy, we would like to outline in very general and simple terms what psychologists believe to happen cognitively when students learn. These mental activities may occur at either conscious or unconscious levels. (You may remember this sequence of learning as it was portrayed in Chapter 2.)

First, students are immersed in a plethora of sensory inputs—sounds, sights, tactile stimuli, odors, and tastes. For learning to occur, students must choose to attend to those stimuli in the learning environment that are related to the learning task and instruction and to ignore competing stimuli, such as the band practicing outside nearby. This process is called _selective perception._ Following perception, information is momentarily stored in working memory. Next, students "take in" the information in the instruction, using things they already know to help them understand the new information. They interpret this new information based on the related content knowledge, values, beliefs, and strategies that they already have available in long-term memory. During this process of relating what they already know to what is new, much of the new information is stored (encoded) into long-term memory, adding to or modifying what students already know. Either immediately or later, students may retrieve from memory their new learning to answer questions, solve problems, or understand yet more new information.

The organizational strategy the designer selects should facilitate these mental operations. Instructional and cognitive psychologists have researched extensively what the characteristics of organizational instructional strategies should be. As mentioned previously, these characteristics may vary according to the type of goal (e.g., declarative knowledge, concepts, and

so on). However, there are some general characteristics of an organizational strategy that seem to facilitate learning, whatever the objective. One of these characteristics is that the organization of a lesson should generally follow this pattern:

- Introduction.
- Body.
- Conclusion.
- Assessment.

Sometimes assessment is not included in an individual lesson but is delayed until a number of goals across several lessons can be assessed at one time. However, the other three sections of a lesson are commonly included in most instructional theorists' lists of the episodes that comprise a lesson organization. What should be included in the introduction, body, assessment, and conclusion? R. Gagné (1972) has suggested that lessons include nine **events of instruction:**

1. Gaining attention.
2. Informing the learner of the objective.
3. Stimulating recall of prerequisite learning.
4. Presenting stimulus materials.
5. Providing learning guidance.
6. Eliciting performance.
7. Providing feedback.
8. Assessing performance.
9. Enhancing retention and transfer.

Traditionally, instruction in training environments, such as military training, has included the following events:

1. Gain attention.
2. Promote motivation.
3. Give overview of lesson.
4. Explain and demonstrate knowledge.
5. Learner practice with supervision.
6. Evaluation.
7. Summary.
8. Remotivation.
9. Closure.

A limitation of these statements is that they make it appear that instruction is something that is _done_ to the learner. There is an alternative way to view these events. The events may be viewed in terms of cognitive processes, and those processes can be performed by learners as well as by external provisions. Consideration of this alternative is at the heart of good strategy design: determination of the _locus of cognitive processing._ But before we look at different possible loci of cognitive processing, let's look first at these processes themselves.

What are the key cognitive processing activities associated with learning? These activities fundamentally take place within the learner and are either *necessary* for learning, for example attending and processing information, or the activity is *substantially helpful* to learning, for example becoming oriented and using learning strategies. Definitions provided for these functions are informal in the interest of clarity:

Attending—being focused and aware of what you are working on

Goal—having an idea of what you would like to do

Motivation—having some good reason to do something, wanting to do it

Orientation—knowing where you are, physically, conceptually

Prior learning—being aware of and using what you already know that is related

Processing information—experiencing new stuff

Focusing attention—homing in on particular parts that are critical

Learning strategies—using things you know about how to learn

Practice—trying to do it yourself, with help as needed, to help you learn it

Feedback—knowing what you did right and wrong, how close you got to good

Consolidation—pulling it all together

Transfer—applying it somewhere else

Remotivation—realizing how having learned this will help you

Assessment—trying to do it yourself now that you've supposedly learned it

Feedback—finding out how well your know it, really

When we think of designing a learning environment, it helps to think carefully about the ways in which these cognitive functions will be accomplished. A particular learning environment may provide support or "scaffolding" for some processing and not others. Other instruction may provide more or less of this cognitive scaffolding.

Two general types of instructional strategy can be described based on the locus of cognitive processing can be *primarily generated* by learners (low scaffolding), *primarily supplied* by instruction (high scaffolding), or any place along the continuum between high and low scaffolding. **Scaffolding** is the cognitive processing support that the instruction provides the learners, allowing them to learn complex ideas that would be beyond their grasp if they depended solely on their own cognitive resources, selectively aiding the learners where needed (Greenfield, 1984). What we call the "expanded events of instruction" (see Figure 7.1) reflects these fundamental alternatives as well as a fully elaborated set of events.

Expanded Events of Instruction	
Generative . . . student generates	Supplantive . . . instruction supplies
Introduction	
Activate attention to activity	Gain attention to learning activity
Establish purpose	Inform learner of purpose
Arouse interest and motivation	Stimulate learner's attention/motivation
Preview learning activity	Provide overview
Body	
Recall relevant prior knowledge	Stimulate recall of prior knowledge
Process information and examples	Present information and examples
Focus attention	Gain and direct attention
Employ learning strategies	Guide or prompt use of learning strategies
Practice	Provide for and guide practice
Evaluate feedback	Provide feedback
Conclusion	
Summarize and review	Provide summary and review
Transfer learning	Enhance transfer
Remotivate and cease	Provide remotivation and closure
Assessment	
Assess learning	Conduct assessment
Evaluate feedback	Provide feedback and remediation

Figure 7.1 The Expanded Events of Instruction

Let us look more closely at the expanded events of instruction. The first statement of each event, such as "Summarize and Review," is couched in a **student-generated** form that is described as the learner carrying the primary load for arranging the condition for learning. Although it may be more customary to think of supplied summaries ("Let's look at what we worked on today. . ."), it is often preferable for students to generate their own summaries ("I want each of you to write a short summary of what we worked with today."). Each event, not just summarizing, can be performed by the student, in which the student performs the primary information-processing called for by the event. The second statement of each event, those in parentheses, such as "Provide Summary and Review," is couched in terms of the instruction-supplied equivalent of the event. It is easy to imagine providing a summary—perhaps a teacher summarizing a lesson, a text chapter providing a summary at the end. For most events, it is easier for novice designers to imagine an instruction-supplied version, but as we will see later in this chapter and throughout this text, the student-generated form has many strengths. We have described the events in this fashion to ensure a balanced treatment of two fundamental approaches to instruction. We will have more to say about these two options, but for now, notice how each event is listed in both "generative" and "supplantive" forms.

We have stated the events in such a way that they can accommodate strategies in which the predominant source of control of processing may be the learner, as well as those situations in which guidance of processing is supplied by the instruction. It is very important for designers to consider that these events may actually be provided by the learner; some instruction may either stimulate learners to generate instructional events themselves or assume that learners will generate the instructional events within themselves. On the other hand, the events may be provided entirely by the instruction, or they may be treated as a shared responsibility between learner and instruction. The events describe instruction that is either more expository or more exploratory. Instruction at both ends of the generative–supplantive continuum can be learner-centered, active, and meaningful.

Lessons and Learning Environments

The overall structure of the events as we present them, with Introduction, Body, Conclusion, and Assessment, smack of a presentation or, at the least, a supplantive lesson of some sort rather than an open or exploratory learning environment. Because we are dealing with fifteen separate instructional events, some form of subdivision seems necessary, and all facilitation of learning, regardless of form has a beginning, middle, and end.

Each of the fifteen events is applicable to learning environments, as well as to more supplantive forms of learning facilitation. Although we will generally use the term "lesson," we hope you realize that lessons are of all sorts and that the term "learning environment" may be always added or substituted. The heart and soul of strategy design lies in devising the best approach for given learners, contexts, and learning tasks. Fortunately, we have a wide variety of approaches to choose from—many ways to engage and support the cognitive processes that will facilitate learning. As you read the remainder of this text, you will see examples selected from this wide variety of approaches, with what we hope is more or less equal representation of supplantive and generative instruction or learning environments, and we will use the label "lesson" most of the time to denote them.

Although these instructional events have been synthesized from a review of research, if you observe master teachers, you often see them including these events whether or not they have heard of them. Teachers probably follow this pattern because they have discovered that students who experience these events tend to learn better than students who do not. The following sections review the expanded instructional events.

Introduction*

The introduction prepares learners for the lesson or learning experience, promoting their selective attention and bringing relevant memories to working memory, where the existing knowledge may aid in making new information understandable. In addition, the introduction establishes an expectancy for a particular learning goal, which aids the learners in employing strategies that will facilitate their learning. Although we typically imagine a presentation of some sort to be associated with the idea of an introduction, we want to ensure that you don't restrict your thinking to presentations or expository instruction. Regardless of the form of instruction, there will be a beginning for any given unit or lesson. Even when instruction is largely self-directed, the introduction and the events described within it are equally appropriate and needed, although they may be learner-generated.

Activate Attention (Gain Attention)

The purpose of this event is for learners to focus their attention on the learning task. As mentioned earlier, there are many stimuli in the learners' environment,

---

*If the term "Introduction" is too freighted with supplantive connotations for your taste, you may wish to add to it or replace it with "Initial Experiences."

so it is important that they attend to the part of the environment that is crucial to the learning task. We have all experienced this event when our teachers said, "Please open your textbooks to page 43 and look at question number 1." Older learners may be able to supply this event for themselves, but even they may benefit from direction to the portion of the learning task that should be attended to at any one time. This is one event that can be similar across all learning outcomes. For example, learners' activation of attention for a principle learning task is much the same as their activation of attention for verbal information learning. Many older learners are able to supply this event for themselves, without much prompting by the instruction. This event is often combined with the other events in the introduction.

Technology-based lessons may gain learners' attention in a number of ways: sounds, graphics (either static or animated), a change in the text on the screen, or verbal information that has high relevance to the learner or appears "attractive" because of its games, fantasy, or human interest aspects. For instance, a program might begin with a short segment of animated graphics to introduce a topic such as the relationship between wavelength and frequency. A major concern of designers is that they include enough stimulation in this event to draw students' attention to the learning task, but not so much stimulation that students' attention is directed only toward the attention-directing device and distracted from the learning task. In addition, designers should weigh the costs in production time and hardware requirements for highly complex presentations such as animated graphics. Just because technology can do some attractive things does not mean that it is always worthwhile to do so. Sometimes an alternative method that is less costly or time-consuming may be just as effective. (Chapter W-3 in the Learning Resources Web site contains more information on gaining and maintaining attention.)

Establish Purpose
(Inform Learner of Instructional Purpose)

In some situations, learners can establish their own purposes for learning. These purposes may or may not be attainable within available instructional materials. Materials that can support multiple purposes, such as data resources on the World Wide Web, library resources, and other reference materials, may provide the best instruction in cases in which the specific goals of learners cannot be anticipated.

For instruction in which goals for learning have been determined, telling students what they are about to learn often facilitates learning. Knowing the learning goal can establish an expectancy in learners,

arousing their interest and giving them a goal toward which to direct their cognitive energies. This event can be easily combined with the event of activating attention by stating the purpose of instruction in a way that attracts students' attention. Only rarely will designers express the learning goals to the learners in the same forms that were used when designing instruction. Goals that are stated in such formal terms may be too detailed, and they may actually interfere with students' learning. The designer may choose to state the goal in terms of a question or to demonstrate what the learner will be able to do after instruction, or the goal may be stated as informally as, "Today you will learn to. . . ."

In general, informing the learners of the purpose of the lesson allows them to "sit in the driver's seat" in the lesson. In informal, voluntary-attendance classes, this information allows the learner to choose whether to attend a particular meeting. In addition, having a clear idea of the purpose of the instruction allows learners to summon from long-term memory prior content and general world knowledge that may be appropriate to the task. It also allows them to recall learning strategies that they have found useful in learning similar kinds of goals. Furthermore, knowing the purpose and goal of the lesson allows learners to monitor their own learning and to actively seek help or clarification when they sense that they are not achieving the goal. There may be occasions when you decide not to inform the learner of the goal because of the strategy you are planning. For example, if you plan to use a discovery or inquiry approach in which the learners induce a principle or concept, you may choose not to reveal the concept or principle in advance. Omitting a statement of the learning goal is acceptable in such circumstances, so long as you ensure at the conclusion of instruction that learners are indeed aware of what they have learned.

The specification of the goal may vary somewhat from learning type to learning type. For example, for declarative knowledge goals, the instruction can specify exactly what the learner must be able to list, summarize, or recall. For intellectual skills goals, the instruction may simply describe kinds of problems learners will be able to solve, or it may demonstrate what learners will be able to do. A demonstration of the desired behavior may also be appropriate for a description of the goal of motor skills or attitude instruction.

It is not uncommon to design materials that are appropriate for multiple purposes. For example, many instructional databases may satisfy a variety of learner purposes. In such cases, the learner takes much of the responsibility in defining the instructional goals and selecting content and sequence that are appropriate to meet these purposes.

Arouse Interest and Motivation (Stimulate Learners' Attention/Motivation)

The critical aspect of this part of the introduction is that learners are cognizant of the importance and relevance of the lesson and/or encouraged to explore the personal relevance of the lesson. The information gained in the learner analysis at this point will be very beneficial in helping you determine why learning may be important to the learner. In courses for which attendance is voluntary, learners may have already made their own determinations as to why the course may be personally relevant, in which case the designer may only need to indicate how this particular lesson relates to the goal of the course. In cases in which learners' attendance is mandatory or a course is required, establishing the importance of the goal may be more of a challenge. In training environments for adults, indicating how attaining the lesson goals may relate to job responsibilities may be sufficient. In other adult learning situations and in many public school environments, the actual application of learning to everyday life may lie in the distant future or may even be unclear. In such cases, the designer may wish to stimulate curiosity in the goal through unusual anecdotes or graphics, or the designer may choose to present a challenging situation in which learning to achieve the goal will allow the learner to resolve the dilemma. (See Chapter W-3 in the Learning Resources Web site for a discussion of creating a motivating lesson.)

Preview Learning Activity (Provide Overview)

In this phase, the instruction itself may summarize the procedure or process that will be followed in the lesson, or the learners may choose or be encouraged to preview the lesson using whatever strategies they already possess. In some cases, learners might be planning the experiences that they believe will allow them to reach the goals of instruction, whether they selected them or "bought into" them.

A very supportive (highly supplantive) lesson might provide an overview that includes a brief content outline as well as an overview of the instructional approach to be used. For example, an instructor might say the following:

> In this lesson, we will first review the portions of the Constitution that allocate powers to the federal government and the state government. Then we will discuss how the contradictions in these two sections of the Constitution lead to an ambiguity that creates two camps of interpretation—loose versus strict constructivism. Finally, you will learn how to recognize positions that represent these two camps. You'll get to practice recognizing these two positions. Next week on our unit test, you'll be tested on your ability to recognize examples of these two diverse interpretations of the Constitution.

Learners engaged in experiential (highly generative) learning experiences will also benefit from knowing something about what they will be doing before they begin. The preview function might be supplied by an explanation (even in an otherwise generative environment) or learners might be guided into exploration that serves a preview function. In problem-based learning, setting the problem, assuring learners that their learning activities will be anchored to it, and supporting the learner in developing ownership of the problem are preview functions in that context. An exploratory, student-centered learning environment (Land & Hannafin, 2000) might look like this:

> On the computer's display monitor, the image of a camera is provided with all of its operating controls in view, along with buttons which are labeled "exposure simulator," "depth of field simulator," "image sharpness simulator," and a button with the caricature of a rumple-shirted fellow loaded down with cameras. A heading at the top of the screen says "Mastering Photography." Although looking at the images on the screen and reflecting upon their function provides a preview (as would tentatively and experimentally clicking on the buttons to see what happens before deciding to actually begin working with the simulator), the designers provided a bit more support for the preview event: the learner does nothing to begin, after a reasonable wait, an additional button appears, labeled "Preview," and when clicked provides a brief explanation that you can learn to make better pictures with your digital camera by taking pictures on this simulated camera, manipulating settings, and comparing results, and that an artificial "expert," Mr. Gomer Lenscap is available to assist when needed.

As we stated earlier, being aware of the instructional purpose helps the learners feel expectant and begin to summon knowledge and strategies that will help them achieve the objective. In addition, previewing the process or procedure that will be followed in the lesson or learning environment will also put the learners "in the driver's seat" by allowing them to anticipate the order and character of the instruction.

Body

RECALL RELEVANT PRIOR KNOWLEDGE (STIMULATE RECALL OF PRIOR KNOWLEDGE). During this phase of instruction, learners are stimulated to retrieve knowledge from long-term memory that is necessary or helpful in learning the new objective. In the case of principle-learning goals, this event may be a review of concepts that comprise the principle to be learned. For declarative knowledge goals, this event may be an advance organizer that relates previously acquired, organized declarative knowledge to new information that will be acquired in the lesson. In the case of motor skills, learners may be reminded of component motor skills they may have acquired that are similar to the skills to be learned. Learners may also be encouraged to recall cognitive strategies that can be employed to learn the new information.

This event may be in the form of a totally learner-controlled review of relevant knowledge in which the learner, being aware of the instructional purpose, searches memory for relevant knowledge and abilities. An experienced student who is beginning to read a text chapter accomplishes this event when, after reading enough of the chapter to get an idea of what it is about, looks up from the text and thinks, "Now let's see, what do I already know about this?" Or the instruction may directly encourage the learner to review particular prior knowledge through use of a comparative advance organizer, an analogy, an expository review, or a questioning of the learners.

A comparative advance organizer (Ausubel, Novak, & Hanesian, 1968) provides a framework, or schema, for new learning by comparing a similar known entity to it. For example, Ausubel mentioned that for a lesson in which Westerners are to learn about Buddhism, a possible organizer might be a review of the features of Christianity and a feature-by-feature comparison to those of Buddhism.

An analogy might compare a known concept (sometimes called the *vehicle*) to the concept to be learned (sometimes called the *topic*). For example, a lesson on the aperture of a camera often compares it to the iris of the human eye (relevant prior knowledge). The similarities (sometimes called the *grounds*) of the aperture and the eye might be discussed. It is also important that the ways in which the eye and the aperture are not similar (sometimes called the *limitations*) be carefully presented.

An expository review might be a simple summary or restatement of relevant prior knowledge that learners have learned in previous lessons. Learners might be guided through questions to recall this information. An entry-level assessment followed by feedback is a rather structured method of reviewing this critical prior knowledge.

The recall of prior knowledge may also be intermixed with the next event, processing information and examples. For example, in lessons in which the learners are encouraged to carry much of the instructional burden, they might be asked to invent appropriate analogies or other comparisons as they are presented with new information. These comparisons are made between concepts that the learners already possess and new information. This mental activity is sometimes called *elaboration*, as the learner is required to elaborate on new information by searching for relevant personal experiences or memories that extend the new information by making it personally meaningful.

In addition to considering helpful and prerequisite prior knowledge, it is often useful to point out to the learners or encourage learners to consider for themselves prior knowledge that is not useful, is incompatible, or may interfere with learning of new information. The application of prior knowledge to situations in which it is not applicable is termed *negative transfer*. The application of English word order rules (particularly for nouns and their adjectives) when learning Spanish is an example of negative transfer.

PROCESS INFORMATION AND EXAMPLES (PRESENT INFORMATION AND EXAMPLES).   During this event of instruction, learners encounter the material they will be learning. This information may be presented in an expository (didactic) form in which generalities such as concept definitions or statements of generalizations are presented prior to their examples. The sequence may instead involve more discovery (inquiry), in which the learners are presented with examples of the concepts or the applications of principles and are encouraged to induce the generality. For example, if students are learning a new defined concept, such as "transparent," they are often presented with the definition of the concept and examples and nonexamples of the concept. This is an **expository sequence.** Learners might, however, be presented with examples and be prompted to induce the concept. This is a **discovery sequence.** Within a discovery sequence learners often take on more of the processing responsibilities, engaging cognitive strategies as well as domain knowledge. However, intermediate levels of instructional support can be provided if learners founder to frustration in an extreme discovery approach. In fact, a strategy that is somewhere between the extremes of "pure generative" and "pure supplantive" may be best. A discovery approach is fundamentally generative, as giving learners the primary responsibility for information processing is the critical attribute of generative strategies. Although inquiry instruction is somewhat less efficient than expository instruction, many educators feel that learners recall and are able to transfer learning more easily when it is acquired from a discovery-type approach.

Although there are many choices to be made in how this event is approached, some general patterns exist for certain types of learning. For example, psychomotor skill instruction may comprise a statement of the procedure, either as a whole or in parts, and a demonstration of the execution of the psychomotor skill. Psychomotor skill instruction seldom follows a discovery sequence. For problem-solving learning, this event may be delivered by simply stating a problem to be solved. Declarative knowledge is simply stated or available to read at this point (either in the form of facts, lists, or organized information) in an expository form.

FOCUS ATTENTION (GAIN AND DIRECT ATTENTION).
Although the learner's attention was invoked at the beginning of instruction, it must be refocused continuously throughout the lesson. This event may be generated by the learners as they highlight or underline critical parts of a textual passage, as they take selective notes, or as they mentally rehearse sections of the instruction. This event may also be scaffolded by the instruction. For example, the instruction might ask leading questions to help students attend to the most critical features of the lesson. Pointing out distinctive attributes of a concept is also an example of focusing attention. (For example, "Notice that in a trapezoid only two sides are parallel.") During psychomotor skills instruction, this event might be supported by an instructor who reminds the learner of the procedure that controls the muscular actions. Textual information either in a print- or computer-based format may direct attention by using boxes, boldfacing, underlining, bulleting, or other attention-directing devices. Video segments may focus attention through such techniques as zooming in on critical portions of a scene. Graphic overlays (such as arrows, boxes, and circles) and cues in the narration are also used to direct the learner's attention.

EMPLOY LEARNING STRATEGIES (GUIDE OR PROMPT USE OF LEARNING STRATEGIES). Throughout the expanded events of instruction, we have pointed out many ways in which the learners might "take charge" of the learning process. When learners do this, they are employing learning strategies they already possess. (Chapter 13 will discuss how to teach these learning strategies.) The purpose of this event is to assist learners to use effective strategies, and that purpose is essentially accomplished by prompting learners to use appropriate learning strategies. Generally during the body of the lesson, this means suggesting to learners how they might encode information so that it can be accurately retrieved. This might involve suggesting to learners that they create mental images of the content, that they take a particular kind of notes, or that they employ a certain kind of mnemonic strategy. Just as the optimal type of content treatment varies from learning outcome type to learning outcome type, so does the appropriate learning strategy. (The following chapters contain information on appropriate strategies for particular learning outcomes.)

Although most media can prompt learners to use learning strategies, few learners can judge the appropriateness of their use. Print and video can suggest that learners employ a strategy, but they cannot assess whether a strategy has been used. Computer-based instruction, including interactive multimedia, can determine if the learner is doing something (entering information); however, it is generally unable to judge the efficacy of the learners' actions as they may or may not

contribute to subsequent learning. Although a human can make this judgment, it is improbable that the instructor can assess all learners' use of strategies across all events with large classes of learners. This difficulty leads many designers to design more scaffolded or supplantive instruction than they might otherwise prefer. Designers sometimes do this to ensure that learners are getting all the assistance they need during instruction.

PRACTICE (PROVIDE FOR AND GUIDE PRACTICE). At this point in the lesson, the learners can be given the opportunity or they may take the opportunity to interact with the material being learned and see if they are ready to proceed to the next part of the lesson. Some learners can and will spontaneously generate problems and questions that "test" their understanding of the content of the lesson and whether they are achieving the identified or their generated learning goals.

It is not the purpose of this event to evaluate the students for grading, but rather to provide for learners' active participation in the learning process and to see how learning is progressing so that remediation may be provided if they are not learning. Remember that some constructivists recommend that for "authentic assessment" this practice activity should be the grounds for assessments. If this approach is taken, learning should be assessed at later points in the learning process as well. Inclusion of the practice event—more than all others—allows the learners to be active participants, rather than passive observers, in learning. Because of its fundamental importance, the opportunity for actual practice should not be left out of any instructional sequence.

It is important that the learner have the opportunity to practice across the range of variability of the learning goal. The designer has defined this range in the assessment specifications (see Chapter 6), so he or she can use these specs to help determine what practice should be made available to the learners. This means that they should have the opportunity to practice across the range of the content with which they should be skilled and that they should be able to practice across the range of difficulty of the goal. Although practice may be sequenced from simpler to more complex items, the need for practicing the complete range of complexity remains. It is not uncommon for designers to feel that since learners are just encountering the content, they should not be required to practice at the level of complexity that will be tested later. However, this decision is predicated on the assumption that learners will experience spontaneous learning over time. Although this is feasible, the active practicing of new learning (especially at more complex levels than those to which learners have been exposed) should not be left to chance. Novices in a content area may not have the experience to imagine how the content might be applied; consequently, provision of instruction with explicit practice items is very important.

The particulars of how practice is provided will vary considerably from learning type to learning type. For example, during concept learning, students may be given a variety of examples and nonexamples of the concept and be asked to identify those that are examples of the concept, or they may be asked to generate their own examples of the concept. For principle-learning goals, students may be asked to demonstrate the application of a principle. Students can practice problem solving if the instructor gives them a problem to solve and has them solve it or if students state which principles seem appropriate for the solution of this particular problem. In learning declarative knowledge students may be asked to state, summarize, recognize, or list part or all of the information they are to learn. Students learning psychomotor skills may be asked to demonstrate the whole or part of the skill as well as to recall the procedure that controls the skill.

When operating under the principles of behaviorism, designers created practice that was almost "error-proof," anticipating that a benefit of totally successful practice would be more motivated learners. More recently, designers have tended to design practice so that it might evoke any misconceptions that learners might have developed. This direct addressing of common misconceptions actually seems to pique learners' interest even more than successful experience. Thus, as you design the practice event, consider the ways that learners might go wrong with the content—how learners might overgeneralize or undergeneralize a concept, or how learners might draw incorrect inferences from declarative knowledge. Then you can design practice experiences that will allow them to confront these "bugs" in their learning.

Learner activity can be elicited in a number of well-known ways. Practice items, whether true/false, multiple choice, short answer, or essay, are probably the most widely used. Simulations, role-playing, or even on-the-job performance opportunities are all methods of practicing learning. Learners should have several opportunities to practice using the knowledge related to a specific goal to promote overlearning and automaticity of skilled performance. In addition, it is often useful to include an extra set of practice problems for learners who may have difficulty during the first set of practice exercises. These learners may benefit from the feedback from the initial set and need another opportunity to practice their skills. Current educational scholars have reminded designers that it is critical that practice experiences be relevant, authentic to the learners and their context, and "anchored" in a familiar situation (Brown, Collins, & Duguid, 1989). This is not a new principle for many instructional designers, or for educators in general. For example, Dewey (1924) recommended the use of community-related class projects to promote learners' application of knowledge. Whether under a traditional or recent rubric, contextualized, relevant problems are central to motivated, meaningful, transferable learning.

Computers are good tools for providing the practice event because they can interact with all learners, asking them to respond and then checking the accuracy of the learners' responses. Software can be designed to be used with individual learners so that they are required to respond in a particular way, eliminating the possibility of their "coasting" on other learners' performance, as can sometimes happen in group-based discussions and practice. A limitation of computer-based software, however, is that it is not generally "intelligent." That is, it cannot think or learn on its own. The computer's lack of intelligence has an impact on practice because the designer must be cautious in the types of questions or other response-eliciting situations the instruction poses. If the designer is to provide learners with accurate and meaningful feedback, she must ensure that the questions or situations posed will produce responses that can be judged by the computer. Intelligent tutoring systems can be developed to deal (to some degree) with production responses, such as short written answers. However, these systems can be very expensive and time-consuming to develop, so they will not be easily available across all content areas for some time (estimates have been offered at four to four-hundred years until such systems may become widely available). For practice in which open-ended responses are required, a teacher or other human will generally be needed to assess the appropriateness of the learners' responses.

EVALUATE FEEDBACK (PROVIDE FEEDBACK). Feedback is a critical event in instruction, and it is one that is too often slighted or overlooked. In fact, feedback is so important that we couldn't even discuss the previous event without mentioning it. Often educators use the term *feedback* to refer to the positive reinforcements, such as "good work," "good for you," and other responses to learners' efforts, that are primarily constructed to encourage. Although this type of reinforcement can be very important, the type of feedback to which we are referring in this event is called **informative** or **informational feedback,** rather than motivational feedback. The purpose of informative feedback is to give learners the opportunity to consider information about the appropriateness of their responses during practice.

In many cases, instruction can be constructed so that learners can, through observation, induce their progress from the natural consequences of their actions. Generative feedback is common to psychomotor skills but can also be fostered in computer simulations, microworlds, and physical or simulated construction kits. In situations in which learners cannot evaluate feedback without instructional support, several types of information can be provided through feedback:

1. Learners may simply be told if they are correct or incorrect. This type of feedback seems particularly appropriate for declarative knowledge learning.

2. If learners are incorrect, they may be given the correct answer. This type of feedback is often used with declarative knowledge and intellectual skills objectives.

3. Learners may be given information so they can determine if they are right or wrong and why they are right or wrong. This type of feedback is particularly appropriate for intellectual skills learning.

4. Learners may be given information about the faulty solution strategies they are using, with hints for more appropriate strategies, without being explicitly told whether they are correct or incorrect. This type of feedback is appropriate for problem-solving learning.

5. Learners may be shown the consequences of their responses. This type of feedback can be used for problem solving or principle learning, particularly with instruction that is delivered via a simulation.

6. Particularly with psychomotor skills, learners may experience proprioceptive (internal sensory) feedback during or after demonstration of a skill. Learners may have to be taught to recognize these sensory cues. Videotape replays, which allow learners to see themselves, are a form of augmentation of sensory feedback.

7. Learners may be given cumulative information on their progress during practice. For example, they might be told what pattern of errors they are making or how close they are to reaching mastery or a pre-stated criterion of performance (Smith & Ragan, 1993).

Feedback may be coupled with second tries at practice items so that if learners are incorrect, they can use the feedback to correct the error on that very problem. For example, all the feedback types just mentioned (except number 2, providing the correct answer) may be used in conjunction with several tries so that learners have the opportunity to apply the feedback to correct their own learning. In contrast to assessment, one expects learning to continue through the practice and feedback events. In other words, practice and feedback are formative, not summative.

As you might surmise, computers are especially good tools for providing individualized and immediate feed-back to learners. Unlike most other instructional media—other than a human tutor—the feedback learners receive from a computer can be adjusted to the answers they gave. With other types of media, such as workbooks and conventional textbooks, you will probably be restricted to the question-and-answer method of feedback. Humans are the best at communicating feedback because of the nature of production responses in which many answers may be equally correct. However, as we mentioned during our discussion of learning strategies, it is unlikely that an instructor can give tailored feedback to each learner in a class after each practice response. This limitation often leads designers to provide more information than some learners might require to ensure that enough feedback is given. In some grouping situations, peers may provide feedback for open-ended questions. The success of this strategy depends on the competence of peers, both in content knowledge and in providing helpful feedback.

As you may have noticed in the preceding treatment of feedback, the range of generative to supplantive approaches to feedback is quite wide, with many techniques employing a mixture of generative and supplantive elements. One example is the third type of feedback, in which information is supplied which learners process in order to generate feedback on their progress. For a more complete discussion of feedback, see Mory (2004) and Dempsey & Sales (1993.)

Conclusion

The conclusion events allow learners to review and elaborate recent learning so that it can be available for further application and use. As time is often short at the end of a lesson, designers have a tendency to abbreviate these events. However, these events are critical in that they support learners' attempts to synthesize and consolidate new learning.

SUMMARIZE AND REVIEW (PROVIDE SUMMARY AND REVIEW). The purpose of the summary is to ensure that the learners recall and synthesize the critical parts of the lesson into a memorable and applicable whole. New learning can be quite confusing, so it is helpful at the conclusion of the lesson to remind learners of what they have just learned. As with many of the other instructional events, lesson summaries may be constructed by the learner or provided by the instruction. It is important that summaries provided to learners not include any new information, but rather restate the gist of the lesson itself. Often with transitory instruction, such as computer-, video-, or lecture-based instruction, learners can be given (or encouraged to produce) a permanent and portable summary in the form of print-based notes.

The actual content of the summary will vary depending on the learning outcome. For example, a review of a procedure might be a restatement of the steps in completing the procedure or a demonstration of the procedure itself. A review of declarative knowledge might include a restatement of a topical outline of main points; development of a concept map, perhaps supported by a computer-based tool such as *Insight*™, or a clustered review of paired information, such as acronyms and the words they represent. A summary of concepts might include a restatement of the definition or the critical attributes of the concepts that have been learned. One particularly useful technique for aiding summarizing is called a *graphic organizer;* it visually and spatially shows the main points in a lesson and how those points are related to one another. You have encountered graphic organizers at the conclusions of the chapters in this book. Designers have found that providing learners with partially completed graphic organizers that the learners must complete can be more effective than providing learners completed organizers or asking them to create the summary from scratch.

Review involves extended practice of the new learning. It can occur in the lesson itself, as an outside class assignment, or as the "review of prior knowledge" event in subsequent lessons. Review may also involve a cumulative practice over several lessons, which allows learners practice in distinguishing among newly learned facts, concepts, or principles. Learners also practice selecting the appropriate information, concepts, or principles from their new repertoire of knowledge to apply to specific situations. It is this ability to appropriately select and apply new learning that supports its integration and usefulness. In the case of declarative knowledge, intellectual skills, psychomotor skills, and perhaps cognitive strategies, spaced (over time) practice of the new learning can facilitate retention and recall. Of all the learning outcomes, declarative knowledge learning and psychomotor skill learning seem to require the most review. Older and more capable learners may be able to construct their own review schedules and their own review items. Younger and less capable learners generally need more assistance in preparing and conducting reviews.

TRANSFER LEARNING (ENHANCE TRANSFER). The process of transfer—the application of new knowledge and skills to a variety of real-life situations and future learning tasks—can be enhanced by giving learners opportunities to apply their learning to a variety of circumstances. Transfer is particularly critical for learning concepts, principles, procedures, problem solving, cognitive strategies, psychomotor skills, and attitudes. The primary transfer task for learning declarative knowledge is the

ability to draw correct inferences from the information. Transfer of learning can be described in terms of a continuum from what is termed *near transfer* to what is termed *far transfer.* Near transfer is the application of learning in a way similar to the manner in which it is applied during learning and to situations similar to those in which it was exemplified and practiced. Far transfer is the ability to apply learning in different ways and in situations that are very different from those in which the learning was acquired and practiced.

For examples of near transfer and far transfer, let's consider a goal in our course on photography: "Given a correct exposure and information on aperture setting, shutter speed, and film speed, and given a description of a change in the situation, the learners can determine a setting in aperture, shutter speed, and/or film speed that can compensate for the change." Examples of the changes that the learners encountered in learning were adjusting to the subject's motion, the light's intensity, and the desired depth of field. Questions that assess the learners' ability to solve problems similar to those practiced and defined in the goal are near transfer. A far transfer task for the photography objective, as envisioned by Bromage and Mayer (1986), might be to describe a situation in which one or more of the components in a camera are malfunctioning and the learners must think of a way to compensate for this malfunction.

With regard to near transfer, the major goal of the transfer event is to enable learners to generalize their new learning to situations in which it is appropriate, but not to overgeneralize the learning to situations in which it is not applicable. This ability requires that learners be able to recognize key features of a new situation that are similar to the critical features of similar situations that they have learned. For learners to be able to do this, they must have experienced many situations in which the noncritical features of the situation varied greatly and the critical features were present. In addition, learners must have been either explicitly instructed or encouraged to explicitly elucidate the critical features of a task that call for application of a particular skill or body of knowledge. For example, learners will be more likely to appropriately transfer cognitive strategies to generalized situations if they are explicitly informed or are encouraged to explicitly express the characteristics of a learning task that might call for a particular strategy.

Encouraging learners to create "rules of thumb" to determine whether particular new learning is appropriate can promote their ability to apply this new learning. Transfer activities may involve asking students to find examples or apply principles in real-life conditions that they would anticipate encountering subsequent to instruction. Research suggests that spontaneous transfer rarely occurs. In many cases learners require prompting to see the connections between prior learning and a new situation.

The factors that contribute to far transfer are somewhat less clearly defined by instructional research. However, Clark and Voogle (1985) suggested several activities that may influence far transfer. These include encouraging learners to develop their own (1) examples and applications, (2) analogies between new learning and prior knowledge, and (3) paraphrases of declarative knowledge lessons. Other aspects of transfer are well described in Butterfield and Nelson (1989).

REMOTIVATE AND CLOSE (PROVIDE REMEDIATION AND CLOSURE). As you will read in Chapter W-3 in the Learning Resources Web site, learners' attitudes toward learning and new content will greatly influence how well the learning will be acquired initially and how well that learning will be retained. That is why we suggest that the lesson conclude as it began: with the learner's realization of the importance of the learning. In particular, learners should be encouraged to explore how they may use this new learning immediately and what future applications they envision. Note how this event supports transfer by allowing learners to consider possible situations to which their new knowledge may, indeed, be transferred. It is not uncommon for learners to be uncertain of the applicability of newly acquired information, so the instructor should be prepared to supply much of this event for the learners. It may also be helpful to point out the learners' success with learning the content to promote their satisfaction with their own learning.

The function of closure is twofold: (1) to let the learners know that, in fact, the lesson is over, and (2) to conclude the lesson on a positive note. Anyone who has ever written something, whether it was an essay, research review, or novel, will remember the difficulties in writing a satisfying conclusion. However, it is important that learners are cued that the lesson is completed so they can consolidate their thoughts and relax their mental efforts. In a video, this is often simply cued with a change in music and rolling the credits. In a textbook, it may be signaled with a listing of references. In teacher-led instruction, closure statements may be as simple as "You've all been very attentive; we'll study a related concept tomorrow. Class is dismissed." Note how ending the lesson positively may seamlessly merge with comments regarding students' successful learning in the remotivation phase. This merging might be accomplished by adding "I can tell that you are able to use concept X very well now" to the previous statement. In generative learning environments, such statements as "time's up" from an instructor or the learner's own schedule or weariness may generate "closure" for a session.

Assessment

ASSESS LEARNING (CONDUCT ASSESSMENT). The purpose of this event is to assess whether learners have achieved the goal(s) of the instruction. Assessment information is critical to the designer, instructor, and the learners. Designers use the information to continuously revise instruction. Teachers use the information to guide their plans for remediation and scheduling. Learners use the information to evaluate the efficacy of their study strategies, as well as to guide their search for remediation. This event differs from practice in two ways: The decisions made as a result of the measures are more summative (conclusive) in nature, for they lead to grading; and assessment instruments are developed more carefully than practice to obtain a reliable and valid measurement of learning. The way the attainment of a goal is assessed is closely related to the statement of the goal. (This relationship will be discussed further in the following chapters.) As discussed earlier, pencil-and-paper tests are only one of many methods of assessing learners' ability to provide evidence of learning. Assessments may include on-the-job performance and simulations of various levels of realism and complexity.

The assess learning event may not occur during the lesson itself. It is a common practice to combine the assessment of several goals into one assessment period, such as a unit test. If assessment is delayed, then it is important to plan review particularly carefully. Also, when many goals are assessed together, instruments can become quite lengthy, and designers may be forced to make tough decisions between practicality and reliability or validity. Consequently, careful planning for the assessment event may result in the specification of more than one assessment period so that adequately reliable and valid measurements can be employed.

EVALUATE FEEDBACK AND SEEK REMEDIATION (PROVIDE FEEDBACK AND REMEDIATION). The feedback learners receive after assessment is often more cumulative—such as a percent correct or a number of objectives mastered—than the feedback accompanying practice. Although item-by-item feedback may be provided upon request, it is not generally designed into the strategy, as the feedback is planned to be more informative than corrective. This evaluation usually leads to a conclusion on the learners' (and often the instructor's) part, such as a grade or an overall judgment of the learners' mastery of the content.

The designer may plan for remediation activities for learners, such as additional practice sets or another presentation of the body of the instruction in an alternate form (e.g., with a more concrete explanation, a different medium, or a more supplantive strategy).

Remediation may address specific goals, or it may address the learning strategies that the learners apparently failed to employ.

A highly generative form of this event could be seen in the learner's thinking, "Now, what do I need to do next?" on the basis of studying information about his learning. Facilitation of this highly self-regulated learning is a worthwhile learning goal and the object of much learning strategy instruction.

Hints on Sequencing the Expanded Events of Instruction

A typical supplantive lesson generally follows this sequence of events:

1. Introduction
2. Body
3. Body
4. Body
5. Conclusion
6. Assessment

The repetition of *body* indicates that in lessons that have several goals/objectives, the goals/objectives could be grouped in such a way that after the lesson introduction, information pertaining to the first group of goals is examined and that learning is practiced; then a second group of goals is presented and practiced, and so on through the groupings of goals. The exact number of goals that should be grouped together for presentation and practice depends on the relationships of the goals, the instructional context, and the characteristics of the learners. After teaching all groups of goals, the instructor provides lesson conclusion. Then he can conduct the assessment of all goals. Sometimes assessment is not conducted during a single lesson but is conducted at the same time for several lesson goals in the form of a unit test. This procedure seems to create efficient instruction.

Of course, many highly generative learning environments,* such as microworlds, simulations, problem-based, or exploratory learning, would not be organized in this way. Learners' efforts on different prerequisite knowledge elements within the instruction would be much more dependent on the learners' own sequencing of concentration on component knowledge needed to be successful in the learning environment. However, when designing the structure of a generative learning environment, attention must be paid to the relationship of goals and their associated activities, and the framework provided by consideration of events and

their possible sequences of encounter is helpful in insuring that the learning environment is an effective one. Jonassen (2000) provides a helpful discussion of the use of activity theory to guide designers in structuring learning environments.

In most lessons, the order from introduction to body to conclusion rarely varies; however, the order of particular items within these events may not follow their numbered order or may be seamlessly combined into fewer perceivable events. They may even be interspersed across lesson sections. For example, the event involving recollection of relevant prior knowledge may start in the introduction and then be addressed more specifically in the body of the lesson. These events should be used creatively and considered a guideline rather than required protocol.

The sequencing of experiences in complex, multitopic or multiskill domains is critically important. The designer will be informed by task analysis (as well as learner and context analysis) in this activity, but must not mistake the sequence in which an expert performs a task with the sequence in which it must be learned. A major criticism of instruction based on traditional Gagné-type hierarchical analysis is that the "bottom-up" instructional sequence that is said to devolve from such analyses is frequently not ideal. We believe (and we think that Gagné would as well) that the sequence of encounter needs to be carefully designed and that such sequences are not always bottom-up. Gagné restricted the applicability of learning hierarchies to intellectual skills (discriminations, concepts, principles, and problem solving). No serious student of instructional design that we can find or think of has suggested that simple-to-complex is the ideal sequence for all material. (Chapter 16 includes practical suggestions for sequencing multitopic content.)

As mentioned earlier in the chapter, the instructional events may be provided by the instruction, prompted by the instruction, or provided by the learner. There are advantages and disadvantages to having the lesson facilitate the learners' processing or in expecting the learners to regulate their own processing. The next section will discuss these advantages and disadvantages.

Following are descriptions of several of the expanded instructional events. Decide which event (or events) is being delivered in each description.

1. A frame states that this lesson is about the "lifeboat ethic," a concept in the study of world ecology. Another frame tells students that they will learn the definition of "lifeboat ethic" and learn to recognize examples of its use.

---

*The concept *generative learning environment* will be defined and discussed in the following section.

2. In the lesson, the student is asked to recall situations in which lifeboats are used. Instruction reminds students of a previous lesson's description of the relationship between (1) waste of natural resources and (2) a nation's dependence on other countries for raw materials.

3. The first frame of the lesson shows an animated graphic, a cartoon of a globe sinking into an ocean with people rowing away. Some people are swimming in the ocean, and some are drowning. Boats are capsizing. Some people seem to be marooned on the sinking globe. A title, *Lifeboat Ethic,* is printed on the frame.

4. A frame points out that the "lifeboat ethic" has been used in this lesson to discuss exploitation of natural resources but that it can apply to national, international, and interpersonal relations in other areas. The lesson suggests that students review current periodicals to find examples of the "lifeboat ethic" in international monetary systems, military relations, and so on.

5. A frame presents a definition of "lifeboat ethic" and subsequent frames present examples in worldwide use of natural resources.

6. Scenarios are given and students are asked to classify them as examples or nonexamples of the concept "lifeboat ethic."

7. Information is given as to whether students' responses during event 6 were correct or incorrect. If they were incorrect, students are told the correct answer and why that answer is correct.

8. Examples and nonexamples of the "lifeboat ethic" are given, and students are asked to highlight portions of the scenarios that give clues as to whether the scenario is an example or nonexample. The student may check a later section to receive a more detailed explanation as to why the scenario is an example or nonexample of the "lifeboat ethic."

9. Students are presented with scenarios that are examples or nonexamples of the "lifeboat ethic," which they are to classify. No cues or explanations are given. After students have answered all questions, they are told which questions they missed, and this information is recorded on score sheets.

ALTERNATIVES IN LOCUS OF INFORMATION PROCESSING

Several years ago, we attended a discussion between Robert Gagné, one of the pioneers of the field of instructional design, and Claire Weinstein, a well-known researcher and writer in the area of learning strategies. The focus of the discussion was whether strategies should be "built" into the learner or into the materials. The issue that they addressed is critical to the field of instructional design: "Which should be the locus of control

of information processing—the instruction or the learners?" Although most of us would immediately respond that it is most desirable that the learners themselves initiate and regulate their own processing, upon careful consideration one will notice that *any* instruction is designed to guide learners' processing to some extent. For example, we do not throw jumbled words at learners for them to decipher; we organize them into sentences and paragraphs. We do not leave students to imagine what a new component of equipment looks like; we provide an illustration. We do not inundate novice learners with unstructured databases from which to interpret procedures; we ensure the availability of procedural steps in a carefully selected sequence. So the question for designers is not which is preferable—learner processing or lesson facilitation of processing—but where on the processing continuum instruction should fall. Earlier we provided examples of varieties in this continuum; now we will look closely at what these alternatives mean to the instructional designer.

The availability of potentially exploratory learning environments, such as hypermedia and some forms of intelligent tutoring systems, has created situations in which implementation of many of the key instructional variables can be placed in the hands of learners. High technology is said to empower learners from a tool-using standpoint so that the learner learns through magnification of his own intellect, not through outside manipulation of material to be learned. Jonassen has used the term "mindtools" in his discussion of this concept (1996). So the question of locus of processing control has become even more pressing because we have the capability to mediate instruction in which the learner has much of the initiative in the learning process. This option has stimulated instructional designers to consider highly generative instructional strategies, which were not seriously utilized by some instructional designers in the past. **Generative strategies** (Wittrock, 1974, Grabowski, 2004) and open learning environments (Hannafin, Land, & Oliver, 1999) are those approaches in which learners encounter the content in such a way that they are encouraged or allowed to construct their own idiosyncratic meanings from the instruction by generating their own educational goals, organization, elaborations, sequencing and emphasis of content, monitoring of understanding, and transfer to other contexts. In other words, learners "generate" the preponderance of information processing during learning by providing much of the events of instruction themselves. Such instruction has low levels of scaffolding (instructional facilitation).

The outgrowth of Wittrock's model has been studies that contrasted supplying learners with "provided instructional devices" (i.e., instructional facilitation of processing), such as summaries, headings, underlining of key ideas, and pictures, which indicate the relationships among ideas for the learner, with asking the learners to generate these devices for themselves (e.g., asking the learners to generate summaries, headings, underlining, or pictures). Generally, studies of this sort have found that learners perform better on comprehension and recall tests if they have generated associations for themselves rather than having the associations supplied. Often, this effect is explained in terms of depth of processing (Craik & Lockhart, 1972): The more the learner is required to relate information to her own cognitive structure (termed *elaboration*), the greater the depth of processing, which results in better learning. In addition to supporting better learning, such strategies for knowledgeable and able students have been purported to be highly motivating by placing learners in an autonomous situation in which they may pursue their own specific interests regarding the content. Generative instructional strategies also allow learners to engage, practice, and refine their learning strategies. However, this approach can place a high cognitive demand on learners' working memory (particularly for less knowledgeable students) by requiring them to acquire new learning while taking the responsibility for structuring that learning situation. This could lead to cognitive overload, emotional frustration, and detract from learning.

SUPPLANTIVE AND GENERATIVE STRATEGIES OF INSTRUCTION

The large amount of processing required of the learner means that successful generative learning may require a large amount of time for learners who are first encountering content. For students who have extensive and frequently used prior knowledge and strategies, generative learning can be almost automatic. Its success highly depends upon the learner's prior knowledge of the content and the breadth of learning strategies the learner possesses. Because of the very nature of the strategy, learning outcomes and interpretations of content from such an approach can be idiosyncratic. Generative strategies do not directly lead to meaningful and motivated learning (or, in other words, just because a strategy is "learner centered," nondidactic, problem-based, or any of a galaxy of generative strategies does not mean it will be effective for facilitating learning). Learners may simply be motivated to complete an activity and not necessarily engage with the content. To promote generative learning, strategies that monitor and prompt learners must be provided.

Traditionally, instructional designers have elected to use relatively **supplantive strategies** (sometimes labeled *mathemagenic**) within their instruction. This instruction, as compared to generative instruction, tends to supplant (Salomon, 1979), facilitate, or scaffold more of the information processing for the learner by providing elaborations that supply all or part of the educational goal, organization, elaboration, sequencing and emphasis of content, monitoring of understanding, and suggestions for transfer to other contexts. In other words, supplantive strategies explicitly and overtly provide much of the events of instruction, actively gaining learners' attention, informing learners of the objective, explicitly providing a preview of the lesson, and so on.

Supplantive instruction tends to conserve novice learners' cognitive capacity for acquiring skills and knowledge related to the learning task by limiting the amount of responsibility they must carry for structuring the learning situation. It may lead to more focused and predictable learning outcomes. For less knowledgeable learners, it may be more efficient than generative learning strategies: More material may be learned in a shorter period of time. Learners with a limited level of prior knowledge and a limited repertoire of learning strategies might be expected to be more successful with this approach. However, if improperly implemented, a relatively supplantive strategy may engage fewer of the learners' mental processes, leading to less complete learning. It may lead to less personally meaningful learning: The meaningfulness of the instruction depends entirely on what kinds of connection the instruction guides the learners to make (and, of course, the connections that the learner actually makes). It may appear too contrived and sterile to the learner and be less challenging and, consequently, less motivating to some learners. Over time it may "short-circuit" learners' critical information-processing skills to the point where learners are dependent rather than independent learners.

It is important to note that instruction on both ends of the supplantive–generative continuum, as well as those combinations in between, can (1) lead to personal interpretations of knowledge, (2) involve high levels of activity on the learner's part, and (3) be interesting, relevant, and motivating. Some designers erroneously infer that the learner is a passive receiver of information in a supplantive lesson. For learning to occur, learners must actively process information. The difference in the two poles is how much scaffolding, support, or prompting is provided to the learner to encourage and bolster this processing.

Mathemagenic refers to processes or events that stimulate learning. The term, coined by Ernest Rothkopf in 1970, is composed of two Greek roots: *mathe* (learning) and *genic* (giving birth to).

Although the comparable advantages of these two diverse forms of environment have not yet been thoroughly empirically investigated, several bodies of theory and research suggest that neither approach is universally superior but that many factors may influence the efficacy of one instructional approach over the other. Among the related research areas are the following: research on generative versus mathemagenic teaching methods (Jonassen, 1985; Osborne & Wittrock, 1985; Wittrock, 1974), learner control in computer-based instruction (Hannafin, 1984; Steinberg, 1977; Tennyson, 1984), discovery versus expository learning (Herman, 1969; Ray, 1961), and cognitive capacity and allocation of mental resources (Britton, Westbrook, & Holdredge, 1978; Burton, Niles, & Lalik, 1986; Craik & Lockhart, 1972; Duncan, 1980; Watkins, 1983).

This research and theory suggests that the decision as to whether to design instruction with more generative or more supplantive strategies is not a simple one. As illustrated in Figure 7.2, the decision is like a balancing act. Generative strategies require greater mental effort and consequently lead to greater depth of processing that results in better learning. However, cognitive capacity in the form of working memory is limited, so if learners are required to carry too much of the instructional burden, they may be overloaded and unable to learn. When designing organizational strategies, the designer must balance these two competing demands: the need to require sufficient mental effort to lead toward learning, and the need to support the learners' processing sufficiently in a way that does not overload their working memory.

TYPES OF LEARNING AND INSTRUCTIONAL STRATEGIES

In Chapter 5, we described the considerable effort that can go into finding out as much as we can about the nature of learning tasks for instruction that we are designing. And, as we previewed in that chapter, this information about the cognitive requirements of different learning tasks has substantial bearing on what sorts of experience would be most helpful in achieving those learning tasks. As we said in Chapter 5, "Some learning tasks are substantially different from others in terms of the amount and kind of cognitive effort required in learning, in the kinds of learning conditions that support their learning, and in the ways to test for their achievement."

Imagine, if you will, one group of students in a physical education class is practicing free-throws on the basketball court, another group of students is learning what different actions are "fouls," and yet another has been challenged by the coach to formulate a strategy for tomorrow's game. As you know from your reading of Chapter 5, each of these learning activities is directed at a different kind of learning task, in this case a psychomotor skill, principles (with new concept learning as well), and problem-solving. As you also already know, the cognitive requirements for these different learning activities are different. Now we want to think about how the different cognitive requirements for different types of learning are reflected in the events of instruction.

When you reflect on an instructional event and a particular type of learning, such as thinking about practice

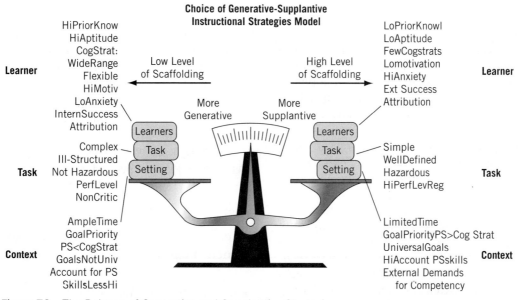

Figure 7.2 The Balance of Generative and Supplantive Strategies

for concept learning, or learning guidance for problem solving, or feedback for psychomotor learning, you are beginning to think at a level for which there is an enormous body of research and practical experience to guide you. Chapters 8 to 15 will make an effort to point out the salient features of facilitating learning for declarative knowledge, concepts, procedures, principles, problem solving, cognitive strategies, attitudes, and psychomotor skills. These chapters explore how events of instruction can best facilitate learning for the learning that is at hand. For more background on the research and theory behind this idea, see Ragan and Smith (2004).

Cognitive Load Theory

A considerable body of research has been conducted on the concept of "cognitive load." (e.g., Renkl & Atkinson, 2003; Mayer & Moreno, 2003; van Merriënboer et al., 2003). The central interest of cognitive load theory is "how constraints on our working memory help determine what kinds of instruction are effective" (Renkl & Atkinson, 2003, p.16).

Complex learning tasks may possess so much "intrinsic load" that overload occurs and learning suffers. Intrinsic load is load resulting from the number of elements a learner must simultaneously attend to in order to understand the material being learned. Mayer and Moreno described this overload as occurring when "the learner's intended cognitive processing exceeds the learner's available cognitive capacity" (Mayer & Moreno, 2003, p. 43). Essential processing refers to cognitive processing that is required by the learning task. Incidental processing is those cognitive processing demands that are built into the instruction, or "primed by the design of the learning task." For example, background music added to a narrated animation requires incidental processing and for that reason may contribute to excessive cognitive load.

Many of the currently popular techniques in technology-using instruction can contribute to overload. Here is Mayer and Moreno's description of a typical event: "A student is interesting in understanding how lighting works. She goes to a multimedia encyclopedia and clicks on the entry for 'lightning.' On the screen appears a 2-min animation depicting the steps in lighting formation along with concurrent on-screen text describing the steps in lightning formation. The on-screen text is presented at the bottom on the screen, so while the student is reading she cannot view the animation, and while she is viewing the animation she cannot read the text" (Mayer & Moreno, 2003, p. 45).

Mayer and Moreno (2003) described a number techniques for reducing cognitive load. All of the these techniques have received extensive treatment for many years in the instructional design and message design lit-

erature. Throughout this text, for example, you will find recommendations for most of these methods, and more. As well, texts on instructional message design such as Fleming and Levie (1993) and instructional text design such as Misanchuk (1992) supply many of the same recommendations as those provided by CLT. However, the focus and theoretic perspective provided by CLT have stimulated a great deal of helpful supporting research, and the following list provides strategy suggestions for which the relationship between cognitive load and the techniques themselves is clear.

Off-loading: moving some essential processing from the visual channel to the auditory channel in cases in which the essential processing in the learner's visual channel is greater than the cognitive capacity in that channel. For example, some things that a designer may wish to place in an already complex display, such as an aircraft instrument set—perhaps additional explanatory material—might be described in narration instead of added to the visual display.

Segmenting: allowing time between successive bit-size segments in cases in which both channels are overloaded by essential processing demands. We have all seen good instructors pause at important times to allow the learners to "absorb" information before moving on, and we've all seen both live instructors and mediated instruction in which the instructor charges on regardless, leaving everyone in the dust.

Pretraining: Providing instruction on prerequisites, such as training in the names and characteristics of components before training in their use.

Weeding: Eliminating interesting but extraneous material to reduce processing of it. Weeding may involve getting rid of the deadwood and superfluous ornamentation, either cognitive or sensory. It may also involve eliminating interesting but extraneous material to reduce processing of extraneous material when the combined load of essential and incidental processing exceeds cognitive capacity.

Signaling: Providing advance cues for how to process the material to reduce the processing demands of extraneous material which may be present.

Aligning: Placing printed words near corresponding parts of graphics to reduce the need for visual scanning.

Eliminating Redundancy: Avoiding the presentation of identical streams of printed and spoken words.

Synchronizing: simultaneous presentation of video with related audio material.

Individualizing: providing instruction in multiple forms, matched to the aptitudes of learners.

Although none of these recommendations is new or unique to CLT, each of them has been supported with research specifically based on the CLT theoretic perspective. CLT is a research-based approach which can help provide guidance on how much or what kind of supplantation may be needed, support which may be needed even within relatively generative learning environments, and the theory has supplied many helpful examples.

Principles for Determining Optimal Degree of Instructional Support

We have proposed some principles for making decisions regarding which side of the balance to lean to in design, depending upon factors within the learners, the learning context, and the learning task. Given the current state of theory and research, we can only hypothesize univariate principles, hence the statement "all else being equal" preceding each principle.* Even these univariate relationships are tentative, given the current status of research and theory with these variables.

LEARNERS' CHARACTERISTICS. Learners' characteristics are the most critical factor influencing the effective balance between generative and supplantive approaches.

1. All else being equal, the higher the level of prior knowledge, the more generative the instructional strategy can be.
2. All else being equal, instruction for learners who have a large and sophisticated repertoire of cognitive strategies can be more generative.
3. All else being equal, instruction for learners with generally high aptitude can be more generative.
3a. When learners possess aptitudes which specifically relate to generative strategy cognitive demands, more generative strategies can be employed (Shute & Towle, 2003).
4. All else being equal, instruction for learners who have a high level of motivation and interest can be more generative.
5. All else being equal, instruction for learners who have high levels of anxiety should have supplantive strategies available.
6. All else being equal, instruction for learners who tend to attribute learning success or failure to factors external to themselves should begin at a more supplantive point on the continuum and gradually move to a more generative level.

*All else is never equal, of course; however, research investigating interactions of these variables is not currently available.

CONTEXT CHARACTERISTICS. Context factors also significantly influence where a lesson falls on the generative–supplantive continuum.

1. All else being equal, when instructional time is limited, the instructional strategy should be more supplantive.
2. All else being equal, when goals for "learning to learn" are given higher priority than goals for domain-specific skills, a more generative strategy should be emphasized.
3. All else being equal, when high achievement of domain-specific goals is a higher priority than "learning to learn" skill, then a more supplantive strategy should be emphasized.
4. All else being equal, when achievement of domain-specific goals is universal for all learners (all learners are expected to learn to at least a minimum level of competence), then a more supplantive strategy should be available.
5. All else being equal, when the educational agency has high accountability, then more supplantive strategies should be available.

LEARNING TASKS. The nature of the learning task should also influence the effective balance between generative and supplantive strategies.

1. All else being equal, the higher in the intellectual skills (closer to domain-specific problem solving), the more generative the strategy.
2. All else being equal, the more complex the problem, the more supplantive the start point of the instruction, and the more critical the progression toward more largely generative instruction.
3. All else being equal, in situations in which learners' misconceptions during the learning process could translate into physical or emotional hazards for themselves or others, a more supplantive strategy should be employed.
4. All else being equal, learning goals that are associated with a critically high level of competence and consistency should utilize somewhat more supplantive strategies.

OVERALL PRINCIPLES. Two overarching principles can guide designers in determining the optimal level of instructional support.

1. An optimal instructional strategy goes as far toward the generative pole as possible while still providing sufficient support for learners to achieve learning in the time possible, with a lim-

ited and acceptable amount of frustration, anxiety, and danger.

2. During instruction in a particular knowledge area/learning task, the instruction should progressively move toward the generative pole, as learners gain skill, knowledge, motivation, and confidence.

We have described the expanded events of instruction in two ways to reflect both generative and supplantive strategy options. Using the events as labeled here, instruction can be designed so that the learners take more responsibility for their processing or so that the instruction itself guides the learners' processing. Of course, the degree of instructional support can be varied from learner to learner and adjusted to class needs as part of formative evaluation. The following chapters will continue to present these options so that you will be prepared to design on either end of the continuum or somewhere in the middle.

Alternatives to Instruction

We cannot leave the topic of instructional strategies without discussing a close relative: performance improvement aids and strategies.

As you may recall, in defining *instruction* as well as *instructional design* in Chapter 1, considerable care was taken to differentiate instruction from other related activities which may be confused with it. Performance support systems are alternatives to instruction and are often preferable because they are typically less expensive to develop and implement than equally effective instruction. Although performance support systems come in many forms, a particularly useful and interesting sort are *electronic performance support systems (EPSS)*. An EPSS is an electronic device, built into a larger device that provides information on how to operate, repair, or use the larger device.

A memorable and historically significant EPSS was one of the first devices of its sort. In the 1970s, Xerox Corporation's staff of engineers, psychologists, and educators at the Palo Alto Research Center (PARC) grappled with the problem of performing routine maintenance and fixing common malfunctions in office copiers, such as replacing paper, fixing a paper jam, and adding toner. Before Xerox's early EPSS, the copier user typically needed to use a manual that was often missing, interpret cryptic flowcharts printed on sheets glued to inside panels, and attend training seminars. The brainstorm was to use the display already in place on the Xerox machine (here, finally, we get to use the term correctly), adding to its function of showing the number of copies selected, collating options, and so forth. The addition was context-embed-ded instructions. The person who is credited with this innovation, John Seeley Brown, was for many years director of PARC, an organization from which has come many significant technological innovations as well as important ideas in learning and instruction (Suchman, 1987).

Fundamental to the concept of a performance support system, and well-exemplified by the Xerox instruction panel, is the idea that if job aids are appropriately situated within the workplace, they can support thinking (cognition) and work in ways that can reduce the amount of learning a person needs to engage in. Because learning to do something is generally more time-consuming than just doing it, performance support systems can save both time and money.

Performance support systems are widely used now to either replace training or supplement it. The concept of the EPSS has expanded from the earliest embodiments to include provision of learning experiences as well as information and advice. (Gery, 1991). An EPSS may also include tools such as word processors, spreadsheets, and databases that can be used *in situ* for learning and problem solving.

In Chapter 3, Context Analysis, the idea was stressed that instruction should only be developed if there is a need for it, and examples are provided there of situations in which something other than instruction was the preferred alternative. And, as noted in Chapters 1 and 20, many people who do instructional design see themselves within a broader context of performance engineering, in which provision of instruction is not the only way to help people function well at a job (see also, Raybould, 1995).

E X E R C I S E S   C

1. Following are descriptions of events that occurred during a lesson. Identify whether the strategy leans more on the side of a generative strategy (G) or a supplantive strategy (S).

a. Students underline key points in a print-based lesson.

b. Students create their own mythical countries that exemplify the concept "fascism."

c. Students watch a video-based summary of factors leading to the Civil War.

d. Students select from a number of instances those that represent the concept "loose constructionism."

e. Students run a number of sample computer programs using subroutines and determine which procedural rules must be used to make programs that don't "crash."

2. Strategy A and Strategy B describe two instructional strategies to teach the same relational rule—the relationship of pitch to length, tightness, and thickness of a plucked string. One of the strategies is more generative; one is more supplantive. Write the type of strategy (A or B) in the blanks, and explain your answers.

_____ More Generative

_____ More Supplantive

STRATEGY A

Materials: Violin, other stringed instruments, tom-tom and other drums, whistle with sliding stopper, piano, xylophone, elastic string, and rubber bands.

Procedures: Teacher statement: We've been talking in this science unit about the "bounce of sound." You will remember that sound is caused by the vibration of the molecules in an object. For instance, when I strike this bell, I set the molecules in the bell vibrating. This causes sound. Yesterday we discussed what causes the pitch of a vibrating object to be low or high. The pitch of the sound an object makes when struck or plucked depends upon how fast the molecules in the object vibrate. Remember when we talk about high and low pitch (demonstrates) that we're not talking about loud and soft (demonstrates). A high pitch can be loud (demonstrates) or soft (demonstrates). Today we'll talk about why when some objects are struck, their molecules vibrate more rapidly and they have a higher pitch, and when other objects are struck, their molecules vibrate more slowly and they have a lower pitch. The pitch of the sound an object makes when struck or plucked depends upon the length, tightness, or thickness of the object. (Writes the words *thickness, length,* and *tightness* on chalkboard.)

Demonstration 1: Teacher demonstrates with running explanation that the thickness of the strings on a violin affects the pitch of the strings. Teacher presents the principle that the thicker the string, the lower the pitch.

Practice 1: Teacher asks students to experiment with various thicknesses and asks such questions as "What will happen to the pitch with that string, Judith?"

Demonstration 2: Teacher demonstrates with running explanation that tightening and loosening a string on the violin affects the pitch of the string. Teacher presents the principle that the tighter the string, the higher the pitch.

Practice 2: Students make predictions about the pitch of various degrees of tightness of a string and then try out their predictions, noting the pitches and the accuracy of their predictions.

Demonstration 3: Teacher has a student shorten or lengthen string and asks students to tell the teacher how this affects the pitch produced. Teacher presents the generalization that the shorter the string, the higher the pitch.

Practice 3: Students make predictions about the pitch with various lengths of string and then try out their predictions, noting the pitches and the accuracy of their predictions.

Demonstrations 4–10: Teacher demonstrates the principle on a variety of musical instruments and has the students predict the effects of changes in length, thickness, and tightness upon the pitch of the instruments. Students try out other instruments on their own. The lesson continues until the principles are obviously learned and the students' predictions are consistently true.

STRATEGY B

Materials: Ukuleles, xylophones, sliding whistles, rubber bands, chimes, drums, and strings.

Procedures: Teacher's statement: I saw many of you at the symphony orchestra's concert yesterday. Which songs were your favorites? Which instruments did you like the best? Have you ever wondered what it is about an instrument that enables it to make higher and lower pitches? Today we have a number of instruments with which you may experiment to try to find out what makes the pitch of instruments go from low to high. Why don't you start with a ukulele? Try to figure out what makes a ukulele string make a higher or lower tone.

Stimulating questions:

- Yes, I can feel that "buzzy" feeling when you strike the chime. What causes that? What happens with the shorter chime?

- Yes, striking harder on the xylophone makes the sound louder. Is that the same as higher? How can you make the pitch higher?

- How can you find out if thicker strings make lower tones?

- Carlos, what do you think of Sheila's idea that the pitch of the whistle has to do with how far the slide is pushed in?

- Zenia, how can you check out your guess about what makes one chime's pitch high and another's low?

- Kenneth, the pitch of your voice is very low, but Sue's voice is high. Why do you think that is so? Where can you go to find out?

Components of Instructional Strategies

Organizational Strategies	Delivery Strategies	Management Strategies
• Macro-Strategies—scope and sequence structures	• Media selection	• Scheduling
• Micro-Strategies—expanded instructional events	• Grouping strategies	• Acquisition of resources

Expanded Instructional Events

Introduction	Body	Conclusion	Assessment
• Activate attention	• Recall prior knowledge	• Summarize and review	• Assess performance
• Establish instructional purpose	• Process information	• Transfer knowledge	• Evaluate feedback and remediate
• Arouse interest and motivation	• Focus attention	• Remotivate and close	
• Preview lesson	• Employ learning strategies		
	• Practice		
	• Evaluate feedback		

Figure 7.3 Summary Diagram for Chapter 7

3. Discuss as completely as you can the comparative advantages and disadvantages of more generative and more supplantive strategies. Use examples from Question 2 to provide a context for your answer.

4. Suppose you were planning the organizational strategy to teach hiring practices that are in accordance with new federal laws to a group of fifty midlevel managers. The managers have only a three-hour class period available for the training. The learners are quite skilled but impatient with anything other than "the facts." The manager who will be delivering the instruction is very knowledgeable in the content but less skilled in modes of delivery other than lecture/discussion. Should you use a more supplantive or more generative strategy for this lesson? Explain your answer.

SUMMARY

During the *Develop the instructional strategy* stage, we take the information that we acquired during the analysis stage and use it to help us make decisions about the instructional strategy. At the lesson level, the designer can use the expanded instructional events as the framework of the lesson. A critical decision that designers make is whether to design the strategy to be more supplantive or generative in nature. At the conclusion of this stage, the designer has developed a strat-

egy for the lesson. The lessons themselves are not produced yet. In other words, they are not in their mediated, or final, form. Figure 7.3 summarizes key points in this chapter.

EXTENDED EXAMPLE

Go to the Learning Resources Web site for a continuation the instructional design of the Photography Basics course. For this chapter, a discussion of instructional strategy approach from the generative–supplantive standpoint will be provided to overview the thinking behind specific instructional strategy decisions that will be illustrated for subsequent chapters which will discuss in detail strategies for different types of learning (Chapters 8 to 15).

READINGS AND REFERENCES

Ausubel, D. P., Novak, J. D., & Hanesian, H. (1968). *Educational psychology: A cognitive view* (2nd ed.). New York: Holt, Rinehart, & Winston.

Beukhof, G. (1986). *Designing instructional texts: Interaction between text and learner.* Paper presented at the meeting of the American Educational Research Association, San Francisco.

Britton, B. K., Westbrook, R. D., & Holdredge, T. S. (1978). Reading and cognitive capacity usage: Effects of text difficulty. *Journal of Experimental Psychology, Human Learning, and Memory, 4*(6), 582–591.

Bromage, B. K., & Mayer, R. E. (1986). Quantitative and qualitative effects of repetition on learning from technical text. *Journal of Educational Psychology, 78*(4) 271–278.

Brown, J. S., Collins, A., & Duguid, P. (1989). Situated cognition and the culture of learning. *Educational Researcher, 18*(1), 32–42.

Bruner, J. S. (1960). *The process of education.* New York: Vintage Books.

Bruner, J. S. (1966). *Toward a theory of instruction.* Cambridge, MA: Harvard University Press.

Burton, J. K., Niles, J. A., & Lalik, R. M. (1986). Cognitive capacity engagement during and following intersperse mathemagenic questions. *Journal of Educational Psychology, 78*(2), 147–152.

Butterfield, E. C., & Nelson, G. D. (1989). Theory and practice of teaching for transfer. *Educational Technology Research and Development, 37*(3), 5–38.

Clark, R. E., & Voogle, A. (1985). Transfer of training principles for instructional design. *Educational Communication and Technology Journal, 33*(2), 113–123.

Craik, F. I., & Lockhart, R. S. (1972). Levels of processing: A framework for memory research. *Journal of Verbal Learning and Verbal Behavior, 11,* 671–684.

Dempsey, J., & Sales, G. (Eds.) (1993). *Interactive instruction and feedback.* Englewood Cliffs, NJ: Educational Technology Publications.

Dewey, J. (1924). *Democracy and education.* New York: Macmillan.

Dick, W. (1986–87). Instructional design and the curriculum development process. *Educational Leadership, 44*(4), 54–56.

Duncan, J. (1980). The demonstration of capacity limitation. *Cognitive Psychology, 12,* 75–96.

Fleming, M., & Levie, W. H. (Eds.) (1993). *Instructional message design: Principles from the behavioral sciences.* (2nd ed.). Englewood Cliffs, NJ: Educational Technology Publications.

Foos, P. W., Mora, J. J., & Tkacz, S. (1994). Student study techniques and the generation effect. *Journal of Educational Psychology, 80*(4), 567–576.

Foshay, W. R., & Foshay, A. W. (1981). A father and son exchange letters. *Educational Leadership, 38,* 621–625.

Gagné, R. M. (1972). *The conditions of learning* (2nd ed.). New York: Holt, Rinehart, & Winston.

Gery, G. (1991). *Electronic performance support systems: How and why to remake the workplace through the strategic application of technology.* Boston: Weingarten Publications.

Grabowski, B. L. (2004). Generative learning contributions to the design of instruction and learning. In D. H. Jonassen (Ed.), *Handbook of research for educational communications and technology* (pp. 719–743). Mahwah, NJ: Erlbaum.

Greenfield, P. M. (1984). A theory of the teacher in the learning activities of everyday life. In B. Rogoff and J. Lave (Eds.), *Everyday cognition* (pp. 117–138). Cambridge, MA: Harvard University Press.

Hannafin, M. J. (1984). Guidelines for using locus of instructional control in the design of computer-assisted instruction. *Journal of Instructional Development, 7*(3), 9–14.

Hannafin, M. J., Land, S., & Oliver, K. (1999). Open learning environments: Foundations, methods, and models. In C. M. Reigeluth (Ed.), *Instructional-design theories and models: A new paradigm of instructional theory* (pp. 115–140). Mahwah, NJ: Erlbaum.

Herman, G. (1969). Learning by discovery: A critical review of studies. *Journal of Experimental Education, 38,* 58–72.

Husic, F. T., Linn, M. C., & Sloane, K. D. (1989). Adapting instruction to the cognitive demands of learning to program. *Journal of Educational Psychology, 81*(4), 570–583.

Jonassen, D. H. (1985). Generative learning vs. mathemagenic control of text processing. In D. H. Jonassen (Ed.), *Technology of text II* (pp. 9–45). Englewood Cliffs, NJ: Educational Technology Publications.

Jonassen, D. H. (1996). *Computers in the classroom: Mindtools for critical thinking.* Englewood Cliffs, NJ: Merrill.

Jonassen, D. H. (2000). Revisiting activity theory as a framework for designing student-centered learning environments. In D. H. Jonassen & S. M. Land (Eds.), *Theoretical foundations of learning environments* (pp. 89–121). Mahwah, NJ: Erlbaum

Jonassen, D. H., & Cole, P. (1993). Learner generated vs. instructor provided analyses of semantic relationships. *Proceedings of AECT Conference, 18,* 426–439.

Kenny, R. F. (1995). The generative effects of instructional organizers with computer-based interactive video. *Journal of Educational Computing Research, 12*(3), 275–296.

Kourilsky, M., & Wittrock, M. C. (1992). Generative teaching: An enhancement strategy for the learning of economics in cooperative groups. *American Educational Research Journal, 29*(4), 861–876.

Land, S. M. & Hannafin, M. J. (2000). Student-centered learning environments. In D. H. Jonassen & S. M. Land (Eds.), *Theoretical foundations of learning environments* (pp. 1–23). Mahwah, NJ: Erlbaum.

Laurillard, D. (1988). The pedagogical limitations of generative student models. *Instructional Science, 17,* 235–250.

Mayer, R. E. & Moreno, R. (2003). Nine ways to reduce cognitive load in multimedia learning. *Educational Psychologist, 38*(1), 43–52.

Misanchuk, E. R. (1992). *Preparing instructional text: Document design using desktop publishing.* Englewood Cliffs, NJ: Educational Technology.

Mory, E. H. (2004). Feedback research revisited. In D. H. Jonassen (Ed.), *Handbook of research for educational communications and technology* (pp. 745–783). Mahwah, NJ: Erlbaum.

Nesbit, J. C., & Hunka, S. (1987). A method for sequencing instructional objectives which minimizes memory load. *Instructional Science, 16,* 137–150.

Orey, M. A., Orey, J. R., Jones, M. G., & Stanley, L. S. (1991). Integrating cognitive theory into Gagné's instructional events. *RTD Proceedings, 16,* 625–630.

Osborne, R., & Wittrock, M. (1985). The generative learning model and its implications for science education. *Studies in Science Education, 12,* 59–87.

Peck, S. (1988). Informal presentation at the University of Texas, Austin, TX.

Posner, G. J., & Rudnitsky, A. N. (1978). *Course design: A guide to curriculum development for teachers.* New York: Longman.

Posner, G. J., & Strike, K. A. (1976). A categorization scheme for principles of sequencing content. *Review of Educational Research, 46*(4), 665–690.

Ragan, T. J. & Smith, P. L. (2004). Conditions theory and models for designing instruction. In D. H. Jonassen (Ed.), *Handbook of research on educational communications and technology* (pp. 623–649). Mahawh, NJ: Erlbaum.

Ray, W. E. (1961). Pupil discovery vs. direct instruction. *Journal of Experimental Education, 29*(3), 271–280.

Raybould, B. (1995). Performance support engineering: An emerging development methodology for enabling organizational learning. *Performance Improvement Quarterly, 8*(1), 7–22.

Reigeluth, C. M. (1979). In search of a better way to organize instruction: The elaboration theory. *Journal of Instructional Development, 6,* 40–46.

Reigeluth, C. M. (1983). The elaboration theory of instruction. In C. M. Reigeluth (Ed.), *Instructional design theories and models* (pp. 335–382). Hillsdale, NJ: Erlbaum.

Reigeluth, C. M. (1987). Lesson blueprints based on the elaboration theory of instruction. In C. M. Reigeluth (Ed.), *Instructional theories in action* (pp. 245–288). Hillsdale, NJ: Erlbaum.

Reigeluth, C. M. (Ed.) (1999). *Instructional-design theories and models: A new paradigm of instructional theory.* Mahwah, NJ: Erlbaum.

Renkl, A., & Atkinson, R. K. (2003). Structuring the transition from example study to problem solving in cognitive skill acquisition: A cognitive load perspective. *Educational Psychologist, 38*(1), 15–22.

Rothkopf, E. Z. (1970). The concept of mathemagenic activities. *Review of Educational Research, 40,* 325–336.

Royer, J. M. (1979). Theories of the transfer of learning. *Educational Psychologist, 14,* 53–69.

Salomon, G. (1979). *Interaction of media, cognition, and learning.* San Francisco: Jossey-Bass.

Shute, V. J. (1993). A comparison of learning enviornments: All that glitters. . . . In S. P. Lajoie and S. J. Derry (Eds.), *Computers as cognitive tools* (pp. 47–73). Hillsdale, NJ: Erlbaum.

Shute, V. J., Glaser, R., & Raghavan, K. (1989). Inference and discovery in an exploratory laboratory. In P. L. Ackerman, R. J. Sternberg, & R. Glaser (Eds.), *Learning and individual differences: Advances in theory and research* (pp. 279–326). New York: W.H. Freeman.

Shute, V., & Towle, B. (2003). Adaptive E-learning. *Educational Psychologist, 38,* 2, 105–114.

Smith, P. L., & Ragan, T. J. (1993). Designing instructional feedback for different learning outcomes. In J. Dempsey & G. Sales (Eds.), *Interactive instruction and feedback* (pp. 75–103). Englewood Cliffs, NJ: Educational Technology Publications.

Snow, R. E., & Swanson, J. (1992). Instructional psychology: Aptitude, adaptation, and assessment. *Annual Review of Psychology, 43,* 583–626.

Steinberg, E. (1977). Review of student control in computer-assisted instruction. *Journal of Computer-Based Instruction, 3,* 84–90.

Suchman, L. (1987). Plans and situated actions: The problem of human-machine communication. New York: Cambridge University Press.

Tennyson, R. (1984). Application of artificial intelligence methods to computer-based instructional design: The Minnesota adaptive instructional system. *Journal of Instructional Development, 7,* 17–22.

Tobias, S. (1982). When do instructional methods make a difference? *Educational Researcher, 11*(4), 4–9.

van Merriënboer, J. J. G., Kirschner, P. A., & Kester, L. (2003). Taking the load off a learner's mind: Instructional design for complex learning. *Educational Psychologist, 38*(1), 5–13.

Watkins, D. (1983). Depth of processing and the quality of learning outcomes. *Instructional Science, 12,* 49–58.

Wedman, J. F., & Smith, P. L. (1989). An examination of two approaches to organizing instruction. *International Journal of Instructional Media, 16*(4), 293–303.

Wetzel, C. D. (1993). Generative aspects of the computer based educational software system. *Instructional Science, 21,* 269–293.

Whitener, E. M. (1989). A meta-analytic review of the effect on learning of the interaction between prior achievement and instructional support. *Review of Educational Research, 59*(1), 65–86.

Winn, W. (1989, March). *Rethinking cognitive approaches to instructional design.* A paper presented at the annual meeting of the American Educational Research Association, San Francisco.

Wittrock, M. C. (1974). Learning as a generative process. *Educational Psychologist, 11,* 87–95.

Wittrock, M. C. (1992). Generative learning processes of the brain. *Educational Psychologist, 27*(4), 531–542.

STRATEGIES FOR DECLARATIVE KNOWLEDGE INSTRUCTION

CHAPTER OBJECTIVES

At the conclusion of this chapter, you should be able to do the following:

- Recognize three forms of declarative knowledge.
- Identify and describe three critical cognitive activities involved in learning declarative knowledge.
- Given a declarative knowledge objective, design strategy plans for that objective.

INTRODUCTION

In this chapter and subsequent ones (particularly Chapters 9 through 12), we will discuss strategies for teaching the components that make up the ability to learn to do domain-specific problem solving. The most basic of the prerequisite knowledge components that make up this type of problem solving is declarative knowledge. Although declarative knowledge may be taught for its own sake, the need for it is often part of a subordinate problem-solving goal. Instruction on declarative knowledge related to a problem-solving goal may precede introduction of the problem-solving instruction, be taught concurrently at the appropriate point in a problem-solving lesson, or be available as a resource during problem-solving lessons. The sequence and organization of this instruction depends on whether the declarative knowledge goals are legitimate goals in their own right or whether they are useful only as they relate to a particular problem-solving goal.

A REVIEW OF DECLARATIVE KNOWLEDGE LEARNING

Declarative knowledge involves "knowing that" something is the case. It is often what we mean when we say we want learners to "understand" a content. You may recall from Chapter 5 that the term *verbal information* is also frequently used to refer to the same sort of learning as declarative knowledge. Words that we often use to describe declarative knowledge performance are *explain, describe, summarize,* and *list*.

Although declarative knowledge learning is sometimes disparaged as mere rote memorization, uninteresting, and unimportant, it is the substance of much of our thinking. Declarative knowledge is a critical part of what we learn throughout life. Although the acquisition of declarative knowledge is often equated with "rote learning," rarely is it or should it be acquired via such a strategy. To the contrary, declarative knowledge is generally acquired within meaningful structures.

When people say that a person is "educated," often what they mean is that the person possesses a large amount of declarative knowledge. During the Persian Gulf War in 1991, surveys indicated that many students were unable to locate countries in the Middle East, an astonishing deficit. The task of locating and labeling the countries in the Middle East is a declarative knowledge learning task. The recent outcry over school students' lack of "cultural literacy" often refers to learners' lack of declarative knowledge.

Declarative knowledge is also strongly tied to other types of learning. For example, the "materials" used in much of concept learning entails the understanding of ideas and how they relate to each other. Such understandings are declarative knowledge. Also, the learning of procedures and psychomotor skills requires another form of declarative knowledge: the recall of a list of steps necessary to complete the skill. Finally, declarative knowledge is necessary to understand problems in order to solve them.

Although declarative knowledge is a major type of learning, there are some important distinctions that can be made within this category of learning. Gagné and Briggs (1979) identified three subtypes, each of which involves slightly different cognitive processes: labels and names, facts and lists, and organized discourse.

The learning of **labels and names** involves pairing of information. This type of learning requires that learners mentally make a connecting link between two elements. This link may be propositional or image-based. Learning of labels is more difficult when the number of labels to be learned increases, when similarity among information pairs increases, or when connections between idea pairs is less meaningful.

The learning of labels and names is sometimes referred to as *paired associate learning* and is somewhat distinct from the other two forms of declarative knowledge. Examples of learning labels and names are foreign language vocabulary learning, learning the names of the state capitols, learning the valences of the chemical elements, and learning to label the parts of a camera. In each case, a pair is linked together, as in "hat" to "sombrero" or "Illinois" to "Springfield" or "oxygen" to "minus 2" or a particular image to "shutter release lever." It is worth noting that learning labels does not necessarily require learning the meaning of the two linked ideas but rather learning that one thing links to the other. In learning that *sombrero* is the Spanish word for *hat*, we aren't necessarily learning what a hat is—that is a concept learning task (which we will discuss in Chapter 9). When learners do not already possess concepts, it makes the learning of labels much more difficult because they lack meaning.

The learning of **facts and lists** is fundamentally propositional in nature. A fact is usually a statement that describes a relationship between or among concepts, such as "Ann Richards was the governor of Texas in 1991." A list is a group of elements that must be remembered together. The order of elements in a list may or may not be important. To be remembered, facts and lists must be made meaningful by integrating them with prior knowledge. The isolated, nonmeaningful memorization of facts is rarely a worthwhile learning goal.

Facts and lists may, however, be learned as individual facts, seemingly apart from other information (e.g., "The discount store closes at 7:00 P.M. on Fridays.") and as networks of interconnected information, such as the local football team's wins and losses. The discount store's closing time is a meaningful thing (for those who shop there), even though it is an isolated fact. The more isolated a fact is, the more difficult it is to learn; consequently, if we manage to remember when the discount store closes on Fridays, it is generally because that is important information to us. Once we have some knowledge, it becomes increasingly easy to add to it. As the network or knowledge base becomes larger and more complex, it also becomes easier to add yet more. This seeming impossibility (the larger and more complex the knowledge base, the easier it is to add to it) is a result of the way in which we learn declarative knowledge—linking, elaborating, and organizing. Having a large knowledge base makes it easier to acquire more knowledge.

The learning of **organized discourse** is also propositional in nature. Whereas facts and lists are discrete, however, the phenomenon of "discourse" itself involves the comprehension of a thread of meaning that runs through an extensive body of information, such as a passage of prose. The archetype for discourse learning is learning through reading a text (typically expository text). For the activity to result in learning, the discourse, which is itself an integrated body of knowledge, must be tied to existing knowledge.

Novice designers often confuse learning connected discourse and learning concepts. As a matter of fact, it is in the midst of conceptual learning that we divide declarative knowledge from intellectual skills. According to Gagné's scheme, which we employ here, much of what is sometimes referred to by others as *concept learning* is described as *connected discourse learning*. For example, "perestroika" is a concept that can be understood in the declarative knowledge sense; the term literally means "building changes" or "redoing construction." With such declarative knowledge, a learner can interpret a conversation or text that uses this word. In addition, having declarative knowledge allows the learner to do the following: (1) explain the meaning and etiology of *perestroika* in its recent use, which refers to economic reforms in Russia; (2) describe the history of the term; and even (3) make inferences, such as making associations between the conceptual knowledge and prior knowledge. The propositional network associated with the concept "perestroika" may be rich and highly differentiated. The strategies to teach this sort of conceptual knowledge are the same as those used to teach connected discourse. But the sort of concept learning that we have categorized under intellectual skills (along with principles and problem solving) is a different kind of learning. It involves pattern recognition productions (i.e., if the presented instance has certain features, then it is an example of *perestroika*). Concept learning as an intellectual skill is a classifying rule.

Neither type of "concept"—declarative knowledge or classifying rule—is a superior kind of learning. Each type of learning meets certain requirements as a basis for future learning or application to life circumstances. The only reason that we make a differentiation between them is that the instructional strategies required for learning are quite different. (To read more about these two ways of looking at "concept," see Tessmer, Wilson, & Driscoll, 1990).

A final point is the sequence in which declarative knowledge and intellectual skills should be learned. We tend to fall somewhere between Anderson (1985) and R. Gagné (1985) regarding the prerequisite relationship of declarative knowledge to intellectual skill (procedural) knowledge. Gagné believes that although declarative knowledge can be useful as prior knowledge for acquiring intellectual skills, it is not essential. Anderson models all procedural learning (i.e., intellectual skills) as being initially represented as declarative knowledge. Through practice, this declarative knowledge is formed into productions (if-then rules). It appears that Anderson believes procedural knowledge must pass through a declarative knowledge stage. We conjecture that in many cases declarative knowledge is essential to learning intellectual skills because the declarative knowledge helps make the intellectual skill meaningful, forming the initial and fundamental memory trace from which all other higher-order uses of the knowledge develop.

As we discuss instructional strategies for declarative knowledge, we will provide separate prescriptions depending on which of these three subtypes (labels and names, facts and lists, and organized discourse) is involved.

Cognitive Processes of Learning Declarative Knowledge

It is important to describe how theorists suggest that declarative knowledge is stored. Since most, if not all, of our knowledge is interrelated in some fashion, the primary form of representation of our declarative knowledge is theorized to be in **propositional networks** (Anderson, 1976). A proposition is somewhat similar to a sentence. For example, the sentence "Pat gave a large bone to Sarah, a smooth collie" contains three propositions:

1. Pat gave a bone to Sarah.
2. The bone was large.
3. Sarah is a smooth collie.

The difference between sentences and propositions is that (1) sentences may contain more than one proposition (as the sentence above does), and (2) propositions *are* the ideas, and sentences are what we commonly use to express the ideas. Propositions may also be expressed as diagrams or illustrations, mathematic expressions, musical notation, and other forms of languaging.* A network of propositions is the collection of many propositions linked together in some fashion. The links that are formed in a propositional network are idiosyncratic to a large extent and are almost as important to the "knowledge" as is the content of the propositions themselves.

Another theoretic construct that has been used to describe knowledge structures is schema theory (Minsky, 1975; Rummelhart & Ortony, 1977), introduced earlier. Schemata (plural of *schema*) are clusters of related ideas. For example, most of us probably have a "restaurant schema," which includes not only the sequence of events that generally occur in a restaurant, but also the objects and people you would expect to see there. Rummelhart (1980) illustrates the operation of schemata in cognition as being like a stage play. Knowledge that an individual possesses is seen to reside in internal structures, which are like play scripts. Although a script specifies characters and events, many particulars vary from performance to performance. The use of a schema involves a process called *instantiation*. Making an instance-based use of a schema can be seen as being analogous to the performance of a play. Memories of instantiated schemata are likened to videos of plays and can be viewed as the basis of recollections. Schemata are also said to have slots, or categories, that can be filled with particular information. For example, on one evening at one restaurant, the "dessert slot" may be occupied by "Baked Alaska"; at another time and place, it may be occupied by "Hot Fudge Sundae with Nuts." In either case, whether we think of them as propositional networks or schemata, the significance of the relatedness of knowledge in memory is the same: To learn declarative knowledge, it must be linked to existing knowledge.

Under schema theory, learning is proposed to take place by three major events: accretion, tuning, and restructuring (Rummelhart & Norman, 1978). Accretion is the building up of factual learning through memory traces—the residue of experience, as it were. Tuning of cognitive structures takes place as a result of accommodating the structure to new information. Restructuring takes place when existing cognitive structures are not sufficient or appropriate for knowledge gained and a new structure must be developed. For example, schema development can take place when a secretary is first exposed to using a computer as a piece of office equipment. As the secretary learns to use the computer as a

word processor, along with various intellectual and perhaps psychomotor skills, she acquires an abundance of specific declarative knowledge including a myriad of labels, names, and facts. Through *accretion*, the secretary's knowledge accumulates, and as a result, her cognitive structures regarding computers engage in *tuning*—the structure modifying slightly, adding as it were leaves and twigs here and there to this main branch, new connections established between the parts like spider webs within the foliage. Then, let's imagine, one day the secretary is exposed to an integrated software package that includes spreadsheet, database, and even graphic development capabilities. This new knowledge could well be enough to cause a *restructuring* for the secretary. The secretary now sees computers in a different light—they are not what the secretary thought they were. Restructuring can be seen as what would happen if we gave sight to the fabled twelve blind men and the elephant. The cycle of accretion, tuning, and restructuring (perhaps not always in that order) goes on throughout our lives.

A refinement to schema theory is provided by the constructivist orientation. Constructivists (e.g., Brown, Collins, & Duguid, 1989; Perkins, 1992) point out that knowledge is never passively "acquired" and would argue with the connotation that the term *accretion* often carries with it in describing the acquisition phase. Even the term *acquisition* would not satisfy some constructivists, as knowledge is seen to be *generated* (or "constructed") by the learner as learning takes place. Although some tenets associated with constructivism are difficult to accommodate within an instructional design perspective, there seems to be no argument with the fundamental tenet of knowledge construction. The very words we use do not possess meaning outside that which users of language attach to them. Therefore, in a fundamental sense, a person must construct meanings. Constructivists stress that language use involves a process of socially negotiated meanings and understandings. Although the schema theory conception of accretion does not appear well suited to expressing this process, the process of knowledge acquisition as theorized by schema researchers and other cognitive scientists is a fundamentally active one, as we will soon see, and does not seem to be inconsistent with constructivism.

Cognitive psychologists widely agree that the learning of all declarative knowledge has certain requirements. E. Gagné (1985) summarizes the process of learning new declarative knowledge in four steps: (1) new knowledge is presented via some medium and apprehended by the learner, (2) the material presented is translated by the learner into propositions, (3) related propositions in the learner's memory are activated, and (4) elaborations are generated by the learner as new connections stimulate the making of inferences. These

---

*Although not in common use, *languaging,* a term from the linguistics field, refers to the engagement of language behavior. The term is used in visual literacy discussions and is a useful one when pointing to language events that involve symbol systems that are not immediately or commonly recognized as "language."

steps underscore the active nature of declarative knowledge learning. The current view about how this learning takes place sharply contrasts with the view of the learner as a passive receiver absorbing material like a sponge. Rather, learners perform certain critical cognitive activities when they are engaged in learning declarative knowledge. These activities are linking, organizing, and elaborating.

Linking with Existing Knowledge

To be easily learned, recalled, and used, new declarative knowledge must be tied to the learner's existing (i.e., prior) knowledge. As a matter of fact, to be stored in long-term memory, incoming information must be meaningful. Incoming information can be meaningful when we have some prior knowledge that links to it. In cases in which there is little prior knowledge to link to, learners have to employ artificial (rather than intrinsically meaningful) links. These links tend to focus on surface similarities, such as similar sounds, shapes, sensory impressions, or motor procedures. When a learner is working in an unfamiliar area, then, early learning may lean heavily on sound associations, similarity in physical features such as letter sequences, or other nonmeaningful sources of connection. When even these "trick" links cannot be made, one has to resort to sheer rote repetition to get the information to be stored in long-term memory.

A result of linking is construction of meaning. In fact, the heart of the process of learning declarative knowledge is this creation of meaning. In this process, we are constructing meaning and, thereby, are acquiring new declarative knowledge. This takes more time than is frequently allowed in instruction. According to Simon (1974), it takes the learner ten seconds to encode one new bit of information. The rate of information presentation in rate-controlled media (such as television, film, and lectures) is frequently too fast for learners to process new information and therefore remember it.

ORGANIZING. Organizing new information is another cognitive activity that facilitates the learning of declarative knowledge. As we receive new information, we actively organize it by clumping (also called chunking) sets together, separating sets from one another, subordinating, and making relationships among sets. Such organization may simplify the cognitive load of handling and remembering masses of data, as seen in the common subdivision of telephone numbers. Which sequence of numbers is easier to learn?

15557568902 or 1 (555) 756 8902

Organization may add meaning by placing new unfamiliar material into some existing "slot." Slots can assist recall by providing a beginning point for recall of

the rest of the schema, or a slot may aid recall by limiting the spread of activation of memory to a smaller and more germane area (only the schema and related schemata).

Although organization is something learners do internally, instruction may either provide organization for the learner or help learners to engage in organization themselves.

ELABORATING. Another activity that is important for declarative knowledge learning is elaboration of information. When we receive new information, such as in reading or listening, we tend to add to that information, partly so that it makes sense to us and partly so that the information will be more retrievable. We elaborate by filling in gaps, making inferences, imagining examples, and so forth. The activity of elaboration is more inevitable in learning—and thus more important to instruction—than was generally acknowledged until recent years. Previously, elaboration was frequently thought of as being analogous to decoration: a nice addition but not necessary. Closer attention to learners' cognitive processes during declarative knowledge learning has led us to realize that elaboration is a basic process by which links are made within information being received as well as for connecting new information to existing knowledge and structures. Computer studies attempting to develop artificial intelligence have provided us with an appreciation for how much of our natural language in speech and writing requires inferences to make sense. The ambiguities of natural language provide an excellent illustration of the need to transcend the words being used. Schank (1984) cited the difficulty of getting a computer to correctly interpret the meaning of the verb *gave* in these sentences:

1. John gave Mary a book.
2. John gave Mary a hard time.
3. John gave Mary a night on the town.
4. John gave up.
5. John gave no reason for his actions.
6. John gave a party.
7. John gave his life for freedom.

If we instruct the computer to infer that "Mary now possesses a book" when it encounters the word *gave* in the first sentence, we can see how the computer (which is less able to actively generate elaborations than humans) would interpret the remaining sentences in the list: "Mary now possesses a hard time," "Mary now possesses a night on the town," "John possesses up," and so forth. Unlike computers, people who are listening or reading with comprehension actively make leaps of inference as a part of the sense-making process of declarative knowledge learning.

Although humans are well equipped to engage in elaboration, it does not mean that they always do so when needed. The unmotivated learner, the learner who is not skilled in employing needed learning strategies, the learner with little prior knowledge, or the learner who is fatigued may not engage in the mental activity needed to learn declarative knowledge being presented, even though the material may be presented clearly and accurately. Hence, instructional strategies need to encourage learners to perform the elaborations required to learn the material.

The three functions—linking, organizing, and elaborating—are the foundation of the information-processing aspect of instructional strategies described later in this chapter.

CONDITIONS SUPPORTING DECLARATIVE KNOWLEDGE LEARNING

The number and variety of possible appropriate strategies for declarative knowledge instruction sometimes present a chaotic picture. There seem to be more specific techniques for assisting the learning of declarative knowledge than for any other type of learning. West, Farmer, and Wolf (1991), for example, present a total of thirty-five specific cognitive strategies, all of which are applicable to declarative knowledge learning. Their eight major categories represent a good set of instructional strategy tools: organization strategies, classification frames, concept mapping, advance organizers, metaphoric techniques, rehearsal strategies, mnemonics, and imagery. These and instructional techniques suggested by other sources can be categorized into three major types of strategies, which correspond to the three critical cognitive activities involved in declarative knowledge learning: linking, organization, and elaboration. We will use these three types of strategies to organize our description of instructional techniques, providing a view of strategy design for declarative knowledge instruction that is both theory-based and functional.

Many events of instruction in lessons for declarative knowledge may be either supplied by instruction or generated by learners. Of the many microstrategies that we present, only one—advance organizers—seems inappropriate for learners to generate for themselves. The vast majority of the strategies can, therefore, be implemented as either supplantive instruction or generative. The decision as to where the strategy is expected to originate should be based on factors such as time available, learner aptitudes, and prior knowledge. The engagement in the appropriate cognitive activity is the critical feature: whether that activity is something controlled and delivered by instruction or whether that activity is something that instruction facilitates the learner to do is

a matter of choice for the designer. If consideration of the factors of time, learner aptitude, and prior knowledge fails to provide a direction, logistical considerations and the need for variety may influence the decision.

Following are two example lessons. The first, from a high school chemistry course, involves learning the names and symbols for 103 chemical elements, and the second, from a college music history course, involves learning the names, composers, and stylistic periods of musical passages from the baroque, classical, and romantic periods.

EXAMPLE A: THE ELEMENTS. LABELS LEARNING TASK.

Setting: High school chemistry class. College prep.

Audience: Teenagers, ages sixteen to eighteen. Class enrollment of twenty-eight.

Task: Given the symbol for a chemical element, the learner can supply the name of the element, or given the name of the element, the learner can supply the symbol.

There are 103 named elements on the periodic table. Here is a sample:

Aluminum	Al
Iodine	I
Barium	Ba
Iron	Fe
Boron	B
Lithium	Li
Bromine	Br
Mercury	Hg

For this instruction we have selected a computer-assisted instruction module as the delivery system.

EXAMPLE B: EUROPEAN MUSIC FROM 1600 THROUGH 1900. ORGANIZED DISCOURSE LEARNING TASKS WITHIN THAT COURSE.

Setting: College elective music history course.

Audience: Adults, undergraduate college students. Class enrollment of twenty-eight.

Tasks:

1. Given a musical passage, the student will be able to recognize it and identify it by title, composer, and stylistic period.

2. The student will also be able to describe the major events and identifying characteristics of music from the baroque, classical, and romantic periods.

For this instruction, we have selected instructor delivery, with audiovisual media (primarily compact discs and an overhead projector) and independent student work involving listening and printed materials.

Introducing Declarative Knowledge Lessons

Deploy Attention / Arouse Interest and Motivation

A variety of techniques is appropriate for attention, interest, and motivation in declarative knowledge lessons. Since the learning of declarative knowledge may be a more onerous task than some other types of learning, it is particularly helpful to plan a strategy to increase curiosity and interest through such techniques as using novel, conflicting, and paradoxical events or providing an abrupt change in stimulus. Throughout the lesson, the use of anecdotes and other devices that interject personal and emotional elements can increase interest, as well as make information relevant by relating instructional goals to learners' life goals, job requirements, and opportunities for advancement. Finally, an important part of motivation, particularly for older learners, can be provided by making it clear how this learning relates to other learning tasks.

In our chemical elements example, an attention-getting introduction might use animated graphics with sound in the computer-assisted instruction, similar to the way computer games begin. Animated sequences of atoms of various structures could spin and interact and then become the title screen. The program could include material related to subsequent instructional events, as well as describe the necessity of knowing the names and symbols for the elements so that the next work with forming compounds will be easier and more meaningful. (For example, if we learn that salt is NaCl, it will be more meaningful if we already know that Na is the symbol for sodium and Cl is the symbol for chlorine.) An additional appeal for college prep students might be the statement, "You can improve your score on the SAT exam by knowing the symbols for the elements."

In our music history class, we can initially attract attention to the subject by playing a short passage of particularly compelling music (e.g., the "Presto" movement of Bach's Italian Concerto, BWV 971), and then change the stimulus by turning off the music. This would immediately shift attention to the instruction. A conflicting/paradoxical event could be supplied by juxtaposing classical composers with the pandering gossip of a supermarket tabloid. The instructor could use humorous headlines to gain students' attention, such as the following: "J. S. Bach won't stop using counterpoint in front of his children," and "Is Amadeus perverting the allegro tempo to please his wife?" and "Beethoven shocks Vienna with the Third!"

Establish Instructional Purpose

Some excellent approaches to establishing the purpose of lessons that are useful for all sorts of learning, not just declarative knowledge, include relating instructional goals to personal life goals or job requirements and encouraging learners to make the instructional goal personally relevant. In addition, there are some considerations for establishing purpose that are particular to this type of learning. Due to the potential for declarative knowledge learning goals to appear more dull than higher-order learning tasks, an effort to present the goal in an interesting, dynamic format may be worthwhile. It is also worthwhile to tie the purpose of the lesson to learning strategies that are effective in learning this particular kind of task.

For example, if students had previously learned to use a mnemonic technique to help them learn the names of state capitals, a good practice would be to remind them of the similarity of learning state capitals to learning chemical element names and symbol. Students could be assisted in seeing the applicability of the strategy used for the previous task, and how it could be used to help learn the new material.

Also, the specific requirements for successful attainment of the learning goal should be pointed out. The learners' expectancy for success can be increased, thereby increasing the likelihood of success. This could be accomplished in our chemical elements instruction with a statement such as "You will be able to write the name of the element for any symbol that I show you, and if I give you the name first, you will be able to write the symbol for it."

It will assist learning if instruction will let learners know in what form they must remember the material (recognize or recall, recite verbatim or paraphrase). Figure 8.1 illustrates the four possible combinations of form of memory. Knowing in advance the performance that is expected will assist learners to activate the appropriate cognitive strategies for the acquisition of the required learning. Consequently, in our chemical elements module, the instruction will explicitly say, "You will be able to write the name of the element," rather than being vague about what the learners will be expected to do.

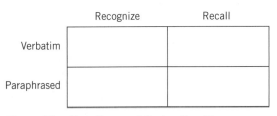

Figure 8.1 Four Forms of Declarative Memory

In our music history course, we will be explicit about the learning that is expected, saying (and providing equivalent information on a printed handout): "You will learn to recognize musical passages and identify their composers and stylistic periods. On an exam, after I play a passage of music, you will write in a blank the name of the composer of that passage and from what musical period that music came. Also you will be able to describe the major events and identifying characteristics of music from three periods in an essay exam." Notice that the wording here is quite similar to that of the objective but with changes made that direct the statement to the learner, rather than talking about the learner. Here we say, "You will learn to . . ." as opposed to "The learner will be able to . . . ."

Previewing the Lesson

Previewing the lesson should include an overview of both what will happen and the nature of the material to be learned. In previewing what will happen in a lesson in which information will be repeated, it is important to ensure that learners know that the information *will* be repeated and reviewed. Learners should know they don't have to grasp it all at once. Knowing what will happen in the lesson gives learners a chance to prepare to use cognitive strategies, even if they are routine.

The overview of the material to be learned in a lesson can be included in an advance organizer. Although advance organizers provide an excellent preview of material to be learned, they have important roles in other instructional events as well. A key point to be communicated in the overview is the way that information in the lesson will be organized. Knowledge of the organization of the material, especially in learning organized discourse, can well be provided through an advance organizer and can clarify the relationships among ideas. Two primary types of advance organizers are expository organizers and comparative organizers.

Expository organizers provide and clarify the hierarchical relationships among ideas. They are best for laying the groundwork for broad areas of new, unfamiliar material for which there is no relevant knowledge to which the new knowledge can be compared.

Comparative organizers make orienting comparisons between current knowledge and material to be learned. They are best for learning for which there are similar bodies of knowledge that can be compared to new knowledge on several major points.

The following example of an advance organizer serves as a preview for our music history course and provides a link between previously learned general history—what was happening in Europe at the time the music under study was being written—and the musical periods under study.

The instructor might begin the class by saying, "Think back to your courses on world history. What were some major figures and events in Europe during the seventeenth, eighteenth, and nineteenth centuries? Let's see, what was happening in the 1600s?" Quickly solicit a few student contributions, relating those to a time-line transparency for the seventeenth century (a graphic organizer). Point out a few memorable events if needed and allow some time for students to look at the chart. "And what was going on in the 1700s?" Similarly conduct recitation and review the time-line transparency for the eighteenth century. "And in the 1800s?" Do similar recitation and review. "In this class, we are going to study what was happening in the world of music in Europe during this period. We will get to know what is now called the baroque period, and we'll get to know the style of music from that period." Play a very short selection from Bach's Brandenberg Concerto no. 2. "We will learn about the music of what is now called the classical period, its composers, and the musical forms that developed. You'll learn what that style is like and how it is different from baroque music." Play a very short selection from Mozart's Symphony no. 36. "And finally, we will learn about the romantic movement and how it came to be." Play a selection from Beethoven's Third Symphony. "We'll also examine what made the romantic period unique and what contributions it made to our world today." Play a selection from Saint-Säens' Third Symphony. The advance organizer described here has elements of both an expository and a comparative organizer. This advance organizer might be most appropriate at the beginning of the first class, coming before the more detailed information on the objective.

An idea related to the advance organizer is the epitome, a concept that is part of Reigeluth's Elaboration Model. An epitome, like an advance organizer, is an initial learning experience covering the whole of a body of material to follow. Unlike the advance organizer, though, the epitome presents the key ideas and has the learners use this knowledge (paraphrasing, making inferences) before moving on to more details. For example, in music, briefly describing each period and how it relates to other periods would be an epitome. Later in the course, the instruction would provide more details for each period.

BODY

Stimulating Recall of Relevant Prior Knowledge

Two powerful techniques for the stimulation (and linking) of prior knowledge to new declarative knowledge are the use of advance organizers and the use of metaphoric devices. A fundamental characteristic of advance organizers is that they bridge old and new knowledge; thus, they are extremely useful in stimulating recall of relevant prior learning. As noted earlier, **advance organizers** frequently apply to more than one event of instruction. Hence, we have seen their applicability in both previewing the lessons and in stimulating recall of relevant prior learning.

Metaphoric devices can provide a link between the known and the unknown as well as provide intellectual stimulation and interest through the figural use of concrete images. Metaphoric devices often include the use of metaphors, in which a known vehicle is used to convey a new topic through setting up an identity, such as "the white blood cells (new topic) are soldiers (vehicle)." Metaphoric devices can also use analogies, in which the vehicle is used to convey the topic through a relationship between pairs, such as "white blood cells attack infections just as soldiers attack their enemy." Although there are dangers in using metaphoric devices (such as the learner generalizing too much or taking the comparison literally rather than figuratively as intended), metaphoric devices can be powerful learning tools, whether used in verbal or visual form (Smith & Ragan, 1990; West, Farmer, & Wolf, 1991).

An example of a metaphoric device for our music history course would be to compare the sonata musical form to the commonly used essay structure of an introduction, a body, and a conclusion.

A final means of stimulating recall of prior learning in declarative knowledge instruction is to perform a straightforward **review** of prerequisite concepts. It is easy to come to the conclusion that concepts are always learned after declarative knowledge. (Bloom's taxonomy mistakenly suggests this relationship.) However, the meaningfulness of declarative knowledge is buttressed by links to previously learned concepts and other declarative knowledge. Without such links, the learner is forced to engage in rote learning if the material is to be learned at all—hardly an efficient or salutary approach in any event.

For our chemistry class instruction, we will stimulate recall of prerequisites by reviewing the previously learned concepts embodied within the periodic table (e.g., the concept of a chemical element and learning from a prior lesson on the organization and structure of the periodic table, including the concepts of atomic weight and atomic number).

Process Information

Many specific techniques are available for the processing of information in learning declarative knowledge. Some techniques are appropriate only for one or two of the three subtypes of declarative knowledge. We will look at each subtype separately.

Some mediation of processing can be provided by instruction, and some should be required of the learner. For example, the use of images is a powerful tool in processing information for learning labels and names. This use of images can be supplied by the instruction, providing learners with images to associate with the content. Or images can be supplied by the learner, as mental images perhaps, with the role of instruction to stimulate the learner to think of appropriate images.

A number of specific techniques are available for assisting the information processing of declarative knowledge learning. One set of techniques assists learners to make associations that aid learning. We will call these **associational techniques**. They include the use of mnemonics, images, and analogies. Another set of techniques helps the learner organize information to be learned. These **organizational techniques** include clustering and chunking by categories, using graphic organizers, generating expository and narrative structures, and using advance organizers. A third set of techniques, **elaborative techniques**, involves making elaborations on the material being learned, including elaboration into sentences and devising rules.

Some of the techniques outlined here apply to one or more of the forms of declarative knowledge and not to others. The techniques will be brought up and discussed as they apply in each category.

LABELS AND NAMES. An organizational technique that is useful in learning labels and names is that of *clustering and chunking into categories*. It is so commonplace to organize information along some structural pattern that we may forget that this is a particular instructional strategy element and a cognitive strategy for learners to employ. The periodic table of elements is clustered in various ways, including columns of elements clustered into categories (metals, nonmetals, noble gases), and the table is frequently color-coded in categories for solids, liquids, gases, and synthetic elements. Clustering and chunking may be employed by learners, for example, by choosing to work on particular subsets of the periodic table, either by columns, by rows, or by some other grouping principle.

An elaboration technique for learning labels and names is the *elaboration of the material into sentences* that make meaningful use of the terms. An example would be an explanation of how Hg became the symbol for mercury. Elaboration of labels into sentences may lead to their being learned as concepts rather than remaining declarative knowledge, depending on a variety of factors, such as the practice available on examples and nonexamples. Note that the instructional event being implemented at this point is "processing information." While elaboration may constitute excellent practice, it can also be used to initially engage the learner with the material. The music history course could make use of elaboration into sentences by having learners write a sentence for each term as it is being explained.

FACTS AND LISTS. A primary associational technique for processing information in the learning of facts and lists is the *use of images*. Many techniques employ images to assist in the memorization of facts and lists. Use of images, either instruction-supplied or learner-generated, includes far too many specific possibilities for us to be able to describe it thoroughly here. Texts on audiovisual media (Heinich, Molenda, Russell, & Smaldino, 1996; Locatis & Atkinson, 1984) do an excellent job of presenting and discussing the use of visuals in instruction, such as use of pictures, graphs, tables, and maps. A few examples of visualization strategies for learner-generated visuals include making mental images of sentences and prose passages, and using the method of loci, in which the locations of objects in an imagined space, such as a room, are associated with points to be remembered.

Organizational techniques for processing information in learning facts and lists include the use of *expository structures and narrative structures*. Expository and narrative structures are more commonly used in connected discourse learning; however, it is possible that lists might be learned by organizing them in such a way that they reflect a common structure. Certainly a chronological structure is commonly employed in recalling lists. We describe expository and narrative structures in more detail in the following sections on connected discourse.

Another organizational technique for processing information in learning facts and lists is *recognizing patterns*. Frequently, patterns exist among facts that are to be learned. These patterns may not be apparent to learners, and, if pointed out by instruction, can assist in the learning of them. For example, the patterns inherent in the columns and rows of the periodic table can be pointed out to learners, making it easier for learners to remember the elements.

An organizational strategy for processing information in learning lists is *clustering and chunking*. (Remember that chunking is the technique that is commonly used to group telephone numbers and social security numbers into smaller subsets that are easier to remember.) Elaboration techniques generally add meaningful information around lists and facts to make them more memorable. For example, information as to why the elements are clustered into the row and column organization that is used in the periodic table may help the learner recall the list of elements.

ORGANIZED DISCOURSE. Just as we have done with the other two forms of declarative knowledge, we will discuss the processing of information for organized discourse in terms of three types of strategies: associative,

organizational, and elaboration. A great deal of the instructional intent of reading organized discourse, such as the material that you are now reading, is reflected in the term *comprehension*. We find *comprehension* used frequently to describe the outcome of processing organized discourse in conventional print, such as books and journals, and in speech, such as lectures. We do not find the term *comprehension* used often in other contexts, such as learning from simulations, computer-assisted instruction (CAI), and video. Comprehension of organized discourse involves apprehending the thread of ideas in prose language and following the flow, much as a surfer rides the crest of a wave. Strategies for information processing for this kind of learning may be supplied in the instruction and thus constitute suggestions for designing instructional prose, or they may be generated by learners and thus constitute suggestions for cognitive strategies.

Associative strategies for processing information for organized discourse include the *use of imagery* and the *use of metaphoric devices*. Imagery has been described previously in the context of learning facts and lists. In the context of organized discourse, considerations change somewhat, even though much of what was noted earlier remains applicable. As a supplantive technique, imagery in organized discourse includes the use of verbal descriptions of images, which sometimes invokes more vivid mental imagery than is possible to achieve on film or video. In part, the power of the printed word to invoke images is illustrated by the fact that given a good novel and a good motion picture rendition of the novel, the mental images created by reading the book are often more vivid and memorable than those that are depicted on film or that remain in the memory after seeing the film. In our high-tech world of film, video, and multimedia, skillfully crafted words remain an exceptionally powerful technique for creating images. Figure 8.2 presents a paragraph from a fiction work, used here to serve as an illustration and reminder of the power of the printed word to invoke images.

In addition to the imagery that words may convey, supplantive uses of images for processing attention in organized discourse include *uses of illustrations in text*. Images can be explicative and represent information, in addition to their uses in attentional and retentional roles (Duchastel, 1978). (Guidelines for selecting and using illustrations in text are provided in Chapter W-2 in the Learning Resources Web site. Further information on using illustrations in text can be found in the references for that chapter, especially Houghton & Willows, 1987; Jonassen, 1982, 1985; Willows & Houghton, 1987).

Metaphoric devices are also applicable as associative strategies to the processing of information in organized discourse. Metaphor use in organized discourse is similar to imagery use: Both are powerful language tools for the subtle, impactful, or memorable conveying of a

My shoes were by this time in a woeful condition. The soles had shed themselves bit by bit, and the upper leathers had broken and burst until the very shape and form of the shoes had departed from them. My hat (which had served me for a night-cap, too) was so crushed and bent, that no old battered handleless saucepan on a dunghill need have been ashamed to vie with it. My shirt and trousers, stained with heat, dew, grass, and the Kentish soil on which I had slept— and torn besides— might have frightened the birds from my aunt's garden, as I stood at the gate. My hair had known no comb or brush since I left London. My face, neck, and hands, from unaccustomed exposure to the air and sun, were burnt to a berry-brown. From head to foot I was powered almost as white with chalk and dust, as if I had come out of a lime-kiln. In this plight, and with a strong consciousness of it, I waited to introduce myself to, and make my first impression on, my formidable aunt.

Figure 8.2 A Passage Illustrating Image-Invoking Prose. (Dickens, C., *David Copperfield*)

message. Often metaphors, analogies, and similes are employed in text that evokes images, such as the sample passage used in Figure 8.2. Although they can be highly useful, metaphoric devices are not without their dangers. Zeitoun (1984) presented critical factors in the use of analogies in instruction, including the need for learners to be familiar with the vehicle of the analogy, to be capable of analogical reasoning, to be able to identify the limitations of the analogy, and to visualize verbally presented analogies. (For additional information on instructional design considerations for using analogies, particularly visual analogies, see Smith & Ragan, 1990.)

Organizational strategies for the processing of information in organized discourse learning include use of expository structures and graphic organizers. **Expository structures** that are often suggested are *description, chronology, comparison-contrast, cause-effect, problem-solution,* and *problem-solution-effects.* In addition, certain contents have common structures that they follow. For example, science content may follow a structure describing a system. Within this structure are common "slots" of function, parts, "how it works," or problems/prevention and solution (Armbruster & Anderson, 1985). Such structures can be supplied by instruction, or the structure may be imposed by the learner as a learning strategy. Selecting the appropriate structure is a constant concern of textbook authors, teachers, and instructional designers. **Narrative structures** can similarly be employed in either a supplantive or generative strategy, placing the information being studied into the structure of a story's events.

Research has suggested that text that is organized using one of these structures is more easily learned (Armbruster & Anderson, 1985; Meyer, 1985; Smith & Tompkins, 1988). In our music history course example, the three historical periods—baroque, classical, and romantic—provide a chronological structure. Further structure may be employed with regard to composers; comparison-contrast is one good alternative. The musical forms, such as minuet and trio, scherzo, rondo, theme and variations, and sonata allegro, lend themselves to a description structure or comparison-contrast structure.

Expository structures have potential relevance in generative instruction as well as their supplantive implications. One research study by Smith and Friend (1986) is an example of generative use of an organizational strategy. Students improved their comprehension of text material by applying a procedure that they were taught to use, that of determining and encoding the text structure of material being studied. Sometimes gifted students discover such strategies on their own; certainly it is unusual for young children to consciously perform structural analyses of material they are reading, yet there is reason to believe that such a skill can be taught to practically anyone.

Graphic organizers can be of great assistance in the information processing of organized discourse learning. Graphic organizers of all sorts may be used for learning facts and lists, but perhaps their most powerful use is in the organization of discourse. Holley and Dansereau (1984) described the use of such graphics as "spatial learning strategies" and included *networking, concept structuring, schematizing,* and *mapping* among such strategies. All strategies are similar in that they require learners to identify and represent ideas presented in instruction and spatially indicate the relationships among these ideas. West, Farmer, and Wolf (1991) called such organizers *frames*. The periodic table is arranged in just such a frame. The composers and periods could be cast into a frame for our music history course (see Figure 8.3).

Another technique involving use of a graphic organizer is *concept mapping*. Concept mapping, like outlining, is a graphic means of depicting relationships among

	Dates	Composers	Forms	Innovations
Baroque				
Classical				
Romantic				

Figure 8.3 Frame Organizer for Music History

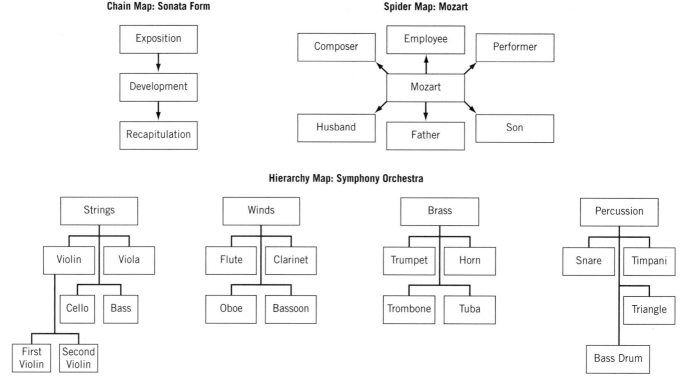

Figure 8.4 Three Forms of the Concept Map

ideas. Like outlines, concept maps may be part of a presentation, or they may be generated by learners. In concept mapping, a wide variety and flexibility exists in arranging elements and depicting their relationships. West, Farmer, and Wolf (1991) described three types of concept maps: spider, hierarchy, and chain, illustrated in Figure 8.4. A supplantive application of concept mapping is employed in the summary diagrams in this text.

In organized discourse, graphic organizers such as frames, networks, and concept maps can assist in the tuning of cognitive structures and, at times, in assisting restructuring. Graphic organizers provide a visible, distanced* pattern on which to build a schema. Graphic organizers may be provided by instruction or generated by learners themselves. An example of learner-supplied graphic organizers is found in the study performed by Smith and Friend (1986). Learning-disabled elementary school students were taught to generate and use visual imagery of text structures to improve comprehension of the text ma-

terial. Teaching students to create and use learner-supplied images—both in creation of concrete visuals such as drawings, photos, and videos, as well as creation of mental images—is a central concern of the Visual Literacy movement (see Heinich, Molenda, Russell, & Smaldino, 1996, pp. 66–71).

Focus Attention

The primary need for attention-focusing in learning labels and names is for focusing on distinctive features. In the learning of facts, attention needs to be focused on key elements. In organized discourse, the learner's attention toward organization of the material is of the most importance. Two particular attention techniques are the procedure of underlining, listing, and reflecting, and the use of questions.

A useful technique for focusing attention in declarative knowledge learning is *underlining, listing,* and *reflecting.* A good example in our chemistry lesson is asking the learner to underline each element name using a computer mouse or other pointing device. The learner could list the elements by name and symbol on paper. Reflection could be stimulated by asking the learner to read through the list of elements, pausing at each element and, with eyes closed, silently saying the name of the element and its symbol before moving on to the next.

*The term *distanced* refers to one of two forms of language: evanescent and distanced. Evanescent language, like the spoken work and sign language, exists in the moment only and is not available for inspection, manipulation, and so forth. On the other hand, distanced language, like the written word and graphics, is available for inspection and manipulation.

Much has been written about the *use of questions* in teaching and in instruction (e.g., Gall, 1970; Rothkopf & Bisbicos, 1967; Wager & Wager, 1985). In addition to other mathemagenic functions that they can serve, questions are a powerful tool for establishing and maintaining attention. Their attention function, in large measure, is accomplished through stimulating information processing on the part of the learner. Questions also have an effect on incidental learning. They tend to focus the learner's attention on related material, reducing the amount of learning in areas not related to the question (Bull, 1973). When learning goals require a substantial amount of exploratory learning of text material, the attention-focusing capability of questions may be more powerful than desired; that is, they may focus attention too narrowly.

Attentional uses of questions can be served by *pre- and post-questions* as well as by *embedded questions*. Pre- and post-questions are perhaps first thought of in their assessment role. However, questions about the content to which the student is expected to respond have the effect of drawing the student's attention to that content, regardless of other uses for the student's response. Embedded questions also serve to hold attention to the material under study. Embedded questions are questions within the body of the instruction—ranging all the way from probing, exploratory questions to simple questions of fact. There is no doubt as to the attentional effect of questions. Schramm (1964) concluded, after an extensive review of the research literature on teaching machines and programmed instruction, that the effect on learning from frequent, active learner response in programmed instruction was substantial, primarily because of the effects of frequent questioning on attention and the subsequent effect of attention on the processing of information following the questions.

In our chemical elements module, embedded questions will form a great deal of the material provided in the computer-assisted instruction. These questions will at the same time serve a practice function.

In our music history course, the instructor will use embedded questions during the classroom lessons. In addition, embedded questions will be provided in the printed materials supplied for individual student use.

Employ Learning Strategies

Learning strategies that are appropriate for declarative knowledge include the use of mnemonics, elaboration strategies, imagery, analogy, organization, chunking, linking, graphic organizers, and rehearsal. All of these strategies, except mnemonics and rehearsal, were previously discussed as information-processing strategies that could either be supplied by instruction or generated and controlled by the learner. When the learner generates and controls a strategy such as elaboration or

imagery to assist in learning desired material, that strategy is being used as a learning strategy. In addition to providing critical training in learning strategies, instruction should guide the learner in the choice of appropriate learning strategies for particular learning tasks. For example, if students were working on the memorization of the names of all the elements in the periodic table, instruction should point them in the right direction, toward use of learning strategies that would be of most assistance in promoting the desired learning. In this case, since the learning task is fact/list, one of the mnemonic techniques, such as single-use coding, pegwords, or method of loci, would be helpful. We will now discuss each of these techniques.

Mnemonic techniques of various sorts are particularly potent associational techniques in processing information for learning of facts and lists, but they should be used as a last resort, only when meaningful associations cannot be made.

A popular mnemonic device, termed **single-use coding** by West, Farmer, and Wolf (1991), involves the use of letters in words or the first letters in sentences to help learn a list. Common examples in music include using the letters in the word *face* to remember the notes on the spaces on a treble clef, and using the first letter of each word in the sentence "Every good boy does fine" to remember the notes on the lines (E, G, B, D, and F). These are examples of mnemonics that instruction could supply. Alternatively, students may be taught to devise their own instead of using a supplied mnemonic. Single-use coding is involved in the use of rhymes, stories, or jingles, such as the poem that begins "Thirty days hath September . . . ." It is also used in any rhyme, story, or jingle that a learner might invent. An example of single-use coding for our periodic table instruction would be learning that the symbol for sodium is Na, associating table salt with sodium and recalling that too much sodium in the diet is not healthy, and then inventing the slogan, "Just say nay (Na) to sodium!"

A complex but powerful mnemonic technique is the use of **pegwords**, in which a list of things is arbitrarily associated with a sequence of numbers beginning with 1, such as "One is for sun; two is for shoe; three is my knee," and so forth. For the list of words to be remembered, the first word is rhymed with the sun, the second with shoe, and so forth. If our list to learn were hydrogen, helium, and lithium, we could first imagine the sun with a big *H* on it, then the shoe being lifted by helium balloons, and finally a knee with lithographic printing all over it (suitable only for those with *lithography* in their vocabulary).

Similar to the pegword technique is the time-honored **method of loci**. The method of loci was a significant part of a memory system used by the Sophists of ancient Greece, a sect known for their amazing ability to memorize large bodies of information. To commit a list of words or topics to memory, one imagines a familiar location, such as a room, including its items, such as furniture. One way to do this is to visualize your own living room. Using a systematic sweep pattern, you scan the living room in your mind's eye, say, in a clockwise direction, beginning with the northeast corner. As each item of furniture or decoration "appears," you make an association between that item and the next topic or word on the list. Given practice in using the method of loci, learners can commit very large amounts of material to memory in a short amount of time (West, Farmer, & Wolf, 1991).

Another mnemonic, the **keyword technique** (Atkinson, 1975; Pressley, Levin, & Delaney, 1982), involves a particular kind of operation to assist in the association of a pair of elements, such as a label or a name. In essence the technique involves creating a memorable image that will stimulate recall of the pair in question. For example, if we wanted to apply the keyword technique to remembering that the symbol for potassium is K, we would need to create images evoking keywords that either sound like or remind us of potassium and the letter K. Keywords can be put together to form a combined image. We will then select potato for potassium and for K we will select kangaroo. The image of a kangaroo playing with a potato (or a potato carved in the shape of a kangaroo) is easy to remember. Studies indicate that although bizarre images have been commonly recommended, either bizarre or commonplace images can be effective. The factors that govern the memorability are interaction of the elements in the image, vividness, uniqueness, and the time spent forming the image (Higbee, 1979).

Although the linking process used in keyword mnemonics may sound complex, it is easy to perform and results in a surprisingly good memory aid with only a modest amount of mental effort. Either the instruction may supply keywords and their images for learners to use, or learners may be assisted in generating these themselves (Higbee, 1979). In general, an advantage of learners generating keyword images themselves is that learners may better remember their own associations. An advantage of instruction-supplied associations is that their use requires less instructional time.

Although fascinating in themselves and highly recommended by many sources, each of which draws from many research studies (e.g., Higbee, 1979; Joyce & Weil, 1986; and West, Farmer, & Wolf, 1991), mnemonic techniques should be used only when equally effective approaches that use meaningful associations have failed. The use of constructed, arbitrary, and artificial meanings, which is required by mnemonics, leaves the learner with a "memorized" learning that is not as lasting or useful as that which is built upon meaningful links.

Rehearsal may be the first and only learning strategy that many learners are able to come up with on their own. Too many schoolchildren and trainees spend countless unnecessary hours engaging in the repeated practice that rote memorization requires. But when rehearsal is placed within the context of use along with other appropriate strategies, it can be quite valuable and appropriate. True rehearsal is not accomplished through meaningless repetition. The concept "rehearsal," as developed in cognitive psychology tradition, involves thinking. A minimalist version of rehearsal would be to think aloud. Many of the previously described techniques involve rehearsal, and they engage it in more powerful and interesting ways than the minimalist version. (However, thinking aloud is often exactly what a person must do to learn a subtle bit or a complex body of declarative knowledge.) Instruction needs to assist the learner in making appropriate use of rehearsal as a learning strategy.

Practice

The strategies discussed to this point require very little rehearsal or practice for mastery of material. Providing for adequate practice is a necessary part of instructional design. One consideration in designing practice is determining whether the learning task requires *recall* or whether it only requires *recognition*. Practice requirements for recognition—all other things being equal (such as learning strategies employed)—are much less cognitively demanding than for recall. Another consideration in determining the amount of practice needed is, if recall is required, whether the recall should be *verbatim* or if it may be *paraphrased*. Again, assuming we use the same learning strategies, a verbatim performance will require more practice than a paraphrased one.

Another factor in practice, particularly for the learning of labels, facts, and lists, is the importance of *spaced practice*. *Massed practice*, as is seen in all-night cram sessions for final exams, is not as efficient as the same amount of time spent in practice spaced over a period of time.

Practice is generally associated with reaching *automaticity* in the performance of a skill. However, automaticity is also involved in declarative knowledge. Some declarative knowledge performances require more automaticity than others. For example, remembering a list requires less automaticity than reciting a poem. The learner must practice material under study until she reaches the desired level of automaticity. In determining the degree of automaticity for declarative knowledge, the designer needs to imagine the context in which the knowledge will be applied. For example, a high level of automaticity will be needed for recalling chemical symbols or elements because this knowledge needs to be available more or less instantly in applying principles and in problem solving.

Practice for labels should involve presenting one of the two elements in the association, such as presenting H and then requiring the learner to provide the other element—hydrogen. Practice for labels is almost always verbatim recall, although it may be verbatim recognition. However, usually the desired end result is that the learner can supply, rather than recognize, the elements, so practice should be at this level. But when learners are practicing supplying labels, if one element is likely to be consistently supplied in use, then that element should always be supplied in practice. For example, when learners learn to label a map with names, usually the map is given and the name must be supplied. The knowledge should be practiced this way. However, in some cases either element is equally likely to be supplied, so practice should be distributed so that each element is supplied and each is recalled.

Practice for facts and lists is generally verbatim recall. With a fact, usually a question is asked that supplies one of the concepts as a cue to elicit recall of the other concept (e.g., "Who is the governor of Texas?" or "In what year did J. S. Bach die?"). A question that asks for recall of a list usually supplies a keyword to cue the list (e.g., "Name the inert gases"). If sequence within the list is important, then the question should remind the learner of its importance (e.g., "Name the planets in the sun's orbit, starting with the planet nearest the sun and moving outward").

Practice for connected discourse is most often in the form of paraphrased recall. Learners are asked to explain, summarize, and describe in their own words content that has been provided in the discourse. Occasionally, learners may be asked to recognize paraphrased statements that best represent the content. They may be asked to determine if a single statement accurately reflects the content. Practice of connected discourse learning usually requires the learners to evidence "understanding."

Practice requirements for our periodic table instruction should involve "overlearning" to reach the required level of automaticity. This means that learners will encounter the material frequently over an extended period of time. The activities involved in the events of instruction, such as processing information, focusing attention, and employing learning strategies, all provide for practice. However, because of the automaticity needed in this learning task, instruction will need to provide for repeated practice over time; this should be individually determined and administered. The use of computer-assisted instruction is particularly suited to satisfying this need. Although "drill and practice" uses of computers are abhorred in some circles, needed practice of the sort required here may be more interestingly and efficiently provided by this medium than other alternatives.

Practice for the periods-of-music-history goal would involve paraphrased and summarized recall of key infor-

mation about the sequence and characteristics of each period of music. This practice could involve a variety of formats, including developing a videotaped "commercial" for a particular period or developing a multimedia presentation describing a music period.

Feedback

For labels, facts, and lists, the requirements of feedback are relatively straightforward. Feedback for labels and facts should evaluate whether information is complete and associations are correct. Lists may have two elements, completeness and sequence, which must be evaluated. If answers reflect an incorrect combination of associations, the feedback might point out the error.

For organized discourse, provision of feedback generally requires that instruction either have an "intelligent" evaluator or provide model responses. An "intelligent" evaluator generally is a knowledgeable human; however, some computer-based intelligent tutoring systems (ITS) may incorporate sufficient natural language processing and "intelligence" to assess a constructed answer. A model response should be constructed with attention to organization and the essential features of a model answer. The marking of essay examinations provides a commonplace example of organized discourse feedback (assuming exams are returned to the student). As all good teachers know, to do a good job of evaluating and providing feedback to students on their essay performances, the instructor must be able to recognize a good answer to the question. This good answer could be either written or in the teacher's head, although we recommend the written version, with levels of quality illustrated (see Chapter 6). The same sort of good answer or model response is needed to provide feedback on practice.

CONCLUSION

Summarize and Review

The summary-and-review process is critical to declarative knowledge learning. As cognitive structures are being tuned and adjusted by new knowledge, summaries are needed as practice and to assist consolidation. Summaries serve somewhat different needs in organized discourse as compared to the other forms of declarative knowledge. A summary of organized discourse, particularly with lengthy and complex material, serves to clarify and ensure the schema-tuning needed to assimilate the material. For the other forms of declarative knowledge, the summary-and-review function will be more related to needs for practice and repetition. So, in learning labels/names and facts/lists, a summary and review can provide an opportunity to work with the material using a different strategy from that which was used in information process-practice-feedback phases. For example, if the designer had chosen to employ a mnemonic strategy for learning a list of technical terms in an electronics course, a summary/review could be conducted using a graphic organizer.

Learners may be more involved in the generation of summary/review activities than has been the case in traditional instruction. The traditional pattern, certainly for didactic, supplantive instruction, has been for the instruction to supply a summary. We are so accustomed to this approach that it might be difficult to imagine summaries being accomplished in any way other than by the instructor or other medium. However, student-processed summaries are a powerful learning tool, particularly for organized discourse. Hidi (1985) devised and studied a technique for training learners in generating summaries of text material. The training proceeds from teaching learners to paraphrase paragraphs in relatively simple material through the summarizing of long, complex bodies of material. The researchers found that although the training required of learners to become proficient at summarizing can be extensive and difficult, students better retained the studied material if they generated the summaries themselves.

A final concern about summaries is the need for them to be employed more than once, over time. Summarizing is not a single event; there is a need, particularly in complex and difficult material, for interim summaries. Interim summaries provide opportunity for consolidation before the material in working memory is replaced by subsequent material. Interim summaries also provide excellent transition vehicles from one subtopic to the next.

A summary of our elements module could be provided by a review of the categories into which elements are grouped. The summary could indicate how the categories are related and could provide a review of the elements and the label for each element.

For our music history course, we might have each student create a musical summary (through editing audio materials onto tape). The summary should be accompanied by a short written verbal explanation.

Transfer

The most critical part of transfer in declarative knowledge learning is that information is available for retrieval to be combined with new information. In other words, to apply a fact or make use of a list, it must come to mind easily so that it can be used. Everyone has experienced being stuck, unable to go on in a conversation or project because the word, phrase, or number needed is on the "tip of the tongue" but not available. Procedures—motor skills and procedural rules—have a declarative knowledge component requiring that learners remember a list of steps. Principles often require declarative knowledge recall, such as a formula or a constant such as the value of pi. Understanding and ability to perform can be stymied by mere lack of ability to remember a simple fact. The governing factor in retrieval of labels, facts, and lists is the strength of the relationships between elements in an association. The more relationships between elements that are established, the easier the retrieval is. Therefore, to enhance transfer, the knowledge should be elaborated in as many different situations as is feasible. Once declarative knowledge is used, it becomes more easily retrieved for further use. The key to connected discourse recall is organization. The organization or structure of a lecture or text provides retrieval cues, much as retrieving a folder in a file allows us to retrieve the information in the file.

Transfer often involves making inferences—bridges between knowledge that have not been made for the learner. Inferences usually involve invoking prior knowledge combined with new information. In building expertise in a body of knowledge, such as a scholar or expert does, one can have the experience of "discovering" links and patterns between sets of information that were learned as separate, distinct entities. College students experience the joy of seeing relationships within their knowledge that seem to deepen and personalize knowledge, making it truly "their own." Opportunities for this sort of transfer to occur are increased when instruction encourages learners to make inferences from the material learned to other possible areas.

In our chemistry instruction, we want learners to be able to apply their knowledge of chemical names and symbols in reading chemical formulas. Practice within instruction or that provided during assessment of recently learned symbols in the context of chemical formulas can assist transfer.

Opportunities for transfer of the learning from our music history course will be available throughout the students' lives and will be actualized, depending on whether the student chooses to do so. Certainly the structure provided by the course can assist recall of the ideas in the course and can provide the learner with building blocks for a richly developed knowledge and appreciation of music.

Remotivate and Close

In remotivation and closure of declarative knowledge instruction, it is important to reemphasize the utility of the knowledge that has been learned. It is also important to encourage the learners to mentally manipulate the information on their own. For facts, labels, and lists, this mental manipulation may be rehearsal. For organized discourse, it may be elaboration with more information or seeking out redundancies, contradictions, or inferences.

Assessment of Declarative Knowledge

Assessment of declarative knowledge objectives involves learners' ability to recall or recognize, either in verbatim or paraphrased form, information that has been presented to them. Items can also be constructed in which the learners must produce a response. Declarative knowledge items should not assess learners' ability to *apply* this knowledge, which would be use of the information as an intellectual skill; rather, they should assess learners' ability to *remember* the information.

These items may take the form of recall items such as fill in the blank or short answer. The information in the stem of the question may be in either verbatim form from its original instructional source (e.g., textbook, film, lecture) or it may be in a paraphrased form that is synonymous in meaning. The response may be accepted in verbatim form only, or a paraphrased response may be acceptable. When using verbatim forms, the designer can only determine that the learner has memorized a response, whereas paraphrased forms may tap learners' *understanding* of the information. The following is an example of a *recall*, declarative knowledge question:

The component of the computer that is sometimes referred to as its "brains" is the _____.

This item happens to be a *verbatim* item, using the exact language from the text. It could be carefully revised to take the form of a paraphrased question:

The brain is to a human as the _____ is to a computer.

Of course, the designer would wish to ensure that the learners were familiar with answering questions in an analogy format like that above, or the reliability of the question would be threatened.

Recognition items are also used to assess the learning of declarative knowledge objectives. These questions require the learner to recognize the correct answer. The stem and foils (options) may be verbatim from the instructional source or paraphrased. Following are examples of verbatim items:

1. Write T for true and F for false.
   RAM is called the "brains" of the computer.
2. Which of the following computer components is called the "brains" of the computer?
   a. CPU
   b. ROM
   c. RAM
   d. DOS
3. Match each term to its definition by writing the letter of the definition beside the term.
   a. CPU   1. Permanent memory
   b. ROM   2. "Brains" of computer
   c. RAM   3. Temporary memory
   d. DOS   4. Binary code
              5. Language of communication between computer and disk drive

These items could be converted to paraphrased questions by carefully revising the language in the definitions to synonymous language:

a. Write T for true and F for false.
RAM is to a computer as brain is to a human.

Constructed answer items may also be written in the declarative knowledge domain. These items are almost always essay questions in a paraphrased form. They require the learner to select, recall, summarize, and synthesize information into a cogent form. Following is an example of a production form declarative knowledge item:

In your own words (100 words or less) summarize the similarities and differences between behavioral and cognitive theories of learning.

EXERCISES

1. Classify the following objectives using LN for labels or names, L for lists, and CD for comprehension of discourse.

In a written paragraph, the student will be able to summarize the newspaper article "City Council Considers Zoning Changes," Norman *Transcript*, 2/29/04.

Given a blank sheet of paper and no other aids or references, the student will be able to name the bones of the human body.

Given an illustration of a human skeleton, the student will be able to identify by name each bone.

The student will be able to draw the organizational chart of the company including names of the officers.

Given an organizational chart of the company, the student will be able to provide the names of the officers.

2. In the following scenarios of declarative knowledge learning, identify the cognitive activity (linking, organizing, or elaborating) that is being engaged and defend your choice by describing how the scenario exemplifies the cognitive activity you selected.

a. As the printed instruction on "The Arethectomy Procedure" describes steps of performing an arethectomy, which uses a tiny rotating blade to open clogged coronary arteries, each step is related in some fashion to corresponding or analogous steps in the commonly practiced angioplasty procedure, which uses an inflatable balloon to open clogged coronary arteries.

Circle the correct response and defend your choice:

Linking   *Organizing*   *Elaborating*

b. The printed instruction on the product called "Animals Alphabet" presents a character of the alphabet along with a picture of an animal on each page, the name of which begins with the alphabet letter in question, such as:

"A is for Annie Alligator" and "B is for Bobby Buffalo" and "C is for Charlie Cat"

Circle the correct response and defend your choice:

Linking   *Organizing*   *Elaborating*

c. The chemistry teacher suggests that students notice the color-coding of sections of the periodic table of the chemical elements. (This example may be relevant in both the sense of the instructor's directing attention to the color-coding as well as the color-coding of the table itself.)

Circle the correct response and defend your choice:

Linking   *Organizing*   *Elaborating*

d. The "top gun" fighter pilots tend to visualize explanations of combat tactics with their own internally generated mental images during explanations of combat maneuvers, even though the explanations provided by the instructor and training materials are generally illustrated richly with graphic displays and animations. The rest of the fighter pilot trainees seem to have equal aptitude and flying skills, but do not generate these imaginary visualized combat engagements as frequently as their more successful comrades.

Circle the correct response and defend your choice:

Linking   *Organizing*   *Elaborating*

SUMMARY

This chapter has taken a close look at designing instruction for the learning of declarative knowledge. Declarative knowledge, also called verbal information, is viewed as being represented in memory as propositional networks, or schemata, linking nodes of information by relationship. There are three kinds of declarative knowledge: labels/names, facts/lists, and organized discourse. Three activities common to all declarative knowledge learning are linking, organizing, and elaborating. Using the expanded instructional events as a framework, we looked at particular instructional techniques for declarative knowledge instruction. Within the discussion of the instructional events, illustrations from two sample applications were provided, one for a module on the periodic table (a facts/list task) and a second involving music history (an organized discourse task). Figure 8.5 recasts the remainder of the chapter's content into a summary frame.

EXTENDED EXAMPLE

Go to the Learning Resources Web site for a continuation the instructional design of the Photography Basics course. The contribution for this chapter is a lesson on f-stops, specifically, learning the common f-stop numbers, involving the learning of facts or a list.

READINGS AND REFERENCES

Anderson, J. R. (1976). *Language, memory and thought.* Hillsdale, NJ: Erlbaum.

Anderson, J. R. (1985). *Cognitive psychology and its implications* (3rd ed.). New York: W. H. Freeman.

Armbruster, B. B., & Anderson, T. H. (1985). Frames: Structures for informative text. In D. H. Jonassen (Ed.), *The technology of text: Vol. 2* (pp. 90–104). Englewood Cliffs, NJ: Educational Technology Publications.

Atkinson, R. C. (1975). Mnemotechnics in second-language learning. *American Psychologist, 30,* 821–828.

Ausubel, D. P. (1968). *Educational psychology: A cognitive view.* New York: Holt, Rinehart, & Winston.

Brown, J. S., Collins, A., & Duguid, P. (1989). Situated cognition and the culture of learning. *Educational Researcher, 18*(1), 32–42.

Bull, S. G. (1973). The role of questions in maintaining attention to textual material. *Review of Educational Research, 43*(61), 83–87.

Duchastel, P. (1978). Illustrating instructional texts. *Educational Technology, 18*(11), 36–39.

Gagné, E. D. (1985). *The cognitive psychology of school learning.* Boston: Little, Brown.

Gagné, R. M. (1985). *The conditions of learning* (4th ed.). New York: Holt, Rinehart, & Winston.

Gagné, R. M., & Briggs, L. J. (1979). *Principles of instructional design* (2nd ed.). New York: Holt, Rinehart, & Winston.

Gall, M. D. (1970). The use of questions in teaching. *Review of Educational Research, 40*(5), 707–721.

Heinich, R., Molenda, M., Russell, J. D., & Smaldino, S. (1996). *Instructional media and technologies for learning.* Upper Saddle River, NJ: Merrill/Prentice-Hall.

Hidi, S. (1985). *Variables that affect how children summarize school texts and the amount they learn during this activity.* Paper presented at the annual meeting of the American Educational Research Association, Chicago, IL.

Higbee, K. L. (1979). Recent research on visual mnemonics: Historical roots and educational fruits. *Review of Educational Research, 49*(4), 611–629.

Introduction	Deploy attention. Arouse interest and motivation.	• Use novel, conflictual, and paradoxical events; interject personal/emotional elements; and make clear how the present learning relates to other learning tasks.
	Establish instructional purpose.	• Relate instructor goals or job requirements, make instructional goals relevant, present goal in interesting format, remind learners of relevant learning strategies, point out requirements for successful attainment of the objective, and let learners know the form in which they need to remember.
	Preview lesson.	• Use advance organizers or epitomes and also outlines or maps, which can be useful forms of preview.
Body	Recall prior knowledge.	• Use advance organizers, metaphoric devices, and revises of prerequisite concepts.
	Process information.	• **Labels/Names** Organization: clustering and chunking. Elaboration: elaboration into sentences. • **Facts/Lists** Association: Images Organization: expository and narrative structures, recognizing patterns, clustering and chunking, and elaboration. • **Organized Discourse** Association: imagery, metaphoric devices. Organization: analysis of expository and narrative structures, use of graphic organizers—frames, concept mapping. Elaboration: elaboration model.
	Focus attention.	• Underline, list, and reflect; questions: pre- and post-, embedded.
	Employ learning strategies.	• Use previously noted strategies (all but advance organizer) • Employ mnemonic techniques such as single-use coding, pegwords, the method of loci, keywords, and the use of rhymes, stories, or jingles. • Rehearse.
	Practice.	• Role of practice; consider different needs for practice for recall vs. recognition learning tasks and for verbatim vs. paraphrased recall, for spaced practice, and the role of automaticity in declarative knowledge.
	Evaluate feedback.	• Consider feedback needed for labels, facts, and lists (evaluate correctness of associations of elements) as contrasted with the feedback needed for organized discourse ("understanding").
Conclusion	Summarize and review.	• Tune cognitive structures, learner generated summaries, interim summaries.
	Transfer knowledge.	• Increase the number of possible connections in the learner's mental map, the role of application in a variety of settings, and learners' inference making.
	Remotivate and close.	• Show how learning can help student.
Assessment	Assess performance.	• Take care to be congruent with objective.
	Provide feedback and remediation.	• Identify and clarify needs for learning.

Figure 8.5 Key Events for Declarative Knowledge Learning

Holley, C. D., & Dansereau, D. F. (Eds.) (1984). *Spatial learning strategies: Techniques, applications, and related issues.* Orlando, FL: Academic Press.

Houghton, H. A., & Willows, D. M. (1987). *The psychology of illustration: Vol. 2.* New York: Springer-Verlag.

Jih, H. J., & Reeves, T. C. (1992). Mental models: A research focus for interactive learning systems. *Educational Technology Research and Development, 40*(3), 39–53.

Jonassen, D. H. (Ed.). (1982). *The technology of text: Vol. I.* Englewood Cliffs, NJ: Educational Technology Publications.

Jonassen, D. H. (Ed.) (1985). *The technology of text: Vol. II.* Englewood Cliffs, NJ: Educational Technology Publications.

Joyce, B., & Weil, M. (1986). *Models of teaching* (3rd ed.). Upper Saddle River, NJ: Prentice-Hall.

Locatis, C. N., & Atkinson, F. D. (1984). *Media and technology for education and training.* Columbus, OH: Merrill.

Meyer, B. J. F. (1985). Signaling the structure of text. In D. H. Jonassen (Ed.), *The technology of text: Vol. 2* (pp. 64–89). Englewood Cliffs, NJ: Educational Technology Publications.

Minsky, M. A. (1975). A framework for representing knowledge. In P. H. Winston (Ed.), *The psychology of computer vision* (pp. 211–280). New York: McGraw-Hill.

Perkins, D. N. (1992). What constructivism demands of the learner. In T. M. Duffy & D. H. Jonassen (Eds.), *Constructivism and the technology of instruction* (pp. 161–165). Hillsdale, NJ: Erlbaum.

Posner, G. J., & Strike, K. A. (1976). A categorization scheme for principles of sequencing content. *Review of Educational Research, 46,* 665–690.

Pressley, M., Levin, J. R., & Delaney, H. D. (1982). The mnemonic keyword method. *Review of Educational Research, 52*(1), 61–91.

Reigeluth, C. M. (1979). In search of a better way to organize instruction: The elaboration theory. *Journal of Instructional Development, 2*(3) 8–15.

Reigeluth, C. M., & Stein, F. S. (1983). The elaboration theory of instruction. In C. M. Reigeluth (Ed.), *Instructional-design theories and models: An overview of their current status.* (pp.335–381). Hillsdale, NJ: Erlbaum.

Rothkoph, E. Z., & Bisbicos, E. E. (1967). Selective facilitative effects of interspersed questions on learning from written materials. *Journal of Educational Psychology, 58,* 56–61.

Rummelhart, D. E. (1980). Schemata: The building blocks of cognition. In R. J. Spiro, B. C. Bruce, & W. F. Brewer (Eds.), *Theoretical issues in reading comprehension* (pp. 33–58). Hillsdale, NJ: Erlbaum.

Rummelhart, D. E., & Norman, D. E. (1978). Accretion, tuning, and restructuring: Three modes of learning. In J. W. Cotton and R. Klatzky (Eds.), *Semantic factors in cognition.* (pp.37–54). Hillsdale, NJ: Erlbaum.

Rummelhart, D. E., & Ortony, A. (1977). The representation of knowledge in memory. In R. C. Anderson, R. J. Spiro, and W. E. Montague (Eds.), *Schooling and the acquisition of knowledge* (pp. 37–53). Hillsdale, NJ: Erlbaum.

Schank, R. C. (1984). *The cognitive computer: On language, learning, and artificial intelligence.* Reading, MA: Addison-Wesley.

Schramm, W. (1964). *The research on programmed instruction: An annotated bibliography.* Washington, DC: U.S. Dept. of Health, Education and Welfare, Office of Education. Publication number OE 34034.

Simon, H. A . (1974). How big is a chunk? *Science, 183,* 482– 488.

Smith, P. L., & Friend, M. (1986). Training learning disabled adolescents in a strategy for using text structure to aid recall of instructional prose. *Learning Disabilities Research, 2*(1), 38–44.

Smith, P. L., & Ragan, T. J. (1990). Designing visual analogies for instruction. *Journal of Visual Language, 10*(2), 60–83.

Smith, P. L., & Tompkins, G. E. (1988). Structured notetaking: A new strategy for content readers. *Journal of Reading, 32*(1), 46–53.

Sternberg, R. J. (1987). The psychology of verbal comprehension. In R. Glaser (Ed.), *Advances in instructional psychology, Vol. 3* (pp. 97–152). Hillsdale, NJ: Erlbaum.

Tessmer, M., Wilson, B., & Driscoll, M. (1990). A new model of concept teaching and learning. *Educational Technology Research and Development, 38*(1), 45–53.

Wager, W., & Wager, S. (1985). Presenting questions, processing responses, and providing feedback in CAI. *Journal of Instructional Development, 8* (4), 2–8.

West, C. K., Farmer, J. A., & Wolf, P. M. (1991). *Instructional design: Implications from cognitive science.* Upper Saddle River, NJ: Prentice-Hall.

Willows, D. M., & Houghton, H. A. (1987). *The psychology of illustration: Vol. 1.* New York: Springer-Verlag.

Zeitoun, H. H. (1984). Teaching scientific analogies: A proposed model. *Research in Science and Technological Education, 2,* 107–125.

STRATEGIES FOR INSTRUCTION LEADING TO CONCEPT LEARNING

CHAPTER OBJECTIVES

At the conclusion of this chapter, you should be able to do the following:

- Given descriptions of several learning tasks, identify those that are concept learning tasks.
- Given examples of an instructional strategy plan for concept learning, identify those that are inquiry and those that are expository.
- Describe the criterial attributes of a given concept.
- Given sets of concepts, identify those that are coordinate concepts.
- Develop a concept map of a given concept, indicating its relationship to superordinate and subordinate concepts.
- Determine a "best example" and a poor initial example for a given concept, and justify your choices.
- Develop a matched example and nonexample for a concept and explain your choice.
- Explain the processes of generalization and discrimination as they apply to concept learning.
- Explain the processes of overgeneralization and undergeneralization as they apply to a provided concept.
- Given a concept objective, design a strategy plan for a concept lesson or learning environment.

A REVIEW OF CONCEPT LEARNING

In Chapter 5, we identified concept learning as one of the intellectual skills, which involves the ability to apply knowledge across a variety of instances or circumstances. Intellectual skills, most often confused with declarative knowledge learning, differ from declarative knowledge learning in that declarative knowledge involves memorizing an association between two or more entities. One example is the association of a dog's appearance with its name. Intellectual skills involve the ability to apply knowledge across a variety of previously unencountered instances—in the case of a concept, the ability to respond "dog" to an infinite variety of usually four-legged, furry, sometimes barking domesticated canines. One definition of concept that we find particularly useful is the following:

> A concept is a set of specific objects, symbols, or events which are grouped together on the basis of shared characteristics and which can be referenced by a particular name or symbol. (Merrill & Tennyson, 1977, p. 3)

Examples of concepts include the following:

computer	Impressionism
house	Cold War
adverb	igneous
theory *Y*	hunter-gatherer
haiku	norm
profit	pulley
cartoon	scapegoat
forehand serve	bull market
triangle	beard
prime number	tax-sheltered annuity
blue	solid
reptile	cumulus cloud

Remember that there are two distinctly different kinds of concepts: concrete and abstract. Concrete concepts are known by their physical characteristics, which may be discerned by any of the senses—sight, smell, taste, touch, or hearing. In the preceding list, "computer," "house," "cartoon," "forehand serve," "triangle," "blue," "reptile," "igneous," "pulley," "beard," "solid," and "cumulus cloud" are most known by their physically perceivable characteristics, so they are concrete concepts. Ideas such as "profit," "haiku," "norm," "bull market," and "tax-sheltered annuity" are not perceivable by their appearance; indeed, some of them, such as "bull market," have no appearance. They are *abstract concepts*, sometimes called *defined concepts*. Members of this category are known only as they fit a particular definition.

Some of the above examples might fall into either category, concrete or abstract, depending upon the level of sophistication of the learners. For example, for a primary school child, a computer is a concrete, physically perceivable object. However, a college student knows that some television sets, dishwashers, and cash registers may also be considered "computers," because they have the built-in capability of processing information digitally. The college student knows the concept "computer" by the definition that includes a function, rather than solely by its physical appearance. The same concrete-to-abstract continuum might be applied to the concepts "cartoon," "triangle," "blue," "acid," and many others.

As you can see, the distinction between abstract and concrete concepts can become quite muddy; therefore, we will not ask you to classify examples of concepts as concrete or abstract. However, in the actual design of instruction, when you know the level of sophistication of your learners, you may wish to consider whether you are teaching a particular concept at the concrete or the abstract level because the way you address the two types is somewhat different.

At this point, it is helpful to review what concept learning is *not*. As we noted earlier, concept learning is frequently confused with learning declarative knowledge. Two misunderstandings are particularly common. One is confusing the learning of a concept with the learning of the definition of that concept. For example, if a child memorized the definition of a triangle as "a three-sided plane figure" but was unable to find the triangles in a set of figures, then the child would only have learned "triangle" at the declarative knowledge level. Another misunderstanding has to do with the labeling of things versus identification of membership in a class of things. A child who points to a dog and says "Gracie" has acquired declarative knowledge. If she points to the dog and says "golden retriever," she has acquired a concept. Declarative knowledge learning enables a person to identify a particular member of the concept category, such as saying, "That is Mt. Kilimanjaro." Concept learning allows a person to identify something when given a picture not previously seen such as saying, "That is an extinct volcano."

Concept learning is also not the application of a principle that contains that concept. For example, learning the concept "the commutative property of addition" would involve recognizing its application. Consider this example:

In which of the following problems is the commutative property applied?

$$2 + 3 = 3 + 2$$
$$2 + 3 = 4 + 1$$
$$(1 + 1) + (2 + 1) = 1 + (1 + 2) + 1$$
$$x + 2 = 14$$

The ability to identify that the first example illustrates the property and the other three do not is a concept level task. The actual application of the commutative property as a principle would require the solution of a particular math problem using the property, such as:

$$2 + 3 = \_\_ + 2$$

A learner who has acquired a concept is able to use that concept to classify previously unencountered instances as members of that concept class or not. We say "previously unencountered instances" because if we assess learners' acquisition of concepts with examples they have encountered in initial instruction or in practice, they may simply have memorized the association rather than actually being able to apply the concept.

Learners who have acquired concepts are also able to supply their own examples of the concepts and apply the concepts appropriately in day-to-day encounters. For example, learners have acquired the concept "bourgeois" if they use it appropriately in speech or writing and understand its meaning when they hear it used. Concepts have both a declarative knowledge aspect and a procedural (intellectual skill) knowledge, pattern recognition aspect (Tessmer, Wilson, & Driscoll, 1990). In this chapter we will discuss the procedural knowledge aspect of concepts.

When we have spoken of "characteristics" of concepts, we have substituted a word that allows you to follow the idea up to this point without using a technical term that requires definition. The technical term for characteristics of concepts is *attributes*. Klausmeier (1992) described three kinds of concept attributes: intrinsic, functional, and relational. An **intrinsic attribute** of a concept is an "invariant property of an observable thing or class of things that typically can be pointed to" (p. 269). Both functional and relational attributes are what we might call *variable attributes*— qualities that can be *possessed by an example* of a concept but which can vary from instance to instance. In other words, the variable attributes of a concept are things that can vary in specific instances or examples of that concept. For example, for the concept "automobile," some variable attributes would be make, model, year, color, owner, and so on. A **functional attribute** relates to how something works and what its use might be, and a **relational attribute** is a quality a concept may possess defined in terms of something else. Klausmeier's approach to the nature of concepts is particularly deep-running and can be extremely useful when a simpler level of consideration is not sufficient. We will limit our consideration of attributes to what Klausmeier calls "intrinsic attributes," and we will use the single term *attributes* to refer to them.

COGNITIVE PROCESSES AND STRUCTURES IN CONCEPT LEARNING

We say that learners have acquired a concept when they have learned to recognize a "pattern" in their surroundings and consistently respond to that pattern, no matter what nonessential features may appear along with that pattern. Learning a concept requires two cognitive processes—generalization and discrimination. When learners are first exposed to a member of a concept, they must learn to **generalize** beyond the single instance of that concept to others that fall into the same category. Generalization is a cognitive process by which we induce generalities from particulars. For example, a young child who sees a picture of cows in a pasture may point to one of the animals and ask, "What's that?" The instructor would respond, "A cow." It is very likely that if the child has not yet learned the concept "cow," then she might point to another of the cows in the picture and ask, "What's that?" The faithful instructor (or parent) will respond again, "A cow." Eventually, the child might point to another animal in the pasture and ask, "Cow?" and receive all of the feedback and encouragement she needs. The child has generalized the concept of "cow" beyond the single first instance encountered to other examples of the concept.

However, when people first learn concepts, they tend to **overgeneralize.** For example, the child who has learned that a large, four-legged animal is a cow may have a tendency to respond "cow" to a picture of a horse, zebra, moose, and many other large, four-legged animals. Gradually, the child learns to **discriminate** between examples of the concept and nonexamples that may share some features with the concept but do not share the critical, or "criterial" attributes that make an instance a member of the class. For example, cows' general body shapes, as well as the shapes of their heads, hooves, and tails, make them distinct from other large, four-legged mammals. The instructor helps the child make these discriminations by saying, "No, that's not a cow. Look at how thin and long the head is. That's not the head of a cow. Look again at the cow's head. It's short and wide."

Please note that it may be possible that in learning concepts, learners first make discriminations that certain entities are similar to each other and that other entities are distinctly different from the group; they then make generalizations. We do know that learners must be able to distinguish differences among entities before they are able to move on to form a concept around one or the other of them. For example, learners must be able to distinguish that a figure that is a circle is different from a figure that is a square before they can acquire the concept "square." It may be slightly more efficient to encourage learners to generalize before they are encouraged to consciously discriminate the distinctive features of a concept. Later you will see that we suggest two slightly different sequences of instruction—one that encourages generalization first and one that encourages discrimination first.

Another necessary generalization of a concept is learners' ability to transfer the concept to settings other than the setting in which they first encountered it. We know that the child has really acquired the concept "cow" when he identifies cows in settings other than the picture in which he first started learning "cow" (for instance, when he points to the billboard advertising a milk company whose logo is a cow and says, "cow," or when he points to a real cow and identifies it as a "cow").

Concept learning can go wrong in two ways. First, learners can continue to overgeneralize, as does the child who continues to say "cow" in response to four-legged animals other than cows, or learners can **undergeneralize,** as with a child who thinks only black-and-white animals with cow features are "cows." In each case, particular instructional strategies can prevent or remediate overgeneralization and undergeneralization of the concept.

Note how critical learning the class label or concept name is to acquiring the concept. While it is theoretically possible that a learner could respond to a class of things without knowing the class's name, the learner must have some label that she uses to mentally represent that class. To have efficient communication, learners must be able to respond to examples of the concept with its name.

Cognitive psychologists theorize that concepts are mentally stored in the form of productions, an if-then representation. For example, the concept "rhombus" might be stored in the following form:

IF the figure is a polygon,

  and the figure is a parallelogram,

  and the figure's sides are equilateral,

THEN the figure is a rhombus.

These productions result from the generalization and discrimination processes. Notice how closely this production mirrors our information-processing analysis of the task of learning the concept "rhombus" in Chapter 5. It is quite possible that these productions do not happen on the conscious level but rather are automatic for learners who are proficient in the application of a particular concept. We often find this automaticity to be the case when conducting an information-processing analysis of a concept learning task. Sometimes quite lengthy and probing questioning is required to ascertain the qualities that an expert uses when assigning entities to categories.

When concepts are grouped together in instruction, all representing one domain, they are generally considered to be either **successive concepts** or **coordinate concepts** (Merrill & Tennyson, 1977; Tennyson & Cocchiarella, 1986). Successive concepts are sets of concepts with a common, superordinate parent concept. Coordinate concepts are sets of concepts in which the characteristics for one concept are in part supplied or defined by others in the set. The production rules for successive concepts are more or less independent, whereas for coordinate concepts, production rules are more dependent on one another. For example, to recognize a coniferous tree when you see it, you have to have had experience seeing not only coniferous trees but also seeing deciduous; so, the concepts are coordinate. However, to know what a biography is, you just need to know what it is—knowing what autobiographies, novels, and short stories are (more precisely, being able to recognize a piece of prose that is unlabeled and you've never seen before as an autobiography) is not necessary to have the concept "biography." In addition, successive concepts have noncritical attributes in common but criterial attributes are not shared, so Ford, Chevy, and Plymouth are successive. Coordinate concepts have criterial attributes in common, so translucent, transparent, and opaque are coordinate (light can pass through both transparent and translucent objects; a clear image cannot be seen through either translucent or opaque objects, and so forth). In teaching coordinate concepts, the examples of one concept can serve as nonexamples for others. Frequently, coordinate concepts require simultaneous presentation of examples and nonexamples to acquire the concepts quickly (Tennyson & Cocchiarella, 1986). Additional examples of coordinate concepts are convex and concave lenses, loose and strict constructionism, stalactite and stalagmite, systolic and diastolic pressures, and synonyms and antonyms.

Another classification of concepts has been provided by Klausmeier (1990, 1992). In this system, concepts are described in terms of increasing depth of processing: concrete, identity, classificatory, and formal. In a sense, these four types of concepts refer to a process of concept development. The first two types, *concrete* and *identity,* refer to the process of discrimination that is part of concept learning. The third, *classificatory,* represents being able to recognize previously unencountered examples and nonexamples of the concept but having limited ability to describe the reasons why one is an example and another one is not. The fourth type, *formal,* represents concept learning as we approach it here, and its attainment requires experiences that are consistent with what we prescribe for instructional conditions. When concept learning has attained a formal level, an individual can identify examples and nonexamples as well as name the concept and its defining attributes, provide a definition of the concept, and specify critical attributes of the concept, even those that differentiate it from closely related concepts. (It is a good idea to review Klausmeier's highly compatible conception of concept learning, enriching your background with the ample research evidence he supplies to support his highly developed theory.)

ESSENTIAL CONDITIONS OF LEARNING CONCEPTS

The essential conditions in a concept lesson or learning environment are the features that promote generalization and discrimination and reduce over- and undergeneralization. Although the most critical features of a concept lesson lie in the events within the body of the lesson, we will describe important features within each of the four main components of the lesson. You will notice that we do not list each of the expanded events in the order in which we first introduced them. This variation further underscores the notion that the order of these instructional events may vary with the learning task, learners, and context.

In this discussion of instruction for learning concepts, we hope you will not only focus on the particular ideas and techniques presented, but also note the differences between what instruction looked like in the previous chapter on declarative knowledge and what it looks like here. A continuing goal you may wish to pursue is to learn how different types of learning can best be achieved through different instructional strategies.

Two General Strategies of Concept Instruction

Concept instruction may follow one of two general strategies: a predominantly generative strategy or a more supplantive one. One type of generative strategy is termed an **inquiry approach.** It is contrasted to a more typically supplantive strategy called an **expository approach.** Neither approach is particularly better than the other, but one may be more appropriate than the other depending upon the context, the learners, and the learning task.

An **inquiry strategy** is often referred to as an *exploratory strategy* or a *discovery approach.* An inquiry strategy presents examples and nonexamples of the concept and prompts the learners to induce or "discover" the concept underlying the instances. Joyce and Weil's (1986) "concept attainment model" is an example of an inquiry approach to teaching concepts. In this strategy, learners are presented with a group of matched examples and nonexamples in verbal, auditory, or visual form. The examples are labeled with the word *yes,* and the nonexamples are labeled with the word *no.*

Learners are invited to join in a guessing game to discover the secret (the concept) as to why some instances are labeled *yes* and others *no.* Learners are encouraged to develop a tentative hypothesis as to the concept underlying the categorization. Then they are presented with more examples and nonexamples labeled *yes* and *no.* Each learner is prompted to confirm his hypothesis by determining if it would predict the categorization of the new instances. Next, learners are invited to state their hypotheses regarding the concept. Some hypotheses may be fallacious, some may be unrelated to the targeted concept (these should be accepted but not further investigated at this time), and others will be correct. These hypotheses should be formalized into a statement of the concept. Finally, learners are encouraged to think of their own examples of the concept and receive feedback regarding the accuracy of their examples. (The example lesson on the concept "art deco" that appears later in this chapter is an example of a slightly different inquiry approach.)

An **expository approach** presents the concept, its label, and its criterial attributes earlier in the lesson sequence than in the inquiry approach. Expository instruction, like inquiry instruction, presents many examples and nonexamples; however, these instances follow a discussion of a best example and how it embodies the characteristics of the concept. In an expository approach learners are encouraged to develop their own examples; however, it is after the attributes of the concept have been carefully discussed. The sequence used in the following discussion of the expanded instructional events employs a more expository sequence. The extended example that teaches the concept "depth of field" in the Learning Resources Web site also uses an inquiry approach.

INTRODUCTION

Deploy Attention/Arouse Interest and Motivation

In text-based concept lessons, learners' attention can be grabbed simply by using boldface type or otherwise highlighting a new term. That term is then further explored in the remainder of the lessons. Inquiry strategies are often highly attention provoking, interest arousing, and motivating. An unusual picture or humorous story relating to the concept may also stimulate interest and attention. Information about the origin or history of the concept to be learned may also promote these two events. The instruction may even present the first matched set of examples and nonexamples of the concept to focus learners' attention on the characteristics of the task, pique their curiosity, and begin to inform them of the objective, all in one step. A matched set of examples and nonexamples is provided by a clear example of the concept and an instance that is similar in some features but is not an example of the concept. For many older learners and adults, information is also provided about how knowledge of this concept will relate to future tasks or problems.

Establish Instructional Purpose

Instructional purpose may be selected by the individual learner ("I'm going to learn the difference between Level 1, Level 2, and Level 3 interactive video."), or it may be provided by the instruction ("Today we're going to learn to distinguish between the legislative, executive, and judicial branches of a government."). A statement of the goal is more typical in an expository form of instruction. A lesson that is structured in an inquiry organization may not inform the learners of the specific purpose of the lesson at its beginning, as this revelation would short-circuit the inquiry process; however, it is critical that within the summary and closure events, it is confirmed that learners clearly understood the purpose of the lesson.

Preview Lesson

The preview of an expository lesson may, if desired, not only provide an overview of the content to be learned but also provide an indication of how the lesson will proceed, such as explaining to learners that they will see examples and nonexamples of the concept under study until they are able to demonstrate that they are able to distinguish examples of these concepts. An inquiry preview may set up the "problem" of the inquiry task, letting learners know that they will be discerning the categories of instances and determining the characteristics by which the instances were placed in these categories, such as a teacher saying, "You will decide what boxes we will make up, and you'll also decide what goes in each box."

Body

Recall Prior Knowledge

The most critical prior knowledge in learning a concept is the knowledge of concepts that comprise the criterial attributes or characteristics of the concept. For example, to learn the concept "rhombus," learners must already possess the concepts "figure," "polygon," "parallelogram," "side," and "equilateral." It is quite likely that before learners reach this point in instruction, they will have already acquired these concepts. If not, these prerequisite learnings must be taught before (or concurrently with) instruction on the concept "rhombus." Teaching the concepts concurrently may be efficient, but

it may sacrifice some clarity, because the concepts are not coordinate and are, therefore, more difficult to teach at the same time.

If the prerequisite concepts have been learned previously, a brief review of these concepts is very useful. This review may take the form of (1) informal questioning of the learners to ensure that they remember the concepts, (2) a formal pretest with feedback, (3) a formal review of each of the prerequisite concepts, or (4) an integrated review of each prerequisite concept as it becomes important in discussing the concept's critical attributes in the Process Information and Examples event.

For concepts that have less esoteric prerequisites (those with criterial prerequisites that come from general world knowledge), the designer may choose to remind the learners of this general world knowledge through the use of an advance organizer. Ausubel, Novak, and Hanesian (1968) suggested the advance organizer as a way to tie prior knowledge to new learning. In particular, the comparative organizer seems most appropriate for teaching concepts. Borrowing from Ausubel's example, suppose a designer wished to teach the concept "Buddhism." One way to bring relevant concepts to working memory is to review the critical characteristics of the dominant religion of the learners in the target audience. These attributes provide a basis of comparison for the new religion being introduced, and the attributes of the new concept can be made more meaningful by being compared to the familiar. In other words, a comparative organizer reviews a coordinate concept that the learners have acquired previously to allow learners to make clear comparisons between the two concepts.

Process Information and Examples

Critical to these necessary cognitive processes are the examples and nonexamples that learners encounter in the initial processing of information about a targeted concept and the practice of that concept. When possible, the first example (sometimes called the *best example* or *prototype*) of the concept should be carefully selected. This example should clearly embody all of the necessary attributes (sometimes called *criterial attributes*) of the concept with few distracting or irrelevant attributes, and it should be familiar to the learners. For example, if the concept to be learned is "transparent," then the first example should concisely represent the concept. A glass window pane is a good best example because (1) it is unequivocally transparent, (2) there are few situations in which a glass window pane would not be transparent, (3) window panes generally vary little in their characteristics, and (4) window panes are familiar objects. A poor example would be a light bulb because clear glass light bulbs are transparent, but some bulbs are frosted and therefore translucent. Another poor example would be the front surface of a typical household mirror. Although it is transparent, this is difficult to visualize as transparent. Later in the lesson, these difficult examples should be used to help the learners refine their generalization and discrimination, but they are not sufficiently obvious to use as first examples.

A procedure that assists in generating and selecting examples is provided by the **rational set generator** technique (Driscoll & Tessmer, 1985). A "rational set" of examples for concepts within a topic area is created (or "generated") by laying out a matrix. On one axis are the criteria for concept discrimination (or the means by which one concept can be distinguished from another) and on the other axis are the criteria for concept generalization (for example, the various contexts in which the concept can be used) (see Figure 9.1). Specific applications are developed that suggest, if not specify, an example in each cell of the matrix. Such a set of examples can be highly useful in both instruction and assessment.

The selection and sequencing of examples can be influenced by whether concepts being taught are successive or coordinate. In our earlier discussion of concept learning, recall that the examples of one concept can serve as nonexamples for others when teaching coordinate concepts, and that simultaneous presentation of examples and nonexamples may be needed as well. With successive concepts, simultaneous presentation of examples and nonexamples is not needed (Tennyson & Cocchiarella, 1986).

Focus Attention

The instruction should point out, either by the definition or a description of the criterial attributes of the concept, why the example represents the concept. Pointing out the criterial attributes is called **attribute isolation.** For some learners—those who possess lower aptitude, those who possess few learning strategies, younger students, or extremely anxious learners—providing visual cues to the attributes as they are isolated may be helpful. These visual cues for concrete concepts could be simplified illustrations to highlight the attributes in the instance that make it an example or a nonexample. For abstract concepts, highlighting may also be used within the defini-

SUBJECT MATTER CLASSES		
Science Physics Chemistry	Technology Industry Engineering	Art Homemaking Business Recreation
Solidification — A physicist uses an oven to convert aluminum to molten aluminum.	A blast furnace converts iron ore to molten steel.	A burning candle heats its wax until the wax runs down the side in drops.
Sublimation — A chemist electrifies a mound of sulfur, which releases sulfur fumes.	A steel factory burns 10 tons of coal a day, which creates a lot of coal fumes.	A ranger burns a bunch of tree limbs to make a smoke signal.
Solidification — A physics student puts some molten lead into the freezer to harden.	A blob of mud poured on a hot sidewalk soon becomes a pile of dirt.	After a volcanic eruption, lava cools to form lava rock.
Evaporation — A bottle of alcohol is heated to release alcohol fumes.	While it runs, a drill engine burns gasoline, which ends up as exhaust.	A glass of soda left outside soon will dry up and become part of the atmosphere.
Liquefaction — A scientist sends electric jolts through a chamber of hydrogen and oxygen to create water.	An engineer uses a compressor to convert alcohol fumes back into alcohol.	When the sky is hit by lightning bolts, rain is often created.
Cohesion — A scientist discovers that glass plates can be joined by sliding one plate over another.	A doctor closes a small wound by pressing one piece of skin onto another one.	After a snowfall, a fresh layer of snow will cling to old layers of snow on the ground.
Adhesion — When a chemist pushes a piece of steel next to a piece of aluminum, they stick together.	A mechanic notices that oil clings to his rubber gloves.	A teacher runs a piece of chalk across a blackboard, which leaves a white mark on the board.

Figure 9.1 Examples of Changes in Matter from a Rational Set Generator.
Source: Tessmer & Driscoll, 1986. Reprinted from *Educational Communications and Technology Journal* by permission of the Association for Educational Communications and Technology. Copyright 1986 by AECT.

tion or within the verbal instance to focus the learners' attention on the criterial attributes of the concept and the relevant features of the instance.

Once the learners understand why the example is an example of the concept, they should encounter a matched nonexample of the concept. The nonexample should be matched with the best example on all the nonrelevant attributes so that criterial characteristics will be distinctive. For example, a wall, which is clearly not transparent, shares many of the nonrelevant attributes with a window (e.g., it is flat and vertical), making it a good matched nonexample. Again, a discussion of why the nonexample is not an example of the concept is essential.

Initial encounters with examples and nonexamples should be followed by the processing of additional examples and matched nonexamples that become more and more difficult, such as the clear light bulb example, the front surface of a mirror, or the glass in front of a television screen. Increasing the complexity of the examples encourages learners to make finer and finer discriminations of the critical and nonrelevant attributes of the concept. In addition, the examples and nonexamples should be as widely dispersed across settings as possible to encourage learners to generalize and transfer the concept to as many appropriate settings as possible. For a more generative strategy, learners may supply this step themselves, if the medium of instruction allows for accurate feedback to the learners as to whether their examples and nonexamples are appropriate. For example, teacher-led instruction can allow for confirmation of the accuracy of learners' examples, while print-based instruction cannot be so accurate. Unless the number of possible examples is fairly limited, computer-based instruction is limited in giving specific feedback to learners.

Practice

Exposure to examples and nonexamples is accompanied by practice, from something very simple to discriminate to a most difficult instance. It is useful if the settings from which the examples and nonexamples are drawn are as random as possible. This practice should include learners distinguishing between previously unencountered examples and nonexamples of the concept, including learners isolating the key attributes of the examples and nonexamples. Learners should occasionally be asked to explain their answers. The examples and nonexamples used should be carefully selected to elicit any misconceptions the learners might have. These examples and nonexamples should provide opportunities for learners to overgeneralize and undergeneralize the concept. In addition, learners should practice producing their own examples (if feedback is possible).

Evaluate Feedback

Feedback provided to the learners should include an explanation of why an instance is classified as an example or nonexample. This explanation may include criterial attribute isolation, which for abstract concepts may refer to the definition. If learners have *overgeneralized* the concept, they should be provided with clear information as to why their examples are not actually examples of that concept. They should be informed of what criterial attributes they are overlooking. If learners have *undergeneralized* the concept, they should be encouraged to determine which features of their examples are not actually criterial attributes of the concept. These learners have narrowed the concept inappropriately in some way and need to recognize that they have done so.

Feedback for production answers—answers in which learners provide their own examples of the concept—may be direct when a person is evaluating the practice answers. For other delivery systems, such as computers, feedback for production answers can be accomplished by providing guiding questions keyed to the criterial attributes of the concept. These questions allow learners to evaluate the adequacy of their own answers: "Is your example of a transparent object an object through which an image can be seen clearly? If so, it is a transparent object."

Employ Learning Strategies

Some strategies that a learner may employ in acquiring concepts have already been mentioned—elaborating by inventing one's own examples and isolating attributes and highlighting these attributes in some way. These strategies may be "built into the instruction" (within the body, conclusion, or remediation events), provided by the learner, prompted by the instruction, or a combination of all three. An approach to concept instruction proposed by Tessmer, Wilson, and Driscoll (1990) emphasizes the use of analogies, learning strategies, and thinking strategies. We will discuss four strategies: the development of concept "trees" or "maps," analogies, mnemonics, and the use of imagery.

Concept trees are hierarchical, graphic representations of a targeted concept that show that concept's relationship to superordinate and subordinate concepts. Figure 9.2 shows an example of a concept map developed by Driscoll and Tessmer (1985) to show the relationship of five easily confused coordinate concepts: positive reinforcement, the Premack principle, negative reinforcement, punishment, and extinction. Note that they included not only the labels for these concepts but also verbal descriptions of their criterial attributes and an example of each. To engage the learning strategy, learners might construct the entire map or complete a partially developed map.

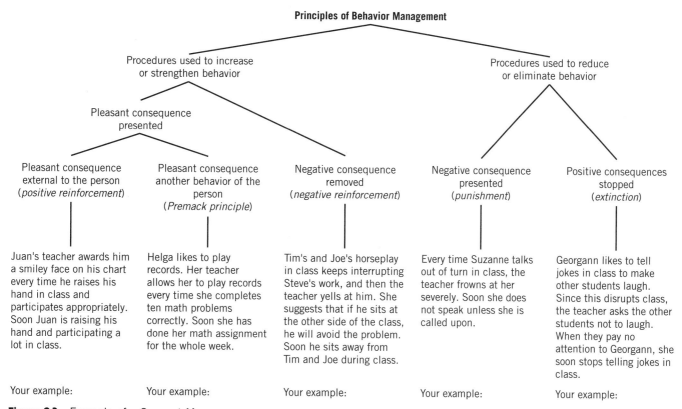

Figure 9.2 Example of a Concept Map.
Source: Driscoll & Tessmer (1985). Paper presented to the annual meeting of the *American Educational Research Association*, Chicago, IL. Reprinted with permission.

Analogies also help learners understand and remember concepts, particularly concepts for which learners possess little related prior knowledge. Analogies may be presented by the instruction, or the learners may be prompted to develop their own verbal or visual analogies. The development of analogies may be useful for both abstract and concrete concepts; however, analogies may be most helpful in making abstract concepts more concrete. An example is the analogy between the iris of an eye and the aperture of a camera. The point(s) of similarity between the new concept and the familiar concept should be related to the criterial attributes of the concept. For example, the similarity between the eye's iris and a camera's aperture is that they both allow light to pass through to a receiving medium (the film or the retina) and that they control the amount of light passing through by expanding or contracting the opening. It is important that learners are encouraged to consider where the analogy breaks down so they do not develop misconceptions about the concept. For instance, one of the differences between the iris and an aperture is in the nature of the receiving medium. Film becomes overexposed if too much light falls upon it; it has a finite limit of the length of time that it should be exposed to light. While the retina can receive too much light, such as when viewing the sun in an eclipse, this overexposure has to do with the intensity rather than the duration of the light falling on the retina.

Mnemonics are more often used to remember verbal information than in concept learning. However, there are verbal information components to learning a concept. One of these components is the association of the concept label to the concept. Particularly when co-ordinate concepts are learned, learners may have difficulty relating the correct label to the correct concept. When these associations cannot be made meaningful easily, use of mnemonics may be helpful. Many of us learned proper associations of the terms *stalactite* and *stalagmite* by remembering that stalactites "hold *tight* to the cave's ceiling" and stalagmites "reach for the cave's ceiling with all their *might*." Mnemonics may also be used to aid learners in remembering the multiple, critical attributes of a concept, and these may be provided by the instruction or created by the learners.

Imagery is another useful strategy for learning certain concepts. Although creating mental images may be easier with concrete concept objectives, some learners may find that developing a visual that concretely represents an abstract concept is very helpful. For example, you can see in Figure 9.3 how the author of a research methods text chose to represent the concepts "validity" and "reliability." Such images, provided by the instruction or pro-

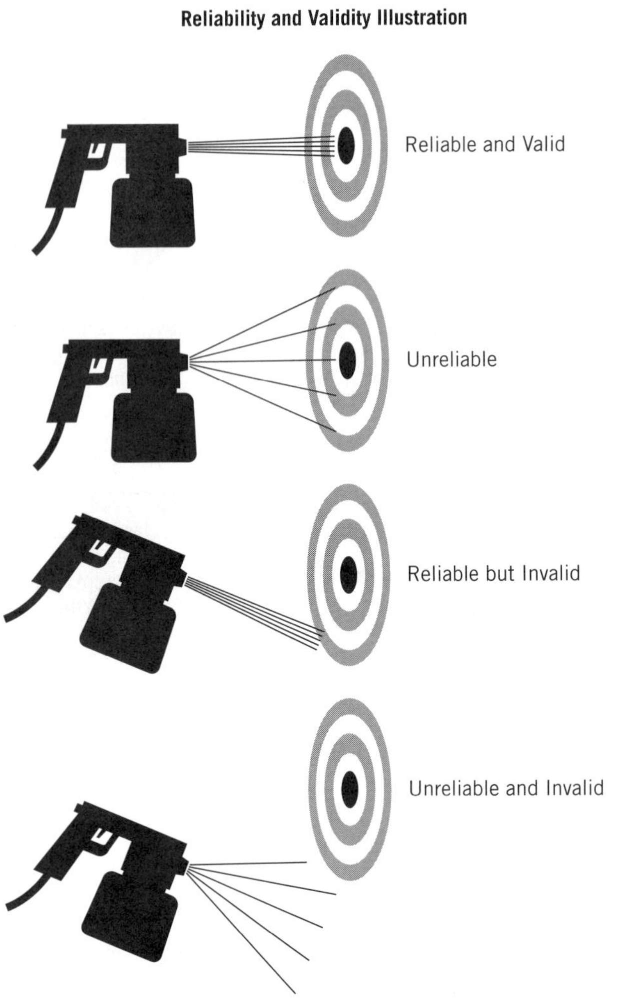

Reliability and Validity Illustration

Reliable and Valid

Unreliable

Reliable but Invalid

Unreliable and Invalid

Figure 9.3 Visual Representation of the Concepts "Validity" and "Reliability"
Source: Patten (2002). Used with permission of Pyrczak Publishing.

duced by learners, may be manipulated mentally or committed to paper or computer for future reference.

Conclusion

Summarize and Review

At this point in the lesson, it is helpful to restate the definition or criterial attributes of the concept as well as the concept name. It is not uncommon for learners to forget the name of the concept they have just spent so much time learning, so emphasizing this association is important. It is also useful, if possible, to paraphrase this statement of the definition rather than present the original statement verbatim so that learners attend to the meaning rather than the exact terms used in the definition. This might be the point where an instructor directs learners to develop or complete a concept map of the concept(s) just learned.

Transfer Knowledge

Learners should be asked to locate examples of the concept they have learned in everyday context, perhaps bringing them up for class discussion and confirmation of their categorization. In addition, learners should be encouraged to use the concept label appropriately in conversation as much as possible. Learners can begin also to make inferences from the concept. For example, if learners have just learned the coordinate concepts "deciduous" and "coniferous," they might be asked, "If Mr. Rogers hates to rake leaves in the fall, what kind of trees should he plant in his yard?"

Remotivate and Close

To experience this event in conjunction with the transfer event, learners may be encouraged to predict how the newly acquired concept may be applied to daily life and how it might be useful in future job responsibilities or learning tasks. Since learning concepts is usually a preamble to learning principles and problem solving, the instruction may preview how this new learning will be useful and what learning task will be addressed in the next class meeting.

Assessment of Concept Learning

Assess Learning

Remember that assessment of concepts may involve learners doing the following:

1. Explaining why a given, previously unencountered instance is or is not an example of a concept.
2. Categorizing given instances as examples and nonexamples of a concept, with or without an explanation of the thinking processes behind the learners' categorization.
3. Producing their own examples of a concept, with or without explanation.

As with practice, learners should be assessed across the range of difficulty of the concept. If recognition items are used, then they should be constructed so distractors represent possible overgeneralization or undergeneralizations of the concept.

In addition, learners may also be assessed on their ability to use the concept to draw inferences, consider the implications of the concept, and use the concept in writing or oral conversation. These transfer items should be separated from the "nearer" transfer items (the performance related to the stated objective), so that learners are not surprised by their appearance.

The assessment may involve a constructed answer, as suggested in point 3 of our list, "constructing their own examples of a concept, with or without explanation." Here are two examples of recognition items:

1. Which of the following is opaque?

    a. Clear water

    b. A white net

    c. A dog in front of a TV set

    d. A frosted mug of soda

2. Write True or False.

    A mirror is translucent.

Of course, to be a valid assessment of a learner's ability to apply this concept, rather than her ability to recall examples given in class, the options given in item 1 and the example given in item 2 should not be examples used during presentation of information or practice in the lesson.

A constructed answer item would ask the learner to supply an instance of the concept that was not presented in class:

3. Give an example of something that is transparent. (Do not use one of the examples that we used in class.)

Concepts cannot be assessed with a recall item because the concept must be applied, rather than recalled, for us to say that the learner has acquired the concept. Related declarative knowledge, such as the definition of the concept, may be tested with a recall item, but this is not an assessment of the acquisition of the concept itself.

Occasionally, to obtain a more reliable assessment of concept learning, we combine the recognition and constructed answer formats into an item that looks like the following:

4. Is chocolate milk translucent? Explain why or why not.

Such an item requires learners to recognize whether chocolate milk is an example of the concept "translucent." It also requires that the learners produce an adequate explanation of their choice. This type of item helps to eliminate the possibility that learners have guessed in answering the question.

Evaluate Feedback and Seek Remediation

Feedback should be given to the learners in terms of whether they appear to have mastered the goal. Their mastery should include not only the ability to identify examples and nonexamples but also the ability to use the concept correctly by developing their own examples. In addition, if transfer items are included, a learner's ability to transfer the concept should be reported separately from his ability to meet the goal as stated.

Remediation should consider a learner's ability to identify examples and nonexamples, her ability to explain their categorization, and whether she is over- or undergeneralizing the concept. Overgeneralization may be remediated by presenting learners with matched ex-amples and nonexamples and isolating the attributes that make the examples viable and the nonexamples not viable. Undergeneralization may be remediated by presenting the learners with an extremely broad range of examples of the concept; attribute isolation should emphasize that despite the variability of the examples, all of them fall into the concept category.

In the discussion of instruction for learning concepts, we hope you will not only focus on the particular ideas and techniques presented, but also note the differences between what instruction looked like in the previous chapter on declarative knowledge and what it looks like here. A continuing goal you may wish to pursue is to learn how different types of learning can best be achieved through different instructional strategies.

E X E R C I S E S

1. Which of the following are concept learning tasks? Justify your answer.

    a. State the definition of *refraction.*

    b. Listen to the following music intervals. Which are fifths?

    c. Explain the kinetic theory of matter.

    d. Circle the pronouns in the sentence.

    e. Read the following sentences. Write the correct form of the verb in the blank in the sentence.

    f. Solve this quadratic equation.

    g. Give an example of a minority.

    h. What is a vegetable?

2. Refer to the examples of generative and supplantive strategies in the Exercises at the end of Chapter 7 (numbers 1 and 2). Which of the examples follows an inquiry approach? Which follows a more expository approach? Explain your answer.

3. Which of the following would be considered criterial attributes of the concept "golden retriever"? Which are irrelevant attributes of the concept? Explain your categorization.

    a. Has a yellow coat with "feathering" at back of legs and tail

    b. Is named "Maggie"

    c. Has a big tail

    d. Good-natured

    e. Drives a Swedish car

    f. Is a dog

    g. Displays a kindly expression

    h. Is female

    i. Is a mammal

4. Which of the following groups of concepts could be considered coordinate concepts? Explain your answer.

- **a.** Inquiry and expository strategies
- **b.** Reptile and snake
- **c.** Perennial and annual flowers
- **d.** Dependent and independent clauses
- **e.** Lever and seesaw
- **f.** Solid, liquid, and gas

5. Construct a concept map representing the relationship of the coordinate concepts "deciduous" and "coniferous" to each other and to superordinate and subordinate concepts.

6. What would be a good best example for the concept "mammal"? Why? What would be a poor best example for the concept "mammal"? Why?

7. Give a matched example and nonexample for the concept "verb." Why do you consider the two instances to be matched?

8. Using the concept "stringed instrument," and the best example "violin," explain what would occur as the learner passed through the phases of generalization and discrimination in learning the concept.

9. Explain what a learner might do if he overgeneralized the concept "bicycle." What might he do or say if he undergeneralized the concept "bicycle"?

10. Read Carl Bereiter's critique of how concepts are thought of and used in school learning (Bereiter, 2002, pp. 306–312). Write a reaction paper, addressing at least "what are concepts good for?", "why should we teach concepts?", and "what would you recommend to improve instruction for concepts?"

EXAMPLE CONCEPT LESSON: ART DECO

Analysis of the Task, Context, and Learners

The next section presents a sample concept lesson on recognizing examples of the concept "art deco." (This is in addition to our extended example on photography in this book's Learning Resources Web site.) To preview the lesson, we will briefly describe the instructional task, the context, and the learners.

Task Analysis

The lesson objective is the following:

> Given a series of color photographs of architectural elements, some of which are examples of art deco and some of which are representative of other art periods, the learner will be able to identify those that are examples of art deco.

This is a concrete concept objective. One can point to an instance of art deco: It is known by its physical attributes.

The production for art deco identification looks something like this:

> IF the object or its decoration includes forms
> that are rectilinear
> and symmetrical
> and streamlined
> and have smooth lines
> THEN the object is art deco.

"Art deco" is an ambiguous concept as it has some common characteristics that are not present in all forms (although not all of these features are required in a form for us to categorize it as "art deco"):

1. Materials
- **a.** Precious stones or metals—obsidian, crystal, onyx, ivory, silver, jade
- **b.** Human-made materials—chrome, plastics

2. Motifs
- **a.** Animals—especially sleek and fleet animals such as deer, antelopes, and gazelles
- **b.** Nude female figures
- **c.** Stylized lightning, leaves, sunbeams, rainbows
- **d.** Geometric patterns

3. Colors
- **a.** orange
- **b.** black
- **c.** silver

4. Form
- **a.** Although the form must include all of the criterial attributes (rectilinear, symmetrical, streamlined, and smooth lines), additional features that aid in the finer distinctions between art deco and other modern forms are the materials, motifs, and colors included in the forms. It is important to include these additional attributes in a discussion of criterial attributes.

Context

This objective is for a lesson in a unit on twentieth-century art and design for high school students in an art class. The unit itself is organized chronologically. The class meets in a classroom that has both typical desks and a lab area. Traditional equipment is available, including a video playback unit, a slide projector, and bulletin board areas.

Learners

Students in this class are high school juniors and seniors who have already taken one year of high school art. The year focused on the production techniques of drawing, painting, and sculpting. The second year includes these production techniques in a more elaborated fashion. In addition, this course attempts to help learners put their work into a context of the history of art. The learners are all quite skilled in production techniques, although there is a range in these skills. Both art classes are electives, so the students are enrolled in the class voluntarily. There are equal numbers of females and males in the class. Many (although not all) of the students anticipate post–high school training in some facet of art. Traditionally, students in this class tolerate the art design and history aspects of the course so they can move on to the related production aspects. The lesson before this one was on the concept "art nouveau" (a period of design that spanned the period from approximately 1890 to 1910), an immediate predecessor to the art deco period. Students in this class learned to identify examples of art nouveau by its major criterial attributes (curvilinear, asymmetrical designs that often included flower- or plantlike motifs as well as flowing female figures). The students saw examples of art deco in their lesson on art nouveau as nonexamples of art nouveau. (Note that these two concepts, art nouveau and art deco, could be taught together as coordinate concepts. To simplify the presentation of the example lesson, we will teach only the art deco concept, but it should be clear how the two concepts might be easily taught together.)

Example Concept Lesson: Art Deco

The lesson will follow an inquiry approach; therefore, you will see how some of the expanded events are resequenced to accommodate this strategy. Although the actual form of mediation may not be finalized until after the strategy design, it is not uncommon for the designer to begin to imagine the appropriate medium to deliver the events. We have selected five media of instruction: video, realia, photographs and line drawings, slides, and a human teacher.

INTRODUCTION
Deploy Attention/Arouse Interest and Motivation

As students enter the class, a videotape will be playing. The videotape includes clips of scenes from films and cartoons of the 1920s that utilize art deco forms, either in the drawings, as with the cartoons, or in the sets, as in the films. The soundtrack is popular music of the period. The videotape is approximately fifteen minutes long. The tape continues to play as

learners prepare for class. Students are directed to notice the style of the sets and the cartoons.

Establish Instructional Purpose/ Preview Lesson

The teacher informs students that today they will study the design style that was popular after the art nouveau period and learn to recognize examples. They are given their first task, which is to discover the key features of this period.

Body
Process Information and Examples

Students are placed into groups of four to six around lab tables. Each group is handed a packet of ten line drawings on cards and given directions to group the cards according to design styles. They are told that one particular style, the style to be studied today, is represented by the most examples. The packet contains ten line drawings, five of which are unambiguous, "best examples" of art deco, and two of which are examples of art nouveau. The remaining three are clearly nonexamples of art deco, including two modern designs and one "arts and crafts" design from the period that followed art deco. These line drawings are of objects that are matched according to function. For example, the two line drawings in Figure 9.4 are included in the packet; one is an art deco teapot, and the other is an art nouveau pitcher. Other objects included vary from jewelry to architectural elements to household decorations.

Students are directed to group the drawings according to style. They are told that there is one predominant style and that the rest of the design periods will vary. When they have the drawings grouped, they are asked to determine the distinguishing features of the design style in the predominant group. When all groups have finished this sorting task, the teacher asks one group to tell how they sorted the drawings. If they failed to sort them according to style but rather by function, they are asked to quickly re-sort them by styles. If they have sorted by style, they are asked to describe the features in the drawings that caused them to sort as they did. (The criterial attributes of the concept relate to the lines of the design, so

Figure 9.4 Art Nouveau Pitcher and Art Deco Teapot

eliminating all irrelevant attributes beyond the lines, such as color and texture, should ensure a predictable sorting by these attributes.) If learners have included drawings from other periods in the art deco pile, they are asked to reconsider according to the attributes they have identified as criterial attributes. If they have included attributes that are not criterial, they should be encouraged to notice that not all of the drawings in their pile include this attribute.

Eventually, when all art deco examples are in one pile, the teacher can ask if any learners know the name of the style represented in the largest pile. If none know it, the teacher can state that the design style is called *art deco.* The teacher can note on the board the criterial attributes of the concept (rectilinear, symmetrical, streamlined forms, with smooth lines). For review purposes the teacher may also ask if learners recognize any familiar styles in the remaining line drawings, which should stimulate a quick review of the features of art nouveau.

Recall Relevant Prior Knowledge

The criterial attribute terms written on the board are concepts that the learners have already acquired, but *rectilinear* may be unfamiliar. If any terms are unfamiliar, they should be reviewed with examples and nonexamples.

Process Information and Examples (continued)/ Focus Attention

The teacher will project (via two projectors to facilitate simultaneous comparison) color photos that relate to each matched pair in the line drawings. The students are asked to point out the critical attributes of art deco in each photo, noting how the attributes are not present in the nonexample. To facilitate this attributes isolation, the line drawing of the image is superimposed over the photo for the first two or three pairs of images. This superimposition will allow students to focus on the critical attributes.

Ten more examples of art deco are projected. These examples may vary considerably in function, setting, and in tightness and length of rectangular lines. Within these examples, common motifs, materials, and colors are represented across several examples. Students are then asked to comment on common motifs, colors, and materials. The teacher points out that though these common features are not necessarily considered art deco, they are common to many examples.

Now the teacher may set the art deco period in chronological perspective by showing on a time-line how the period followed the art nouveau period. The period may also be set in conceptual perspective by students or by the teacher pointing out that the clean, sleek lines of the art deco movement may have been a reaction to the intricacies and fussiness of the art nouveau period. The teacher may also inquire if learners see the influence of any other art movements on art deco. If no students notice, the teacher can point out the effects of cubism in the rectilinear forms.

To set the art deco movement into historical context, the teacher may also point out that this movement occurred at the height of the Industrial Revolution and that the art deco movement was an attempt to rectify a failure of the art nouveau movement. One of the goals of art nouveau designers was to create a style that was appropriate for mass production. However, the intricacies of the nouveau style did not facilitate mass production. The elongated, simple lines of the deco style were appropriate for mass production. (The teacher may elaborate the context of the period more; however, this contextual information should be focused on how the period influenced the particular criterial attributes of art deco. Too much background information can interfere with the targeted objective, which is recognizing examples of art deco.)

Employ Learning Strategies

As these are second-year art students, and possibly highly visual learners, they may have difficulty with recalling the verbal label of the concept with the visual attributes (especially since they will be learning many such labels in an art and design history unit). They are encouraged to develop their own mnemonic to tie the label to the criterial attributes. If they are unable to do so, the teacher may supply a mnemonic. One such mnemonic might be a rhyme, formed by the tie between the influences of Aztec art and art deco. The instruction might suggest that the students remember the rhyme of AzTEC and art DECo. To emphasize this relationship, learners can be shown the visual of an Aztec pyramid and the stepped shape of an art deco radio (sometimes known as an *Aztec radio,* as shown in Figure 9.5). This was inspired by Hillier's (1968) text on art deco.

Practice and Feedback

Practice 1 Students are asked to write the numbers from 1 to 15 on a sheet of paper. They are then presented with fifteen slides of images, ten of which are previously unencountered examples of art deco, ranging in function, colors, motifs, materials, and difficulty of identification. Five are nonexamples, all modern styles, including at least two examples of art nouveau. Each slide is numbered. Some of the nonexamples should include art deco motifs, materials, or colors. Students are asked to write "yes" beside the number of the slide if it is an example of art deco and "no" if it is not. They are asked to be prepared to justify their answers.

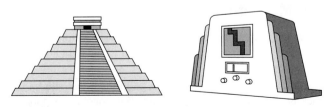

Figure 9.5 Aztec Temple and "Aztec" radio

Feedback 1 Students are asked to reveal their decisions and explain their answers. Explanations should include how the criterial attributes are represented. In addition, students may discuss the other common features that may be included in art deco style. If students overgeneralize these common features, the teacher points out that the common features do not constitute the criterial attributes. If students undergeneralize, they should be encouraged to notice the range of the examples that are indeed art deco, and the teacher should try to discover and remediate the misconceptions of irrelevant attributes that students mistakenly consider to be criterial.

Practice 2 The teacher asks students to think of any examples of art deco that they may have seen. Examples may be local: the carpet at Radio City Music Hall, skyscrapers such as the Chrysler Building in New York City, Boston Avenue Methodist Church in Tulsa, Oklahoma, and so forth.

Feedback 2 If the teacher is unfamiliar with the examples, the students are encouraged to sketch their examples. In each case, the example is compared to the criterial attributes of art deco.

Conclusion

Summarize and Review/Remotivate and Close/Transfer Knowledge

The videotape that was used at the beginning of the lesson is replayed, and students are asked to point out examples of the art deco style. (The tape can be paused. The students are asked to explain their answers by stating how the criterial attributes that distinguish art deco from other design styles are represented in the tape.)

At the close of the lesson, students are reminded that they now can identify the art deco style and the art nouveau style and distinguish the difference between them. Students are encouraged to find examples, either realia or photos, of the two styles and bring them into the classroom to an interest area, which is separated into deco and nouveau areas. They are also assigned to design (draw) one of the following in art deco style: bookends, a stained glass window, or a book cover. (No examples of these items were shown in the examples in the body of the lesson, so students must actually apply the concept in their production.) The students are reminded that 60 percent of the grade on this design project will be based on how nearly the design embodies the criterial attributes of the style. Forty percent of the grade will be derived from the quality of the rendering of the drawing.

Assessment

Assess Learning/Evaluate Feedback and Seek Remediation

Assessment will be delayed until the end of the unit. Part of the assessment of this objective will be the assessment of the adequacy of the design project that was just discussed. The teacher uses a checklist that details the criterial attributes of art deco,

as well as criteria for production derived from course goals, to evaluate the project. Feedback will take the form of written comments regarding the match between the attributes and the design, as well as the adequacy of the rendering. (The teacher may also wish to consider the adequacy of any examples that learners bring to the interest area as part of the assessment.)

The second aspect of the assessment will be a more conventional exam in which students are shown slides of all the styles learned during the unit. The learners will identify each style on paper. At least ten examples from the art deco style should be allowed so that the teacher has a reliable measure of the learners' performance on this objective. In addition, careful attention should be given to selecting these examples so that they cover the range of nonrelevant and common attributes. Learners should be asked to justify at least some of their answers.

Learners are provided with not only a summary score from the entire assessment but also a score on mastery in identifying each of the specific design styles. Patterns of overgeneralization and undergeneralization are identified and remediated as students are shown the slides as a group and are asked to identify the styles. As with the feedback following practice, isolating the criterial attributes in the examples and pointing out their absence in the nonexamples can encourage remediation of any misconceptions the learners may have developed.

SUMMARY

Figure 9.6 highlights the chapter's key points in a summary frame.

EXTENDED EXAMPLE

Go to the Learning Resources Web site for a continuation the instructional design of the Photography Basics course. The contribution from this chapter is strategy design for a text-based concept lesson: the concept of depth of field.

READINGS AND REFERENCES

Ali, A. M. (1981). The use of positive and negative examples during instruction. *Journal of Instructional Development, 5*(1), 2–7.

Andre, T., & Thieman, A. (1988). Level of adjunct question, type of feedback, and learning concepts by reading. *Contemporary Educational Psychology, 13,* 296–307.

Ausubel, D. P., Novak, J. D., & Hanesian, H. (1968). *Educational psychology: A cognitive view* (2nd ed.). New York: Holt, Rinehart, & Winston.

Introduction	Deploy attention. Arouse interest and motivation.	• Highlight concept label, use unusual picture or humorous story regarding concept, provide interesting information on origin or history of concept, and present first matched example and nonexample. Use inquiry approach.
	Establish instructional purpose.	• State explicitly in expository lesson, delay statement in inquiry lesson.
Body	Preview lesson.	• Conduct overview process of inquiry approach; point out importance of examples and nonexamples and practice in lesson.
	Recall prior knowledge.	• Review concepts constituting critical attributes of concept, use techniques such as informal questioning, formal pretest, advance organizer, or analogy.
	Process information.	• Expose to best example and/or definition; emphasize criterial attributes; consider matched examples and nonexamples; present concept in range of settings. with diversity of nonrelevant attributes.
	Focus attention.	• Isolate criterial attributes in examples with highlighting such as boldface type, color, or a simplified drawing.
	Employ learning strategies.	• Generate concept maps, analogies, mnemonics, or images.
	Practice.	• Identify examples from previously unencountered instances, which range in difficulty and settings; explain categorizations; generate samples.
	Evaluate feedback.	• Provide feedback that contains attribute isolation.
Conclusion	Summarize and review.	• Restate criterial attributes. • Repeat or paraphrase key information.
	Transfer knowledge.	• Apply outside classroom. • Provide further examples.
	Remotivate and close.	• Show how learning can help student.
Assessment	Assess performance.	• Test ability to isolate criterial attributes in examples and point out their absence in nonexamples. • Test range of common and nonrelevant attributes.
	Provide feedback and remediation.	• Provide score or other performance summary. • Identify problems of over- and undergeneralization.

Figure 9.6 Key Events for Concept Learning

Bereiter, C. (2002). *Education and the mind in the knowledge age.* Mahwah, NJ: Erlbaum.

Dijkstra, S. (1988). The development of the representation of conceptual knowledge in memory and the design of instruction. *Instructional Science, 17,* 339–350.

Driscoll, M. P., & Tessmer, M. (1985). The rational set generator: A method for creating concept examples for teaching and testing. *Educational Technology, 25*(2), 29–32.

Driscoll, M. P., & Tessmer, M. (April, 1985). *The effects of design methods for teaching coordinate concepts via concept trees and testing concept learning via rational set generators.* Paper presented to the annual meeting of the American Educational Research Association, Chicago, IL.

Gagné, R. M. (1985). *The conditions of learning* (4th ed.). New York: Holt, Rinehart & Winston.

Gorsky, P., & Finegold, M. (1994). The role of anomaly and of cognitive dissonance in restructuring students' concepts of force. *Instructional Science, 22,* 75–90.

Hamilton, R. (1989). Role of concept definition, teaching examples, and practice on concept learning from prose. *Contemporary Educational Psychology, 14,* 357–365.

Hillier, B. (1968). *Art deco.* New York: Schocken Books.

Joyce, B., & Weil, M. (1986). Attaining concepts. In B. Joyce and M. Weil (Eds.), *Models of teaching* (3rd ed), pp. 25–39. Upper Saddle River, NJ: Prentice-Hall.

Klausmeier, H. J. (1980). *Learning and teaching concepts.* New York: Academic Press.

Klausmeier, H. J. (1990). Conceptualizing. In F. F. Jones, & L. Idol (Eds.), *Dimensions of thinking and cognitive instruction* (pp. 93–138). Hillsdale, NJ: Erlbaum.

Klausmeier, H. J. (1992). Concept learning and concept teaching. *Educational Psychologist, 27* (3), 267–289.

Mason, L. (1994). Cognitive and metacognitive aspects in conceptual change by analogy. *Instructional Science, 22,* 157–187.

Medin, D. L. (1989). Concepts and conceptual structure. *American Psychologist, 44* (12), 1469–1481.

Merrill, M. D., & Tennyson, R. D. (1977). *Teaching concepts: An instructional design guide.* Englewood Cliffs, NJ: Educational Technology Publications.

Newby, T. J., & Stepich, D. A. (1987). Learning abstract concepts: The use of analogies as a mediational strategy. *Journal of Instructional Development, 10*(2), 20–26.

Patten, M. L. (2002). *Understanding Research Methods.* Los Angeles: Pyrczak Publishing.

Ranzijn, F. J. A. (1991). The sequence of conceptual information in instruction and its effect on retention. *Instructional Science, 20,* 405–418.

Schimmel, B. J. (April, 1983). *A meta-analysis of feedback to learners in computerized and programmed instruction.* Paper presented at the annual meeting of the American Educational Research Association, Montreal, Quebec, Canada. ERIC Document Retrieval Service ED 233 708.

Schimmel, B. J. (April, 1988). *Patterns in students' selection of feedback in computer-based instruction.* Paper presented at the annual meeting of the American Educational Research Association, New Orleans, LA.

Smith, M. A., & Smith, P. L. (1991). The effects of concretely versus abstractly illustrated instruction on learning abstract concepts. In M. Simonson (Ed.), *Thirteenth annual proceedings of selected research paper presentations at the 1991 annual convention of the Association for Educational Communications and Technology* (pp. 804–815). Ames, IA: Iowa State University.

Tennyson, R. D., & Cocchiarella, M. J. (1986). An empirically based instructional design theory for teaching concepts. *Review of Educational Research, 56*(1), 40–71.

Tessmer, M., & Driscoll, M. P. (1986). Effects of diagramming display of concept definitions on classification performance. *Educational Communications and Technology Journal, 34,* 195–205.

Tessmer, M., Wilson, B., & Driscoll, M. P. (1990). A new model of concept teaching and learning. *Educational Technology Research and Development, 38*(1), 45–53.

Vermette, P. J. (1986). The identification and evaluation of exemplar intensity in the classroom teaching and learning of concepts. *Contemporary Educational Psychology, 11,* 90–106.

Wilcox, W. C., Merrill, M. D., & Black, H. B. (1981). Effects of teaching conceptual hierarchy on concept classification performance. *Journal of Instructional Development, 5*(1), 8–13.

Wilson, B. G. (1987). What is a concept? Concept teaching and cognitive psychology. *Performance and Instruction, 25*(10), 16–18.

Wilson, B. G., & Tessmer, M. (1990). Adult's perception of concept learning outcomes: An initial study and discussion. In M. Simonson and C. Hargrave (Eds.), *Twelfth annual proceedings of selected research paper presentations of the 1990 annual convention of the Association for Educational Communications and Technology.* (pp. 689–700). Ames, IA: Iowa State University.

STRATEGIES FOR INSTRUCTION LEADING TO LEARNING PROCEDURES

CHAPTER OBJECTIVES

At the conclusion of this chapter, you should be able to do the following:

- Determine whether a procedure is simple or complex.
- Design a strategy plan for the procedure lesson.

A REVIEW OF LEARNING TO APPLY A PROCEDURE

Procedures are often strictly defined—all steps are included and each step is unambiguous. Another term for such a strictly defined procedure is *algorithm.* Many procedures are algorithms. For example, mathematics operations are procedures that are algorithmic. The procedure for subtracting by "borrowing" is an algorithm: The steps in the procedure usually do not vary. Procedures may be simple, with only one set of steps that the learner follows linearly, or they may be complex, with many decision points. Decision points are points in a procedure at which the learner must determine which of two (or sometimes more) situations exist. Each decision point could lead to a different path, or branch, through the algorithm. Making decisions at these points requires a kind of concept recognition. An example would be "Is the battery charging?" Based upon this determination, the learner follows one branch or another of the procedure.

Some procedures may be somewhat less clearly prescribed. In such cases, there may be incomplete knowledge of the steps involved, unreliable consequences of the application of the procedure, or a mass of steps with much ambiguity at decision points. Dealing with situations in these areas may require the application of "rules of thumb" or heuristic knowledge. Two examples are techniques for reducing cholesterol level and protocols for treating certain illnesses. In such cases, teach the procedures in these areas as problem-solving tasks rather than as procedures.

Some examples of procedures are the executive subroutines for psychomotor skills, such as throwing a javelin or performing the broad jump. Many tasks in mathematics that we term *problem solving* are really applications of procedures. Some of these tasks are dividing fractions, finding the average of a series of numbers, determining the area of a polygon, constructing a pentagon within a circle, and solving a quadratic equation. Many training goals are application of procedures, such as those tasks for operating a piece of equipment, readjusting the timing of an engine, or doing an if-then analysis on a spreadsheet.

As will be described in Chapter 11, "Strategies for Instruction Leading to Principle Learning," it is not uncommon for a learner to learn a procedure to complete some task (such as solving for an unknown in an equation) and, as a product of applying the procedure, learn the principle that underlies the procedure. The reverse sequence—learning the principle first and then the procedure—may also occur. For example, learners learn the principle that states that the amount of current flow in an electrical current is related to volts of electricity put into the circuit and the resistance of the current ($I = V/R$). However, learners will discover or be taught a procedure for solving such problems quickly: First, determine what values are known, and then determine which form of the equation will solve for the unknown. With this approach, learners can acquire an efficient means to deal with solving for an unknown (by applying a procedure), but at the same time they will truly "understand" what occurs when the procedure is employed through learning the principle that relates the relevant concepts. The instructor should tie the two types of instruction together, teaching procedures so that learners have efficient means of dealing with a given circumstance; but the instruction should also explain the procedure in the context of the underlying principle so the information is more meaningful and, therefore, more memorable and transferable.

Remember that the ability to list or describe the steps in a procedure is declarative knowledge learning. The learning of the procedure involves the ability to *apply* that procedure to a variety of previously unencountered situations. The ability to state the steps in a procedure may be helpful in learning to apply it; however, stating the procedure is not sufficient evidence that it has been learned. Demonstration of knowledge of a procedure requires actual application of it.

Like concepts and principles, the mental operations involved in applying procedures are called *productions* (Anderson, 1985), which are hypothesized mental operations that generally take the form of if-then representations. Productions are implicit in all of the intellectual skills—concepts, principles, procedures, and problem solving. Later we will look at examples of productions for this type of learning.

When procedures are being learned, a fundamental "internal condition" of the learner is that the concepts that are part of the procedure must be in the learner's possession *as concepts.* There is less certainty about the prerequisite nature of the declarative knowledge aspect of procedures. Clearly all procedures have a declarative knowledge component—knowledge of the steps (knowing what to do)—but it does not appear necessary that this knowledge be gained by the learner before meaningful procedural learning can proceed. However, the learner must possess the concepts within the procedure before learning can proceed. This is one of the few instances where a "bottom-up" sequencing is necessary, and even here, the bottom-up sequence is only partial in that we are not including declarative knowledge as a necessary prerequisite.

COGNITIVE PROCESSES INVOLVED IN THE LEARNING OF PROCEDURES

Procedures require that productions be learned. Following is a generic format for productions involved in using procedures:

IF the situation contains certain distinguishing features X, Y, Z (usually understood as concepts),

THEN follow procedure P.

Although the both procedures and principles are described by cognitive psychologists as forms of *rules,* an information-processing analysis for procedural rules is somewhat different from that for relational rules (principles). Following is a general information processing analysis for a procedure:

1. Recognize a situation in which the procedure is applicable.
2. Recall the procedure.
3. Apply the steps in the procedure.
4. If required, make decisions at the decision points.
5. If required, choose correct branch(es).
6. Complete steps in required branch(es).
7. Ascertain that the procedure has been applied appropriately.

An example of such a procedure might be the procedural rule of applying cardiopulmonary resuscitation (CPR).

1. Determine if the person is unconscious. (There is an entire subprocedure to determine this.)
2. Open an airway. (This is another subprocedure.)
3. Determine if the person is breathing (another subprocedure). If there is no breathing, go to step 4; if the victim is breathing, go to step 5.
4. Give four breaths (another subprocedure).
5. Determine if there is a pulse (another subprocedure).
6. If there is no pulse, provide CPR (another subprocedure).

In addition to recognizing an initial situation that calls for the use of a procedure, many procedures have decision points within them that also require classification of situations and branching into alternate paths depending upon the decisions. Step 3 above is an example of a decision point.

Use of procedures requires that a learner (1) determine if a situation requires that she learn to do a particular procedure for cognitive tasks (i.e., concept recognition); (2) recall the steps in the procedure (i.e.,

declarative knowledge); (3) complete the steps in the procedure; and (4) analyze the completed procedure and confirm/disconfirm that the procedure has been correctly applied. In addition, if the procedure is complex, procedures require that the learner make decisions within the procedure.

Steps in a procedure may be "decision" steps or "operation" steps. Decision steps are those like step 3 above that require the learner to determine whether a certain set of circumstances exists and to follow alternate pathways depending upon the decision. Procedures that do not have decision steps are termed *linear* or *serial.* Procedures with decision steps are termed *branching* or *parallel.*

Procedures may be classified as simple or complex, depending on the type and number of steps to be completed. Simple procedures are taught somewhat differently from complex procedures. A linear procedure may be considered simple if it only has a few (five to seven) steps (Schmid & Gerlach, 1990). The age, sophistication, and prior knowledge of the audience, as well as the difficulty of each step, should help a designer determine whether to use five or seven steps. Simple procedures with no decisions may be taught and practiced as a unit. The procedure for calculating an average is simple:

1. Add the values together.
2. Determine the number of values.
3. Divide the sum of the values by the number of values.

A branching procedure is considered to be a complex procedure. Our CPR example is a complex procedure. The following discussion outlines how to vary instruction for complex procedures.

CONDITIONS SUPPORTING THE LEARNING OF PROCEDURES

General Design Decisions

WRITING THE PROCEDURE. Before teaching a procedure, the designer must clarify it and list its steps and decisions in an unambiguous form. Some guidelines for verbally describing the procedure are:

- Steps should be described in clear sentences.
- Steps should result from a careful cognitive task analysis.
- Each operation step should represent a single, elementary action.
- When possible, each decision should be dichotomous, resulting in the selection of one of two possible paths. If the decision must result in more than

two options, the branches resulting from a decision should not exceed five.

- Decision steps should be stated in the form of a question.
- Operation steps should be stated as imperative sentences (beginning with a verb).

Figure 10.1 presents an example of a procedure description for selecting film of an appropriate speed.

SIMPLE VERSUS COMPLEX PROCEDURES. Simple procedures may be taught straightforwardly, with a step presented and demonstrated and then practiced. It may sometimes be useful to present and practice the procedure by presenting the last step first; then the learners will learn and practice the next to the last step, and so on (Gilbert, 1978). This gives the learners the satisfaction of completing the procedure over and over.

Complex procedures must be simplified for their initial instruction. Later the procedure can be elaborated into its more complex form. Some methods for simplifying (adapted from Wilson, 1985) are to teach the following items first:

- The simplest or most common path.
- The major branches.
- A simplified initial case.

It is possible also to provide output of difficult or time-consuming steps and/or chunk related steps together.

One popular way to simplify a complex procedure is to choose the *simplest or most common path* through the procedure and teach that first. The procedure is taught with its decision steps; however, there is only one route through the procedure, so it is initially linear. In such a case, the learners need not learn all the branches and steps in the first stages of learning. What they do learn can be built upon in subsequent elaborations of the procedure. An example of this approach would be to instruct on the most common repair for a piece of malfunctioning equipment first and then move on to more difficult repairs.

Providing instruction and practice on separate *major branches* is also a common simplifying procedure. In complex procedures, a first decision point is often one that sends the learner through two or more separate and distinct paths. One approach to teaching a procedure of this kind is to teach one branch from beginning to end before moving to other branches. (Our sample lesson in this chapter includes an example.)

A third method of simplifying a complex procedure is by *simplifying* the original instructional case. When we teach concepts, we select best examples that embody critical characteristics; we also can begin instruction on a procedure with a simple case. The instruction may limit the sheer volume of the original case so that the entire procedure can be demonstrated in a short period of time. This is the approach we use when we have students apply the instructional design procedure to a single objective lesson. It is also the method math teachers use in explaining the procedure of borrowing in subtraction.

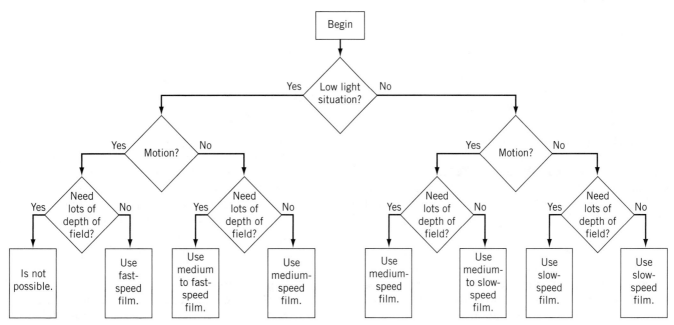

Figure 10.1 Selecting Film of an Appropriate Speed

When the completion of individual steps in a procedure is extremely time-consuming, tedious, or otherwise complex, it may be helpful in initial presentation and practice to provide learners with the output of individual steps. In such a case, the learners can complete the entire procedure as a whole, without becoming frustrated or distracted with the details of completing any single step. For example, when we teach students to use a page-processing software program, we initially provide them with a text file and a graphics file. This is so that they initially do not have to go through the extended process of creating these files, but they still have the experience of completing the page processing related to the software. Another example is instruction on completing a tax form. An initial pass through the instructional events might provide the learners with some of the calculated values so that completed calculations are needed only on the most critical and meaningful parts of the form.

If a particular procedure is made complex by the sheer number of steps, one way to simplify the instruction originally is to chunk the steps into stages or phases. Then the learners can learn to complete and practice those individual steps together, rather than being overwhelmed by the entire task. Ultimately, the individual steps in a stage may be mentally "compiled" so that they represent one cohesive unit (Anderson, 1985). Thus, they are easily dealt with in the entire procedure. We could use this approach with students in a car mechanics class learning to tune up a car. First, we provide instruction on tuning up the ignition system. Learners can practice this procedure before moving on to learn how to adjust the valves. Finally, they can learn to tune up the carburetion system. Eventually, learners can be given instruction and practice on completing all three phases of a tune-up.

In general, it appears that distributed practice (spaced practice) facilitates cognitive processing of procedures, whereas massed practice makes a greater contribution to associative learning (Mumford, Costanza, Baughman, Threlfall, & Fleishman, 1994) and with complex tasks may only be appropriate for certain instances of psychomotor instruction.

EXPOSITORY OR DISCOVERY STRATEGY. A relatively supplantive, didactic, expository approach, rather than a highly generative, discovery approach, seems to be best for teaching procedures. Because procedures are efficient means for the repeated solution of situations that might otherwise be solved by the application of a principle or through problem solving, it makes sense to teach the procedure as efficiently as possible. The best strategy appears to be a straightforward presentation of the procedure with demonstrations of the applications of the procedure, rather than having learners struggle with discovering the procedure for themselves.

However, Landa (1983) suggests that in some cases it may be useful to support learners' discovery of their own procedures, which may be somewhat idiosyncratic. We believe that such a discovery approach may be appropriate if one of the primary goals of the instructional system is for learners to acquire skills in generating procedures. However, such an instructional task would more appropriately be considered a problem-solving task than a procedure application task.

The following section discusses how the expanded events of instruction may be adapted for teaching procedures.

SPECIFIC DESIGN DECISIONS—EVENTS

Introduction

Deploy Attention

The instructor may gain learners' attention to the instructional task by asking a question that presents a situation requiring the application of the procedure or through demonstrating the actual application of the procedure itself. Attention may also be encouraged by pointing out the efficiency of the procedure over trial-and-error techniques.

Establish Instructional Purpose

Learners may be informed of the purpose of the lesson both in terms of which procedure is to be learned and its range of applicability. In addition, it is important that learners are aware of the efficiency of learning a procedure instead of continuing to respond to each situation with a trial-and-error approach. In many cases the procedure may be demonstrated to clarify the purpose of the lesson (and to preview the lesson).

Arouse Interest and Motivation

Learning procedures can be intrinsically motivating because they allow learners to complete tasks more efficiently and more reliably than they did using trial-and-error approaches before instruction. Since learning procedures may be rote and meaningless to the learner, it is important that the purpose of learning a procedure (in terms of its efficiency and reliability) be emphasized. This efficiency might actually be demonstrated to the learners. If learners have experienced the situations as trial-and error tasks, they may have already begun to formulate their own procedures to deal with these tasks more efficiently. Learners should be encouraged to compare any procedures they have developed to the procedure being taught on the basis of efficiency and effectiveness.

Preview Lesson

The procedure should be previewed during this phase of the lesson. If the procedure is fairly simple, with approximately seven steps or fewer (even fewer steps for younger learners) and has no or few decision points, then the complete procedure should be demonstrated. If the procedure is complex, with many steps and decision points with related branches, then the overview may be a summary of the procedure with several steps grouped together, such as our description of the complex CPR procedure. Such an overview may be made concrete with a verbal or visual outline of the steps.

It is important that learners be told that the demonstration is an overview and that they are not expected to learn the entire procedure at this point. Learners can become very anxious if it is not made abundantly clear that they will be taught the procedure's individual steps.

Body

Sequencing and clustering of the steps of the procedure are important decisions at this stage in the strategy plan. A very simple procedure may be taught first in its entirety and then practiced. However, most procedures must be simplified in some way and be taught and practiced in segments. Teaching the procedure in stages will require that the events in the body of the lesson be repeated for each stage of the procedure.

Recall Relevant Prior Knowledge

Prior knowledge that can support the acquisition of a procedure may be concepts that are known and that must be used in recognition of a situation, such as the concept "pulse" in the CPR procedure. Concept knowledge may also be involved in completing a step of the procedure, such as recognition of certain tools in the procedural repair of equipment. These concepts should be reviewed.

As we stated earlier, learners may have learned a principle (such as the relationship of distance, time, and rate) and later learn a procedure to efficiently and reliably solve problems involving these variables. It is helpful to review the principle underlying the procedure to make the procedure meaningful.

Often, learners have previously learned less complex procedures that will be combined with other procedures to form a new and complex procedure. For example, learners may have already learned to take a pulse in another context before taking a course on CPR. This procedure should be reviewed at the appropriate time in the CPR course.

Process Information and Examples

Remember that to learn a procedure, learners must learn to recognize situations that require a particular procedure, complete its steps, recall the steps in the procedure, and determine if the procedure has been properly applied. In addition, if the procedure is complex, the learner must learn to make decisions within the procedure by classifying situations and choosing branches of it depending upon the decisions that are made. Although we suggest that the instructional sequence occur in the following order, other sequences may also be appropriate.

1. *Learning to determine if the procedure is required.* To make the procedure meaningful, the first information that should be processed is the context or situation(s) in which the procedure is applicable. This is a prerequisite "pattern recognition" or concept learning that should be learned and practiced first in the lesson. A strategy for teaching concepts will be appropriate for this phase: Learners should see examples of the variety of situations in which the procedure is applicable and the characteristics of the situations that make them appropriate for the application of the procedure. Situations that have similar nonessential features should be contrasted so that learners can clearly identify the attributes of the situations that are critical to the use of the procedure. For example, part of learning the procedure for changing the oil in a car is knowing how to recognize that the car is low on oil. The presentation of these matched examples and nonexamples should be followed with practice and feedback.

2. *Learning to complete the steps in the procedure.* This phase of presenting and processing information differs, depending on whether the procedure is a simple procedure or a complex procedure. Simple procedures may be learned in a single pass through the process information event and practiced as a whole, or each individual step may be learned and then practiced. Complex procedures may be taught in an elaborated instruction (see the discussion of Reigeluth's Elaboration Model in Chapter 16) in which learners move through the events multiple times with increasingly complete experiences. For example, if the designer uses a most common path simplification of the procedure, then each iteration of the events might present instruction on steps that are in less and less common paths.

Each step of the procedure may be presented as a live demonstration, a video, or, in some cases, audio representation, computer frames, or illustrated textual materials. Generally, each individual step should be considered and demonstrated separately. The importance of this principle becomes apparent when we consider examples of print-based instruction, such as that developed to teach the assembly of equipment.

Designers often are tempted to save space and cost by combining steps when teaching and illustrating them. This almost always leads to learners' confusion about the sequence of steps. Although presentation and processing of individual steps can be tedious and costly, such thoroughness is generally beneficial.

Recall that in our discussion of concepts and principles, we suggested using matched nonexamples. There has been some controversy among designers as to the utility of presenting nonexamples when teaching procedures. Based upon the scanty research that is currently available, we suggest that it *is* useful to show learners common errors in completing individual steps. This presentation should occur only after the correct application of a step has been clearly demonstrated with several examples. This will avoid possible confusion about the correct procedure. The statement of the error should be couched in a general form rather than in terms of the specific error in a particular example. For example, the study on which this suggestion is based taught the procedure for constructing a musical interval on a scale (Marcone & Reigeluth, 1988). The researchers used the following warning: "BE CAREFUL: You should begin counting on the note given and NOT the line or space above it. THIS IS THE MOST OFTEN MADE MISTAKE!!!" The study found that it was more beneficial to state the warning and show the error exemplified on a staff than to show the error without the warning.

After each step is demonstrated, the learners should have the opportunity to practice that step until they are proficient. Then the next step should be presented and practiced along with the previous step.

3. *Learning to list the steps in the procedure.* After learners have seen steps demonstrated and practiced, they must learn to combine the steps into an articulated whole. This integration is partly a result of practicing the steps together as a whole. It is also a result of learners acquiring a mental representation of the sequence and nature of the steps. For simple procedures, a recollection of the order of the steps and what each step entails may be easy; practicing the procedure with spaced review on the order and nature of the steps will generally be sufficient for learning the steps.

Complex procedures will be more difficult to remember because of the number of steps and the branching possibilities. It is important for a designer to determine whether the learner must actually remember the order and nature of the steps. Memorizing the steps may not be necessary for the following types of procedures: (1) those that are exceedingly complex with multiple decision points, (2) those that are rarely executed, (3) those that will always be completed in one particular location, (4) those that do not have to be completed speedily, and (5)

those that are very similar and easily confused with related procedures. Such procedures may be supported with a printed list of steps and decisions, often in the form of a checklist or flowchart. Research on use of flowcharts and other visual depictions has been found to be helpful in learning procedures (Phillips & Quinn, 1993). Checklists, flowcharts, and other printed material can be used as job aids in addition to their utility in assisting explanations. For example, the procedures for troubleshooting malfunctioning equipment are often exceedingly lengthy and involve many branches. It is very common to support these procedures with flowcharts that repair persons carry with them. If job aids are to be used in the application setting, then learners should have them available to them during all the events of instruction (including assessment) and be taught to use them. Instructing learners to use job aids effectively involves modeling the use of the job aid and feedback to the learners.

The following types of procedures must be recalled without the help of a job aid: (1) procedures that must be completed in crisis situations, (2) those that may be required in many and unexpected locations, and (3) those that must be completed often and routinely. Occasionally, especially with complex procedures, initial instruction may include a job aid to support the learners' first practice attempts. If this support is provided, however, the instruction should include transition instruction that teaches learners how to develop a mental representation of the information on the job aid. Learners should practice without the job aid until they are proficient. The instruction should also include spaced practice without access to the job aid.

Another strategy that may enhance the retention of these steps is a discussion of the meaningfulness of the particular sequence of the steps as they appear (i.e., why the steps are ordered as they are). If this information can be made personally meaningful to the learners, they may remember the steps more easily.

4. *Learning to check the appropriateness of a completed procedure.* Part of learning a procedure is learning to determine whether it has been applied correctly. This skill depends upon the learner being able to mentally review the procedure (after it has been applied) and confirm that each step and decision was completed appropriately. The previously described instruction in concert with practice in reviewing procedures completed by others will support this learning. In addition, learners should receive instruction on how to judge the adequacy of the output of a procedure. For example, learners could be given input and then practice estimating the output of a mathematical procedure. This would give them a feel for the range of acceptable outputs of the calculation. Other types of procedures may have specific cues to signal a correct application of a procedure, such as auditory cues of a correctly tuned car or the appearance of a correctly baked soufflé. Most of us were taught to check the result of subtraction by adding the difference (answer) to the bottom number (subtrahend). This skill is an example of instruction on monitoring the successful completion of a procedure. Direct instruction on judging the adequacy of the output of a procedure should be included in the instructional events so that learners may become good monitors of their own performance.

Focus Attention

1. *Learning to determine if the procedure is required.* As with other pattern recognition (i.e., concept) learning tasks, it is important that the critical features of the situation that requires the application of the procedure be highlighted and contrasted to noncritical features within the situation. These features can be emphasized by pointing out the critical features in a comparison of examples and nonexamples of situations that require the procedure.

2. *Learning to complete the steps in the procedure.* As the students learn to complete each step in the procedure, it is important that their attention be focused on the key cues that indicate when a particular step should be initiated and when it has been completed correctly. These cues may be visual, auditory, tactile, or olfactory. In addition, the students should be presented (or encouraged to develop) keyword summarizers of each step. These keywords, which should generally be verbs that signal the learners' performance during each step, should be emphasized during instruction and review.

3. *Learning to list the steps in the procedure.* The important features that should be emphasized during this part of instruction are sequence and keyword performances. If a job aid is used and its continued use is anticipated, then sequence and keyword verbs should be highlighted.

4. *Learning to check the appropriateness of a completed procedure.* As in learning to complete individual steps, learners' attention should be focused upon the cues within the situation that signal the successful completion of the procedure. Examples of these cues would be the correct threading of paper through a printer, the cessation of blood leaving a wound, and having all blanks filled in on a form.

Employ Learning Strategies

It may be useful to provide the learners with a mnemonic device to aid them in recalling the critical steps of the procedure. Learners may also be encouraged to develop their own mnemonics. For instance, CPR training often includes the mnemonic ABC to remind the learners to first establish an airway (A), next commence breathing (B), and then begin cardiac massage (C). Learners might also be encouraged to develop visual mnemonics or other visual images that represent the sequence of steps in the procedure.

Instead of providing learners with a job aid, it may be useful to encourage them to develop their own job aids. This will help them to consolidate their own learning and may make the learning more memorable. If they have not had previous experience in developing job aids, time should be set aside to provide guidance and instruction in the purpose and possible formats of a job aid. In addition, instructors should provide feedback on the usefulness and efficiency of the job aids that the learners have developed.

The monitoring of output of a procedure is a learning strategy that applies beyond the characteristics of this type of learning. As with other learning, it is important that learners acquire the habit of estimating the results of their actions. Then they can compare the actual end results of their actions with their estimates. If the conclusion is far off the estimate, they can either revise the estimate or reapply the procedure. This monitoring of progress may also be employed at the conclusion of some individual steps. For example, when learning to fill in blanks on an income tax form, learners may learn to monitor whether each of the values "makes sense" in the context of the procedure.

Practice

Although the ultimate goal of learning a procedure is the ability to perform all four of the components of completing a procedure, it is helpful to practice each of these components before moving on to the next component.

1. *Learning to determine if the procedure is required.* This skill, which is prerequisite to performing the entire procedure, may be practiced by presenting situations in which the procedure might be useful. Learners should then decide whether or not the procedure should be applied. It is also critical at this point that learners justify their answers so the instructor knows that they have truly identified the situation by its critical attributes. Learners' practice should begin with situations that clearly require the procedure. Then they can move on to situations that are less clear because of extraneous details. If learners have previously learned other procedures that are easily confused with the new procedure, they should be presented with some of these situations (or encouraged to propose such situations) to have practice in distinguishing between these potentially confusing situations.

2. *Learning to complete the steps in the procedure.* In general, each individual step of the procedure should be practiced immediately after it is presented. This may be practicing a decision step by determining which of two or more conditions exists, or it could be practicing an operation step by completing a performance step in the procedure. Landa (1983) suggested that the first step be demonstrated and practiced, then the next step be demonstrated and practiced, and then steps 1 and 2 be practiced together. Next, step 3 is demonstrated and practiced, and then it is practiced with steps 1 and 2. Landa proposed that this "snowballing" effect of practicing new steps with previously learned steps would enhance learners' learning the entire procedure as a whole. Gilbert (1978) suggested a similar approach to practicing procedures that underlie psychomotor skills. He, however, suggested that it may be helpful to learn and practice the steps of some procedures in a reverse order. In such an approach, the last step would be learned and practiced, then the next-to-last step would be learned and practiced, and then the two steps would be practiced together. For some procedures and some learners, this "backward chaining" may be very effective and motivating, especially for tasks in which completing the last step is highly satisfying.

After practicing the individual steps, learners should have practice in completing the entire procedure a number of times. With a complex procedure, this practice might, after initial instruction, involve only simplified cases. However, after instruction with more complex cases, the practice should occur across a wide range of possible situations. These should include some situations that require the simplest or most common path, some that require a more complex and extensive path, and some that do not require the procedure at all.

For procedures that are to be performed without a job aid, practice should proceed without a job aid or the instructor should remove the job aid toward the end of the practice event. For procedures in which the job aid will be employed during the projected actual application of the procedure, practice should include use of the job aid. In addition, some practice items may ask learners to note the portion of the job aid that is relevant to a portion of the procedure to ensure that the learners are able to use the job aid as a guide and reference.

3. *Learning to list the steps in the procedure.* After learners have practiced executing the procedure, it is critical that they practice recalling the sequence and nature of the steps in the procedure. If learners are learning to complete a procedure that is supported by a job aid, of course, this type of practice will not be necessary. However, if they will be required to remember the steps of the procedure in the correct order, then they must be provided ample opportunity to recall this order. In addition, they should be able to recall critical keywords that summarize the performance in each step. It will also be useful to require learners to expand on these keywords to ensure that they do indeed denote the entire proce-

dure to the learner. (This type of recall is a declarative knowledge learning task and will profit from suggestions for practice presented in Chapter 8. Of these suggestions, the suggestion for spaced review and practice is particularly important in learning procedures.)

4. *Learning to check the appropriateness of a completed procedure.* Practice should also include an opportunity for learners to view the process and/or product of a procedure and determine whether the procedure was correctly performed. This practice should include their overt reviewing of their own performance, as well as the opportunity to review the performance of others. Reviewing others' performances or products allows the learners to note errors that they may not have made yet in their executions of the procedure but might commit later in their performance. As a part of this practice, learners may be encouraged to identify the source of the error and suggest approaches for rectifying the problem.

Evaluate Feedback

1. *Learning to determine if the procedure is required.* Of course, the instructor should first provide feedback that confirms whether the learner has appropriately identified the situations that require the application of the procedure. In addition, some explanatory feedback should tell the learner why a particular situation does or does not require the application of the procedure. Such feedback should include a discussion of the critical attributes of the situation and a mapping of these attributes onto the situation, indicating where the attributes do or do not match.

2. *Learning to complete the steps in the procedure.* Learners should be provided with feedback about the accuracy of their completion of each step of the procedure. During initial learning phases when each step is first learned, this feedback may be more detailed than in later practice of the entire procedure. Feedback on decision steps will include information as to whether the learner correctly assessed the nature of the situation and made the correct decision, leading to choosing the correct path in the procedure.

Feedback on completion of operation steps should include not only dichotomous information as to whether the step was correctly completed but also qualitative information as to (1) whether they selected the inputs into the operation appropriately, (2) whether the outputs of the operation reached any prescribed criterion, and (3) whether the step was completed with acceptable precision and efficiency.

The instructor should videotape procedures with operation steps that have a significant observable motor component so that learners can observe their own behavior while reviewing any written or spoken feedback. In addition, learners can be taught to judge the adequacy of the completion of individual steps in the procedure, just as they can be taught to judge the adequacy of the completion of the entire procedure. For some procedures that have a motor component, learners can also learn to recognize the kinesthetic feedback when an operation step is completed appropriately.

3. *Learning to list the steps in the procedure.* For procedures that must be completed without a job aid, useful feedback includes whether all the steps of the procedure were remembered in the correct order. In initial practice this feedback may be in response to a declarative knowledge exercise, such as, "List the steps of *X* procedure in the correct order." Later, when the entire procedure is practiced, this feedback may be included. Additional feedback might include such hints as to what characteristics of an antecedent step cued the step that followed.

4. *Learning to check the appropriateness of a completed procedure.* Feedback for this type of practice should include correct answer feedback as to whether the given procedure has been correctly completed. The learners can then compare this judgment to their own assessments of whether a demonstrated procedure has been executed properly. This general feedback might be followed with a detailed explanation of why a particular decision was made.

Conclusion

The conclusion should give learners an opportunity to compile their representation of the procedure across all of the variations of the procedure that they experienced during the instruction.

Summarize and Review/Transfer Knowledge

The summary of a procedure lesson often begins with a review of the types of problems, goals, or situations to which the procedure applies. This review will also support the transfer of this learning. The instruction or the learners may supply these situations; however, it will be helpful if the situations are classified into categories. For instance, some situations require a simple form of the procedure, while other situations require a more complex form.

A summary may also include a reiteration of the relationship between the procedure and a principle (or principles) from which it is derived. This review will add meaningfulness, which might not have been as apparent at the beginning of the lesson when this relationship was first described. Any increase in meaningfulness should enhance retention of the procedure.

Next, the form, nature, and variations of the procedure should be summarized and reviewed. This summary can be supplied by the learners, perhaps by their creation of a graphic organizer, or the summary can be provided by the

instruction. For example, the instruction might present the sequence of steps for a simplest case and then add overlays to outline the procedures for increasingly complex cases. The presentation of these procedural steps might also be presented in clusters to aid learners' compilation of the steps into larger units. This compilation will enhance retention and automaticity, particularly within clusters. The instruction should also review any particularly difficult or confusing steps within the procedure and the features that indicate a correctly completed procedure.

As there is a considerable declarative knowledge component in learning a procedure, spaced review and practice of the procedure—including the variations of the procedure—should be planned for subsequent lessons. This spaced practice may encourage greater efficiency or precision in execution of the procedure. This spaced practice might be combined with instruction that encourages transfer of the procedure to other learning tasks. The procedure, or parts of the procedure, may be incorporated in other tasks, such as incorporating the Heimlich maneuver into a CPR procedure. Cognitive strategies acquired while learning a procedure, such as self-monitoring techniques, may be incorporated into a procedure. In addition, a simpler procedure may be elaborated in later lessons.

Remotivate and Close

Part of the remotivation may occur in the previous event as learners are reminded of the breadth of utility of the new procedure. In addition, here at the conclusion of the lesson, the learners should again be reminded of the usefulness of the procedure over other ways of solving problems: the efficiency and the reliability of the outcome if the procedure is correctly applied. They should also be reminded of its limitations, situations that would nullify the utility of the procedure. The closing statement of the lesson should include a name for the procedure to ensure that the learners can recall it by its label.

Assessment of Procedure Learning

Assess Learning

The ultimate assessment for a procedure is the learner's ability to correctly apply the procedure across as diverse a range of difficulty and situations as the designer has prescribed. If possible, the designer will develop several items across this range in order to obtain a reliable and valid assessment of the learner's skill. It is often desirable to assess component (prerequisite) knowledge—the identification of situations that call for the procedure, the listing of steps in correct sequence, and the evaluation of a completed procedure as to its correctness. If this component knowledge can be assessed, their results can provide information if remediation is required.

Occasionally, it is possible to gather information as to learners' knowledge of these components by observing learners' demonstration of the procedure—by having them "show their work"—or by reviewing their final product to determine their correct use of the process.

Assessment of application of a procedure may include the following types of items:

1. Listing the steps in the procedure.
2. Recognizing situations in which the procedure is applicable.
3. Applying the procedure.
4. Determining whether a procedure has been correctly applied.

Of course, item type 3 can be constructed to include the other three types. Both recognition and construction items may be used to assess the application of a procedure. For example, a recognition item may be used to assess ability to apply a procedure for restating negative exponents.

In solving the problem $1/2^{-2} =$ _____, what should you do first?

    a. Multiply $1/2 \times 1/2$
    b. Divide $1/2$ by $1/2$
    c. Invert the fraction $1/2$ to 2.
    d. Multiply the fraction times itself three times

Or a similar question may be asked in a constructed response format.

In solving the problem $1/2^{-2}$ what should you do first?

Type 3 items assessing the procedural rule involving negative exponents could also be assessed through a constructed answer by asking the following:

$1/2^{-2} =$ _____

Or as a recognition item:

What is the answer to the problem $1/2^{-2} = ?$

    a. 2
    b. 4
    c. 1/4
    d. 16
    e. 1/8

Evaluate Feedback and Seek Remediation

Feedback can inform learners about their skill in completing the procedure at its various levels of complexity and common errors they have made when applying the procedure. When learners' performance is poor, it can also inform them of what specific component knowledge has not been mastered.

EXAMPLE PROCEDURE LEARNING LESSON: SCIENTIFIC NOTATION

TASK ANALYSIS. The procedure for this lesson is to convert numbers from standard notation to scientific notation. For purposes of brevity, we will limit the objective to positive numbers. The objective for the lesson is the following: "Given a number greater than one in standard notation, the learner can convert the number to scientific notation."

The production for this task is:

    IF a number is in standard notation,
        And IF the number is greater than ten thousand,
        Or IF it is necessary to report the number compactly,
        THEN convert to scientific notation by using the following procedure.

(See Figure 10.2 for a flowchart of this procedure.)

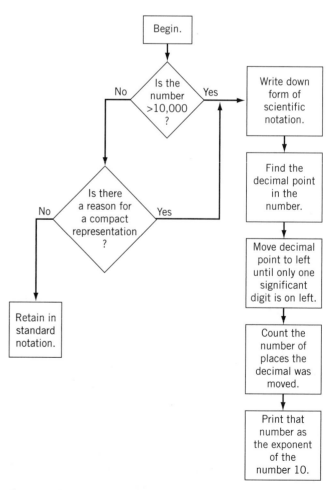

Figure 10.2 Conversion to Scientific Notation

Learners and Content

The learners for this example lesson are eighth-grade students in general science classes, which include a survey of earth science, physics, biology, and chemistry. This lesson occurs early in the year-long course.

In the learners' mathematics classes in both sixth and seventh grades, students learned the meaning and use of exponents. They also learned the concepts of place value and base ten numbers.

This lesson will be mediated in print because it is a simple, straightforward procedure. Feedback for this particular objective can be presented even for constructed response items. Notice that, as in previous lessons, we have re-sequenced the expanded instructional events as needed for this particular lesson and these particular learners.

EXAMPLE PROCEDURE LEARNING LESSON

Introduction

Deploy Attention/Establish Purpose/Arouse Interest and Motivation

The lesson will begin by presenting scenarios in which scientists and students must present very large numbers used in science, such as the distance between planets, the number of bytes of information the human brain can store, or the mass of the Earth. These scenarios should be portrayed as humorously as possible. Other scenarios should depict situations in which large numbers must be presented compactly. Instruction should state that the purpose of this lesson is for students to learn to represent large numbers in a more compact form. This compact form is called *scientific notation*. Instruction points out that learners will learn to follow a procedure for converting numbers to scientific notation. Students could find the answer without using the procedure, but they will reach the answer more reliably and efficiently with this procedure.

Preview the Lesson

The overview should indicate that the instruction will answer the following questions:

- What is scientific notation? What is standard notation?
- When should I use scientific notation?
- How do I convert a number from standard to scientific notation?

Notice we do not review the steps of the process here because some concepts must first be learned for the process to make any sense.

Body

Process Information/Employ Learning Strategies/Focus Attention/Review Prior Knowledge

The instruction lists several large numbers in standard notation and labels them as such. It then defines *standard notation*. The lesson points out that *standard* usually means "common" and that *notation* comes from the word *note*. Then the lesson lists a series of numbers and labels them as *standard notation*.

Next the lesson presents these same numbers in scientific notation. It juxtaposes the same values in scientific and standard notation. It highlights the form of scientific notation:

$$\_\_ \times 10?$$

The lesson asks the learners to notice that the value in the blank is a number between 1 and 10. It may contain fractional parts in the form of a decimal. Then the lesson emphasizes that the value of the exponent tells how many times the 10 would be multiplied by itself. The lesson also states that in standard notation the base must always be 10.

Practice

Several numbers are presented, including numbers in standard notation, scientific notation, and numbers (not 10) with exponents. The learners are asked to label the numbers as *scientific notation, standard notation,* or *other.*

Evaluate Feedback

The instructor must provide numbers with correct labels and explain why numbers with exponents in which the base number is not 10 are not scientific notation.

Recall Prior Knowledge

The instructor must take one of the examples from earlier and show how the number in scientific notation actually represents the number. Then the instructor must review place value to show how this notation actually works (reviewing principles and concepts underlying the procedure).

Process Information

The instructor should discuss the two types of numbers for which scientific notation is preferable: numbers larger than 10,000 and numbers smaller than 10,000 that must be presented compactly, pointing out that later in their studies learners will be introduced to additional reasons. The instructor then reviews several situations in which scientific notation would be appropriate and contrasts those with somewhat similar situations in which scientific notation would be unnecessary. The instructor emphasizes that scientific notation can be used with any numbers, but that it is generally unnecessary to make the conversion except in the situations just mentioned.

Practice

The instructor presents a variety of situations in which scientific notation is and is not necessary. (The instructor must be creative and make the practice fun by presenting humorous number problems.) The instructor then asks students to label the situations and explain their decisions.

Evaluate Feedback

The instructor gives the learners feedback by presenting each number in both forms and then discussing which is the preferred form. Each decision should be briefly explained.

Preview the Lesson

The instructor previews the process for converting to scientific notation. The instructor emphasizes the keywords for each step and reminds students that each step will be explained and practiced later.

1. Write the shell for scientific notation.
2. Find the decimal point in the number in standard notation.
3. Move the decimal point to the left until only one number is to the left of the decimal. Write this number in the first blank.
4. Count the number of places the decimal was moved to the left. Write this number as the exponent of the 10.
5. Check the number mentally by converting it back to standard notation.

The lesson should be in a parallel, two-column format to demonstrate the conversion of a number beside each step.

Process Information

The first step should be labeled with the heading *1. Write the shell*. The instructor reviews the term *shell* from students' computer literacy classes, and shows the form of the shell:

$$\_ \times 10?$$

The instructor explains that two values must be added to complete the scientific notation and reviews the nature of these two numbers.

Practice

The instructor has students write the form of the shell, circle the two places where the number will be added, and explain the nature of the numbers that should appear in these two places.

Evaluate Feedback

The instructor provides a shell with locations for two additional values circled and an explanation of these two values.

Process Information/Focus Attention

The instructor begins this section with the heading *2. Find the decimal*. The instructor presents several numbers, some of which contain decimals and some of which have "understood" decimals. He highlights the location of the decimals.

Practice/Evaluate Feedback

The instructor presents several numbers, some of which contain decimals and some of which have "understood" decimals. He then asks students to locate the decimal and then presents these numbers with decimals highlighted.

Summarize and Review

The instructor lists the first two steps of the procedure, using a sample problem and taking learners through the first two steps:

1. Write the shell for scientific notation.
2. Find the decimal point in the number in standard notation.

Practice

The instructor gives several numbers in standard notation that are appropriate for standard notation. He asks students to complete the first two steps in converting to scientific notation.

Evaluate Feedback

The instructor shows each step and labels them explicitly for each number.

Process Information/Focus Attention

The instructor presents the third step with the heading *3. Move the decimal,* emphasizing the object of this step, to get only one number to the left of the decimal. The instructor offers several examples with the first two steps completed and the third step demonstrated. The number written in the first blank of the shell should be highlighted. The lesson should emphasize that this number must be between 1 and 10 (but will never *be* 10). The lesson also emphasizes that the movement is to the left, not the right.

Practice/Evaluate Feedback

The instructor presents several numbers suitable for scientific notation, giving the learners the first two steps completed for each number and asking them to complete the third step by entering the value of the number in the first blank of the shell. The instructor provides feedback by showing the third step for each practice number.

Practice

The instructor presents several numbers suitable for scientific notation, asking the learner to complete the first three steps of the procedure for converting to scientific notation.

Feedback

The first three steps of the procedure should be presented for each of the practice numbers.

Process Information/Focus Attention

The instructor labels this step *4. Count the moves* and offers a visual example with the first three steps completed. The procedure of moving the decimal is emphasized with a dotted line stopping at each place the decimal is moved. An arrow points to the location where the decimal will now appear. The arrow indicates that the movement was to the left. The number of moves is indicated with a number below the dotted line. The connection between the number of moves and the exponent is visually emphasized. The shell is completed with the exponent of the 10 completed. Following several examples, the learner reads the text, which explains that this step is just a procedural way of determining the place value of the significant digit that is given in the first blank. It should also be emphasized that the count stands for the moves, not the places the decimal is moved.

Practice/Evaluate Feedback

The instructor presents several numbers that are appropriate for scientific notation with the first three steps completed. He directs the learners to complete the fourth step by entering the exponent for the 10 and provides feedback, including the completed shell.

The instructor presents more numbers that are appropriate for scientific notation, asking learners to complete the first four steps of the procedure. He offers feedback in the form of a completed shell for each number.

Process Information/Focus Attention/Employ Learning Strategies

The fifth step, *5. Confirm answer,* is introduced as a critical step in all procedures. Learners are presented with some examples of numbers in standard and scientific notation, some of which have been converted correctly and some of which have the correct form but an error in conversion. Some of these numbers contain zeros in both the initial and in medial positions. The instructor suggests three approaches for checking the answer: checking the format of the number, reapplying the procedure, or converting the number back to standard notation. The instructor demonstrates the procedure for converting a number from scientific to standard notation with appropriate graphic devices that emphasize the procedure.

Practice

The learners are presented with several numbers written in scientific notation with their standard notations. Some of these are incorrectly computed, with moves incorrectly counted, more than one number as a significant digit, and other common errors. Learners are asked to mark each conversion as correct or incorrect. Beside those that they mark as incorrect, they are asked to explain their answers.

Feedback

Feedback includes the number in its given standard notation and scientific notation, with the note "correct" or "incorrect." Each incorrect answer is explained with a statement of which approach would be most likely to locate a problem: checking the format of the number, reapplying the procedure, or converting the number back to standard notation.

Practice/Feedback

Several numbers are presented in an application context, some of which are appropriate for conversion and some of which are not. The instructor directs students to determine which numbers should be converted and then to convert them. The instructor's feedback indicates the numbers that should be written in scientific notation in that form, with a brief explanation as to why some numbers were not converted.

Practice/Feedback

The instructor asks learners to list the five steps in converting a number to scientific notation in their own words. His feedback provides a list of these steps.

Conclusion

Summarize and Review/Employ Learning Strategies

The five steps for conversion to scientific notation are presented with the keywords emphasized. Learners are encouraged to shut their eyes and visualize these steps either in words or in representative pictures. The situations that require scientific notation are reviewed. The process is demonstrated with one last number.

Transfer Learning

The instructor informs learners of a number of situations in which they will be asked to use scientific notation in future units. They are asked to locate numbers in texts and other publications in which scientific notation is used or should have been used. They are given a number that is negative (but with an absolute value of 1 or more), asked to convert it to scientific notation, and then provided with feedback. The instructor might also give them a number that is less than 1 (and appropriate for scientific notation) and ask them to guess how it might be converted, providing feedback.

Remotivate and Close

The instructor gives learners an exciting, interesting, or humorous scenario in which they must convert a number to scientific notation. They are encouraged to explain why this is a useful skill to have.

Assessment

Assess Learning

If learning from this lesson is to be assessed independently from other objectives, then several separate items may be included to assess if learners can do the following: (1) identify situations in which scientific notation should be used, (2) apply the procedure to convert a number from scientific notation to standard notation, (3) list the steps for the procedure, and (4) determine whether the procedure has been correctly applied. If assessment time is limited, only components 2 and 4, or perhaps just 4, may be assessed.

Evaluate Feedback and Seek Remediation

The instructor should provide feedback in a generalized form. Information can be provided as to whether the learners have difficulty in identifying situations appropriate for scientific notation, applying the procedure, listing the steps, or monitoring an answer. Even if separate items of each type were not administered individually, the grader may be able to view the learners' responses and draw some inferences about the source of the problems. In addition, the grader may be able to identify for the learners any common or consistent errors they are making.

E X E R C I S E

1. Which of the following are procedures?

_____ listing the steps in making an omelet

_____ careful and complete description of the procedure for making an omelet

_____ being able to identify egg, whisk, butter, skillet, and spatula

_____ making an omelet

_____ determining the best times and situations in which to serve omelets to guests of differing tastes and preferences

_____ washing the dishes

2. Classify the following procedures as simple or complex procedures:

_____ long division

_____ adding two-digit numbers

_____ writing a check

_____ completing a U.S. Income Tax return using the long form and instructions provided by the I.R.S.

_____ installing spark plugs in a car

_____ measuring blood pressure using a sphygmomanometer and stethoscope

S U M M A R Y

Figure 10.3 provides a summary of the particularly appropriate application of events of instruction for instruction intended to lead to the learning of procedures.

Introduction	Deploy attention. Establish instructional purpose. Arouse interest and motivation. Preview lesson.	• Ask question, demonstrate procedure, describe efficiency. • Describe procedure to be learned and range of applicability. • Emphasize efficiency and reliability of procedure. • Preview procedure in chunks.
Body	Recall prior knowledge. Process information. Focus attention. Employ learning strategies. Practice. Evaluate feedback.	• Review component concepts, subprocedures, or related principle. • Simplify complex procedures, situations that require procedures, steps in procedure, order of steps, how to evaluate correctness of application. May elaborate over several iterations. • Identify critical characteristics of situations requiring procedure, key cues to transitioning between steps, keywords for each step, cues for correct completion of procedure. • Use job aid, mnemonic for order of steps. • Identify situations requiring procedure, order of steps, completion of steps, correct completion of procedure. • Correct answer with explanation, checklist or rating scale, video feedback.
Conclusion	Summarize and review. Transfer knowledge. Remotivate and close.	• Review major steps in procedure related to principle, appropriate situations for application. • Relate to problem solving, more complex procedures. • Emphasize utility of procedure in terms of reliability and efficiency.
Assessment	Assess performance. Provide feedback and remediation.	• Identify to which procedure applies, correct order and completion of steps, recognize correctly completed procedure. • Identify common errors and misconceptions.

Figure 10.3 Key Events for Learning Procedures

EXTENDED EXAMPLE

Go to the Learning Resources Web site for a continuation the instructional design of the Photography Basics course. The contribution from this chapter is strategy design for instructor-led instruction leading to the learning of a procedure: focusing a zoom lens to achieve best focus at any focal length.

READINGS AND REFERENCES

Anderson, J. R. (1985). *Cognitive psychology* (2nd ed.). New York: W. H. Freeman.

Gagné, R. M. (1985). *The conditions of learning* (4th ed.). New York: Holt, Rinehart & Winston.

Gilbert, T. (1978). *Human competence: Engineering worthy performance.* New York: McGraw-Hill.

Graham, S., Wedman, J. F., & Garvin-Kester, B. (1993). Manager coaching skills: Development and application. *Performance Improvement Quarterly, 6*(1), 2–13.

Landa, L. N. (1974). *Algorithmization in learning and instruction.* Englewood Cliffs, NJ: Educational Technology Publications.

Landa, L. N. (1983). The algo-heuristic theory of instruction. In C. M. Reigeluth (Ed.), *Instructional design theories and models* (pp. 163–221). Hillsdale, NJ: Erlbaum.

Marcone, S., & Reigeluth, C. M. (1988). Teaching common errors in applying a procedure. *Educational Communications and Technology Journal, 36*(1), 23–32.

Mitchell, M. C. (1980). The practicality of algorithms in instructional development. *Journal of Instructional Development, 4*(4), 10–16.

Mumford, M. D., Costanza, D. P., Baughman, W. A., Threlfall, K. V., & Fleishman, E. A. (1994). Influence of abilities on performance during practice: Effects of mass and distributed practice. *Journal of Educational Psychology, 86*(1), 134–144.

Phillips, T. L., & Quinn, J. (1993). The effects of alternative flow-charting techniques on performance on procedural tasks. *Performance Improvement Quarterly, 6*(1), 54–66.

Reigeluth, C. M. (1987). *Instructional theories in action.* Hillsdale, NJ: Erlbaum.

Scandura, J. M. (1983). Instructional strategies based on the structural learning theory. In C. M. Reigeluth (Ed.), *Instructional design theories and models* (pp. 213–246). Hillsdale, NJ: Erlbaum.

Schmid, R. F., & Gerlach, V. S. (1990). Instructional design rules for algorithmic subject matter. *Performance Improvement Quarterly, 3*(2), 2–15.

Wilson, B. G. (1985). Techniques for teaching procedures. *Journal of Instructional Development, 8*(12), 2–5.

STRATEGIES FOR INSTRUCTION LEADING TO PRINCIPLE LEARNING

CHAPTER OBJECTIVES

At the conclusion of this chapter, you should be able to do the following:

- Determine whether a learning task requires the application of a principle.
- Given a principle, identify its component concepts.
- Given a principle application objective, design a strategy plan for the rule lesson.

A REVIEW OF PRINCIPLE LEARNING

Remember from Chapter 5 and 10 that rules may be of two types: procedural rules (procedures) and relational rules (principles). Principles prescribe the relationship(s) among two or more concepts. These relationships are often described in the form of an if-then or cause-effect relationship. Boyle's law is an example of a principle: When the temperature of a gas remains constant, if pressure increases, then volume decreases (and vice versa). Other terms that have been used for principles are *propositions, laws, axioms, theorems,* and *postulates.* Equations from mathematics and science are abbreviated forms of principles because they state the relationships between concepts. We find examples of principles in every content area, including mathematics, science, the social sciences, and language learning, as well as in the arts, such as music. Here are some examples of principles:

- *Mechanics:* Power = Work/Time (e.g., if a certain amount of work is expended in a certain amount of time, then a certain amount of power is used; for example, if you halve the time and keep work constant, you will double the power).
- *Sociology:* If a society undergoes industrialization, then the population will grow rapidly at first and then level off as a result of successive reductions in death rates and birth rates.
- *Statistics:* If the mean, median, and mode of a distribution are the same, then the distribution is normally distributed.
- *Optics:* The greater the curvature of a convex lens, the shorter the focal length.
- *Mathematics:* The associative property in addition can be represented as follows:

  $(a + b) + c = a + (b + c)$
- *Economics:* The principle of diminishing marginal utility is as follows: The more units of a certain economic product a person acquires, the less eager that person is to buy still more (of that product).

You can see how a principle describes the relationship between the concepts in the principle. These concepts are often in the form of variables—factors that can have many values. The application of a principle enables learners to predict what will happen if one of the variables is changed. Principles also allow the learner to explain what has happened. For example, why did sales of yo-yos decline during the late 1950s? (The principle of diminishing marginal utility can help you explain this situation.) Finally, knowing a principle allows you to control the effects of variables upon each other. For example, using the principle from optics describing the relationship between lens curvature and focal length,

consider John, who needs new glasses. What lens curvature does he need—more or less than his current lenses—if he cannot focus as closely as he needs to in order to read?

The acquisition of a principle should not be confused with the ability to state that principle. The ability to state a principle is declarative knowledge learning. The acquisition of a principle involves the ability to *apply* that principle to a variety of previously unencountered situations. The ability to verbally state the relationship between concepts may be helpful in learning to apply a rule; however, stating the principle is not sufficient evidence that the rule has been learned. A principle must be applied to show that it has been learned. The failure to recognize this distinction is very common in both training and educational settings. Instruction often fails to allow for sufficient experience in applying a principle for learners to learn to apply it with unfamiliar instances. A real benefit of thinking of types of learning during the analysis phase is determining how learners will need to be able to use new knowledge: in this case, whether being able to explain the relationship of the concepts is enough or whether learners must be able to apply this principle to explain, predict, or control the effects of one variable on others.

The mental operations involved in applying principles are called *productions* (Anderson, 1985). As you may recall, productions are hypothesized mental operations that generally take the form of if-then representations. Productions are implicit in all of the intellectual skills. (We will see examples of productions involved in applying principles later in this chapter.)

Remember that principle learning is central to domain-specific problem solving. In fact, they are the "engines" of the processing required in problem solving: To find and solve problems in a content domain, learners must have a repertoire of principles that explain the relationships between critical concepts within that domain. Problem solving, then, is the selection of the appropriate principles to combine to solve a problem that requires application of several principles, often concurrently, to solve it. In Chapter 12, we will discuss the pros and cons of learners mastering the application of individual principles before learning to apply them in combination to solve complex problems. This chapter will consider the features of instructional support that can facilitate principle learning, whether that principle learning is accomplished prior to the problem-solving instruction or embedded within it.

Principle learning is distinct from learning procedures. Procedures are a generalizable series of steps initiated in response to a particular class of circumstances to reach a specified goal. Often, using a procedure is a simplified alternative to using a principle. The learning of arithmetic and the learning of statistics is full of examples of the choice between learning the same thing as a procedure or a principle, with the trade-off typically emphasizing relative ease and simplicity when the procedural learning route is taken and meaningfulness and breadth of application emphasized when the principle learning route is taken. Even so, some learners may learn to apply principles as efficiently as they can apply a procedure. We discussed this relationship between principles and procedures in Chapter 10, along with strategies for supporting learning procedures.*

E X E R C I S E S

Write *PRI* in the blank if the outcome is an example of principle learning. Write *PRO* if it is an example of application of a procedure. Write *X* if it is neither a principle nor a procedure. Explain your answer.

_____ 1. Demonstrating the technique for jump-starting a car.

_____ 2. Determining the amount of energy released from a nuclear reaction with the equation $E = mc^2$.

_____ 3. Stating the law of supply and demand.

_____ 4. Recognizing examples of deviant behavior.

_____ 5. Determining what to do when a traffic light is red.

_____ 6. Deciding whether to use *a* or *an* before a noun.

_____ 7. Showing how to make bread.

_____ 8. Soldering two wires together.

_____ 9. Determining the length of a hypotenuse of a triangle given the length of the two sides.

_____10. Conjugating a regular verb in Spanish.

COGNITIVE PROCESSES OF LEARNING PRINCIPLES

Just as with procedures, principles require that productions be learned, but an information-processing analysis for principles is somewhat different from that for procedures. The cognitive processes underlying the intellectual skill of applying a principle can be identified in the productions associated with those cognitive processes:

IF the situation described involves key concept *A*

   and IF the situation described involves key concept *B*,

THEN rule *Q* applies in this case (concept recognition).

*Some fairly fierce educational debates have at heart only the choice between considering a learning task as a principle or as a procedure.

The principle explains the relationship of these two concepts:

IF concept *A* changes in direction *R* with magnitude of *Z*,

THEN concept *B* will change in direction *M* with a magnitude of *N*.

Prior knowledge of the concepts represented in the principle (here identified as concepts *A* and *B*) is prerequisite to learning a principle. If you will recall the general *information-processing analysis* for applying a principle (from Chapter 5, see page 87–88), one of the main cognitive tasks in learning to apply a principle is learning to recognize the situation in which these two or more concepts are related so that the principle applies. This recognition requires the generalization of the principle to more than the first context. It also requires discrimination in which the learner learns to recognize occasions in which the principle does not apply. The learner must be able to state the relationship of these concepts (a declarative knowledge component of the task). Next, the learner must determine which concept or concepts have changed and the magnitude and direction of the change. Finally, the learner must determine what effect these changes will have on the other concept(s).

An example of this cognitive operation is the task of learning Ohm's law, which most of us learned in general science. It is prerequisite to learning many advanced principles and concepts in electronics. Ohm's law states that voltage is directly related to both current and resistance.

1. Determine what variables are involved in the situation.
2. Determine which principle applies. (If the situation relates current, voltage, and resistance, then Ohm's law applies.)
3. Determine which variables' values are known.
4. Determine which variables' values are unknown.
5. Determine the direction and magnitude of the known variables.
6. Using the principle (Ohm's law), determine the effects of the known variables on the unknown variables by determining the value of the unknowns.
7. Determine if the value makes sense.

The final step in the task analysis is critical for learners to complete to demonstrate fundamental understanding of the relationships underlying the task. For example, voltage is directly related to both current and resistance: One symbolic relationship of these variables is $V = I \times R$. For example, in one problem the current is

2 amps and resistance is 60 ohms. A calculation of 10 volts would clearly not make sense. The importance of understanding the principle underlying this relationship is one reason why principles should be learned as principles rather than as procedures (although you can see how easily we could convert the information-processing analysis into a procedure to follow for solving problems involving Ohm's law).

CONDITIONS SUPPORTING LEARNING PRINCIPLES

The design for principle lessons is quite similar to the design of concept lessons. Just as with designing concept lessons, when designing a strategy for principles, the designer can choose between an inquiry or an expository approach. An inquiry strategy for teaching principles involves presenting learners with examples and nonexamples of the application of the principle and encouraging the learners to discover the principle (i.e., the relationships between the concepts in the situation). Both Taba (1967) and Suchman (1961) suggested ways in which inquiry methods may be used in teaching rules. In his Model of Inquiry Teaching, Suchman suggests the following instructional process:

1. Present the learners with a puzzling situation that shows the relationship between the variables. Such a situation may be a demonstration or description.
2. Allow learners to ask the teacher (or an "intelligent" computer) questions about the situation that can be answered in the form of "yes" or "no." Students' questions should eventually move through questions verifying the nature of the situation, to gathering more data about the situation, to isolating the relevant variables in the situation, to forming hypotheses about the situation, to testing their hypotheses to confirm cause-effect relationships.
3. At the conclusion of the experience, learners should be able to state a formal principle or rule about the relationships of the concepts involved.
4. Learners should also be encouraged to discuss the inquiry process itself, including those approaches that were fruitful and those that were not. (This practice will encourage the development of cognitive strategies, discussed in Chapter 13.)

Although an inquiry approach may be extremely useful for teaching principles, especially for extremely abstract principles or in situations where learners are particularly skilled in prior knowledge or cognitive strategies, such a strategy can be more time-consuming and potentially confusing to unskilled learners than an expository approach. On some occasions, the optimal sequence of instruction is more expository: The princi-

ple is presented and demonstrated, and learners have an opportunity to practice the principle's application. We will describe each of these approaches in more detail.

INTRODUCTION

Deploy Attention

Learners' attention should be directed toward investigating the relationships between key concepts in the principle. This may be done by highlighting the concepts verbally or visually. An inquiry strategy can gain learners' attention quite quickly by presenting an anomalous situation involving the key concepts and their relationships. For both inquiry and expository strategies, attention may be piqued through demonstrations or scenarios of the application of the principle.

Establish Instructional Purpose

In an inquiry strategy, the purpose may be originally defined as a puzzle to solve. Before the lesson is concluded, it is important that the purpose of the lesson be explicitly stated in terms of the acquisition of the principle. For more expository lessons, the purpose may be stated explicitly by verbally stating the rule that relates two or more particular concepts together, such as "Today, you will learn how to determine the change in volume of a gas when given a specified change in pressure." Or the instructor may ask a question regarding the nature of the relationship between concepts and point out that the purpose of the lesson is to determine this relationship.

Arouse Interest and Motivation

An inquiry approach itself may sufficiently stimulate interest. Move directly into the puzzling situation to promote such interest. Puzzling situations may also be posed in an expository lesson. In addition, learners may be shown previous experiences that have involved the rule or principle. Students may be motivated when they hear how the rule can be used in explaining, controlling, or predicting everyday situations. Older learners and learners with high aptitude may be motivated by a discussion of how the rule will be later combined with other rules to solve problems.

Preview Lesson

For instruction using an inquiry strategy, this event will involve giving directions to the solution of the puzzle as well as an overview of how the entire lesson will progress. In a more expository lesson, the preview may involve an outline of how the lesson will allow the learners to solve a puzzle or resolve a scenario that has been presented.

Body

Recall Relevant Prior Knowledge

The most critical prior knowledge to acquisition of a principle is acquisition of the concepts underlying the principle. Learners should have more than declarative knowledge of the concepts (i.e., they should be able to apply the concept, not just state its definition or characteristics). For example, the principle that gas expands when heated has three concepts—"gas," "heated," and "expands."

It is not uncommon for the concepts that are incorporated in a principle to be taught in the same lesson as the principle itself. In most cases, learners should experience instruction on the concepts, including practice and feedback, until they are skilled with the concepts, before instruction on the principle begins.

Principle analogies may be used in tying prior knowledge to new learning. For example, in BASIC programming, consider teaching the use of the "GOTO" command as opposed to the "GOSUB" command. (This involves if-then principles.) An analogy to flipping pages in a book may be used to distinguish the differing needs of a programming situation. (For example, if you plan to return to the page, you put your finger in that page. That's a GOSUB. If you don't plan to return, then you flip the pages over completely. That's a GOTO command.)

Process Information and Examples

At this point in the instruction, the learners may be presented with a statement of the principle and with subsequent examples of the principle's application, or the learners may be presented with examples of the principle's application and asked to induce the principle. If the principle is stated first, it is usually stated in an if-then form, although other ways of stating this generality are also acceptable. Examples of statements of a principle include the following:

- If a stamp has complete perforations, then it is more valuable than if it has incomplete perforations.
- If a musical phrase contains a crescendo, then begin the phrase singing at the volume indicated and gradually increase the volume to the level indicated by the music (or by the director).
- If a plant's leaves are drooping and its soil is dry to the touch, then water it.
- If a fire breaks out on the kitchen stove and the material that is burning is grease, then don't spray it with water, but do cut off the oxygen to the fire.
- When incorporating material written by others in your own writing, clearly designate those ideas that are directly borrowed from others.
- To get wax out of your ears, use drops to break down the wax, and then use a gentle spray of water to wash out the wax.

In expository instruction, these principles will be stated in a form that is appropriate for the audience in terms of vocabulary and sentence complexity. It helps to display a statement of the principle on a poster, bulletin board, transparency, or chalkboard for learners to refer to during the initial portion of the lesson. Later, the designer can remove the statement of the principle so that learners will rely on their own memory.

It is often useful to explain the *whys of* a principle to make it meaningful and, therefore, more memorable. For example, in the stated principle about a grease fire, an explanation as to why you should not spray water on it is necessary. The explanation should be at a level that is understandable to members of the audience, based upon their prior knowledge. It should help them to remember and apply the principle. Often, this explanation uses knowledge of principles that the learners have already acquired. Inquiry strategies will, of course, not state the principle immediately but will lead the learners to develop a statement of the principle after they have observed the action of the concepts in examples.

Once learners have been exposed to the statement of the principle in expository strategies, or initially in inquiry strategies, they should experience applications of the principle. These applications can be directly experienced or demonstrated. For example, the tighter a string is pulled, the higher its pitch when plucked; this principle could be demonstrated by the instructor or directly experienced by learners who are given string or rubber bands. Often, instruction may include demonstration first and then direct experience. Generally, learners find direct experiences more engaging and interesting. However, the context, characteristics of the learners, and characteristics of the instructional task may dictate whether direct experience is possible. For example, if molecules are heated, they move more rapidly. This principle cannot be directly observed; it may only be simulated (for example, through video animation).

Applications may show how the principle can be used to predict effects (Will the pitch be higher or lower than the previous pitch?), to explain outcomes (Why was the pitch lower than the previous pitch?), or to control the outcomes of a situation (How can I make the pitch lower?). As with concept learning, it may be helpful for learners to first experience a best example of the principle. This example should clearly demonstrate the application of the principle, with few extraneous (noncritical) aspects in the situation. It is very helpful if this example has some features such as humor, analogy, novelty, or personal relevance to make it more memorable.

The outcomes of a principle application may be discrete, as in the correct conjugation of a verb; it may be continuous, as in the result from applying Ohm's law to calculate the amount of current in a circuit when given the voltage and resistance; or it may be general, as when predicting the effects of industrialization on population growth. Learners should encounter sufficient examples of the application to have a clear idea of the character of the answers that can be acquired when applying the principle.

Unlike learning concepts, matched nonexamples may not be critical to learning principles. For example, it may not be possible to think of a reasonable nonexample for the principle relating the tightness of a string and its relative pitch when plucked. On the other hand, it is important to use contrasting examples and nonexamples when teaching learners about how to select from the nominative and subjective forms of pronouns in a sentence ("Tim brought the present to Gracie and *I*" versus "Tim brought the present to Gracie and *me*").

When a principle guides a clear choice from several alternatives, matched examples and nonexamples should be experienced early in learning to apply the principle. If, however, the application of the rule yields multiple outcomes, such as varying pitches in our rule example, or multiple values of volume of a gas when pressure on that gas changes (Boyle's law), then often there is not a reasonable match in terms of results of application. Once the learners have begun to learn to apply the principle, the designer can point out to them common errors or misconceptions regarding the relationship of the concepts in the principle. For example, there is a common misconception that plucking a string harder will change its pitch. (Those learners are confusing pitch with volume: To change the volume of the sound coming from a plucked string, pluck it softer or harder.) With regard to Boyle's law, a common misconception is that pressure and volume of a gas are directly (rather than inversely) related. These misconceptions may be directly addressed or evoked and corrected during practice.

As learners experience the application of a principle, it is important that they identify which features of the situation suggest that a particular principle should be employed. For example, learners should be able to identify that the critical features in the plucked-string situation are the following:

- There is a string.
- The string will be plucked.
- We wish to change the pitch of the sound resulting from the plucked string.

So that the learners can be aware of the breadth of the domain to which the principle is applicable, they should also be encouraged to identify noncritical aspects of the principle application. For example, in the plucked-string situation, the principle is equally applicable if the strings are different colors, attached to instruments or unattached, or of different materials and thicknesses (although this does introduce another principle as well) from those with which the learners practiced.

Focus Attention

Learners may require assistance in determining which concepts are being related by the principle and how the concepts are related. These features may be highlighted in the principle statement by inflection (if the principle is stated orally) or by typography (if the principle is in written form). In addition, as learners experience applications of the principle, they should be encouraged to focus on these key features in each application. Learners also should be encouraged to note the direction and magnitude of changes in one variable (concept) when another variable has been changed.

Employ Learning Strategies

To support retention of the principle statement, learners may be asked to develop their own mnemonic, or if they are unable to do so, a mnemonic may be suggested to aid them in recalling a principle. For example, many of us were taught the mnemonic "*i* before *e* except after *c*" to help us remember a spelling principle. Learners may also be taught techniques to support application of the principle. When given the sentence "Ben gave the horn to Molly and me," removing the noun *Molly* from the sentence will allow the learner to determine the appropriate form of the pronoun. Learners might also be encouraged to illustrate or diagram the relationships of concepts as presented in the principle.

Practice

Learners should practice principles at four levels. First, they should practice stating the principle. Although research results are somewhat mixed regarding the necessity of actually being able to state a principle to apply it, it is very useful for learners to practice stating the principle at the point of learning it. Learners may also be encouraged to state the principle in their own words, with the instructor providing feedback as to whether their statements accurately reflect the intention of the principle. Instructors can often gain useful information about learners' misconceptions by observing their paraphrased statements of a principle.

Second, they should practice recognizing situations in which the principle is applicable. For example, after studying Boyle's law, learners might practice using items in which pressure and volume of liquids are changed, temperature and pressure of gases are changed, and pressure and volume of gases are changed. Students could be asked to identify situations in which Boyle's law is applicable. If students have previously learned related principles that might be easily confused with the application of the current principle, this practice may include questions that require the learners to distinguish between them.

Third, they should practice applying the principle to predict, explain, or control the effects of one concept on another. This practice should be across the range of difficulty and applicability of the principle so that learners are exposed to the range of situations in which the principle is applicable. The situations should vary as much as possible on noncritical aspects. Some of the practice items should require learners to explain their answers. Depending upon the availability of a medium that can provide feedback to production questions—a human or an "intelligent" computer system—some items may ask students to provide their own examples of the application of the principle.

And finally, learners should practice determining whether a principle has been correctly applied. It is important that learners do not practice at this level until they are skilled at applying the principle because they should not be confused by incorrect applications of a principle before they are skilled in its correct application. However, it is important that they be able to scan a solution to a situation in which the principle has been applied and determine if the solution is reasonable and appropriate. They must have this skill to "check" their own solutions; therefore, it can be helpful for them to be presented with carefully constructed incorrect solutions and be asked if the answers are reasonable. The incorrect solutions could represent common misconceptions or errors that learners make when applying a particular principle. After learners have identified whether the principle has been properly applied, they should be asked to explain their decisions. This explanation is important in this situation because with a dichotomous answer (yes/no), learners have a strong possibility of guessing the answer correctly without actually being able to apply the principle. Requiring an explanation ensures that learners must truly be able to apply the principle.

Evaluate Feedback

Feedback varies for each type of practice question. For items that practice stating the principle, feedback should provide information as to whether learners' statements contain the key concepts of the principle and relate these concepts appropriately. Feedback might also include identification of any extraneous or incorrect information included in the statement of the principle. With some media, such as print or computer-based instruction, feedback might be limited to a model answer, with a highlighting of critical features of the statement. Such feedback might also include identification of common errors and factors that should not be included in the answer.

Items that offer practice recognizing situations in which the principle is applicable should be followed with feedback that identifies whether the principle under consideration is applicable and what features of the situation make the principle applicable or not applicable.

For items in which learners actually practiced applying the principle, feedback should provide the outcome of the application of the principle. This may be a single answer, as in the case of the determination of an appropriate pronoun form, or it may describe the direction and magnitude of the change in one concept (variable) when there is a change in another variable. It is also helpful to provide explanatory feedback in the form of a step-by-step solution of the item, a highlighting of critical features in the item that influence the application of the principle, or a graphic illustrating how the solution can be drawn by applying the principle to the information given.

Feedback for items in which the learners determined whether a principle has been correctly applied should include a clear indication of the correct answer. For situations in which the principle has not been correctly applied, the feedback should point out the error and state how the principle should have been applied.

Conclusion

The conclusion of a principle learning lesson should allow learners the opportunity to consolidate their learning into a form that can be readily applied in a variety of circumstances and that can be transferred to higher-order learning tasks, such as problem solving.

Summarize and Review

A summary and review of a rule-learning task should include a paraphrased restatement of the principle from the original statement in the lesson. The review may present this principle in a graphic format, such as an illustration or diagram that shows the relationship of the concepts that are associated in the principle. The instruction may also refer to any best example that was presented earlier in the instruction, with a clear review of why this example epitomizes the application of the principle.

Transfer Knowledge

The most common transfer of a principle is its application in concert with other rules in problem-solving situations. It can be quite helpful to support this transfer by suggesting in the conclusion of the lesson how this principle may be applied later in combination with other principles. Students should also be encouraged to locate the principle's application in their daily lives. An area of the classroom, such as a bulletin board, may be set up to document these observations.

Remotivate and Close

Remotivation in the lesson may be supported by learners identifying the relevance of the principle's application in their later instruction or in their daily lives.

Assessment of Principle Application

Assessment of principle application may include the following types of items:

1. Stating the principle.
2. Recognizing situations in which the principle is applicable.
3. Applying the principle.
4. Determining whether a principle has been correctly applied.

Of course, the items represented by item 3 most nearly assess the intention of the goals of most principle learning lessons. Items 1, 2, and 4 represent knowledge that support the application of the principle. Therefore, the majority of the items should involve application of the principle to predict, explain, or control the influence of one variable on another. In assessments in which it is practical, you may wish to also assess 1, 2, and 4 because these items may provide information as to learners' ability in knowledge that supports the application of the principle.

An example of a type-2 item—recognizing when to apply the principle of pronoun usage—can be assessed with the following item:

1. *What grammar rule is violated in the following sentence?*
   The doghouse was built by Tim and myself.

   a. Subject-verb agreement.
   b. Pronoun reference.
   c. Reflexive pronoun.
   d. No rule is violated.

A constructed answer item of the same type would be this:

1. What grammar rule is violated in the following sentence?
   The doghouse was built by Tim and myself.

Of course, a constructed answer item involving the use of the principle would have the learners actually solve the problem using a principle, as in a type-3 item:

1. You and Tim have built a doghouse. Complete the sentence below that tells this thought. (Do not use your name in the blank.)

The doghouse was built by Tim and _____.

You can combine recognition and constructed answer in item types 2 and 3 as in the following:

1. The directors of reading curriculum in the No Waste School District are favorably impressed by Schank and Minsky's work on "scripts and plans" and their impact on learning to read. The director develops a module about these models. He expects that the reading teachers will learn to use these models while teaching reading. When the director observes reading classes six months later, there is no evidence that the model is being incorporated into the reading instruction.
   What principle of dissemination and diffusion have the directors violated? What might the directors have done differently?

Type-3 principle application problems can often be assessed with a recognition format:

1. *Which of the following sentences is grammatically correct?*
   a. The doghouse was built by Tim and I.
   b. The doghouse was built by Tim and me.
   c. The doghouse was built by me and Tim.
   d. The doghouse was built by Tim and myself.

One limitation of this type of recognition item is its limited number of options, which makes it possible for learners to determine the answer either through guessing or elimination while being unable to solve the item in a production form. It is also sometimes difficult to develop plausible foils. In constructing recognition problems for assessing principle application, the designer should determine the common errors that learners make in solving such items and then create foils that represent each of them.

Of course, as with assessing concepts and discriminations, when assessing principles, items should be examples that were not presented during the instruction, including practice items. If an instructor used these old instances, she would be assessing recall of declarative knowledge, not the ability to apply the principle.

Principle use cannot be assessed with recall items because recall items test strictly recall of information, not its application. However, principle use has component declarative knowledge, such as the verbal statement of a principle that can be tested in a recall format.

The items should assess across the range of applicability and difficulty levels of the principle. Several related and/or easily confused principles may profitably be assessed at the same time to ensure that the learners know how to differentiate between applications. However, the designer must be careful not to develop items that require the selection and multiple application of several principles, as this is problem-solving learning.

Evaluate Feedback and Seek Remediation

Feedback for assessment should generally be in the form of cumulative information, such as whether the learner has or has not acquired the ability to apply the rule. Correct answer feedback may also be helpful after assessment.

Remediation should address misconceptions the learners have evidenced in their responses. For instance, learners may indicate that they have overgeneralized the rule. Remediation can highlight and review the features of the situations that call for the application of the rule. Remediation of overgeneralization should also involve more practice in identifying situations that require application of the rule.

Remediation may also be necessary for undergeneralization. Learners who evidenced this problem can be helped with practice across the full range of the applicability of the rule.

EXAMPLE PRINCIPLE APPLICATION LESSON: USE OF WHO, WHICH AND THAT

TASK ANALYSIS

This lesson focuses on the grammar rule that guides the selection of *who, which,* or *that* in a sentence such as "The Mozart Mass in C, (who/which/that) is sometimes called the *Coronation Mass,* was written in 1779." Following are the objective and productions associated with this principle.

Objective   Given a sentence with a blank in it, the learner will determine whether the pronoun *who, which,* or *that* is appropriate for filling in the blank.

Productions

> IF the noun referent is a person,
> THEN use the pronoun *who.*
> IF the noun referent is an animal, object, or idea, and IF the pronoun begins a nonrestrictive clause,
> THEN use the pronoun *which.*
> IF the noun referent is an animal, object, or idea, and IF the pronoun begins a restrictive clause,
> THEN use the pronoun *that.*

Learners   The learners for this lesson are undergraduate college students in a technical writing class. This class is an elective course for programs from such diverse subject matter areas as science, sociology, nursing, and English. All learners in the class have passed an exam that assesses high school graduate-level skills in punctuation, grammar usage, and composition.

Context   The technical writing course follows a PSI (Personalized System of Instruction) instructional management system in which students receive individualized instruction for some components of the course and group-delivered instruction for other segments. The current lesson will be designed for a segment of individualized instruction on pronoun usage. For the purposes of this example, we will predetermine the medium to be computer-based instruction (although ideally we would delay making a media selection decision until after we had determined how the expanded instructional events might be implemented).

An Example Lesson for Relational Rules

Although an inquiry approach could be used for this lesson, we will use an expository approach (see Figure 11.1).

INTRODUCTION

Deploy Attention

The supermarket _____ has the freshest produce will be our supplier.

WHO? WHICH? THAT?

Establish Instructional Purpose—Arouse Interest and Motivation

The ability to select the appropriate pronoun to use in a descriptive pronoun phrase, particularly to select between the pronouns which and that, is a distinctive skill of technical writer.
Many writer are unaware that the words which and that are not interchangeable.
In this lesson you will learn to determine which relative pronoun to use in sentences in which you must choose among *who*, *which*, and *that*.

Figure 11.1   Example Principle Lesson

Preview Lesson

In this lesson you have some options as to the order of the lesson. Here is how the lesson is arranged. Click on the point in the lesson where you would like to begin.

Use of "Who"	Use of "Which"	Use of "That"	Review of "Restrictive" and "Nonrestrictive"

Review of Lesson

Practice

BODY

Recall Relevant Prior Knowledge

Relative Pronouns
As you recall from the previous lesson, relative pronouns are the pronouns *who* (or *whom*), *which*, and *that*. A relative pronoun is a pronoun that does two things:
* Takes the place of a noun.
* Connects a dependent clause and a main clause.

Process Information and Examples—Focus Attention

The Use of Who
You use the pronoun *who* when you are writing a phrase to describe a person.
For example, here are some correct uses of *who*.
* The driver *who* drove persistently in the left lane was a menace on the road.
* Bob Fields, *who* designs cardboard houses, lives in Rockport, Maine.
* The carousel operator *who* went to sleep at the controls gave the children a long ride.
Is it *incorrect* to use the pronoun *who* to begin a phrase that describes an animal, an event, or an idea.
The collie who lives in the corner house sat in the shade of the oak tree.
The Chevrolet truck who was going 80 mph was stopped by the highway patrol.
The parade who turned the corner onto Sixth Street was drenched by a sudden shower.

Employ Learning Strategies

Notice that *who* should not be used:

The collie who lives in the corner house sat in the shade of the oak tree.

The Chevrolet truck who was going 80 mph was stopped by the highway patrol.

The parade who turned the corner onto Sixth Street was drenched by a sudden shower.

Practice

Directions: Click on the boxes beside the sentences in which the word *who* could fill the blank.
☐ a. The meteorologist____had been up 26 hours stumbled over his words in the emergency broadcast.
☐ b. Make sure that you put the cat____is on a special diet in the front cage.
☐ c. Chuckles the Clown,____entertained children on TV for years, has retired to Pago Pago.
☐ d. Mother Theresa was a person____we all respect.
☐ e. The town of Rolla____is in the rolling hills of Missouri is near Fort Leonard Wood.

Evaluate Feedback

☑ a. The meteorologist____had been up 26 hours stumbled over his words in the emergency broadcast.
☐ b. Make sure that you put the cat____is on a special diet in the front cage.
☑ c. Chuckles the Clown,____entertained children on TV for years, has retired to Pago Pago.
☑ d. Mother Theresa was a person____we all respect.
☐ e. The town of Rolla____is in the rolling hills of Missouri is near Fort Leonard Wood.

Figure 11.1 *(continued)*

Review Relevant Prior Knowledge

To understand the correct use of *which* and *that*, you must be able to determine whether a phrase or clause that modifies that noun is restrictive or nonrestrictive.

A *nonrestrictive* phrase or clause is a phrase or clause that
- Modifies a noun.
- Does not limit (i.e., restrict) the meaning of the noun.
- Can be removed from the sentence without changing the essential meaning.
- Is often separated from the remainder of the sentence by commas.

Here are some examples of *nonrestrictive* phrases and clauses:
- The paper, *which was due yesterday*, was to be 10–12 pages long.
- The agent, *who lives in Anaheim*, arranged contracts for two authors.
- The car, *which had flame decals on the sides*, was stuck in the carwash.

Notice how the meaning of the sentences would not be substantially changed if the nonrestrictive phrases were omitted.

Restrictive phrases and clauses have the following characteristics:
- Restrict or limit the meaning of the noun they modify.
- Cannot be removed without substantially changing the meaning of the sentence.

Here are some examples of *restrictive* phrases and clauses.
- All students *who fail to turn in the final project* will receive Fs.
- The classes *that did not "make"* were canceled.
- Cats *that have not been immunized* are at risk of catching distemper

Notice how the meaning of the sentences would not be substantially changes if the restrictive phrases were omitted.

Process Information—Focus Attention

The Use of *Which*

Use the relative pronoun which to begin phrases/clauses that
- Describe animals, ideas, or events (any noun other then a person).
- Are nonrestrictive.

For example, these are some some correct uses of *which*:
- The paper, *which was due yesterday*, was to be 10–12 pages long.
- The car, *which had flame decals on the sides*, was stuck in the carwash,
- The computer, *which was purchased with department funds*, required additional memory to run the software.

The Use of *That*

Use the relative pronoun that to begin phrases/clauses that
- Describe animals, ideas. or events (any noun other then a person).
- Are restrictive.

For example, these are some correct uses of *that*:
- The classes *that did not "make"* were canceled.
- Cats *that have not been immunized* are at risk of catching distemper.
- The TV program *that began at 4 o'clock* was not finished until 9 o'clock.

Employ Learning Strategies

Comparison of *which* and *that*
- Organizations *that* follow the plan can expect to experience improved employee relations.
- Organizations, *which* often are built from a "Mom and Pop business," can apply for information regarding the new tax laws.
- This instrument, *which* is called a 3-bar roller, can be used to straighten twisted pipeline.
- The instrument, *that* the burglar used to pry open the window was left in the bathroom.

Practice

Directions: Type in the correct pronoun, *which* and *that*.
1. The bear,____entered the room through the window, knocked the canisters off the kitchen shelves.
2. The book____was listed as a required text was not available in the bookstore.
3. The computer,____Dad purchased for the family, was surrounded by 15 children from the neighborhood.
4. The law,____had been long forgotten by many, prohibited teachers from dating.
5. I have been writing books____are modern versions of Greek tragedies.

Figure 11.1 *(continued)*

Feedback

1. The bear, *which* entered the room through the window, knocked the canisters off the kitchen shelves.
2. The book *that* was listed as a required text was not available in the bookstore.
3. The computer, *which* Dad purchased for the family, was surrounded by 15 children from the neighborhood.
4. The law, *which* had been long forgotten by many, prohibited teachers from dating.
5. I have been writing books *that* are modern versions of Greek tragedies.

CONCLUSION

Summarize and Review

In review, the following are the uses of *who*, *which*, and *that*:
- Use *who* in the phrases/clauses that describe people.
- Use *that* in phrases/clauses that are restrictive (i.e., the meaning of the sentence would be substantially changed without phrase or clause).
- Use *which* in phrases/clauses that are nonrestrictive (i.e., the meaning of the sentence would not be substantially changed without the phrase or clause).

Transfer Knowledge

The punctuation has been intentionally omitted from these sentences. Fill each sentence with *who*, *that*, or *which*. Then punctuate the sentence correctly.
1. The cat____broke its leg is unable to move from the bed.
2. The minister____wore a robe entered the sanctuary from the side door.
3. The soda____was in a red can was tucked into the rear of the refrigerator.
4. The photograph____was printed on glossy paper created a glare when it was filmed.
5, Sally____was the first first on the scene of the accident administered first aid.
6. The disk____was stuck in the disk drive was warped from the heat.

Feedback

1. The cat *that* broke its leg is unable to move from the bed.
2. The minister *who* wore a robe entered the sanctuary from the side door.
3. The soda *which* was in a red can was tucked into the rear of the refrigerator.
4. The photograph *that* was printed on glossy paper created a glare when it was filmed.
5, Sally, *who* was the first first on the scene of the accident administered first aid.
6. The disk *that* was stuck in the disk drive was warped from the heat.

Remotivate and Close

An Assignment:
Look for examples of the use of who, which, and that in newspapers, magazines, and textbooks. Can you find instances in which they are used incorrectly?

Practice using these relative pronouns correctly in your own writing. Soon you will find that using them correctly will require little thought and seem automatic to you.

Figure 11.1 *(continued)*

Introduction	Deploy attention. Establish instructional purpose. Arouse interest and motivation. Preview lesson.	• Identify curiosity-evoking situation/problem. • Understand/apply principle, relationship between concepts. • Identify curiosity-evoking situation. • Inquiry equals directions; expository equals outline.
Body	Recall prior knowledge. Process information. Focus attention. Employ learning strategies Practice. Evaluate feedback.	• Review component concepts. • Present/induct relationship; state in principle form; demonstrate application. • Note the direction and size in change of one variable when another variable(s) changes. • Make a mnemonic rule statement, diagram of relationship. • Predict, explain, control changes in concept(s) based on change of another; recognize situations where rule applies; determine whether rule correctly applied. • Obtain information on whether rule applicable, outcome of application.
Conclusion	Summarize and review Transfer knowledge. Remotivate and close.	• Note change in symbol system; restate principle. • Point out how principle will be incorporated into problem solving; identify life situations. • Identify relevance to daily lives or current problems.
Assessment	Assess performance. Feedback and remediation.	• Recognize whether principle applicable; apply principle to predict, explain, control. • Identify misconceptions, over- or undergeneralization.

Figure 11.2 Key Events for Principle Learning

SUMMARY

Figure 11.2 summarizes key points from the chapter.

EXTENDED EXAMPLE

In the Learning Resources Web site you will find this chapter's contribution to our photography course. The example for this chapter is strategy design for a multimedia lesson on a principle, specifically, the relationships among depth of field, shutter speed, and aperture opening.

READINGS AND REFERENCES

Anderson, J. R. (1985). *Cognitive psychology* (2nd ed.). New York: W. H. Freeman.

Gagné, R. M. (1985). *The conditions of learning* (4th ed.). New York: Holt, Rinehart & Winston.

Gilbert, T. (1978). *Human competence: Engineering worthy performance.* New York: McGraw-Hill.

Joyce, B., & Weil, M. (1986a). Teaching inductively: Collecting, organizing, and manipulating data. In B. Joyce and M. Weil (Eds.), *Models of teaching* (3rd ed.) (pp. 40–53). Upper Saddle River, NJ: Prentice-Hall.

Joyce, B., & Weil, M. (1986b). Inquiry training. In B. Joyce and M. Weil (Eds.), *Models of teaching* (3rd ed.) (pp. 55–69). Upper Saddle River, NJ: Prentice-Hall.

Reigeluth, C. M. (1987). *Instructional theories in action.* Hillsdale, NJ: Erlbaum.

Scandura, J. M. (1983). Instructional strategies based on the structural learning theory. In C. M. Reigeluth (Ed.), *Instructional design theories and models* (pp. 213–246). Hillsdale, NJ: Erlbaum.

Schmid, R. F., & Gerlach, V. S. (1990). Instructional design rules for algorithmic subject matter. *Performance Improvement Quarterly, 3*(2), 2–15.

Suchman, J. R. (1961). Inquiry training: Building skills for autonomous discovery. Merrill-Palmer Quarterly, 7, 147169.

Taba, H. (1967). *Teacher's handbook for elementary social studies.* Reading, MA: Addison-Wesley.

Tennyson, R. D., & Tennyson, C. L. (1975). Rule acquisition design strategy variables: Degree of instance divergence, sequence, and instance analysis. *Journal of Educational Psychology, 67*(6), 852–859.

STRATEGIES FOR PROBLEM-SOLVING INSTRUCTION

CHAPTER OBJECTIVE

At the conclusion of this chapter, you should be able to do the following:

- Given a problem-solving objective, design strategy plans for that objective.

A REVIEW OF PROBLEM-SOLVING LEARNING

The term *expert* is used to describe someone who can apply knowledge to solve problems in a particular field of endeavor. In contrast to some educators' use of the term, we define *problem solving* as a specialized skill within a domain of knowledge rather than a generalized skill that applies across a variety of content areas. **Problem solving** is the ability to combine previously learned principles, procedures, declarative knowledge, and cognitive strategies in a unique way within a domain of content to solve previously unencountered problems. This activity yields new learning as learners are more able to respond to problems of a similar class in the future. This type of problem solving is often described as "domain-specific" or "semantically rich" problem solving because it emphasizes learning to utilize principles in a specific content area. The sort of problem solving that this chapter addresses encompasses a great deal of what is meant by the term *expertise*.

For some time, educational psychologists have attempted to describe problem solving and identify aspects that might be transferable to various domains of endeavor (Dewey, 1933; Newell & Simon, 1972; 1945). A number of curricula (e.g., the Productive Thinking Program, Covington, Crutchfield, Davies, & Olton, 1974; and the *Cognitive Research Trust*, or "CoRT," de Bono, 1973) have been developed to teach generic problem-solving skills. (We will describe some of these in our discussion of cognitive strategies in Chapter 13.) Cognitive strategies are the outcome in Gagné's category system, which is similar to generic problem solving. However, it has become more and more clear that the key ingredient to skill in problem solving in any domain is knowledge within that domain, particularly knowledge of relational and procedural rules and how these principles relate to each other. Attention is thus concentrated on how experts in particular fields are able to solve problems and on identifying appropriate instructional strategies for domain-specific problem solving, rather than trying to identify and teach generic problem-solving skills.

Problem solving differs from principle learning because problem solving requires the selection and combination of multiple principles in order to solve a problem, rather than a single principle. Problem solving as we describe it is often not what is termed *mathematical* problem solving. Mathematical problem solving can be application of single principles or procedures, rather than selection and application of multiple principles. For a learning goal to be termed *problem solving* according to our criteria, it must involve the almost simultaneous consideration of principles and procedures within a domain, the careful selection of the principles that are applicable, and the sequencing of the application of the principles so a problem is solved.

This category of learning is congruent with what is called *heuristic* problem solving, or problem solving for which no clear procedural rule exists. Application of a procedural rule is sometimes termed *algorithmic* problem solving, but we have chosen to include algorithmic problem solving in the procedure learning category because its instruction is quite different from heuristic problem solving. One thing that may make the distinction between procedural rule learning and problem solving difficult is the following: A learning task may be taught first as a problem-solving objective, and then later learners may form their own solution algorithm or they may be taught one so that they may employ a procedure to accomplish work rather than use the more taxing problem-solving process. How the learning is initially approached (with or without algorithm) helps us decide what type of learning it is and, therefore, what the instructional strategy should be.

Solving a problem as a result of random activity or trial and error is possible, and, under certain circumstances, it is a desirable activity. However, problem solving that results from uninformed trial and error does not generally produce the kind of learning that can be applied in the future. Thus, this kind of problem solving is not useful in learning about effective ways to solve problems either in a subject domain or in a general sense.

Examples of Problem Solving

Goals that require the application of multiple principles and that are generally taught as problem-solving outcomes include learning to do the following tasks:

- Construct geometry proofs (selection and application of appropriate laws and theorems in the correct sequence).
- Read music.
- Teach school.
- Design instruction.
- Write computer programs.
- Design a house or, more simply, select and position the windows in a house.
- Plan and conduct an experiment.
- Make a medical diagnosis.
- Troubleshoot malfunctioning equipment when no algorithm is provided.
- Practice law.
- Respond to an emergency call as a police officer.

Problem-solving tasks can be complex or simple. Problem solving is simpler when fewer principles must be considered (e.g., designing the windows for a house versus designing a house). Another feature that relates to complexity in problem solving is the clarity of the problem: Some problems are much "fuzzier" than others. To understand what makes a problem unclear, we need to define some common terms related to problem solving.

According to Duncker (1945), a *problem* is present when one has a goal but does not know immediately how this goal can be reached. The goal cannot be reached without a "search process" (Gilhooly & Green, 1989). To solve problems, learners must search their long-term memory for relevant principles, knowledge, and strategies that might apply to this problem. In so doing, they begin to clarify the "problem space." The problem space (Anderson, 1985) includes the goal state (i.e., the desired end state of the situation; what conditions would be like if the problem were solved), the given state (the current situation, including its restrictions and obstacles), and the intermediate states that must be overcome to move from the given state to the goal state. The clearer the given state and the goal state, the less "fuzzy" the problem. A clear given (or initial) state has all the relevant information explicitly provided, requiring that less information be inferred or researched. A clear goal precisely states the criteria for determining if the problem has been solved.

Problem situations for which given and goal states (as well as the principles to transform a situation from its initial state to goal state) are clear are often termed **well-defined (or well-structured) problems.** Problems for which much of the given and goal states (and the transforming principles) are unknown, vague, or extremely situation-dependent are termed **ill-defined (or ill-strucured) problems.** Well-defined problems have a single solution or a finite, definable range of solutions. Ill-defined problems often have multiple, correct solutions with the appropriateness of the solution dependent upon the rationale for solution. Well-defined and ill-defined problems do not appear to be separate, distinct categories of problems, but rather problems appear to fall somewhere on a continuum between these two poles. Of the problems listed as examples of problem solving earlier in this chapter, developing geometry proofs, troubleshooting malfunctioning equipment, and reading music are closer to the well-defined pole. The other examples—writing computer programs, designing a house, planning an experiment, making a medical diagnosis, practicing law, and responding to an emergency call—are more ill-defined. Jonassen (2000) provides more examples along the continuum of well- and ill-structured problems.

The example lesson at the end of this chapter, which requires problem solving in order to develop a simple application in Java, can be viewed as instruction for well-defined problems—that is, problems that have a definite correct range of answers. However, if we placed the Java programming in the everyday context of a computer application developer's work, we might find that correct solutions to the problems vary widely, depending on the context or perspective from which the programmer views the problems. If the programmer views the programming problem from a code-efficiency standpoint, the principles that will be applied will differ considerably from the principles that might be used by a programmer who is preparing a computer-based learning environment and places a high priority on clarity of the user interface. Even from these varying contexts, certain principles must be applied, as well as the general principles that allow the solution of well-defined problems in programming. However, once these additional contexts are added, the adequacy of the solution, to some degree, depends on the rationale of the programmer.

COGNITIVE REQUIREMENTS OF PROBLEM-SOLVING LEARNING

To solve problems in a domain, learners must possess and apply three kinds of knowledge: principles, declarative knowledge, and cognitive strategies (R. Gagné, 1980, 1985; de Jong & Ferguson-Hessler, 1986). The ability to apply principles seems to be the most critical component to problem solving; however, it is clear that without declarative knowledge and cognitive strategies, the learner may not be able to adequately identify or search the problem space or be able to identify the class of problem at hand (Jonassen 2000, 2003). These types of knowledge are used in varying degrees to support four components of cognitive processing in problem solving: Knowledge representation, solution planning, solution implementation, and solution evaluation.

Problem Representation

In the first stage of problem-solving processing, the learner develops a representation of the problem by defining and decomposing the problem into subproblems. For well-defined problems, definition involves identifying the appropriate problem schema. **Problem schemata** are superordinate productions in the if-then form, with the *if* representing the salient conditions for a particular class of problems (along with all the related declarative knowledge and principles related to this condition) and the *then* representing the cognitive strategies and principles to support the solution of the problem. Identifying the problem schema for a well-defined problem can be relatively straightforward: The problem may have distinctive features that make it clear that the principles and strategies from a particular domain must be selectively applied. In well-defined problem solving, the problem itself is unambiguous. A skilled problem solver recognizes that the current situation is analogous to a previous problem situation, "Oh, this is one of those!" The learner "maps" the features of the current problem on to the critical features of the problem schema that is stored in long-term memory. The more this mapping is related by "deep structure" (i.e., with meaningful and conceptual links) rather than by similarities on "surface features" (e.g., similarities in actual wording, or similarities in contexts in which learning occurred), the more the knowledge will support facile problem solving.

Occasionally, the learner may recognize a problem as being analogous to a similar but simpler situation or problem in a very different context for which a solution is apparent and then applies that same solution to the problem at hand. For example, students could use an analogy strategy to solve Duncker's (1945) problem:

> Suppose you are a doctor faced with a patient who has a malignant tumor in his stomach. It is impossible to operate on the patient, but unless the tumor is destroyed, the patient will die. There is a kind of ray that can be used to destroy the tumor. If the rays reach the tumor all at once at a sufficiently high intensity, the tumor will be destroyed. Unfortunately, at this intensity the healthy tissue that the rays pass through on the way to the tumor will also be destroyed. At lower intensities the rays are harmless to healthy tissue, but they will not affect the tumor either. What type of procedure might be used to destroy the tumor with the ray, and at the same time avoid destroying the healthy tissue? (pp. 307–308)

In Gick and Holyoak's (1980) study, students were given a hint in the form of an analogy: An army is attempting to take over a fortress that is surrounded by mined roads. The mines detonate only when large forces travel on them. The solution is dividing the forces and having them all converge upon the fortress from different directions. Ninety-two percent of the students who were given this analogy as a hint were able to solve the tumor problem. Only ten percent of the students who were not given the analogy hint were able to solve the problem.

Decomposition of the problem into subproblems may be similarly straightforward for well-defined problems because such problems often have analogous subproblems. For example, photography problems generally have subproblems dealing with exposure, focus, and motion/depth-of-field of the subject.

Definition of an ill-defined problem may require skilled strategy to determine *what* the problem actually *is*. Ill-defined problems may be difficult to identify because of the problem of (1) having multiple perspectives, such as the photography example we alluded to earlier, with each of the perspectives representing the problem in a different way; (2) requiring multiple domains in order to articulate the problem, such as some instructional design problems; or (3) being pre-

sented as a problem, when no actual problem exists. To clarify an ill-structured problem, learners must identify the alternative perspectives of individuals affected by and affecting the solution. Learners also clarify what is known, what can be found out, and what must remain unknown. They must also identify factors, other than lack of knowledge, that constrain possible solutions.

Learners may activate problem schemata to solve ill-defined problems, as well as well-defined ones; however, the "fit" between the ill-defined problem and existing problem schemata may be imperfect. The learner may have to construct a new problem schema that combines knowledge from existing schemata or keep several viable problem schemata active through trial solutions to see which problem schema is most productive. Decomposing an ill-defined problem into subproblems may be quite cognitively demanding because different perspectives or problem schema may suggest different subproblems.

Solution Planning

Solution planning requires searching, selecting, combining, and sequencing relevant knowledge. Solution planning for well-defined problems is activated when an appropriate problem schema is engaged. These problem schemata often include causal models that relate individual principles together. These models may be multitiered, with some overarching principles subsuming less generalized principles. These causal models are particularly apparent in learners' representations of the mechanisms of both artificial and real systems. Johnson-Laird (1983) conjectured that knowledge is stored in a "mental model" of the information related to a domain. This mental model interweaves declarative knowledge propositions and principle-based productions. The mental model is subject to restructuring with experience, additional learning, and the type of problem presented. Problem schemata or mental models suggest a range of principles that, when applied in some combination and sequence, will solve the current problem. However, the learner must select those principles that address the current problem and the order in which they must be applied. This selection of principles and their ordering may be unique to each problem in a class of problems. If the learner has sufficient knowledge to decompose the problem into subproblems, the subproblems will suggest the principles to be applied and their order. Learners who have not achieved this level of expertise, without instructional scaffolding, may depend on some generic and weak strategies to guide their plan for solution, such as means-ends, difference reduction, and working backwards.

A learner employing the means-ends strategy mentally jumps back and forth between the desired end and the current state, identifying intermediate states and the principles to convert each state to the next intermediate state. We prepare dinner using this strategy. Our goal is to have a hot meal. The difference between the initial state and the final state is hot, prepared food. How do we get hot, prepared food? Well, we must go the store and buy it. How do we get to the store? We travel in a car. What do we have to do to use the car? Fill it with gas. How do we fill it with gas? Go to the gas station. And so on.

The difference-reduction strategy attempts to select principles to enact upon the current state to get it to look more and more like the desired state. You may have seen this strategy used by a sculptor who carves away clay and adds material to make the image resemble the desired figure. The process is repeated many times. This may not be the most efficient problem-solving strategy for this task, but it is a very common and effective one. A learner employing the working-backwards strategy starts with the desired end state and then selects and applies the principles that will back up to the intermediate state just before the desired state. Then the learner moves to the next-to-next-to-last step, and so on until the intermediate state is reached. You've probably employed this strategy in solving mazes.

Specific cognitive strategies developed for a particular domain tend to be more potent and efficient than generic strategies. One example of a specific strategy is Schoenfeld's (1979) problem-solving heuristics for solving problems in mathematics: (1) Draw a diagram; (2) if there is an integer parameter, look for an inductive argument; (3) consider arguing by contradiction or contra-positive; (4) consider a similar problem with fewer variables; and (5) try to establish subgoals (cited in Mayer, 1987, p. 38).

The search for solutions for ill-structured problems is less prescribed by a problem schema or mental model because no single representation adequately describes the problem nor proposes the causal model for solution. Jonassen (1997) suggested that during this phase of ill-defined problem solving that learners (1) "generate possible problem solutions, (2) assess the viability of alternative solutions by constructing arguments and articulating personal beliefs, and (3) monitor the problem space and solution option" (p. 81). As ill-defined problem solving is often context-bound with multiple perspectives representing alternative solutions, the problem solver must examine her own perspective and personal benefits from various solutions, as well as her beliefs about the nature of "truth" and what provides evidence for truth. Such processes require examination of both alternative problems and alternative solutions for these ill-structured problems. The strategy that Jonassen recommends for resolving which problems and which solutions are viable is through the development of a defensible, cogent argument.

Solution Implementation

To apply multiple principles, learners must know those principles. They must be able to identify situations in which the principles can appropriately be applied; they must be able to apply the principles; and they must be able to confirm that the principles have been correctly/appropriately applied. Some instructional strategies assume that learners can learn/discover the principles while they are learning to problem solve. For example, many instructional strategies use simulations or other types of problem-based learning environments for learners to practice problem solving in a domain without giving learners prior experience with the principles that must be considered and sequentially applied to solve the problem presented in the simulation. It is possible to learn principles in the same lesson as problem solving. However, such an approach has a high cognitive demand because it requires that learners acquire domain-specific principles to the application level at the same time that they learn to identify problems that require applications of multiple principles. The advantage to such an approach is that it provides an immediate relevancy for why such principles must be learned. To limit the cognitive load of instructional strategies that engage learners with new problem solving and principle learning simultaneously, the designer may wish to carefully limit problems so that learners have few principles to consider.

In one lesson, a learner might first learn to apply the principles singly and then to select and apply the principles in concert. In many cases, it may be preferable that a learner learn to apply these principles automatically prior to trying to apply them in a problem-solving situation. The whole issue of how to deal with prerequisite learning in problem-based learning environments has been discussed at length by Dick (1992) and Perkins (1992) in the context of constructivism.

As you have read in Chapters 10 and 11, principles and procedures are theorized to be stored in memory as productions. These productions have an if-then structure. For example, in the photography content in our extended example, there are principles relating to (1) how to adjust exposure with shutter speed and aperture, (2) how to select film types and speeds in particular conditions, (3) how to obtain particular effects through composition, and (4) how to adjust field of view and size of image through lenses. To solve photography problems, these principles must be considered almost simultaneously because they are so interrelated. Those principles that are pertinent to the particular problem conditions must be selected from among all the interrelated principles. Then these principles must be applied in the correct order. Once the photograph is produced, it must be evaluated to see if it solves the identified "problem."

Solution Evaluation

Cognitive processing is not complete until the learner has confirmed that her solution correctly or appropriately solves the problem. To get to this solution may require multiple iterations between solution implementation and solution evaluation, with the learner trying out multiple solutions until one works. Confirmation for well-defined problems may be quite simple because the system itself provides feedback that the problem is solved. For example, when troubleshooting a malfunctioning printer, if the printer begins working correctly, then the learner has a good indication that the problem is solved. Learning to determine whether a solution is appropriate for an ill-defined problem may be more difficult. Jonassen (1997) suggested some questions to guide the learners' evaluation of the solution to an ill-defined problem, such as "Does it produce an acceptable solution to the involved parties?" and "Is it elegant and parsimonious?" (p. 82).

PROBLEM-SOLVING TASK ANALYSIS

What *is* the generic task analysis for problem solving? Now that you know a bit more about problem solving, you can tackle our task analysis from Chapter 5, which now has more precise terminology and additional steps. Although a single approach is not clearly identified in the research or theoretical literature, it seems that in problem-solving conditions, the following stages often occur. They may not occur in the same sequence as described as follows and may vary depending on how well-defined the problem is.

1. Clarify the given state (conditions), including any obstacles or constraints.
2. Clarify the goal state, including criteria for knowing when the goal is reached.
3. Search for relevant prior knowledge and declarative, principle, or cognitive strategies that will aid in solution.
4. Determine if conditions and goal state imply a known class of problems.
5. Decompose the problem into subproblems with subgoals.
6. Determine a sequence for attacking subproblems.
7. Consider possible solution paths to each subproblem using related prior knowledge.
8. Select a solution path and apply production knowledge (principles) in the appropriate order.
9. Evaluate to determine if the goal is achieved. If not, revise by returning to step 1 above.

In a specific content area, this schema may be employed with specific content knowledge filling in the "slots." We do not suggest that instruction teach this strategy in a content-free context. These nine steps can be used in analyzing specific problem-solving tasks within content domains, helping the designer to find and structure the primary subtasks.

THE DIFFERENCES BETWEEN EXPERT AND NOVICE PROBLEM SOLVERS

Psychologists have spent much of the past thirty years trying to describe the processes of expert and novice problem solvers. Psychologists have studied problems in the domains of chess (Chase & Simon, 1973; de Groot, 1965), physics (Chi, Glaser, & Rees, 1982; Larkin, 1989), mathematics (Schoenfeld & Herrmann, 1982), political science (Voss, Greene, Post, & Penner, 1983), and medical diagnosis (Norman, 1985) to name but a few. These studies and others (de Jong & Ferguson-Hessler, 1986; Frederiksen, 1984; Larkin, 1980; Mayer, 1983; Simon, 1980; Simon & Chase, 1973) have marked the following differences between novice and expert problem solvers, indicating that experts have the following:

1. A "perception-like" recognition of problem types (i.e., pattern recognition).
2. More domain-specific knowledge.
3. Better organized and integrated domain-specific knowledge.
4. The ability to represent problems and their similarities to other problems by abstract, "deep structure" (semantically), rather than by surface features (e.g., similarities in unimportant physical or spatial properties).
5. Compiled knowledge, so application of principles is more automatic.
6. Related principles chunked together in memory.
7. The ability to recognize when a problem is solved and solved appropriately.
8. A tendency to use a working-forward strategy rather than a working-backwards strategy.
9. The ability to develop solution hypotheses quickly but delay acting upon them.
10. More schema-driven than search-driven solution strategies.

Although we have quite a refined description of the differences between novices and experts, we have few research-based principles regarding how to facilitate the transformation from novice to expert. In the remainder of the chapter, we will describe some principles of instruction for problem solving. Some have been tested with research; others seem logical given what we know about the cognitive processes of problem solving. Hopefully, future research will provide empirical validation of our recommendations.

INSTRUCTIONAL EVENTS FOR A PROBLEM-SOLVING LESSON

Often when novice instructional designers begin to design the instructional strategies for a problem-solving objective, they imagine that there is really nothing to "teach," as all of the principles may have been learned prior to the problem-solving lesson. They suggest that the only thing remaining is for learners to practice combining the principles. Indeed, practice is a critical part of a problem-solving lesson; however, there are additional instructional events that can support the acquisition of problem-solving skill. The design of problem-solving instruction will vary depending on how well defined the problem is (Jonassen, 1997, 2004).

Remember that the prerequisites (principles and their associated concepts, declarative knowledge, and cognitive strategies) for problem solving can be taught in lessons prior to problem-solving lessons. Or instruction on principles, concepts, declarative knowledge, and strategies can be taught in sets interspersed with instruction on how to combine this knowledge for problem-solving. The question of sequencing prerequisite learning is perhaps the most critical unknown at issue today in the area of fostering problem-solving learning. Van Merriënboer, Kirschner, and Kester (2003) do an excellent job of comparing whole-task and part-task approaches in their discussion of sequencing alternatives from the perspective of cognitive load (see especially pp. 6–7), and a close reading of this discussion along with other discussions of the issue such as Jonassen (2000) will make it clear that despite occasional claims to the contrary that you might run across, the best approach to this question is simply not known. Consequently, we will discuss illustrate both approaches and emphasize that in practice, you have options as you *design* learning environments for problem solving.

INTRODUCING PROBLEM-SOLVING LESSONS

Deploy Attention

Presenting an interesting and challenging problem that the learners will learn to solve can gain attention and begin to identify the purpose of the instruction. If novel stimuli, such as graphics or video, are used to present the problem, learners are likely to be more interested.

Establish Instructional Purpose

The instructor or learning materials may describe the nature of problems that the students will learn to solve. If a challenging problem has been presented to promote motivation and attention, the instructor may explain how this problem is representative of the class of problems to be learned. If the strategy being employed is inductive, or if the instructor feels that overtly stating this information at this point may reduce the learners' interest in the problem, this event may be accomplished in a generative fashion and the learners can be asked to demonstrate their induction of the characteristics of this class of problems during the conclusion.

Promote Interest and Motivation

Suggesting how problem solving in this domain may assist learners in everyday problems can promote interest. Problem solving, if completed successfully, can be motivating in itself. The instruction should be constructed to provide successful practice as quickly as possible. If a relatively short simulation is to be used within the instruction, learners might view a portion of the simulation.

Preview Lesson

If a simple-to-complex approach will be employed, the instruction should inform the learners that they will be going through a succession of problems with increasing complexity. The instruction may preview the primary strategies that will be employed and the learners' responsibilities within the strategies. A lesson does not have to be expository or didactic for there to be a need for some form of preview or orientation to the learning experience.

Body

The events described within this section will be cycled through several times in a problem-solving lesson.

Reviewing Relevant Prior Knowledge

The conception of prior knowledge that the designer should hold for problem solving is more critical and complex than for other types of learning, especially when working with ill-structured problems. A more comprehensive, context-related "inventory" of domain knowledge may be needed, as suggested by Jonassen (1997). Such inventories, otherwise known as task analyses, can be based on activity theory (Leont'ev, 1978) and will include the goals behind the actions of problem solvers.

If declarative knowledge, concepts, principles, or strategies appropriate to the task have been previously learned and applied, then the knowledge can be overtly reviewed by doing the following:

- Review declarative knowledge related to the area: This should cause learners to bring to working memory the information needed to understand the nature of the problem.

- Review general problem-solving strategies, directly suggesting an appropriate structure for attacking the problem and suggesting any modifications that are particularly appropriate to this domain.

- Review the type and source of principles (and their associated concepts) related to this problem, ensuring that learners have access to principles and examples of their application.

If the instruction on this knowledge was recent and learners evidenced a high level of skill with it, the recall of this knowledge could be interspersed in places that are immediately appropriate. This knowledge could be reviewed less directly, with the instructor modeling problem solving or using guiding questions as learners practice solving problems.

If learners have acquired the prerequisite knowledge over a period of time or if it is likely that they have knowledge structured in a manner that will not facilitate problem solving, they could be encouraged to restructure their knowledge so that it is appropriate to solve the new class of problems. The extended example illustrates a way to do this by using a spatial strategy, a networking technique, to show the relationships of concepts or principles, with the instruction imposing a new structure on previously learned concepts or principles. Mayer (1989) called such visuals "conceptual models." The learners would then fill in the network with additional concepts, knowledge, and principles. Diagrams or visuals could be added to this spatial representation to make it more concrete. This reorganization of knowledge should be in a form that emphasizes the underlying generalities of the concepts, principles, and their relationships rather than their surface similarities (such as the use of similar terms in two principles). This rearrangement may show hierarchical relationships among concepts and/or principles, or it may be organized functionally, as illustrated in the extended example.

If learners have solved problems that have similarities to the current class of problems, then this similarity should be explicitly mentioned and the differences between these classes of problems should be clearly identified.

Strategies that intersperse acquisition of principles and concepts with problem solving should review the knowledge relevant to them at the point when the instruction occurs.

Processing Information

The instruction, whether computer-based or human, must determine whether a more supplantive or a more generative approach should be used to support the events of processing information, focusing attention, and employing learning strategies. If the learners have well-organized and extensive content knowledge, good cognitive strategies, high aptitude, high motivation, and a sufficient amount of time, then a more generative, low-scaffolding strategy would be appropriate. If learners' prior knowledge is limited and not organized well, cognitive strategies are limited, aptitude is not high, motivation is low, time is short, and a high level of skill is required by all learners, then a more supplantive, high-scaffolding strategy would be appropriate.

The most generative strategy that we recommend is presenting sets of increasingly complex problems for the learners to solve, with the guiding questions of the instruction used to evoke the processing, attention focusing, and strategies described in these events. A slightly more supplantive approach would be to present a problem and have the instructor (whether computer or human) model the solution to the problem by thinking aloud, as in initial stages of a cognitive apprenticeship. This approach is somewhat analogous to Jonassen's (1997) recommendation that well-defined problems be taught with "worked examples." The model should utilize the processing, attention focusing, and strategy techniques that seem appropriate. Using this level of support, the students would next be provided with a problem in which they would do some of the processing and the instructor would also provide some. Finally, the learners would solve this type of problem with only the support of guiding questions. This sequence would be repeated with increasingly complex problems and decreasing external support. The efficacy of such an approach, involving worked examples in the early phases of problem solving learning and phasing out support in latter phases is supported by research conducted from a Cognitive Load Theory perspective reported by Kalyuga, Ayres, Chandler, and Sweller (2003) and Renkl & Atkinson (2003). Kalyuga et al. conclude: ". . . when fully guided instructional material is presented to more experienced learners, a part of all of the provided instructional guidance might be redundant. In contrast, that same material may be essential for less experienced learners" (p. 29).

The most supplantive strategy that we recommend is for the instructor to present an example problem, modeling the solution with a full explanation of each step of the solution to the problem. Practice might be broken into smaller chunks, such as merely clarifying and verbalizing the given state of the problem. After this deliberate and careful presentation and explanation of a solution (and practice with individual steps along the way), the learners would be provided practice with complete problems and guided through a solution with the instructor's explicit instructions or guiding questions.

Regardless of which approach is taken, the following main aspects of presentation of information and processing must occur.

1. *Presentation of the problem.* Problem presentation should employ a simplified version first. A simple-to-complex sequence for problem-solving learning seems reasonable and has support from Cognitive Load Theory-based research (e.g. Van Merriënboer, Kirschner, and Kester, 2003).* The problem may be simplified in a number of ways: limiting the number of principles that must be accessed, providing external representations of these principles as cues, providing the solutions to parts of the problem, limiting the extraneous information presented in the problem, or clarifying the given state or goal state. The simplified problem should be prototypical of problems of its class, with clear delineation of attributes that make the situation typical, and it should contain a minimum of distracting information. Problems may be presented in case studies, simulations, or in written or graphic formats. Use of causal modeling techniques (Jonassen et al., 1996) can be helpful in selecting appropriate cases and other problem representation devices.

2. *Problem space.* Learners must learn to recognize the problem space (although we would not use the term *problem space* with students because it would confuse more than clarify for them). The instructor should encourage the learners (perhaps by modeling) to do the following:

- Review the task instructions for relevant information by verbalizing and elaborating on the characteristics of the goal state. This is done by inspecting the solved problem and systematically scanning the task instructions for situational cues and other relevant information regarding the given state.
- Construct a network of relationships of the variables in the given state with those in the goal state, either mentally or with a diagram.
- Analyze the relationship of the given and the goal states for a pattern that is recognizable as identifying a given set of problems.
- Identify what is not known, what learners can make inferences about, and what topics about which learners must seek more information. Decide if sufficient information is provided to solve the problem, what inferences must be drawn, what assumptions must be made.

- Decompose the problem into intermediate states (subgoals) between the given state and the goal state. This usually involves recognizing where particular principles can operate on the givens to transform them to the point where another principle can be employed.

3. *Appropriate principles.* Learners must also receive direct instruction or guidance on how to select appropriate principles to move from each intermediate state to the next state.

Focusing Attention

The instruction can use guiding questions or direct statements to focus learners' attention on key aspects of the problem state or the given state, relevant principles, or problem-solving strategies. Learners may also need assistance in focusing their attention during the pattern-recognition task of identifying the critical features of the given state and the goal state.

Employing Learning Strategies

Both general and specific strategies may be suggested. If learners are successful and their strategies are not faulty or inefficient, they should be encouraged to continue to use them. If their strategies are ineffective (or may prove to be with more complex problems) or inefficient, then the instructor may promote the acquisition of new strategies. Learning strategies may be taught through direct instruction, modeling, or guiding questions. The initial strategies taught might not be the strategies that experts would use, as their knowledge is consolidated and organized differently from novices. However, the strategies that are taught should be effective given the state of their representations of knowledge and principles. The instruction may supply learning strategy assistance by providing any of the following:

1. Alternate ways of representing the problem—graphic, analogy, etc.
2. Ways of limiting the number of alternative approaches.
3. Hints at the general form of the solution or subsolutions.
4. Search strategies for retrieving relevant information.
5. Monitoring techniques for appraising the appropriateness of the solution.
6. Mental imagery tactics for recognizing problem types or solution types.
7. Methods for providing external storage to deal with memory limitations, such as creating job aids or graphics.
8. Generic strategies such as hypothesis and test, working forward, working backward, and means-ends.

*Not all theorists recommend this problem simplification approach (Spiro & Jehng, 1990).

9. Specific strategies for representing problems or retrieving solutions for the particular domain.
10. Worked examples.
11. Completion tasks.

Many of the above recommendations have found research support in research on reducing cognitive load (see Mayer and Moreno, 2003 for an excellent summary of this research).

Practice

Chase and Chi (1980) suggest that thousands of hours of practice may be needed to transform a novice into an expert problem solver. After learners have experienced the solution of example problems, they should have the opportunity to solve problems of similar difficulty. Instructional guidance, such as hints, guiding questions, presentation of a database of principles, and suggestions for strategies, should be phased out gradually. Sufficient practice should be provided so that (1) knowledge can be reorganized and elaborated in a manner that supports problem solving, (2) pattern-recognition skills become automatic even with complex or ill-structured problems, (3) identification of subgoals and related principles becomes automatic, and (4) selection and application of strategies is automatic. For ill-structured problems, various argumentation techniques can assist learners in applying domain knowledge so as to clarify underlying concepts.

Initial practice may involve performance of only one stage of problem solving, such as (1) identifying the goal state, (2) identifying important information in the problem, (3) identifying relationships between variables, (4) constructing a representation of variables in given and goal states, (5) identifying pertinent principles that should be applied, and (6) confirming the appropriateness of a solution. Each phase should be followed by feedback, rather than having the learner apply the entire process. Later, following initial practice and feedback, learners should practice solving the entire problem before receiving feedback.

Practice should start with problems that have easily recognizable, distinctive features in given and goal states, with little extraneous detail. More ill-structured problems should be introduced gradually (Van Merriënboer, Kirschner, & Kester, 2003).

Many strategies for facilitating problem-solving learning have been developed that relate to how practice is structured. Here is a helpful list of these strategies, presented in order appropriateness for well-structured (at the beginning) to more appropriate for ill-structured problems (at the end): logical problem, algorithms, rule-using problems, decision making, troubleshooting in closed system, diagnosis-solution in open system, strategic performances, case analysis, design problems, and dilemmas.

Processing Feedback

Initial feedback may be in the form of hints or guiding questions, if the learner's solution has gone awry. Feedback may also be specific in terms of information used or misused.

Feedback should include information regarding not only the appropriateness of the learners' solutions but also the efficiency of the solution process. As learners make the transition from novice to expert, their problem solving will become more automatic. Therefore, as learners become more and more expert in their approaches to problems, their solutions should be more and more streamlined. Feedback on the efficiency or speed of problem solving is necessary to the extent that genuine expertise is often expected as part of the learning goal. Feedback information, especially early in the instructional process, may also include whether the learner has correctly identified the problem, correctly defined the goal state, appropriately decomposed the problem, considered the relevant alternatives, selected a viable approach, and reached the goal state.

One way to provide feedback regarding effectiveness and efficiency is to present a model of the solution process. If the solution process produces artifacts of the stages of the solution (such as intermediate written solutions), the learners may be given a written or visual model answer to the solution. This model may include a description of how the solution led from the given state to the goal state and how the solution represents the goal state.

Conclusion

Summary and Review

The summary and review, whether provided by the learners or the instruction, should include the following:

1. A review of the characteristics of problems that make them members of the class of problems that can be solved in a similar manner.
2. A summary of effective strategies for this domain of problems.
3. Suggestions of methods for organizing the problem schema for storage and later retrieval.

Transfer

Transfer of problem-solving skill, particularly transfer of strategies, does not occur spontaneously. For transfer to occur, learners need explicit hints that point to the utility of this learning to similar and dissimilar problems from this lesson. They also need reminders in subsequent instruction, of which knowledge, principles, or strategies may be useful. In general, the more and varied the problems encountered in practice, the better the transfer to related problem tasks.

The guided discovery approach that we have recommended (with three levels of processing support) tends to encourage transfer of specific and, to some degree, general problem-solving skills. In addition, learners should be encouraged to identify similar kinds of problems in real-life situations or within more complex problems.

Learners can also be encouraged to develop their own problem descriptions that fall into this same class of problems and construct their own solutions. Learners may be encouraged to give the problems to fellow students.

During subsequent instruction, transfer can be explicitly supported by hinting that strategies used in this lesson can be applied to the new one. Learners can be reminded of knowledge representations that they constructed in this lesson, and then those representations can be elaborated upon during new instruction.

Remotivation and Conclusion

A product of problem-solving learning is frequently knowledge of how to use knowledge, so the function of remotivation may be generated by learners as part of successful learning. If there is reason to believe remotivation may not occur, learners may be sufficiently remotivated and the lesson successfully concluded by reminding learners of the amount and utility of the knowledge that they have acquired in the lesson.

Assessment of Problem-Solving Learning

The assessment of problem-solving skills should require learners to solve problems of the class that the instruction has targeted. The problems should be from contexts similar to those that were used as examples and practice in the lesson. Task instructions should also be similar to those provided in instruction. However, the problems themselves should be novel and previously unencountered. Simulations and case problems may be used during assessment. Frequently, the same argument-construction activities discussed earlier under "Practicing" may be appropriate as assessment activities.

A key difficulty in evaluating problem-solving skills is that often the time required to solve a single problem may be extensive. It is, consequently, difficult to provide a sufficient number of items during an assessment period to feel confident in the reliability of the measure. In such cases, designers of assessment instruments may wish to include some partial problems, such as problems in which the learners must evaluate the appropriateness of a provided solution, in addition to the one or two complete problems that the learners must complete.

Domain-specific problem solving involves identifying the knowns and unknowns in a problem, selecting principles to solve the problem, applying a procedure defining the order in which these principles should be applied, confirming the correct application of principles, and "fixing up" if the principles have not been correctly applied. Although the principles differ across domains, problem-solving tasks generally involve these common steps. Each of these steps can be assessed separately as recognitions or constructed responses, or all of the steps can be assessed together in a recognition or constructed response form.

Following are examples of a recognition type of item that could be used in assessment of skills in chemistry.

Below is a balanced equation.

$$2HCl + Ba(OH)_2 \longrightarrow BaCl_2 + 2H_2O$$

It has been converted to a net ionic equation. Which of the conversions is correct?

  a. $2Cl^- + 2OH^- \longrightarrow BaCl$
  b. $2H^+ + 2OH^- \longrightarrow 2H^2O$
  c. $2H^+ + 2Cl^- + Ba^{2+} + 2OH^- \longrightarrow Ba^{2+} + 2Cl^- + 2H_2O$
  d. $Ba^{2+} \rightarrow 2Cl^-$

This item is similar to the confirmation step in problem solving. The item also requires that the learners actually solve the problem, so it assesses whether they can correctly select and apply the principles. The item is somewhat less demanding than a constructed response problem that requires the solution of the problem; however, it may, in some cases, be a more practical format for assessment. Here is a recognition problem that assesses whether the learners can select from available principles those that are applicable to a particular problem:

Below is a balanced equation.

$$2HCl + Ba(OH)_2 \longrightarrow BaCl_2 + 2H_2O$$

Which of the following principles for converting must you apply to convert the equation to a net ionic equation?

  a. Rule of binary acids
  b. Rule of ternary acids
  c. Rule of polyprotic acids
  d. Rule of (writing) gases

This chemistry problem is a problem-solving task rather than a principle-using task because the learner must choose from several principles and apply them in the correct order to solve the problem. However, it does not assess whether the learners can actually solve the problem. The first constructed response item *does* assess this skill.

Constructed response problems could resemble the following:

Below is a balanced equation.

$$2HCl + Ba(OH)_2 \longrightarrow BaCl_2 + 2H_2O$$

Convert the above equation to a net ionic equation. Write your answer in the space below.

You could also combine these formats in a number of ways to create an item that is both recognition and constructed response:

Below is a balanced equation.

$$2HCl + Ba(OH)_2 \longrightarrow BaCl_2 + 2H_2O$$

It has been converted to a net ionic equation. Which of the conversions is correct?

a. $2Cl^- + 2OH^- \longrightarrow BaCl$
b. $2H^+ + 2OH^- \longrightarrow 2H_2O$
c. $2H^+ + 2Cl^- + Ba^{2+} + 2OH^- \longrightarrow Ba^{2+} + 2Cl^- + 2H_2O$
d. $Ba^{2+} \longrightarrow 2Cl^-$

List below the principles that you used to determine your answer.

MACROSTRATEGIES FOR PROBLEM-SOLVING INSTRUCTION

Educators and trainers often employ one of two equally ineffective strategies for teaching problem solving. The first is to teach the relevant principles for problem solving (sometimes only in their declarative form, without any instruction in their actual application) and assume that learners can select and combine these principles for problem solving without any instruction, including practice, in problem solving in the domain. The second, more common strategy is to provide opportunities for problem solving without any instruction on the principles that must be applied to solve problems; this makes the assumption that the learners can induce the principles from the context. Each of the approaches might be effective with very bright learners who have a great deal of prior knowledge on which to draw, good cognitive strategies, and successful experience in filling in the gaps left by faulty instruction. However, both of these teaching approaches should be considered with caution. With such incomplete instruction, slower learners will not learn to problem solve, and the most able learners may have to struggle and worry more than is profitable.

This does not mean that we recommend didactic, expository instructional strategies for teaching problem solving. It simply means that we feel that the prerequisites for problem solving should be taught and that problem solving itself is new learning that should also be taught using appropriate instructional strategies. (Both the sample lesson on computer programming in this chapter and the Extended Example contribution from this chapter on the Learning Resources Web site employ a combination of supplantive and generative instructional strategies.) A highly generative strategy may be selected, or a more scaffolding strategy may be more appropriate, depending on many factors that the designer should consider.

A second concern, in addition to instructional strategy type, is the sequencing of the related principle learning with regard to problem-solving learning. It is possible to provide instruction on prerequisite principles first and then just teach how to integrate the knowledge, principles, and cognitive strategies to solve problems using the principles. The extended example at the end of this chapter will use this approach. Or the instruction on principles and problem solving can be interwoven, providing instruction on a certain subset of principles, along with instruction on how these principles can be used to solve a certain subset of problems within the content domain. The example on computer programming later in this chapter employs this approach. There are advantages and disadvantages to each approach, and the superiority of one approach over the other has not been established by research.

A number of exciting macrostrategies are available for teaching problem solving. Most of them are amenable to a "guided discovery" approach; that is, the learners must discover how the principles and knowledge can be combined to solve problems, but the instruction hints and occasionally directly teaches the appropriate principles, knowledge, or strategies to use along the way. The hints and direct teaching can gradually be dropped out during practice, requiring learners to do more and more of the information processing for themselves. This guided discovery approach with diminishing amounts of guidance should be motivational and effective in promoting transfer of problem-solving skills. Thus, with the amount of prior knowledge of content that learners usually possess before they begin a problem-solving lesson when guided discovery of prerequisite knowledge has been employed, designers can usually use a more generative strategy for problem-solving instruction itself.

Although any of the following eight macrostrategies may be a good candidate for assisting the learning of well-structured problem solving, they vary when it comes to assisting the learning of ill-structured problem solving. The strategies are presented in a rough, hypothetically based sequence, with the least applicable to ill-structured problem solving first and the most applicable last. Also, although the following eight macrostrategies are described separately, elements of several strategies might be combined to create a strategy uniquely suitable to a particular learning goal.

Socratic Dialogue

The Socratic dialogue is a method of teaching in which a student is guided to attainment of desired learnings through interaction with an expert or mentor whose role it is to provide instances and guiding questions. Our prototype example of this approach is the instructional strategy that the Professor Kingsfield character used in the movie/TV series *The Paper Chase*. You may remember that in trying to teach his students to apply contract law, Professor Kingsfield described a problem and then required students to use laws in order to unsnarl the legal problem.* His pointed questioning guided the learners in both the selection of the appropriate laws (principles) and their application to the particular problem.

Socratic dialogue is a powerful technique for teaching problem solving. It is very demanding for the teacher, requiring exceptional skills in attention to learners, the ability to infer the learners' line of reasoning, and a clear conception of the ultimate goal of the instruction. It is easy for a less-skilled teacher to be distracted by unimportant details or to be unable to construct a question (rather than a lecture) to guide the learners' reasoning. Another negative aspect of Socratic dialogue is that the questioning can involve only one student at a time. Other learners may vicariously experience the interactions, but the line of questioning may not really address their own misconceptions or faulty lines of reasoning. Computer-based programs (often described as "intelligent tutoring systems") that engage learners in Socratic dialogue have been developed in a number of domains. Although experimental and limited at the moment (primarily because of computers' inability to understand natural language), this technology ultimately has the potential for giving all learners in a class the opportunity to experience this instructional interaction intimately. Collins and Stevens (1983) suggested several types of interactions that the teacher may originate (or the teacher may guide the learners to generate) in Socratic dialogue: positive or negative examples of principles, counterexamples of principles, hypothetical cases, hypotheses, tests of a hypothesis, predictions and alternate predictions, entrapping of students, tracing consequences to contradiction, and questioning authority. A variant of Socratic dialogue was described by Fosnot (1989) using the term "coaching," in which care is taken to ensure that the mentor is open to accepting alternative perceptions from the protégé.

*If the reference to these Paper Chase performances made over thirty years ago are not familiar to you, you may wish to either: a) consult someone born before 1960, b) rent a video, or c) imagine old Prof. Kingsfield and move on.

Expert Systems

Expert systems are computer-based programs which, when given data, are able to solve problems within a limited domain of expertise. Expert systems were originally developed to substitute for expertise within esoteric domains of expertise in which the number of humans who possess the expertise is limited. For example, two expert systems were developed—one related to the repair of steam-driven train engines and one related to the cleaning of chemical tanks—when it became clear that the experts in these two areas were nearing retirement and no one had been specifically trained to solve problems in these two areas. As they are developed, expert systems are designed to preclude the need for problem-solving instruction within a domain. The development of expert systems is extremely time-consuming, even with the assistance of shells (Grabinger, Wilson, & Jonassen, 1990). Of course, the broader the domain of problem solving and the more complex the potential problems, the more difficult the development will be.

Expert systems are composed of two components: a knowledge database and an inference engine. The knowledge base is composed of domain-specific declarative knowledge and principles. The inference engine is composed of generic and domain-specific strategies that determine how the knowledge base should be combined. When an individual uses an expert system to solve a problem, the expert system asks the individual for information about the given and the goal state. If this information is adequate, the system can provide the user with a solution. If the information is inadequate, the principles are incomplete, or the domain is "fuzzy," the system can provide the user with information as to how probable its solutions are.

If they are available or feasible to develop, expert systems can be used in problem-solving instruction. Simply using an expert system to help solve problems probably will not teach the learner to solve problems independently. If a learner could induce the principles and cognitive strategies, it would be a very inefficient instructional strategy because the original role of the expert system is to avoid instruction. There are at least three ways in which expert systems could be used to teach problem solving in a domain: sequenced problem sets, intelligent tutoring systems, and building an expert system.

Use of sequenced problem sets is one way in which expert systems can be used to assist instruction in problem solving. When queried, some expert systems will display the principles that were used to solve a problem and the sequence in which the principles were employed. Some systems also show the declarative knowledge within the system and the information provided by the user that was used to solve the problem. Problem-solving instruction that uses an existing expert system may wish to ensure that learners already can apply the principles individually. Then it should provide learners with carefully selected and sequenced problem sets to give to the expert system. Learners should be taught how to access, read, and interpret the system's explanation of its reasoning. Learners should have the system solve problems in the first problem set (the simplest class of problems in the domain). They should study and explain the reasoning of the system. Learners should solve similar problems on their own and then give the problems to the system for feedback. Finally, they should solve problems in the set independently and evaluate the adequacy of their solutions. Then they can move on to the next problem set and follow the same pattern. For more information on expert systems, read Goodyear and Tait (1991), Lippert (1988), and McFarland and Parker (1990).

Intelligent tutoring systems (ITS) are computer-based instructional systems that include not only a knowledge base and an inference engine but also a teacher model and a student model. The teacher model (sometimes called the *pedagogical component, tutor,* or *coach)* contains knowledge and principles regarding instruction. The student model contains a model of the principles and knowledge that the learner has acquired. As the learner learns more, the student model is updated to reflect the learners' new knowledge. ITS programs are designed to be self-contained and sufficient in teaching learners a particular content. ITS programs are very complex, expensive, and time-consuming to develop and, at present, are mostly used for research rather than implemented as instruction in schools and training facilities. Some ITS programs have been developed to teach problem solving in very narrow areas of content, such as programs designed to teach solving specific types of problems in programming, physics, or medical diagnosis. Others teach declarative knowledge or concepts. Considering the cost and complexity of ITS development, developers will probably reserve them for research and for the most critical and difficult-to-learn skills; these would be skills for which learners may have very diverse prior knowledge and for which it is difficult to predict how learners' prior knowledge will interact with the new content. For more information on ITS systems, we suggest you read Lajoie (2000), Lajoie and Derry (1993); Nguyen-Xuan, Nicaud, and Gelis, (1995), and Polson and Richardson (1988). A promising approach is found in Merrill and Associates' *ID Expert* (Merrill & ID2 Research Group, 1998), which is an expert system designed to decrease the time needed to design and develop instruction as well as providing a delivery system for the materials developed from within *ID Expert.*

A third strategy for using expert systems to teach problem solving is to have the learners develop an expert system that can solve problems in the specific content domain that they are learning. Expert system shells are available that allow nonprogrammers to develop a simple expert system. Using these shells varies in difficulty, and their power also varies (Grabinger, Wilson, & Jonassen, 1990). However, educators have reported their successful use with both high school and college students (Starfield, Butala, England, & Smith, 1983; Wideman & Owston, 1988) and with adult learners as well (Shute, Torreano, & Willis, 2000). Such an endeavor would require intense teacher training and considerable time and resources. In general, students would need to be skilled in the application of individual principles before developing the system. For more information on instructional expert system, we suggest you read Grabinger, Wilson, and Jonassen (1990).

Sequenced Problem Sets

One of the best macrostrategies for teaching problem solving involves the presentation of carefully sequenced problem sets. The first set of problems should be the most fundamental of those to be learned. Reigeluth (1992) suggested a technique for selecting these fundamental principles through a filter of "simplifying conditions." Students may learn these principles far in advance of the problem-solving instruction or just prior to the problem-solving instruction. If the instruction of the principles occurs just prior to instruction on combining the principles in problem solving, the designer should definitely ensure that sufficient examples and practice have been incorporated so that the application of each independent principle is fairly automatic. After learners have received instruction on selecting and combining the principles to solve a class of problems, then instruction may move on to learning additional principles and combining these principles with the old ones to solve a larger class of problems. You may recognize this approach as an adaptation of the Elaboration Model (Reigeluth & Stein, 1983). We will use this approach later in this chapter in our description of a computer programming course.

Simulations

A simulation can also be used effectively as a macrostrategy for problem-solving instruction. A *simulation* is an activity that attempts to mimic the most essential features of a reality but allows learners to make decisions within this reality without actually suffering the consequences of their decisions. Instructional simulations generally provide a problem situation through depiction of a system in operating form and then require the learner to interact with the problem. With every action of the learner, there is a response within the simulation. Simulations are often computer-based so that the quality of the feedback to the learners' response can be lifelike and immediate. An example of a computer-based simulation to teach problem-solving skills was the "Fruit Fly Simulation" that was originally delivered on the PLATO system (Hyatt, Eades, Tenczar, & Denault, 1968). It was devised to give learners the opportunity to apply multiple principles of genetics for predicting and controlling inheritance of factors for the fruit fly. The learners could see the effects of their manipulations of parents on the offspring for several generations within a few minutes rather than waiting to see the actual effects of a live genetics experiment.

Simulations can occur with written material, such as an in-basket simulation in which a learner must deal with all the mail that has built up in an in basket within an environment. Simulations can also be group-based, as with simulations in which the learners must role-play within a prescribed environment. Tennyson (1988) listed the advantages of simulations, noting that simulations can do the following:

1. Portray a meaningful context.
2. Be quite complex.
3. Expose learners to alternative solutions.
4. Require problem solving in situations in which there is no single correct answer.
5. Allow learners to see the consequences of their solutions.
6. Require learners to predict the effects of their actions.

Another advantage of simulations is that they can be constructed so that in initial phases, the problem and goal state are simplified; it is then within the capabilities of the learners early in the instruction to solve the problem. The problem and related solution can be made more and more complex (as in real life) to require the learner to employ more selection and processing strategies. Simulations, particularly those that are computer-based, may be run a number of times by learners so that they have multiple practice opportunities.

Unfortunately, good simulations can be quite difficult and time-consuming to create. In designing a simulation, the designer must carefully plan the description of the environment, the actors within the environment, and the principles that govern (1) when and how the actors may act, (2) how these actions will affect the environment, and (3) how the environment will react to the actors' actions. All of the elements in the design must mirror reality. The cause-and-effect principles governing the actors and the environment should be those principles that the learners are learning to manipulate in problem solving. Towne (1995) described guidelines for designers of simulations. These guidelines include sys-

tem representation and modeling, learner support, representing the invisible, generating directed and diagnostic environments, and using development systems and tools. Other sources that provide guidance for developing simulations are Greenblat and Duke (1981), Maidment and Bronstein (1973), Shirts (1975), and Walcott and Walcott (1976).

Once a simulation is developed, it is imperative that designers carefully outline the suggested use of the simulation within instruction. For example, it is extremely critical that prior to encountering simulations, learners acquire the principles that must be combined in the simulation and an instructor be prepared to provide a high level of scaffolding for students in initial passes through the simulation. Even with multiple passes through a simulation, learners cannot be expected to induce the principles that have been interacting within a simulation. As noted earlier, although the most able or gifted learners may be able to perform the mental leaps necessary to induce unknown principles from working with multiple problems, such an approach may be inefficient for even the best students and will not work for the vast majority of students in any event. Also, the debriefing following the simulation is critical. It is quite possible for learners to have been successful within a simulation and still not have acquired the ability to apply the principles in concert to other cases. Their behavior within the simulation may have been trial-and-error or based on faulty, albeit successful, reasoning. During the debriefing, learners should be required to explain their understanding of the given state, the goal state, their selection of principles to solve the problem, and how their actions moved the situation from the given state to the goal state. Joyce and Weil (1986) and Kozma, Belle, and Williams (1978) presented suggestions for the actions of a teacher during a simulation. As designers develop their simulations and related teacher/trainer guides, the activities of teachers or other media that introduce and conclude the instruction should be carefully considered and explained because introduction and conclusion are very critical to the effectiveness of the simulation. Additional readings in simulation design and use include Brant, Hooper, & Sugrue, 1991; Duchastel, 1991; Gorrell, 1992; Gredler, 2004; Lierman, 1994; Matoon & Klein, 1993; Njoo & DeJong, 1991; Reiber & Kini, 1993; Rieber, 1996a; Thomas & Hooper, 1991; and Wager, Pokinghorne, & Powley, 1992.

Microworlds

The concept of *microworld* is quite similar to that of simulation, except that the central idea of simulations is the representation of a system, and the central idea of a microworld is a learner centered construction (Rieber, 1996b). Seymour Papert (1980) is generally considered to be the originator of the idea, in which children's use of the LOGO programming language to create "turtle graphics" could assist in generation of deep-running and sophisticated mathematical understandings. With its emphasis on learner construction rather than system representation, the microworld concept stimulates local-level development of computer-based learning environments. Using relatively approachable development tools such as Authorware™, Flash™, or Director™, it is feasible for schools and training agencies to develop microworlds to assist problem-solving instruction.

As a macrostrategy for learning problem solving, microworlds offer particular assistance in providing a learning environment that is intrinsically motivating and cognitively challenging. However, it is a mistake to assume that a learner's natural impulses in interaction with the microworld will provide the best learning environment. Sufficient learning guidance and appropriate handling of other events of instruction may be absent unless designers consciously attend to them in design of the microworld. For example, in a study of learning from a LOGO microworld, Cope & Simmons (1994) found that limiting feedback was an important aid to learning. The immediate feedback offered by the turtle graphics to keyboard input encouraged learners to engage in relatively mindless trial-and-error problem solution, whereas restricted feedback in which rotation of the turtle on the screen was not shown until completion of the problem encouraged a more mindful approach and contributed to students' development of more efficient solutions of the problems. Honebein (1996) provided another example of a microworld in a computer-based model of a biotechnology building. Within this building, learners may practice sociological research skills, particularly investigating how social, architectural, and scientific forces influence the design of a biotech research center. In this microworld, students may ask questions and then search data within the building and its layout for the answers. See Rieber (2004) for additional information on microworlds.

Anchored Instruction

Another conception of improved instruction that focuses primarily on the learning of domain-specific problem solving based on situated cognition is that of "anchored instruction." Instruction is described as "anchored" if it provides a meaningful context and realistic, interesting problems for the learners. A fertile source of ideas and development in this area has been the Cognition and Technology Group at Vanderbilt (1990). The Vanderbilt group has developed a great deal of extremely high quality instructional materials, focusing on the interactive videodisc format (notably, *The Adventures of Jasper Woodbury*), and have studied the use and effectiveness of their products with unusual thoroughness.

We find the interpretations of constructivism that have been reflected in their materials as well as in their writing to be highly compatible with our own views. As discussed in Chapter 2, one area of concern with situated cognition is transfer; however, the Vanderbilt group indicates a full understanding of the threats to transfer from use of a single situation and recommends the use of many. Further reading in this area can be found in Barab, Evans, & Baek (2004), Choi & Hannafin (1995); Winn (1994); and Young (2004), all of which offer interesting and helpful perspectives.

Case Studies and Case Problems

Case studies can be similar to simulations in that they present a realistic situation and require the learners to respond as if they were the person who must solve a problem. Case studies also require learners to select and manipulate multiple principles in order to solve problems. Hudspeth and Knirk (1989) described case materials as follows:

> [Case materials are] problem oriented descriptions of a believable event which provide sufficient detail to allow the reader to analyze the problem/solution process. A complete case describes an entire situation and includes background information, the actions and reactions of persons involved, the solution, and the possible consequences of the actions taken. Case materials should have enough background information and detail so that they are readable and believable. (p. 31)

An example of a case study might be developed to teach problem-solving skills in an instructional design class, such as application of the principles involved in selecting instructional media. A single case study or multiple case studies might be written that provide a full description of the instructional environment (including time and resources available for the development project), the potential learners, and the instructional task. Given this information, learners in the class could examine the givens, identify the goal state, select the principles that would be appropriate for determining optimal media, apply the principles to determine optimal media, and evaluate the quality of their solutions.

Case studies are particularly useful in learning to problem solve in situations in which there is more than one correct solution to the problem or in the more complex and subtle world of ill-structured problems. As with simulations, case studies can by written in sets with increasing levels of detail, complexity, and irrelevant information so that learners can manipulate more and more principles and employ more cognitive strategies as they proceed through instruction. Case studies may be completed individually or in cooperative learning groups. Another advantage of case studies is that they aid transfer to real-life situations. They are also a highly motivating strategy.

Case studies are more difficult to develop than might be immediately apparent. If the designer begins with a problem and attempts to invent a situation for its context, the designer will find that "fleshing out" the situation so that it appears realistic and has sufficient irrelevant detail can be tedious. The result can appear very contrived. If, in contrast, the designer models the case study on a real-life problem, the designer will find that real problem situations can be too complex to use, at least in initial problem-solving instruction. We find it to be most effective to begin with a known case and simplify it by eliminating some of the problems or omitting some of the extraneous detail. We occasionally combine characteristics of two known situations to make one clear problem case. For guidance on development of case materials, see Hafler, 1999; Hudspeth & Knirk, 1989; Hudspeth & Knirk, 1991; Shulman, 1992; Stolovitch & Keeps, 1999; Wassermann, 1994; and a set of publications by Harvard Business School Case Services (no date) (see especially publications in this series by Culliton, Laurence, Sanford, and Towl). For additional reading on the use of case studies, see Ertmer & Russell (1995) and Kolodner, Owensby, & Guzdial (2004).

Problem-Based Learning

Considerable interest has developed in an approach to instruction that structures courses and entire curricula on problems rather than subject content. Such an approach to curriculum organization is by no means new (see Chapter 16), but the emphasis of application to professional education rather than K–12 schooling marks a change. Under a problem-based approach, a professional preparation curriculum is organized about fundamental or critical problems encountered in professional practice (Boud & Feletti, 1991; Schmidt, 1995). The most common arena of application appears to be medical schools, although the approach should have equal utility in law, business, education, and other specialties in which professional preparation includes the need for substantial learning of domain-specific problem-solving skills. In a sample of studies in medical schools (Boreham, Ellis, & Morgan, 1985; Geerligs, 1995; Schmidt, Van der Arend, Kokx, & Boon, 1995; Wilkerson, 1995), topics of investigation ranged from curriculum-wide questions of sequence to staff development issues to group and tutorial interactions. A primary benefit that can be expected from well-conceived and problem-based learning is high student interest and motivation. Problems can be anticipated in instructional management. Interestingly, the structures of schools providing professional education may be more suited to successful problem-based learning than

were (and are) the K–12 public schools in which such ideas were developed and applied in the 1920s and 1930s (see Chapter 16). Readers may find more specifics for designing problem-based environments in Barrows (1985) and Boud and Feletti (1991).

Cognitive Apprenticeships

A traditional apprenticeship involves a learner working under the supervision of an expert or master to learn the skills of a trade, particularly procedures and motor skills. However, because of social and workplace changes in recent years, such as increasing technical complexity in the workplace and less time available during the workday for learning, the apprenticeship has fallen out of favor as a method of learning (Brown, Collins, & Duguid, 1989; Collins, Brown, & Newman, 1989; Gott, 1988). At the same time, the newer *cognitive apprenticeship* has been developed as a method of teaching. Essentially, a cognitive apprenticeship involves placing a learner in an authentic work environment as a partial participant.

Collins, Brown, and Newman (1989) proposed six primary elements of cognitive apprenticeships: modeling, coaching, scaffolding, articulation, reflection, and exploration. Some scholars point to a reduction in the importance of the "master-apprentice" relationship (Duffy & Cunningham, 1996), while others emphasize relationships between the content knowledge and thought processes experts employ to perform complex tasks (Choi & Hannafin, 1995). Designers of cognitive apprenticeships should pay particularly close attention to the learning goals of the apprenticeship (What is the expected learning benefit to the learner?), the cognitive tools that the learner is expected to apply (Does the learner already have the tools needed in the apprenticeship, and if not, how will the learner acquire the needed tools?), how access to the community of practice will be provided, and how will learning from the apprenticeship will be assessed. A sample of further information available on cognitive apprenticeships can be found in Dennen (2004).

Other Macrostrategies

A number of other suitable macrostrategies may be most appropriate for problem solving in particular domains of content. For example, Suchman's Inquiry Training and the Biological Sciences Curriculum Inquiry Model (Joyce & Weil, 1986; Schwab, 1965) are most appropriate to problem solving in the sciences. They outline methods for teaching science through experimentation. The Jurisprudential Inquiry approach (Joyce & Weil, 1986; Oliver & Shaver, 1966) and the Social Science Inquiry approach (Joyce & Weil, 1986;

Massialas & Cox, 1966) were developed especially for problem solving in the social sciences. The Jurisprudential model would be appropriate for problem solving with human-made principles, such as laws, which may have values and attitudes attached to them. For a fascinating and helpful treatment of powerful strategies involving computers directed primarily at learning problem solving see Lajoie & Derrry (1993) and Lajoie (2000).

EXAMPLE PROBLEM-SOLVING LESSON—JAVA PROGRAMMING

Audience: The class consists of undergraduate and graduate students, most of whom are education majors. Learners are heterogeneous in their experience with computers and scripting or programming. Some have prior knowledge of scripting or programming; however, many report that they have forgotten what they learned in previous programming courses. Few have used any programming skills in the previous year. Usually, almost all of the class has used a computer for applications, such as word processing. A few students are fearful of using the computer for any purpose and when forced to, do not particularly like it. Every semester there are some students who describe themselves as "not very analytical" and are uncomfortable with analytical approaches to problems. Two-thirds of the class are instructional technology students who are seeking an advanced degree. The instructional technology majors will also take coursework involving use of authoring systems to develop software.

Setting: The class meets weekly for 3 hours for 15 weeks in a classroom with 25 networked personal computers. Usually the class has 15 to 24 students. The classroom has a display system for demonstrations that allows the instructor to show the output of his computer to the entire class. The networking includes both an in-building intranet supported by a department file and application server as well as high-speed connection to the Internet.

Learning Task: The goals of the course are that learners can do the following: (1) interpret and "debug" Java code; (2) given an instructional problem, code, compile, and debug an application that will solve the instructional problem; (3) implement fundamental principles of instructional design in the development of an instructional program; (4) use programming and computer-based instructional development terminology appropriately; (5) appreciate the tediousness and time-consuming nature of programming on the one hand and the precision of control which programming potentially provides; and (6) given a desired characteristic of an instructional application, estimate the feasibility,

difficulty, and amount of time that it would take to code that part of the application.

The objective for the problem-solving lesson that will be described in the following example lesson is as follows: Given specifications for a simple Java application, the learners can edit, save, compile, execute, and debug (if necessary) an application program which meets the specifications.

A Description of Problem-Solving Lesson

Before we describe the lesson, we will briefly describe the entire course because each lesson is a problem-solving lesson that leads to the skills represented by the course goals. The macrostrategy for the lesson in context of the course is the Elaboration Model. The course begins with a lesson in which the students learn to apply the most basic programming statements and fundamental coding principles. For the first six weeks, each subsequent lesson elaborates a single, relatively simple Java application designed to teach the concepts "transparent," "translucent," and "opaque." Each lesson in the course adds some additional instructionally sound elaboration to the computer-based lesson and teaches the Java coding needed to program the new part of the transparent-translucent-opaque concept lesson. For the most part, each Java lesson follows the same structure as the lesson described here, except that as the course progresses the lessons become more and more generative, with the learners supplying more and more of the processing as they build up knowledge, principles, and strategies. Lessons earlier in the course, such as the one to follow, provide more support or supplantation, even though the core of the problem-solving learning is and must be generative.

Because the students are learning to develop instructional software, varieties of instructional strategy and learning environment designs are modeled to provide students with examples. These model programs are Java adaptations of model programs in texts such as Ragan and Smith, (1989), Myers and Lamb (1992), and Hooper (1999). Handouts have been prepared to take the place of a text. The Web-based tutorial from Sun Microsystems (developers and distributors of Java) at http://java.sun.com is used for Java basics content. Each lesson is divided into four major sections: (1) design of the computer-based lesson (instructional design with its consequent programming structure), (2) programming of the computer-based lesson (a line-by-line description of the function of the code), (3) summary, and (4) exercises.

The first lesson in the semester provides needed background for functioning within the particular environment of the classroom and laboratories, such as system login, network capabilities and operating procedures. It also introduces the concepts of "code," "application," and "applet" and provides two examples in Java. The first lesson ends with an overview of the entire semester and a viewing of sample final projects from the previous semesters.

The following paragraphs describe the second class in the semester.

INTRODUCTION

Deploy Attention / Establish Purpose / Promote Interest and Motivation / Preview Lesson / Review Relevant Prior Knowledge

For these parts of the lesson, the instructor does the following:

- Tells students that today they will learn a few fundamental Java statements and keywords from the Java Class Libraries and how to put them together in application programs to solve problems.

- Tells students that once these keywords and statements are learned along with learning to find and use appropriate Java libraries, they will have overcome a substantial hurdle and will have skills they can build on for the rest of the course.

- Explains that during the lesson, the student will analyze an application program to see what it does, enter it into the computer, learn what each individual statement does, and do some exercises that require the student to write some programs of his or her own.

- Compares the instructional strategy that he will use to meaningful approaches to learning to read and write. (Children are taught a few words by sight so they can read sentences very quickly.) This technique is similar in that the learners will learn a few statements with which they can make useful programs after today's lesson.

Body

Review Relevant Prior Knowledge

The instructor asks learners to explain what a computer application is (reviewing relevant concepts). The instructor also reminds them of experiences with programmable toys they may have operated and discusses how specific application code must be to get desired results (reviewing analogous strategies).

Process Information (Relational Rules Principles: Statements) / Practice / Employ Learning Strategies / Focus Attention

Materials consist of two orienting, beginning computer applications: one entitled "Hello World" on Sun's Java Web site, and a second entitled "Sampler," which is supplied on the local intranet server. Each application is provided with a printed listing and a brief description of what the applications do. The applications themselves are trivial, yet they provide a beginning point for what an application is, its main parts and the concepts that underlie them (comments, methods and variables, classes and objects, main method, beginning statements, and putting statements together).

The learners run the applications several times, using the strategy suggested by the instructor. The first time they view an application, they notice what it does in general. During the second run of the application, the students are to note the different things (operations) that the application does. The third time they view it, they note the sequence of events within it. Learners run the application additional times, answer the displayed questions in different ways, and notice how the application responds to different answers.

Feedback

The instructor runs the Sampler application and asks the students to explain generally what the application does, the major operations of the application, the sequence of operations, and how the application execution varies with different inputs.

The instructor also points out operations that learners often fail to identify, such as calling new methods in such a way as to present the intended display for the user.

Review Relevant Prior Knowledge/Process Information (Principles: Syntax)/Focus Attention

For these parts of the lesson, the instructor does the following:

- Reminds the students of how explicit they had to be in programming programmable toys in terms of sequence, correctly spelling statements, and including all desired operations.

- Explains that they must employ that same care in writing Java source code statements to execute.

- Asks learners to note the spacing of words and the use of uppercase letters in the application source code. Point out that Java is case-sensitive, and display the keywords that are capitalized in Java. Remind students that not using proper case will generate errors in the application program.

- Explains the principles relating to use of spaces, indents, and line feeds when typing in code. Point out that white space is used to increase readability of programs. Therefore, students should include enough spaces and indents when editing (typing) the program.

- Explains: comments, methods and variables, classes and objects, main method, beginning statements, and putting statements together.

Review Relevant Prior Knowledge (Variable)/ Practice/Focus Attention

For these parts of the lesson, the instructor does the following:

- Asks the learners to note how each line of code is constructed and runs each line of code to show the students what each line does.

- Reviews what each statement does and how each statement works within the application.
- Gives hypothetical questions requiring the use of only one statement and asks learners to provide the code.
- Asks students to explain what a variable is, to find a variable in the application, and to detail the function of the variable.
- Introduces the concept "instance variable," explains its function, gives examples and nonexamples of the use of variables, and asks the learners to give examples and nonexamples of the use of variables.
- Explains the syntax of variable names, gives examples and nonexamples, and asks students to give examples and nonexamples.

Process Information (Procedural Rules)/Review Relevant Prior Knowledge/Practice/Focus Attention

In these parts of the lesson, the instructor demonstrates the following:

- The function of source files and bytecode files and explains their role in Java coding, compiling, and interpreting.
- How to enter and edit lines of code, how to correct typing errors, and how to insert lines of codes.
- How to save the application, reminding students that this is a operating system function and why it is so classified. Tell students that they must save the application with a .java extension.

The students enter and edit the sample application. The instructor answers questions and reminds students of coding structure principles.

Process Information (Problem Solving) / Practice / Focus Attention / Employ Learning Strategies

The students run the application and attempt to debug it. The instructor helps with debugging, asking guiding questions that stimulate the students to recall statement use, syntax principles, and procedural rules for operating the computer. The instructor also suggests debugging strategies.

Practice

The students complete exercises that require them to employ the statements, procedural rules, and syntax principles *to new problems*. In other words, each student develops a new Java program from scratch. The exercise provided assists students in selecting a purpose and scope for their programs which is feasible given their current knowledge and the time available. The students develop, compile, run and debug their applications. (Note: It is at this point that learner activities are directly engaged in problem-solving learning. Other activities before and after this assist the learner in being oriented

and able to do this work, as well as better remember and apply what has been learned.)

Feedback/Focus Attention/Employ Strategies

In these parts of the lesson, the instructor does the following:

- Asks guiding questions that help learners recall principles.
- Suggests strategies for planning the solutions to the problems.
- Praises students who solve problems and encourages those who have difficulty.
- Answers questions.

The computer provides feedback as to whether problems are solved correctly.

Conclusion
Summary and Review/Remotivation and Conclusion

Here, the instructor reviews the following:

- The concepts program readability, comments, methods and variables, classes and objects, main method, editing, compiling, debugging, and proper saving procedures for Java.
- Statements and their functions.
- Principles of Java coding and why they are important.
- The means for setting up a new application, compiling, saving, and executing it.

The instructor also reminds the students of how much they have learned in just one day and previews the next week, when additional functions will be learned. The students read the handout, which restates the principles learned during class and previews the upcoming topics of object oriented programming, language basics for handling different data types, operators, and control flow, and interfaces and packages.

Transfer

For homework, the students develop written descriptions of problems that require the functions learned in this lesson, and they write a paper solution. Next week they will try their solutions in the computer and try to stump other students with their problems.

Assessment

The instructor provides ungraded review of programming exercises as an ongoing assessment. A midterm examination and final project are used in postassessment, exams requiring the development of Java applications under "open book" individual work conditions.

1. Using the expanded instructional events as a framework, describe the design of a lesson to provide instruction for the following situation. Make sure you describe any preceding instruction.*

Setting: This is a high school biology class (college prep).

Audience: Class enrollment is twenty-eight students, ages sixteen to eighteen.

Task: Given the phenotype and genotype of a parent generation, the learner can determine the phenotype and geno-type of the offspring and explain the answer using principle statements.

Sample Problem: Suppose a woman with normal vision is a carrier of color blindness. She marries a color-blind man. What is the probability of their having a color-blind son or daughter? Show the possible phenotypes and genotypes for all possible offspring. Explain how you determined your answer.

This should be approximately a one-hour lesson. Using the events of instruction, outline the sequence and content of the lesson.

RELATED PRINCIPLES

1. If an organism's genotype has one dominant and one recessive gene, the organism's phenotype will show the dominant trait.

2. If an organism's genotype has two dominant genes, then the organism's phenotype will show the dominant trait.

3. If an organism's genotype has two recessive genes, then the organism's phenotype will show the recessive trait.

4. If a member of a human generation is a male, then it has both an X (from the mother) and Y (from the father) chromosome.

5. If a member of a human generation is a female, then it has both an X (from the mother) and an X (from the father) chromosome.

6. If a human is color-blind, (s)he carries that recessive gene on an X chromosome.

7. If a male is color-blind, he carries the recessive color-blind gene on the X chromosome.

8. If a female is color-blind, she carries recessive color-blind genes on both X chromosomes.

9. Previous events do not affect the probability of later occurrences of the same event.

10. The probability of independent events occurring together is equal to the product of the probabilities of these events occurring separately.

11. If the task is to determine phenotype and genotype of offspring from the parents' phenotype and genotype, then use a Punnet square.

S U M M A R Y

Our definition of *problem solving* is the ability of a learner to combine rules and principles from a content domain to solve novel problems in that domain. This definition refers to *domain-specific* problem solving. Although many psychologists have struggled to identify generic problem-solving skills that can transfer to multiple domains, we agree with those who suggest that even these generic strategies should be taught as part of domain-specific problem solving.

Experts are those who are able to combine their knowledge to solve problems within a particular domain. There appear to be numerous differences between the way experts and novices solve problems. One of the most striking differences between novices and experts is the amount of domain-specific knowledge that they possess. Learners are unable to solve problems unless they have content knowledge in the form of declarative knowledge, principles, and associated concepts. Learners also must acquire cognitive strategies that enable them to manipulate this knowledge.

Although research has clarified to some degree how people solve problems, many questions remain as to the qualities of instruction required to teach people to solve problems. Eight macrostrategies appear to be useful: cognitive apprenticeship, anchored instruction, the Elaboration Model, Socratic dialogue, simulations, microworlds, expert systems, problem-based learning, and case studies.

A number of issues continue to remain unresolved regarding the design of domain-specific problem-solving instruction. These are (1) what to do about instruction on prerequisite principles, concepts, declarative knowledge, and cognitive strategies; (2) the value and limitations of beginning instruction with simplified problems; and (3) the number of problems or cases that learners should encounter to become competent at problem solving. A summary of our suggestions for how the expanded instructional events might be delivered for problem solving is presented in Figure 12.1.

*You may have difficulty with this exercise. Finding subject matter that is appropriate for problem-solving exercises and that is familiar to all potential users of the text has proved to be impossible. You may wish to review the subject using a high school science text or discuss the topic with a subject matter expert, or select a content area with which you are familiar and a problem-solving goal for which you would like to develop a design plan.

Introduction	Deploy attention. Arouse interest and motivation. Establish instructional purpose. Preview lesson.	• Present a challenging and interesting problem that is represented in a novel manner. • State class or problem that learners will learn to solve. • Delay statement in inquiry lesson. • Point out that problems will become increasingly complex throughout lesson.
Body	Recall prior knowledge.	• Explicitly review relevant prior knowledge; rules, declarative knowledge, or strategies. • Suggest ways that learners can reorganize knowledge in a more conducive from. • Attend to similarities and differences with other problem-solving learning..
	Process information.	• Encounter simplified, prototypical versions of problem first. • Verbalize task requirements. • Provide model think-alouds. • Decompose problem into subgoals.
	Focus attention.	• Isolate critical attributes in given state and goal state. • Generate networks and analogies. • Monitor success of solutions. • Ask guiding questions and provide hints. • Represent problem in alternate forms. • Use print or other media as a form of external storage.
	Practice.	• Practice identifying and clarifying given and goal states. • Practice decomposing problem. • Practice evaluating adequacy of a provided solution. • Practice with well-defined problems first.
	Evaluate feedback.	• Model solution of process or provide models of solution. • Give hints to ask questions. • Provide information on efficiency as well as effectiveness of solution.
Conclusion	Summarize and review.	• Restate criterial attributes of problem class. • Summarize effective strategies. • Suggest ways to organize knowledge for storage and retrieval.
	Transfer knowledge.	• Find similar problems outside of classroom. • Explicitly state when strategies may transfer to other problem types.
	Remotivate and close.	• Review the importance and breadth of what has been learned.
Assessment	Assess performance.	• Test ability to solve similar but novel problems, both well defined and poorly defined. • Test ability to isolate criterial attributes' goal and given states. • Test ability to evaluate others' solutions. • Test ability to justify solutions.
	Provide feedback and remediation.	• Identify whether problems are in pattern recognition, decomposition, explaining solution, etc.

Figure 12.1   Key Events for Domain-Specific Problem-Solving

EXTENDED EXAMPLE

This chapter's installment to the Extended Example on the instructional design of a photography course is strategy design for instruction leading to the learning of domain-specific problem solving, in this case an ill-structured problem, the taking of pictures with good composition, exposure, and focus. You will find the Extended Example in the Learning Resources Web site.

READINGS AND REFERENCES

Alexander, P. A., & Judy J. E. (1988). The interaction of domain-specific and strategic knowledge in academic performance. *Review of Educational Research, 58*(4), 375– 404.

Anderson, J. R. (1985). *Cognitive psychology and its implications* (2nd ed.). New York: W H. Freeman.

Atkinson, M. A., & Burton, J. S. (1991). Measuring the effectiveness of a microcomputer simulation. *Journal of Computer-Based Instruction, 18*(2) 63–65.

Barab, S. A., Evans, M. A., & Baek, E. (2004). Activity theory as a lens for characterizing the participatory unit. In D. H.

Jonassen (Ed.), *Handbook of research on educational communications and technology* (pp. 199–214). Mahwah, NJ: Erlbaum.

Barrows, H. D. (1985). *How to design a problem-based curriculum for preclinical years.* New York: Springer.

Boreham, N. C., Ellis, M. R., & Morgan, C. H. (1985). The effect of sequence of instruction on students' cognitive preferences and recall in the context of a problem-oriented method of teaching. *Instructional Science, 13,* 329–345.

Boud, D., & Feletti, G. (Eds.) (1991). *The challenge of problem-based learning.* New York: St. Martin's Press.

Brant, G., Hooper, E., & Sugrue, B. (1991). Which comes first, the simulation or the lecture? *Journal of Educational Computing Research, 7*(4), 469–481.

Brown, J. S., Collins, A., & Duguid, P. (1989). Situated cognition and the culture of learning. *Educational Researcher, 18* (1), 32–42.

Carlsen, D. D., & Andre, T. (1992). Use of a microcomputer simulation and conceptual change text to overcome student preconceptions about electric circuits. *Journal of Computer-Based Instruction, 19*(4), 105–109.

Catrambone, R. (1995). Aiding subgoal learning: Effects on transfer. *Journal of Educational Psychology, 87*(1), 5–17.

Chase, W. G., & Chi, M. T. H. (1980). Cognitive skill: Implications for spatial skill in large-scale environments. In J. Harvey (Ed.), *Cognition, social behavior, and the environment* (pp. 111–136). Potomac, MD: Erlbaum.

Chase, W. G., & Simon, H. A. (1973). Perception in chess. *Cognitive Psychology, 4,* 55–81.

Chee, Y. S. (1995). Cognitive apprenticeship and its application to the teaching of Small Talk in a multimedia interactive learning environment. *Instructional Science, 23,* 133–161.

Chi, M. T. H., Glaser, R., & Rees, E. (1982). Expertise in problem solving. In R. Sternberg (Ed.), *Advances in the psychology of human intelligence* (pp. 161–183). Hillsdale, NJ: Erlbaum.

Choi, J. I., & Hannafin, M. (1995). Situated cognition and learning environments: Roles, structures, and implications for design. *Educational Technology Research and Development, 43*(2), 53–69.

Cognition and Technology Group at Vanderbilt (1990). Anchored instruction and its relationship to situated cognition. *Educational Researcher, 19*(30), 2–10.

Collins, A., Brown, J. S., & Newman, S. E. (1989). Cognitive apprenticeship: Teaching the crafts of reading, writing, and mathematics. In L. B. Resnick (Ed.), *Knowing, learning, and instruction: Essays in honor of Robert Glaser* (pp. 453–494). Hillsdale, NJ: Erlbaum.

Collins, A., & Stevens, A. L. (1983). A cognitive theory of inquiry teaching. In C. Reigeluth (Ed.), *Instructional-design theories and models* (pp. 247–278). Hillsdale, NJ: Erlbaum.

Cope, P., & Simmons, M. (1994). Some effects of limited feedback on performance and problem-solving strategy in a Logo microworld. *Journal of Educational Psychology, 86*(3), 368–379.

Covington, M. C., Crutchfield, R. S., Davies, L. B., & Olton, R. M. (1974). *The productive thinking program: A course in learning to think.* Columbus, OH: Merrill.

Culliton, J. W. (n.d.). *Case method.* Boston, MA: Harvard Case Service, Harvard Business School.

Culliton, J. W. (n.d.). *Handbook on case writing.* Boston, MA: Harvard Case Services, Harvard Business School.

de Bono, E. (1973). *CoRT thinking materials.* London: Direct Education Services.

de Groot, A. E. (1965). *Thought and choice in chess.* The Hague: Mouton.

de Jong, T., & Ferguson-Hessler, M. G. M. (1986). Cognitive structures of good and poor novice problem solvers in physics. *Journal of Educational Psychology, 78*(4), 279–288.

Dennen, V. P. (2004). Cognitive apprenticeship in educational practice: Research on scaffolding, modeling, mentoring, and coaching as instructional strategies. In D. H. Jonassen (Ed.), *Handbook of research for educational communications and technology* (pp. 813–828). Mahwah, NJ: Erlbaum.

Derry, S. J., & Kellis, A. (1986). A prescriptive analysis of low-ability problem-solving behavior. *Instructional Science,* 15, 49–65.

Derry, S. J., Hawkes, L. W., & Tsai, C. (1987). A theory for remediation problem-solving skills of older children and adults. *Educational Psychologist, 22*(1), 55–87.

Dewey, J. (1933). *How we think.* Boston: D. C. Heath.

Dick, W. (1992). An instructional designer's view of constructivism. In T. M. Duffy & D. H. Jonassen (Eds.), *Constructivism and the technology of instruction* (pp. 91–98). Hillsdale, NJ: Erlbaum.

Duchastel, P. (1991). Instructional strategies for simulation-based learning. *Journal of Educational Technology Systems, 19*(3), 265–276.

Duffield, J. A. (1991). Designing computer software for problem-solving instruction. *Educational Technology Research and Development, 39*(1), 17–29.

Duffy, T. M. & Cunningham D. J. (1996). Constructivism: Implications for the design and delivery of instruction. In D. M. Jonassen (Ed.), *Handbook of research for educational communications and technology* (pp. 170–198). New York: Macmillan.

Duncker, K. (1945). On problem solving. *Psychological Monographs, 58* (Whole No. 270).

Ertmer, P. A., & Russell, J. D. (1995). Using case studies to enhance instructional design. *Educational Technology, 35*(7), 23–31.

Foshay, W. R. (1991). What we know (and what we don't know) about training of cognitive strategies for technical problem-solving. In G. J. Anglin (Ed.), *Instructional technology: Past, present, & future* (pp. 344–353). Englewood, CO: Libraries Unlimited.

Fosnot, C. T. (1989). *Enquiring teachers, enquiring learners: A constructivist approach to teaching.* New York: Teachers College Press.

Frederiksen, N. (1984). Implications of cognitive theory for instruction in problem solving. *Review of Educational Research, 54*(3), 363–407.

Gagné, E. D. (1985). *The cognitive psychology of school learning.* Boston: Little, Brown.

Gagné, R. M. (1980). Learnable aspects of problem solving. *Educational Psychologist,15,* 84–92.

Gagné, R. M. (1985). *The conditions of learning* (4th ed.). New York: Holt, Rinehart, and Winston.

Geerligs, T. (1995). Students' thoughts during problem-based small-group discussions. *Instructional Science, 22,* 269–278.

Gick, M. L. (1986). Problem-solving strategies. *Educational Psychologist, 21*(1 & 2), 99–120.

Gick, M. L., & Holyoak, K. J. (1980). Analogical problem solving. *Cognitive Psychology, 12,* 306–355.

Gilhooly, K. J., & Green, A. J. R. (1989). Learning problem-solving skills. In A. M. Colley & J. K. Beech (Eds.), *Acquisition and performance of cognitive skills* (pp. 85– 111). New York: Wiley.

Glaser, R. (1989). Expertise and learning: How do we think about instructional processes now that we have discovered knowledge structures. In D. Klahr and K. Kotovsky (Eds.), *Complex information processing* (pp. 269–282). Hillsdale, NJ: Erlbaum.

Goodyear, P., & Tait, K. (1991). Learning with computer-based simulations: Tutoring and student modeling requirements for an intelligent learning advisor. In M. Carretero, M. Pope, R. Simons, and J. I. Pozo (Eds.), *Learning and instruction, Vol. 3* (pp. 463–481). Oxford: Pergamon.

Gorrell, J. (April, 1990). *Effects of cognitive monitoring and implicit rule presentation on problem solving.* Paper presented at the annual meeting of the American Educational Research Association, Boston, MA.

Gorrell, J. (1992). Outcomes of using computer simulations. *Journal of Research on Computing in Education, 24*(3), 359–366.

Gott, S. P. (1988). Apprenticeship instruction for real-world tasks: The coordination of procedures, mental models, and strategies. In E. Z. Rothkopf (Ed.), *Review of research in education, 15,* 97–169.

Grabinger, R. S., Wilson, B., & Jonassen, D. H. (1990). *Building expert systems in training and education.* New York: Praeger.

Gredler, M. E. (2004). Games and simulations and their relationship to learning. In D. H. Jonassen (Ed.), *Handbook of research for educational communications and technology* (pp. 571–581). Mahwah, NJ: Erlbaum.

Greenblat, C. S., & Duke, R. D. (1981). *Principles and practices of gaming/simulation.* Beverly Hills, CA: Sage Publications.

Greeno, J. G. (1978). A study of problem solving. In R. Glaser (Ed.), *Advances in instructional psychology, Vol. 1* (pp. 13–76). Hillsdale, NJ: Erlbaum.

Greeno, J. G. (1989). Situations, mental models, and generative knowledge. In D. Klahr and K. Kotovsky (Eds.), *Complex information processing* (pp. 285–318). Hillsdale, NJ: Erlbaum.

Hafler, J. P. (1991). Case writing: Case writers' perspectives. In D. Boud & G. Feletti (Eds.), *The challenge of problem-based learning* (pp. 150–158). New York: St. Martin's Press.

Heller, J. I., & Hungate, H. N. (April, 1984). *Theory-based instruction in description of mechanics problems.* Paper presented at the annual meeting of the American Educational Research Association, New Orleans, LA.

Honebein, P. C. (1996). Seven goals for the design of constructivist learning environments. In B. Wilson (Ed.), *Constructivist learning environments: Case studies in instructional design* (pp. 11–24). Englewood Cliffs, NJ: Educational Technology Publications.

Hooper, S. (1999). *Authorware: An introduction to multimedia.* Upper Saddle River, NJ: Prentice Hall.

Hudspeth, D., & Knirk, F. G. (1989). Case study materials: Strategies for design and use. *Performance Improvement Quarterly, 2*(4), 30–41.

Hudspeth, D., & Knirk, F. G. (1991). Introduction to special issue on case studies. *Performance Improvement Quarterly, 4*(1), 2.

Hyatt, G., Eades, D., Tenczar, P. J., & Denault, J. M. (1968). *Drosophila genetics.* Urbana, IL: University of Illinois Computer-Based Education Research Laboratory.

Ingram, A. L. (1988). Instructional design for heuristic-based problem-solving. *Educational Communications and Technology Journal, 36*(4), 211–230.

Johnson-Laird, P. (1983). *Mental models.* Cambridge, MA: Harvard University Press.

Jonassen, D. H. (1997). Instructional design models for well-structured and ill-structured problem-solving learning outcomes. *Educational Technology Research and Development, 45*(1), 65–94.

Jonassen, D. H. (2000). Toward a design theory of problem solving. *Educational Technology Research and Development, 48*(4), 63–85.

Jonassen, D. H. (2003). Instructional design for learning to troubleshoot. *Performance Improvement Quarterly, 42*(4), 34–38.

Jonassen, D. H. (2004). *Learning to solve problems: An instructional design guide.* San Francisco: Jossey-Bass.

Jonassen, D. H., Mann, E., & Ambrusco, D. J. (1996). Causal modeling for structuring case-based learning environments. *Intelligent Tutoring Media, 6,* 103–112.

Joyce, B., & Weil, M. (1986). *Models of teaching* (3rd ed.). Upper Saddle River, NJ: Prentice-Hall.

Kalyuga, S., Ayres, P., Chandler, P., & Sweller, J. (2003). The expertise reversal effect. *Educational Psychologist, 38*(1), 23–31.

Kantowitz, B. H. (1987). Mental workload. In P. A. Hancock (Ed.), *Human factors psychology* (pp. 81–121). North-Holland: Elsevier.

Kigrt, E. (1991). What we know (and what we don't know) about training of cognitive strategies for technical problem solving. In G. J. Anglin (Ed.), *Instructional technology: Past, present, and future* (pp. 344–352). Englewood, CO: Libraries Unlimited.

Klein, G. A., & Weitzenfeld, J. (1978). Improvement of skills for solving ill-defined problems. *Educational Psychologist, 13,* 31–41.

Kolodner, J. L., Owensby, J. N., & Guzdial, M. (2004). Case-based learning aids. In D. H. Jonassen (Ed.), *Handbook of research for educational communications and technology.* Mahwah, NJ: Erlbaum.

Kotovsky, K., & Fallside, D. (1989). Representation and transfer in problem solving. In D. Klahr and K. Kotovsky (Eds.), *Complex information processing* (pp. 69– 108). Hillsdale, NJ: Erlbaum.

Kozma, R. B., Belle, L. W., & Williams, G. W. (1978). *Instructional techniques in higher education.* Englewood Cliffs, NJ: Educational Technology Publications.

Lajoie, S.P. (Ed.) (2000). *Computers as cognitive tools volume II: No more walls.* Mahwah, NJ: Erlbaum.

Lajoie, S. P., & Derry, S. J. (Eds.). (1993). *Computers as cognitive tools.* Hillsdale, NJ: Erlbaum.

Larkin, J. H. (1980). Teaching problem solving in physics: The psychological laboratory and the practical classroom. In D. T. Tuma & F. Reif (Eds.), *Problem solving and education: Issues in teaching and research* (pp. 111–125). Hillsdale, NJ: Erlbaum.

Larkin, J. H. (1989). Display-based problem solving. In D. Klahr & K. Kotovsky (Eds.), *Complex information processing* (pp. 319–342). Hillsdale, NJ: Erlbaum.

Lawrence, P. R. (n.d.). *Preparation of case material.* Boston, MA: Harvard Case Services, Harvard Business School.

Leont'ev, A. N. (1978). *Activity, consciousness, and personality.* Upper Saddle River, NJ: Prentice-Hall.

Lierman, B. (1994). How to develop a training simulation. *Training & Development, 48*(2), 50–52.

Lippert, R. C. (1988). Expert systems: Tutor, tools, and tutees. *Journal of Computer-Based Instruction, 16*(1), 11–19.

Maidment, R., & Bronstein, R. H. (1973). *Simulation games: Design and implementation.* Columbus, OH: Merrill.

Massialas, B., & Cox, B. (1966). *Inquiry in social studies.* New York: McGraw-Hill.

Matoon, J. S., & Klein, J. D. (1993). Controlling challenge in instructional simulation. *Journal of Educational Computing Research, 9*(2), 219–235.

Mayer, R. E. (1983). Can you repeat that? Qualitative effects of repetition and advance organizers on learning from science prose. *Journal of Educational Psychology, 75,* 40–49.

Mayer, R. E. (1987). The elusive search for teachable aspects of problem solving. In J. A. Glover and R. R. Ronning (Eds.), *Historical foundations of educational psychology* (pp. 327–347). New York: Plenum.

Mayer, R. E. (1989). Models for understanding. *Review of Educational Research, 59*(1), 43–64.

Mayer, R. E., & Wittrock, M. C. (1997). Problem-solving transfer. In D. C. Berliner & R. C. Calfee (Eds.), *Educational Psychology Handbook* (pp. 47–62). New York: Macmillan.

Mayer, R. E. & Moreno, R. (2003). Nine ways to reduce cognitive load in multimedia learning. *Educational Psychologist, 38*(1), 43–52.

McFarland, T. D., & Parker, R. (1990). *Expert systems in education and training.* Englewood Cliffs, NJ: Educational Technology Publications.

McNair, M. P. (n.d.). *McNair on cases.* Boston, MA: Harvard Case Services, Harvard Business School.

Merrill, M. D., & ID2 Research Group (1998). ID Expert: a second generation instructional development system. *Instructional Science, 26*(3, 4), 234–262.

Myers, D., & Lamb A. (1992). *HyperCard Authoring Tool* (2nd ed.) Orange, CA: Career Publishing.

Newell, A., & Simon, H. A. (1972). *Human problem solving.* Upper Saddle River, NJ: Prentice-Hall.

Nguyen-Xuan, A., Nicaud, J., & Gelis, J. (1995). An experiment in learning algebra with an intelligent tutoring environment. *Instructional Science, 23,* 25–45.

Njoo, M., & DeJong, T. (1991). Learning processes of students working with a computer simulation in mechanical engineering. In M. Carretero, M. Pope, R. Simons, and J. I. Pozo (Eds.), *Learning and Instruction, Vol. 3* (pp. 483–495). Oxford: Pergamon.

Norman, G. R. (1985). The role of knowledge in teaching and assessment of problem solving. *Journal of Instructional Development, 8*(1), 7–11.

Oliver, D., & Shaver, J. P. (1966). *Teaching public issues in the high school.* Boston: Houghton-Mifflin.

Papert, S. (1980). *Mindstorms: Children, computers, and powerful ideas.* New York: Basic Books.

Perkins, D. N. (1992). What constructivism demands of the learner. In T. M. Duffy & D. H. Jonassen (Eds.), *Constructivism and the technology of instruction* (pp. 161–165). Hillsdale, NJ: Erlbaum.

Perkins, D. N. (April, 1988). *Understanding and expertise: The double helix of mastery.* Paper presented at the annual meeting of the American Educational Research Association, New Orleans, LA.

Pillay, H. K. (1994). Cognitive load and mental rotation: Structuring orthographic projection for learning and problem solving. *Instructional Science, 22,* 91–113.

Polson, M. C., & Richardson, J. J. (1988). *Foundations of intelligent tutoring systems.* Hillsdale, NJ: Erlbaum.

Polson, P. G., & Jeffries, R. (1985). Instruction in general problem-solving skills: An analysis of four approaches. In J. W. Segal, S. F. Chipman, & R. Glaser (Eds.), *Thinking and learning skills, Vol. 1* (pp. 417–455). Hillsdale, NJ: Erlbaum.

Polya, G. (1945). *How to solve it.* Princeton, NJ: Princeton University Press.

Ragan, T. J., & Smith, P. L. (1989). *Programming instructional software.* Englewood Cliffs, NJ: Educational Technology Publications.

Reigeluth, C. M. (1992). Elaborating the elaboration model. *Educational Technology Research and Development, 40*(3), 80–86.

Reigeluth, C. M., & Stein, F. S. (1983). The elaboration theory of instruction. In C. M. Reigeluth (Ed.), *Instructional-design theories and models: An overview of their current status* (pp. 335–381). Hillsdale, NJ: Erlbaum.

Renkl, A., & Atkinson, R. K. (2003). Strucuring the transition from example study to problem solving in cognitive skill acquisition: A cognitive load perspective. *Educational Psychologist, 38*(1), 15–22.

Rieber, L. P. (1996a). Animation as feedback in a computer-based simulation: Representation matters. *Educational Technology Research & Development, 44*(1), 5–22.

Rieber, L. P. (1996b). Seriously considering play: Designing interactive learning environments based on the blending of microworlds, simulations, and games. *Educational Technology Research and Development, 44*(2), 43–58.

Rieber, L. P. (2004). Microworlds. In D. H. Jonassen (Ed.), *Handbook of research for educational communications and technology.* Mahwah, NJ: Erlbaum.

Rieber, L. P., & Kini, A. S. (April, 1993). *The effects of computer simulations on children's inductive learning in science.* Paper presented at the annual meeting of the American Educational Research Association, Atlanta, GA.

Riesbeck, C. (1996). Case-based teaching and constructivism: Carpenters and tools. In B. Wilson (Ed.), *Constructivist learning environments* (pp. 49–64). Englewood Cliffs, NJ: Educational Technology Publications.

Rosati, P. (1985). Experimental use of a computer problem-solving tutorial in engineering statics. *Journal of Educational Technology Systems, 14*(1), 15–21.

Roth, W. (1990). Short-term memory and problem solving in physical science. *School Science and Mathematics, 90*(4), 271–282.

Sanford, M. J. (n.d.). *Case development and teaching notes.* Boston, MA: Harvard Case Services, Harvard Business School.

Savery, J. R., & Duffy, T. M. (1996). Problem-based learning: An instruction model and its constructivist framework. In B. Wilson (Ed.), *Constructivist learning environments* (pp.

135–150). Englewood Cliffs, NJ: Educational Technology Publications.

Schmidt, H. G. (1995). Problem-based learning: An introduction. *Instructional Science, 22,* 247–250.

Schmidt, H., Van der Arend, A., Kokx, I., & Boon, L. (1995). Peer versus staff tutoring in problem-based learning. *Instructional Science, 22,* 279–285.

Schoenfeld, A. H. (1979). Can heuristics be taught? In J. Lockhead & J. Clement (Eds.), *Cognitive process instruction* (pp. 315–338). Philadelphia: Franklin Institute Press.

Schoenfeld, A. H., & Herrmann, D. J. (1982). Problem perception and knowledge structure in expert and novice mathematical problem solvers. *Journal of Experimental Psychology: Learning, Memory, and Cognition, 8,* 484–494.

Schwab, J. J. (1965). *Biological sciences curriculum study, biology teachers' handbook.* New York: Wiley.

Sfondilias, J. S., & Siegel, M. A. (1990). Combining discovery and direct instruction strategies in computer-based teaching of mathematical problem solving. *Journal of Computer-Based Instruction, 17*(4), 130–134.

Shirts, R. G. (1975). Ten "mistakes" commonly made by persons designing educational simulations and games. *SAGSET Journal, 5,* 147–150.

Shulman, L. S. (1992). Toward a pedagogy of cases. In J. H. Shulman (Ed.), *Case methods in teacher education* (pp. 1–30). New York: Teachers College.

Shute, V. J., Torreano, L. A., & Willis, R. E. (2000). DNA: Toward an automated knowledge elicitation and organization tool. In S.P. Lajoie (Ed.), *Computers as cognitive tools, Vol 2.* (pp. 309–335). Mahwah, NJ: Erlbaum

Simon, H. A. (1980). Problem solving and education. In D. T. Tuma & R. Reif (Eds.), *Problem solving and education: Issues in teaching and research* (pp. 81–96). Hillsdale, NJ: Erlbaum.

Simon, H. A., & Chase, W. G. (1973). Skill in chess. *American Scientist, 61,* 394–403.

Spiro, R. J., & Jehng, J. (1990). Cognitive flexibility and hypertext: theory and technology for the nonlinear and multidimensional traversal of complex subject matter. In D. Nix and R. Spiro (Eds.), *Cognition, education and multimedia* (pp. 163–205). Hillsdale, NJ: Erlbaum.

Starfield, A. M., Butala, K. L., England, M. M., & Smith, K. A. (1983). Mastering engineering concepts by building an expert system. *Engineering Education, 74,* 104–107.

Steinberg, E. R., Baskin, A. B., & Matthews, T. D. (1985). Computer-presented organizational memory aids as instruction for solving Pico-formi problems. *Journal of Computer-Based Instruction, 12*(2), 44–49.

Stewart, J., & Hafner, R. (1991). Extending the conception of "problem" in problem-solving research. *Science Education, 75*(1), 105–120.

Stolovitch, H. D., & Keeps, E. J. (Eds.). (1999). *Handbook of human performance technology,* 2nd Edition. San Francisco, CA: Jossey-Bass.

Suchman, J. R. (1962). *The elementary school training program in scientific inquiry.* Report to the U.S. Office of Education, Project Title VII. Urbana, IL: University of Illinois.

Tennyson, R. D. (April, 1988). *Problem-oriented simulations to develop and improve higher-order thinking strategies.* Paper presented at the annual meeting of the American Educational Research Association, New Orleans, LA.

Thomas, R., & Hooper, E. (1991). Simulations: An opportunity we are missing. *Journal of Research on Computing in Education, 23*(4), 497–513.

Towl, A. R. (n.d.). *Case-course development: The case method of learning administration.* Boston, MA: Harvard Case Services, Harvard Business School.

Towne, D. M. (1995). *Learning and instruction in simulation learning environments.* Englewood Cliffs, NJ: Educational Technology Publications.

Trollip, S., & Lippert, R. (1988). Constructing knowledge bases: A promising instructional tool. *Journal of Computer-Based Instruction, 14*(2), 4448.

Trone, D. M. (1995). *Learning and instruction in simulation environments.* Englewood Cliffs, NJ: Educational Technology Publications.

Van Joolingen, W. R., & DeJong, T. (1991). Supporting hypothesis generation by learners exploring an interactive computer simulation. *Instructional Science, 20,* 389–404.

Van Merriënboer, J. J. G., Kirschner, P. A., & Kester, L. (2003). Taking the load of a learner's mind: Instructional design for complex learning. *Educational Psychologist, 38*(1), 5–13.

Voss, J. F., Greene, T. R., Post, T. A., & Penner, P. C. (1983). Problem solving skill in the social sciences. In G. H. Bower (Ed.), *The psychology of learning and motivation: Advances in research and theory, Vol. 17* (pp. 165–213). New York: Academic Press.

Vygotsky, L. S. (1978). *Mind in society: The development of higher psychological processes.* Cambridge, MA: Harvard University Press.

Wager, W. W., Pokinghorne, S., & Powley, R. (1992). Simulations: Selection and development. *Performance Improvement Quarterly, 5*(2), 47–64.

Walcott, C., & Walcott, A. (1976). *Simple simulations: A guide to the design and use of simulations/games in teaching political science.* Washington, DC: American Political Science Association.

Wassermann, S. (1994). *Introduction to case method teaching: A guide to the galaxy.* New York: Teachers College.

Wedman, J. F., & Smith, P. L. (1989). An examination of two approaches to organizing instruction. *International Journal of Instructional Media, 16*(4), 652–660.

Wideman, H. H., & Owston, R. D. (1988). Student development of an expert system: A case study. *Journal of Computer-Based Instruction, 15*(3), 88–94.

Wilkerson, L. (1995). Identification of skills for the problem-based tutor: Student and faculty perspectives. *Instructional Science, 22,* 303–315.

Wilson, B. (Ed.). (1996). *Constructivist learning environments.* Englewood Cliffs, NJ: Educational Technology Publications.

Wilson, B., & Cole, P. (1991). A review of cognitive teaching models. *Educational Technology Research and Development, 39*(4), 47–64.

Winn, W. (1994). Why I don't want to be an expert sitar player. *Educational Technology, 34*(10), 11–13.

Young, M. (2004). An ecological psychology of instructional design: Learning and thinking by perceiving-acting systems. In D. H. Jonassen (Ed.), *Handbook of research on educational communications and technology* (pp. 169–177). Mahwah, NJ: Erlbaum.

STRATEGIES FOR COGNITIVE STRATEGY INSTRUCTION

CHAPTER OBJECTIVES

At the conclusion of this chapter, you should be able to do the following:

- Given a cognitive strategy technique, identify the cognitive process type of which it is an example (organizing strategy, elaborating strategy, rehearsing strategy, or comprehension monitoring strategy).

- Given a cognitive strategy objective, design strategy plans for a cognitive strategy lesson.

A REVIEW OF COGNITIVE STRATEGY LEARNING

As we discussed in Chapter 5, cognitive strategies are those techniques that learners use to control and monitor their own cognitive processes. R. Gagné (1985) has identified two primary kinds of cognitive strategies: those for learning and those for thinking. Cognitive strategies for learning are mental tactics for attending to, organizing, elaborating, manipulating, and retrieving knowledge. Cognitive strategies for thinking are mental tactics that lead to discovery, invention, or creativity.

Cognitive strategies that support learning are sometimes called *learning strategies*. These are the same skills that we have suggested in our expanded instructional events, which instructional designers explicitly plan to prompt or encourage. The cognitive strategies that we call *thinking strategies* are of a different sort than previously discussed in this book. We have described these thinking strategies as "generic problem-solving skills." These general problem-solving skills are a form of thinking strategy that is different from the domain-specific problem solving discussed in Chapter 12. In this chapter, we will discuss the nature of both learning strategies and thinking strategies, and how both learning and thinking strategies may be taught so that they are within a learner's repertoire and available for use. We will give more attention to learning strategies, primarily because they have been more clearly described and their related instructional strategies have proven to be more successful than more general thinking strategies. We will include integration into the expanded instructional events and a sample lesson for learning strategies only.

Learning Strategies

Cognitive strategies may control the processing of information that does not lead to learning (as *learning* was defined in Chapter 2), such as a strategy for recalling a phone number long enough to dial it. However, much cognitive strategy instruction is instruction to support acquisition of learning strategies. Learning strategies are those tactics employed by learners to facilitate the acquisition of knowledge and skills. When learning strategies are employed, the learners guide their own processing, rather than having the processing guided or supplied by the instruction (Davidson, 1988; Derry & Murphy, 1986; Gagné & Driscoll, 1988; Weinstein, 1982). We have suggested that processing strategies can be "built into" the instruction or "built into" the learners. In other words, portions of cognitive processing can be supplanted by the instruction or generated by the learners. Learning situations in which the learner takes the major responsibility for processing are termed *self-regulated learning* (Butler & Winne, 1995; Schunk & Zimmerman, 1994).

The instructional designer must consider a number of factors in determining how much cognitive processing can be supplied by the learner. One of these factors is whether learners possess appropriate strategies. Learning strategies are not often directly taught (Norman, 1980): They are more often discovered by good students. Unfortunately, they are seldom discovered by poorer students (Brown, 1978; Torgesen, 1979). Therefore, it appears that for many learners, direct instruction on cognitive strategies may be beneficial. To date, several studies have indicated that training in cognitive strategy use can be effective (Brown, Campione, & Day, 1981; Dansereau, 1985; Weinstein, Cubberly, Wicker, Underwood, Roney, and Duty, 1981; Weinstein & Mayer, 1986).

Although strategies are by nature cognitively based processes, they are often categorized as cognitive or affective. **Cognitive domain strategies** are used to support information processing; these include selecting information to attend to, promoting the encoding and storage of information, and enhancing retrieval. Weinstein and Mayer (1986) categorized cognitive strategies as organizing strategies, elaborating strategies, rehearsing strategies, and comprehension monitoring strategies. *Organizing* strategies are used to structure information in memory and to store new information in memory within an appropriate structure (e.g., within an appropriate schema). Examples of organizing strategies are techniques such as grouping similar information together, developing graphic organizers, or outlining content. *Elaborating* strategies are used to establish associations between new information and previously acquired knowledge. Tactics such as mental imagery, analogies, the keyword method, paraphrasing, generating personal examples, and generative note taking are examples of elaborating strategies. *Rehearsing* strategies assist in the encoding and retrieval of information that is not easily structured or elaborated. An example of such strategies would be a learner actively reciting or naming items. *Metacognitive* strategies relate to a learner's awareness, monitoring, and regulation of cognitive processes. Evidence strongly suggests that these strategies and their application to improvement of learning can be taught (Haller, Child, & Walberg, 1988). Also known as *comprehension monitoring strategies,* metacognitive strategies help learners determine whether they are understanding or learning. An example of a monitoring strategy would be self-questioning. **Affective domain strategies,** sometimes called *support strategies,* are those self-motivational skills that influence an individual's active engagement in a learning task and maintain a psychological attitude conducive to learning (Dansereau, 1978; McCombs, 1984). Examples of such strategies are time management, stress reduction techniques, and positive self-talk (McCombs, 1984; Weinstein & Underwood, 1985). A promising line of work that includes both cognitive and affective factors, called "Approaches to Learning," has been developed out of extensive research by Miller, Greene and associates (e.g., Greene & Miller, 1996; Greene, DeBacker, Ravindran & Krows, 1999; Miller, Behrens, Greene, & Newman, 1993; Miller, Greene, Montalvo, Ravindran, & Nichols, 1996). In Approaches to Learning, students' goal-setting, self-efficacy, and learning strategy use have been investigated, and ways of facilitating effective learner-instructor interaction are explored.

Instruction in cognitive strategies—especially if it is appropriately "situated" within a continuing discussion of cognition—can enhance the development of metacognition (Brown, Campione, & Day, 1981; Flavell & Wellman, 1977). Metacognition involves students' awareness of their own cognitive processes, their ability to control these processes by selecting among cognitive strategies, and their ability to monitor, evaluate, and revise their strategy use (Brown, 1978; Flavell, 1977; Weinstein & Mayer, 1986).

Learning strategy instruction has been increasingly advocated, particularly for learners in public schools. In addition, even in training environments, such as the military, increasing attention has been given to developing skills in "learning how to learn" (Dansereau, 1985; McCombs, 1981–82). This chapter will consider the most effective instructional strategies for the teaching of learning strategies and promoting their transfer.

Divergent Thinking Strategies

The category of cognitive strategies that we label *thinking strategies* includes techniques and strategies intended to help learners solve problems or generate new ideas, regardless of the domain of application. In many cases, such strategies are directed at assisting in something Bruner (1973) found to be a critical attribute of people who were good at problem solving, something he termed "problem finding." As noted above, this "creative problem solving" or "general problem solving" is quite a different matter from domain-specific problem solving. Whereas domain-specific problem solving involves application of rules from within a subject area to problems within that domain, creative problem solving involves techniques or skills that may be applied to a variety of situations requiring invention. A commonly used framework for creative problem solving is what has been labeled "divergent-production" (Polson & Jeffries, 1985). Approaches to improving thinking skills that employ this paradigm focus on divergent thinking and the generation of many possible hypotheses. These approaches usually employ the general problem-solving heuristics developed by Polya (1957).

A variety of thinking strategies have been proposed and studied. Stein (1974) describes various individual proce-

dures: techniques used to exert influence from a personality standpoint, including role-playing, hypnosis, and psychotherapy; techniques used to assist hypothesis formation, such as Osborne's "brainstorming," Zwicky's "morphological analysis," and Crawford's "attribute listing"; techniques of forced relationships; Taylor's nine-step "PakSA" technique; General Electric's Input-Output technique; and miscellaneous techniques such as "use of the ridiculous," "modification," and "fresh eye." Group procedures for stimulating creativity include brainstorming; Parnes's Creative Problem-Solving; Gordon's Synectics; and Crutchfield et al.'s "Productive Thinking Program." The four primary divergent-production problem-solving strategies identified by Polson and Jeffries (1985) are Crutchfield et al.'s "Productive Thinking Program"; deBono's "CoRT Thinking Lessons"; Rubenstein's "Patterns of Problem Solving"; and Wickelgren's "How to Solve Problems." Techniques from the information-processing perspective, also as identified by Polson and Jeffries, include work by a variety of researchers on search strategies such as the "generate and test" strategy and "means-ends analysis." They also include techniques involving both understanding and search, such as "planning by abstraction," "decomposition," and various techniques for acquiring of problem-solving skills through enhancing one's awareness of self as a problem solver.

One serious limitation of much of the work in thinking strategies (particularly work from the divergent-production perspective) is a lack of sufficient attention to the need for knowledge in the area or topic in which the learner is to become creative or to which area general problem-solving skills will be applied. Successful inventors, musical composers, architects, artists, and good problem solvers in business and industry all tend to be very knowledgeable in the area in which they are working. Domain-independent thinking strategies tend to grossly underemphasize the need for expertise in the domain to which the strategies are to be applied. Stein (1974) noted some elements of divergent thinking for which no technique appears to exist in the creative problem-solving literature: inspiration, intuition, and selecting the "good possibility." In describing the lack of direct investigation on inspiration, Stein stated that "It might be said that to achieve a state of inspiration an individual would have to prepare himself intensively in his field and devote himself sincerely to the work he has undertaken" (p. 202). Similar statements can be made of how individuals come to possess the talent for making shrewd guesses, proposing good hypotheses, and selecting the best possibilities from among a variety of hypotheses. It is interesting to note that Newell (1980), in discussing the importance of search strategies in problem solving, classifies the two "general" search strategies previously noted (generate and test; means-ends analysis) as "weak methods." Newell wrote that their weakness derives from their generality—trading the power of a domain-specific search for the generality of an approach that can be used across many tasks. This may be a good characterization of thinking strategy instruction and its role in instructional design. Approaches to assisting learners' creative problem-solving skills that claim great power and at the same time neglect the importance of knowledge in the area of application should be viewed with extreme caution.

Within the domain of instructional technology, Bruce (1989) studied the relationship between use of technology in education and creativity. He concluded that use of technology, in and of itself, neither encouraged nor inhibited creativity, but that certain uses of technology can enhance creativity. An interesting comment on creativity in instructional design was provided by Dick (1995), who wrote that particular conditions surrounding the design process—such as client criteria for products, work climate, participatory design environments that include not only designers and subject matter experts but also students, and technology use in implementation—all influence the creativity of designers and their products more than design models or even philosophies held by members of the design team.

An Example of a Thinking Strategy Instruction Model

The Synectics approach, developed by Gordon (1961), was selected by Joyce and Weil (1986) as a model for teaching creativity and is an instructional strategy for promoting divergent thinking strategies. The Synectics approach emphasizes the use of metaphoric thinking, primarily through generation of analogies. Joyce and Weil presented one strategy derived from Synectics that involves six phases, directed toward helping learners generate new ideas, or new ways of looking at a familiar concept:

1. The first step is description of the present condition; that is, clarifying the task at hand. This phase is generally initiated and directed by a teacher, with student involvement.
2. The second phase is generation of direct analogies. In this phase, students are stimulated to generate analogies that relate to the problem, select one analogy, and explore that analogy further.
3. In the third phase, students generate personal analogies. Students are assisted in translating the direct analogy into a personalized form—they "become" the analogy selected in the first phase.
4. In phase four, students engage in what is described as "compressed conflict," which involves generating two-word descriptions of an object that contradict; that is, oxymorons. Examples include "dark brightness" and "prideful modesty." Joyce and Weil (1986) cite two from Gordon:

"life-saving destroyer" and "nourishing flame." Compressed conflicts used in this process are to be taken from analogies generated in phases three and four. Students are directed to select one compressed conflict from the set created.
5. The fifth phase involves developing of another direct analogy, but this time it must come from the compressed conflict selected in phase four.
6. Phase six reexamines of the original task in light of the last analogy developed or helpful products from any of the previous phases.

The Synectics model can add richness and variety to students' thinking about a topic. Used by a skillful teacher, it can stimulate new ideas about a familiar topic, increasing the quality of thinking and helping cut through stereotypes and clichés.

COGNITIVE REQUIREMENTS OF COGNITIVE STRATEGY LEARNING

An information-processing analysis of the procedure that is involved in applying a cognitive strategy clarifies the requirements of the learning task. This analysis was developed from an extensive review of literature and identifies the overarching cognitive processes involved in applying a cognitive strategy:

1. Analyze the requirements of the learning task.
2. Analyze one's ability to complete the task, including the predictable demands on and limitations of memory.
3. Select an appropriate strategy.
4. Apply the selected strategy.
5. Evaluate the effectiveness of the strategy used.
6. Revise as required.

This overarching process, which is mentally employed by the learner, strongly resembles the information-processing analysis of traditional problem solving. Selection, application, and evaluation of a cognitive strategy is indeed very similar to problem solving. However, cognitive strategies tend to be applicable across a variety of domains of content, rather than domain specific. Step 4 in this process is the application of a procedural rule, which varies depending on the specific cognitive strategy. The learner's analysis of the task and her own ability to cope with the task, the selection of an appropriate strategy, the evaluation of the success of the strategy use, and the revision of the process depending upon this evaluation are all metacognitive skills that must be learned along with the ability to apply a particular cognitive strategy. Learners' evaluation of strategy use and revision based on feedback is reviewed in Butler and Winne (1995).

Pressley, Snyder, and Cargilia-Bull (1987) reviewed the learning strategies literature and categorized six alternative approaches to strategy instruction. We have added the seventh approach:

1. *Discovery and guided discovery.* Typically, the discovery approach is the way most students learn cognitive strategies, as formal instruction in strategies is not common. The guided discovery approach involves a more direct instructional technique, in which the instructor, through questioning, leads the learner to discover a particular strategy.

2. *Observation.* Observation of a model demonstrating the use of a cognitive strategy is a technique suggested by social learning theory (Bandura, 1977). According to Pressley et al., the delivery system for an observation strategy might involve cooperative application of cognitive strategies with paired learners, expert demonstration by a teacher, or symbolic modeling by a fictional character, which is presented visually or textually.

3. *Guided participation.* Guided participation depends heavily upon a teacher who guides students through the use of a strategic procedure in day-to-day school tasks. As tasks are encountered, the learners and teacher together determine the characteristics of a learning task, identify strategies to facilitate the learning task, and determine effective ways to employ the strategy. This type of activity normally does not involve direct instruction regarding the strategy.

4. *Strategy instruction in books and courses.* This category describes "prepackaged" instruction on strategies (some of which were noted earlier in our discussion of thinking strategies), such as de Bono's (1983) CoRT thinking skills program, Feuerstein et al's Instrumental Enrichment Programme (1980), Higbee's (1977) text on cognitive skills, and Covington et al.'s (1974) Productive Thinking Program. Pressley et al. suggested that one disadvantage of this approach is that it may lack practice in applying the strategies to the types of materials that the learners encounter in their school tasks and may, consequently, fail to promote transfer to the very contexts in which the strategies must be applied.

5. *Direct explanation, largely teacher directed.* This type of instruction not only teaches learners the procedure of the strategy but also provides them with information on when and where the strategy should be applied. Direct instruction includes "concrete examples, modeling, and practice" (Pressley et al., p. 97).

6. *Dyadic instruction.* Dyadic instruction involves a one-to-one interaction between the learner and a knowledgeable adult. The adult demonstrates strategy application, making thought processes as obvious as possible to the learner, perhaps through think-aloud procedures. The technique also involves the learner reciprocating by demonstrating the strategy to the adult, and the adult providing advice and supervision of this strategy application.

7. *Self-instructional training.* Although not described by Pressley et al., Meichenbaum's (1977) self-instructional training is clearly an approach to teaching cognitive strategies. The approach includes (in addition to self-instruction) active interactions with a teacher who may also model strategy use and provide feedback to the learners. A critical part of the approach (and the characteristic that makes it "self instructional") is the encouragement of learners to engage in private speech, perhaps initially overtly, and later covertly. Another self-instructional training approach is described by Puntambekar (1995), who reported development and use of a computer-based ITS (intelligent tutoring system) for metacognition to improve learning from text.

Although Pressley et. al. detailed advantages of these instructional techniques, they suggested that direct explanation may be the most successful and the most applicable in classroom situations. This position is supported by many, including Weinstein (1978), who found that students who received explicit training in strategy use outperformed students who were informed that a use of a particular strategy would be helpful.

Analysis of these seven instructional strategies reveals that they vary in their relationship to instruction on content-related objectives (Rigney, 1980). Certain strategies may be characterized as "embedded," in which instruction on the technique in question is part of (or embedded within) instruction on content-related objectives. For example, strategy 3, "Guided participation," would always be employed within the context of a lesson on some particular topic. Other strategies may be characterized as "detached," in that instruction on the learning strategy stands alone—it is the topic at hand. An example of a detached technique is 4, "Strategy instruction in books and courses."

Each approach (embedded or detached) has general advantages and disadvantages. Embedded training can be superior to detached training in transfer to real-life tasks (Resnick, 1987). In addition, strategies taught in an embedded setting, such as problem solving taught in science courses, can be applied across domains, something more likely to occur given explicit instruction and practice in application to other domains (Niaz, 1995). On the other hand, the embedded training may suffer from insufficient attention to the learning strategy caused by pursuing it at the same time as content objectives. Detached training may provide more time and emphasis on learning the strategy itself but may not be as readily transferred to real application. Here we will approach cognitive strategies as "detached" strategies; however, the same techniques that we are teaching can be used in an "embedded" approach. The extended example for Chapter 12 includes an application of embedded cognitive strategies, in which instruction on a "networking" strategy—which helps learners make use of previously learned concepts and rules—is provided within the problem-solving lesson.

In the final analysis, instruction that is designed to involve both embedded and detached approaches may be ideal (Derry & Murphy, 1986). Initial learning may best be acquired through a direct approach. As learners acquire the fundamentals of a learning strategy, their application can be encouraged and prompted in content instruction. Over a period of time, prompting of applications can be faded to the point where learners determine to use the strategy when needed. Such an approach is completely consistent with instruction in cognitive strategies as suggested here. Using strategies in lessons directed at achievement of other objectives, as in the expanded instructional events throughout this text, is consistent with the idea of embedded strategy learning.

Davidson and Smith (1990) found in the recommendations of many scholars seven specific events that are recommended for instruction in a cognitive strategy (Deshler, Alley, Warner, & Schumaker, 1981; E. Gagné, 1985; Meichenbaum, 1977; Pressley, Snyder, & Cargilia-Bull, 1987; Weinstein, 1981). Those events are the following:

- Specific identification of the utility of the strategy—when and where to use it.
- Overview of the specific steps in the strategy.
- Demonstration or modeling of the strategy.
- Examples and nonexamples of application of the strategy.
- Practice using the strategy across a wide variety of appropriate situations with graduated difficulty of situations requiring the strategy.
- Corrective feedback.
- Explicit encouragement to transfer the strategy to appropriate contexts.

These critical attributes of successful instruction in cognitive strategies highlight the more detailed treatment of instructional events that follows.

EVENTS OF INSTRUCTION FOR TEACHING COGNITIVE STRATEGIES

The learning of cognitive strategies an interplay that may be best supplied through the rapid and complex analysis and processing that is available through a live teacher. It is quite possible, however, that many instructor demonstrations might be videotaped in order to obtain a practiced and replicable model.

INTRODUCTION

Deploy Attention/Establish Instructional Purpose/Arouse Interest and Motivation

One way to begin instruction on a specific strategy is to give learners a task that requires use of the particular strategy and then ask them to complete it. In doing so, the learners demonstrate their prior knowledge of the requirements of the task and particular strategies that they currently have available, enabling the teacher/ trainer to diagnose the learners' level of knowledge and skill and build upon that knowledge and skill. A discussion of the utility and efficiency of the strategies that the learners used can lead into a statement of the purpose of the current lesson—to learn a particular strategy that can be applied effectively to a certain category of tasks. The active involvement of the learners at this point and the attention to relevancy of the task should activate the learners' attention to the lesson. If there is a clear mismatch between learners' current approach and the requirements of the task, learners may choose to change their tactics and learn to employ the new strategy.

To arouse motivation, the specific strategy being learned should be discussed within the context of metacognition and executive processes. This discussion can include the importance, effectiveness, and efficiency of active, purposeful learning. Pressley, Borkowski, and Schneider (1987) suggest that the introductory message include the points that good strategy users know that many strategies can be used and that all are useful in attaining specific goals, and that they are aware that good performance is tied with effort. In particular, with regard to effort, learners should know (and perhaps believe) the following: "(1) personal effort often increases the likelihood of success; (2) although effort per se is important, effort channeled into strategic activity is better than working hard; (3) specific strategies are not tied to one task but can be matched to new situations; and (4) if strategic actions and plans are to be successful, they should be shielded from competing behaviors, distractions, and emotions" (pp. 1, 25–28).

Preview Lesson

The steps in the cognitive strategy can now be overviewed and a model can demonstrate the use of the strategy for a straightforward situation appropriate for the strategy. The model might be the teacher/ trainer, a knowledgeable student, or a fictitious student presented in a video. The model can follow a think-aloud procedure that explicitly points out the critical features of the strategy, including which aspect of the learning task cued the use of this particular strategy. This presentation allows the learners to gain a perspective as to what is meant by the strategy; explicitly, what the steps to the strategy procedure are, and how the various steps fit together.

Body

Review Relevant Prior Knowledge

If other strategies have been taught or if other strategies that include similar steps are already in the learners' repertoire, then these strategies may be contrasted with the new strategy. Later, such a comparison may also be made on the utility of the strategy as compared to other strategies.

Process Information and Examples/Focus Attention

The next information to be presented to the learners is when and where the strategy can be appropriately applied. First, the instructor can provide an explicit description of the learning tasks to which this strategy is applicable. Then, the instructor can present the learners with situations that are appropriate for the strategy, asking them to point out what characteristics of the situation suggest the strategy. To promote transfer, these examples should vary on as many noncriterial attributes as possible, including content, task type, time length of task, and context of task. Next, the instructor can give the learners examples in which the strategy is inappropriate. These nonexamples should be as "matched" on noncriterial attributes (such as content) as possible. (Notice that recognizing the context appropriate to a particular cognitive strategy is a concept performance, sometimes termed *pattern recognition task*. The instructional strategy for learning to determine when a particular cognitive strategy should be used is similar to the instructional strategy for teaching concepts identified in Chapter 9.)

The instructor may ask learners to point out why certain situations are inappropriate for the application of the strategy, as the instructor confirms and corrects their comments. The learners can be asked to supply example situations in which the strategy is appropriate and situations in which it is inappropriate. The instructor, in collaboration with the other learners, may provide feedback and correction as to the appropriateness of the examples that are presented.

Employ Learning Strategies

This new strategy may be contrasted with other strategies that have been taught or already exist in the learners' repertoire. Other strategies that may have similar application may be compared as to their efficiency or effectiveness and the purpose of the instructional task or other aspects that may make the new strategy superior to other strategies.

Practice/Evaluate Feedback

Learners can now be provided with example situations in which they specify whether or not the new strategy is appropriate. They should be encouraged to substantiate their answers based on the requirements of the learning task and the utility of the strategy. If learners have learned related strategies or have other strategies in their repertoire, they should be encouraged to explain why this strategy may be superior to others as they identify a strategy as appropriate to the situation. As with other pattern recognition practice, some of the instances should be very easy and obvious, while others should involve fine discriminations in order to determine that the learners are neither undergeneralizing nor overgeneralizing the utility of the strategy. The instructor should give feedback that not only informs the learners of the correctness of their responses but also provides information as to why a particular response is correct or incorrect. The instructor might also provide the learners with a video of an age-appropriate student applying the strategy in a particular context. The learners might be asked to appraise whether the student is appropriately applying the strategy and be asked to explain their answers.

Process Information/Focus Attention

The sequence of instruction that is followed next depends upon the complexity of the cognitive strategy being taught. If the strategy is complex, involves many steps, or involves many decision points with alternate steps that depend on the decision, then a part-whole technique for presentation and practice would be appropriate. If the strategy steps are few, with few decision points, then the strategy may be presented and practiced in its whole from the outset.

The instructor (or another model) can again demonstrate a part of a complex strategy or the entire simple strategy. In this demonstration, the instructor can use a think-aloud procedure that emphasizes the cognitive processes required of the strategy. In addition, he should demonstrate the steps in the metacognition relating to this strategy: The instructor should think-aloud the analysis of the requirements of the task, the selection of this strategy as appropriate to the task, the application of the strategy, the evaluation of the strategy in terms of its effectiveness, and any "fix-up" techniques involved in revising the strategy use.

Employ Learning Strategies

The instructor may find a self-questioning pattern appropriate to represent this metacognitive processing, particularly monitoring success of the strategy (e.g., "What is it that I'm supposed to do with this task? Have I fulfilled the requirements of the learning task?").

Practice/Evaluate Feedback

The learners now should be given the opportunity to practice applying the strategy (or the part of the strategy). This practice may be supported with a checklist or flowchart that reminds the learner of the steps to follow. This practice may involve reciprocal teaching in which learners are paired. One learner can demonstrate the strategy with its accompanying metacognition in a think-aloud mode, while the second learner plays the role of a coach-evaluator, using a checklist as a guide. Then the roles can be reversed.

The materials for the learning task in this second practice should be reduced to simple, straightforward, and short situations to which the strategy is clearly applicable. After the learners have each had an opportunity to practice, the instructor may provide group feedback (through demonstration), learner demonstration, or attention to specific aspects of the strategy with which the learners displayed difficulties. This feedback may involve reviewing any artifacts of the strategy (such as notes) as good and poor models of the outcomes of strategy application. The instructor can encourage the learners to contribute their observations acquired during the dyad practice to this feedback.

Process Information/Focus Attention/Employ Learning Strategies

If the strategy is complex and was broken up into a part-whole presentation, the instructor should present the next part of the strategy following steps previously described through each of the individual parts, and then through the entire strategy. Following this complete part-whole presentation or instruction on the entire simple strategy, the next presentation of information should be an instructor's (or other model's) think-aloud demonstration of the strategy with more complex and naturalistic tasks and materials. There should also be a presentation with tasks and materials that do not require the strategy at all. The entire metacognitive sequence, from assessing the task to evaluating the success of the strategy use and "fix-up" techniques, should be shown in these demonstrations.

Practice/Evaluate Feedback

Here, perhaps in dyads again, the learners should be provided the opportunity to practice the strategy on more naturalistic, complex materials across a variety of contents and tasks. The practice should also in-clude some tasks to which the newly acquired strategy is not applicable in order for the learners to practice this decision point in the metacognitive process. This practice may extend across several days, or even weeks, depending upon the scope of the application of the strategy, the time each application takes, the amount of interchange among dyads, and the complexity of the feedback. After each application, there should be opportunity for feedback and discussion of the strategy.

Conclusion

Summarize and Review/Transfer Knowledge

This event is perhaps the most critical to the development of the executive control and metacognition processes. This event can extend over many months or even years. As learners acquire other learning strategies and the contexts in which they should be used, the learners should be encouraged to consider whether previously learned strategies are viable alternatives to the newly learned strategy, or whether the new strategy is useful in learning situations that are unique.

In addition, the instructor may move the newly learned strategy from a detached strategy to an embedded strategy by prompting or the use of the checklist or flowchart detailing the strategy. All instructors that interact with the learners, whether they explicitly teach the strategy or not, should be skilled in the strategies being taught and aware of the schedule upon which the strategies are taught so that they can explicitly and consciously prompt the learners to employ the strategies appropriately. The instruction should explicitly review how the learners may monitor and evaluate the effectiveness of the strategy use. It should suggest modifications of the strategy that may be appropriate when the strategy does not seem to be effective. Gradually, the instructor and external prompts should be "faded" so that the learners are depending upon their own cognitive processes to evoke and employ the strategy. When there is evidence that the learners are not using the appropriate strategies, the strategy should again be "detached" and reviewed. This event should be done carefully and conscientiously, even to the point of being organized into a curricular scope and sequence. This event is critical to the success of strategy and metacognitive development.

Assess Performance/Feedback/Remediation

The ideal assessment of the learners' ability to apply the strategy would be individual assessments of the learners' think-aloud protocols by the instructor or other skilled strategy users. However, realistically, the use of the strategy may require assessment at a less direct level of evaluation, such as evaluation of the concrete artifacts of the strategy use or learners' evaluation and suggestions for a videotape of a learner applying the strategy. This assessment should be ongoing and may be included in the teaching of subsequent strategies (by including the strategy and tasks to which it is appropriate as the nonexamples for the new strategies). Feedback might include whether the strategy was applied to appropriate learning tasks, whether the strategy was applied correctly, and whether appropriate monitoring of strategy use and adaptation to problems was used.

EXAMPLE COGNITIVE STRATEGY LESSON: NOTE-TAKING

The following example of strategy instruction was developed to teach a note-taking technique involving the use of graphic organizers for typical text structures found in expository prose (e.g., chronology, cause-effect, problem-solution). Intended for high school students, the instruction is to be used in content area classes such as English or social studies. Although it is especially beneficial for low-ability students, we have found that average and above-average students also feel that this note-taking strategy facilitates comprehension and retention of content area reading materials. Prior to this instruction, the students have already learned to recognize the major types of text structure and their graphic representations; students are now learning the strategy that employs these structures. The instructional procedure involves the following processes.

Deploy Attention/Establish Instructional Purpose/Arouse Interest and Motivation

The instructor assigns a naturalistic reading assignment. Students are asked to read and study the assigned section as they normally would. After students have completed the assignment, the teacher leads a discussion of the techniques that they employed and the relative success or lack of success of the strategies. The objective of the lesson—learning a note-taking strategy—is presented.

The teacher and students discuss the purposes for taking notes. Students are encouraged to discuss note-taking tech-niques and problems that they have in taking notes. The teacher points out that many students have difficulties taking notes, such as trouble in deciding what to include or trouble in organizing notes. Students are told that they will be learning a strategy that may help them when taking notes.

The teacher points out to the learners that students frequently think that merely trying hard will lead to success. The instructor emphasizes that effort does promote success, but that success in learning also requires the use of appropriate strategies.

Body

Review Relevant Prior Knowledge

The teacher reviews the content structures and their graphic representations that students learned to recognize in prior lessons: time-order, comparison-contrast, problem-solution, problem-solution-results, cause-effect, description, and definition-example.

Process Information and Examples/Focus Attention/Employ Learning Strategies

The teacher points out that the strategy of read-think-aloud is appropriate for expository reading assignments. (The instructor should review the concept "expository" with examples as required.) The teacher also points out that this strategy is most appropriate when the learning task is to "understand" main ideas and interrelationships of ideas, rather than to recall isolated facts. She then discusses the utility of this strategy for taking notes over written passages and well-organized and overviewed lectures. The instructor tells students that this strategy can be used for recopying less-structured lecture notes and emphasizes that this strategy requires time. She compares this strategy to the known strategy of note taking—outlining—and discusses the types of assignments and purposes for which the new strategy and the outlining strategy are each appropriate.

The learners view a video in which a model (a student approximately their age) demonstrates the use of the entire note-taking strategy, thinking aloud all the cognitive steps in the strategy, including determining that this particular strategy is appropriate to the task. The steps in the strategy are listed and displayed for later reference:

1. Determine that the task requires fitting ideas together and understanding the whole, rather than the recall of isolated facts.

2. Determine that the passage is expository.

3. Skim the passage to determine its overarching structure.

4. Represent this structure in a graphic on the notes page and fill in the main ideas for this structure.

5. Read the passage carefully, determining the underlying structures, representing these structures graphically, and filling in key words to explain these ideas.

6. Check comprehension of how ideas in the passage relate to one another.

7. If comprehension is spotty, scan back through the passage to find key connecting ideas, and then repair notes.

Practice/Evaluate Feedback

The teacher provides learners with example passages in which students must determine whether the strategy is appropriate to use. They should substantiate their answers by stating whether recall and understanding of main ideas or individual details are required. The teacher provides feedback on the correctness of students' responses; if errors occur, she provides an explanation of appropriateness.

Process Information and Examples/Focus Attention/Employ Learning Strategies

The learners view a videotape of a student using an explicitly structured passage from a content area textbook, approximately five to ten paragraphs in length. The student models the note-taking strategy using a read–think-aloud procedure (Flower & Hayes, 1981). The student states a purpose for reading the passage, scans the passage, and comments upon the overarching structure when it becomes evident. Then the student uses the structure to predict subsequent content and rectify misconceptions within predictions as he encounters new information. The student continuously scans back and forward to check on ideas that support the structure. After reading in this manner, the student in the videotape creates a structure-based graphic organizer, filling in main ideas and detail information, fleshing out the graphic summary by referring back to the text, and adding pictorial cues to represent main idea or important detail information. When filling in the organizer, where possible, he paraphrases rather than using verbatim wording from the text.

Practice

Evaluate Feedback

The teacher provides learners with one explicitly structured and one implicitly structured three- to five-paragraph expository passage. They are then asked to break up into pairs and practice the note-taking strategy using the read–think-aloud procedure, starting with the explicitly cued passage. One student in each pair should read the passage aloud and take notes, describing his mental processes orally. The other student should provide feedback and encouragement. Then students should switch roles and work with the implicitly cued passage.

Process Information/Focus Attention/Employ Learning Strategies

The instructor introduces a chapter-long segment of expository material that has explicitly cued, clear combinations of structures. It may be necessary to revise existing materials to have

such a clear-cut example for this learning experience. The instructor can model the note-taking strategy using the read–think-aloud technique, underlining or creating marginal notes to highlight the structure. This process should generate a graphic organizer that embodies the combinations of structures included in the chapter. The instructor can point out that there is no single correct form of organizer but that the organizer that is developed should present the top-level structure as well as the other structures used in the passage.

Practice/Evaluate Feedback

The instructor provides students with chapter-length, explicitly cued, and clearly structured expository material that they have not encountered previously. In pairs, they use the note-taking strategy to generate a graphic organizer. The instructor collects and reviews structured notes that the learners produced. The instructor can choose two or three sets of notes to discuss and evaluate in a subsequent lesson. In the discussion, the instructor provides feedback on the selection of structures, layout on page, selection of main ideas, and details included on the organizer. Next, the learners complete a similar activity independently.

Conclusion
Summarize and Review

The learners review the steps involved in applying the strategy. The emphasis is on understanding the strategy rather than memorizing verbatim the steps in the strategy. Learners explain how each step leads naturally into the next. The learners should also review the occasions for which the strategy is appropriate and how to monitor the effectiveness of the strategy.

Transfer Learning

One way to promote transfer is for the instructor (or another model) to demonstrate the read–think-aloud procedure using the note-taking strategy with implicitly structured and poorly organized materials. In this demonstration, learners are presented with alternative structures that might be used in creating graphic organizers, and they discuss how selection of alternate structures yields emphasis on different points. Then the learners can practice the note-taking strategy with implicitly organized and poorly organized chapter-length materials.

Another way to promote retention is to discuss how the level of detail of the content in the notes and the amount of elaboration within notes may vary depending upon the purpose for reading. The instructor can present two sets of structured notes created over a chapter that students read earlier. One set should include a high level of detail and be verbatim from the text, reflecting the type of notes suitable when students are preparing for an exam composed of multiple-choice and short-answer types of questions. The second set should show an emphasis on main ideas and the integration of information with prior knowledge (such as a comparison-contrast structure, comparing new information in the text to information obtained in other sources). The second set of notes would be more appropriate for preparation for class discussions and essay-type exams.

Remotivate and Close

The lesson concludes with a restatement of why the strategy is important and an emphasis on the significance of both effort and selecting the appropriate strategies in learning.

Assess Learning

The teacher prepares a test situation in which the students are to use the read-think-aloud procedure. Chapter-length expository material most appropriately evaluates their ability to transfer the strategy to natural settings. This time students are asked to complete the task using the strategy on an individual basis. The notes are collected and reviewed for accuracy. The assessment may also include observation as to how students are performing. If appropriate, this strategy could be tested using videotaped or audiotaped sessions.

IMPEDIMENTS TO STRATEGY USE

Throughout the chapters on instructional strategies, we have included in our expanded instructional events learning strategies that are appropriate for learners to employ while engaged in a lesson for a particular kind of learning outcome. Within a lesson, learners may be prompted with a greater or lesser degree of directness to employ these strategies. Research suggests that many learners do not employ cognitive strategies spontaneously; there are factors that inhibit the use of strategies:

1. *Low skill in strategy use.* Remember that instruction on cognitive strategies must be provided; most learners do not "discover" the most effective strategies, and most do not induce metacognitive information regarding the application of the strategy. For example, one of the greatest problems in strategy application is transfer. Learners tend to have difficulty in recognizing similarities between a current situation and situations in which a strategy was learned. Consequently, when confronted with a new learning task, they may have an appropriate strategy in their repertoire but they may not recognize its usefulness. Direct instruction and practice help in identifying critical characteristics of a learning task that suggest a particular learning strategy. If an instructor pays attention to this aspect of strategy training, transfer should be enhanced.

2. *Low motivation.* Although strategy use can become automatic, it generally requires the learner's conscious, willful effort. Employment of strategies is a very private matter. It often presents no observable evidence of activity. Therefore, strategy use may not be subject to social reinforcement by teachers or fellow students. There must be high internal motivation to achieve the learning task in order for learners to engage in what they may perceive as the "extra" effort of applying strategies. To encourage such motivation, designers should consider employing tactics that encourage attention, relevancy, confidence, and satisfaction.

3. *Learners' feelings of self-efficacy are low, and attributions of success are external.* For learners to use cognitive strategies, they must believe that the additional effort they expend in using the strategy will pay off. This factor is closely related to motivation, but is sufficiently important and distinct for us to mention it separately. If learners tend to perceive themselves as poor learners, and/or if they ascribe extreme success or failure in learning to factors external to themselves (external locus of control), then they may tend to believe that the effort required for cognitive strategy use is pointless. Learners who employ strategies tend to be more successful and, consequently, tend to acquire greater self-esteem. They also tend to become more internal regarding their learning attributions. Learners who are impeded by feelings of low self-efficacy or external attributions may need more prompting to employ strategies. They may also benefit from more explicit and overt reward systems. They should be encouraged to note the causative relationship between their use of strategies and their success with a learning task. A classroom situation should encourage learners to externalize their cognitions and provide social reinforcement for cognitions that employ appropriate strategies; this will promote strategy use by learners with feelings of low self-efficacy or external attributions.

4. *Learners' lack of awareness of their own memory and processing characteristics.* Learners must be sufficiently aware of their own cognitive capabilities to determine when strategy use will be needed. They must be able to reflect on their own cognitions and predict when a learning task or learning context will require the additional support of a strategy. They must be able to monitor their own learning and determine when strategic behavior must be employed. This type of metacognitive knowledge takes time, both in terms of purposeful instructional attention to it (such as with a teacher modeling prediction and monitoring) and in terms of the years of experience and practice required to become learners who are aware of their own metacognition.

5. *Lack of knowledge of task characteristics.* For learners to assess the match between (1) their memory and processing characteristics, and (2) the learning task, they must be aware of the learning task, and they must be able to assess the cognitive demands of the learning task. If learners are uninformed as to what they are to learn and to what degree or depth they must learn, they will have difficulty in ascertaining whether strategies must be engaged and which strategies are appropriate. In addition to having a knowledge of instructional goals, learners must be able to analyze a goal in terms of its cognitive demands. In our chapters on each of the types of learning outcomes, we have outlined what appears to be the required cognitions, and we have related them to the characteristics of the instructional strategy. In a similar, although perhaps simplified fashion, as part of describing the learning task, the instruction may suggest the type and depth of cognitive activity that is required for successful acquisition of the learning goal.

6. *Devoting/allocating insufficient time.* The dual-level processing that is required in order to employ strategies and process new content may take more time than more superficial processing of content. (Of course, this time-on-task variable is often a confounding factor in studies on the efficacy of cognitive strategies.) Learners must have enough time to engage strategies and reflect on their cognitions. The newer the strategy is for learners, the more time that must be allocated to a lesson in which they will be encouraged to use it. This demand for time often leads designers, particularly in training situations, toward supplanting more of the processing in order to proceed through the instruction more rapidly. Of course, this supplantation can lead to more superficial processing and ultimately, less learning.

7. *Insufficient content knowledge.* To make sense out of the learning task and thereby determine the cognitive demands of the task and the consequent appropriate strategies, the learners must have some prior content knowledge. In addition, the more foreign the content is, the more cognitive capacity that must be allocated to comprehending the instruction; this also means that there will be less available capacity for employing the strategy. Therefore, in initial contacts with new content, if the designer expects the learners to engage cognitive strategies, then he must set aside much additional time and support for the instruction. The designer might also plan more supplantive instruction as learners are encountering initial concepts and principles, and more generative instruction later, capitalizing on cognitive strategies that have been learned.

When analyzing the task, the learners, and the context during the process of designing the instructional strategy, the designer should carefully examine whether any of these inhibiting factors is present. If these factors are present, the designer may devise a method to ameliorate them or may either facilitate the use of the strategies with more direct prompting or supplant the particular processing with more complete and direct instruction.

ASSESSMENT OF COGNITIVE STRATEGY LEARNING

Although an example assessment earlier provided application of events of instruction, we need to take a more detailed look at assessment for instruction leading to this type of learning. In practice, cognitive strategies are not often assessed, because they are rarely explicitly taught. However, should they be taught (a practice we strongly encourage), their assessment can very closely resemble the assessment of problem-solving objectives. As you may recall from Chapter 5, application of a cognitive strategy requires the following steps: analysis of the requirements of the learning task, selection of an appropriate strategy, application of the selected strategy, monitoring and evaluation of the effectiveness of strategy use, and revision of strategy use as required. Each one of these steps or the total use of the strategy may be assessed. A designer might assess whether the learners can perform each of the individual steps by giving them a task and then prompting them to perform each step. For example, learners who have been taught a strategy for studying prose materials might be given the following problem:

The attached chapter from a geography text describes the topography, culture, economy, and politics of Peru, comparing it to Brazil, which you read about in the previous chapter. The test that you are preparing for will ask you general questions about major characteristics of Peru and how it compares to Brazil, as well as specific factual questions about the topography, culture, economy, and politics of Peru. Answer the following questions based upon the "structured notes" strategy that you have learned in the past weeks.

1. What is the reading task?
2. Why is the structured notes strategy appropriate?
3. What overall text structure is used in the chapter? What are the clues to this structure?
4. What other text structures are used in the text?
5. Outline the chapter using structured notes. Which parts of this information should you review most carefully?

Although this assessment evaluates whether the learner can perform each step of a strategy when prompted, it does not evaluate the learners' ability to select from all the strategies that have been learned the one that is most appropriate, or to perform the strategy when not prompted. A designer can develop such an assessment in either recognition or constructed answer formats. For example, learners who have been taught several cognitive strategies for dealing with prose may be given the following recognition item:

1. Jane was given the attached history chapter to study for a unit exam. The teacher has told Jane's class that they must remember the main ideas from the chapter and how these ideas relate together, but they do not need to recall all the dates and facts in the chapter. Here is a copy of Jane's

notes and a videotape of Jane studying. Has she selected the appropriate study strategy? Is she applying it correctly? Circle the correct answer:

a. Jane has selected the appropriate strategy, but she is not applying it correctly.

b. Jane has selected the appropriate strategy, and she is applying it correctly.

c. Jane has not selected the appropriate strategy, but she is applying her selected strategy correctly.

d. Jane has not selected the appropriate strategy, and she is applying her selected strategy incorrectly.

Note that this item could be adjusted to become a combination of recognition and constructed response by asking the learners to explain their answers or to suggest an alternate strategy to Jane's approach, if it is not appropriate.

A constructed response item to assess the use of cognitive strategies might look like this:

> Here is a chapter in a history book on which you will be tested later. The test will consist of items that require you to remember main ideas and how those ideas are related to each other. Here is an example of the type of item that might be asked: "How did the introduction of the automobile contribute to the changing morals of rural people in the 1920s?"
>
> Select a strategy that is appropriate for studying and note taking. Study the chapter using this strategy. When you have finished, write down a description of the strategy that you used and why you selected it, and predict how well you will perform on the exam. Turn in this description and a copy of your notes to your teacher.

In addition to the learners' written products, the instructor might use a checklist or a rating scale to observe the learners' study behaviors to confirm that they are applying the strategy appropriately. This observation might not be practical, however, if there are many students in the class or if several observers are not available. See also O'Neil and Abedi (1996) for additional suggestions on assessment of cognitive strategy use.

E X E R C I S E S

Identify the cognitive processing type of the following strategies. In the blanks provided, write O for organizing strategies, E for elaborating strategies, R for rehearsal strategies, and CM for comprehension monitoring strategies.

_____ In reviewing his notes on statistical techniques, Mike decided that it would help him understand as well as remember the techniques if he made a chart that grouped similar aspects of the techniques together in subsections. (Grouping similar information.)

_____ Amy made a diagram of the material she read on causes of World War I. (Developing a graphic organizer.)

_____ Theresa developed her own outline of the material as she read her text on adolescent development, even though an outline is provided in the text's table of contents. (Outlining content.)

_____ Xun was having difficulty getting the Gagné types of learning straight, and she decided it would help her if she made a chart that compared the Gagné types with Bloom's taxonomy, with which she was already very comfortable. (Establishing associations between new information and previously acquired information.)

_____ As Doug was working on Boolean logic principles, he found it useful to make pictures in his mind, visualizing the different Boolean operations. (Mental imagery.)

_____ Cal, a graduate of the University of Nebraska, found it helpful in learning the many-faceted and complex nature of immune system functions in his advanced microbiology class, to make analogies between immune system elements and football team positions. Although some of his analogies were a bit strained, they were helpful to him. (Making analogies.)

_____ While she was working on learning the somewhat involved and technical definitions of emotional disorders in her counseling class, Barbara found it helpful to restate the definitions in shortened form in her own words. (Paraphrasing.)

_____ When Pat was studying Erikson's Eight Ages of Man, she found that it helped her remember the stages and their meaning by writing down examples of the stages from her own experience and that of family members whom she had observed. She found she could come up with a pretty good example for each stage and that the examples were extremely helpful in remembering the stages. (Generating personal examples.)

_____ As he is driving to work, Steven speaks his lines and signs his part as Don Alhambra in the Gilbert & Sullivan opera, *The Gondoliers,* using a tape recording to cue him when he gets stuck. (Actively reciting.)

_____ Ray looked up from his reading and asked himself, "Now, Raymond, old boy, what was that last paragraph about?" (Monitoring awareness.)

S U M M A R Y

Figure 13.1 highlights the chapter's key points in a summary frame.

Introduction	Deploy attention. Arouse interest and motivation. Establish instructional purpose. Preview lesson.	• Experience task that requires the strategy. • Discuss role of strategic thinking in learning. • Demonstrate entire strategy needed.
Body	Recall prior knowledge.	• Recall previously learned strategies or tasks that seem similar.
	Process information.	• Experience situations for which application of the strategy is appropriate and inappropriate. • Model demonstration strategy with think-aloud.
	Focus attention.	• Identify critical attributes of tasks to which strategy is appropriate. • Identify cues that indicate successful application of strategy.
	Employ learning strategies.	• Think aloud about cognition and monitor effects of the strategy.
	Practice.	• Identify contexts/tasks to which strategy is appropriate and explain why. • Apply strategy to increasingly difficult tasks. • Use reciprocal practice.
	Evaluate feedback.	• Use peer evaluation. • Provide group feedback: model appropriate application: examine artifacts of strategy use.
Conclusion	Summarize and review.	• Summarize steps and review tasks to which strategy is appropriate.
	Transfer knowledge.	• Move from attached to embedded with prompts; withdraw prompts. • Compare strategy to others learned later.
	Remotivate and close.	• Identify importance of effort coupled with strategy use.
Assessment	Assess performance.	• Directly observe. • Examine artifacts of strategy use.
	Feedback and remediation.	• Was appropriate strategy selected. • Was strategy applied correctly. • Were success of strategy monitored and "fix-up" strategies employed?

Figure 13.1 Key Events for Cognitive Strategy Learning

EXTENDED EXAMPLE

Go to the Learning Resources Web site for a continuation the instructional design of the Photography Basics course. The contribution from this chapter is strategy design for teaching a cognitive strategy of conceptual networking (Dansereau, Collins, McDonald, Holley, Garland, Diekhoff, & Evans, 1979), a strategy which can be applied by the students to the large number of new concepts that they are learning in the photography course.

READINGS AND REFERENCES

Bandura, A. (1977). *Social learning theory.* Upper Saddle River, NJ: Prentice-Hall.

Battig, W. F. (1979). Are the important "individual differences" between or within individuals? *Journal of Research in Personality, 13,* 546–558.

Brown, A. L. (1978). Knowing when, where, and how to remember: A problem of metacognition. In R. Glaser (Ed.), *Advances in instructional psychology, Vol. 1* (pp. 77–165). Hillsdale, NJ: Erlbaum.

Brown, A. L., Campione, J. C., & Day, J. D. (1981). Learning to learn: On training students to learn from text. *Educational Researcher, 10,* 12–14.

Brown, A. L., & Smiley, S. S. (1978). The development of strategies for studying texts. *Child Development, 49,* 1076–1088.

Bruce, R. (1989). Creativity and instructional technology: Great potential, imperfectly studied. *Contemporary Educational Psychology, 14,* 241–256.

Bruner, J. S. (1973). *The relevance of education.* New York: W. W. Norton.

Butler, D. L. & Winne, P. H. (1995). Feedback and self-regulated learning: A theoretical synthesis. *Review of Educational Research, 65*(3), 245–281.

Covington, M. C., Crutchfield, R. S., Davies, L. B., & Olton, R. M. (1974). *The productive thinking program: A course in learning to think.* Columbus, OH: Merrill.

Dansereau, D. (1978). The development of a learning strategy curriculum. In H. F. O'Neil (Ed.), *Learning strategies* (pp. 1–29). New York: Academic Press.

Dansereau, D. (1985). Learning strategy research. In J. W. Segal, S. F. Chipman, and R. Glaser (Eds.), *Thinking and learning skills, Vol. 1* (pp. 209–239). Hillsdale, NJ: Erlbaum.

Dansereau, D. F., Collins, K. W., McDonald, B. A., Holley, C. D., Garland, J., Diekhoff, G., & Evans, S. H. (1979). Development and evaluation of a learning strategy training program. *Journal of Educational Psychology, 71* (1), 64–73.

Dansereau, D. F., McDonald, B. A., Collins, K. W., Garland, J., Holley, C. D., Diekhoff, G. M., & Evans, S. H. (1979).

Evaluation of a learning strategy system. In H. F. O'Neil and C. D. Spielberger (Eds.), *Cognitive and affective learning strategies* (pp. 3–45). New York: Academic Press.

Davidson, G. V. (1988, January). *Training children to use learning strategies to improve their ability to attain concepts.* Paper presented to the Association for Educational and Communications Technology, New Orleans, LA.

Davidson, G. V., & Smith, P. L. (1990). Instructional design considerations for learning strategies instruction. *International Journal of Instructional Media, 17*(3), 227–243.

de Bono, E. (1983). *CoRT thinking: Notes.* Oxford: Pergamon Press.

Derry, S. J., & Murphy, D. A. (1986). Systems that train learning ability. *Review of Educational Research, 56,* 1–39.

Deshler, D. D., Alley, G. R., Warner, M. M., & Schumaker, J. B. (1981). Instructional practices for promoting skill acquisition and generalization in severely learning disabled adolescents. *Learning Disabilities Quarterly, 4,* 415–421.

Deshler, D. D., Warner, M. M., Schumaker, J. S., & Alley, G. R. (1983). Learning strategies intervention model: Key components and current status. In J. McKinney & L. Feagans (Eds.), *Current topics in learning disabilities* (pp. 245–283). New York: Ablex.

Dick, W. (1995). Instructional design and creativity: A response to the critics. *Educational Technology, 35* (7), 5–11.

DiVesta, F. J., & Finke, F. M. (1985). Metacognition, elaboration, and knowledge acquisition: Implications for instructional design. *Educational Communications and Technology Journal, 33* (4), 285–293.

Feuerstein, R., Rand, Y., Hoffman, M., & Miller, R. (1980). *Instrumental enrichment.* Baltimore, MD: University Park Press.

Flavell, J. H. (1977). *Cognitive development.* Upper Saddle River, NJ: Prentice-Hall.

Flavell, J. H., & Wellman, H. M. (1977). Metamemory. In R. V. Kail & J. W. Hagen (Eds.), *Perspectives on the development of memory and cognition* (pp. 3–33). Hillsdale, NJ: Erlbaum.

Flower, L., & Hayes, J. R. (1981). A cognitive process theory of writing. *College Composition and Communication, 32,* 365–387.

Gagné, E. (1985). *Cognitive psychology and school learning.* Boston: Little, Brown & Company.

Gagné, R. M., (1985). *The conditions of learning* (4th ed.). New York: Holt, Rinehart, & Winston.

Gagné, R. M., & Driscoll, M. A. (1988). *The essentials of learning for instruction.* New York: Holt, Rinehart, & Winston.

Garner, R. (1990). When children and adults do not use learning strategies: Toward a theory of settings. *Review of Educational Research, 60* (4), 517–530.

Garner, R., & Alexander, P. A. (1989). Metacognition: Answered and unanswered questions. *Educational Psychologist, 24*(2), 143–158.

Gordon, W. J. (1961). *Synectics: The development of creative capacity.* New York: Harper & Row.

Greene, B. A., DeBacker, T. I., Ravindran, B., & Krows, A. J. (1999). Goals, values, and beliefs as predictors of achievement and effort in high school mathematics classes. *Sex Roles, 40*(5), 421–458.

Greene, B. A., & Miller, R. B. (1996). Influences on course performance: Goals, perceived ability, and self-regulation, *Contemporary Educational Psychology, 21,* 181-192.

Haller, E. P., Child, D. A., & Walberg, H. J. (1988). Can comprehension be taught? A quantitative synthesis of "metacognitive" studies. *Educational Researcher, 17*(9), 5–8.

Higbee, K. L. (1977). *Your memory: How it works and how to improve it.* Upper Saddle River, NJ: Prentice-Hall.

Holley, C. D., & Dansereau, D. F. (1984). Networking: The technique and empirical evidence. In C. D. Holley and D. F. Dansereau (Eds.), *Spatial learning strategies: Techniques, applications, and related issues* (pp. 81–108). Orlando, FL: Academic Press.

Jonassen, D. H. (1985). Learning strategies: A new educational technology. *Programmed Learning and Educational Technology Journal, 22*(1), 25–34.

Joyce, B., & Weil, M. (1986). *Models of teaching* (3rd ed.). Upper Saddle River, NJ: Prentice-Hall.

Levin, J. R. (1986). Four cognitive principles of learning-strategy instruction. *Educational Psychologist, 21*(1), 3–18.

Mannes, S. (1994). Strategic processing of text. *Journal of Educational Psychology, 86*(4), 577–588.

Mayer, R. E. (1980). Elaboration techniques that increase the meaningfulness of technical text: An experimental test of the learning strategy hypotheses. *Journal of Educational Psychology, 72,* 770–784.

McCombs, B. L. (1981–82). Transitioning learning strategies research into practice: Focus on the student in technical training. *Journal of Instructional Development, 5*(2), 10–21.

McCombs, B. L. (1984). Processes and skills underlying continuing intrinsic motivation to learn: Toward a definition of motivational skills training interventions. *Educational Psychologist, 19,* 199–218.

McCombs, B. L., & Marzano, R. J. (1990). Putting the self in self-regulated learning: The self as agent in integrating will and skill. *Educational Psychologist, 25*(1), 51–70.

Miller, R. B., Behrens, J. T., Greene, B. A., & Newman, D. (1993). Goals and perceived ability: Impact on student valuing, self-regulation, and persistence. *Contemporary Educational Psychology, 18,* 2-14.

Miller, R. B., Greene, B. A., Montalvo, G. P., Ravindran, B., & Nichols, J. D. (1996). Engagement in academic work: The role of learning goals, future consequences, pleasing others, and perceived ability. *Contemporary Educational Psychology, 21,* 388-422.

Meichenbaum, D. M. (1977). *Cognitive behavior modification.* New York: Plenum.

Newby, T. J., & Stepich, D. A. (1990). Teaching cognitive strategies. *Performance and Instruction, 29*(1), 44–45.

Newell, A. (1980). One final word. In D. T. Tuma & F. Reif (Eds.), *Problem solving and education* (pp. 175–189). Hillsdale, NJ: Erlbaum.

Newell, A., & Simon, H. A. (1975). *Human problem solving.* Upper Saddle River, NJ: Prentice-Hall.

Niaz, M. (1995). Enhancing thinking skills: Domain specific/domain general strategies: A dilemma for science education. *Instructional Science, 22,* 413–422.

Norman, D. A. (1980). Cognitive engineering and education. In D. T. Tuma & F. Reif (Eds.), *Problem solving and education* (pp. 97–107). Hillsdale, NJ: Erlbaum.

O'Neil, H. F., & Abedi, J. U. (1996). Reliability and validity of a state metacognitive inventory: Potential for alternative assessment. *Journal of Educational Research, 89*(4), 206–218.

Perkins, D. N., & Salomon, G. (1989). Are cognitive skills context-bound? *Educational Researcher, 18*(1), 16–25.

Polson, P. G., & Jeffries, R. (1985). Instruction in general problem-solving skills: An analysis of four approaches. In J. W. Segal, S. F. Chipman, & R. Glaser, (Eds.), *Thinking and learning skills, Vol. 1: Relating instruction to research* (pp. 417–455). Hillsdale, NJ: Erlbaum.

Polya, G. (1957). *How to solve it* (2nd ed.). Garden City, NJ: Doubleday Archer.

Pressley, M., Borkowski, J. G., & Schneider, W. (1987). Cognitive strategies: Good strategy users coordinate metacognition and knowledge. In R. Vasta & G. Whitehurst (Eds.), *Annals of child development, Vol. 4* (pp. 89–129). Greenwich, CT: JAI Press.

Pressley, M., Snyder, B. L., & Cariglia-Bull, T. (1987). How can good strategy use be taught to children? Evaluation of six alternative approaches. In S. M. Cormier & J. D. Hagman (Eds.), *Transfer of learning* (pp. 81–120). San Diego, CA: Academic Press.

Puntambekar, S. (1995). Helping students learn "how to learn" from texts: Towards an ITS for developing metacognition. *Instructional Science, 23*, 163–182.

Resnick, L. B. (1987). Instruction and the cultivation of thinking. In E. deCorte, H. Lodewijks, R. Parmentier, & P. Span (Eds.), *Learning and instruction: European research in an international context, Vol. 1* (pp. 415–442). Leuven, Belgium: Leuven University Press.

Rigney, L. B. (1978). Learning strategies: A theoretical perspective. In H. F. O'Neil (Ed.), *Learning strategies* (pp. 165–205). New York: Academic Press.

Rigney, L. B. (1980). Cognitive learning strategies and dualities in information processing. In R. E. Snow, P. Federico, & W. E. Montague (Eds.), *Aptitude, learning and instruction, Vol. 1* (pp. 315–343). Hillsdale, NJ: Erlbaum.

Rohwer, W. D. (1980). An elaborative conception of learner differences. In R. E. Snow, P. A. Federico, & W. E. Montague (Eds.), *Aptitude, learning and instruction, Vol. 2* (pp. 23–46) Hillsdale, NJ: Erlbaum.

Ross, S. M., & Rakow, E. A. (1982). Adaptive instructional strategies for teaching rules in mathematics. *Educational and Communication Technology Journal, 30*, 67–74.

Salomon, G., & Perkins, D. N. (1989). Rocky roads to transfer: Rethinking mechanisms of a neglected phenomenon. *Educational Psychologist, 24*(2), 113–142.

Schmitt, M. C., & Newby, T. J. (1986). Metacognition: Relevance to instructional design. *Journal of Instructional Development, 9*(2), 29–33.

Schnotz, W. (1991). Metacognition and self regulation in text processing: Some comments. In M. Carretera, M. Pope, R. Simmons, & J. I. Pazo (Eds.), *Learning and instruction: European research in an international context, Vol. 3* (pp. 365–375). Oxford: Pergamon.

Schunk, D. H. (1990). Goal setting and self-efficacy during self-regulated learning. *Educational Psychologist, 25*(1), 71–86.

Schunk, D. H., & Zimmerman, B. J. (Eds.). (1994). *Self-regulation of learning and performance: Issues and educational applications*. Hillsdale, NJ: Erlbaum.

Siegler, R. S., & Jenkins, E. (1989). *How children discover new strategies*. Hillsdale, NJ: Erlbaum.

Singer, R. N., & Gerson, R. F. (1979). Learning strategies, cognitive processes, and motor learning. In H. F. O'Neil & C. D. Spielberger (Eds.), *Cognitive and affective learning strategies* (pp. 215–247). New York: Academic Press.

Smith, P. L., & Friend, M. (1986). Training learning-disabled students in a strategy for using text structure to aid recall of instructional prose. *Learning Disabilities, 2*, 38–44.

Stein, M. I. (1974). *Stimulating creativity, Vol. 1: Individual procedures*. New York: Academic Press.

Stein, M. I. (1975). *Stimulating creativity, Vol. 2: Group procedures*. New York: Academic Press.

Sternberg, R. J. (1986). Intelligence, wisdom, and creativity: Three is better than one. *Educational Psychologist, 21*(3), 175–190.

Taylor, I. A., & Getzels, J. W. (1975). *Perspectives in creativity*. Chicago: Aldine.

Tennyson, R. D. (1981). Use of adaptive information for advisement in learning concepts and rules using computer-assisted instruction. *American Educational Research Journal, 73*, 326–334.

Thiede, K. W., & Dunlosky, J. (1994). Delaying students' metacognitive monitoring improves their accuracy in predicting their recognition performance. *Journal of Educational Psychology, 86* (2), 290–302.

Thomas, J. W., & Rohwer, W. D., Jr. (1986). Academic studying: The role of learning strategies. *Educational Psychologist, 21*(1), 19–42.

Torgesen, J. K. (1979). Factors related to poor performance on memory tasks in reading disabled children. *Learning Disability Quarterly, 2*, 17–23.

Torrance, E. P. (1979). *The search for satori and creativity*. Buffalo, NY: Creative Education Foundation.

Weinstein, C. E. (1978). Elaboration skills as a learning strategy. In H. F. O'Neil (Ed.), *Learning strategies* (pp. 31–55). New York: Academic Press.

Weinstein, C. E. (1981). Learning strategies: The metacurriculum. *Journal of Developmental and Remedial Education, 5*, 6–10.

Weinstein, C. E. (1982). Training students to use elaboration learning strategies. *Contemporary Educational Psychology, 7*, 301–311.

Weinstein, C. E., Cubberly, W. E., Wicker, F. W., Underwood, V. L., Roney, L. K., & Duty, D. C. (1981). Training versus instruction in the acquisition of cognitive learning strategies. *Contemporary Educational Psychology, 6*, 159–166.

Weinstein, C. E., & Mayer, R. E. (1986). The teaching of learning strategies. In M. C. Wittrock (Ed.), *Handbook of research on teaching* (3rd ed.) (pp. 315–327). New York: Macmillan.

Weinstein, C. E., & Underwood, V. L. (1985). Learning strategies: The how of learning. In J. Segal, S. Chipman, & R. Glaser (Eds.), *Learning and thinking skills, Vol. 1* (pp. 241–258). Hillsdale, NJ: Erlbaum.

Winn, W. (1983, April). *Learning strategies and adaptive instruction*. Paper presented at the meeting of the American Educational Research Association, Montreal, Quebec, Canada.

Winn, W. (1986, February). *Emerging trends in educational technology research*. Paper presented at the meeting of the Association of Educational and Communications Technology, Las Vegas, NV.

Zimmerman, B. J. (1990). Self-regulated learning and academic achievement: An overview. *Educational Psychologist, 25*(1), 2–18.

Zimmerman, B. J., & Schunk, D. H. (Eds.). (1989). *Self-regulated learning and academic achievement: Theory, research, and practice*. New York: Springer-Verlag.

STRATEGIES FOR ATTITUDE LEARNING

CHAPTER

14

CHAPTER OBJECTIVES

At the conclusion of this chapter, you should be able to do the following:

- Translate broad goals that involve affective learnings into specific affective objectives that can be used in designing instruction for their achievement.

- Given an affective goal, devise a hierarchy of affective objectives related to it.

- Given an attitude objective, design a strategy plan for that objective.

- Given an attitude objective, describe three possible approaches to assessment of it, select a "best approach," and defend the selection in terms of the fit between assessment characteristics and salient characteristics of learners, task, and setting.

- Relate three instructional conditions (role model, role-playing, and reinforcement) to the learning components to which they lead.

- Describe techniques to promote interest and motivation in lessons for all learning outcome types.

- Given an instructional activity or instructor's statement, categorize that activity/statement as to motivational strategy type, attention, relevance, confidence, or satisfaction.

INTRODUCTION

Chapters 8 through 13 discussed instructional strategies for achieving learning objectives in the cognitive domain; Chapter 15 will address instructional strategies for objectives in the psychomotor domain. This chapter is concerned with the affective domain, which has been relatively neglected over the years in educational practice. We hope to redress the balance by devoting this chapter to instructional strategies for objectives in the affective domain and the affective component of lessons in the cognitive and motor domains.

In this chapter, we will treat designing instructional strategies for learning within the affective domain, particularly learning that has to do with attitude formation or change. In the Learning Resources Web site for this book, an additional chapter related to the affective domain is provided. That chapter looks at a body of theory and some specific techniques for enhancing the motivational qualities of instruction for all domains.

INSTRUCTION FOR ATTITUDE OBJECTIVES

Although attitude objectives are not as frequently stated in explicit form as cognitive or even psychomotor objectives, there are times when we want to form or change an attitude. In public education, such objectives are seen in drug education, sex education, health education, and in the "informal curriculum" that implements many of the schools' socially derived goals such as cooperating to achieve common goals, democratic values and processes, and so forth (McCaslin & Good, 1996). The exercise at the end of this section presents public school goals that are attitudinal in nature and that illustrate just how pervasive attitude objectives are in schoolwork, even when they may not be explicitly stated. (Several of these goals are very similar to much of corporate America's training needs and goals.)

Before going further, we should point out that the traditional separability of "cognitive, affective, and psychomotor domains" is very much under question and for good reason. In point of fact, any "cognitive" or "psychomotor" objective has some affective component to it if at no deeper level than a willingness to sufficiently interact with learning resources to achieve the learning. The roles that learners' intentions and achievement goals play in conceptual change make affect inseparably related to cognitive learning (Sinatra & Pintrich, 2003). Relationships between the three domains work the other way as well (so-called "affective" objectives have important cognitive components, and so forth). Rather than view the domains as completely separate, practitioners should strive to integrate them as they design instruction.

However, for purposes of clarity—as a place to begin—it is appropriate to work specifically on learning and instruction in what is called the "affective domain," knowing full well that a strict division or separation in instructional practice is not intended. As you will see, our treatment of attitude learning (see especially "Components of Attitude Learning" later in this chapter) reflects the multidimensional nature of affective learning.

In addition to school learning, more goals of higher education and training environments involve attitudes than might be anticipated. In something as seemingly cut and dried as an engine mechanics unit in an aircraft mechanics course, building appropriate attitudes and dispositions toward work and tasks may be the most difficult and important part of the training design problem. Likewise, in another training environment—managerial training—attitude objectives form a large portion of the actual intent of training. Many educators and trainers frequently assume, in both education and training settings, that the affective domain is somehow "off limits"—that it cannot be dealt with through instruction. This is not the case. There *are* viable instructional strategies to promote attitude formation and change. If a designer finds it difficult to identify affective objectives in the setting with which she is most concerned, she should look toward the more general goals or mission statements of the organization or agency. A school's broadest goals will, upon close examination, often be almost entirely affective. In translation to specific objectives, because of such factors as tradition and lack of imagination, many designers fail to do justice to needs for development in the affective domain.

We hope that this chapter will help you recognize and translate broad goals that involve affective learnings into specific affective objectives. These objectives can be used in designing instruction for their achievement. We also hope that the chapter will help you design effective and appropriate instructional strategies for attitude instruction by increasing your understanding of attitudes and attitude learning, as well as specific strategies and the application of expanded events of instruction to designing attitude instruction.

E X E R C I S E   A

Read the set of goal statements in Figure 14.1, and identify those that represent or involve attitude formation or change. The source of these goals is a statement of educational goals for U.S. public schools from the National Education Association (Educational Policies Commission, 1938). Although these statements appear to us now to be goal statements, their original form was as "objectives."

Label	Objective Statement
The Objectives of Self-Realization	
__The inquiring mind:	The educated person . . . has an appetite for learning.
__Speech:	speaks the mother tongue clearly.
__Reading:	reads the mother tongue efficiently.
__Writing:	writes the mother tongue effectively.
__Number:	solves his problems of counting and calculating.
__Sight and hearing:	is skilled in listening and observing.
__Health knowledge:	understands the basic facts concerning health and disease.
__Health habits:	protects her own health and that of her dependents.
__Public health:	works to improve the health of the community.
__Recreation:	is a participant and spectator in many sports and other pastimes.
__Intellectual interests:	has mental resources for the use of leisure.
__Aesthetic interests:	appreciates beauty.
__Character:	gives responsible direction to his own life.
The Objectives of Human Relationships	
__Respect for humanity:	The educated person . . . puts human relationships first.
__Friendships:	enjoys a rich sincere, and varied social life.
__Cooperation:	can work and play with others.
__Courtesy:	observes the amenities of social behavior.
__Appreciation of home:	appreciates the family as a social institution.
__Conservation of home:	conserves family ideals.
__Homemaking:	is skilled in homemaking.
__Democracy in home:	maintains democratic family relationships.

Label	Objective Statement
The Objectives of Economic Efficiency	
__Work:	The educated producer . . . knows the satisfaction of good work.
__Occupational information:	understands the requirements and opportunities for various jobs.
__Occupational choice:	has selected her occupation.
__Occupational efficiency:	succeeds in his chosen profession.
__Occupational adjustment:	maintains and improves her efficiency.
__Occupational appreciation:	appreciates the social value of his work.
__Personal economics:	plans the economics of her own life.
__Consumer judgment:	develops standards for guiding his expenditures.
__Efficiency in buying:	is an informed and skillful buyer.
__Consumer protection:	takes appropriate measures to safeguard her interests.
The Objectives of Civic Responsibility	
__Social justice:	The educated citizen . . . is sensitive to the disparities in human circumstance.
__Social activity:	acts to correct unsatisfactory conditions.
__Social understanding:	seeks to understand social structures and social processes.
__Critical judgment:	has defenses against propaganda.
__Tolerance:	respects honest differences of opinion.
__Conservation:	has regard for the nation's resources.
__Social applications of science:	measures scientific advance by it's contribution to general welfare.
__World citizenship:	is a cooperating member of the world community.
__Law observance:	respects the law.
__Economic literacy:	is economically literate.
__Political citizenship:	accepts his civic duties.
__Devotion to democracy:	acts upon an unanswering to democratic ideals.

Figure 14.1 A Set of Educational Goals
Source: Educational Policies Commission (1938), p. 41.

In the following pages, we will look at instructional design that has attitude change or formation as its goal. We will discuss how attitudes are learned and the components of attitude learning. Then we will present a framework for attitude learning involving use of a taxonomy of objectives in the affective domain. Next we will look at three instructional conditions for learning attitudes, and finally we will apply the expanded instructional events to attitude learning as a structure for design of attitude instruction.

A REVIEW OF ATTITUDE LEARNING

The basic idea of attitudes is captured in the idea of choosing to do something. The most salient influence that an attitude has on an individual's behavior is on choices that he or she makes. No matter if the topic is practicing "safe sex," or practicing conservation, or settling arguments nonviolently, or voting, whether or not we have made an influence on our students' attitudes will be evidenced by what our students *choose to do* with those attitudes. It's clear, then, that attitude learning is fundamental. Many psychological theories have dealt with attitude change and formation over the years (Simonson & Maushak, 1996). Martin and Briggs (1986) summarized five theories of attitude change that have instructional implications:

1. *The Yale Communication and Attitude Change Program.* This is a reinforcement-based approach that stresses, in addition to the use of reinforcement, the necessity to address the cognitive elements of beliefs and opinions.

2. *Festinger's Cognitive Dissonance Theory.* This theory stresses the importance of the cognitive element of dissonance—a tension created by inconsistencies in an individual's beliefs—and the need to reduce that dissonance.

3. *Cognitive Balancing.* This resembles Cognitive Dissonance theory, a theory that involves balancing and accommodation, but Cognitive Balancing uses both affective and cognitive components.

4. *Social Judgment Theory.* This theory describes how attitudes change through a judgment process involving internally held subjective reference scales of acceptability that people use to judge their own positions or values in contrast to competing values offered by persuasive communications.

5. *Social Learning Theory.* This approach describes attitude change through learning from (a) direct experience (as a consequence of one's own behavior); (b) vicarious experience (through observation of a model) or experience through reading or hearing about; or (c) through emotional associations. (pp. 118–138)

In their text, *Instructional Message Design,* Fleming and Levie (1993) presented a listing and description of principles of attitude change derived from research. The authors presented twenty-two principles involving three fundamental sources: persuasion, modeling, and dissonance. Figure 14.2 presents a summary listing of the principles, which may be used as a reminder of motivational techniques that you have previously learned, or they may stimulate you to further study. In the Fleming and Levie text, each principle is discussed in terms of both its research basis and application.

Research on belief change, which is related to that of attitude change, draws upon and has cross-validated many attitude change principles. For example, Kardash and Scholes (1995) found that causal arguments were effective in a study of changing beliefs about AIDS. The high comprehensibility of the text used to convey the arguments was found to contribute to the belief of change. Other factors included in Fleming and Levie's principles (1.1 and 1.3) were also found to contribute. In addition, Eagly & Warren (1976) found that ease of comprehension contributes to persuasion. Another factor in the Kardash and Scholes study relates to principle 1.11: The audience was highly motivated and willing to think deeply about the issue at hand (Petty & Cacioppo, 1986). The study of belief change is a highly germane area for instructional designers and illustrates well the often blurry line between outcomes we call "cognitive" and those we label "affective."

Components of Attitude Learning

Even though they are generally "affective" in nature, attitudes have three components that we can derive from the previous review of attitude learning: cognitive, behavioral, and affective. If, for example, we wanted students to learn the attitude of "safe driving," they would have more to do than just acquire an affective disposition toward driving safely.

1. The *cognitive component* consists of "knowing how." Before the student can practice any attitudes about safe driving, he or she must know how to drive. Although it is reasonable to think of the cognitive component as prerequisite learning, it is a prerequisite that will always be present in all examples of attitude learning; therefore, it is something we can think of as being part of the attitude itself.

2. The *behavioral component* of attitude learning is seen in the need to apply the attitude—to engage in behavior. Thus, to actually internalize the attitude of safe driving, it will be necessary for the students to do it—to drive safely and receive feedback about it.

3. The *affective component* is the "knowing why," the urge or desire to drive safely. The most fundamental

1. Persuasive Messages

1.1 High-credibility sources exert more persuasive influence than low credibility sources.

1.2 Sources perceived by the receiver as attractive are more influential.

1.3 The quality and structure of the arguments in a persuasive message are more critical for credible sources than for attractive sources.

1.4 Be sure the receiver is informed of the expertise of a high-credibility communicator.

1.5 To enhance communicator attractiveness, establish belief congruence with the receiver by arguing in favor of positions the receiver is known to hold.

1.6 Arguments are more effective if they are relevant to the receiver's needs.

1.7 Generally, two-sided arguments are slightly more effective than one-sided messages.

1.8 It is almost always advisable to state the conclusion explicitly rather then to allow receivers to draw their own conclusions.

1.9 Repetition helps, but only one or two repetitions are likely to have any additional effect.

1.10 No one media type has been explicitly shown to have greater persuasive effectiveness than any other media type. Face-to-face communication, however, is more effective in promoting acceptance than mediated communication, particularly in difficult cases.

1.11 It is very difficult to change the attitudes of receivers who are highly committed to their positions on an issue.

2. Modeling

2.1 High-credibility models exert more persuasive influence than low-credibility models.

2.2 For modeling to be effective, the learners must comprehend the presentation as demonstration of specific behaviors.

2.3 In addition to observing the model demonstrating the behavior, learners should observe the model being reinforced for that behavior.

2.4 Role-playing can have a powerful persuasive impact.

2.5 Active participation produces more attitude change than passive reception of information.

3. Dissonance

3.1 If a person can be induced to perform an important act that is counter to the person's own private attitude, attitude change may result.

3.2 When a person is induced to perform an attitudinally discrepant act because of promise of reward or punishment, attitude change will occur only to the extent that the person feels the magnitude of the reward or punishment was insufficient to justify the attitudinally discrepant behavior.

3.3 Demonstrate the social acceptability of the desired attitude and the reward available socially for behavior consistent with the attitude.

3.4 Alternate between presenting information discrepant with existing beliefs and inducing behaviors discrepant with existing attitudes to maximize dissonance.

3.5 Structure attitude-change lessons so that attention is paid to the cognitive (information), affective (feeling), and the behavioral (acting) elements of the attitude.

3.6 Use successive approximations to move attitudes gradually between a current status and a desired state.

Figure 14.2 Principles of Attitude Change.
Source: Fleming & Levie, *Educational Technology Publications* (1978), pp. 199–242. Reprinted by permission of Macmillan Publishing Company.

condition for achievement of the affective component is provision of a role model. A role model is a respected person who demonstrates the desired behavior. Thus, in the case of learning to drive safely, a person the student respects must demonstrate (or "model") safe driving.

A particularly insightful discussion of the relationships among cognitive, behavioral, and affective components in learning attitudes is provided by Kamradt & Kamradt (1999).

The Cognitive Component in Attitude Change and Formation

It is important to remember the existence of the cognitive component in attitude learning (it is equally important to attend to the affective component of cognitive objectives—see Chapter 5). Many failures and difficulties in attitude learning are mistakenly attributed solely to the affective component; often, a deficit in the cognitive component needs to be remedied first. For example, when a student displays poor study habits, it is common to place the blame on the student's lack of desire to study; but often the student does not know how to study. An attitude includes both knowing how to do something and choosing to do it. Later we will see how the three components of attitude learning can be provided in a single lesson, although much attitude instruction is interwoven with other lessons for longer spans of time than individual lessons.

Attitudes are but one of many types of affective objectives that can be objects of instruction. There have been many attempts to describe and categorize types of learning outcomes in the affective domain (Brandhorst, 1978; Gephart & Ingle, 1976; Krathwohl, Bloom, & Masia, 1964; Martin & Briggs, 1986; Nunnally, 1967). For our purposes, the most suitable categorization scheme is the taxonomy developed by Krathwohl et al. because it shows a wide range of objectives, not just attitudes. The Krathwohl taxonomy also lends increased precision to our descriptions of affective learning outcomes, including attitudes, since commonly used affect-related terms such as *attitudes, values, appreciations,* and *interests* are broader and less precise than the terms set forth and described by the taxonomy.

The Krathwohl taxonomy has five major categories, each of which comprises subcategories. Figure 14.3 presents a summary of the taxonomy. To illustrate the meanings of each of its categories, let's select a topic area, "appreciation of classical music," and see how that topic might be reflected in activities and learning outcomes throughout the taxonomy. Although some of what the taxonomy addresses is far beyond the idea of "appreciation," this is a commonly understood way to start. We will begin with this scenario: We have taken on a mission to convert our friend George, who hates

1.0 Receiving (or "attending")	1.1 Awareness
	1.2 Willingness to receive
	1.3 Controlled or selected attention
2.0 Responding	2.1 Acquiescence in responding
	2.2 Willingness to respond
	2.3 Satisfaction in response
3.0 Valuing	3.1 Acceptance of a value
	3.2 Preference for a value
	3.3 Commitment
4.0 Organization	4.1 Conceptualization of a value
	4.2 Organization of a value system
5.0 Characterization by a Value Complex	5.1 Generalized set
	5.2 Characterization

Figure 14.3   Summary of the Taxonomy of Educational Objectives in the Affective Domain.
Source: Krathwohl, Bloom, & Masia (1964).

classical music, into a person who has, at the very least, a positive attitude about classical music.

1. *Attending.* In the attending category, we begin with the small, but real, achievement of just getting George to be *aware* of the music (1.1 in Figure 14.3), to be *willing* to actually listen to it (1.2), and to even be able to *focus* in on parts of it—to pay close attention to the music (1.3). The attending level is where we always begin, in any instructional situation, and if we were thorough in our learning task descriptions, we would include it as a prerequisite or part of all of our instruction. Although attending is an implicit part of all instruction, rarely would we expect to see attending as the actual objective of instruction. When our objective is in the affective domain, attending will be a prerequisite—part of an affective learning hierarchy.

2. *Responding.* It's one thing for George to be willing to listen to the classical music, and it's another for him to actually take satisfaction in it. We can observe the difference—even though it is difficult to detect sometimes—between George's mere attention to and his responding to the music. George may perhaps move from *acquiescence* (2.1) to *willingness* to respond (2.2) to taking *satisfaction* in response to the music (2.3). When he achieves this level of affective learning with regard to classical music, we may observe subtle evidences of his response, perhaps with facial expression and bodily movements.

The responding level is right at the center of what is generally meant by *appreciation* in common language. As you can see, *responding* is a more precise description, one that we may use in a performance objective. In our mission to convert George, this may be as far as we had intended to go when we started, but as we will see, this goal may be extended into how deeply and pervasively George internalizes (or "appreciates") classical music.

3. *Valuing.* If George finds himself enjoying classical music in one or more instances, we are likely to find that he achieves the next level in the hierarchy: valuing. Like the other categories treated so far, valuing has subcategories that George may experience. He may begin with *acceptance* of the value of classical music (3.1). For example, when asked, "Do you think classical music is any good?", he may change his response from "No" to "Yes, I guess some of it is." Then he may experience *preference* (3.2), in which, for example, he goes to the record store and finds that he looks for the classical section first. Finally, he may experience *commitment* (3.3), in which, for example, he chooses to spend time or money on his classical music interest, such as buying season tickets to the symphony orchestra concerts, taking time off from other activities to go to a concert, or helping the orchestra in its annual fund-raising drive.

Many school and training affective objectives will be in the valuing category. We want the learners to not only respond positively to our topic but to internalize an interest in the topic so that it becomes something that they value. The final two categories in the Krathwohl taxonomy take the idea of valuing and deepen or extend it.

4. *Organization.* George's mind is full of conflicting and contradictory value structures and systems. He doesn't have all of his values organized into a consistent, carefully constructed system. We can see that just having achieved the valuing level does not automatically mean that George will make the mental effort of *conceptualizing* (4.1) his valuing of classical music. For example, he might become a "true believer" in classical music and shun good jazz in a snobbish fashion, as is often the case with those who have acquired commitment to a value but have not yet conceptualized it. Having conceptualized his valuing of classical music, George can take one step deeper and begin to form an *organized value system* (4.2). At this point, George goes beyond his newfound eclecticism and links with other values outside classical music itself. Now George is reading literature of a higher quality than he formerly did, he has joined an ethics and philosophy discussion group, and he has begun to study computer programming for aesthetic reasons. His views on politics have even changed.

Organization goes beyond what we typically attempt to do in school or training situations, although our most general goals often reflect this level of achievement. The goals of graduate study, for example, seem to involve this level of functioning, especially with respect to the field of study itself. It is important that the student (1) know things, (2) have skills in the field, and (3) acquire particular affective learnings tied to particular skills and knowledge. And, for the health of the field itself, it is important that the student have the organized system of beliefs, commitments, and preferences that one associates with a person in that particular field.

5. *Characterization.* It would be hard to imagine George going any further with this classical music business than he already has, but the characterization level gives us an opportunity to take him even further. At the characterization level, we see an individual who not only possesses certain organized sets of values, but also someone whom we would look to as a source of those values—a model. Over time, given the behaviors and affective states that we saw George experiencing at the organization level, we may see George take on what is known as a *generalized set* (5.1). The clichés such as the tweed sport coat with elbow patches, the dignified gray beard, and the Tudor-style home with a grand piano in the living room begin to communicate at a superficial level what is meant by a generalized set—all of the things associated with being a connoisseur of classical music. More technically, *generalized set* refers to a predisposition or consistent response to a wide variety of situations. Thus, rather than just being completely obsessed by his "classical music jag," we hope that George now possesses an orientation that is made up of organized sets or clusters of related values. The final level that George could aspire to is itself called *characterization* (5.2). At this level, we would look to George to find a reflection of interest in classical music. In fact, the last we heard of George, he was teaching a music appreciation class with great success. The characterization level is the level we hope our teachers and professors have achieved with regard to the subjects and fields they are teaching. People functioning at this level are our actual, genuine role models. Perhaps this need is one that underlies the need for classroom teachers who have undergone extensive teacher education as well as excellent subject matter preparations. Certainly we hope for professionals—physicians, lawyers, teachers, and others—to possess the depth of knowledge and commitment reflected by the characterization level. Rather than blindly wishing for professionals to randomly reach this level of functioning, we can draw upon the Krathwohl taxonomy and other concepts to design instruction that will intentionally educate for this goal.

E X E R C I S E   B

For the following goal statements from the 1938 Educational Policies Commission report, develop a learning hierarchy related to each goal. Use the Krathwohl taxonomy as a guiding framework.

1. The educated person has an appetite for learning.

2. The educated person protects her own health and that of her dependents.

3. The educated person observes the amenities of social behavior.

4. The educated citizen acts to correct unsatisfactory (social) conditions.

INSTRUCTIONAL CONDITIONS FOR ATTITUDE OBJECTIVES

From our review of attitude learning, we have derived three key instructional conditions for its attainment. Although many variations are possible, we would offer these three conditions as primary and critical: (1) demonstration of the desired behavior by a respected role model; (2) practice of the desired behavior, often through role-playing; and (3) reinforcement of the desired behavior. Other conditions include persuasive communications, dissonance establishment and reduction, and use of group discussions (see pp. 137–140 of Martin and Briggs [1986] for more information on these latter conditions).

As we elaborate on three primary conditions for attitude instruction, the three components for learning an attitude should be recalled: the cognitive component (knowing how), the affective component (knowing why), and the behavioral component (opportunity to practice). As we describe the instructional conditions for forming or changing attitudes, you can see how these learning components relate to the design of instruction that leads to learning.

1. *Demonstration of the desired behavior by a respected role model.* We have already seen how important a role model is in our discussion of the Krathwohl taxonomy. Gagné (1985) underscores the utility of modeling as an instructional technique by noting, "One of the most dependable methods of establishing attitudes is by means of a set of learning conditions that includes human modeling" (p. 241). Conditions that Martin and Briggs (1986) present as essential to the use of role models include how important it is that the learners "comprehend and see the model demonstrating the behavior *and* being reinforced" (p. 139). Gagné (1985) presents a four-step procedure for the use of human models in attitude learning:

a. Establish the appeal and credibility of the model.

b. Stimulate the learner's recall of relevant knowledge and concepts.

c. Demonstration or communication of desired action by the model.

d. Demonstration or communication of reinforcement of the model as a result of the action taken. (p. 238)

2. *Practice of the desired behavior (role-playing).* As pointed out earlier in the discussion of attitude learning, learner activity with regard to the attitude in question is a powerful tool in attitude formation and change. Role-playing offers the opportunity for learner activity within an instructional environment and constitutes another means by which modeling can be employed. In the case of role-playing, the actor (the learner or another person) "plays out" the role rather than using an actual role model. According to Gagné (1985), in addition to particular role-playing methods that may be employed, such as case studies and simulations, conventional group discussion is also a legitimate means for practice of a desired behavior. In a discussion, as each student contributes from the point of view of the attitude at hand, that student serves as a role model for the attitude. The discussion leader has the opportunity to provide reinforcement for the discussion participant/role model, and as the discussion progresses, the attitude may be expressed with more and more precision.

3. *Provide reinforcement for the desired behavior.* Behavioral techniques have remained a substantial part of instruction for attitude learning. Even in role-model use (and role-playing), reinforcement is an integral part of the process. In these circumstances, the reinforcement, as well as the role model *per se*, is thought to function in a surrogate or vicarious fashion for the learner. Research from the social-learning standpoint has pointed out that reinforcement is such a potentially powerful tool in these situations that even observing a model being reinforced can be a condition for attitude formation or change (Martin and Briggs, 1986). However, the most powerful reinforcers will be those that apply directly to the learner as a product of the learner's own behavior. That behavior may be a demonstration of the desired behavior in an actual situation, in role-playing, with discussions, or in other contrived situations.

Reinforcement is a slippery concept, and defining what reinforcers actually *are* turns out to be somewhat circular. No particular type or category of event may be guaranteed to be a reinforcer. A **reinforcer** is technically defined as a stimulus that increases the probability of the preceding behavior reoccurring. In day-to-day use, reinforcers are generally thought to be rewards, but not all rewards are reinforcing. In the case of reinforcement for taking an action of choice, the most powerful reinforcers seem to be those that we can call "natural consequences." The thanks from someone you have helped, the safe passage through a dangerous situation, and observation of the benefit gained from help you supplied are all much more direct and powerful reinforcers than praise or reward from a teacher. In fact, in many situations, praise and reward can be

worse than no attempt to reinforce at all. A teacher's role in providing reinforcement can be seen as assuring that learners are put in contact with and comprehend the feedback resulting from their actions.

E X E R C I S E   C

For each of the three instructional conditions for attitude learning previously discussed, describe which learning components (cognitive, behavioral, affective) are being provided.

ASSESSMENT OF ATTITUDE LEARNING

When engaged in instructional design, it is less common for the designer to have affective objectives than cognitive objectives. One reason for this is that it is more difficult to assess affective objectives than cognitive objectives. In assessing affective objectives we hope to determine learners' attitudes, values, preferences, or interests regarding objects, people, or ideas. Often in instructional arenas we hope to not only develop a skill in a particular area, such as mathematics, but also a positive attitude or interest in that area. We often evaluate whether the learner has acquired a skill (the cognitive component of the attitude objective) and whether the learner is now predisposed to use that skill (the affective component of the attitude objective). Occasionally, the focus of instruction is primarily to *change* an attitude rather than form a new attitude. In either case, we generally need to assess two things when assessing attitudes, values, or interests: Can the learner perform the skill or demonstrate the knowledge desired? and Is the learner predisposed to use this skill or knowledge? (With the second question, the designer tries to discern whether the learner will *choose* to use this skill or knowledge.)

Three general types of instruments can be used to assess affective objectives: direct self-report, indirect self-report, and observation. The first two approaches are similar to recognition items, and the latter resembles a constructed response item. Each of these types of instruments has advantages and disadvantages, which we will discuss and exemplify in the following paragraphs.

Direct Self-Report

In assessment of attitudes, we attempt to devise instruments that predict whether learners will behave in a desired manner (the manner dictated by the precepts of the attitude). One way to assess these predispositions is direct self-report; that is, to ask learners how they currently perform or how they would perform in the future.

For example, if we had just completed a unit on protecting the environment and wished to assess learners' attitudes (as indicated by behavior) toward recycling, we might use the following questions in an instrument that is administered several weeks after instruction.

Directions: In the following questions circle the descriptor that best describes your current level of activity in recycling household products. There are no right or wrong answers, so answer as honestly as you can.

1. We recycle aluminum cans.
Always   Often   Occasionally   Rarely   Never
2. We recycle glass products, such as bottles and jars.
Always   Often   Occasionally   Rarely   Never
3. We recycle newspapers and other paper products.
Always   Often   Occasionally   Rarely   Never
4. We recycle oil products, such as car engine oil.
Always   Often   Occasionally   Rarely   Never

You might change the directions by asking learners to compare their level of activity prior to instruction with their current level, or you might administer one questionnaire prior to and one following instruction to determine changes. Immediately following instruction, you might also ask learners how they plan to behave in the next month.

Indirect Self-Report

The primary problem with direct self-reported attitude questionnaires is that people tend to respond in the manner that they believe will be seen as the most socially acceptable—in other words, how they think they are supposed to respond. Thus, such questionnaires give us a reading of how much learners think they are supposed to perform in a certain way, but the questionnaire is susceptible to learners giving a designer what they think he wants. Therefore, we often choose to use a somewhat less direct measure than the straightforward questionnaire form. For example, we might devise a questionnaire that presents scenarios in which there is some competition for the main character's time or other resources, to determine the learners' level of commitment toward recycling. For example, the following items might be used to assess these predispositions toward recycling behaviors:

Directions: Read each of the following scenarios and decide the extent to which you agree or disagree with the behavior of the main character. This behavior is underlined in the scenario. Circle the descriptor that most nearly reflects your level of agreement or disagreement.

1. It is Tuesday morning and Greg is getting ready to go to school. Tuesday is the morning that the recycled newspapers and bottles must be placed in separate boxes on the curb for pickup. Greg's friend Skip arrives to walk to school with him, but Skip is in a hurry because he wants to talk to the science teacher before school. Greg decides that it won't hurt to forget recycling this one week, so he throws all of the bottles and newspapers in the regular dumpster in the alley and leaves for school with Skip.

Strongly agree   Agree   Disagree   Strongly disagree

As it is sometimes difficult to discern why a learner chooses a particular position toward a behavior, you may obtain a more valid "reading" of the learners' attitude by asking the learners *why* they circled the responses that they did.

Observation

The indirect self-report, unlike the direct self-report, is less susceptible to error from responding with the most socially acceptable answer. However, the indirect self-report is still vulnerable to learners responding more in line with how they think they should respond, rather than how they would actually respond if they were in the situation themselves. Therefore, often it is desirable to actually observe learners' behaviors to see what they actually choose to do. For example, to assess learners' actual behavior regarding recycling, a teacher might set up a recycling center in the corner of the classroom and observe the frequency and duration of each learner's contribution to the recycling effort. A checklist instrument might be used, in which the teacher unobtrusively observes the recycling center for a specified amount of time each day over the period of a month. The checklist might look something like this:

Directions to observer: Beside each student's name for each occurrence in which the learner properly contributes to the recycling center, enter the date of the contribution.

Name	Paper	Plastic	Cans	Bottles
Terry Schritt			2/14	
David Lieber				
Kathryn Arenque	2/18	2/18	2/18	2/18
Mildred Zuni				
Jim Jardinero	2/14			
Tom White			2/19	

Obviously, observational measures require a lot of time, effort, and persistence to obtain a reliable measure of an attitude for a group of learners. However, it is the most valid measure of how learners choose to perform. Assessment of attitudes is so difficult that we often try to use more than one measurement to obtain a clearer picture of the learner's actual attitude. For example, with the recycling example, we might wish to employ one self-report and one observational measure and combine the two measures in some way to get a final measure of learners' attitudes. In general, these changes in attitude are not reflected in learners' grades, primarily because of the difficulty in validly measuring attitude learning and difficulties in determining what is an acceptable level of performance. However, we commonly use aggregated group measures to assess the overall effectiveness of our instruction during formative or summative evaluation.

E X E R C I S E   D

Carol and Larry are safety engineers for a chemical manufacturer, duRiviére. They are working on a variety of approaches to improve worker safety in the plants. Among their activities has been the design and development of improved safety training, in which they have tried to both improve employee knowledge and skills of safe handling procedures and increase employee commitment to always employ safe procedures. They have developed instruction involving print materials, virtual reality simulations, and a series of Safety Seminars that include both persuasive, large-screen multimedia presentations and small-group discussions. Their current concern is assessment of employee learning from the program, including the affective goals of the program. In a team effort with Quality Improvement personnel, Carol and Larry will have access to whatever they need to implement their assessment. Describe three possible forms of assessment for this program, select one, and defend your selection in terms of salient characteristics that you can derive from this scenario relating to learners, learning task, and setting.

EXAMPLE ATTITUDE LESSON

Now we will expand on the basics of attitude learning and put together an example lesson that employs both the fundamentals discussed to this point, as well as the expanded instructional events as a strategy development framework for an entire lesson.

Our example attitude lesson will use the following objective: Given an interpersonal conflict situation, the student will choose to respond in a nonviolent manner, resolving the conflict, if possible. (This objective arose out of a personal experience one of the authors had as a classroom teacher in an elementary school in which there was a definite and clear need for the students to

achieve this particular learning objective.) We would classify the objective in the Krathwohl taxonomy as a valuing objective, either at the level of preference for a value (3.2) or at the commitment level (3.3).

INTRODUCTION

Deploy Attention/Establish Instructional Purpose/Arouse Interest and Motivation/

Preview Lesson

Our instruction in "nonviolent solutions" might begin with the teacher showing a videotape that depicts a common classroom conflict situation, perhaps a conflict between two elementary students over a pencil:

"You've got my pencil!"

"No I don't!"

"Oh yes you do!"

As the argument becomes truly heated, the teacher stops the video and asks, "What would you do?"

Although it does not follow a strict set of steps, the introduction to this lesson seems to be an appropriate one and fulfills the functions of gaining attention, arousing interest, and in a vague, perhaps dramatic way, establishing a direction.

One important characteristic of the videotape is that at least one of the characters on the tape is a person who functions as a role model for the students. If the tape is locally produced, the person might be an older student whom students in this class would probably respect. If the tape is commercially produced, it will help if the character is portrayed by an actor who is particularly popular with students in the class.

Body

Recall Relevant Prior Knowledge/Process Information and Examples

When the teacher stops the tape, a class discussion may focus on answering the question "What would you do in this situation?" The teacher will need to have in mind (or on a lesson plan used as notes) anticipated responses from the students, some of which might include "I would hit him and get my pencil back," and "I would get the teacher to settle it," and "I would see if we could figure out whose pencil it was and where the other pencil went." For each case, the teacher needs to be able to discuss what the results of this type of response are likely to be. For example, if the suggestion is to hit the other student and take the pencil back, what is likely to happen if that action is taken? If we call in the teacher, what is likely to happen? If we negotiate or talk it out, what is likely to happen?

In attitude change, if a persuasive communication is used and discussion is also employed, the persuasive communication should happen before discussion, in order to minimize public commitment to the old attitude and lessen the resistance to change (Hoban & Van Ormer, 1950). This principle would suggest that before the discussion begins, the entire videotape should be shown because the role model demonstrates the desired choice.

Focus Attention/Employ Learning Strategies

There are two different approaches, both potentially effective, for continuing the lesson. The teacher could employ a persuasive communication technique to describe the consequences of the desired nonviolent approach, if the students have not already done so in their discussion. The other alternative would be to continue viewing the videotape, depicting the hero (role model) settling the difference in a nonviolent fashion. It is important that the dramatization end with the role model receiving reinforcement for having chosen the action taken. Depiction of acceptance and admiration by peers is an appropriate reinforcer for all age groups.

Practice/Evaluate Feedback

The group discussion could be considered as practice and feedback; it certainly is for the cognitive component of the objective. However, additional practice and feedback is completely feasible in this example and should be used. Role-playing by students in a variety of contrived (but believable) situations could be an excellent part of the instruction. (This is not a discussion of an individual lesson because we anticipate this work to go on for a period of time.) One of the goals of the role-playing would be to help students gain a repertoire of nonviolent responses to a variety of situations, experiencing the learning in all three components: cognitive (knowing some ways to respond to conflict situations other than violently); affective (knowing why—gaining the disposition to choose to respond nonviolently); and behavioral (practice in responding nonviolently with feedback experienced for that behavior).

Conclusion

Summary/Transfer Knowledge/Remotivate and Close

It is appropriate to end each session or lesson with a conclusion that includes the events of summary, transfer knowledge, and remotivate and close. The specifics of each conclusion would vary with what has been done during the particular session. A clear restatement of the desired behavior by a respected model would be a good summary, leaving learners with no doubt regarding the purpose of the instruction. (We *do* believe that the purposes of affective instruction should be stated explicitly at some point to lessen the impression of manipulation.)

Assessment

Assess Learning/Evaluate Feedback and Seek Remediation

The primary and fundamental assessment would be in observation of the students' future behavior in conflict situations. Even so, other forms of assessment are appropriate—their gain in reliability offsets the losses in validity from the ideal (of actually observing what each student does in all future conflict situations). Role-playing, again, would appear to be an excellent means of assessment. The role-playing situation may not adequately bring out the affective component of the objective. (This is because students may make different choices when they are out of the teacher's sight.) However, observations of role-playing situations can do a good job of providing for assessment of the cognitive and behavioral components of the objective.

S U M M A R Y

In this chapter, we have considered instructional design for the learning of attitude objectives. We began by discussing attitude learning from a variety of theoretical standpoints, involving both learning theory and a communication perspective. Following a discussion of the components of attitude learning, we broadened our scope somewhat and looked at a variety of kinds of objectives in the affective domain using the Krathwohl taxonomy. Then we presented instructional conditions for attitude learning and a sample attitude change lesson that illustrated use of the expanded instructional events in designing attitude instruction.

Figure 14.4 outlines key instructional events for attitude learning

EXTENDED EXAMPLE

In the Learning Resources Web site, you will find this chapter's contribution to our photography course. The example for this chapter is strategy design for teacher-led (either face-to-face or online) instruction on an affective learning goal, that of appreciating black and white photography.

R E A D I N G S A N D R E F E R E N C E S

Bednar, A., & Levie, W. H. (1993). Attitude-change principles. In M. Fleming & W. H. Levie (Eds.), *Instructional message design: Principles from the behavioral and cognitive sciences* (2nd ed.) (pp. 283–304). Englewood Cliffs, NJ: Educational Technology Publications.

Introduction	Deploy attention.	• Use an engaging situation.
	Arouse interest and motivation.	• Identify with character or situation.
	Establish instructional purpose.	• May be direct or indirect but to withhold for whole lesson is manipulative.
	Preview lesson.	• May be indirect or withheld.
Body	Recall prior knowledge.	• Present persuasion before expression of old attitude.
	Process information.	• Use persuasion, discussion, role playing, or simulation.
	Focus attention.	• Use respected role model if persuasion technique is used; role model should be seen to receive valued reward.
	Employ learning strategies.	• Use acronyms, mnemonics, and slogans for cognitive component as appropriate.
	Practice.	• Practice cognitive, behavioral, and affective techniques; know what to do, and know how it feels.
	Evaluate feedback.	• Emphasize natural consequences. • Include cognitive, behavioral, and affective aspects.
Conclusion	Summarize and review.	• Offer clear restatement of desired behavior; purpose of instruction should be clear.
	Transfer knowledge.	• Discuss applications, situations. • Role-play, use simulations.
	Remotivate and close.	• Realize how new learning can be used.
Assessment	Assess performance.	• Ideal is behavior in actual free choice situation. • Practical is role-play or simulation of situations.
	Feedback and remediation.	• Emphasize natural consequences. • Include cognitive, behavioral, and affective aspects.

Figure 14.4 Key Events for Attitude Learning

Bohlin, R. M. (1987). Motivation in instructional design: Comparison of an American and a Soviet model. *Journal of Instructional Development, 10*(2), 11–14.

Brandhorst, A. R. (1978). *Reconceptualizing the affective domain* (No. ED 153 891). Williamsburg, VA: ERIC Document Reproduction Service.

Cennamo, K., & Braunlich, E. (1996, February). *The effects of relevance on mental effort.* Paper presented at the meeting of Association for Educational Communications and Technology, Indianapolis, IN.

Eagly, A. H., & Warren, R. (1976). Intelligence, comprehension, and opinion change. *Journal of Personality, 44,* 226–242.

Fleming, M., & Levie, W. H. (1978). *Instructional message design: Principles from the behavioral sciences.* Englewood Cliffs, NJ: Educational Technology Publications.

Fleming, M., & Levie, W. H. (Eds.). (1993). *Instructional message design: Principles from the behavioral and cognitive sciences* (2nd ed.). Englewood Cliffs, NJ: Educational Technology Publications.

Gagné, R. M. (1985). *The conditions of learning* (4th ed.). New York: Holt, Rinehart & Winston.

Gephart, W. J., & Ingle, R. B. (1976). *Evaluation and the affective domain.* Proceedings of the National Symposium for Professors of Educational Research (NSPER) (No. ED 157 911). Phoenix, AZ: ERIC Document Reproduction Service.

Graham, S., & Weiner, B. (1996). Theories and principles of motivation. In D. C. Berliner & R. C. Calfee (Eds.), *Handbook of educational psychology* (pp. 63–84). New York: Macmillan.

Greene, B. A., & Miller, R. B. (1996). Influences on achievement: Goals, perceived ability, and cognitive engagement. *Contemporary Educational Psychology, 21,* 181–192.

Hoban, C. F., & Van Ormer, E. B. (1950). *Instructional film research, 1918–1950.* Pennsylvania State University Instructional Film Research Program (Tech. Report No. SDC 269-7-19). Port Washington, NY: U.S. Naval Training Device Center, Office of Naval Research.

Howe, M. J. A. (1987). Motivation, cognition and individual achievements. In E. deCorte, H. Lodewijks, R. Parmentier, & P. Span (Eds.), *Learning and instruction: European research in an international context, Vol. 1* (pp. 133–145). Leuven, Belgium: Leuven University Press.

Images of Man. (1972). (Filmstrip Kit). New York: Scholastic.

Kamradt, T. F., & Kamradt, E. J. (1999). Structured design for attitudinal instruction. In C. M. Reigeluth, *Instructional-design theories and models II: A new paradigm of instructional theory* (pp. 563–590). Englewood Cliffs, NJ: Erlbaum.

Kardash, C. M., & Scholes, R. J. (1995). Effects of preexisting beliefs and repeated readings on belief change, comprehension, and recall of persuasive text. *Contemporary Educational Psychology, 20,* 201–221.

Katzell, R. A., & Thompson, D. E. (1990). Work motivation theory and practice. *American Psychologist, 45*(2), 144–153.

Kiesler, C. A., Collins, B. E., & Miller, N. (1969). *Attitude change: A critical analysis of theoretical approaches.* New York: Wiley.

Krathwohl, D. R., Bloom, B. S., & Masia, B. B. (1964). *Taxonomy of eductional objectives: The classification of educational goals: Handbook II. Affective domain.* New York: Longman.

Martin, B. L., & Briggs, L. J. (1986). *The affective and cognitive domains: Integration for instruction and research.* Englewood Cliffs, NJ: Educational Technology Publications.

Mason, R. G. (Ed.). (1970). *The Print.* New York: Time-Life Books.

McCaslin, M., & Good, T. L. (1996). The informal curriculum. In D. C. Berliner & R. C. Calfee (Eds.), *Handbook of educational psychology* (pp. 622–670). New York: Macmillan.

Merrill, M. D. (1972). Taxonomies, classifications, and theory. In R. N. Singer (Ed.), *The psychomotor domain: Movement and behavior.* (pp. 385–414). Philadelphia: Lee & Febiger.

Miller, R., Behrens, J., Greene, B., & Newman, J. (1993). Goals and perceived ability: Impact on student valuing, self-regulation, and persistence. *Contemporary Educational Psychology 8,* 2–14.

National Special Media Institutes. (1972). *The affective domain: A resource book for media specialists: Handbook 1 Contributions of behavioral science to instructional technology.* Washington, DC: Gryphon House.

Newby, T. J., & Stepich, D. A. (1990). Teaching attitudes. *Performance & Instruction, 29* (3), 48–49.

Nunnally, J. C. (1967). *Psychometric theory.* New York: McGraw-Hill.

Petty, R. E., & Cacioppo, J. T. (1986). *Communication and persuasion: Central and peripheral routes to attitude and change.* New York: Springer-Verlag.

Simonson, M., & Maushak, N. (1996). Instructional technology and attitude change. In D. J. Jonassen (Ed.), *Handbook of research for educational communications and technology* (pp. 984–1016). New York: Macmillan.

Sinatra, G. M. & Pintrich, P. R. (Eds.). (2003). *Intentional conceptual change.* Mahwah, NJ: Erlbaum.

Weiner, B. (1991). Metaphors in motivation and attribution. *American Psychologist, 46*(9), 921–930.

Zimbardo, P. G., & Leippe, M. R. (1991). *The psychology of attitude change and social influence.* Philadelphia, PA: Temple University Press.

STRATEGIES FOR PSYCHOMOTOR SKILL LEARNING

CHAPTER OBJECTIVES

At the conclusion of this chapter, you should be able to do the following:

- Design a strategy for a psychomotor lesson.
- Determine whether spaced or massed practice is needed for a particular situation.
- Determine whether part or whole practice is needed for a particular situation.

INTRODUCTION

We will now look at guidelines for designing instruction for psychomotor learning. It is important to consider psychomotor learning as a separate skill area because this domain is commonly misunderstood in practice. On the one hand, learning tasks in this domain are frequently ignored or treated as if they were cognitive tasks (such as ignoring the motor skill aspect of learning to drive a car). On the other hand, we frequently see learning tasks that are not actually psychomotor tasks treated as if they were (such as writing an essay or doing long division with pencil and paper). Another reason motor learning is important to study is its relative neglect in the instructional design literature. Relatively little emphasis has been given to the specifics of instructional design for motor learning, but a great deal of research in this area has been done in the physical education and music education fields. We can draw upon and use this research in the instructional design process.

On the following pages, we will look at what psychomotor learning is and how to accurately identify learning tasks in this domain. We will also look at instructional concerns and specific instructional strategies that are effective for psychomotor learning tasks, along with the critical instructional events of performance and feedback for this type of learning task. We will then return to our photography unit, looking at a motor skill that is part of our unit and showing how this skill could be taught using the guidelines presented in the chapter.

A REVIEW OF PSYCHOMOTOR LEARNING

Chapter 5 introduced the type of learning called *psychomotor skills* and used Gagné's (1985) characterization of them as "coordinated muscular movements that are typified by smoothness and precise timing" (p. 62). Let us begin our review of psychomotor learning by looking first at what is meant by the idea of skills; then we will look more specifically at psychomotor skills as learning tasks.

The concept of "skill," in the broad sense, may be defined as a "completion of a task with ease and precision" (Robb, 1972, p. 39). Generally, when we think of skills, we have psychomotor capabilities in mind. Psychomotor tasks involve skills that are physical in nature. We are using the term *psychomotor* rather than *motor* to emphasize the fact that there is a cognitive part to all motor skills. This cognitive component to a skill may be thought of as a schema that underlies the skill. Once we become actually skilled in a psychomotor capability, the cognitive or "thinking" part of the skill becomes automatic and we are no longer conscious of that part of the skill. Yet in learning a psychomotor skill, the cognitive part of the skill is an important part of the learning task.

Designers frequently have difficulty classifying psychomotor tasks accurately, mistaking the physical manifestations of intellectual skills for the physical part of psychomotor skills. Learning to write an essay, for example, is not a psychomotor objective, even though physical movement may be observed as the student writes. The critical, distinguishing feature of the objective is the *new* learning that is involved. In learning to write an essay, the student's new learnings are not of a physical nature. The handwriting or typing involved in writing the essay is a psychomotor task—an important but distant prerequisite learning.

To demonstrate that they possess an intellectual skill, learners generally must use some muscular movement. For example, if you are asked to demonstrate your skill in long division, you must move your hand to write or your mouth to speak the answer. You may even engage in movements as you solve the long division problem. In fact, good instruction of the concepts and rules involved in long division can involve manipulating objects and doing a lot of physical activity. But what is being learned—the new learning involved in learning long division—is a mental, not a physical skill. When the learner works on a long division exercise or test item with paper and pencil, the manipulations of the pencil, although necessary, are not what we are interested in. At some earlier point in time, we were interested in the learner's manipulation of the pencil as a learning task. At that time, when the youngster was learning to write with a pencil, we *were* concerned with a psychomotor learning task.

Skills that are of a psychomotor nature have their own particular characteristics. In general, a learning task can be said to be a psychomotor task if it requires learning to perform coordinated muscular movements. Examples of psychomotor learning tasks include learning to dribble a basketball, form letters and words with a pencil, parallel park a car, and use a mouse to select objects on a computer screen. Psychomotor tasks are skills that involve learning new muscular movement.

Researchers have developed various categories of psychomotor skills (Magil, 1985; Oxendine, 1984; Singer, 1980). One means of categorizing psychomotor skills—as discrete versus continuous—relates to the distinctiveness of the beginning and ending points of skills. **Discrete skills** consist either of a single step or a few steps and have distinct, task-determined beginnings and endings, such as using a key to unlock a door, clicking the mouse button on a computer, or hammering a nail.

Continuous skills are those for which the beginning and ending points are more subtle and performer-determined, such as dribbling a basketball, swimming, and steering a car to stay within a traffic lane. A sub-category of discrete skills, *serial skills,* is a series of sub-skills assembled to form a major skill. Forming letters to write words, parallel parking a car, and playing a violin are examples of serial skills. A particularly interesting and frequently encountered task that has characteristics of both continuous and serial skills is the tracking task, such as aiming at a moving target. The stimulus of a tracking task may be continuous—such as a steadily moving target—but research has revealed that acquisition of the target (aiming at it) frequently involves a complex series of decisions and actions rather than one continuous fluid motion as we subjectively experience it (Travers, 1977). Since it takes approximately one-quarter of a second to initiate movement in a direction, only two or three adjustments can be made in a second. Expert performance in tracking tasks demanding particularly fast response requires anticipation.

Another means of categorizing psychomotor skills—as closed versus open—involves determining how the skill relates to the environment. **Closed skills** are performed without active influence from the environment. **Open skills** are used when the environment causes the performer to make continuous adjustments. Thus, bowling and golf involve closed skills, whereas playing basketball and hockey involve open skills. If all of basketball comprised doing slam-dunk demonstrations without contending with other players, then basketball would be a closed-skill sport. Since those pesky opponents and the player's interactions with them do have a way of making the exact situation of making any shot unpredictable, we find that basketball involves open skills—skills performed in interaction with changing and dynamic external situations.

A third means of categorizing psychomotor skills involves classifying **person and object motion** (Fitts & Posner 1967; Merrill, 1972): The person may perform the skill either at rest or in motion, and the object may either be at rest or in motion. The two conditions of the person and the two conditions of the object are cast in a matrix in Figure 15.1. The four cells of the matrix represent four types of motor skills. Each of these types has different learning and performance concerns. Type I skills, used when both the performer and the object are at rest, such as clicking the mouse button on a computer or using a key to open a lock, are concerned primarily with consistency of response, with little need for quickness of adjustment. Type II skills, used when a stable performer works with a moving object, such as aiming at a moving target from a stationary platform, are partially dynamic tasks. Type III skills, used when a moving performer is working with a stable object, such as making a slam-dunk shot in basketball, are also partially dynamic tasks. Practice requirements for Type II and Type III skills are greater than for Type I skills due to the need to be prepared for the variety of situations that can be encountered. General recommendations include the use of standard, "most probable" situations for initial practice until some competence is developed, such as might be seen in batting practice with a pitching machine. This should occur before encountering the more complex and demanding situations, such as batting to a big-league pitcher (Singer, 1980). Type IV skills, used when both the performer and the object are in motion, such as a spirited volley in badminton or catching a ball while running, involve the most complex dynamic interaction. Learning these skills is generally a long process, involving prior practice at levels II and III.

Environmental Object	
At Rest	**In Motion**
Type I Driving a golf ball Picking up a pencil Threading a needle	**Type II** Hitting a baseball Aiming a gun at a flying duck Following a rotary pursuit
Type III Shooting a layup (basketball) Throwing to first base (the shortstop in baseball)	**Type IV** Aiming at an aircraft from a bobbing ship Running while throwing a football to a moving receiver

(Body: rows labeled At Rest and In Motion)

Figure 15.1 Psychomotor Tasks Classified by Movement of Performer and Object
Source: M. D. Merrill, (1972), p. 403. Used with permission.

Clearly, each of the three approaches to categorizing skills sheds a somewhat different light on the nature of psychomotor skill learning and on individual learning tasks as well. One task may be viewed under each of the three approaches because each way provides new insights into the learning requirements for that task.

As we mentioned previously, in addition to learning to control a muscular movement, psychomotor learning tasks have a cognitive component to them. This component is the *psycho-* part of the *psychomotor* combination. Remember that psychomotor skills usually contain within them a procedural rule that organizes the kind and sequence of actions performed. Thus, we see psychomotor learning as a process involving the acquisition of two basic components—muscular movements and a procedural rule.

E X E R C I S E   A

Classify the following skills, using each of the three categorization schemes. In the three blanks, label each skill as discrete (D), continuous (C), or serial (S); as open (O) or closed (C); and as Type I, II, III, or IV.

_____ _____ _____   **1.** Touch-typing on a keyboard.

_____ _____ _____   **2.** Ice-skating.

_____ _____ _____   **3.** Returning a serve in tennis.

_____ _____ _____   **4.** Shooting a clay pigeon.

_____ _____ _____   **5.** Writing the letter *g* in cursive script.

_____ _____ _____   **6.** Playing kettle drums in an orchestra.

_____ _____ _____   **7.** Grabbing the brass ring on a carousel ride.

CRITICAL ELEMENTS OF PSYCHOMOTOR SKILLS

The two components of a psychomotor skill, as characterized in the research literature on human skilled behavior, provide a foundation for prescribing the instructional strategy for this type of learning. Two primary characteristics distinguish skilled behavior from other activities. First, the act employs *executive subroutines* to control decisions and supply subordinate skills in a hierarchical organization or plan (Miller, Galanter, & Pribram, 1960; see Robb, 1972). Second, the act employs *temporal patterning* of skills to integrate the sequence of performance over time in which the skilled performer employs pacing and anticipation to enable the act to be performed with ease and smoothness (Robb, 1972).

Competing lines of theory in the specialty of motor learning include the "closed loop" theory (Adams, 1971) and a schema theory (Schmidt, 1982). Both theories

attempt to describe the cognitive component of skills, often called *motor programs,* the role of internal feedback, and knowledge of results, or *KR* ("information about the correctness of response from an external source such as . . . a teacher or coach" [Magil, 1985, p. 68]).

Much of what we do in providing instruction for psychomotor skills involves (1) a demonstration and explanation that leads to the verbal information and procedural rule learning that form the basis for the executive subroutines, and (2) practice with feedback that leads to temporal patterning. (Chapter 10 described instructional strategies for learning procedural rules, and more about the cognitive component of psychomotor learning will be provided later in this chapter.) The other critical factor is practice. Two issues deserve attention here: distribution of practice (massed versus spaced) and chunking of skill elements (whole versus part).

Massed versus Spaced Practice

In *massed practice,* the learner engages in one or a few intensive, extended periods of practice with little or no rest in between. The alternate form of practice, called *spaced practice,* is the form in which many relatively short practice sessions are distributed over time.

Mumford, Costanza, Baughman, Threlfall, and Fleishman (1994) studied distribution of practice and found that interactions existed between learner abilities, task complexity, and best form of distribution of practice. In general, they found that spaced practice facilitates cognitive processing, and massed practice contributes to associative learning. Their results point to situations in which massed practice is sometimes preferable in learning psychomotor skills. Matching of practice with primary factors that contribute to best distribution should be performed with care.

The primary factors that interact with practice distribution are learner characteristics (such as age, skill level, and prior experience) and the type of skill to be learned (whether the skill is simple or complex, has few or many elements, is fatiguing, or demands close attention to detail). Harrison and Blakemore (1989) described typical conditions under which spaced practice would be advisable:

> Younger students and students with low ability levels fatigue easily and have shorter attention or concentration spans, and lower interest levels. Distributed practice sessions in which several skills are practiced during a class period are usually preferred for these students. . . . Strenuous activities often must be scheduled for shorter periods of time due to the effects of fatigue. (p. 95)

Figure 15.2 summarizes factors that affect decisions on practice distribution.

	Shorter and More Frequent	Longer and Less Frequent
If the Task	Is simple, repetitive, or boring Demands intense concentration Is fatiguing Demands close attention to detail	Is complex Has many elements Requires warm-up Is a new one for the performer

If the Learner	Is young or immature
	  (unable to sustain activity)
	Has short attention span
	Has poor concentration skills
	Fatigues easily
		Is older or more mature
		Is able to concentrate for long
		  periods at a time
		Has good ability to focus attention
		Tires less easily

Figure 15.2 Factors in Practice Distribution.
Source: Rothstein, A., Catelli, L., Dodds, P., and Manahan, J. (1981), p. 40. Used with permission of American Alliance for Health, Physical Education, Recreation and Dance.

Whole versus Part Practice

Another issue regarding practice that has been the object of a great deal of research is the question of how best to "chunk" the parts of a skill. A skill may be practiced as a *whole,* such as practicing a tennis serve, or it may be practiced in *parts,* such as practicing first the toss of a tennis serve, then separately practicing the swing and the follow-through. In part practice, each separate part of a skill is mastered before assembling the parts into a whole. The concern here is with the chunking of practice; demonstrations and explanations of a skill may be chunked into separate parts even when whole practice is employed.

As with massed and spaced practice decisions, the primary factors that influence decisions about whole versus part practice are found within the learner and the learning task. The number, complexity, and relationship of the subroutines in a skill can vary from relatively independent and isolated, such as tying a knot, to relatively integrated and simultaneous, such as riding a bicycle. Likewise, learner differences in attention span, memory span, and skill level help determine how much part practice will be necessary. Figure 15.3 summarizes primary factors that interact in decisions on whole versus part practice.

Even when part practice is necessary because of learning task and learner factors, there is a drawback to it: Learners may experience difficulty in putting the parts together. One technique that has been developed to overcome this problem is called the **progressive part method,** in which learners practice the first step, or part 1 of a skill, and then practice part 2 together with part 1. Then they practice part 3 along with parts 1 and 2, and so forth. Music ensemble rehearsals often

	Emphasize Wholes	Emphasize Parts

If the Task	Has highly dependent
	  (integrated) parts
	Is simple
	Is not meaningful in parts
	Is made up of simultaneously
	  performed parts
		Has highly individual parts
		Is very complex
		Is made up of individual skills
		Requires limited work on parts or
		  different segments

If the Learner	Is able to remember long sequences
	Has a long attention span
	Is highly skilled
		Has a limited memory span
		Is not able to concentrate for a long
		  period of time
		Is having difficulty with a
		  particular part
		Cannot succeed with the whole method

Figure 15.3 Factors in Chunking a Skill for Practice.
Source: Rothstein, Catelli, Dodds, & Manahan (1981), p. 38. Used with permission of American Alliance for Health, Physical Education, Recreation and Dance.

make use of progressive part practice to facilitate mastery of long, complex musical compositions.

A further refinement in progressive part practice can be seen in a technique called **backwards chaining,** in which the learner is exposed to and practices each step from last to first, in a progressive part fashion but in reverse order. For example, in teaching a young child how to tie her shoes, we would first show the whole operation as an overview. Then we would quickly tie a shoe up to the last step in the process and direct the child's attention to that last step: "Now watch me pull the loop through the hole." After two or three repetitions of this demonstration, we would give the child the shoe with the knot all tied except for this last step, which the child would get to perform. We would then demonstrate and practice the next-to-last step, and then the third-to-last step (along with the next-to-last and last steps), and so forth. The last thing we'd show and practice with her would be the first step. Backwards chaining compensates for the forgetting problem between explanations and demonstrations when there are many steps in a skill, each one of which requires practice.

Feedback Issues

In performing a motor task, the individual experiences feedback from internal sources called *proprioceptive feedback* and other sensory feedback such as vision. The nervous system, which sends commands to muscles to move, also sends signals back to the brain from the muscles and organs such as the skin. We experience a mild form of proprioceptive feedback loss when under anesthetic during dental work. Sometimes we find we have chewed our tongue or cheek badly, something that proprioceptive feedback would have prevented had the nerves in the mouth not been temporarily deadened. An expert performer of a skill depends heavily on the feedback that engagement in the task provides—visual, auditory, and proprioceptive sensations that performance of the task (and the situation) generates.

A great deal of the expertise in psychomotor functions lies in the skill of "reading" feedback generated by performance of a task. When a person is learning a new psychomotor skill, the sensation of having properly performed the skill is not present because the person can't properly perform the skill yet. External (or instructionally provided) feedback may supplement the learner's built-in feedback (the learner may think, "My swing was three inches too high"), or instruction may provide guidance to the learner on what to look for or be sensitive to (the teacher/coach may say, "Feel it on the balls of your feet when you receive the serve").

Two forms of feedback can be provided in psychomotor learning: feedback about the product (or "quality of response outcome") and feedback about the process or causes of the response outcome (Magil, 1985). During early stages of learning, feedback about process may be most helpful to learning; during later learning, feedback on outcome alone may be sufficient. Instruction-supplied feedback may not always be needed or even helpful. Early learning of simple motor tasks has been found to be improved by providing feedback on less than every response (Ho & Shea, 1978; Newell, 1974). Precision of instruction-supplied feedback can affect learning. It is possible to provide feedback that is too precise to be useful, such as describing a distance in millimeters when centimeters would be more meaningful (Rogers, 1974). The precision offered by quantitative feedback has been found in some cases to be superior to qualitative feedback, such as "you're holding the ball two inches too high" versus "you're holding the ball too high" (Smoll, 1972).

EXERCISE B

For the following scenarios, label the practice distribution as massed (M) or spaced (S). Also label the practice chunking as whole practice (W), part practice (P), progressive part practice (PP), or backward chaining (BC).

___ ___ **1.** Terri and Danny, both seven years old, are each going to assemble a model airplane. Neither of them has ever built a model airplane. The kit has balsa wood pieces that must be fit together and glued. To complete the model, one must apply wet tissue paper to the wooden framework. Both children have the desire to build the plane, but the task will be a challenge because of their age. (Consider the task of building the whole kit, as well as the subtask of papering. Think of the children's learning, not just the successful completion of the kit.)

___ ___ **2.** Jean and Ray, both ten years old, have joined a beginner's soccer team. They will be learning all aspects of the game of soccer over the four-month season.

___ ___ **3.** Amy and Abbas are graduate students in piano; they want to improve their playing technique to the concert level. They are learning to control the cross from left to right hand in loudness changes, with each hand playing a rhythmic pattern. They are both practicing George Gershwin's "Rhapsody in Blue," a long piece that is extremely difficult to play. Amy has excellent technique, but her hands are not very strong. Abbas has very strong hands but is less coordinated than Amy.

_____ _____ **4.** Barbara and Mark, both in their late twenties, are new employees at a chemical manufacturing plant. Their jobs involve moving large amounts of material from one part of the plant to another. Although aided by equipment, their jobs involve a great deal of strenuous work; they also must learn to operate hoisting and rolling equipment.

Task Analysis of a Psychomotor Skill

Earlier we noted that the learning of a psychomotor skill includes a cognitive component. The importance of the cognitive component of psychomotor skills is underscored by the "knowledge structures" approach to analyzing and describing skills (Vickers, 1990). The foundation for instructional design for physical activities that Vickers employed is a form of learning task description that emphasizes the *structure of knowledge* in a specialty.

Let's look at an example skill description, one that includes consideration of the cognitive component of the skill as subroutines in the skill:

> The task of beginning bowling can be divided into three subroutines. These are (1) the approach, (2) moving the ball, and (3) the release of the ball. Further examination of each subroutine reveals that the approach consists of steps that get progressively longer and faster and end with a slide. Since this is not the way a person normally walks, the subroutine of walking will have to be modified. Conscious effort and practice will be needed to overcome this habitual walking pattern.
>
> The second subroutine involved in the task of bowling is moving a ball through space. Although the performer is accustomed to swinging his arm, he is not familiar with moving a ball that weighs between 12 and 16 pounds.
>
> The third subroutine involves the release of the ball. A smooth release is characterized by a roll of the ball rather than a drop or throw. Thus the beginner must learn to bend his left knee (assuming he is right-handed) and release the ball smoothly on the lane, not on the approach area. The ball should land on the lane like an airplane landing on a runway. (Robb, 1972, p. 143)

Some authorities break down the learning of a psychomotor skill into three phases: cognitive phase, associative phase, and autonomous phase (Fitts & Posner, 1967; Singer, 1982). We can analyze the bowling example from this three-phase standpoint to better understand the role of the cognitive component in psychomotor learning.

During the beginning or cognitive phase of learning a psychomotor skill, learners begin to acquire the verbal information and procedural rule components of that skill. They learn what they are to do and in what sequence. Note that the learners learn *what* is to be learned; at this time they do not learn *how* to do it in the physical sense. Explanations and demonstrations are part of what is required to achieve the cognitive learning requirements for psychomotor skills. In addition, learners may need repetition and rehearsal to remember the steps of the skill. Depending on the requirements of the skill at hand, repetition along with practice during the second and third phases might be sufficient, or the cognitive component may require its own repetition and application as one grouping of objectives in a lesson design. (Refer to Chapter 10 to review the design of instruction for learning procedural rules; many of that chapter's recommendations are pertinent to learning a procedural rule that is a part of a psychomotor skill.)

During the second (or associative) phase of learning a psychomotor skill, learners begin to learn how to physically perform the skill. In bowling, learners will at some point engage in their first few practice rounds. Actual performance is required during this phase of learning, in which the learner associates the cognitive knowledge of the skill with the muscular movements required to perform it. At this stage, the procedural rule is deepened and made meaningful by the actual physical activity that accompanies each step in the procedure, but a smooth, highly skilled performance is not likely.

During the autonomous phase, practice and feedback allow the learner to progress from the jerky or fumbling efforts of the novice to the smooth, controlled, apparently effortless actions that characterize the expert performance of a psychomotor skill. The student bowler becomes more proficient at the skill, reaching what is called *automaticity*. As automaticity is attained, the performance of the cognitive component is less and less conscious, with each physical movement cueing the next physical movement. Automaticity may be parallel to schematization. When thinking about and studying the phenomenon of a skill becoming automatic, a good explanation for what goes on may be found in thinking about schema. The same networking and unifying process that underlies schematization of knowledge and rules would appear to be a good explanation for the cognitive component of psychomotor skill learning in moving from novice to expert.[*]

Novice designers are often seduced into employing a simple "bottom up" sequence for instruction based on a "simple to complex," hierarchical task analysis. The structure of complex psychomotor skill learning is rarely so straightforward, as should be learned from performing an information-processing analysis (see Chapter 5). Vickers (1990) provided an excellent example of the need for designers to avoid simplistic sequencing:

---

[*]This linking of schema with automaticity is not the same idea as that held by Schmidt (1982) described earlier in this chapter. Yet there appears to be no contradiction between our discussion and Schmidt's "Schema Theory of Motor Learning." We are indebted to Rita Richey for this concept.

Consider a two-on-two situation in basketball. Students can learn the rudiments of strategies that accompany this maneuver (give and go, screen to, post play) at the same time or even before they have mastered the intricacies of the prerequisite individual skills (dribble, pass, shoot). In addition, students often learn these skills independent of one another and not in a set, simple-to-complex progression. It is not unusual to be adept in what is considered a complex skill (e.g., shooting), but deficient in what is often considered an underlying or simpler skill (e.g., footwork). Requiring learners to move in a lockstep manner from one simple skill to the next can be a debilitating design strategy when used exclusively. (p. 36)

A GENERAL PROCEDURE FOR TEACHING PSYCHOMOTOR SKILLS

Singer (1982) provides a three-phase approach to the teaching of psychomotor skills that dovetails with the three phases of learning described above. Singer's three phases for instruction are prior to practice, during practice, and after practice. We will now elaborate these three phases to form a general procedure for teaching psychomotor skills, using our expanded instructional events as a framework.

Instruction prior to practice prepares the learners for learning the skill and engaging in the initial learning of the skill itself. To begin, learners need to know what is being learned, they need to know why they must learn it, and they need to know how they are going to go about learning this skill. In addition, during this stage of instruction explanations and demonstrations are provided, supplying the conditions for achieving the cognitive phase of learning the skill.

If we apply our expanded instructional events, we can see that events that occur prior to practice include those from both our Introduction and Body phases. From the Introduction phase we deploy attention to the lesson, establish instructional purpose, arouse interest and motivation, and obtain a preview of the lesson. Events during the Body of the lesson (but still prior to practice) include the recall of relevant prior learning, processing information and examples associated with an explanation and/or demonstration (at this stage of instruction, verbal and visual, not tactile), focusing attention to the demonstration/explanation, and employing learning strategies. Using our bowling example, let's examine the instruction.

Attention

The student's attention may be directed to bowling by merely being in the bowling alley, yet many distracting sights and sounds make it likely that the instructor will need to actively and explicitly direct the student's attention to the learning task frequently within the instruction. As an aid to continued attention, it will help to make the learner aware of how she will benefit by learning the skill that is to be taught. Much of the value in the following two events is found in helping the learner continue to pay attention to and invest effort in the lesson as it proceeds.

Purpose

Establishing the purpose can be done in many ways, but somehow the learner must be apprised of what is to be learned now. For this lesson, the instructor might say, "Today, we are going to begin to learn to bowl," and the instructor might even demonstrate what will be learned. The direction will be further refined when the instructor actually previews the lesson.

Interest and Motivation

The learner should determine why she should learn the material at hand. Placing the material into a larger scheme (particularly when the learnings for the current lesson have a prerequisite function for subsequent lessons) can be sufficient for learners who are generally motivated in the course or program. For learners who are not such "self-starters," direct and personalized relating of how the material can help them may be required, including appeals to personal-social needs of the learners. For high school learners in our bowling lesson, some relationship of being skilled in bowling to being popular with peers might somehow be devised. Appeals to health and fitness might not be sufficient for high school students but might well hit home with a middle-aged population.

Preview

The preview should include both an overview of *what* will be learned, as well as *how* the lesson will proceed. For example, the instructor might give an overview of the content of a bowling lesson by saying the following:

In today's introductory lesson in bowling, we will learn three main steps. First, we will learn the approach, in which we will see that we walk toward the line with steps of increasing length and increasing speed. Second, we will learn how to move the ball during the approach. Third, we will learn the release, in which we will learn to roll the ball out of the hand rather than drop or throw it.

Notice that a preview of exactly what is to be learned is presented. Next, the instructor would preview how the lesson will proceed by saying something like the following:

We'll proceed like this: First, I will show you each of the steps and point out things to focus on. Each of you will have a chance to see what is involved in each of the steps—how to do it right. Then you'll have a chance to practice. I will be watching you and helping you. I'll offer correction if I see you're not doing something right. Then, after we've had a chance to practice the skill, I'll have each of you roll the ball a few times without help. At this point I'll be watching you to see how well you can do it. OK, let's begin.

Recall Relevant Prior Knowledge

The skills of bowling build upon previously learned skills. The approach in bowling, for example, is a special form of walking. Immediately prior to the demonstration of the approach, the instructor might find it helpful to remind learners that what the instructor is doing as she performs the approach is simply walking. During the practice phase, as well, learners can be assisted in their first tries at the approach by being advised to walk. The instructor might include verbal tips such as the following:

Walk to the line now. Just pretend you're on a stroll in the park. This time, though, just imagine that you're walking up to something with longer and longer and faster steps as you near your goal. That's it.

Process Information and Examples

In our psychomotor skill lesson, this event is accomplished by the explanation/demonstration of the skill itself. Still prior to practice, the instructor presents the skill itself. In some lessons, an explanation should precede a demonstration, and in others, the explanation and demonstration should occur simultaneously. The decision will depend on the specifics of the skill being learned and is a fairly self-evident one. The instructional medium used for information and examples does not always have to be a live teacher; a videotape will frequently be a superior medium for delivering this event. Advantages of video include its ability to show close-up details, to employ techniques such as slow motion, and to provide the opportunity for individualized instruction. Regardless of the delivery medium employed, the explanation/demonstration should be clearly and explicitly organized in terms of the steps (or subroutines) of the skill, perhaps even providing verbal cues, such as *pause, left, right, left and back, release, slide,* and *follow-through.* In the bowling lesson, the instructor will demonstrate and explain simultaneously, repeating demonstrations that focus on each of the three bowling steps. In addition to live demonstration, a videotape will be used that shows the bowler from different angles (from the side, back, and front) and presents close-ups of the release itself in slow motion as well as normal speed.

Focus Attention

The learner's need to attend to instruction will be present throughout the lesson, but lapses of attention during presentation of information and examples are a frequent contributor to unsuccessful instruction. The learner's attention will be enhanced by the quality of the introduction, as well as by characteristics of the explanation/demonstration itself. Also, during and after the practice phases of the lesson, the learner activity that is intrinsic to psychomotor skill lessons is potentially a built-in attention aid, but learner attention should not be taken for granted, even in psychomotor skill lessons.

Attention takes on particular importance in many psychomotor skill lessons, which involve skills that we can call *critical skills.* Critical skills are those that involve potentially life-threatening situations, such as piloting aircraft, performing surgery, and packing parachutes. Just because instruction involves potentially life-threatening situations does not necessarily mean that learners will be paying sufficient attention during all phases of instruction. The importance and relevance of the activities at hand should always be clear to the learner. Specific techniques for maintaining attention should be considered and employed as needed. Often with psychomotor skill instruction, attention-directing can be included as a part of carefully performing demonstrations. The instructor might say, "Notice that I . . ." or "See how he . . ." and so forth.

Employ Learning Strategies

Learners can be assisted in their acquisition of new skills by employing learning strategies. The instrudction in the new skill may include assistance or suggestions that can lead the learner to employ learning strategies that he may not otherwise devise. In our bowling lesson, the instructor might suggest a visualization strategy by saying the following:

Before you step up to the lane, briefly close your eyes and try to visualize yourself executing the steps in bowling, smoothly and skillfully.

Another example of a possible learning strategy for our bowling lesson could be the use of a mnemonic or oral rehearsal of what the learner should be doing. One such mnemonic that has been used in tennis instruction for the steps in returning a tennis serve is SBSSF: "*S*ide to the net, racket *B*ack, *S*tep and *S*wing through the ball, and *F*ollow through." Analogies can also be used to support the recall of the steps in the procedural rule supporting the motor skill. For instance, many of us learned to tie a bow knot through an analogous story about a rabbit going around a tree, in a hole, and so forth.

Practice

During practice, instruction primarily needs to support appropriate practice. Here is where decisions about the distribution (part/whole) and scheduling (massed/spaced) of practice are made, as well as sequencing. Practice is a fundamental aspect of learning and perfecting psychomotor skills. Complex skills such as musical performance and athletics are refined over long periods of time involving repeated practice.

From the standpoint of our expanded instructional events, we can see that *all* of the events may legitimately take place in the "during practice" phase, but that the predominant events are practice and feedback.

Practice will involve the student actually grasping the bowling ball, walking to the line while beginning the arm swing, and so forth. During practice, guidance may be provided by a coach talking the learner through his first attempts or by providing hints and suggestions on holding the ball, placing the feet, and so forth. Provision of learning guidance may also be seen in ensuring that the learner participates in repeated practice, appropriately scheduled and chunked. Much of the traditional role of a good athletic coach may be seen as an excellent example of the provision of learning guidance.

During this event, we also have the opportunity to specifically apply what we know about practice distribution, scheduling, and sequencing. In the case of our bowling example, spaced practice will be required because of fatigue and task complexity factors. Many athletic skills are of this nature because the concept of "mastery" does not apply, and practice can lead to improvement over a period of years. In learning a skill such as bowling, practice will be required until the learner reaches automaticity.

Feedback

Feedback is obtained not only externally by the comments and suggestions provided by a coach or videotape replay but also internally by the learner's own built-in proprioceptive feedback mechanisms and senses of hearing and vision. The internal feedback that we receive from kinesthetic "feel" and from sensory systems is fundamental to learning psychomotor skills. For this reason, feedback is considered to be a "during practice" event rather than an "after practice" event. Learners may have to be taught to recognize proprioceptive feedback. For example, a coach might throw the ball at the "sweet spot" of the learner's tennis racket many times before the learner begins to recognize the "feel" of hitting the ball properly.

After practice, we are primarily concerned with evaluation and conclusion of the lesson. We will reverse our usual instructional events sequence in this example. As noted in the introduction to the expanded instructional events in Chapter 7, the sequence provided is nominal, not strictly prescriptive. In this example's bowling lesson, the instructor will include an assessment of the learners' skills within the lesson itself, followed by the conclusion phase of the lesson.

Assessment of Psychomotor Skill Learning

The *psycho-* or cognitive portion of psychomotor tasks can be assessed in the manner we have described in Chapters 8 through 14. For example, many psychomotor tasks involve the learners' ability to apply a procedural rule or rules, such as the mental procedure of selecting the appropriate place to stand, the proper placement of the body, and the procedure for getting the racket back, connecting, and following through when performing a serve in tennis. There are also many declarative knowledge, concept, and rule objectives related to following the rules and scoring in many sports that involve psychomotor skills. All of these can be assessed in a manner similar to the categories described in the previous chapters.

However, the *motor* portion of these skills must be assessed in a somewhat different manner. Generally, these skills must be assessed by learners' demonstrating or producing the behavior (constructing a response). This type of assessment will be the most valid. Generally, learners are given a number of instances or trials to perform the behavior. This ensures a reliable measure. Checklists or rating scales are often used to evaluate the learners' performance. For example, the following rating scale is based upon a portion of Rink's (1985) task analysis of the psychomotor skill of dribbling in basketball:

Directions to observer: *Learner should be observed dribbling during the course of a regular game of basketball. Rate learners on the frequency of their performance of each of the desirable behaviors listed below.*

1. Effectiveness
Keeps the ball away from the defense.
Always   Often   Occasionally   Rarely   Never
Uses the dribble to put the team in a better position.
Always   Often   Occasionally   Rarely   Never
2. Efficiency
Uses pads of fingers and wrist action.
Always   Often   Occasionally   Rarely   Never
Keeps ball close and slightly to the side of the dribbling hand when stationary.
Always   Often   Occasionally   Rarely   Never
Keeps ball close and out in front when traveling with more speed.
Always   Often   Occasionally   Rarely   Never
Keeps knees flexed when stationary.
Always   Often   Occasionally   Rarely   Never

The previous rating scale was based upon the frequency of learners performing in a certain way. It might also have been based upon degrees of acceptability. For example, the anchors might be labeled *Excellent, Good, Fair, Poor,* etc., or simply *Acceptable* and *Unacceptable.* Your subject matter expert should be able to help you determine what features and anchors are most critical for the skill and the level of the learner. Other factors that might be evaluated in assessing motor skills are accuracy, time or duration, speed in completing the task, distance (such as in shot put throws), and height or weight (e.g., in pole-vaulting and weightlifting, respectively). A valuable resource in finding, developing, and using measurement of psychomotor skills is found in a text by Clarke and Clarke (1987), *Application of Measurement to Physical Education.*

You may choose to use recognition assessment items upon occasion, such as asking a learner to recognize whether a performer's body position is correct or incorrect. However, this assessment will not substitute for learners actually demonstrating the movement themselves. It may evaluate prerequisite skills, such as a learner's ability to recognize correct or incorrect body motions, but not the ability to perform the skill.

Using an informal observation as a basis for assessment in our bowling example, the instructor could tell a learner that he is doing well on the approach but that the release needs some improvement. Another learner might be told that she is doing everything properly and should continue practicing.

Summarize and Review

The summary should recap the main points of the lesson. In our bowling example, the summary might go something like this:

> Today we had our first lesson in bowling. You all learned to throw the ball correctly, which as you recall involves three things: first, the approach, where we learned to walk to the line with steps of increasing length and speed; second, we learned how to move the ball as we approach; and third, we learned the proper way to release the ball.

In the summary, it is important to emphasize the material that has already been covered. New material should be resisted; at the very least, it should not be allowed to interfere with the consolidating and clarifying function of the summary.

Transfer of Learning

Transfer is primarily accomplished by additional practice with accompanying learning guidance and feedback. Our bowling instructor might prescribe practice twice weekly for the next six weeks, with observation and feedback twice within the practice period. This is to reinforce what was initially learned during the first session. A further example of transfer could be to bowl in different alleys.

Remotivate and Close

At the very last of our bowling lesson, the instructor will briefly remind learners, now that they know the skill, how they can apply it in the future. The closure of the lesson will let the students know that the lesson is over:

> So, now you have another alternative to going to the movies or watching TV. When you do go bowling with friends or on a date, you won't need to feel embarrassed at not being able to bowl—even if you're not an expert yet. Just remember how you did it. Go through the steps in your mind, and then let your body's memory do what it remembers. OK, see you Thursday.

Evaluate Feedback and Seek Remediation

Here, the learner processes what he knows about how well he can perform the skill and takes appropriate action. For example, one learner will need further instruction on the release of the ball. Another learner who is performing quite well will not need to concentrate on making any particular corrections, only to deepen and perfect the skills he has developed. An instructional system, such as a computer-managed instruction system, might take on some of the job of processing evaluation results and prescribing remediation.

SUMMARY

This chapter began with a review of psychomotor learning. We looked at what kind of learning characterizes psychomotor learning tasks—skills involving physical activity. We learned to look for the distinguishing feature of "what new learning is involved" to assist in accurately discriminating psychomotor tasks from other types of learning tasks.

In our review of psychomotor learning, we also looked at psychomotor learning from the "skilled performance" viewpoint. We also reviewed issues in psychomotor learning regarding practice: massed versus spaced practice and whole versus part practice, including two techniques for improving part practice—progressive part practice and backward chaining.

Next we reviewed the task analysis of a psychomotor skill (using the example of bowling), in which we saw that the major steps of the skill, or major subroutines, form the basis of the skill. Also, we looked at the phases of learning of a psychomotor skill: the cognitive phase, the associative phase, and the autonomous phase. In addition, we discussed sequencing issues that point to the need to consider "top-down" sequences rather than "bottom-up" sequences in learning psychomotor skills.

We presented a three-phase approach to the teaching of psychomotor skills, in which we looked at the instructional events that should take place prior to practice, during practice, and after practice. We used the expanded events of instruction to examine strategy decisions by using the bowling example.

Finally, we discussed the assessment of psychomotor learning, emphasizing the need for observation of performance and indicating ways to increase the reliability of such observations.

Figure 15.4 summarizes key points from the chapter.

EXTENDED EXAMPLE

In the Learning Resources Web site you will find this chapter's contribution to our photography course. The example for this chapter is strategy design for a lesson on a psychomotor skill, specifically, the skill of panning with a moving object.

Introduction	Deploy attention.	• Focus on task.
	Arouse interest and motivation.	• Determine how skill will help (may be implicit from preview or may need context of larger skill).
	Establish instructional purpose.	• The skill to be learned now should be clear.
	Preview lesson.	• Provide overview of what will be learned and how.
Body	Recall prior knowledge.	• Point out the known skills that new skill uses.
	Process information.	• Offer explanation and then demonstration. • Offer explanation and demonstration together. • Always organize by steps (subroutines) of the skill.
	Focus attention.	• Provide learner activity during practice. • Pay special attention to critical skills (dangerous, etc.).
	Employ learning strategies.	• Offer visualization of performance, mnemonics, analogies.
	Practice.	• Distribution (whole/part) Scheduling (mass/spaced) • Should be sufficient for automaticity and desired skill level.
	Evaluate feedback.	• External: suggestions, comments. • Internal: proprioceptive, sensory.
Conclusion	Summarize and review.	• Include recap of the steps in consolidating and clarifying fashion.
	Transfer knowledge.	• Extended practice—maintain proficiency; use as fundamental in many skills.
	Remotivate and close.	• Demonstrate how to apply in future and when to use.
Assessment	Assess performance.	• Observe performance; use performance rating.
	Feedback and remediation.	• Learner needs clear idea of how well he or she can perform the skill and understand what to do next.

Figure 15.4 Key Events for Psychomotor Learning

READINGS AND REFERENCES

Adams, J. A. (1971). A closed-loop theory of motor learning. *Journal of Motor Behavior, 3,* 111–150.

Briggs, L. J. (Ed.). (1977). *Instructional design.* Englewood Cliffs, NJ: Educational Technology Publications.

Clarke, H. H., & Clarke, D. H. (1987). *Application of measurement to physical education* (6th ed.). Upper Saddle River, NJ: Prentice-Hall.

Fitts, P. M., & Posner, M. I. (1967). *Human performance.* Belmont, CA: Brooks/Cole.

Gagné, R. M. (1985). *The conditions of learning* (4th ed.). New York: Holt, Rinehart & Winston.

Harrison, J. M., & Blakemore, C. L. (1989). *Instructional strategies for secondary school physical education* (2nd ed.). Dubuque, IA: Brown.

Ho, L., & Shea, J. B. (1978). Levels of processing and the coding of position cues in motor short-term memory. *Journal of Motor Behavior, 10,* 113–121.

Jonassen, D. H., & Hannum, W. H. (1986). Analysis of task analysis procedures. *Journal of Instructional Development, 9,* 2–12.

Magil, R. A. (1985). *Motor learning concepts & applications* (2nd ed.). Dubuque, IA: Brown.

Merrill, M. D. (1972). Taxonomies, classifications, and theory. In R. N. Singer (Ed.), *The psychomotor domain: Movement and behavior* (pp. 385–414). Philadelphia, PA: Lea & Febiger.

Miller, G. A., Galanter, E., & Pribram, K. (1960). *Plans and the structure of behavior.* New York: Henry Holt.

Mumford, M. D., Costanza, D. P., Baughman, W. A., Threlfall, K. V., & Fleishman, E. A. (1994). Influence of abilities on performance during practice: Effects of mass and distributed practice. *Journal of Educational Psychology, 86*(1), 134–144.

Newell, K. M. (1974). Knowledge of results and motor learning. *Journal of Motor Behavior, 1,* 235–244.

Oxendine, J. B. (1984). *Psychology of motor learning.* Upper Saddle River, NJ: Prentice-Hall.

Rink, J. E. (1985). *Teaching physical education for learning.* St. Louis, MO: Times Mirror/Mosby.

Robb, M. D. (1972). *The dynamics of motor-skill acquisition.* Upper Saddle River, NJ: Prentice-Hall.

Rogers, C. A. (1974). Feedback precision and post-feedback interval duration. *Journal of Experimental Psychology, 102,* 604–608.

Rothstein, A., Catelli, L., Dodds, P., & Manahan, J. (1981). *Basic stuff series I: Motor learning.* Reston, VA: American Alliance for Health, Physical Education, Recreation, and Dance.

Schmidt, R. A. (1982). *Motor control and learning: A behavioral emphasis.* Champaign, IL: Human Kinetics.

Singer, R. N. (1980). *Motor learning and human performance.* New York: Macmillan.

Singer, R. N. (1982). *The learning of motor skills.* New York: Macmillan.

Singer, R. N., & Dick, W. (1974). *Teaching physical education: A systems approach.* Boston: Houghton Mifflin.

Smoll, F. L. (1972). Effects of precision of information feedback upon acquisition of a motor skill. *Research Quarterly, 43,* 489–493.

Stepich, D. A., & Newby, T. J. (1990). Teaching psychomotor skills. *Performance & Instruction, 29*(4), 47–48.

Travers, R. M. W. (1977). *Essentials of learning* (4th ed.). New York: Macmillan.

Vickers, J. N. (1990). *Instructional design for teaching physical activities: A knowledge structures approach.* Champaign, IL: Human Kinetics.

MACRO STRATEGIES: INTEGRATION OF TYPES OF LEARNING

CHAPTER

16

CHAPTER OBJECTIVES

At the conclusion of this chapter, you should be able to do the following:

- Identify examples as "macro-level strategy" or "micro-level strategy," and explain why.
- Recognize examples of world-related, inquiry-related, concept-related, utilization-related, and learning-related macro-organizational strategies.
- Explain how a given content could be organized according to the Elaboration Model.
- Identify the type of curriculum organization—separate subjects, correlated, fused, or integrated—given descriptions of various curricula.

INTRODUCTION

Michael was an excellent designer, working in a medium-sized corporation as the "workshop specialist." Mike's workshops had that wonderful combination of effectiveness and appeal: People learned what they needed, and they liked his workshops a lot. He received an offer from a vocational-technical school system that he couldn't refuse, so he moved to a new job in a large VoTech center. One of Mike's first assignments was a redesign of the entire curriculum on digital robotics. He was panicked: He had never thought about, much less done, any development at the "macro-level." Where should he start? What recommendations can you make to him?

Our emphasis to this point has been on "micro-level" strategies: ways to approach instruction on particular topics or learning goals. Typically, a design and development task for either education or training involves more than one goal or topic. In most cases, larger chunks such as units, chapters, courses, and multicourse curricula are part of the learning context. These larger units are candidates for design work, just as are the individual elements. Developing instruction at the macro level is frequently referred to as *curriculum development*. The function of a curriculum has been described by Apple (1979) as *providing access to knowledge*. How this access is to be supported and organized is a central curriculum question. Macro-level concerns are in many ways parallel to those at the micro level, as we will see in this chapter. There are concepts and tools, however, that are used only at the macro level, and these concepts and tools are the major focus of this chapter.

The expanded instructional events provide an excellent organizational structure for designing a lesson that may range from one to a few class meetings. However, the events are not an adequate macro-organizational pattern for organizing an entire course or unit (although you may see some valuable suggestions for introducing or closing a course within those events).

Novice designers commonly assume that there is one "best" way to sequence content or organize learning experiences within courses or larger instructional scopes, and that this best sequence will be obvious to the designer once all of the learning goals are identified. On the contrary, many organization alternatives exist, many of which are not intuitively obvious. Finding the best curriculum organization should be the result of the designer's problem solving as he takes under consideration salient attributes of goals, learners, and context.

It is important to point out that many excellent texts on curriculum are available, and this chapter does not attempt to replace them. We will introduce a few of the most critical concepts in curriculum design, particularly for individuals whose specialty *will not* be curriculum design but *will* be the design of instruction. We have also treated curriculum in a way that is not currently available in the curriculum literature. In so doing, we have developed a few prescriptive principles for designing curricula, particularly that related to curriculum organization. As it is unusual for instructional design texts to consider the topic of course design, this chapter has something unique to offer instructional designers. Excellent concise treatments of curriculum planning and course design issues can be found in Posner (1996) and Kessels and Plomp (1996).

This chapter describes curriculum organization patterns, key curriculum design tools and concepts, alternative views of curriculum design, assistance that technology provides to curricula, and guidelines for curriculum design.

CURRICULUM SEQUENCING STRUCTURES

Curriculum design is concerned with making decisions about the scope, organization, and sequence of content at the macro level. The term *curriculum* comes from a Latin word that referred to chariot race courses. A small shift in meaning has given us our current term, which in its most fundamental sense refers to a "course of study." As a rule, curriculum designers are more concerned about *what* to teach as opposed to *how to* teach (see Dick, 1986–87; Foshay & Foshay, 1981; and Laska, 1984). Hannum and Hansen (1989) present a straightforward approach to curriculum design:

> The starting point in organizing and sequencing instructional content for education and training programs is to assign large units of related content to courses. Then the related content within each of the courses is grouped into several individual lessons. Finally the content of each lesson is analyzed to determine the necessary supporting content or prerequisites. Once the content of individual lessons has been determined, the instructional events that are the component parts of a lesson are generated and sequenced. (p. 123)

Although this description provides a succinct overview of curriculum design, alternative approaches to curriculum organization can inform the instructional designer in ways to integrate learning at the macro level by organizing more by goals than by content.

After reviewing numerous curricula over all content areas and across a variety of age groups, Posner and coworkers (Posner & Strike, 1976; Posner & Rudnitsky, 1994) classified curriculum sequencing structures into five major categories: world-related structure, inquiry-related structure, utilization-related structure, learning-related structure, and concept-related structure. We will discuss each of these briefly and examine in greater detail two approaches to macro-level strategy development that have grown out of the instructional design specialty, learning enterprises and the Elaboration Model.

World-Related Structure

In a world-related structure, content is clustered and sequenced according to the way things in the world seem to be organized—by time, space, and physical characteristics. An example of organizing by time or chronology would be teaching music history with units organized by historical periods and sequenced from the time of the earliest known music through the Renaissance, Baroque, Classical, Romantic, and Contemporary periods up to the present day. An example of organizing by spatial relationships (grouping and sequencing according to how things occur spatially in the world) would be teaching world geography by grouping units by continent and teaching geography of all countries one continent at a time. When content is organized by physical characteristics, content that is similar in its physical attributes is clustered together. Generally, then, the entities with the least complex physical attributes are taught first. For example, a biology class might be organized by beginning with the least complex units—cell and subcell levels—then moving into more complex organisms (which might also be perceived as chronological for those using an "evolution" pattern). A course in chemistry might be organized around the clustering of elements into their groups, such as inert gases, metals, nonmetals, and so on.

Inquiry-Related Structure

An inquiry-related sequence and organization teaches ideas together because they represent similar phases of inquiry. Following this scheme, a designer would sequence and organize instruction by the steps of inquiry that the scientists in that field pursue. For example, a course in educational research would be organized and sequenced according to the steps that an educational researcher would follow in studying a question: the formulation of a question, review of the literature, statement of hypotheses, design of a study, collection of data, analysis of data, and drawing conclusions. Often instructional design classes are organized following problem-finding and problem-solving sequences of instructional design models.

The curriculum revision projects of the 1960s were designed to teach children to "think like a scientist," while mathematics curricula were developed to help children "understand arithmetic as a mathematician does," and so forth. Although a difficulty with many of the products of 1960s curriculum reform was their lack of attention to needed prerequisite learnings (attempting problem solving without knowledge of the concepts and principles with which to work), the general raising of the level of attainment expected of students and a change in purpose-setting injected a needed vitality and rigor into many school subjects often unappreciated by the public at large.

Utilization-Related Structure

A utilization-related organization groups ideas together according to how skills will be used in the future, either personally, socially, or vocationally. Following this orientation, groups of concepts, facts, procedures, or theories are grouped together and taught in a such a manner that the first to be taught are those topics that will be used first, the next topics taught are the next used, and so forth. For example, this text is sequenced in a general order that a professional designer follows in designing instruction, starting with analysis, continuing with strategy development, and concluding with evaluation of developed instruction, with a great deal of reference back and forth among chapters to indicate the interrelatedness of activities. Using another form of utilization-based sequence, we teach the most frequently used knowledge first. For example, instruction for statistics might be organized so that the most commonly used statistics, such as descriptive statistics, correlation, t-tests, and ANOVA would precede introduction to more specialized and less frequently used tests such as path analysis.

Learning-Related Structure

Learning-related structures organize information in such a way that new learning builds on relevant prior knowledge. One way to use a learning-related structure is through a prerequisite-based organization. If a designer conducted an information-processing analysis of the tasks related to all of the goals for an entire course, the outcome of that analysis would indicate the prerequisite relationships of all the information and skills in that course. An investigation of this analysis would reveal that there are some fundamental concepts, skills, or knowledge that are foundational for the entire course. Using a strictly prerequisite-based organization, these skills would be taught first; however, care should be taken not to overgeneralize what is known about learning hierarchies. Only the intellectual skills—concepts, rules, and problem solving—have been found to benefit from a prerequisite sequence (Gagné, 1985). Other learning tasks—declarative knowledge, attitudes, psychomotor skills, and cognitive strategies—must follow sequences derived by an other-than-prerequisite basis. A prerequisite-based structure, for example, might be found in a computer programming course in which the knowledge of commands and ability to combine commands into data structures are prerequisite to later hands-on programming experiences that involve problem-solving.

A second perusal of the task analysis would reveal a second tier of concepts, rules, or information that is prerequisite to later, more complex skills. There may be several groupings of these ideas within the second tier of analysis. The information and skills in this tier would be taught next. For example, in the prerequisite-structured computer programming course, the next ideas to be taught might be the concepts relating to program structure, such as the program body and subroutines and related commands. The pattern of "moving up" the hierarchy of the task analysis is followed until learners are taught to achieve the most complex skills in the course. Such an approach has been described as *bottom up*.

The prerequisite-based structure is a commonly utilized macro-organizational strategy in the field of instructional design. A disadvantage of prerequisite-based structure, even when the nature of learning tasks (by type of learning) suggests the possibility of its use, is that learners have a tendency to lose the "big picture" as they acquire skill with individual prerequisites. They may lose sight of how the prerequisites relate to each other and to the goal of the course. For this reason, prerequisite-based organization may be less motivating than other forms of structure. Often designers organize the course by some other curriculum structure and use a prerequisite structure within units. (We have referred to this approach in Chapter 12.)

A less formal approach to prerequisite-based instruction is predicated on teaching the familiar before the unfamiliar. For example, in a religion class, the aspects of the more commonly prevailing religion might be studied before moving on to the more unfamiliar. In a world geography class, the study of the geography of one's own country might precede the study of more distant locales.

The **knowledge structures** idea as seen in *learning enterprises* is another example of a learning-related structure. Recall from Chapter 5 that learning enterprises present an example of a learning-related structure that integrates multiple learning objectives (Gagné & Merrill, 1990). The unifying element in an enterprise is a declarative knowledge representation of the enterprise itself. A strong emphasis is placed on the purposeful and interrelated qualities of the knowledge, and hence, various theories related to schema formation and use are employed, including frames (Minsky, 1986), mental models (Gentner & Stevens, 1983), schemata (Rummelhart & Ortony, 1977), and work models (Bunderson, Gibbons, Olsen, & Kearsley, 1981). The declarative knowledge of the enterprise is referred to as an *enterprise schema*, and three kinds of enterprise schemata are described: denoting, manifesting, and discovering.

A **denoting schema** is appropriate for enterprises that require the *naming* of entities, knowledge of the *classes* to which entities belong, and the *functions* served by entities. A **manifesting schema** is called for when

enterprises involve processes. A **discovering schema** is needed for enterprises in which discovery reveals a *previously unknown or novel* entity.

The prescription for instructional designers that Gagné and Merrill provided from learning enterprises is to make explicit provision for the learning of enterprise schema that integrate specific learning required by an overall goal. Consequently, a course with enterprise goals might have a first tier of organization structured by the enterprises themselves, organized according to their schemata and sequenced accordingly. For example, a concept-related organization (see the following section) would be appropriate for denoting schema, a chronological organization for manifesting schema, and inquiry for discovering schema. The second tier of organization might employ an inquiry or utilization structure.

Concept-Related Structure

Concept-related structures use the structure of the discipline to organize the content. The most superordinate, all-inclusive concepts or principles are taught first, and then the more specific cases of the concepts or applications of the principles are taught later. One of the advantages of this structure, in contrast to the prerequisite-based structure, is that the resulting learning may be integrated, with clearer relationships of ideas. Jerome Bruner was an educational theorist whose thinking had a major impact on the K–12 curriculum project movement of the 1960s in which the *structure of knowledge* within disciplines and the idea of the *spiral curriculum* guided curriculum development (Bruner, 1960, 1966). Many of the science programs developed during the 1960s curriculum reform movement in the United States, such as BSCS biology, were developed based upon the concept-related macro-structure. An example of such an organization in a general science class would be teaching about the properties of matter before teaching about atoms, and teaching about atoms before teaching about electricity. Reigeluth's Elaboration Model is a particular example of a concept-related macro-structure.

THE ELABORATION MODEL. Concept-related structures have many advantages; in particular, they employ a sequence that is consistent with the manner in which many cognitive theorists suggest that information is stored, with more specific information being subsumed under superordinate concepts. However, their disadvantage—and the reason why instructional designers often structure courses according to prerequisites—is that they may not consider types of learning (discriminations, concepts, rules, problem solving) and how these types relate to one other. This failure to consider prerequisites can lead either to learners' encountering material for which they lack a background or to them only encountering the information at the declarative knowledge and concept levels, never working at higher levels of learning, such as principle using or problem solving. Reigeluth devised an organizational pattern to take advantage of positive aspects of both the concept-related and prerequisite-based macro-strategies and to diminish the disadvantages of each with his Elaboration Theory (Reigeluth, 1979, Reigeluth & Stein, 1983; Reigeluth, Merrill, Wilson, & Spiller, 1994).

Reigeluth focused on organizing an entire course according to one of three major types of outcomes: concepts, principles, and procedures. He suggested that a particular content may be taught by setting out to achieve any of the three goals. (For example, statistics may be taught by emphasizing the concepts in statistics, the principles of statistics, or the procedures for calculating statistics.) He stated that one of the first actions of the designer was to determine which of the three content structures—conceptual, theoretical (principle-based), or procedural—should be emphasized in a particular unit or course. Recent discussion of the Elaboration Model has recommended a broader view of outcomes, noting that this restrictive view is not necessarily helpful (Wilson & Cole, 1992). Reigeluth (1992) has, in fact, expanded his theory to allow for a "simplifying conditions method," which has an epitome that is a simplified case problem. The Elaboration Model may be described as a *top-down* approach.

Reigeluth suggested that following identification of outcomes and content structure, the designer identify the most overarching, fundamental concepts, principles, or procedures (depending upon which structure is selected). These overarching generalizations should be taught first at the application level in what Reigeluth called an *epitome*.

Reigeluth described three primary types of epitomes, corresponding to different goals for learning: conceptual, procedural, and theoretical. Each type of epitome is characterized by a type of synthesizer and by the instructional conditions necessary for understanding the synthesizer. A *conceptual epitome* has as its synthesizer the "top" layer of material, consisting of an orientation structure that reflects as much of the breadth of the material to be learned as is possible in an orienting class session. The synthesizer for a *procedural epitome* is a simplified "parallel procedural structure," which allows an entire procedure to be grasped at an orienting level in a single introductory session. A *theoretical epitome* may be developed in similar manner to the conceptual, in which the top layer is an overarching principle that is fundamental to theory. Frequently, a theoretical epitome may be developed in a manner similar to development of the simplified parallel structure of a procedural epitome.

An intriguing aspect of the epitome is the idea that it might be an orientation to the entire content developed at the most concrete level of application possible, including, if possible, application-level work with the content. Such an epitome is particularly attractive when study of a large body of highly unfamiliar material is to be undertaken. The difficulty with a traditional "overview" with such subject matter is that a verbal survey of totally unfamiliar terrain will leave the student "confused at a higher level." Our first contacts with computer programming in the 1960s involved an overview with data structures and memory use, including an analogy of data locations to mail slots in a mail room. With no knowledge of what a computer program might look like and what fundamental operations were involved in developing one, our confusion was total and complete. We constructed enormous misunderstandings that lasted almost the entire semester. How much better it would be to begin such a course with an epitome, in which the act of programming—all the way from developing specifications for a program, developing code, entering it, running the program, and debugging it—could actually be done by the learner in an initial class period, providing a very simple programming problem and a great amount of guidance (Ragan & Smith, 1989).

After the epitome is taught and practiced at the application level, more detailed instruction—an "elaboration" of the content—is encountered. For example, in a photography lesson based on theoretical structure (Wedman & Smith, 1989), learners participated in instruction on the functions and relationships of f-stops, shutter speeds, and film speeds in the first level of elaboration. In the photography unit this meant that learners were taught about how motion interacts with shutter speed and how depth of field relates to aperture size. In the final elaboration, learners investigated the actual number values for f-stops, shutter speeds, and film speed, and how these values were related (e.g., an f-stop of 5.6 lets two times as much light in a camera as f/8). This continuing elaboration of general ideas is similar to Bruner's concept of the "spiral curriculum" (1960), Ausubel's concept of "progressive differentiation" (1968), and Norman's concept of "web learning" (1980). Within each level of elaboration, information is sequenced according to prerequisite relationships. Instruction at each level of elaboration is tied to the other levels with synthesizing and summarizing statements that integrate the levels of elaboration. Reigeluth likened this form of instruction to the "zooming in" of a camera to pick up details in a visual field and then "zooming out" to give the viewer a perspective of the whole picture.

Reigeluth predicted that when used with large bodies of content, such as units or courses, elaborated instruction will result in more integrated and motivated learning. However, studies of short segments of instruction (one to several lessons) have failed to substantiate these predictions (Beukhof, 1986; Wedman & Smith, 1989). While not intended to validate the theory, a more recent study (English & Reigeluth, 1996), characterized as a "formative evaluation" study, provided substantial evidence of effectiveness in college undergraduate coursework in electrical engineering. Nevertheless, the model has such intuitive appeal that designers continue to use it to organize large segments of instruction. We recommend it as a structure for designing units and courses. For more information on the particulars of design, read Reigeluth's own description of the model (Reigeluth & Stein, 1983) and his example of the model's application (Reigeluth, 1987), along with revisions to the model (English & Reigeluth, 1996; Reigeluth, 1992). Revisions have placed greater emphasis on the epitome and have provided useful suggestions on improving the effectiveness of the epitome as well as recommendations regarding sequencing, refinements for learning procedures, and problem solving (consistent with strategy recommendations presented in this text in Chapters 10 and 12).

E X E R C I S E   A

1. The following are descriptions of course structures. Beside each, write the type of macro-structure employed: world-related (WR), inquiry-related (IR), utilization-related (UR), learning-related (LR), or concept-related (CR).

a. Teach anthropology from the earliest appearance of humankind on the earth to present day.

b. Teach the concept of "velocity" before teaching the concept "acceleration," a change in velocity.

c. Teach biology in the sequence that a researcher follows in the scientific method: examine data, construct hypotheses, select a likely hypothesis, test the hypothesis, examine data, and accept the hypothesis or consider alternate hypotheses.

d. Teach math by teaching the most commonly used operations first, followed by the next most commonly used operations.

e. Teach phonics skills before teaching students how to read sentences.

2. Explain how you might teach an instructional design or a computer programming class following the Elaboration Model.

INTEGRATIVE CURRICULUM TOOLS AND CONCEPTS

Some tools and concepts have particular utility to instructional designers working at the macro level. We will discuss *scope and sequence* and *object-orientation* as both tools and concepts. After introducing "articulation," we will discuss alternative forms of *curriculum organization* that have been devised to solve articulation problems.

Scope and Sequence

A fundamental curriculum tool is the scope and sequence chart. Scope and sequence have relevance regardless of the approach taken to learning: subject-based or experiential, pragmatist or constructivist. The *scope* of a curriculum, typically displayed on a chart on the horizontal axis, describes the "what." A large-scale curriculum scope, such as that for a technical training course, for work at a grade level, or for an entire school, will obviously reflect more than one topic or experience. Although curriculum designers traditionally organize scope in terms of subject matter or topics, it is equally feasible and often quite appropriate to organize scope on the bases of experience units, problems, or other bases. The term *strand* is often used to indicate individual elements of content in a scope that is neutral with regard to the basis of organization. Thus, a curriculum will reflect the relationship between multiple strands. The *sequence* is typically displayed on the vertical axis, indicating what is planned for each strand. The sequence may be merely ordered, or, more often, related to a schedule such as an academic year, semester, or course calendar. An example of a scope and sequence chart is presented in Figure 16.1

Object-Oriented Curriculum Architecture

Business and industry has been a fertile source of thinking and tools that can increase the efficiency of training programs. In keeping with this tradition, the object-based design model from computer science has been applied to instruction at the macro level in the form of learning objects (Friedlander, 1996; Wiley, 2002). Commonly used components of an instructional system, such as instructor guidelines, handouts, student guides, presentation materials, assessment materials, and other materials may be viewed as *learning objects* (also referred to as *educational objects* and *curriculum objects)*. Learning objects are not entirely different from

The Student will . . .	Grade			
	9	10	11	12
H. Identify and use figurative language and sound devices (e.g., metaphor, simile, personification, rhythm, rhyme, alliteration, onomatopoeia, hyperbole, and analogy).				
1. Hyperbole	I	I	I	I
2. Metaphor	R	r	r	r
3. Personification	R	r	r	r
4. Onomatopoeia		I	M	R
5. Imagery	M	M	R	R
6. Alliteration	I	M	R	r
7. Rhythm	R	R	r	r
8. Rhyme	R	R	r	r
I. Demonstrate a knowledge of literary elements and techniques and how they affect the development of a literary work (to include plot, character, setting, theme, conflict, point-of-view, symbolism, imagery, flashback, foreshadowing, irony, tone, and allusion).				
1. Recognize the difference between the assumed "I" of narrator and the author himself/herself.	I	I	I	M
2. Know when an author takes a satirical approach to a subject and can explain possible reasons for that approach.		I	M	R
3. Identify an ironical statement of situation encountered in a literary work.		I	M	R
4. Explain the effects of the author's selection of negative point-of-view on the telling of the story.	R	r	r	r

I = Introduced; M = Major topic; R = Review, major; r = review, minor

Figure 16.1 Portion of a Scope and Sequence Chart in Language Arts.
Source: Courtesy Norman Public Schools, used with permission.

the widely used *instructional modules,* but the concept is enriched by application of the standard set of characteristics for an "object" from object-oriented programming to define the characteristics of learning objects. A learning object must possess independence (not depend upon another object for its delivery), reusability (constructed in such as way as to be reusable), inheritance (be able to be combined into larger objects with the larger object inheriting qualities from the parent objects), and polymorphism (be able to be reconfigured for different uses without substantial change to the content). Like its contribution to computer programming, the object orientation facilitates the reuse of modules. A training or educational organization can reap substantial development savings by employing an object orientation to its overall design and development effort. Again, analogous to applications in the computer arena, the object orientation requires adjustments and may not see immediate payoff, but over time, and particularly with large-scale efforts, the reuse through recombination can be a powerful tool for efficiency. Wiley

(2002) contains many helpful chapters contributed by a variety of scholars and experts in the design and use of re-usable learning objects.

One of the essential elements to making learning objects available is some form of organization system which supports the cataloging and retrieval of learning objects. The most widespread and successful effort this sort is called "metadata." Metadata are tags, small strings of data, which can be made part of a learning object. Metadata tags enable searches, even when the object is not text-based, such as an illustration. Examples of metadata systems include the IEEE standards body Standard1484.12.1, for learning objects metadata, the U.S. Office of Education-sponsored Gateway to Educational Materials (GEM), and Recker, Walker, and Wiley's Altered Vista system (2002) which includes a collaborative element to provide, improve, and broaden the utility of learning objects through metadata filtering. The current status of the IEEE learning object metadata standard, GEM, and Altered Vista as well as other information on metadata and learning objects can be checked at this text's Learning Resources Web site.

A good example of practical application of learning objects is the U.S. military services use of a form of object-orientation to organize the vast amount of knowledge and training materials under their purview (Curda & Curda, 2003). The Department of Defense acronym for this effort is SCORM (Shareable Content Object Reference Model). SCORM supports the retrieval and interoperability of learning objects within the Advanced Distributed Learning environment. In addition to Web-based materials, print, audio/videotapes, CD-ROM and other media are supported.

Another example may be found in a particularly useful white paper on authoring reusable learning objects developed by Cisco Systems, Inc. (Cisco, 2003). This white paper describes a procedure for developing courses, lessons, modules, and topics in an object-based fashion. The paper uses concepts and language that will be comfortable and familiar for students of instructional design.

The technology of design, development, and implementation of learning objects is changing rapidly. A weakness of some metadata systems as of this writing is lack of information on a learning object's goals and objectives as well as information on effectiveness of the object in facilitating intended learning and information on contexts for which the object is appropriate. In practice, your evaluation, use, and improvements on learning object technology can be supported and strengthened by a careful and reflective application of your instructional design knowledge.

Designers must be prepared to make intelligent use of databases of learning objects if they are to avail themselves of the potential contribution of object-oriented curriculum architecture. In addition, however, your knowledge of the macrostrategy tools and concepts for structuring and integrating a curriculum that are also described in this chapter will help you put those objects to best use.

Articulation

A fundamental curriculum concept is **articulation:** how content segments relate to one another within a curriculum or course of study. Articulation of two primary forms, vertical and horizontal, is of constant concern for curriculum developers. *Vertical articulation* refers to designing curriculum so that one unit builds upon the next, leading to vertical transfer (e.g., from concepts to rules to problem solving) as knowledge develops and experiences progress. Concern with prerequisites and sequencing are fundamental vertical articulation issues. *Horizontal articulation* refers to linking across topics of the same level of complexity, leading to lateral transfer (e.g., from application of a rule in

one domain or situation generalized to use in another). Inspection of practically any scope and sequence chart will reveal a wealth of articulation issues—problems solved and problems remaining. Attempts to solve the problems of achieving articulation as well as others such as interest, motivation, and relevance have stimulated the development of varied forms of curriculum organization.

The following curriculum organization patterns overlap, to some extent, the five forms of curriculum sequencing structures described earlier. However, these organization patterns make distinctions on a different basis and reveal alternatives that we have not previously considered. Whereas the Posner classification reviewed earlier is the product of an analytic and logical investigation, the following classification arises from description of public school practices in the United States that have been historically identified. The curriculum organization patterns that follow were developed by educators over the years in efforts to increase articulation of learning within classes and across a school. The four major types, in order of increasing unification, are (1) separate subjects, (2) correlation, (3) fusion (or broad fields), and (4) integration. Three primary forms of integration—student-centered, social functions–centered, and experience-centered—have been described.

The **separate subjects** curriculum organization is best known for its widespread use and the high level of criticism it engenders. Under it, subject matter concerns, as generally defined in schools by traditional academic fields and knowledge areas, define the main strands. Thus, a high school curriculum generally contains courses in mathematics, including geometry, algebra, trigonometry, and so on. Although not from traditional academic sources, many training organizations similarly organize their curricula by subject matter strands. (The second type of curriculum organization, correlation, is actually as commonplace as separate subjects.) In fact, few examples of pure separate subjects curricula exist in American elementary schools, even when strands are subject-related.

Correlation is achieved through efforts to teach two or more subjects simultaneously. Thus, if an institution organizes its teacher education curriculum with correlation, student teachers would take a course in assessment development techniques during the same semester as they take a teaching methods course in which a short unit of instruction is developed, taught, and assessed. An effort to assist correlation among the faculty might result in the instructor of the measurement course ensuring that students learn the primary test development techniques before they complete the teaching unit in the methods course, which provides for application of those techniques.

Fusion occurs in a curriculum when two or more subjects are combined into one course or other packaging unit. A good example of a fusion innovation that has now become standard practice in schools is the area called *social studies*. This area is the product of curriculum planners' fusion of such fields as history, geography, political science, anthropology, sociology, and other social sciences. Another example is the fusion of the separate subjects of writing, rhetoric, and literature. In American public schools these and other subjects were fused into English and later, in a more encompassing fusion, into "Language Arts." These and other common examples of fusion partially explain why it is difficult to find a "pure separate subjects" curriculum in American public education, even though the curriculum may be subject-based.

Integration as a form of curriculum organization refers to the integration of subject content through some vehicle other than a content-based structure. Most forms of integrated curriculum organization are to some extent reflections of the thinking of the philosopher and educational reformer, John Dewey (1938). Three commonly described forms of integration are student-centered, social functions–centered, and experience-centered.

A **student-centered** form of organization takes the interests of students as its cue. Guided by these interests and teachers' expectations for students (which may include goals for learning), projects are developed that provide a vehicle for student learning. One of the more vivid descriptions of such a curriculum is found in Ellsworth Collings's book *An Experiment with a Project Curriculum* (1923), which details student-centered teaching in McDonald County, Missouri, in 1917. Student-centered curriculum organization in its pure form is quite uncommon because it is difficult to implement. Its extreme form, espoused in the late-eighteenth century by Rousseau, holds that young children possess a purity of thought and spirit that the external interventions of society and school only corrupt; therefore, education should only extend a child's natural tendencies.

A **social-functions** basis for curriculum organization takes its structure from persistent life situations or common social enterprises. Stratemeyer et al. (1957) developed an extremely sophisticated curriculum pattern for public education based on age-appropriate problems and situations in such areas as (1) living in the home as a family member, (2) living in the community as a participant in civic activities, and (3) at work, as a member of an occupational group. Using these and other persistent life situations as a framework, the Stratemeyer group developed an entire K–12 curriculum that includes the traditional skills but is placed within a social context and organization. An example of a common social enterprises curriculum was seen in the Virginia Course of Study for Elementary

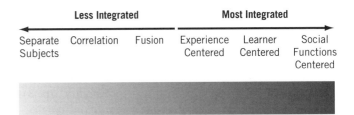

Figure 16.2 Curriculum Organization Continuum

Schools (1934). Similar to Stratemeyer's approach, the Virginia schools curriculum was structured around such enterprises as conservation, production, consumption, transportation, and communication.

The **experience-centered** conception of curriculum will be discussed at greater length in a discussion of contrasting views of curriculum. In this moderate style of integration, there is no particular form or theme that the curriculum must reflect. The requirement is only that curriculum plans be made that focus on experiences that carry out intentions for learning (W. B. Ragan, 1953). This form of organization, labeled "neo-progressivist," was highly popular in American public education in the 1960s and 1970s, and currently sees renewed interest under other labels (e.g., "open learning environments"). Trainers who examine the traditions of adult learning curricula will see the same trends under the labels "experiential" and "problem-based" learning. Figure 16.2 presents curriculum organization alternatives in a least- to most-integrated continuum.

ALTERNATIVE VIEWS OF CURRICULUM DESIGN

The traditional view of curriculum is as a sequence of topics or content, yet that is not the only way to organize a curriculum. Let us reflect first on the traditional content-centered view of curriculum and then explore an integrated curriculum. Discussion of these points of view draws us into closer relationship with a number of current issues within instructional design.

A content-based view of curriculum is obvious upon inspection of a college transcript. The student's course of study is reflected in content-based course titles. These courses are generally organized on the transcript by subject-based concerns such as major, minors, and requirements as well as electives, which themselves are often defined in content-related terms (e.g., "at least two courses in computer applications . . ."). Some curriculum theorists insist that a curriculum is seen in documents: course descriptions, outlines of units of study, plans of instruction, and catalogs (e.g., Beauchamp, 1956). When asked about the curriculum of a school or an educational system, many people would refer to the documents.

Other curriculum theorists (e.g., W. B. Ragan, 1953) preferred to view curriculum as an integrated set of experiences, which are only partially reflected by the documentation and subject-based descriptions. Ragan defined curriculum as "all of the experiences of the student for which the school accepts responsibility" (p. 3). This broad experience-centered conception of curriculum is applicable to all of the integrated curriculum organization forms: experience centered, learner centered, and social functions centered. An integrated approach to curriculum organization does not rule out the making of syllabi, courses of study, and other documents needed for instructional and administrative purposes. However, an integrated view places emphasis of a school's curriculum on what *happens* in the school rather than verbal descriptions. Consequently, if a person wished to evaluate the curriculum, it would be necessary to observe the activities taking place in the school, not merely its documents.

Focusing on learner experience rather than content as the fundamental reflection of curriculum places a greater emphasis on instructional strategy from the outset of curriculum design. If the designer thinks in terms of content from the outset, major decisions of the design process will be determined by default. To the extent that content is a vehicle for achieving learning, a view that *begins* with content may tend to limit consideration of learning goals and how learning will be facilitated. However, when viewing instruction from an experiential frame of reference, the designer must determine what intentions for learning are and what sort of experiences would best facilitate that learning—essentially strategic decisions.

An integrated curriculum remains open to any of the five sequencing options described earlier but facilitates the organization of problem-based, project-based, and other strategies that are based on learner experience and activity rather than on academic subject-matter containers. The goal in either case is learning. When designers make decisions about curriculum organization alternatives, they are determining the kind of structure they wish to use to facilitate it.

It is important to remember that integrated approaches are not content-less, nor, on the other hand, are content-centered approaches devoid of learner experience. The question should never be whether or not "content" will be learned (or alternatively, whether or not students will have experiences). Alternative views color our thinking, and hence, can influence decision-making. A primary reason for the emergence of non-traditional thinking about curriculum and instruction was a desire to improve student learning over that which is achieved under existing practices.

In the case of the Progressive Education movement of the 1920s and beyond, the practice of packaging the content of school learning in traditional academic subject areas was replaced by the use of *projects* that were to be generated out of *student interests* as vehicles by which to organize the curriculum. Many of the same goals for school learning were pursued by both progressivists and traditional educators: reading, writing, arithmetic, history, fine arts, and so forth. However, the progressive educator sought to both integrate learning from many fields and make learning interesting and meaningful through use of experience units. For example, the production of a school play can involve reading (of scripts, background material, and procedural instructions for such things as set building), writing (of scripts, promotional materials, programs, and so forth), arithmetic (involving measurement in set construction, time calculations in production planning, addition and subtraction in budgeting and accounting), history (in such activities as character and setting research), and fine arts (in the acting, directing, set construction, music, lighting, and other aspects of production and delivery of a play).*

There is no doubt that traditional learning tasks can be learned quite effectively through experience- and project-centered approaches. In addition, learning beyond the traditional subject areas was also important to progressivists, particularly learnings related to the individual's social and emotional growth and adjustment within a "democratic" and "experimentalist/scientific" context (for more information on progressive education, see Dewey, 1916, 1938). Within training environments we see parallels as illuminated by the contrast between "human resource development" and "training" within the organization.

However, the reader may have discerned a major difficulty with the progressivist approach while reading the description of a teacher guiding the pursuit of many academic learning tasks subsumed within one activity with responsibility for a classroom full of learners: Most teacher/trainers are not up to it! To use the activity of putting on the school play outlined above for purposes of learning in many areas, the teacher must ensure that the play selected is something in which the learners are interested or something the teacher can get them interested in. The teacher must consciously and continuously draw each student's learning of important skills into the project while managing the whole thing. She must be able to assess each student's learning within the context of the activity. The teacher must adjust and adapt conditions continuously, and the teacher must use her knowledge of what each individual student learned to inform the teacher on learning guidance that each student will need in the next project. And finally, the teacher must not abandon the goals for learning

---

*It is easy to substitute "constructivist" for "progressivist" in this and most illustrations of progressivism.

which, though more difficult than to manage the activity for its own sake, are the reason for the activity to begin with. While a few gifted teacher/trainers have been able to do this, possessing the talent and energy required is a rare commodity indeed. The downfall of the Progressive Movement can be attributed to the impossible demands that its successful implementation placed on teachers, particularly given tools available in the early- and mid-twentieth century.

Now, technology is available, both in the form of the process technology of instructional design and in product technologies, notably computers, that can help make real the dreams of the progressivists. Such techniques and approaches as microworlds (Rieber, 1992, 1996), interactive video-based situated cognition (Cognition and Technology Group, 1992), exploratory learning environments, and phenomenaria (Perkins, 1992) clearly reflect progressivist ideas that are not at all unlike the constructivist thinking with which they are currently associated. These tools and others, such as computer management, computer-assisted assessment tools, multimedia development tools, and the World Wide Web, make experience-centered learning environments feasible. This was not so until recently except in rare, isolated instances.

Instructional design is beneficial to all three integrated curriculum organization patterns. Although the tradition that generated social-functions-centered curriculum organization, for example, was a different one from that which generated instructional design, the tools of instructional design are as applicable as if the two had come from the same source. A point of view that an instructional designer will bring to a curriculum problem is that all three forms of integrated curriculum organization (as well as other alternatives organization forms) are less than ideal.

Technology has made implementation of major innovations in curricula feasible, but still not widespread. Computers see a fair amount of use in school settings (particularly to teach computer skills), but the curricular reforms that computers and other technology make possible and that have been demonstrated repeatedly (e.g., Cognition and Technology Group, 1992; Wilson, Hamilton, Teslow, & Cyr, 1994; Wilson, 1996) have not seen common use as of this writing. Interestingly, education and training in other settings such as business and military environments have seen a greater influence from technology than in American public education. In other words, technology (particularly computer technology) has made possible large-scale improvements in school curricula and instructional practices that have not yet been *implemented* on a large scale (Walker, 1996).

What accounts for the low level of widespread implementation of technology in schools? In order to fully enjoy the benefits of technology, a restructuring of public education in the United States will be required. Current school system organization is based on (1) independent, virtually autonomous school districts established and maintained at the township level, and (2) reliance on a teacher-in-classroom functional organization for delivery and management of learning experiences. Commendable school restructuring work is well underway that emphasizes empowerment of teachers (Peterson, McCarthey, & Elmore, 1996; Jenlink, Reigeluth, Carr, & Nelson, 1998). However, a reorganization of public schools in the United States may be required that reduces their autonomy in curriculum and instructional resources. Such reduction in autonomy may be needed to increase the scale at which costly development can be used. Certainly structural changes in the system of public education will be required to make nontrivial applications technology on a widespread basis.

The problem of costs, by itself, may force changes before educators are ready. If school restructuring would take instructional technology into consideration, the change could be better accomplished through planning than through reaction. An excellent discussion of the relationship between the structure of education and use of technology can be found in Heinich, Molenda, Russell, & Smaldino (1996, pp. 350–357).

TECHNOLOGY'S ASSISTANCE TO INTEGRATED CURRICULUM DESIGNS

The most interesting and powerful uses of product technology in both education and training appear to be in those that clearly fit within integrated curriculum designs. The World Wide Web is most widely viewed as an exploratory learning environment; interest in computer-based instruction has been supplanted by interest in computer-based learning environments; educational video is considered passé, while interest is high in interactive multimedia that supports exploration and interaction with microworlds and simulations. There is no lack of interest in the design and development of technology-based instruction of a highly generative sort.

Recall the plight of the 1930s schoolteacher in a progressive school, teaching the entire third grade curriculum through projects; the genius and effort required was beyond the capacities of most mortals. Reconsider the same scenario with inclusion of the best technology can offer. Fitting a project with student interests can be facilitated with information on learners that was not feasible to gather before computer-based testing and recordkeeping. Project descriptions and materials to support projects can be made available on the Web in a variety that would not have been available to all but perhaps an extremely fortunate handful only a few years ago. Assistance in tracking student progress and other aspects of instructional management can be delivered by computer. The mechanics of script development, set design, and even set construction can be facilitated by computer. The performance itself might be virtual, with the development of a multimedia presentation accessible by millions in a Web site.

The process technology of instructional design has an enormous benefit to offer in large-scale projects such as those suggested here. The tools of goal finding and setting, context analysis, learner analysis, task analysis, appropriate assessment design, appropriate strategies design, and formative and summative evaluation are what is needed to make large-scale projects work.

PRESCRIPTIONS FOR CURRICULUM DESIGN

Educators' choices between curriculum organization alternatives have traditionally been made on the basis of allegiance to one or another world view or educational philosophy. Consequently, learner-centered curricula tend to be recommended and adopted not by any problem-solving or design process but by association with individuals who are advocates of that form of organization. Subject-centered curricula are sometimes the result of default or are based on belief systems such as "back to the basics" movements whose advocates are unaware of or hostile to alternatives.

We propose that decisions on sequence, structure, and organization of curricula be the result of a problem-solving design process, analogous to that which drives the design of micro-level strategies discussed in this text. Thus, we conceive of curriculum design to be a process involving "macro strategies."

Primary considerations in determining curriculum organization should be: (1) context, (2) learners, (3) learning tasks (typically, goals), and (4) purpose of the curriculum. Although the specifics are somewhat different from employing these same factors at the micro level, the general approach is the same. We would, in addition, make decisions on macro strategy as we do at the micro level. Whereas at the micro level, a guiding principle is "make the strategy as generative as setting, learners, and task characteristics allow," the analogy at the macro level is:

Make curriculum organization as integrative as setting, learners, and goal characteristics allow.

Application of this principle does not mean that all curricula are destined to employ integrated curriculum organization. A similar trade-off can be anticipated with curriculum organization alternatives as that which we saw in the trade-offs between generative and supplantive micro-strategy alternatives. Some of the trade-offs in curriculum organization decisions may be hypothesized as follows:

1. AOTBE,* more time, resources, and educational design expertise are required to successfully implement more integrated curricula in public schools. In practice, context constraints are the biggest reason for adoption of less integrated curricula. Regarding AOTBE, a major unequalizer can be technology. If used on a wide-enough scale, technology can facilitate development of very high-quality instruction more inexpensively than local, small-audience, duplication-of-effort development.

(The following hypotheses are consistent with practice and seem reasonable; however, we are not aware of empirical evidence to support them.)

2. a. AOTBE, younger learners need a more integrated curriculum than older learners. Older learners can be expected to benefit from integrated curricula but AOTBE, their need for assistance in seeing relationships of subject matter is not as great as younger learners.

  b. AOTBE, learners with higher intrinsic motivation require less integrated curricula.

3. AOTBE, critical learning goals—goals that involve hazard to human safety—may be better served with less integrated curricula (again, this hypothesis is consistent with practice, but we are not aware of evidence to support it). When less variation in experience can be tolerated, as in training in areas that involve danger, a more tightly structured, subject- or topic-based organization provides greater assurance of consistent and predictable training.

4. AOTBE, the more pluralistic or vague that an organization's purposes for education or training are, the more integrated curriculum organizations will be needed. (Conversely, agencies with clear and agreed-upon single-purpose missions may tolerate a less integrated curriculum organization).

| E   X   R   C   I   S   E   B |

For the following scenarios, identify the type of curriculum organization that is reflected and discuss its appropriateness given setting, learner, and learning tasks described or implied. Suggest alternatives that you believe are better, and describe why.

1. Training for the operations engineers and operations management personnel for a statewide system of seven electrical-generation nuclear power plants in the state of Bohrland has recently been overhauled. Because of some close calls caused by human error, higher management has committed to a major overhaul involving

*AOTBE is an acronym for "All Other Things Being Equal."

millions of dollars for development of a new curriculum and learning resources. In keeping with the latest in educational practice, the engineers are given access to a database containing everything known about nuclear power plant design, construction, operation, and maintenance, including a rich library of multimedia demonstrations, video clip archives, and access to the World Wide Web. To empower the engineers for their own learning, cooperative learning groups are established that determine the problems in which they are interested and what resources they will use. Instructors are used only as facilitators, assisting groups in location of resources they wish to use and helping in the process aspects of working in cooperative groups.

2. Rob Harris, Superintendent of Schools in Hutchins, New York, has spent the past ten years reforming the curriculum of the school system. He began the work because he and most of the constituency in his school system were fed up with the superficiality of today's youth; disgusted with the lack of understanding and appreciation for the Great Dialogue; horrified with moral relativism; appalled by the lack of knowledge of geography, history, and the great works of the western world; and encouraged by a large and vocal segment of the community who had little patience with the mediocrity resulting from application of "educationist" practices. The community is a prosperous one, and the school budget has allowed the hiring of excellent fac-

ulty, consisting of bright and able young scholars in the arts and sciences from the finest private liberal arts colleges in the United States, as well as a strong cadre of overseas graduates from Oxford, Cambridge, and the University of Heidelberg. Curriculum materials used are books that contain the actual sources, not textbooks, and a substantial collection of excellent editions has been collected. Children in all of the Hutchins elementary schools spend mornings with one hour each in grammar, rhetoric, and dialectic (logic). In the afternoons, arithmetic, geometry, astronomy, and music are studied in rotating four-week blocks throughout the semester. Block examinations over topics clearly outlined in syllabi are administered at the end of the autumn semesters, and a week of comprehensive exams is provided at the end of each school year. Junior high and high school students study a similar curriculum, with more emphasis on discussion and writing related to the subjects studied.

SUMMARY

From project method curricula of the 1920s to problem-based instruction in the 1990s, experience-centered approaches are reflections of educators' desire to see learning integrated in ways that are personally meaningful, significant, and life-changing for learners.

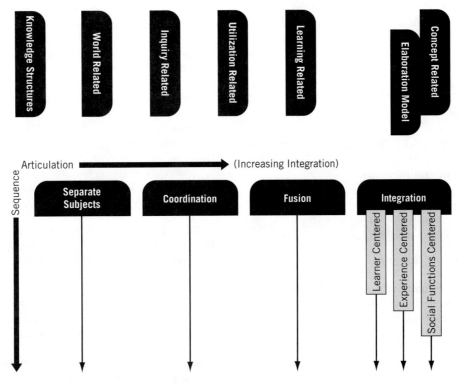

Figure 16.3 Summary Diagram for Macro Strategies

Many ideas about the organization of learning experiences that stem from educators' thinking primarily of public school learning have utility in such other settings as business and industry. In fact, education and training in industrial settings have traditionally been more learning-centered and less subject-centered in their organization than schools have often been. We see it as unfortunate that attributions of tools (ID), settings (business), and methodologies (all supplantive) have developed. Such attributions are neither fair nor accurate. (We discuss this topic and ideas related to it at greater length in Chapter 2.)

This chapter presented six general methods of sequencing content: world-related, inquiry-related, utilization-related, learning-related, knowledge structures, and concept-related (including a discussion of the Elaboration Model). The chapter also introduced curriculum tools and concepts that can be used to integrate learning experiences: the scope and sequence chart and object-oriented architecture. In addition, curriculum-based concepts were introduced: articulation (vertical and horizontal), and curriculum integration (separate subjects, correlation, fusion and integration). Forms labeled as "integrated" were experience-centered, learner-centered, and social functions–centered.

The chapter concludes with some prescriptions for curriculum design that parallel to some extent the approach that has been developed throughout this text: a problem-solution orientation to curriculum design as opposed to design through loyalty to one belief system about "best" forms of curriculum organization. Figure 16.3 provides a graphic summary of the main ideas of this chapter.

EXTENDED EXAMPLE

In the current installment to the Extended Example in the Learning Resources Web site, we select a macro-strategy for our photography course.

READINGS AND REFERENCES

Apple, M. (1979). *Ideology and curriculum.* London: Routledge and Kegan Paul.

Ausubel, D. P. (1968). *Educational psychology: A cognitive view.* New York: Holt, Rinehart & Winston.

Beauchamp, G. A. (1956). *Planning the elementary school curriculum.* New York: Allyn & Bacon.

Beukhof, G. (1986). *Designing instructional texts: Interaction between text and learner.* Paper presented at the annual meeting of the American Educational Research Association. ERIC NO.: ED274313.

Bruner, J. S. (1960). *The process of education.* Cambridge, MA: Harvard University Press.

Bruner, J. S. (1966). *Toward a theory of instruction.* Cambridge, MA: Harvard University Press.

Bunderson, C. V., Gibbons, A. S., Olsen, J. B., & Kearsley, G. P. (1981). Work models: Beyond instructional objectives. *Instructional Science, 10,* 205–215.

Cisco Systems, Inc. (2003). Reusable learning object authoring guidelines: How to build modules, lessons, and topics. White Paper, Cisco Systems, Inc. Available at http://business.cisco.com.

Cognition and Technology Group at Vanderbilt. (1992). The Jasper experiment: An exploration of issues in learning and instructional design. *Educational Technology Research and Development, 40*(1), 65–80.

Collings, E. (1923). *An experiment with a project curriculum.* New York: Macmillan.

Curda, S. K., & Curda, L. K. (2003). Advanced distributed learning: A paradigm shift for military education. *Quarterly Review of Distance Education, 4*(1), 1–14.

Dewey, J. (1916). *Democracy and education.* New York: Macmillan.

Dewey, J. (1938). *Experience and education.* New York: Macmillan.

Dick, W. (1986–1987). Instructional design and the curriculum development process. *Educational Leadership, 44*(4), 54–56.

English, R. E., & Reigeluth, C. M. (1996). Formative research on sequencing instruction with the elaboration theory. *Educational Technology Research and Development, 44*(1), 23–42.

Foshay, W. R., & Foshay, A. W. (1981). A father and son exchange letters. *Educational Leadership, 38,* 621–625.

Friedlander, P. (1996). Competency-driven, component-based curriculum architecture. *Performance & Instruction, 35*(2), 14–21.

Gagné, R. M. (1985). *The conditions of learning.* (3rd ed.). New York: Holt, Rinehart, & Winston.

Gagné, R. M., & Merrill, M. D. (1990). Integrative goals for instructional design. *Educational Technology Research & Development, 38*(1), 23–30.

Gentner, D., & Stevens, A. L. (1983). *Mental models.* Hillsdale, NJ: Erlbaum.

Hannum, W., & Hansen, C. (1989). *Instructional systems development in large organizations.* Englewood Cliffs, NJ: Educational Technology Publications.

Heinich, R., Molenda, M., Russell, J. D., & Smaldino, S. E. (1996). *Instructional media and technologies for learning.* Upper Saddle River, NJ: Prentice-Hall.

Jenlink, P. M., Reigeluth, C. M., Carr, A. A., & Nelson, L. M. (1998). Guidelines for facilitating systemic change in school districts. *Systems Research and Behavioral Science, 15*(3), 217–233.

Kessels, J. W. M., & Plomp, T. (1996). Course design. In T. Plomp & D. P. Ely (Eds.), *International encyclopedia of educational technology* (2nd ed.) (pp. 143–152). Tarrytown, NY: Elsevier.

Laska, J. (1984). The relationship between instruction and curriculum: A conceptual clarification. *Instructional Science, 13,* 203–212.

Minsky, M. (1986). *The society of mind.* New York: Simon and Schuster.

Newell, A., & Simon, H. A. (1975). *Human problem solving.* Upper Saddle River, NJ: Prentice-Hall.

Norman, D. A. (1980). What goes on in the mink of the learner. In W. J. McKeachie (Ed.), *Learning, cognition, and college teaching: New directions for teaching and learning* (pp. 37–49). San Francisco: Jossey-Bass.

Perkins, D. N. (1992). Technology meets constructivism: Do they make a marriage? In T. M. Duffy & D. H. Jonassen (Eds.), *Constructivism and the technology of instruction.* Hillsdale, NJ: Erlbaum.

Peterson, P. L., McCarthey, S. J., & Elmore, R. F. (1996). Learning from school restructuring. *American Educational Research Journal, 33*(1), 119–153.

Posner, G. (1996). Curriculum planning models. In T. Plomp & D. P. Ely (Eds.), *International encyclopedia of educational technology* (2nd ed.) (pp. 137–142). Tarrytown, NY: Elsevier.

Posner, G. J., & Rudnitsky, A. N. (1994). *Course design: A guide to curriculum development for teachers* (4th ed.). New York: Longman.

Posner, G. J., & Strike, K. A. (1976). A categorization scheme for principles of sequencing content. *Review of Educational Research, 46*(4), 665–690.

Pratt, D. (1980). *Curriculum design and development.* New York: Harcourt Brace Jovanovich.

Ragan, T. J., & Smith, P. L. (1989). *Programming instructional software.* Englewood Cliffs, NJ: Educational Technology Publications.

Ragan, T. J., & Smith, P. L. (1996). Conditions-based models for designing instruction. In D. H. Jonassen (Ed.), *Handbook of research for educational communications and technology* (pp. 541–569). New York: Macmillan.

Ragan, W. B. (1953). *Modern elementary curriculum.* New York: Dryden.

Recker, M. M., Walker, A., & Wiley, D. A. (2002). Collaboratively filtering learning objects. In D. A. Wiley (Ed.), *The Instructional Use of Learning Objects: Online Version.* Retrieved February 8, 2004, from the World Wide Web: http://reusability.org/read/chapters/reckerdoc.

Reigeluth, C. M. (1979). In search of a better way to organize instruction: The elaboration theory. *Journal of Instructional Development, 6,* 40–46.

Reigeluth, C. M. (1987). Lesson blueprints based on the elaboration theory of instruction. In C. M. Reigeluth (Ed.), *Instructional theories in action* (pp. 245–288). Hillsdale, NJ: Erlbaum.

Reigeluth, C. M. (1992). Elaborating the elaboration theory. *Educational Technology Research and Development, 40*(3), 80–86.

Reigeluth, C. M., & Garfinkle, R. J. (Eds.). (1994). *Systematic change in education.* Englewood Cliffs, NJ: Educational Technology Publications.

Reigeluth, C. M., Merrill, M. D., Wilson, B. G. & Spiller, R. T. (1994). The elaboration theory of instruction: A model for sequencing and synthesizing instruction. In M. D. Merrill & D. G. Twitchell (Eds.), *Instructional design theory* (pp. 79–102). Englewood Cliffs, NJ: Educational Technology Publications.

Reigeluth, C. M., & Stein, F. S. (1983). The elaboration theory of instruction. In C. M. Reigeluth (Ed.), *Instructional design theories and models* (pp. 335–381). Hillsdale, NJ: Erlbaum.

Rieber, L. P. (1992). Computer-based microworlds: A bridge between constructivism and direct instruction. *Educational Technology Research and Development, 40*(1), 93–106.

Rieber, L. P. (1996). Seriously considering play: Designing interactive learning environments based on the blending of microworlds, simulations, and games. *Educational Technology Research and Development, 44*(2), 43–58.

Rousseau, J. (1950). *Emile.* (Trans. by B. Foxley.) New York: E. P. Dutton.

Rummelhart, D. E., & Ortony, A. (1977). The representation of knowledge in memory. In R. C. Anderson, R. J. Spiro, & W. E. Montague (Eds.), *Schooling and the acquisition of knowledge* (pp. 37–53). Hillsdale, NJ: Erlbaum.

Stratemeyer, F. B, Forkner, H. L., McKim, M. G., & Passow, A. H. (1957). *Developing a curriculum for modern living* (2nd ed.). New York: Teachers College.

Vickers, J. N. (1990). *Instructional design for teaching physical activities: A knowledge structures approach.* Champaign, IL: Human Kinetics.

Virginia State Board of Education. (1934). *Tentative course of study for Virginia elementary schools.* Richmond, VA: State Board of Education.

Walker, D. F. (1996). New information technology in the curriculum. In T. Plomp & D. P. Ely (Eds.), *International encyclopedia of educational technology* (2nd ed.) (pp. 539–545). Tarrytown, NY: Elsevier.

Wedman, J. F., & Smith, P. L. (1989). An examination of two approaches to organizing instruction. *International Journal of Instructional Media, 16*(4), 293–303.

Wiley, D. A. (Ed.) (2002). *The instructional use of learning objects.* Bloomington, IN: Association for Educational Communications and Technology. Also available from the World Wide Web: http://reusabilityorg.

Wilson, B. G. (Ed.). (1996). *Constructivist learning environments: Case studies in instructional design.* Englewood Cliffs, NJ: Educational Technology Publications.

Wilson, B., & Cole, P. (1992, April). *Returning the "theory" to elaboration theory: Strategies for organizing instruction based on cognitive conceptions of learning.* Paper presented at the annual meeting of the American Educational Research Association, San Francisco, CA.

Wilson, B. G., Hamilton, R., Teslow, J. L., & Cyr, T. A. (1994). *Technology making a difference: The Peakview Elementary School study.* Syracuse, NY: ERIC Clearinghouse on Information and Technology.

IV

IMPLEMENTATION, MANAGEMENT, AND EVALUATION

Three separate but related topics are treated in this section. Each presents another set of tools and techniques that improve the process and increase the success of instructional design efforts.

Chapter 17, "Implementation," provides a brief but helpful introduction to concepts, principles, and techniques for getting good use out of what we design. A key technique, the CBAM approach, is introduced and placed into context of instructional design efforts.

Chapter 18, "Management of Instruction," involves two sides of management that are relevant: one the management of instructional design projects and the other the management dimension, or management strategies that are part of instruction that we design.

Chapter 19, "Formative and Summative Evaluation" treats processes that are extremely helpful to the development of high-quality instruction. In the formative evaluation section, an approach to improving instruction is presented that ties together the task analysis and strategy development work studied earlier. Summative evaluation designs that help assess the quality of instruction are also discussed.

IMPLEMENTATION

CHAPTER OBJECTIVES

At the conclusion of this chapter, you should be able to do the following:

- Given descriptions of stages of the adoption process, identify the stage.

- Generate an example of a situation in which an instructional design project might need implementation work.

- Given terms and definitions related to implementation—diffusion, dissemination, adoption, adaptation, integration, and stakeholders—match the term with its definition.

- Given scenarios depicting implementation problems, identify what principles the designer failed to observe and describe a plan for improving implementation based on the CBAM model and other implementation principles ("open book"—use notes or references on CBAM and other implementation principles as needed).

OVERVIEW OF IMPLEMENTATION

Consider the fictitious case of Language Arts at Gutenberg High School. Brad Wiley was about the best English teacher they ever had at Gutenberg. His first year of teaching was marked with remarkable success, with his students doing unusually well and having amazingly good attitudes. During his second year of teaching, he spent extra time checking out where the biggest learning problems were in English classes and over the following summer developed an integrated system of writing exercises based on a modified "Whole Language" approach, including feedback models, and "initiator modules" to stimulate interest, assist in topic selection, and provide guidance on a process approach to writing. During Wiley's third year he fine-tuned his writing improvement system through a carefully designed series of trial uses with increasingly large groups of students. The system was, by the end of the year, amazingly helpful and well-liked by students.

During the following summer, as Brad worked as a roofer, he thought about how much good his system could do if other teachers used it, not only at Gutenberg but also at other schools in town. As the summer wore on, he dreamed of even wider use, fame, and glory.

In the first week of school, Brad made copies of the materials he developed and gave them to his fellow English teachers at the first Language Arts Department Faculty Meeting. He made a short presentation about what success he had had with his system and made it clear to the language arts faculty that anyone who did not use it was sadly out of step and probably not a very good teacher.

With visions of fame and glory dancing in his head, Brad checked with his fellow English teachers just before Christmas break. Of the five other English teachers at Gutenberg, two said they hadn't had a chance to use it yet, one said, "what system?", one reported she had used it for a week but got stuck on how to use the feedback modules, and the last reported that he used it and thought it was about the dumbest collection of stuff he had ever seen.

Brad learned a hard lesson about implementation. The movie *Field of Dreams* popularized the phrase: "If you build it, they will come." Although the implied automaticity of implementation may in rare and miraculous occasions come to pass, usually it does not. If designers expect their work to be used and to be of the kind of help to learning that they had anticipated during design and development, careful work in the area of implementation is generally needed.

This chapter is about what implementation means, why it is needed, how to facilitate successful implementation, and issues surrounding implementation that can impact on your efforts.

WHAT IS IMPLEMENTATION?

A dictionary defines *implementation* as "to put something into effect or action." With regard to instructional design, implementation involves successfully putting designs into use in the contexts for which they are intended.

WHAT IS THE ROLE OF IMPLEMENTATION IN INSTRUCTIONAL DESIGN?

The result of engaging in instructional design is typically an innovation, something new, a new way to solve a learning problem. New materials, new insights, and new ways of engaging learners: these are the products of instructional design efforts. If the use of the innovation is restricted to the person who created it, as can be the case when a teacher engages in design to improve the learning in her own classes, then implementation concerns may be limited to "am I using what I developed in the way I had in mind when I developed it?" and "are there adaptations that I should make to my plans or materials based on changes in conditions that existed when I originally developed and evaluated my materials?"

If the results of design are to be used by people other than the designers themselves, implementation becomes a more difficult and extensive process, often involving organizational change. Potential users must be aware of a problem that the innovation can solve, be aware of the innovation itself, believe that that innovation can solve the problem, be in favor of the innovation, and see a role for themselves in using or adopting the innovation.

Key concepts in implementation, in addition to the concept of innovation include:

- *Diffusion:* a process by which innovations spread to members of a social system.
- *Dissemination:* the same as diffusion with the addition of an intentional diffusing effort.
- *Adoption:* a decision to make full use of a new idea as the best course of action available. The primary phases of adoption when viewed as a process may generally be described as: 1) Awareness, 2) Interest, 3) Evaluation or Appraisal, 4) Trial, 5) Adoption, and 6) Integration (these stages are defined and described further on in the chapter).
- *Stakeholders:* people with vested interest in an innovation, such as the learners themselves, teachers and trainers, administrators and managers, support personnel, designers, other impacted people, and so forth.

IMPORTANCE OF CONSIDERING IMPLEMENTATION

Since people vary greatly in their response to innovations, ranging from being innovators and early adopters to being resistant or violently opposed to any sort of change (Rogers, 1995), and since the policies, practices, and "corporate culture" of organizations themselves vary greatly with regard to innovation and change (Reigeluth & Garfinkle, 1994), implementation must often be given considerable attention and effort if the innovation has any chance at being successfully accomplished.

Seven cases in Ertmer and Quinn's *I/D Casebook* (2003) have implementation as a primary issue (the cases of Sam Bell, Carla Fox, Suzanne Garner, Jim Huggins, Jacci Joya, Michelle Nguyen, and Brent Wilson and May Lowry). Only for the issue of "instructional strategies" are more cases presented.

Our case of the unfortunate English teacher, Brad Wiley, illustrates many of the results of unsuccessful implementation: apathy, failure to use the innovation, misuse of the innovation—a failure to use the innovation as intended or use as intended in an inappropriate context, and active dislike of the innovation with accompanying resistance to its adoption. Anyone who has had a job in an organization of any size has most likely experienced all of these reactions, either first hand or by observation.

TIMING OF IMPLEMENTATION

A traditional approach to the timing of implementation is to begin working on dissemination and other implementation activities when development work is finished. What some have called an "integrated model" begins work on dissemination at the beginning of the overall project. Figure 17.1 illustrates the distribution of effort under both approaches. Advantages of the integrated model include potential to improve project quality by increasing attention to context factors which concern with implementation can provide, potential reduction of time from project inception to full implementation, and more even distribution of effort throughout a project's life cycle.

STAGES OF THE ADOPTION PROCESS

If we view implementation as a process of facilitation of the adoption of an innovation, our understanding of the way in which the adoption process works is a helpful component. It seems well-established that adoption follows a fairly predictable, developmental process. Although the particulars vary slightly among different theorists (e.g., Havelock & Zlotolow, 1995; Rogers,

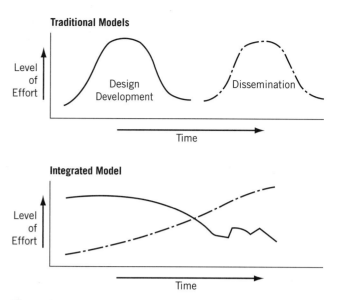

Figure 17.1 Development–Dissemination Models

1995), the following six stages are generally representative of a consensus:

Stage 1: Awareness. An innovation may be available and even present without potential adopters even being aware of it. Awareness includes both exposure to and consciousness of an innovation. Awareness is a prerequisite to any further possible adoption processes. Awareness is a more or less passive interest and does not mean that the individual will seek further information about the innovation.

Stage 2: Interest. Interest typically results in active information seeking about the innovation. Interest does not mean that the individual has made a judgment about the value of the innovation, only interest in learning more about it. At this point, the individual may begin to make tentative positive and negative options about the innovation.

Stage 3: Evaluation. Before doing a behavioral (or actual) trial, people generally perform a mental trial of innovations they are considering. The individual applies the innovation to her own situation and decides whether it is worth the effort or not to try it out.

Stage 4: Trial. In performing a trial, the individual uses the innovation on a small scale in order to find out how it will work in his own situation. In-service or staff development training often offers this opportunity and can provide support and encouragement, helping a user to evaluate his own experience, since results of use may not always be immediately or obviously apparent.

Stage 5: Adoption. The decision to make full use of the innovation, Adoption may be the result of weighing and considering results of a post-trial evaluation.

Although this sounds formal, the process is well-reflected in a decision to buy a new minivan after reading about minivans, test driving many, and consulting with the spouse.

Stage 6: Integration. Integration is the use of an innovation until it becomes routine. Using our minivan example above, integration would be using the minivan as a primary family transportation solution. A failure to integrate, using this example, would be if nobody liked to drive it or didn't want to be seen in it, other vehicles were used, and it sits in the driveway most of the time (highly unlikely, but possible).

At the end of the chapter, an exercise will assist in application of these concepts of stages of adoption.

PRINCIPLES FOR ENCOURAGING IMPLEMENTATION

The following principles are pragmatic, practical recommendations that can be helpful to instructional designers in getting their work put to good use.* Although it is difficult to accept, it is likely that implementation strategies for diffusion and dissemination have more effect on the adoption and continued use of learning environments and instructional materials than the products themselves.

General Rules. The beginning of an instructional design project, not the end of it, is time to begin making decisions about implementation. Tools and ideas from management, such as Gantt charts (see Chapter 18), will help in accomplishing this planning. Second, early in the project, if it appears that the project is going to self-destruct eventually, it is best to make it self-destruct as soon as possible. This will save everyone a lot of time, money, and anguish in the long run. A third general rule is to remember that a single change or innovation affects every other part of the learning environment or system of which the innovation is a part. New instruction can change the role of instructors, the structure of classrooms, and so forth, even to the storage of materials.

The Adopting System. It is important to analyze the potential adopting system to determine: a) the organizational and decision-making structure, b) the rules and policies regarding adoption of instructional materials, and c) the resources available in the adopting system such as time, money, and expertise.

The People. It is a good idea to get a representative of everyone who is directly affected by the project (the

stakeholders) involved in some way in the project. Potential blockers and politically influential individuals are particularly important to include. Although there are many ways in which to involve stakeholders, a frequently-used approach is the establishment of an advisory board. For an institution to change, the people within it must change, so it is critical to build a good relationship with those directly affected by the innovation. Many books have been written on building good relations, but these five concepts may help: 1) reciprocity (a give and take approach with emphasis on information); 2) openness (especially to new ideas, seeking out ideas and opinions); 3) realistic expectations (including avoidance of overselling the innovation's benefits); 4) expectations of rewards (a realistic association between adoption and benefits); 5) minimum threat (since change is threatening, minimizing perception of threat can be helpful in acceptance).

A prominent change theorist (Rogers, 1995) has recommended that potential adopters be identified by adoption category: innovators, early adopters, early and late majority, and laggards. In situations in which persuasion is needed and appropriate, strategic planning of engagements can be based on these classifications. For example, innovators do not need to be persuaded to change because they are doing the innovating; whereas efforts to persuade laggards are not likely to be successful; and early adopters are often the most important individuals to persuade since they are the most likely to both accept an innovation and they are also often opinion leaders for the majority.

The Instructional Material. The innovation itself should be congruent with the attitudes and values of most members of the client system (good context analysis will increase the likelihood of this criterion being met), the innovation should be capable of being easily and convincingly demonstrated as well as being tried out on a limited basis (pilots, demo versions, etc.), and any physical materials should be adequately packaged and labeled. Low user cost can be a significant factor in adoption, and products that replace existing materials than merely supplement existing materials are more likely to be adopted and integrated. If a product is seen as a solution to a specific, high-priority, recognized problem in the system, it is more likely to be adopted.

Awareness. A common error by developers is to begin awareness too soon. Complex technology-using projects often evolve, and premature awareness by potential users can be confusing and lead to rejection, even when the early problems have been worked out. Also, it is helpful to make the perceived advantage ("what's in it for me?") obvious for each level of adopters including administrators/managers andteacher/trainers.

---

*The primary source for these principles was instruction from Prof. Ernest Buckman at Florida State University, whose depth of knowledge, insight, and willingness to share them are deeply appreciated by the authors.

Trials. Field testing may be used as a dissemination process, as well as a part of the design process. Field tests should involve early adopters if possible. Also, adaptation to materials to particular environments will assist the success of implementation.

Teacher/Trainer Training. A common mistake in training is to begin with the theory behind the new materials. It is generally more effective to begin with "what's in the box" and what teachers/trainers can do with the materials in the classroom. It is also helpful, if possible, to allow teachers/trainers to take the materials with them. Ideally, training should take place over time, with several staff development sessions to check for problems.

AN APPROACH TO FACILITATING IMPLEMENTATION: CBAM

Although there is a rich literature related to implementing innovations in education (e.g., Berman & McLaughlin, 1975; Ely, 1990; Fullan & Stiegelbauer, 1991; Havelock & Zlotolow, 1995; Rogers, 1995; Zaltman & Duncan, 1977) we will present a summary of the Concerns-Based Adoption Model (Hall & Hord, 1987) as an example approach that has high utility and is widely used. Many of the principles for encouraging implementation described previously are incorporated into to this approach.

The *Concerns-Based Adoption Model* (CBAM) looks at the implementation process from the standpoint of the users of an innovation, focusing on the concerns or viewpoints which potential users have and the kinds or levels of use they make of the innovation. Over the years since its inception, the CBAM has grown into a comprehensive approach to facilitating implementation, including not only concepts and principles but also data collection instruments which proponents of an innovation may use to assist in their efforts.

One CBAM instrument, the *Stages of Concern Questionnaire* (SoCQ), is used to find out the attitudes or concerns of stakeholders about the innovation. (Hord, Rutherford, Huling-Austin, & Hall, 1987) Six stages of concern have been conceptualized in a developmental framework, from earliest to most well-integrated: awareness, informational, personal, management, consequence, collaboration, and refocusing. These stages move through three general categories, from self-focused concerns, through task-related concerns, to impact-centered concerns.

A second instrument, the *Levels of Use Questionnaire* (LoUQ) provides information on what sort of application users of the innovation are making. The levels of use which the instrument identifies roughly correspond to the stages of adoption described previously in this chapter. Responses to the questionnaire are scored to identify which of eight developmental levels of use best characterize an individual's engagement with the innovation: 0, Non-use; 1, Orientation (in which the individual takes the initiative to learn more about the innovation); 2, Preparation (in which the individual makes plans to use the innovation); 3, Mechanical (in which the individual makes organizational changes which will make room for use of the innovation); 4a, Routine (an established pattern of use); 4b. Refinement (makes changes to increase benefit from use of the innovation); 5. Integration (makes deliberate efforts to coordinate with others who use the innovation); and 6, Renewal (the user seeks alternatives to make more effective use).

A third instrument in CBAM, the *Innovation Configuration Matrix* ICM), is a framework for measuring and describing the operational characteristics of an innovation. An ICM for an innovation is displayed as a two-dimensional matrix with the operational elements of the innovation on one axis and a scale of use levels from ideal through acceptable through minimal to unacceptable use. In developing an ICM, each cell of the matrix provides a description of what events will have occurred regarding adoption of an innovation.

A fourth instrument, like the ICM, is one that is developed by the innovation project personnel using guidelines supplied by CBAM literature. The *Intervention Taxonomy* describes specific actions that can be undertaken to support the change process that will facilitate successful implementation of the innovation.

The general approach in using CBAM to facilitate implementation is to target assistance to users in an organization based on their interests and needs. CBAM views organizational change from a developmental standpoint and is particularly helpful when the innovation is complex and represents substantial change for the adopters. The CBAM approach employs a system of instruments and techniques, and it is a well-established and widely used implementation methodology.

This brief introduction is not intended to be sufficient guide for application, only an introduction to a powerful tool that deserves further study and application. The CBAM approach is described in greater detail in many sources, a selected set of which appears in the Readings and References section of this chapter. As a next step for those considering use of CBAM with forthcoming projects, a good start would be to read Hord et al. (1987). An example of an adaptation of CBAM's ICM to develop a tool for analysis of the quality of implementation of computer-based instruction may be seen in Mills & Ragan (2000).

FIDELITY OF IMPLEMENTATION

As we have noted earlier, innovations may be applied, even enthusiastically at times, in ways that the designers had not intended. Concerns with fidelity of implementation reflect this possibility. For an innovation to be successfully implemented, it typically needs to be used in a manner congruent with the ways it was intended to be used. (Fullan and Pomfret, 1977) The term "fidelity" might remind you of a comparison between an old, scratchy wax cylinder recording and a CD played on high-quality audio reproduction equipment. High fidelity, whether in music or instructional implementation, is about being closer to the original event or idea. As mentioned above and in Chapter 19 on Evaluation, the degree of fidelity of implementation can be measured using CBAM's ICM.

It is widely known that a teacher or trainer can sabotage any instructional system or learning environment. As we discussed earlier in Chapter 3, "Context Analysis," it is vital that designers know a great deal about who will implement any new instruction that is designed and developed. In addition to designing to fit the context, efforts at encouraging implementation such as those described above can make an enormous difference in the extent to which learning systems are used as intended.

The degree of fidelity of implementation can be measured. In other words, it is possible to measure the extent to which an innovation is being used the way it was intended. As mentioned earlier and in Chapter 19, "Formative and Summative Evaluation," the degree of fidelity of implementation can be measured. One approach to accomplishing this measurement is to use CBAM's "innovation configuration matrix (ICM) technique. For more information on using the ICM to measure fidelity of implementation, see Mills & Ragan (2000).

ADOPTION, ADAPTATION, AND INTEGRATION

A complicating factor in implementation is the role of adaptation in the process of adoption. To understand this, it is helpful to use a "tool" metaphor. Most instructional innovations can be thought of as tools—technology devised to assist in accomplishing a task. When we put a tool to good use, whether it is a screwdriver or an exploratory learning environment, we must not only select the right tool for the job—as in using a #2 Phillips screwdriver only for screws it fits and using an exploratory learning environment in contexts, for tasks and learners for which it fits—we not only select it but we put it into use in an appropriate way . . . we adopt

the tool for the task. **Adoption** is a decision to make full use of a new idea as the best course of action available. The concept of fidelity of implementation addresses use from the standpoint of use as intended, such as using the tip of the screwdriver on the screw rather than the handle and pressing down on the screw with sufficient force to prevent the blade from slipping out.

The concept of **adaptation** addresses use from the standpoint of what changes need to be made to make the tool work. Continuing our screwdriver analogy, an adaptation that a mechanic may need to make is to wrap the handle with a sticky rubber strip to improve her grip in a hot, sweaty environment. Although in general, the more suited a tool is for the job, the less adaptation will be required, adaptation is a perfectly legitimate activity. "From a teacher's point of view, the critical question for successful use of technology is not so much how to implement it as design, but how to adapt it so that it fits within the teacher's instructional approach." (Mills & Ragan, 2000, p. 22).

There are countless examples of adaptation and the need for it in education and training settings. Some familiar, easy-to-remember examples include: Ms. Lewis assigning algebra homework to complete problems 1, 2, 4, and 7 rather than all provided in the text; Ms. Chisolm allowing thirty minutes for group work on the Constitutional Amendments project rather than the fifteen minutes specified based on prior experience which suggests that her students will get learning benefit from the additional time; Ms. Dunham adding an example of a nonparallel sentence construction to those provided in the writing text; and Mr. Huddleston providing an explanation and demonstration of the use of the ball peen hammer in addition to the state curriculum's recommendation of claw hammer treatment for Grade 6 Industrial Arts.

Adaptation may add, delete, resequence, or provide any of a wide variety of instructional strategy elements in a fashion different from what is provided or specified. The Expanded Events of Instruction can give you a good framework for consideration of possible areas for adaptation. Notice, as well, that adaptation is a good term for the "highest" level of use described in the CBAM Levels of Use Questionnaire, described previously.

Nothing we design or develop is perfect or is perfectly suited to application in all environments for which it may be suitable. Adaptation will always be a legitimate part of the adoption process.

Integration, as we defined earlier while discussing stages of adoption, is the use of an innovation until it becomes routine. Many useful and helpful innovations are given use, sometimes ongoing use, but fail to be integrated into a school or training environment. Such is often the case with technology-based changes. The concern in K–12 schools with "technology integration" is one sign that on the one hand there is interest and effort being expended to implement technology solutions in schools, on the other hand, such solutions are not fully implemented. The ultimate goal of full implementation is integration.

The goal of an instructional designer is to solve learning problems. If we reflect for a moment on the main ideas of Chapter 3, "Context Analysis," we can recall the role of a needs assessment . . . to find out if there is a problem for which development of appropriate instruction would be a good solution (and if so, to continue on to determine more about the problem, the setting, the learners, and so forth). In the end, our goal is beyond implementing a system. It is that the system actually helps.

EMBODIMENT AS PART OF IMPLEMENTATION

A dimension of implementation that we have not yet considered is the actual physical embodiment of the instruction or learning environment. Two primary forms in which instruction manifests itself are media and groupings. Reigeluth (1983) called these embodiments "delivery strategies." All learning activities are embodied in some form. The major forms or media which are employed in practice include the Web, print, interactive multimedia, video, and teachers. These alternatives and others are discussed at length in Chapter W-1, provided on the *Learning Resources Web Site*. This online chapter discusses media attributes and selection of appropriate media, including exercises which provide practice application of context, learning task, and learner considerations in media selection. In addition, the online chapter treats the second aspect of delivery strategies, grouping. Alternatives for grouping include individual learners (both individual exploratory and adaptive individualized) two-person, small group (including cooperative learning), and large group.

E X E R C I S E S

1. Given below are descriptions of stages in the adoption process. Write the name of each stage beside its description. The stages are: awareness, interest, evaluation, trial, adoption, and integration.

a. Elizabeth Price considers how the "Geometry for Grade School Students" units would work in her third grade, lower socioeconomic class. _____

b. Jerry Murray of Big'N' Round Tire Company listens to a convention presentation by the developers of a learning environment that is a new approach to training die-cast troubleshooters. _____

c. The use of the Web search tool, "Google," has become routine in Patricia Tillman's eleventh-grade social studies classes. Patricia keeps her own skills in using Google sharp by reading magazine articles and attending technology training sessions on effective Web search techniques. _____

d. Gracie Pough has read an interesting article in her special education journal about instructional materials that claim to teach emotionally disturbed children how to monitor their own behavior. The program sounds like it has potential, so Gracie writes to the developers for more information. _____

e. Bill, Troop Leader of Boy Scouts Troop #118, uses the first module in a new series designed to teach use of hand-held GPS units in orienteering. He wants to see how the training program will work with Bravo Squad, one of his groups of new scouts. If the system works well with Bravo Squad on a weekend outing, he will consider using it in all the units of all of his courses. _____

f. Bill looks at his notes for Bravo Squad's highly successful week end outing and compares these data with Alpha and Charlie Squad's from the previous two weekends in which they both became lost multiple times. He considers the cost of the training program materials and the time he must spend preparing lessons using the materials. He decides that in his Troop, the benefits are worth the costs and that he will use the training program in Troop #118. _____

2. Match the term with its definition

_____ Diffusion	**A.** Deciding to really use something
_____ Dissemination	**B.** People who tend to be the first to use innovations
_____ Adoption	**C.** How innovations spread from one person to another
_____ Adaptation	**D.** Premature awareness
_____ Integration	**E.** Fine-tuning changes made by users
_____ Stakeholders	**F.** Routine use of an innovation
	G. Intentional spreading of innovation
	H. Those individuals who would be affected by the innovation

3. Using the case of Brad Wiley at the beginning of this chapter, identify what principles of good implementation were ignored or violated and write a short implementation plan for Mr. Wiley's project.

4. Given below are descriptions of diffusion/dissemination problems. In your own words, state at least one principle that was violated. Then, in your own words state what should have been done to avoid the problems or what could be done now to remediate the problem.

a. The Instructional Development Corporation of Norman (IDCN) developed a set of instructional materials to teach sociology. Materials include texts in four-color, videos provided in both tape and DVD, and a Web and intranet server to support authentic learning activities. Once the materials were developed, many school systems were interested in the materials, but only three school systems adopted them.

What principle has this corporation violated?

What might the developers have done differently?

b. The director of reading curriculum in the Northwest City School district was favorably impressed by Schank and Minsky's work on scripts and plans and their impact on learning to read. The director developed a module about these models. He expected that the reading teachers would learn to use and apply the models while teaching reading. When the director observed reading classes six months later, there was no evidence that the model was being incorporated into the reading instruction.

In your own words, what implementation principle has the director violated?

What should the director do to remediate the problem?

c. Another activity of the IDCN (Instructional Development Corporation of Norman) has been to develop modules of instruction to teach licensed practical nurses (LPNs) how to be patient educators. When the materials were distributed to LPNs in town, Maggie King, president of the local LPN professional association, complained bitterly about the addition of these materials and recommended to other LPNs that the materials not be used. The materials were not adopted by local or regional hospitals for staff development training.

In your own words, what implementation principle have the developers at IDCN violated this time?

What should the developers have done?

d. The Saskatchewan Education Agency (SEA) developed instructional materials to teach students how to deal with rapid change. They have published an article about the new materials in the Saskatchewan Teacher's Association newsletter which is sent to every teacher in the province.

During their formative evaluation stage, the developers find that their materials do not teach the students to cope with change, as a matter of fact, the students seem to be more anxious after studying the materials than before using them. The SEA decides to scrap the project.

In your own words, what implementation principle did the SEA violate?

What should the developers have done differently?

e. The Director of Human Resources at Paynes Auto Rental Company developed a new check-out training program for rental agents worldwide to correct the high error rate in check-outs which the company had been experiencing. Instructors from each region were sent to a two-day training session in Boston to learn how to teach the new program to all agents in their regions. Three months later the error rate had not improved in most regions, and observation of training being conducted by the regional instructors revealed that most of them were making many errors in their presentations and demonstrations of the system, and some were not even teaching the new system.

In your own words, what implementation principles did the HR Director violate?

What should the Director have done differently?

SUMMARY

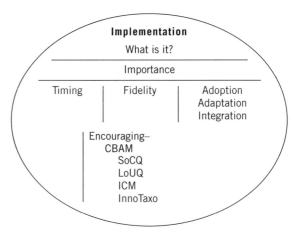

Figure 17.2 Summary Diagram

READINGS AND REFERENCES

Berman, P. & McLaughlin, M.W. (1975). Implementation of educational innovation (Rand Study). *The Educational Forum, 40* (3), 345–370.

Ellsworth, J. B. (2000). Surviving change: A survey of educational change models. Syracuse, NY: ERIC. (ED 443 417)

Ely, D. (1990). Conditions that facilitate the implementation of educational technology innovations. *Journal of Research on Computing in Education, 23*(2), 298–305.

Ertmer, P. A., & Quinn, J. (2003). *The ID case book: Case studies in instructional design.* Upper Saddle River, NJ: Merrill.

Fullan, M., & Pomfret, A. (1977). Research on curriculum and instruction implementation. *Review of Educational Research, 47,* 335–397.

Fullan, M., & Stiegelbauer, S. (1991). *The new meaning of educational change.* New York, NY: Teachers College Press (ED 354 588).

Hall, G., & Hord, S. (1987). Change in schools: Facilitating the process. Albany, NY: State University of New York Press.

Havelock, R. G., & Zlotolow, S. (1995). *The change agent's guide to innovation in education* (2nd ed.). Englewood Cliffs, NJ: Educational Technology Publications.

Hord, S. M., Rutherford, W. L., Huling-Austin, L., & Hall, G. E. (1987). *Taking charge of change.* Alexandria, VA: ASCD Publications.

Loucks, S., & Pratt, M. (1979). A concerns-based approach to curriculum change. *Educational Leadership,* 212–215.

Mills, S. C., & Ragan, T. J. (2000). A tool for analyzing the implementation fidelity of an integrated learning system. *Educational Technology Research & Development, 48*(4) 21–41.

Reigeluth, C. M. (1983). The elaboration theory of instruction. In C. M. Reigeluth (Ed.), *Instructional design theories and models* (pp. 335–382). Hillsdale, NJ: Erlbaum.

Reigeluth, C., & Garfinkle, R. (1994). *Systemic change in education.* Englewood Cliffs, NJ: Educational Technology Publications.

Rogers, E. M. (1995). *Diffusion of innovations* (4th ed.). New York: The Free Press.

Zaltman, G., & Duncan, R. (1977). Strategies for planned change. New York: John Wiley and Sons.

MANAGEMENT
OF INSTRUCTION

CHAPTER OBJECTIVES

At the conclusion of this chapter, you should be able to do the following:

- Describe components of ID project management in general.
- Identify the elements of ID project management relevant to a given ID project.
- Describe the management issues that should be considered regarding a given ID project.
- Identify some of the organizational and institutional characteristics that are likely to enable or constrain the success of an ID project.
- Given the specifications and context of an instructional intervention, analyze the implementation and management issues relevant to that instruction.
- Given the plan for an instructional design project, identify some cost-benefit tradeoffs and potential risks relevant to the success of that project.
- Identify the potential utility and tradeoffs of utilizing integrated learning systems for a particular instructional project.

OVERVIEW OF MANAGEMENT OF INSTRUCTION

What are the ways in which management concerns intersect with instructional design? Although there are many, we will treat two primary aspects of management here: 1) management of instructional design projects, and 2) management concerns related to the instructional process itself, as an instructional strategy element. We will treat project management first, providing a relatively thorough discussion, followed by a more brief treatment of instructional management.

WHY SHOULD A DESIGNER KNOW PROJECT MANAGEMENT?

A regional university wants its professors to develop Web pages to broaden outreach to potential students. The administration wants every professor to have something of quality on the Web within one academic year. The budget has to be allocated across multiple departments, an evaluation done, and some consistency of look-and-feel maintained. Who will be in charge of making sure these goals are achieved?

The city school district received a grant to create professional development training modules for teachers at all of its sites. Do they use direct classroom or multimedia instruction? What topics will be covered, and on what schedule? Who will manage the decision-making process, guide the development, and make the final report to the district administration and to the funding agency?

An independent design company has landed the contract for a series of government training modules deliverable over two years. Producing them will require both internal and external technical expertise, periodic work with multiple subject matter experts, and communication between collaborating teams in the company's three offices, located in different states. The contract includes a tight schedule, complex tasks, frequent handoffs, and strict evaluation standards. How will the company ensure that nothing is missed on this lucrative contract?

In each of these cases, these organizations need project managers, trained to assess organizational needs, plan and schedule communication, manage interactions among and between people and teams, budget and allocate resources, and evaluate and report project outcomes. Project managers have a broad range of skills that together help to ensure that work gets done, on time and within budget. Without effective project management, it's entirely possible that even well-conceived training will fail to be developed or delivered, or that a Web presence intended to enhance the image of a company will harm its image instead.

DEFINING PROJECT MANAGEMENT

To understand Project Management, we should first understand its two component terms. By one definition a *project* is, "a one time, multi-task job with definite start and end, clearly defined scope of work, budget, and usually a temporary team" (Lewis, 2001; p. 5). From a different perspective, J. Juran referred to a project as, "a problem scheduled for solution" (in Lewis, 2001; p. 6). *Management* is the organization of tools, people and systems (Lewis, 2001), not limited to just scheduling or resource management, though these are a large part of it.

Project management (PM) is the synthesis of a diverse set of skills. Some of these skills are generalizable; that is, they apply to nearly any kind of management role. Others are highly contextualized to project type and organization. There are skills and applications that tend to apply more to project-level management than to other management roles, and some that apply to a special subset of PM, such as to managing projects in instructional technology and instructional design (versus to noninstructional projects). Project management, "has become a highly sought-after" skill set (Murch, 2001), for which employers across contexts advertise constantly and pay well.

Project management involves, "the application of knowledge, skills, tools, and techniques to project activities to meet project requirements" (ANSI, 2000). Similar to instructional design, project management involves several iterative and sequential phases: analysis (of needs and risks), design (planning of activities and tasks), development (coordination, allocation, acquisition, creation of tools and structure to get work done), implementation (execution and control), and evaluation (of progress and outcomes).

A project manager is concerned with groups of variables represented by four basic constraints:

1. Quality/Performance (specifications)
2. Cost (budget)
3. Time (linear time and human resource collective hours), and
4. Scope (size of the task)

There are always tradeoffs between these constraints. They are interdependent (like the sides on a triangle) so that change in one results in change in the others. They exist in a systemic relationship such that no PM decision is ever made in isolation. An additional factor that managers need to consider is risk, anticipating problems that can arise in the course of the project that reduce or constrain any of the other four factors.

Projects are generally conducted in teams, because more minds can consider more ideas and perspectives, and teams can bring more diverse skills to project tasks. A project team is a collaboration of experts with the skill sets necessary to achieve the goals of a project. Some project tasks are achieved individually, while others are achieved by a series of handoffs from one team member to another until all of the skill are applied to a given product. The success of a team project is measured by more than numbers, representing quantity or even quality. Project success is often judged upon a complex set of process and product measures. Even so, the bottom line is to achieve the established goals, for both quantity and quality, on time and on budget.

There is not just one "right way" to manage a project, but there are core requisite skills and best practices. These skill sets are adaptive to the specific requisites of the task and context, which results in various approaches to applying them. Important differences in management practices exist by culture and context, such as the division between corporate and educational institutions. People management skills are a dominant skill set of the project manager, yet different parameters and strategies useful when team members are employees versus when they are volunteers in a not-for-profit organization.

Effective documentation is critical. While "seat-of-the-pants" management can work, like "seat-of-the-pants" instructional design, it is inconsistent and is often not replicable. Documentation is important for planning the course and tracking the progress of a project, providing points of comparison against the targets on all of the key variables (quality, cost, time, and scope). It is possible to overplan and overdocument, but far more often the opposite mistake is made. As with instructional design generally, underplanning is far more common than overplanning. How does a project manager, especially a novice, know how much documentation is necessary and appropriate?

A commonsense principle is: The bigger the project, the more documentation is necessary to control it effectively. The term "bigger" here refers to project scope, in the forms of organization, timeline, and number of personnel involved, as well as the geographic distance between team members. This principle is true because the bigger the project, the more variables are interacting, and the more chances there are to lose control!

The range and nature of documents necessary for a project obviously vary, yet some general principles apply here, too. In any project there are both internal (team) and external (organization/administration/stakeholder) documents. The internal ones are "team management" documents, while the external ones are "report" documents. Internal documents tend to be more malleable, and function for tracking and direct management. External documents tend to be more stable/static, and function for output/updates beyond the team itself. Documents' number and nature may be organizationally-determined, or manager-chosen, and most often a project includes some of both.

Though the precise format of documents differs widely, most instructional design projects will have, at minimum, some version of the following documents:

- Proposal (defines the project as a whole)
- Resource Analysis (identifies the requisite resources to achieve project goals)
- Schedule (defines chronological timeline and critical path of project)
- Budget (identifies and itemizes the monetary resources for the project)
- Risk Analysis/Troubleshooting Plan (identifies potential problems and solutions/alternative methods for achieving goals if problems occur)
- Assessment and Evaluation Plan (establishes measures of goal achievement and product quality)
- Project Report/Summary (reports success on goals and summarizes project activities of interest to stakeholders)

Beyond the current project, clear and appropriate documentation enhances organizational knowledge management, so that information, methods, tools, and strategies can be rolled over from one project to the next, saving money, time, and other valuable resources.

PROJECT MANAGEMENT IN INSTRUCTIONAL DESIGN

Instructional design occurs most often in teams, either internal or external, and often a mix of internal professionals and external contractors. Someone must keep tasks coordinated and deadlines met. This is the role of the project manager. Sometimes the project manager is a member of the organization (internal) and in other cases the manager is a consultant or contractor (external).

A big part is planning, the pre-launch part of project management. As with ID generally, thorough front-end analysis and planning makes all the difference in eventual success, and in the need for rework and problem-solving on the way to project goals. In addition, even a well-conceived, well-planned project often fails without effective process management.

Companies are hiring instructional design professionals with PM skills because projects fail without effective, efficient managers. If there is nobody to take care of planning, progress, resources, and challenges that arise, any project can fail. Having a capable manager in charge of the big picture means that the experts on a team can focus on using their skills to achieve project goals and not worry about potential problems "blindsiding" them.

Although the characteristics identified so far are not limited to instructional design projects, there are some elements of instructional design projects, and more particularly multimedia projects, which define the project management process in particular ways. One example is that the software development life cycle defines a specialized type of evaluation plan characterized by a design evaluation, then a prototype evaluation, and often a modular release cycle for multiple-module projects. Alpha-testing and beta-testing of media-based instruction should be built into the evaluation plan and project timeline. These specialized elements of evaluation (and their consequent time-critical resource-management) are not characteristic, for instance, of direct-instruction training materials design. Similarly, Web site design dictates a specific series of approvals by stakeholders, generally approval of concept, then storyboards/organizational design, and then general content approval (by clients or SMEs) as precontingent to materials production/development. Thus, the nature of the product being designed dictates elements of the documentation and management process, even as the dictates of the management process drive some elements of design and production.

In all cases, the eventual targets of project management are to *control* money cost, time in development, and time to market, while *maintaining* product quality. As in instructional design, the goals are efficiency and effectiveness, doing the best job with the least requirements, or (in management terms) optimizing return on investment.

STANDARDS FOR PROJECT MANAGEMENT

Within the International Board of Standards for Training, Performance and Instruction's *Instructional Design Competencies* (Richey, Fields, & Foxon, 2001), is a set of ID competencies relevant to project management. Some of these competencies focus on the design process and strategies, while others either span both design and management, or focus on the management role within ID practice.

Although an ID project manager should be a competent designer first, and thus practice all of the general ID competencies, some of the *essential* ID competencies that focus on the specific demands of PM include:

- Communicate effectively in visual, oral and written form
- Facilitate meetings effectively
- Present, receive, seek, and share information to facilitate project success
- Update and improve one's knowledge, skills and attitudes
- Determine how organizational features influence project outcomes

- Modify the design and development model if project parameters change
- Identify and resolve ethical and legal implications of design in the workplace
- Identify and describe the characteristics of the organizational environment
- Evaluate and assess instruction and its impact on the organization
- Manage the evaluation process

Among the *advanced* ID competencies are more that focus on management skills in ID:

- Establish project scope and goals
- Use a variety of tools to develop a project plan and write proposals
- Develop project information systems
- Monitor multiple ID projects simultaneously
- Allocate resources to support project plans
- Troubleshoot project problems
- Reflect on project success and debrief project teams
- Identify need for collaborations and partnerships
- Analyze stakeholder needs and involvement
- Build and promote effective relationships to promote project success
- Promote and manage productive interactions among team members
- Plan for distribution or diffusion of products from project
- Link design efforts to organizational goals
- Establish strategic and tactical goals for design functions
- Establish standards of quality for design products
- Recruit, retain, and develop human resources within project goals
- Provide financial plans and project controls
- Maintain management and stakeholder support of project
- Market services and manage customer relations
- Design instructional management systems

In addition to the ID standards relevant to PM, the field of Project Management has a set of national knowledge and performance standards. If you will be actively engaged in ID PM, you should know and practice these more specialized standards, as detailed in the *Guide to the Project Manager's Body of Knowledge* (ANSI, 2000). They include both essential and advanced standards in the following areas:

- Project Integration Management
- Project Scope Management

- Project Time Management
- Project Cost Management
- Project Human Resource Management

These global areas represent critical skill sets that an effective ID project manager is constantly practicing and refining. Even if an instructional designer or developer thinks, "I'll never manage a team," knowing how PM functions and what to expect from managers is useful to every member of a team. It can, help team members to function as team players so the whole project runs more smoothly.

PROJECT INTEGRATION MANAGEMENT

Project integration refers to managing the interactions among the many factors that comprise the project. This skill set is overarching in the management process, and includes many of the other areas of management. The project manager needs to ensure that the various elements of a project are effectively coordinated, from planning to final reporting. An ID project manager needs to allocate, utilize, adjust, share, and otherwise arrange the use of resources that include people and their skills, time, technology, tools, and anything else it takes to get the job done, to achieve the goals of the project. This may include not only arranging the sharing of resources between individuals working on one project, but also managing the sharing of centralized resources between multiple projects being conducted by different teams, under the direction of several managers.

Project integration is demanding and requires the manager to know the team and its resources well, to know the organization and context in which the project is being designed and developed, and to have thoroughly identified potential risks surrounding the essential interfaces within project flow. It also includes management considerations dealing with change, both in the project demands and in the larger organization and culture. Thus, project integration management is the "big picture" skill set of the ID project manager.

PROJECT SCOPE MANAGEMENT

Project scope refers to how big and complex the ultimate end goal of the project is. If it is an instructional multimedia package, then scope may be articulated as the number of modules and the types and quantity of media events and interactions in each module and in the package overall (Alessi & Trollip, 2001). On a Web-based instructional project, scope may be expressed as number of pages, graphics and other media content, overall site size, and number and types of interactive and evaluative events. For direct-instruction training, scope may be expressed as hours, manual contents, and job aids and other support materials (including the scope and type of each of those).

Project scope management involves making sure that all of the specified project work (and only the specified work) gets done, to complete the project successfully. Without effective scope management the result could be a "runaway project" that keeps changing as clients try to add "just one more" feature. The key to effective scope management is to specify scope at the outset of the project and stick to the specifications throughout. Sometimes changes beyond the control of clients will influence a change in needs, and in those cases the PM can negotiate and manage change that is responsive but controlled.

PROJECT TIME MANAGEMENT

Time is a mission-critical component of nearly every project. Time management influences all of the other variables, because it interacts with resource management and can constrain project scope. The project manager needs to plan and track time in at least two ways: 1) cumulative hours, and 2) linear time. Managing cumulative hours means planning and tracking time allocated and committed to the project by all team members, across all phases. Managing linear time means checking that progress is maintained on various tasks and phases, so that handoffs and deliverables occur on schedule.

Time management requires not only that the manager generate the project timeline and allocate resource hours, but that the manager communicates those to all team members and keeps track of progress relative to time allocated through the life of the project. For these tasks, a project manager needs a complex and powerful tool, and typically the Gantt Chart is the PM's tool of choice.

Probably the most universal of project management tools is the Gantt Chart, created by Henry Gantt (1861–1919). The *Gantt Chart* is a planning timeline that not only identifies the component parts of a project, but also represents, in graphic form, the relationships between various phases and products of the project. The Gantt Chart concept can be represented in a very simple form, using a table or grid diagram produced either by hand or with common drawing tools in a word processing program, or a very sophisticated interactive Gantt Chart can be made with custom software. The Gantt-type planning timeline is an essential tool because it enables the manager to identify the critical path of dependencies and track any lag in handoffs relative to those dependencies. Figure 18.1 provides an example of a Gantt chart.

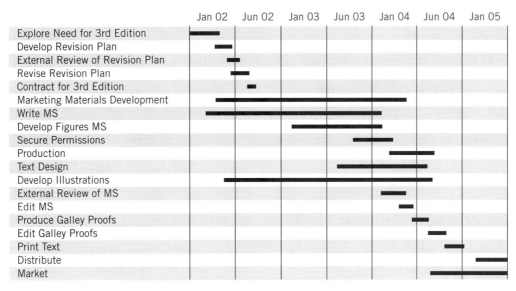

Figure 18.1   A Simple Gantt Chart for a Hypothetical Textbook Project

Another charting methodology to aid project time management is *PERT/CPM:* Program Evaluation and Review Technique/Critical Path Method. The PERT methodology was developed in the 1950s by the General Dynamics Corporation, the general contractor for the Polaris nuclear submarine weapons system design and development. That project was of such complexity, with so many sub-systems and sub-contractors, that a new project management technique had to be developed in order to successfully complete the project. Project diagrams which use the PERT technique depict events and processes. Events take no time (such as "finish first draft" and "begin review") and are displayed with circles. Processes occur over time (such as "develop

first draft" and "review manuscript") and are displayed with lines. A statistical technique is used to assist in the development of reliable time estimates for processes, and the diagramming technique can display multiple, concurrent processes and events. CPM adds the capability to make more efficient use of resources by identifying the "critical path" to which most attention must be paid in management and activities in which "slack" may allow reallocation of resources to focus effort to activities that need it most. Although PERT/CPM is most valuable in highly complex projects, informal PERT charts can be useful in planning and managing smaller projects. Figure 18.2 provides an example of a simplified PERT chart from a portion of a hypothetical project.

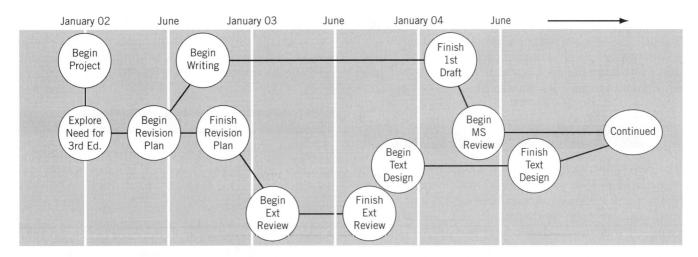

Figure 18.2   Simple PERT Chart from a Hypothetical Textbook Development Project

It is important that the manager is aware of dependencies, that is, tasks that have prerequisite tasks. These are represented differently in the planning documents from tasks that are concurrent, those that can be completed simultaneously. A task that is prerequisite to another project task will generate a handoff, a point at which it is critical for one team member to give some incremental version of the product or documentation to another team member. An example of this is that in multimedia design a structural template must be prepared before content can be inserted, though the content (both text and graphics in raw form) may be designed concurrently. The schedule for the template and raw content to be prepared for integration into the functional module is a handoff that the project manager will schedule carefully. It is the manager's job also to notify all of the team members involved, and track their progress to ensure that the handoff occurs on time.

A single handoff missed can set the entire project back and require the rescheduling of future dependencies. To guard against a rescheduling crisis, the manager should build in what various experts call "float time" or "slack." Essentially this means building in a small amount of extra time into the project timeline to allow for small errors or unexpected events, ranging from a missed handoff to a member of the team becoming ill. Learning to build in float time is necessary because with the number of variables extant in any given project, errors are eventually bound to happen.

Scheduling of any project is domain-specific, organizationally-defined, and goal-sensitive. The bottom line is to see all of the possibilities and make informed decisions about tradeoffs that exist. Even so, some general guidelines can help the novice project manager to plan and schedule projects. First, focus on tasks, scheduling based on requisite work, and let dates follow (don't tie your hands). Second, schedule task work in typically longer time increments, and knowledge work in smaller time increments. Third, publish the timeline to team members and update it frequently, so people can plan their time ahead, especially if they are lending expertise to multiple projects with multiple teams simultaneously.

PROJECT COST MANAGEMENT

The development of instruction is a more costly activity than most people realize. A national board reported that a single online Advanced Placement course "takes a 15-member team approximately eight months and $100,000 to $200,000 to develop." (NASB, 2001, p. 43) As long ago as the 1960s, one year's programming of "Sesame Street" cost the Children's Television Workshop over one million dollars* (Bogatz & Ball, 1971). Examples abound of the cost and complexity that instructional design projects can involve. As a practicing instructional designer, the likelihood is high that you will at some point in the future become involved with a project for which cost management is crucial.

Project cost management includes the processes that ensure that a project is completed within the established budget. Across projects and organizations, the degree to which the project manager controls the budget varies from almost totally to hardly at all. In general, a project manager should know how to resource plan, estimate project costs, and control project costs during design and development. Whether the ID group (and consequently the ID project manager) is internal or external to the client organization may have important implications for the degree to which a manager controls the budget and the criticality of budget control by project. Both sets of circumstances require the same global goals of PM budget management, but they tend to be characterized by different degrees of control and therefore present different types of decision-making tradeoffs.

When instructional design is external to the client organization, the project manager typically has more direct budget responsibility, since the budget is externally contracted, and resources allocated to that project must be billed to the client. Once the budget is set, any additional project costs that result from management oversights must be absorbed by the ID provider, which reduces project profit for the company.

When the instructional design service is internal to the client organization, the project manager typically has less direct budget responsibility, since the budget is internally billed, and resources allocated to that project are managed within the home organization. Once the budget is set, the manager still needs to be attentive and control any tendency of the project to "balloon" out of control, but small adjustments in budget reallocation can usually be managed. However, when a project uses in-demand internal expertise or equipment, even a small shift in project scope can disrupt the critical path not only for that project, but potentially for other in-house projects, also resulting in important losses for the ID group.

PROJECT HUMAN RESOURCE MANAGEMENT

Human resource management requires the manager to identify and make the most of the people resources essential to project success. People and their

---

*In case you were worried about a wastefully high cost, given the number of children who viewed "Sesame Street" in its second year and the number of hours viewed, the program cost was a penny per child per hour.

skills are the most important and the most challenging resource that the PM is responsible for, the primary resource in a project team and the key commodity on the ID market. People possess ideas, creativity, subject matter expertise, design skill, development skills, all of the raw materials of success in the field. Yet people get sick, injured, hired away by other companies, or reallocated to more urgent needs within the organization, and if the project manager has not planned for contingencies, the entire project can grind to a halt.

Every team member can help or hinder the management of a given project, either intentionally or unintentionally, and support or disrupt smooth team functioning. Sometimes people hinder out of ignorance, or busy-ness, or because they fail to see the utility or importance of tools and systems. An example is communication systems such as those implemented to keep team members and management apprised of progress and workflow related to project tasks. If an individual fails to enter information in a timely fashion, then others on the team may have unrealistic expectations of when their time and expertise is needed, and may be unprepared to contribute. Whether information is shared in face-to-face meetings or in electronic systems, the manager must ensure that every team member is clear and is participating in information sharing. If team members are unwilling or unable to keep information updated, then the PM may need to step in and facilitate the process.

One factor that often surprises novice managers is the fact that a "full-time" employee can only be allocated actual work time equaling about 60 percent of the work week. The reason is that myriad events get in the way of a person's work cycle: setup, cleanup, interruptions and restarts, antecedent and incidental tasks, meetings, paperwork, and life in general combine to reduce "full time" to part time. Knowing this and planning for it can prevent frustration and project stall by overallocating people hours on a project to fit an ideal instead of a realistic set of human resource expectations. Beyond the challenge of the people-to-task interface is the challenge of the people-to-people interface, an additional element of the project team manager's potential range of responsibility. People challenges to project success include miscommunication, varying perspectives, and interpersonal differences in understanding.

As with cost management, human resource management is influenced by whether the ID management is internal or external to the client organization. When ID is internal to the larger organization, then the support structure generally includes in-place human resource allocation. In educational organizations they tend to be centralized, either in an HR (human resources) department or in a faculty development center. In corporations ID groups tend to be decentralized, with designers assigned to support various departments. The project manager for an ID group within a department generally reports to the department manager, or to a training manager who reports to the department manager. ID organized this way can be specialized to the needs of the department and its subgroups. The processes and documentation can also be tailored to the department's needs. Within a department-level ID group, the PM has a set budget, staff are salaried, and reporting is directly to internal stakeholders or to the training manager. What varies is the degree of control that the PM has over project parameters and human resource allocation. In such cases, the PM may have a set team of in-house experts assumed to have appropriate expertise to meet any need, and that team may be handed project assignments approved by upper management, without being given much control of the schedule, specifications, and outcomes.

When ID is external to the client organization, then generally multiple ID providers compete for contracts to other companies and organizations. In some cases new requests for proposals (RFPs) are generated for each project, and in other cases a company has an ongoing (e.g., annual) contract with the larger organization, to design and develop or deliver frequent and varied instructional projects and materials. There may be one manager and an in-place team, as is frequently the case in a small ID group, or in a larger company there may be a large staff with diverse expertise and experience. In the latter case, the project manager may select different teams for each project, based on project needs. For instance, a government contract for the military may require at least one designer with specific military contract experience, while a contract for a K–12 educational organization may require a designer with teacher training expertise.

The nature of the project content itself also drives human resource selection. A multimedia project requiring complex video content should include a team member with specialized skills in video design and development, while a project with primarily still graphics would require a graphic designer on the team. Clark and Spohr (2002) provide a helpful guide to management of video-based projects.

RISK, CHANGE, AND CRISIS MANAGEMENT

Special types of management that confront every PM are risk, crisis, and change management. As leader and facilitator for the project, the manager is responsible for dealing with anticipated or unanticipated problems that may arise. Risks are potentially foreseeable but not absolutely predictable concerns that may arise during the life of the project. Risks may be very large or trivial in their scope and impact on the project. Since risks are potentially foreseeable, the manager should have contingency plans in place to address them if they do occur. Crises are large-scale problems, whether foreseeable or not, that may threaten the success of the project. While crisis is often not manageable by specific contingencies, it is often up to the project manager to handle it, at least to some degree, which may mean creative use of all of the resources available. Change management refers to responding to alterations in the organizational or market conditions under which the project was originally undertaken. Often the most challenging part of project management is dealing with the number of variables that are constantly changing in any system, then seeing into the future to be aware of and anticipating how to deal with new potential changes.

Skill Sets and Toolkits

In summary terms, what a project manager needs to be able to do is to:

1. Analyze the needs and goals of a project,
2. Plan for how to utilize resources (including people and their expertise) in achieving those goals,
3. Maintain productivity under constraints such as time and budget,
4. Anticipate the potential problems that could sidetrack a project,
5. Figure out how to work around those problems if they should arise,
6. Know how to evaluate outcomes and report those outcomes to stakeholders.

Software packages to assist project managers abound in the field. Some are effective in developing the manager's plan into clear, effective documents for communication and reporting. Others are limited in their range and flexibility, producing externally less useful documents and tools. A danger for the novice project manager in grabbing software tools too soon is to become dependent on the tool rather than refining skills and capacity for advanced management thinking. New managers should resist "plugging into" software until they have mastered deep-level project management skills "on manual," with the old technology of the brain. In the digital age it is too easy to buy into the deception that software thinks for you. As James Lewis points out, using software tools before learning to manage well only enables you to "document your failures with great precision" (Lewis, 2001, p. 259).

Generic project planning tools, such as *Inspiration*™, Microsoft *Project*™, and Omni *Graffle*™, provide assistance in developing flow charts, Gantt charts, and other project management visualizations. In addition to the generic tools, there are those specialized ID tools such as Allen Communications' *Designer's Edge*© and David Merrill's *ID Expert*©. Though they are not "management" tools *per se*, these aids are useful in facilitating design and development practice via replicating design analysis and application across instructional units and projects. More on these and other design and management tools can be obtained elsewhere (online and via professional organizations).

MACRO-LEVEL AND MICRO-LEVEL MANAGEMENT ISSUES

The external contractor versus the internal employee: Both may be project managers, but they have different levels of control over the variables that influence project outcomes. Macro-level management is essentially having control of the whole, big-picture issues of the project. Micro-level project management is organizing and troubleshooting individual considerations, like the mission-critical handoffs and production-side HR commitments. Both are important, and both levels of management are legitimately within the range of the PM's job. Micro-level project managing is a positive characteristic, not to be confused with the negative business term "micro-managing," which refers to managers who overmanage the people subordinate to them in a team or department.

Depending on the size of the organization and his or her location in it, the instructional designer my wear either a micro or a macro management "hat." Sometimes an instructional designer will have micro-level management responsibility for a project or subproject, typically managing tasks and incremental deliverables, while a supervising manager has global (macro-level) responsibilities for budget, deadlines, and issues of organizational interface management (such as shared organizational resource allocation).

Various analogies have been used to try to capture the work of the project manager. Alessi and Trollip (2000) use the analogy of an orchestra conductor to represent the role of the PM, "one who pulls together diverse talents to form a harmonious group" (p. 530). This representation focuses on integration and human resource management. They also use the analogy of the general contractor on a new building, the on, "who has to ensure that the right materials are available when needed, and that the painters are only scheduled after the walls are up" (p. 530). This analogy focuses on time management.

Peters (1992) has said that most of the work done in organizations has the characteristics of projects. That is, tasks tend to need to fit with other tasks, and often involve people working together in teams to meet specified deadlines. Project managers work in every field and type of organization at every level of design, production and administration. In fact, every administrative role includes PM tasks at one time or another. For all of these reasons, instructional designers should know and appreciate the field of project management. Many designers will need to wear a project management hat one day. The job of the PM is complex and challenging, and the PM's expertise can very clearly determine the success or failure of an instructional design project.

INSTRUCTIONAL MANAGEMENT

Instructional management strategies are those strategies that guide the orchestration of organization and delivery for implementation of instruction. These are the overarching strategies that guide the scheduling of instructional events and the mechanisms for delivering these events. Management also coordinates the articulation among various delivery systems. Examples of managing multidelivery instruction include a course that is taught primarily as direct-instruction but has independent learning components, and courses with both lecture and laboratory components that must align with shared objectives. With the amount of assessment and scheduling information inherent in many instructional systems, management strategies must also devise means of organizing and reducing this assessment information to interpretable units and getting this information to the proper people in a timely fashion. Management strategies also involve techniques for getting instructional resources to learners who need them.

At the class or group level, instructional management functions such as resource distribution can be implemented by the teacher or facilitator, and in many cases by computer. A teacher's or instructor's guide may be developed by the designer to give critical information about appropriate sequencing of presentation and delivery of content elements and interactions. At the course implementation level, instructional management may occur in an amazingly broad range of contexts.

Instructional management (IM) is more than just sequencing events and activities for a single classroom with unique outcomes. It includes consideration of special needs for course consistency, replicability, access flexibility, and authenticity. For example, IM may include efforts to standardize content and sequencing across multiple instructors and learner groups, at multiple sites within an organization. These needs arise whenever many individuals need comparable knowledge and skills to do the same work equally well and with very similar products. This is true in higher-education math, science, and engineering classrooms, where several thousand learners each year must be prepared in each course with entry-level knowledge and skill for each next course in sequence. It is true in corporate industry and manufacturing, where hundreds of geographically distributed professionals must periodically be updated on methods for doing the same tasks, and they must do those tasks efficiently and effectively to make handoffs to the next sequential phase of production. It is true in health care and social service organizations when new government regulations require that skills be updated to meet specified requirements—yesterday.

Instructional management requires the designer-manager to consider both traditional and non-traditional instructional models and methods of producing, presenting, checking and controlling, and supporting learning and instruction, to meet specified needs. Solutions to IM challenges may include mass single-site training events, train-the-trainer and multi-site training solutions, individualized mentored instruction, standardized online instruction, and combinations of any of these and other approaches. Options and requisites differ broadly by content, context, and needs; the key point here is that IM is an additional consideration of instructional implementation that includes not only delivery of instruction but often follow-up and maintenance of skills, and ongoing performance support.

Two commonly used IM approaches are described in the following sections: Integrated Learning Systems and Course Management Systems. Although both involve computers and both reflect the dimension of management of instruction, they are highly distinct in approach.

Integrated Learning Systems

One widely-used IM approach focuses on the management of individual learners over extended periods of time. Such systems are generally referred to as *integrated learning systems* (ILSs). Integrated learning systems include both instructional software and an assessment and management system that provides computer-based tests and record-keeping of test results for individual students, along with a tracking and advisement capability. Commonly used ILSs are published by the Computer Curriculum Corporation, founded by mathematics education researcher Patrick Suppes, Jostens Learning Corporation, and others.

For example, imagine Sandy is a fourth-grade student in a class that goes to a networked computer lab twice a week for one-hour ILS sessions. Sandy logs into an available computer. After Sandy has logged in, the computer display welcomes her and notes that she is doing very well with multiplication but might benefit from some more work on long-division. Sandy's records within the ILS database include not only her performance on long-division practice exercises and quizzes in great detail reflecting knowledge of subskills in a learning hierarchy but also when those data were gathered and how long it took Sandy to complete each exercise. Such detail allows the ILS to advise Sandy and provide examples and practice that are closely-targeted to Sandy's individual learning needs. Over time, the database can reflect an increasingly sophisticated picture of what Sandy knows and what her strengths and preferences are. The ILS that Sandy's school is using can help her learn arithmetic and mathematics through college algebra and calculus, in an articulated curriculum.

Human tutors can provide such attention to individual student learning requirements in an expository, supplantive instructional style only on an individual basis. Teachers responsible for groups of students cannot individualize at the level of detail that a computer can, prescribing and supplying different teaching materials that supply information, practice and feedback along with associated quizzes, keeping track of practice and assessment data, and making instructional management decisions using these data. The primary strength and contribution of ILSs are found in their instructional management capabilities.

The conceptual roots of ILSs go back to programmed instruction and the earliest work with computer-based instruction, for example the PLATO project at the University of Illinois beginning in 1960 (Price, 1989). The significance of the ability of tutorial software to provide effective facilitation of learning lie not only in that effectiveness but in the potential to meet the learning needs of individual learners in groups of students whose needs may vary widely. Among the earliest efforts to combine computer-based management of learning along with tutorial instruction were the Program of Learning in Accordance with Needs (PLAN) developed by the American Institutes for Research (AIR) and Westinghouse Learning Corporation, and the Advanced Instructional System (AIS) developed by McDonnell-Douglas Aircraft Corporation for the United States Air Force in the early 1970s. In both PLAN and the AIS, a central computer provided tests, scoring, diagnosis, prescription, and reporting to aid teachers in keeping track of student learning progress. Contemporary ILSs have built on this heritage to provide instructional management within systems that include not only tutorial computer-based instruction but also other strategies including Web use.

ILSs are typically used in K–12 schools on a site-license basis. Depending on the kind of use made and the organization of the school, an ILS may be either horrendously expensive or a cost-reduction tool.

The effectiveness of ILSs is not clear-cut. On the one hand, a meta-analysis of 22 evaluation studies involving CCC materials revealed a consistent learning improvement, with an average effect size of .40 (Kulik, 1994). On the other hand, critics have cited weaknesses in assessments used and transfer issues (Becker, 1992).

As of this writing, major challenges to developers of ILSs lie in the areas of providing consistently high quality instruction throughout a system leading to not only isolated skill learning but also consolidation and transfer to new application settings. Another important element in the success of ILSs is their implementation, thought by some to be a critical variable in ILS success (Mills & Ragan, 2000). You may recall from Chapter 17 the need for attention to implementation, especially with regard to complex innovations in large organizations—a situation for which use of ILSs in schools is a good example.

Course Management Systems

Another widely-used IM approach focuses on online instructional implementation of courses. Such systems come in many variations and called by several names. Among these are: course management systems (CMSs), instructional management systems (IMSs), and learning management systems (LMSs). These are alternative terms for digital, generally Web-based systems designed to translate, facilitate, and support implementation functions (e.g., information delivery, communication, assessment, and feedback), to readily accessible online instruction. For the sake of clarity here, we will refer to the whole group as course management systems (CMSs). While these types of CMSs have different tooling and purposes, in general they are all pre-programmed instructional shells in which the designer can customize content and interactions.

One group of CMSs that is familiar and increasingly popular for both workplace and school-based instruction is a group generally called learning management systems (LMSs). These systems include Web Course Tools (WebCT©) and Blackboard©, and a number of others. Learning management systems are not project management tools. They are password-protected, self-contained course-delivery systems with some interactive elements embedded in them. At this writing, they still tend to be somewhat limited in their interactivity, and do not (yet) offer the full range of structural options for content organization (such as is possible with direct programming). However, they do offer document delivery and exchange features, and some built-in communication tooling (such as internal email, chats, and threaded discussions) that are useful to managing and implementing self-contained or complex instruction online, without advanced programming skills. The more advanced versions of LMSs can integrate audio, video, and multimedia files, and include browsable graphic collections. Some are equipped with highly interactive communication tools, including email, discussion forums, chat rooms, and collaborative development tools such as white boards that enable real-time group access.

A benefit for the designer or manager choosing CMSs for multiuser instruction (such as for a course program taught by several teachers with different development skills) is that they are built with WYSIWYG development tools, so the developer needs no high degree of Web development savvy or programming knowledge. However, the developer must be fairly familiar with the interface and recognize the specific requisite sequence of actions necessary to create and set options for each tool and module. Another potentially time-saving feature of CMSs is that the major proprietary systems have developed partnerships with publishers to provide textbooks and premade learning support materials on a variety of subjects in CMS-ready formats. These, like all other enhancements to the CMS are available—for an additional fee.

Such systems offer potential for designer-managers to increase design and production efficiency over total course creation. Some of these systems also offer opportunities to generate beta test data and evaluation information either prior to course launch, or during the launch phase with real and remote members of the target learner group. From a project management perspective, utilizing online course management systems to develop and deliver instruction presents significant cost-benefit tradeoffs. First, such systems tend to carry very large licensing fees, not only for the hosting organization or institution, but based on the number of users. Within a major educational institution, such fees may be absorbed when spread across hundreds or thousands of users, but for an individual designer to justify CMS licensing for a project is unusual. Further, if the instructional project is expected to have a long lifespan, CMSs generally require ongoing renewal and maintenance costs as well. Thus, expense saved in hiring programmers to create security and interactivity features may be offset by long-term costs to support the interface.

In general, two factors tend to drive overall cost of licensing a CMS: 1) tool sophistication (power, versatility, complexity), and 2) ownership. It is mostly the sophistication of the CMS itself that drives price. However, ownership should be considered, since commercially-owned systems can cost as much as ten times the price of tools owned by educational organizations, even those equipped with similar functionality. Part of the reason for this cost difference is the degree of technical support available, so the manager should consider support needs in cost-benefit analysis as well.

The success of instruction delivered (or supported) via CMSs is dependent on effective design of both instructional and management components. All of the content, whether designed and developed originally, or uploaded from preexisting instruction, must:

• Fit with the teacher's or organization's instructional approach,

• Align with the objectives of instruction,
• Match the target context of instruction and transfer expectations, and
• Offer fidelity, authenticity, clarity, and efficiency.

The systems mentioned here and others like them all present different potential benefits and constraints.

With new CMSs emerging constantly, those mentioned above represent just a few examples of what is available in these systems, and only a hint of what may soon be available. It is offered to enable designers to recognize the potential value, utility, and cost-effectiveness of selecting and developing materials for preprogrammed management systems.

EXERCISES

1. In general terms, the PM is responsible to:
   a. Analyze _____ and _____
   b. Plan how to _____
   c. Maintain _____ under _____
   d. Anticipate potential _____
   e. Figure out how to _____
   f. Know how to _____ and _____ outcomes

2. Match the following areas of PM to the brief examples below:
   a. Project Human Resource Management _____
   b. Project Scope Management _____
   c. Project Integration Management _____
   d. Project Cost Management _____
   e. Project Time Management _____

   i. Controlling the size of the project in elements, hours, and total product
   ii. Keeping track of human resource commitments and linear project deadlines to deliver on schedule
   iii. Allocating, coordinating, and managing people skills within the organization and among project phases and tasks
   iv. Controlling fiscal resources, inflow and outflow, and making adjustments as needed
   v. Ensuring that the various elements of a project are effectively coordinated

3. The director of a university's technology training program decided that last year's training design for basic undergraduate user technology workshops can be recycled pretty much as it was created and used before, without redesign. What conditions must be true, for this to be an appropriate design management decision? What are the benefits of the technology director's decision? What are the potential risks of the same decision?

4. You are project director in a not-for-profit environmental organization that uses large numbers of volunteers. A new federal environmental legislation just instituted the requirement that you train and assess the six-hundred volunteers distributed across the state in a complex set of policy and procedures within six months. What characteristics of the organization and its specific circumstances make this ID project especially challenging? How will you address each of the challenges presented?

5. Previously a mid-level administrator in a large university medical center, you were just handed management responsibility for the implementation and evaluation of the organization's Health Information Patient Privacy Act (HIPPA) compliance online training system. This Web-based training consists of six instructional modules with built-in assessments of learning objectives. The audience for implementation is 2000 doctors, nurses, medical students, counselors, and support staff over the next three years, and then ongoing training of new staff to meet federal requirements. If you can't demonstrate compliance, the hospital could be closed. What issues are especially important in your role as manager of this project? What specific expertise do you need on your team? What potential risks can you anticipate, and how might you address each of them?

6. Your office neighbor has just been given the task of managing a short-term project team for a contract-based single-event training seminar package. Her seriousness and excitement about this new responsibility is obvious, but she has never managed a project team. She knows that you have studied project management, so she has come to you for help. What advice would you give this new ID project manager?

7. Teachers in a school district need skills updates on integrating Web-based resources into their classroom instruction. What are some of the project management issues that would arise for the manager of this training?

8. An instructional materials development company has an ongoing contract for supplying HR support resources for a large manufacturing corporation. You have been designated the project manager for the latest project, producing a multicultural awareness package. How do you see each of the five global design areas fitting into this type of project's demands?

9. The University's College of Fine Arts needs to increase its Web presence and wants it to originate with the faculty, but the professors don't think they should have to "do technology." As the internal project manager handed this challenge, what are your main concerns and key decisions?

SUMMARY

Project managers assess organizational needs, plan and schedule communication, manage interactions among and between people and teams, budget and allocate resources, and evaluate and report project outcomes. A project is a specific, multifaceted instructional task with a defined beginning and end, and management is the organization of tools, people and systems to carry out that project. Instructional design occurs most often in teams, either internal or external, and often a mix of internal professionals and external contractors. Someone must keep tasks coordinated and deadlines met. This is the role of the project manager.

Project management (PM) is the synthesis of a diverse set of skills A project manager is concerned with groups of variables represented by four basic constraints: performance, cost, time, and scope. There are always tradeoffs between these constraints. They are interdependent (like the sides on a triangle) so that change in one results in change in the others. They exist in a systemic relationship such that no PM decision is ever made in isolation.

There is not just one "right way" to manage a project, but there are core requisite skills and best practices. These skill sets are adaptive to the specific requisites of the task and context, which results in various approaches to applying them. Important differences in management practices exist by culture and context, such as the division between corporate and educational institutions. Effective documentation is critical, to keep management effectiveness replicable and track progress. Though the precise format of documents differs widely, most instructional design projects will have, at minimum, some version of the following documents: proposal, resource analysis, schedule, budget, risk analysis, evaluation plan, and project report.

Five essential components of the project manager's role are managing project: integration, scope, time, cost, and human resources. Project integration refers to managing the interactions among the many factors that comprise the project. Project scope refers to how big and complex the ultimate end goal of the project is. Project scope management involves making sure that all of the specified project work (and only the specified work) gets done, to complete the project successfully. Time management requires not only that the manager generate the project timeline and allocate resource hours, but that the manager communicates those to all team members and keeps track of progress relative to time allocated through the life of the project. Project cost management includes the processes that ensure that a project is completed within the established budget. Human resource management requires the manager to identify and make the most of the people resources essential to project success.

MANAGEMENT AND INSTRUCTION

Product Management

Standards   Product Integration

Scope   Resource
Time   Cost

Risk, Change, and Crisis

Instructional Management

Integrated Learning Systems (ILS)

Course Management Systems (CMS)

Figure 18.3 Summary Diagram for Chapter 18

Software packages to assist project managers abound in the field. A danger for the novice project manager in grabbing software tools too soon is to become dependent on the tool rather than refining skills and capacity for advanced management thinking. New managers should resist "plugging into" software until they understand project management skills and requisites without them.

Integrated learning systems (ILSs) of various kinds may be useful both in implementation of instruction and in management of instructional projects. The success of any instruction, however it is developed, delivered, or managed, depends on the quality and clarity of its design.

Figure 18.3 summarizes the key points of this chapter.

EXTENDED EXAMPLE

Go to the Learning Resources Web site to see the Extended Example contribution from this chapter. Instructional management issues relating to our photography course's development and the management of the course's delivery will be discussed.

READINGS AND REFERENCES

Alessi, S. M., & Trollip, S. R. (2001). *Multimedia for learning: Methods and development* (3rd ed.). Boston: Allyn & Bacon.

American National Standards Institute (ANSI) (2000). *A guide to the project management body of knowledge*. Newtown Square, PA: Project Management Institute.

Becker, H. J. (1992). Computer-based integrated learning systems in the elementary and middle grades: A critical review and synthesis of evaluation reports. *Journal of Educational Computing Research, 8*(2), 1–41.

Bogatz, G. A., & S. Ball. (1971). *The second year of Sesame Street: A continuing evaluation (Vols. 1–2).* Princeton, NJ: Educational Testing Service. (ERIC Document Reproduction Service Nos. ED 122 800, ED 122 801)

Clark, B., & Spohr, S. (2002). *Guide to postproduction for TV and film: Managing the process* (2nd ed.). Burlington, MA: Focal Press.

Kulik, J. (1994). Meta-analytic studies of findings on computer-based instruction. In E. L. Baker & H. F. O'Neil, Jr. (Eds.), *Technology assessment in education and training* (pp. 9–33). Hillsdale, NJ: Erlbaum.

Lewis, J. P. (2000). *The project manager's desk reference.* NY: McGraw Hill.

Lewis, J. P. (2001). *Project planning, scheduling & control: A hands-on guide to bringing projects in on time and on budget.* NY: McGraw Hill.

Mills, S. C., & Ragan, T. J. (2000). A tool for analyzing implementation fidelity of an integrated learning system. *Educational Technology Research & Development, 48*(4), 21–41.

Murch, R. C. (2001). *Project management: Best practices for IT professionals.* Upper Saddle River, NJ: Prentice-Hall.

NASB (2001). *Any time, any place, any path, any pace: Taking the lead on e-learning policy.* Alexandria, VA: National Association of State Boards of Education.

Price, R. (1989). An historical perspective on the design of computer-assisted instruction: Lessons from the past. *Computers in the Schools, 6* (1/2), 145–157.

Peters, T. J. (1992). *Liberation management: Necessary disorganization for the nanosecond nineties.* New York: A. A. Knopf.

Senge, P. (1990). *The Fifth Discipline.* NY: Doubleday.

Vroom, V., & Jago A (1988). *The new leadership.* Englewood Cliffs, NJ: Prentice Hall.

Richey, R. C., Fields, D. F., & Foxon, M. (with M. M. Spector and T. Spannaus). (2001). *Instructional Design Competencies: The Standards* (3rd ed.) Syracuse, NY: ERIC Clearinghouse on Information and Technology.

Journals in Project Management

Project Management Journal, professional research, training and development journal published by the Project Management Institute, Headquarters Four Campus Boulevard, Newtown Square, PA, 19073–3299. Email: pmihq@pmi.org; Online at: http://www.pmi.org/info/PIR_PMJournal.asp.

Useful Web Sites on Project Management

Web site of the Project Management Institute, a leading professional organization dedicated to research, training, and development in the field. Available at: http://www.pmi.org.

Web site of the Lewis Institute, includes tools and information useful to managers, from novice to expert. Available at: http://www.lewisinstitute.org.

Web Sites on Course Management Systems

EduTools, a not-for-profit site developed under a grant from the Hewlett Foundation, to provide information about online instructional development tools. Available at: http://www.edutools.info/ about/index.

WebCT home site, with detailed information on Web Course Tools system features and licensing options. Available at: http://www.webct.com.

Blackboard home site, with detailed information on Blackboard Course Management System features and licensing options. Available at: http://www.blackboard.com.

FORMATIVE AND SUMMATIVE EVALUATION

CHAPTER OBJECTIVES

At the conclusion of this chapter, you should be able to do the following:

- Contrast the purposes of formative and summative evaluation.
- Identify the purposes, procedures, data sources, designer's role, materials, participants, and timing of each of the stages of formative evaluation.
- Compare the procedures, materials, and timing for formative evaluation of different media.
- Display formative evaluation data for each phase.
- Interpret given formative evaluation data.
- Identify the purposes, procedures, data sources, designer's role, materials, participants, and timing of each of the stages of summative evaluation.

EVALUATING INSTRUCTIONAL MATERIALS

The evaluation of an individual student's performance tells us "whether we're there" with regard to the individual student's learning. After evaluating the performance of a group of students, the designer knows whether they have achieved the objectives of instruction. There is yet another kind of evaluation that is critical and essential in the design of instruction: the evaluation of the instructional materials. This evaluation occurs during two separate points in the instructional development process for two different purposes. At one point, the designer evaluates the materials to determine the weakness in the instruction so that revisions can be made to make them more effective and efficient. Then she knows whether the instructional materials are "there" yet, or whether she needs to continue the design process. This is called **formative evaluation**. Later, after the materials have been implemented into the instructional contexts for which they were designed, designers may be involved in the process of evaluating the materials in terms of their effectiveness in order to provide data for decision makers who may adopt or continue to use the materials. This is called **summative evaluation**.

OVERVIEW OF FORMATIVE EVALUATION

Although the evaluation of instruction often appears to come late in the design/development process, both formative and summative evaluation should be planned early in the design process. Indeed, as the designer is gathering information to substantiate the problem to be solved via instruction, she is already documenting the indicators that could be evaluated to indicate that the intervention was successful, meaning that it solved the problem. Throughout this chapter, we will point out the aspects of formative evaluation that can be conducted as the project is designed. However, that does not mean that the designer completely forgets about the summative evaluation. As she conducts analysis, she drafts plans for both formative and summative evaluation of the instructional intervention.

At the conclusion of the phase in which the instructional strategy is developed, the designer has created prescriptions for instruction. These prescriptions are in the form of outlines (for text-based instruction), storyboards (for video- or slide-tape-based instruction), frame planning sheets, or prototypes (for computer-based instruction). In any case, the prescriptions show what the instruction will look like and how it will be sequenced. The prescriptions include both the instruction and plans for all of the assessments that we described in the previous section. These prescriptions are built upon principles of learning and instruction. Based upon the instructional theory that these principles represent, we hypothesize that the instructional systems they prescribe will instruct effectively. However, instructional theory is not an absolute science: There is still much we do not know about setting up conditions for students to learn. If instructional theory is still incomplete and our interpretations of it are sometimes inaccurate, it is essential that we try out the instruction with representative members of the target audience before using materials with many learners or going through the expense of mass-producing the materials. Therefore, formative evaluation is considered to be fundamental to the instructional design process.

Commercial publishers of instructional materials (software or textbooks) are not well known for conducting such formal evaluations. They do send copies of instructional materials to potential teachers/trainers for their opinions, but usually the materials are already in the final form, not in a form in which revisions are possible. At any rate, research indicates that teachers/trainers are not the best sources of information for predicting whether materials will be effective (Rosen, 1968; Rothkopf, 1963). The best source of such information is the learners themselves. Although learners' opinions of the quality of the instruction are important, the key is their learning as a result of the instruction.

Trying out materials with learners can help instructional developers determine where revisions are necessary. As a matter of fact, materials that have been tried out with only one or two representative students and then revised based upon the information gained are substantially more effective than the original instruction. Unfortunately for public education, publishers are often unwilling to commit the time and effort to do such evaluations. This is particularly the case with producers who wish to get their products quickly available for sale. Some states, such as Florida, Texas, and California, are beginning to demand that materials considered for state adoption provide evidence of "learner validation" (i.e., formative evaluation). In business and industry as well, formative evaluation is frequently skipped because of the cost. However, such policies may be shortsighted because more effective training (which frequently results from formative evaluation) can result in more profitable operations in the long run.

An advantage of large-scale projects, for schools or training, is that their budgets may be able to absorb the cost of a fully implemented formative evaluation. When design and development costs can be spread across a large number of courses and learners served by the instruction, the benefits of the instruction make the cost low. The ability to perform a thorough formative evaluation is one example of how an economy of scale can contribute to the quality of instruction.

Not all educational materials are amenable to formative evaluation as we will describe it; however, we believe that all products of systematic instructional design should be. Formative evaluation (as we describe it) would not be appropriate for those materials that were not designed to foster achievement of specified learning goals. Such materials include the traditional textbook that is written as an aid to learning a variety of objectives. Increasingly, textbooks are written with specific learning goals in mind and stated; for those texts, a full formative evaluation is appropriate. For traditional texts, only the first phase of the four that we will describe (expert review) has been traditionally employed by the publishing industry. More and more, particularly with texts intended for the K–12 public school market, texts are being viewed as media of instruction tied to specific learning goals, and such texts should be created and evaluated using instructional design principles and techniques.

Formative evaluation is especially important to include in the instructional design process when (1) the designer is a novice, (2) the content area is new to the designer, (3) the technology is new to the designer or design team, (4) the audience is new to the designer, (5) the designer is using a unfamiliar instructional strategy, (6) task performance is critical, (7) the design agency's accountability is high, (8) the client is expecting that formative evaluation will be conducted, (9) the instruction will disseminated widely and in large quantities, and (10) opportunities for later revision are slim.

PHASES OF FORMATIVE EVALUATION

The following sections will briefly discuss the procedures of formative evaluation and revision. Four stages of formative evaluation will be described: design reviews, expert reviews, learner validation, and ongoing evaluation. The first two stages are less traditionally considered to be part of formative evaluation. Design reviews occur prior to the actual development of any instructional materials. Expert review of materials often occurs after the completion of the materials but prior to their actual use with learners. The latter two phases involve the use of the actual instructional materials with learners who represent the target audience.

Design Reviews

The output of each stage of design—goals, learner and context analyses, task analysis, and so on—can all be submitted to formative evaluation in order to make revisions prior to any actual development of materials. These reviews may be conducted as each phase of design is completed. They serve to confirm the accuracy of

the design process at each stage. During this phase of formative evaluation, the designer attempts to answer questions such as the following:

- Does the instructional goal reflect a satisfactory response to the problems identified in the needs assessment?
- Do the environment and learner analyses accurately portray these entities?
- Does the task analysis include all of the prerequisite skills and knowledge needed to perform the learning goal, and is the prerequisite nature of these skills and knowledge accurately represented?
- Do the test items and resultant test blueprints reflect reliable and valid measures of the instructional objectives?
- Do the assessment instruments and their related mastery criteria reliably distinguish between competent and incompetent learners?

GOAL REVIEW. Goal review confirms that the goals that have been established are representative of a real instructional need and congruent with the client's expectations. Conducting a formal needs assessment will ensure that the goal meets an instructional need, and having the client (or client's representative) review the learning goal once it is stated in formal performance terms will ensure that there is agreement as to the purpose of the instruction.

REVIEW OF ENVIRONMENT AND LEARNER ANALYSIS. The designer will have gained much data as he developed his analysis of the environment and the learners. At the conclusion of these analyses, he needs to review their adequacy. He may wish to collect further information after the original draft in order to confirm or extend his analysis. For example, he may wish to collect survey or aptitude data to confirm his analysis of the targeted learners; he might wish to give a reading test to sample members of the target audience to confirm his estimates of their reading grade level, or he might wish to survey managers within the organization to confirm that the attitudes regarding training that he gathered during his analysis of the learning environment are indeed representative of that group.

REVIEW OF TASK ANALYSIS. The task analysis can be confirmed using a number of techniques. The prerequisite relationship of skills may be confirmed by testing groups of learners who do and do not possess the targeted skills and determining if the learners who can achieve the terminal objective can indeed perform all those listed as subordinate and vice versa. The designer might refer to White and Gagné (1978) to see the procedure that they followed in order to confirm their learning hierarchies. He might also ask content experts and other instructional designers to review his task analysis for accuracy and completeness.

He may also wish to confirm that the point at which he identified objectives as entry level is accurate. He may assess a sample of his target audience's ability on these entry-level skills in order to confirm the accuracy of his estimates. (He might also want to give a pretest on the skills to be learned.)

REVIEW OF ASSESSMENT SPECIFICATIONS AND BLUEPRINTS. Assessment items can be formatively evaluated for their validity by having content and testing experts review the assessment item specifications and blueprints. The reviewers can evaluate the congruence of the objective and the item specifications. They can determine if the type of items outlined by the specifications adequately describes the domain of items that the objective might cover. They can also determine if the number of items in the item specifications and blueprints is sufficient to adequately sample the range of the domain of the content that the objectives might cover.

The assessment instruments may also be administered to skilled learners prior to the development of the materials to determine the practicality and the reliability of the instruments. Traditional statistical tests of reliability often do not work well with instruments developed on a criterion-referenced plan because often they do not have the variability (spread) of scores for the statistics to work. Therefore, methods of reliability analysis based upon "mastery" learning have been developed. One way to assess reliability of a criterion-referenced test is to determine the consistency of the test in certifying learners as "masters" or "nonmasters." (Refer to Chapter 6 for a brief description of this procedure and Shrock and Coscarelli [1989] for more complete procedures.)

Expert Reviews

Before instructional materials are used by learners in the latter stages of formative evaluation, it is often helpful to have experts review materials: content experts, instructional design experts, content-specific education specialists, or experts on the learners, such as teachers. During one type of expert review—a content review—the designer has a subject matter expert examine the content of the instructional material for accuracy and completeness. For example, if the instructional materials are on the principles of physics, then an expert in physics should review the instruction. An individual who knows the target audience may also be called in to review the materials for appropriateness. This may involve an examination of the vocabulary, examples, and illustrations that are included. A content-specific educator (in this case a science education specialist) would

also be a good reviewer because such an educator could evaluate the congruence of the presentation of content with current educational theory in the specific content areas. During expert review, depending upon the expertise of the reviewer, the designer is attempting to answer questions such as the following:

- Is the content accurate and up-to-date?
- Does the content present a consistent perspective?
- Are examples, practice exercises, and feedback realistic and accurate?
- Is the pedagogical approach consistent with current instructional theory in the content area?
- Is the instruction appropriate for the target learners?
- Are the instructional strategies consistent with principles of instructional theory?

The materials given to the reviewers at this stage are in draft form. The comments of particular experts should be considered in terms of their expertise. For example, it is not uncommon for content experts to make suggestions regarding the instructional strategy used in the materials. While certainly this information should be carefully considered for its value, the expert's advice on the accuracy of the content will be much more valuable. Inaccuracies should be eliminated at this time. However, the designer may wish to delay following up on suggestions about instructional strategies until information is obtained on learner performance.

It is a good idea to divide context experts' comments into three categories: revisions that should be made immediately, questions for which data should be collected during subsequent phases, and suggestions that should be ignored. In the case of items that fall into the second category, the designer should design explicit questions either to ask of the learners during subsequent one-to-one evaluations or to use as particular items on assessment instruments in order to be certain that actual information is gathered regarding the unresolved issue.

The best indication of whether learners can learn from the instruction is to try out the instruction with representative learners to see how well they do learn and what kinds of problems arise as actual learners go through the instruction. This **learner validation** is reflected in the following three phases: one-to-one evaluation, small-group evaluation, and field trials.

One-to-One Evaluation

During one-to-one evaluation, the designer tries out the instructional materials with two or three members (sometimes more) of the target audience. The purpose of this stage is to determine and rectify any gross problems in the instruction. The types of problems that may be located in this stage are typographical errors, unclear sentences, poor or missing directions, inappropriate examples, unfamiliar vocabulary, mislabeled pages or illustrations, illustrations that do not communicate intent, and frames in incorrect sequences, to name but a few. During one-to-one evaluation, the designer is attempting to answer questions such as the following:

- Do the learners understand the instruction?
- Do learners know what to do during the practice and tests?
- Can learners interpret graphics in the text?
- Can the learners read all of the textual material?

The designer sits down with one student at a time, asking the student go through the instruction in its draft form, including the tests. This draft form may be print materials with hand-drawn illustrations, frame sheets for computer-based instruction, a storyboard for a video presentation, or other drafted materials in a particular medium. It is not typical to use one-to-one evaluation for teacher-mediated instruction, except for any components based on other media.

DESIGNER'S ROLE. The designer's role in one-to-one evaluation is to query the student about any problems that she is having and to clear up these problems by restating the instruction or correcting misconceptions. The designer makes notes in his own copy of the materials about the kinds of problems that the learner has encountered and ways to correct these problems. It is a useful practice for the designer to develop a list of questions about aspects of the materials: Is certain vocabulary in the instruction familiar to the learner? Is the intent of a particular practice question clear? Does the learner understand a particular explanation? Can the learner understand the use of a particular analogy? If the learner does not comment on these features, the designer can ask questions regarding them.

LEARNERS' ROLE. As some learners will be reluctant to criticize the materials, the designer should emphasize that if the learner is having difficulty with the instruction, it is not the learner's fault, but the material's, and the designer should ask particular probing questions if the learner does not volunteer problems. The designer may also wish to distance himself from the materials by saying something such as "I've been asked to try out these materials with learners to see how they work." The evaluation of materials is something like a taste-test of scientific inquiry with learners. Learners used in one-to-one evaluations should represent learners of average, slightly above average, and slightly below average ability. The more verbal the learners are, the better the information will be. It is not uncommon to need to "prime"

the learners with specific questions. These questions should remind the designer of pending issues regarding the materials. The designer should ask the questions at the ends of sections so as to not interrupt the flow of the learners' processing within a continuous section.

PROCEDURES. One approach that may be useful in conducting one-to-one evaluations is the use of a "read-think-aloud" technique (Smith & Wedman, 1988). When using this approach, the designer asks the learner to read and think aloud while interacting with the instructional materials. This approach is particularly appropriate when evaluating instruction that has a print- or computer-based component, but it may also be used when having learners review storyboards for video-mediated instruction. The learner is asked to express aloud any thoughts she has as she reads a particular instructional passage. The learner is not asked to explain these thoughts, only to say them aloud, and then to continue reading orally. These oral utterances can be tape-recorded and transcribed, creating a permanent record of the learner's comments. These transcriptions, called *protocols,* provide information not only as to whether the learner can read the materials, but also as to the learner's actual thought processes. These thought processes often give clues about the misconceptions or difficulties that the learner is encountering. As thinking aloud is not a natural action for most learners, it is a good idea to demonstrate the procedure and ask the learner to practice the technique before beginning the actual evaluation of the materials.

One way to give learners an idea of the kind of utterances the designer wants is to remind them of how they may talk aloud as they interact with a new computer program or how young children talk aloud as they complete a task. Some learners become very good at this process; others find it impossible to externalize their thought processes. Designers will find that they must frequently prompt learners by saying, "Tell me what you are thinking." If thinking aloud seems to be too great a task for the learner, the designer can simply ask the learner to read aloud. Although hearing students read aloud is not as informative as "think alouds," learners' phrasing and misreading of words give some subtle hints about their thoughts.

Assessments should be included in the one-to-one process, primarily to obtain information about the learners' ability to respond to the directions and individual items. As trying out materials can be rather time-consuming, it is a good idea to try out entry-level tests and pretests on a day prior to the evaluation of the actual instructional materials. During the administration of the pretests (or even the entry-level tests, if your estimate of entry skills is inaccurate), the designer may sense that the learners are becoming frustrated. It is also a good idea to construct the tests with the simpler (prerequisite) skills first on the instrument and the more difficult items sequenced later. With this approach, the designer can determine the point at which the learners' skills fall off. Designers can encourage the learners to try later items, in case their analyses of prerequisite skills is not correct.

Some of the problems that the learners encounter may be of sufficient magnitude and their revisions may be sufficiently apparent that the designer may make revisions immediately after the evaluation with a single learner. Other problems may appear to be idiosyncratic to the learner, or the designer may have insufficient information as to how to solve the problem. Some designers wait until all one-to-one subjects have completed the instruction. However, at the completion of the one-to-one evaluations, it is likely that the designer will revise numerous aspects of the instruction. As one-to-one data are more qualitative than quantitative, we suggest that one-to-one data and the revision decisions based upon them be presented in the form as shown in Figure 19.1.

DISPLAYING AND INTERPRETING ONE-TO-ONE DATA. Designers should include the source of revision decisions in the "data source" category, as it is important that revisions at this stage come directly from learners' problems. It is also important to tie the revisions to the actual problems that the learners encountered. We rarely include one-to-one posttest scores as data for guiding decisions,

as these scores really do not reflect the interactions of the learner and the instruction, but of the learner, the designer, and the instruction. Making decisions based upon the posttest scores, therefore, can be very deceptive.

The designer makes the revisions in the instruction that are indicated by the one-to-one evaluation. The output of this stage of formative evaluation is an instructional lesson that has been revised to eliminate gross problems in the instruction and tests. If there were many problems in instruction and the revisions were substantial, the designer may wish to go through another round of one-to-one evaluations before proceeding to the next stage. If money or time is not available for further evaluation, the designer has still obtained information that helps eliminate most severe problems. This allows for a product that is substantially more effective than it was before the revisions. If time and money are available, the designer should move to the small-group evaluation stage. Small-group evaluation data provide additional information that may clarify the breadth and severity of any problems that the designer has already found.

Small-Group Evaluation

The purpose of this stage of formative evaluation is to check the efficacy of the revisions based on one-to-one data, to ascertain how well the instruction works with more varied learners, and to see how well the instruc-

Objective	Data Source	Information Gained	Revision Decision
G	Pretest	Some students were able to multiply out the numbers greater than one, obtaining the correct answer while unable to complete the targeted process.	Provide workspace on pretest and posttest. Do not count correct where work indicates students have not followed targeted process.
A, B	Pretest/Posttest	Directions to items 1 and 2 are confusing.	Reword directions to read "Circle the letter of the phrase (or number) . . ."
Entry skill	Student comments on pretest	Students knew what a decimal point was. They felt that asking such an obvious question was confusing. They wondered if I was asking a more complex question.	Students definitely possess this entry skill. Delete this question from entry assessment.
A	S's comments, observations	S1 and S2 had no difficulty with the concept of exponents. S3 had difficulty, but a brief review within the lesson corrected the problem. The concepts of negative and positive exponents were discussed in two separate places in the lesson, S's tended to ignore this discussion.	Instruction should be resequenced and consolidated to produce a short review of the concept of exponents (both negative and positive) at the beginning of the lesson.
All objectives	S's comments, observations	S's had difficulty separating information and procedures regarding negative exponents from those regarding positive exponents. No obvious formatting distinction was made in the materials.	Add subheadings "Numbers Greater Than 1" and "Numbers Less Than 1" to make the two sets of procedures more distinct.

Figure 19.1 Display of One-to-One Data and Interpretation

tion teaches without the designer's intervention. In this phase, designers are asking the following questions:

- Do the learners have the anticipated entry-level skills?
- If so, did they succeed in the instruction? If they didn't succeed, what revisions are needed?
- If they did not have predicted entry-level skills, did they succeed in the instruction?
- If they did not succeed, what skills were they lacking?
- Did the learners have additional skills that were not predicted?
- How long does it take for the learners to complete the instruction?
- How do the learners feel about the instruction?
- If their feelings are negative, how do these feelings affect their performance?
- What revisions are necessary to improve attitudes toward the instruction?
- Are the revisions made as the result of one-to-one evaluations satisfactory?

In this stage, the designer steps back and observes, supplying help only when problems arise that students cannot solve without assistance (an unusual circumstance when revisions based on one-to-one evaluations have been made). Despite the fact that this evaluation is called *small-group*, not all members of the group must go through the instruction at one time in one room—unless small-group activities, such as listening to a lecture or participating in group discussions or activities, are part of the instructional strategy. Enough students should go through the instruction at this point to give the designer confidence that the materials have been used with a fairly representative group of students.

LEARNERS' ROLE. Of course, the more students who participate in the small-group evaluation, the more representative the group and the more accurate the data and the consequent revisions will be. The designer should use eight to twelve students during this stage. If there are some differences within the target audience in terms of general or specific characteristics that he anticipates might make a difference in the effectiveness, efficiency, or appeal of the instruction, individuals that represent these differences should be included in the small-group evaluation. It can be useful to administer a learner analysis questionnaire to obtain general demographic data about the learners who are participating. This questionnaire might assess any initial attitudes or experiences that you think might influence the effectiveness of the instruction.

During this phase, students should sit down with the instruction and go through it as if they were in the real learning environment. They should take any entry-level tests, pretests, or posttests provided. As with one-to-one evaluations, if the designer is worried that the learners will be fatigued by the initial testing and the tryout of the materials, the entry-level tests and pretests may be given on a day prior to the evaluation of the actual instruction. The designer must also be confident that the learners will not "bone up" on the content in the interim.

DESIGNER'S ROLE. In this stage of formative evaluation, the designer is an observer, making notes of any nonverbal cues that may be picked up about the effectiveness or interest level of the instruction and any problems that the learners may volunteer. The designer may assist the learners only in cases in which the instruction cannot proceed without intervention. In cases of group-based instruction, it may be useful for the designer to videotape the instruction (after receiving written permission from the participants, of course).

PROCEDURES. This is a good time to address a question that many beginning designers have. You may recall that in Chapter 6 we suggested that the ideal in entry-level tests, pretests, and posttests is that each prerequisite objective is assessed and assessed with sufficient items so that a reliable decision regarding an individual's skill on that objective can be made. We also noted that this thoroughness can result in extremely lengthy assessment instruments and that sometimes these instruments must be shortened for practical purposes. During formative evaluation, if at all possible, it is important to have learners respond to complete instruments assessing all objectives. The designer may construct shortened forms for actual use when the instruction is implemented, but it is important during formative evaluation to gain all of the information possible in order to gain an accurate profile of the effects of the instruction. Hence, comprehensive assessment instruments are critical. Therefore, initial testing may require additional times for administration, and the designer may feel that he is using an inordinate amount of time in testing. If he becomes bothered by this, he should remember that the processes that he uses during formative evaluation will ensure good evaluation of the materials. The procedures for actual instruction might change as a result of this evaluation.

Although lengthy testing may be involved, the procedures for small-group evaluation are fairly straightforward. Learners should be informed as to their roles and encouraged to perform at their best level. Initial entry-level tests and pretests should be administered. (Remember: These two initial experiences may occur on days previous to the actual interaction with the instruction.) Learners should then interact with the instruction and receive the posttest and the attitude questionnaire. Then learners should engage in a group debriefing with the designer. The designer may use the attitude questionnaire as a guide for this discussion or ask more probing questions regarding the learners' feelings toward the instruction. Many designers find that useful information comes from this debriefing because learners are more willing to explain their opinions orally than to laboriously write them. Also, they have a tendency to "piggyback" on each other's ideas, and they are more willing to express critical ideas if they hear peers being critical.

Small-group evaluation is conducted with all forms of mediation: print-based texts, prototype computer programs, rough-edited videotapes, and check-disks for interactive video. Small-group evaluation may also be conducted with teacher delivery. Particularly in training environments, agencies may have the resources in terms of time, learners, trainers, and facilities to conduct a small-group trial with teacher-led instruction. It is useful to have a small-group trial with teacher-led training, particularly if the instructional strategy depends heavily on group activities or discussions, or if anything about the instruction is highly complex or problematic. The advantage of limiting the first delivery of teacher-led instruction to a small group is that it allows the teacher to concentrate on the content and delivery, and it limits the possible negative effects of untried instruction to a very small number of learners.

COLLECTING AND DISPLAYING DATA. The primary data obtained in small-group formative evaluation are the scores on the entry-level test, pretest, practice items, and posttest. In addition, attitude questionnaire data and time data are gathered. The designer uses these data to identify weak spots in the instruction. For example, if the designer finds that all students can perform at mastery level on some of the objectives tested on the pretest, then the instruction can be made more efficient by eliminating the portions of the lesson that address these objectives. If most or all students fail to reach mastery on some of the objectives on the posttest, the designer can seriously examine both the test items and the instruction for those objectives. If time data are well beyond the expected requirements, then the designer may consider dividing the instruction into segments of different sizes. If attitude data indicate a poor motivation level or a bad attitude toward the instruction, additional interest or motivation tactics may be included.

PERFORMANCE DATA. The designer should collect an assessment of learners' retention and transfer of learning with a parallel form of the posttest because such data may suggest revisions that learners' immediate performance did not indicate. The amount of the delay before the retention test should be dictated by the anticipated length of time that the learners will need to retain the learning before using it in the next learning context. This may be one day in K–12 situations or several weeks in training environments.

Reducing the data obtained during small-group evaluation so that conclusions can be drawn can be something of a task. Performance data can be displayed in two different ways: (1) using a chart that displays performance on all tests, listed by objective, and (2) recording pre- and post-data on a task analysis diagram. The first method involves displaying learners' mastery of each individual objective on pretest, practice, and posttest (as well as entry-level and delayed posttest, if the designer administered them). Mastery criteria for each objective were developed when the designer wrote his test specifications. If the designer either abbreviated or expanded the number of items, he may have to slightly adjust his percentages for mastery from those that appear in the test specifications.

Figure 19.2 includes the criteria for mastery performance on pretest, practice, and immediate posttest for an example lesson we evaluated. The figure shows the pretest, practice, and posttest scores for ten students who participated in small-group evaluation of instruction on converting numbers into scientific notation. Eight objectives, A through H, were taught in the lesson, with A being the simplest and E and H being the terminal objectives. Here are abbreviated objectives for objectives A through H:

A. Concept of exponent.

B. Concept of scientific notation.

C. Procedure to convert numbers from standard notation to scientific notation—numbers greater than 1.

D. Procedure to convert numbers from standard notation to scientific notation—numbers less than 1.

E. Procedure to convert numbers from standard notation to scientific notation—any number.

F. Procedure to convert numbers from scientific notation to standard notation—numbers greater than 1.

G. Procedure to convert numbers from scientific notation to standard notation—numbers less than 1.

H. Procedure to convert numbers from scientific notation to standard notation—any number.

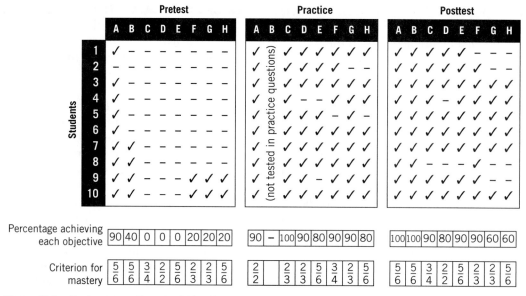

Figure 19.2 Performance Data by Objective Across Tests

The criterion for mastery gives the number of items used to assess the objective and the number of items that must be correct in order for learners to be considered skilled, or "masters," in the objective. For example, for a learner to be considered a master in objective H on the pretest, the learner must get five of the six items correct. In addition, the figure indicates what percentage of the ten learners evidenced mastery of the objective. It may seem a bit odd for a mastery level to be indicated on practice items; however, it is important for us to be able to conclude whether learners were skilled with the objective immediately after instruction on that particular objective. Then, from the posttest performance, we can determine whether that skill was retained for any period of time.

From the data in Figure 19.2, we can conclude the following:

1. Learners already knew the concept of exponent, as evidenced by objective A on the pretest.
2. Although students 2, 4, and 5 had some difficulty in the practice exercises, overall the students achieved quite well during practice, with at least 80 percent achieving mastery on each objective.
3. Although student 8 had some difficulty throughout the posttest, overall the students' performance was quite good except for their performance on objectives G and H. Students' performance fell on these objectives from practice to posttest. It would have been useful to have delayed posttest scores to see if performance fell on other objectives over time.

4. The poor performances of learners 1 and 8 on the posttest may be due to interest factors or prior knowledge factors that should be examined with demographic and questionnaire data. (The entry-level tests were omitted after four subjects evidenced overwhelming skill during one-to-one trials. Upon reflection, that may not have been a good decision.)

The second method of displaying performance data is to record pretest and posttest data on a task analysis diagram that indicates the prerequisite relationships of objectives (a hierarchy). Figure 19.3 is an example of such a display.

Pretest and posttest data on the hierarchy may indicate where the breakdown in skill occurred. In our example of the scientific notation lesson, we conclude that the breakdown in skill occurs in objectives G and H, as suggested by the data in Figure 19.2 when placed into the learning hierarchy in Figure 19.3. Since objective G is prerequisite to H, it is highly likely that the poor performance in H is due to the poor performance in G. (The entry-level skill was not assessed during the small-group evaluation because the one-to-one evaluations indicated that it was a skill mastered by all learners in the target group.)

ATTITUDE DATA. As we discussed in Chapter 14, learners' attitudes have a critical impact on their learning, so it is important to include a measurement of their attitudes in formative evaluation. The attitude questionnaire also can provide helpful information to explain

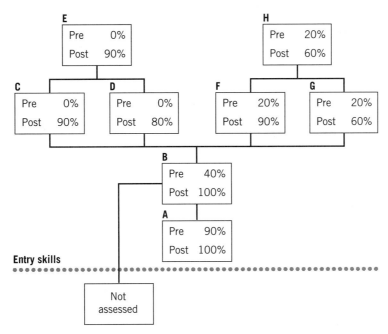

Figure 19.3 Pretest and Posttest Percentages of Learners Mastering Objectives

problems that are evidenced as performance problems on practice and posttests. The format and the vocabulary of the questionnaire will, of course, vary depending upon the characteristics of the learners participating in the formative evaluation. For example, with small children the anchors on the questionnaire may be a smiling face, a neutral face, and a frowning face, and the questions may be read to the learners or audiotaped. For adult learners the forms may be quite extensive with a larger number of anchors. Figure 19.4 presents an attitude questionnaire that may be modified or used as is in many formative evaluation efforts. (Such a questionnaire should include plenty of room for comments.)

Questionnaire data may be tallied on a clean copy of the form or entered in a computer in an electronic copy of the form. Comments can be summarized and written in as well. Any related comments from the debriefing may be also added. (Consider coding these debriefing comments in a separate font or color.)

TIME DATA. The time required to complete each of the tests and the actual instruction should be recorded as part of small-group formative evaluation. If the instruction is individualized, then each individual's time can be recorded. It is often feasible for computer-assisted instruction modules to be programmed so that they gather time data as they are being used, making use of the clock that is built into most computers. If the instruction is group-paced, then the total time for the les-

son should be recorded, along with each individual's time for completing the tests. Time data may be indicated for each test, the instruction itself, and total learning time. Averages and ranges can be indicated. Figure 19.5 is an example of such a display.

INTERPRETING SMALL-GROUP DATA. Determining what revisions are needed based upon the data can occasionally be difficult. Following are some general principles that can guide your decisions.

If performance on practice and posttest for the same objectives are both low, then the designer should do the following:

1. First look at the directions and format of items for those objectives to ensure that the vocabulary and intent are clear to the learners. Refer back to any data from the one-to-one evaluations that might provide hints as to problems that exist in practice or tests.

2. If the test directions and item formats are clear, look at the task analysis to determine where the breakdown of skills occurred. Consider whether objectives are sequenced incorrectly or whether there is a missing prerequisite skill or knowledge. Refer back to one-to-one evaluations to determine any indications of sequence or prerequisite problems.

3. If the above two solutions do not solve the problem, examine the instruction itself. Look for in-

Directions: Please place a check mark by the phrases below that match your opinion of the "Powers of Ten" unit. Write down any comments you have about any of the questions. Please be candid in your comments. Help me to get the "bugs" out if this lesson.

1. How difficult was this lesson?
   _____Too easy   _____About right   _____Too difficult
   COMMENTS

2. How was the vocabulary in the lesson?
   _____Too easy   _____About right   _____Too difficult
   COMMENTS

3. How was the length of the lesson?
   _____Too long   _____About right   _____Too short
   COMMENTS

4. How were the practice exercises?
   a._____Too easy   _____About right   _____Too difficult
   b._____Too few   _____About right   _____Too many
   COMMENTS

5. How were the test questions?
   a._____Too easy   _____About right   _____Too difficult
   b._____Too few   _____About right   _____Too many
   COMMENTS

6. Did the test questions match the things taught in the lesson?
   _____Too easy   _____Some did,   _____Too difficult
                        but some didn't
   COMMENTS

7. How were the directions on the practice items and tests?
   _____Confusing   _____O.K.   _____Very clear
   COMMENTS

8. What did you think about the examples given?
   a._____Confusing   _____O.K.   _____Very clear
   b._____Too few   _____About right   _____Too many
   COMMENTS

9. How did you like the pictures in the lesson?
   a._____Weren't needed   _____O.K.   _____Very helpful
   b._____Distracting   _____O.K.   _____Very important
   c._____Too silly   _____O.K.   _____Very humorous
   COMMENTS

10. Would you like to receive instruction in this form again?
    _____No   _____Maybe   _____Absolutely
    COMMENTS

11. Would you recommend this instruction to a friend who wanted to learn about scientific notation?
    _____Confusing   _____Maybe   _____Absolutely
    COMMENTS

12. How do you like math?
    _____Hate it   _____It's O.K.   _____Love it
    COMMENTS

13. Would you like to use scientific notation?
    _____No   _____Maybe   _____Sure
    COMMENTS

14. Do you think you could explain how to use scientific notation to a friend?
    _____No   _____Maybe   _____Sure
    COMMENTS

Figure 19.4   Example Attitude Questionnaire

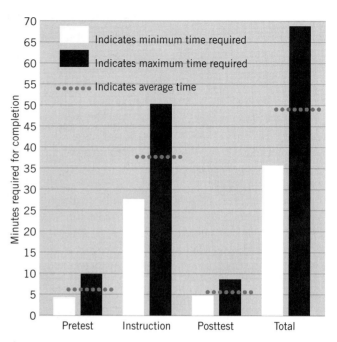

Figure 19.5   Range and Average of Completion Times for Instructional Components

complete or ambiguous explanations, examples, practice, or feedback. Consider alternate display modes such as illustrations or other graphics. Review other events of instruction related to deficient objectives. Refer back to one-to-one evaluations for any indications of need for alternate or more complete information.

4. If the previous steps provide no clear solution, refer to the attitude questionnaire data and to the debriefing information for any learners' insights or attitudes that might indicate problems with those particular objectives.

If practice performance is adequate, but posttest performance is low, then the designer should do the following:

1. Examine the items assessing deficient objectives on both practice and posttest to ensure that items for both tasks are of the same range of difficulty and level of applicability. Ensure the same weighting of items across these ranges as per the assessment item specifications. If such a problem exists, eliminate it by ensuring that each assessment follows the item specifications.

2. Consider any prompting that may be occurring during practice that is not being presented in the posttest. Either eliminate the prompts or provide some additional practice without the prompts.

3. Consider the feedback that accompanies practice. Determine whether feedback is prompting later

responses or being previewed by learners prior to response in the practice. If so, consider adding some practice that does not include feedback. (We do not suggest eliminating feedback from all the items, as feedback is such an integral part of instruction.)

4. Consider adding additional items of practice in later practice sessions in the lesson to encourage retention and automaticity.

5. Consider whether fatigue might have influenced posttest performance. If such a possibility appears likely, consider breaking down the instruction into sections.

6. Consider adding motivational reinforcement comments during feedback.

If practice performance is low and posttest performance is adequate, then the designer should do the following:

1. Examine the items assessing deficient objectives on both practice and posttest to ensure that items for both tasks are of the same range of difficulty and level of applicability. Ensure the same weighting of items across these ranges as per the assessment item specifications. If such a problem exists, eliminate it by ensuring that each assessment item follows the item specifications.

2. Consider learners' questionnaire data and non-verbal behaviors to ensure that any initial frustrations during practice did not produce predictable long-term negative attitudes toward the subject matter or the mode of instructional delivery.

If attitude data is low and posttest performance is adequate, then the designer should do the following:

1. Consider the implications for the long-term effects of negative attitudes. If these attitudinal concerns are not an important consideration of the institution or training organization, do nothing.

2. If long-term effects of negative attitudes are of concern, consider specific comments on questionnaires and debriefing for suggestions for revisions.

3. Consider adding additional motivating and interest-provoking devices, such as relevancy statements, curiosity-provoking scenarios, or relevant human interest stories. (See Chapter 14 for additional suggestions.)

4. If the problems are serious, consider alternate, "easier" media for some segment(s) of the instruction.

The output of the small-group stage of evaluation is an instructional lesson that has been revised based upon time, performance, and attitude data from representative members of the target audience. If evaluation has revealed substantial problems, then the designer may

choose to conduct another small-group evaluation with the revised materials before proceeding to the field trials.

Field Trials

The purpose of this stage of evaluation is to (1) determine the effectiveness of the revisions made during small-group evaluation, (2) ascertain any problems that might arise in the administration of the materials in a real instructional environment, and (3) validate the instruction with a large enough sample of the target audience to make a confident prediction of its effectiveness. The revised instructional materials, including tests, should be used in this stage. Instructional materials should now be in a more final form than they were during small-group evaluations. While it is optimal to use the complete entry, pretest, and posttest assessment instruments (as well as a possible delayed posttest), the test instruments may have to be abbreviated to include only the major objectives of the instruction. Documentation that prepares the teacher/trainer to integrate the instruction provided in the materials with other instruction in the class (e.g., teacher/trainer guides) should also be included.

Field trials are intended to design revisions based on the answers to questions such as the following:

- Can the instruction be implemented as it was designed?
- What types of administration problems are encountered?
- Does the teacher/trainer guide present the needed information in a form that can be easily used?
- Do the learners have the expected entry-level skills?
- Can the learners attain the objectives of the instruction?
- Are the time estimates for completion of the instruction accurate?
- How do the learners feel about the instruction?
- Are the revisions made as a result of small-group evaluations effective?
- How do the teachers/trainers feel about the instruction?
- Do teachers and learners implement the instruction as it was designed?
- What changes or adaptations do teachers/trainers make in the instruction?

LEARNERS' AND TEACHERS'/TRAINERS' ROLES. The instructional materials should be tried with at least thirty students during this stage. To obtain information about administration problems, which may vary from instructional environment to instructional environment, it is a good idea to conduct field trials in several different instructional sites, such as rural and urban, high and low socioeconomic status, well-funded sites and poorly funded sites, and multiple regions of the country, with approximately thirty learners at each site. Of course, the number and range of sites for field trials depends on the target audience. If the target audience is local, then the field trial sites should be local. The learners should respond to tests, instruction, and questionnaires.

Teachers and trainers should be involved in the instruction as their role is planned for the actual implementation, whether that role is presenting lectures, managing individualized instruction, or facilitating group activities. Training should be provided to the field trial teachers and trainers. This may include group training sessions, individual consultation, and teacher/trainer manuals. Teachers/trainers should be asked to respond to extensive questionnaires on the actual use of the instruction and any administrative problems associated with the trial of the instruction.

DESIGNER'S ROLE. Quite often the designer is not even present during the field-trial stage, especially if the instruction is of considerable length and there are many field trial sites. It is helpful if the designer can actually observe the trials because it is useful to gather information on whether the instruction has been implemented the way it was designed to be implemented. Such information is especially useful in instruction that has a component of lecture or other group-based activity.

The designer should coordinate the collection of the data, making the administration of tests and instruction as easy as possible. In addition, the designer must analyze and interpret the data from the field trials and conduct any follow-up data collection, such as interviews that may be needed. The designer may also conduct teacher/trainer training and create the teacher/trainer manuals.

DATA COLLECTION, DISPLAY, AND INTERPRETATION. Learners' performance, attitude, and time data may be collected and displayed in the same form that small-group data are collected and presented. In addition, information should be gathered from the teacher/trainer regarding the administration of the instruction. Figure 19.6 is an example of a teacher/trainer questionnaire that is appropriate for field trial data gathering. (Such a questionnaire should include plenty of room for comments.)

Within field trials, the designer should collect data on the degree of implementation of the designed program. We have already discussed ways to assess the effects of the instructional program that is being evaluated. Too often designers assume that these effects are the product of the program as defined by the materials and the teacher/trainer guide rather than the program as im-

plemented. In other words, designers frequently assume that the program is implemented as it was designed to be implemented. This may be a faulty and dangerous assumption. Instead of assuming that the program is being implemented as described, the designer/evaluator should assess the actual level of implementation of the instructional program. This form of evaluation is sometimes called *process evaluation* or evaluation of the *fidelity of implementation*, a concept you may recall from Chapter 17, "Implementation." If an evaluator can measure the degree to which the instructional program has been implemented as intended—a description of the program as it actually occurred—then he can be much clearer in determining what revisions in the materials should be made. For example, if one field trial site's data show an unexpectedly low percentage of learners achieving the learning goal of a lesson, it would be very helpful to have information as to whether the lessons were implemented as designed. Although we mention this here in the section on field trials, degree of implementation information might also be useful during small-group evaluations, and it is certainly necessary for summative evaluations.

To develop an instrument to measure the level of implementation of the instructional program, the designer needs to develop a clear description of the distinctive features of the program. To assess these features, the designer must describe them in terms of observable features. Instructional designers are often the best people to develop this description because they have developed the program based on some key principles or theory that they predict will positively affect learning. Fitz-Gibbon and Morris (1975) suggested that the evaluator (designer) develop this list by asking: If a stranger viewed the instructional program in operation, what distinctive features would be seen? The evaluator must also answer the following questions: What specifically would students be doing? How would teachers be acting? What would parents and administrators do? When identifying the key features to be sought, the evaluator should pick out observable manifestations of the instructionally robust features that were built into the instruction. For example, a reading program designer might identify such features as a specific technique for teaching the blending of sounds when decoding words; this should be manifested by the teacher when teaching and the learners when attempting to decode a word orally. The program might also include a required half hour of silent reading each day. Another critical feature might be that the learners take a book home each evening and read a minimum of twenty minutes with an adult. The distinctive features may be something that should be *left out* of a program as well as features that should be present. For example, a reading program might emphasize the absence of phonics instruction. Since use of phonics is

Directions: Please indicate with a check mark the degree to which you agree with the following statements regarding the administration of the unit "Powers of Ten." Any additional comments you provide will be very helpful in interpreting the results of this questionnaire. Your responses will enable us to improve the quality of this instruction as well as subsequent units. Please be as candid as possible.

Strongly Agree	Agree	Disagree	Strongly Disagree

1. The teacher/trainer guide and the accompanying materials provided all the information I needed in order to teach the unit.

_____   _____   _____   _____

COMMENTS

_____

_____

2. All of the materials and equipment that I needed to teach the unit were available to me.

3. The personnel support that I needed to teach the unit was available to me.

_____   _____   _____   _____

4. The facilities that I needed to teach the unit were available to me.

5. The intention and perspective of the instruction were clear to the learners.

_____   _____   _____   _____

6. The intention and perspective of the instruction were clear to me.

7. The time estimates provided in the teacher/trainer guide were accurate for my class(es).

_____   _____   _____   _____

8. My class(es) is(are) very similar to the target audience for the instruction that is described in the teacher/trainer guide.

_____   _____   _____   _____

9. The instruction required adaptation to fit my class(es) and this context.

_____   _____   _____   _____

Strongly Agree	Agree	Disagree	Strongly Disagree

10. The instructional materials were used as described in the teacher/trainer manual.

_____   _____   _____   _____

11. Learners who were present on the days of the instruction completed all instructional materials.

_____   _____   _____   _____

12. The information that I needed to know was easy to find in the teacher/trainer guide.

_____   _____   _____   _____

13. I found the unit easy to teach.

_____   _____   _____   _____

14. I found the unit interesting to teach.

_____   _____   _____   _____

15. I feel that the students learned from the unit.

_____   _____   _____   _____

16. I would like to teach other units with designs similar to this one.

_____   _____   _____   _____

17. I would recommend this unit of instruction to other teachers/trainers.

_____   _____   _____   _____

18. The teacher in-service training prepared me well to teach this unit of instruction.

_____   _____   _____   _____

19. Additional suggestions for improvement of the instruction that are not contained in my previous comments follow:

_____

_____

Figure 19.6   Teacher/Trainer Questionnaire for Field Trials

something that is fairly fundamental to many teachers, the assessment of implementation should report the degree to which this prohibition is observed.

A measurement of the degree to which these features are being implemented may be gathered in several ways. It is usually helpful if several measures are used. Extant data, such as teachers' lesson plans, students' papers, notes to and from parents, and administrators' records, may provide evidence of the program's implementation. These data may be examined by an evaluator using a carefully devised checklist that allows him to note the degree to which the distinctive features of the program are being implemented. One obvious but

extremely useful way to measure implementation is through observation of instruction actually occurring. Evaluators may periodically observe classrooms using the instructional program and record observations of the implementation of distinctive program features. Interviews or surveys of students, teachers, parents, and administrators may also yield key information about the implementation of the program. However, this information is subject to the limitations of "self-report" data. (People have a tendency to report what they think others wish them to say.) For a more detailed description on developing such instruments, readers may refer to Heck, Steigelbauer, Hall, and Loucks (1981).

ANALYSIS AND INTERPRETATION OF FIELD TRIAL DATA.
Learners' performance, attitude, and time data from field trials can be analyzed and interpreted in a manner very similar to data from small-group evaluations. The data from each individual class should be reviewed, analyzed, and interpreted separately before information is collapsed across separate classes or sites. This will enable the designer to be sensitive to any aberrant groups or patterns that occur with learners from particular regions or backgrounds. Problems that occur across all sites should be interpreted and revisions should be designed using the principles we suggested in our discussion of small-group evaluation. Administrative problems that consistently occur, such as lack of specific equipment or materials, may require revision in the instructional materials, development of alternate mediation, or provision of suggestions for adaptations.

Problems that were idiosyncratic to particular sites should be interpreted in conjunction with the teacher/trainer questionnaire. In addition, such sites may require visits or interviews in order to establish whether the following is true: (1) the learner population actually matched the target description, (2) the instruction was implemented as designed, and (3) additional special problems existed that affected the effectiveness of the instruction. After obtaining this information, the designer (in conjunction with the original client or client agency) must determine how representative the aberrant sites are of the actual target audience. This decision will determine whether alternative materials should be constructed to deal with the problems that the learners and/or their teacher/trainer encountered.

Teacher/trainer information should be tallied on a clean copy of the questionnaire, with comments summarized on this same form. This summarization should be done first for individual sites if there are several teachers/trainers in one site. Finally, summarization could be organized by groupings that appear to have similarities in patterns related to the characteristics of the sites. If all groups appear to have similar response patterns, summarization can occur across all sites. Problems that seem to be common across all sites should be addressed; problems that result from incomplete or inaccurate information in the teacher/trainer guides can be revised; and problems in the instruction itself that seem to have confirmation in learners' attitudes or performance should be addressed in a revision of the instruction. However, these changes should be considered cautiously; the designer must ensure that they are consistent with the strategy designed into the materials and that they specifically address performance or attitude problems. Questions or suggestions that occurred consistently across trial sites but that are deemed inappropriate should be addressed; their inappropriateness should be explained diplomatically in the teacher/trainer guide or during teacher in-service training or "train the trainer" sessions.

Implementation data should be carefully examined for consistent non-implementation of specific features. This non-implementation should be investigated to determine whether the feature is necessary, why the feature was not implemented, and what instruction was used in place of the missing feature.

As with the learners' data, if there are radical differences in responses related to certain types of sites, the designer must consult with the client regarding the centrality of these sites to the target audience.

ONGOING EVALUATION

Data collection for the purpose of revision of that instruction (formative evaluation) should not cease even when the instruction has been implemented in the target systems. Teacher/trainer guides and training on the use of the instruction should include encouragement to take a data-based perspective toward improving the quality of the instruction. To ensure that the revisions teachers make are consistent with the design strategies originally incorporated in the instruction, some of the teacher/trainer training time should be allocated to pointing out the critical features of the instructional strategies and explaining their importance in the learning process.

Instruction, other than teacher-led instruction, may be difficult to revise because of the expense involved. However, materials that are anticipated to have an extended period of implementation may be revised several times over that period. In some cases these revisions may not be incorporated in the more expensive media, such as an interactive video lesson; however, they will be incorporated in some accompanying media that are less expensive, such as print-based material. On other occasions, the expensive medium itself may be revised in an inexpensive way, such as revising the computer software (rather than the video materials) in an interactive video lesson or changing and redubbing the audio track on a video presentation.

Long-term implementation projects should develop methods for gathering effectiveness information into their evaluation plans. Subsequent revisions of the instruction may be dictated by many factors, some of which are changes in the entry-level skills of the targeted learners, changes in the content, and changes in the facilities, equipment, or social mores of the learning context. Some of this data gathering may dovetail with information gathering for summative evaluation, which we will discuss in the next section.

Ongoing evaluation attempts to answer questions similar to the questions addressed in field trials and additional questions that can lead to revisions in the instruction, such as the following: Are the revisions made as a result of field trials effective? Do learners' characteristics change over time?

Devising a Formative Evaluation Plan

Chapter 3 suggested that as designers develop learning goals on the basis of a needs assessment, they use the needs and goals to begin devising an evaluation plan. The evaluation plan should include not only plans for summative evaluation, but also plans for formative evaluation. Tessmer (1993) recommended that an evaluation plan include the following components: learning goals, analysis of resources and constraints, a task analysis, a description of learning environment, questions to be answered, indicators and measures to provide evidence for answers, identification of parts of the instruction to be evaluated, and stages of formative evaluation to be conducted and questions to be answered at each stage. As design continues from the activities relating to the needs assessment, revisions may be made to adjust to constraints or resources of the design context, questions about the learners, concerns about the task analy-

sis, issues with the assessment instruments, or ambiguities regarding the instructional strategy. As formative evaluation may be started with reviews of the needs assessment instruments and documents and learning task analysis, it is critical for the designer to plan early for the types of information he will require.

1. Which stage of the formative evaluation procedure does each of the following statements describe?

a. Teachers/trainers report on the appropriateness of the documentation that accompanies a package of computer-based instructional software.

b. Experts in the content area for which a slide-tape set was developed review the materials for accuracy and to ensure that they are up to date.

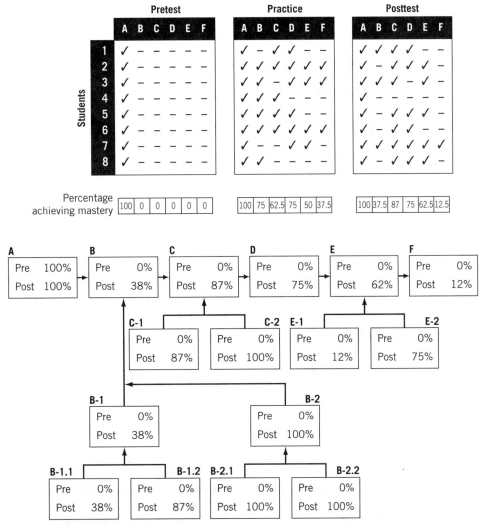

Figure 19.7 Data from Small-Group Evaluation
Used with permission, K. Cennamo, Macmillan Publishing Company.

c. Individual students review the storyboards of an instructional videotape with the designer.

d. At least thirty students go through the instruction.

e. The designer only assists students when they encounter severe difficulties.

f. Students read and think aloud as they interact with written instructional materials.

g. Test materials are tried out with groups of individuals—some of whom are "masters" of the content, and some of whom are not.

h. Data are collected regarding problems with the instruction after the instruction is implemented in the target contexts.

2. Figure 19.7 shows the data that resulted from a small-group evaluation of an instructional package on learning to use Logo™, a graphic-based programming language (Cennamo, 1986). The learning task was a procedure in Logo programming. Analyze the findings and plan a sequence of actions to plan revisions.

3. Develop a chart that describes the following for each of the six stages of formative evaluation: purpose, stage of development of instruction, role and characteristics of learners, role of designer, and procedures.

4. The situation: Maribelle Sanders is a training specialist for an international company, Big Boards, which produces building materials. New recommendations from the EPA, FDA, and the World Health Organization in conjunction with other international agencies have a strong and immediate impact on the safety precautions for Big Boards employees. New guidelines have just been published pertaining to the use of certain chemicals used in the manufacturing process of some of the processed wood products that Big Boards produces. The training will include new techniques for handling chemicals and using new safety equipment. This training, which will target all nine-hundred employees of the company who work line production positions in six plant locations, must be completed within six months. Documentation must be maintained on the date each employee received training and the performance score on a written test. Big Boards has excellent training centers with all equipment at three U.S. and three international sites. Maribelle is in the process of completing context, learners, and task analyses. She is tentatively planning trainer-led instruction that is supported by video clips and print-based materials.

The problem

a. Given the goals and resources/constraints of this situation, suggest a tentative formative evaluation plan, including stages, personnel, form of materials, and important questions to be answered.

b. Identify other information that you might need to assist you in making your plan and the potential sources of this information.

c. Identify any assumptions you're making in developing your plan.

AN OVERVIEW OF SUMMATIVE EVALUATION

Within the context of instructional design, the purpose of summative evaluation is to collect, analyze, and summarize data to present to decision makers in the client organization so that they can make a judgment regarding the effectiveness, and perhaps appeal and efficiency, of the instruction. This judgment usually leads to decisions regarding continued use of the instruction. Other users of summative data are agencies that fund instructional development and potential adopters of the instruction. There are occasions when the evaluators are also the clients and even the deliverers of the instruction. An example would be a teacher who had developed instruction and after a time collected data in order to decide whether to continue using this instruction. Summative evaluation occurs after the instruction has been implemented into the target contexts.

For systematically designed instruction, often the judgment of effectiveness is criterion-referenced and attempts to answer this question: Does the instruction adequately solve the "problem" that was identified in the needs assessment and that resulted in the development of the instructional materials? In such a criterion-referenced evaluation, the criterion of how well the problem must be solved for the instruction to be deemed successful should be established prior to the beginning of the evaluation. Indeed, this criterion should be established in conjunction with the needs assessment, in which the "ideal" attainment is established. These criteria may be stated in terms of payoff from the desired performance of the system, such as "reduction of error rates from 21 percent (in needs assessment terms, 'what is' prior to the initiation of the newly designed instruction) to 10 percent or less ('what should be' after the full implementation of the instruction)." Another example would be "reduction in the number of high school dropouts from 42 percent to 20 percent or less."

Sometimes the question is comparative: Which of several programs of instruction best addresses the problem that was identified in the needs assessment? This comparative question may involve comparing the effects of an existing instructional program to those of a newly designed program(s). Even with a comparison of several programs, a summative evaluation following systematic design should refer back to the original needs assessment and identify which of the alternative programs best solves the problem identified in the needs assessment.

Following are more specific questions, the answers to which may help determine whether the problem identified in the needs assessment has been solved:

- Do the learners achieve the goals of the instruction?
- How do the learners feel about the instruction?
- What are the costs of the instruction?
- How much time does it take for learners to complete the instruction?
- Is the instruction implemented as it was designed?
- What unexpected outcomes result from the instruction?

ALTERNATIVE APPROACHES TO SUMMATIVE EVALUATION

Currently, two approaches to summative evaluation are used in the fields of education and training: objectivism and subjectivism. These two approaches mirror the alternative modes of inquiry that are popular in educational research as well as evaluation. We will briefly discuss these, but Worthen and Sanders (1987) provide a more comprehensive description.

Objectivism relies on empiricism, answering questions based upon observation and data. The major advantage of an objective evaluation is that the results are replicable, meaning that trained individuals, given the same questions and a similar methodology, will gather similar data and draw similar conclusions. An objective evaluation usually employs the scientific method: setting hypotheses, designing an experiment to control extraneous variables, collecting data, and drawing conclusions. In general, such evaluations tend to depend upon the collection of quantitative data. Objective evaluations are often goal-based, focused on determining the degree to which the goals of the instructional program have been obtained. Traditionally, the majority of educational evaluations and evaluation texts have employed an objective basis for evaluation. Most federal agencies require such quantitative "impact data," data that indicate the impact of the instructional innovations on learners, as part of reports from funded materials development projects. The major limitation of objective evaluations is that because they are focused upon the goals of the program, they use designs to control extraneous variables, and they examine only a limited number of factors. Therefore, the evaluation may not examine some of the most critical effects of the instructional program, particularly if those effects are from unanticipated sources.

Subjectivism employs expert judgment as the criterion of evaluation. The accuracy of a subjective evalua-

tion depends upon the experience and knowledge of the evaluator(s). Subjective evaluations often employ qualitative methods such as observation and interviews to examine the instructional context. In addition, subjective evaluations are often "goal-free." Goal-free evaluations, as suggested by Scriven (1972), do not start from the goals of the program. Indeed, evaluators employing a goal-free evaluation do not wish to be biased by being informed of the goals of the program. They wish to describe the program and its effects as they perceive it, not as they have been predisposed to perceive it. The advantage of subjective evaluations is that they are more likely than objective evaluations to highlight unexpected results of an instructional program. The limitation of a subjective evaluation is that it may not be replicable. The results of the evaluation may be more biased by the idiosyncratic experiences, perspectives, and biases of the individual who conducts the evaluation. An example of a subjective evaluation is Eisner's (1979) educational connoisseurship model. This model employs the tactics of art criticism and literary criticism for evaluating instructional programs.

No evaluation is totally objective or totally subjective; all evaluations fall somewhere on a continuum between the two. Posavac and Carey (1997) suggested that an evaluation may tend toward the subjective end of the continuum if any of the following factors exist: unclear or complex program goals, disagreement regarding goals and processes of the program, a complex instructional context, or disagreement in perspectives or philosophies among those in or influenced by the instructional context.

As you might expect, summative evaluations of systematically designed instruction have traditionally tended toward the objective end of the evaluation continuum. Systematic design is consistently based upon the goals of the instructional program. It also depends on collecting quantifiable data to make decisions, such as revisions as a result of formative evaluation. Therefore, a summative evaluation for a systematically designed program will often take a more quantitative, goal-based approach. However, it is often appropriate and desirable to add goal-free and more qualitative aspects to the evaluation in order to examine unexpected outcomes of a program. It if often even likely that the questions that guide the evaluation may require more qualitative methods and less quantifiable answers. For example, what are the unexpected outcomes of the instruction? These unexpected outcomes may be positive, or they may be negative. In any event, findings of subjective evaluation may be of utility in estimating the merit of an instructional program or system from a standpoint somewhat outside the instruction's goals.

Designer's Role in Summative Evaluation

The role of an instructional designer in summative evaluation has been a somewhat controversial issue. Many educators believe that the instructional designer has a strong investment and consequent bias to find the instruction effective. Therefore, the designer is too biased to give a fair evaluation of the instruction. Others feel that no one knows the instructional program and its potential strengths and weaknesses better than the designer and, therefore, the designer is in the best position to most efficiently design an evaluation that probes deeply into the ultimate effectiveness of the program in its target context.

It is probably ultimately less problematic to hire an external evaluator to conduct at least part of a summative evaluation of an instructional program. However, it is *not* impossible for the designer to obtain an objective evaluation of a program, especially if the evaluation tends toward the objective end of the evaluation continuum. Often an organization is not in a position to hire an external evaluator; therefore, an internal evaluator, even the designer of the program itself, must be used. In such a case, it is *most important* to document the evaluation procedure carefully and completely so that the measures and procedures employed are known, and any biases that may be involved in these procedures and their implementation are open to scrutiny. However, the goal-free part of the evaluation may be conducted by an external evaluator. It may be difficult for an instructional designer to ignore the goals of an instructional program that he designed and conduct an adequate goal-free evaluation.

If designers do not actually direct the summative evaluation, they will be active in providing information to the evaluator. Most of the documentation from context analysis (including needs assessment procedures and conclusions) through learner and task analysis, statement of goals, assessment item specifications, assessment instruments, and strategy plans should be made available to the evaluator.

Timing of Summative Evaluation

One common error in conducting summative evaluations that causes them to yield fallacious data is conducting the evaluation too early in the implementation of the instructional program. If at all possible, the summative evaluation of a program should not occur in the first implementation of the instructional program. This means that if an instructional program is a year's curriculum, then the program should not be evaluated in its first year. If the program is a six-week training program, then it should not be evaluated in the first six weeks' offering. Rarely are programs delivered in the first implementation as they were designed to be delivered; often, the teacher/trainer learns how to deliver the instruction during the first administration.

PROCEDURES FOR SUMMATIVE EVALUATION

The following sections will summarize the steps in completing a goal-based summative evaluation. These steps are similar to procedures recommended by Morris (1978), Popham (1988), and several authors within Borich's (1974) text. The Morris text in particular is a more complete source for designers who must design a summative evaluation.

DETERMINE GOALS OF EVALUATION. The foremost activity in this stage is to identify the questions that should be answered as a result of the evaluation. These questions will direct all of the subsequent procedures. These questions should be identified by the client organization and often may be defined by the requirements of funding agencies or interests of other stakeholders. Here is the list of questions we suggested earlier in the chapter:

- Does implementation of the instruction solve the problem identified in the needs assessment?
- Do the learners achieve the goals of the instruction?
- How do the learners feel about the instruction?
- What are the costs of the instruction? What is the "return on investment" of the instruction?
- How much time does it take for learners to complete the instruction?
- Is the instruction implemented as it was designed?
- What unexpected outcomes result from the instruction?

Often, more questions are identified than can be economically and efficiently answered. In this case, evaluators can select the questions to be answered via the evaluation by considering the following issues, which have been adapted from lists by Flagg (1990) and Worthen and Sanders (1987):

- What decisions must be made as a result of the evaluation? Which questions will provide the best information to answer these questions?
- How practical is it to gather the information to answer this question?
- Who wants the answer to this question? Are these individuals key to the future success of the program?
- How critical is the information gained from this question to the continued use of the program?
- How much uncertainty is associated with the answer to this question?

The evaluator and the client organization should agree on the exact nature of the questions before moving to the next steps in the evaluation procedure. This is not to say that, as the planning advances, additional questions may not be added, priorities changed, or questions clarified. However, in a goal-based evaluation, such a clear direction for evaluation is possible.

SELECT INDICATORS OF SUCCESS.   The evaluator, in collaboration with his clients, must determine where to look for evidence of the impact of the instructional program. Answering the following questions is an effective technique to focus on the program's impact: If the program is successful, what will we observe in instructional materials and learners' activities? In teachers'/trainers' knowledge, practice, attitudes? In learners' understanding, processes, skills, attitudes?

SELECT ORIENTATION OF EVALUATION.   As the questions are identified, the evaluator and clients will agree on the orientation that is most appropriate in answering the evaluation questions. The decisions on orientation will address such issues as the following:

- Will the approach be more goal-based or goal-free?
- If one perspective predominates, will there be aspects of the other orientation?
- Are quantitative or qualitative data appropriate as evidence to answer the questions?
- Will a more experimental or naturalistic approach be used?

SELECT DESIGN OF EVALUATION.   Evaluation designs describe what data will be collected, when the data should be collected, and under what conditions data should be collected in order to answer the evaluation questions. Designers should begin to develop this plan during the needs assessment activity while the learning goals and the reasons for identifying the learning goals are clearly recalled. The evaluation design must be developed to allow the client(s) to draw the necessary conclusions and make the necessary decisions. Three issues must be considered in determining what design an evaluation should utilize:

- How much confidence must we have that the instructional program actually caused any effects found in learners' performance or attitudes?
- How important is it that we can generalize the conclusions of the evaluation to learners or contexts not involved in the evaluation?
- How much control can we have over the instructional situation?

The issue of causation is generally termed *internal validity.* There are many things that can cause changes (both positive and negative) in learners' performance and attitude that may have nothing to do with the new instructional program. For example, learners grow older, and this can change their behavior. They may realize that they are part of a study, and this awareness alone can change their effort and performance. Students can be influenced by learning as a result of something that occurs outside the instructional context. If these rival sources of causation are likely, there are ways to organize an evaluation so that these possible effects can be eliminated from consideration. Actually there are many possible rival sources of causation. Most evaluation texts or research design texts will discuss these factors. Or, you might wish to read one of the primary sources on internal validity, Campbell and Stanley (1963).

The issue of generalizability is termed *external validity.* Although Campbell and Stanley mention a number of factors that can threaten external validity, there are three threats that are often of particular consideration for systematically designed instructional programs. The first is the effect of pretesting, which may alert or sensitize the learners in some way that will make the instruction more effective with a pretested group than with students who did not have a pretest. This is not usually a problem if the instructional program itself is designed to include a similar pretest (as is often the case with systematically designed instruction). The second threat to generalizability is that the learners involved in the evaluation may not be representative of the learners who will use the instruction in the future. In such a situation the learners might perform better, worse, or differently than the students in the evaluation group. The third rival causative factor is that students in the evaluation group may respond differently from students in future implementations because they realize they are in an "experiment." The second threat is probably the greatest problem, but it can be dealt with in the design of the instruction: The solution is to design instruction that is suitable for a wider target audience than was originally anticipated.

The issue of control allows the evaluation designer to determine the limits of what can be done with internal and external validity. The two basic ways that the evaluation design can deal with the threats to internal and external validity are comparison groups and randomization. Comparison groups allow us to exclude a number of rival sources of causation by comparing the performance and attitudes of learners who have experienced the instructional program to the performance and attitudes of learners who have had the same basic experiences with the exception of the instructional program. This is very similar to research studies that employ a research group and a control group.

Randomization allows the evaluator to eliminate threats that may be due to a situation in which the learners who were evaluated were "special" in some way and were—if a control group was employed—"better" (or "worse") than the students in the control group or "better" (or "worse") than students in subsequent "real" implementations of the instructional program. There are two types of randomization. First, students may be randomly *selected* to participate in an evaluation study. Secondly, students may be randomly assigned to receive alternate instructional materials in an evaluation. Some evaluation studies may use both forms of randomization.

Dealing with the three issues of causation, generalizability, and control is a balancing act because there are always trade-offs involved when designing an evaluation that accounts for each issue. Many times in evaluation studies, it is not possible to eliminate all of the factors that might threaten internal and external validity. In these cases, the evaluation designer must carefully consider whether the threats are real or only possible. When there are threats that cannot be controlled in the evaluation, they must be acknowledged in a discussion of the limitations of the evaluation in the evaluation report.

To systematically employ control groups and randomization, a number of alternative designs have traditionally been employed. We will present only those that have been most commonly employed in evaluations of systematically designed instruction. They vary in terms of whether randomization and control groups are used. In addition, they may vary as to whether a pretest is employed.

ALTERNATIVE DESIGNS

Instruction, Posttest. In this design, sometimes called the *case study* design, a single group is presented with the instruction, followed by a posttest. This design is limited in that it does not control for threats to conclusions of causality and threats to the ability to generalize. For example, suppose that the performance of the learners is very high. An individual examining such evaluation data might ask, "How do you know that they didn't already know how to perform the tasks on the posttest?" or "How do you know that you didn't just have a bright set of learners?" or "How do you know that it wasn't the series on television this semester that led to the learning shown on the posttest?" There is no information provided by this design to counter these suspicions. Although this is a weak design, there may be occasions when there are no reasonable threats to drawing conclusions of causality and to generalizing the conclusions to similar groups. In such a case you might use a case study design.

Pretest, Instruction, Posttest. The first design of this type is termed the *one-group pretest-posttest* design, the use of which we suggested in formative evaluation. In

contrast to the case study design, this design can establish that there is an improvement in performance over time. Unfortunately, it cannot establish that the improvement is due to the instruction. It cannot refute the allegation that the learners involved in this study were unusually bright or motivated. To counter such rival sources, a control group design must be employed.

G1   *Pretest* ——————> *Instruction* ——————> *Posttest*
G2   *Pretest* ———————————————————————> *Posttest*
     or
G1   *Pretest* —————> *Instruction X* ——> *Posttest*
G2   *Pretest* —————> *Instruction Y* ——> *Posttest*

A second pretest, instruction, posttest design is termed the *nonequivalent control group* design. The control groups are considered nonequivalent because the study does not employ random assignment of learners to groups. This is the control group design most commonly used because it is quite common to be unable to randomly assign learners to a class for an evaluation study. In this design, one group receives the newly designed instruction, and the other group (the control group) receives no related instruction at all. The two groups are pretested. This pretest serves two purposes. First, it allows the designer to discard the argument that the instructed group performed better because it was somehow sensitized by the pretest. It also allows him to establish some degree of equivalence, even without randomization. If the two groups perform similarly on the pretest, the designer can at least say that the groups were similar in specific prior knowledge. He cannot conclude that they were similar in other factors that might also impinge on learning and attitudes. The second design (Instruction *X* and *Y*) is the design that is often employed when a designer has a second instructional program that he is comparing in terms of effectiveness. It uses a "comparison" group rather than a "control" group.

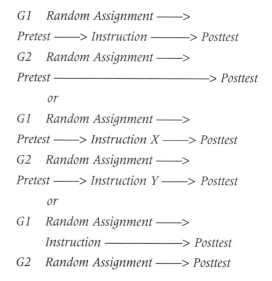

G1   *Random Assignment* ——>
Pretest ——> *Instruction* ——————> *Posttest*
G2   *Random Assignment* ——>
Pretest ———————————————————> *Posttest*
     or
G1   *Random Assignment* ——>
Pretest ——> *Instruction X* ——> *Posttest*
G2   *Random Assignment* ——>
Pretest ——> *Instruction Y* ——> *Posttest*
     or
G1   *Random Assignment* ——>
     Instruction ——————————> *Posttest*
G2   *Random Assignment* ——> *Posttest*

A more rigorous pretest, instruction, posttest design, just as with the nonequivalent groups design, the *pretest-posttest control group* may use a control group or an alternate instruction comparison group. Because it randomly assigns learners to groups, using it is a good argument against the charge that the effectiveness of the newly designed instruction is due to some important differences in the groups whose posttest scores are compared. An alternate form is the *posttest-only control group* design, useful when it is not advisable to use pretests. Perhaps as it is most powerful as a research design, the posttest-only design has limited usefulness in evaluation of instruction, in which pretests are a regular part of the instructional system.

Pretest, Instruction, Posttest, Posttest, Posttest. The *interrupted time-series* design is often used with a single group when one wants to examine trends prior to and after instruction. Such a design might be extremely useful when examining the "payoff" criteria after all learners have received the instruction. For example, a designer might examine the error rates in a particular job task prior to and following instruction. This design can also be used with a comparison or control group when there are possible rival sources of causation.

Within a single evaluation study more than one design may be employed. Designs may vary for different measurement instruments. For example, a nonequivalent pretest-posttest control group design could be used for learning and attitude outcome measures, and an interrupted time-series design might be used for examining payoff criteria. Of course, the various designs must be compatible with each other. It would not make much sense, for example, to use both a nonequivalent and an equivalent control group design. If a designer can obtain an equivalent control group, it should be used since it is a more desirable design for supporting conclusions involving causation and generalization.

Design or Select Evaluation Measures

This section will describe the particular considerations involved in designing measures of payoff outcomes, learning outcomes, attitude outcomes, level of implementation, and cost effectiveness in evaluation studies. In most evaluation studies, the evaluator plans for multiple measures of the effectiveness of the instructional program in each of the following categories: payoff, learning, attitude, implementation, and cost. In addition, it is common to utilize multiple measures within any one category. There are occasions in which an existing standardized test may meet the assessment needs of the evaluation. Often, new measurement instruments must be developed using the principles suggested in Chapter 6.

PAYOFF OUTCOMES. One of the most critical measurements that should occur in evaluation is a measure that allows the evaluator and the client to determine if the problem identified in the needs assessment—the problem that led to the development of the instruction—has been solved. This measure is a measurement of the *payoff* outcomes. Payoff outcomes may be measured in any number of ways, depending on the problem to be solved. Some examples include the number of errors identified by quality assurance in a manufacturing division, the number of dropouts from a high school, the number of customer complaints from a service agency, the number of National Merit Scholars from a school system, and so on. Kearsley (1986) listed several factors that may be considered by training agencies as payoff criteria: costs avoided as a result of problems such as overruns, overtime, or employee turnover; increased output in sales/orders, production rate, or the number of transactions processed; improved quality, evidenced in customer satisfaction, better safety records, and higher success/lower failure rate; and improved efficiency in such things as reduced equipment repair time, faster delivery service, or more customers handled. In many instances, payoff data may be routinely collected and made available as extant data. The task of the evaluator may be to simply identify these data as relevant and obtain access to them. In some cases the evaluator may have to arrange to have the data collected more systematically and more frequently than might be routine. Evaluation of payoff is also identified as a *Level-4 evaluation* by Kirkpatrick (1983). Level-4 evaluations determine the impact of the instruction on the mission of the organization or agency.

LEARNING TRANSFER. Transfer is the application of new learning to other situations. The next measure to be described, "learning outcomes," usually measures *near transfer*, such as the ability to solve similar problems in similar situations. *Far transfer* can mean a variety of things, such as to job performance, to other subjects, or to future learning tasks. Evaluation studies rarely include far transfer measures, usually due to the cost and difficulties of longitudinal follow-up. However, as far transfer is often the real goal of instruction, it is often worth the effort to organize a way to obtain these data. Kirkpatrick labeled evaluations that gather job performance data or other far transfer data as *Level-3 evaluations*.

LEARNING OUTCOMES. Principles to consider in developing measures of learning outcomes were discussed thoroughly in Chapter 6. These principles should, of course, be followed when designing assessment instruments for evaluations. In addition, it is critical to have a logical relationship among the payoff outcomes, the goals of the instructional program, and the learning outcomes measured. For example, if through needs assessment and analysis it was established that students' dropping out of a school was related to their inability to read and a reading comprehension program was consequently developed, then the learning outcome that should be measured is reading comprehension ability.

Of course, learning outcome measures can take any of the forms suggested in Chapter 6. The instruments should meet all of the criteria of good assessment instruments: reliability, validity, and practicality. The exams used as a part of the actual instruction can be used as data sources in summative evaluation. Two situations might preclude such use. The assessment should reflect the effects of the entire program. Many units and exams of even larger scope assess prerequisite skills in order to provide information for remediation. This thoroughness may limit the adequate (reliable) measurement of the end goal of the program. A special exam may be required to reliably evaluate learners' performance on the learning goal of the program. A second reason that a special exam may be required would be a situation in which two or more programs with similar but not identical learning goals are being compared for the evaluation. In this case, the assessment instruments for neither of the two (or more) versions may be a fair evaluation of the other program. A separate instrument that reflects the performance identified in the needs assessment but is not biased toward the particular focus of any of the alternate programs should be developed for the summative evaluation. Evaluations of these near transfer measures are often termed *Level-2 evaluations.*

ATTITUDES. Rarely are attitude objectives the primary payoff goals for instructional programs. However, it is not uncommon for attitude outcomes to be clearly related to the payoff criterion. Our previous example of the reading program for school dropouts must absolutely include assessment of attitudes in the evaluation of the program. Even for programs in which attitudes are not so clearly related to goals of the program or to the problem identified in the needs assessment, it is usually critical to evaluate students' attitudes toward the program. In evaluating those attitudes, the evaluator may formulate questions that ask about learners' attitudes toward learning, the instructional materials themselves, or the subject matter. When comparing two or more programs in an evaluation, learners' attitudes to the programs may differ significantly enough to influence decisions about the materials. When evaluating a single program, information on the appeal of the instruction should be factored into the decision as to whether the instruction solves the problem identified in the needs assessment. The evaluator should be cautious in planning an evaluation that makes a comparison of pretest and posttest attitudes. Attitudes are slow to change. If the instruction is not lengthy, it is unlikely that a comparison of pre to post attitudes will yield significant and important differences.

Flagg (1990) suggested several indices of appeal that might be considered for assessment in an evaluation: attention, likableness, interest, relevance, familiarity, credibility, acceptability, and excitement (arousal). Although a single evaluation might not examine all of the indices, it is quite possible that the evaluator might plan to examine several of them. These factors might be assessed through self-report interviews, questionnaires, or observation. Evaluations that collect only attitude data are described as *Level-1 evaluations* (Kirkpatrick, 1983).

LEVEL OF IMPLEMENTATION. As suggested in our discussion of field trials, it is extremely useful in both formative and summative evaluation to obtain a measure of the degree to which the instructional program has been implemented as designed. You can see from the careful discussion of evaluation designs that it is important in evaluation to ascribe the effects of an instructional program to the program itself, rather than to some additional source (such as superior students in the sample of students receiving the instructional program). In addition, in drawing the line of causation from the instruction to the results, it is critical to be able to identify the degree to which the description of the program represents what actually occurred during instruction with the new program.

If the instructional program to be evaluated has been systematically designed according to some clearly espoused principles, the identification of the distinctive features should be fairly easy. Then the evaluator can design the observation, interview, and materials review forms to use when assessing the level of implementation of the program. If two or more programs are being compared in the evaluation, the features to be evaluated should be those features that are distinctively and critically different in the programs.

COSTS. When evaluators estimate costs during summative evaluation, they usually consider the costs to implement and continue the program. These costs include personnel, facilities, equipment, materials, any other inputs, as well as any inputs required of the students (e.g., calculators, books, lab equipment). For inservice training (training of individuals already on the job), costs also include production time lost from the employees who must be off the job during training. Regardless of whether the materials were developed "in house" (a case in which the costs of design, development, and production must be accounted for) or whether the instruction is purchased, the costs for the instructional program itself are usually considered under the "materials" category.

Most techniques for analyzing costs in relation to effectiveness are devised on a comparative basis. One approach is the "benefits forsaken" comparison (Popham, 1988), in which an evaluator compares the benefits for the cost of a particular program to the hypothesized benefits of other ways in which the money could be spent. Another approach is to compare the relative costs and benefits of two programs. When evaluating systematically designed instruction, comparison programs are sometimes used. The instruction may be compared to a traditional way of presenting the same content or even a new alternative program. However, many times there is no comparison program. The question in such a case is "Will the ultimate outcome of this program be worth the cost?" We will review three types of cost studies recommended by Popham: cost-feasibility, cost-effectiveness, and cost-benefit.

Cost-feasibility is usually stated in terms of the cost for the instructional program per student (or per student hour). Feasibility indices do not consider effectiveness but rather report the cost (or relative costs if two or more programs are being evaluated).

Cost-effectiveness information is usually reported in a ratio of cost for the program divided by some measure of the effectiveness of the program (e.g., per ten-point gain on a standardized exam). Two programs may be compared using a cost-effectiveness ratio if the programs have similar goals and can, therefore, be legitimately measured using the same measure.

The third index for evaluating costs is *cost-benefit*, which is usually measured in terms of program costs divided by some monetary estimate of the benefits of the program. (Examples would be estimated monetary value in production rate, estimated value of customer satisfaction, or savings because of better safety records due to the new instruction.) The factor evaluated in terms of monetary benefit should be related to the problem identified in the needs assessment (e.g., slow service, employee turnover, or error rate). In public school environments, it is difficult to assess a monetary value to some learning effects, but for certain programs (e.g., programs to reduce dropouts or to reduce drug use) dollar estimates of the benefits of the program might be appropriate.

A more recent term used to examine cost benefit is *return on investment (ROI)*. This term is frequently used in business, governmental, and other training agencies. Basically, as do cost-benefit indices, the ROI measure attempts to compare the financial benefits of a training project to its costs. Historically, ROI is calculated as pretax earnings divided by average investment. Often, in the case of training to solve a particular problem, ROI may be calculated as annual savings (due to training) divided by investment costs in the training. Phillips (1991) listed some values that can be considered in the annual savings category: value of increased output, value of cost savings, value of time savings (wages and salaries, better service, penalty avoidance, opportunity for profit, training time), value of improved quality (savings due to lessening of scrap/waste, rework, customer/client dissatisfaction, product liability, inspection and quality control, internal losses, employee morale). Phillips suggests additional indices that might be used in the calculation of values similar to ROI. He also provides several examples of such calculations. (Readers interested in this particular measure should review Phillips's text on training evaluation and measurement methods, as well as other references on ROI listed at the end of this chapter.)

Collect Data

Once the evaluator has selected the outcomes and other characteristics of the program that should be measured and has selected or developed appropriate measurement instruments, he should devise a plan for the collection of data. Included in this plan should be appropriate scheduling of data collection periods, which are partially dictated by the evaluation design and partially dictated by the types of payoff and implementation measures desired. Of course, the evaluator must ensure that all policies regarding the collection of information from individuals within the organization are scrupulously followed.

Analyze Data

Data should be analyzed in such a way that it is easy for the client (and other decision makers who will examine the evaluation data) to see how the instructional program affected the problem presented in the needs assessment. In some cases simple descriptive statistics (e.g., means, standard deviations, range, and frequency distributions) may be sufficient to show these effects. In other cases inferential statistics may be required. It is beyond the scope of this text to discuss inferential statistical analysis; however, in cases in which differences in outcomes are found and reported the designer should be cautious. These may be either differences between two programs or differences from pretest to posttest in a single program. Numerical differences could be caused by the effects of programs, but these differences *may* be caused by chance. Inferential statistics allow the evaluator to determine whether differences can be legitimately ascribed to programs rather than chance.

Report Results

Morris (1978) suggested that the summative evaluation report contain the sections outlined below. Instructional design documentation should provide information for Section 2 (Background). Information needed for the remaining sections can be gleaned by following the suggestions for conducting a summative evaluation as described in this chapter.

1. Summary
2. Background
   Needs assessment and goal
   Learner description
   Context description
   Description of program
3. Description of evaluation study
   Purpose of evaluation
   Evaluation design
   Outcome measures
   Implementation measures
   Cost-effectiveness information
   Analysis of unintentional outcomes
4. Results
   Outcomes
   Implementation
   Cost-effectiveness information
   Unintentional outcomes
5. Discussion
   Causal relationship between program and results
   Limitations of study
6. Conclusions and recommendations

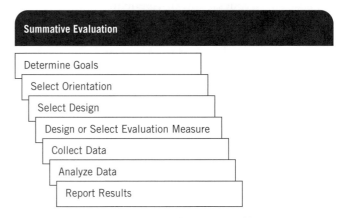

Figure 19.8 Summary Diagram for Chapter 19

SUMMARY

During the six stages of formative evaluation, the decisions that were made during the earlier design phases are tested. Problems that learners encounter during instruction are analyzed, and revisions are made. Designers should conduct as many stages of evaluation as possible to ensure a quality product. However, if time and money for evaluation are limited, then evaluation should proceed at the very least through one-to-one evaluation.

Evaluators conduct summative evaluations to determine the effectiveness of the instructional program for solving the instructional problem identified in the needs assessment. In conducting a summative evaluation, the evaluator may assess payoff outcomes, learning outcomes, attitude outcomes, level of implementation of the program, and costs. In addition to goal-based evaluation (which is focused on examining the degree to which the instructional problem is solved), the evaluation may also include an assessment of unintentional outcomes. Such goal-free evaluation uses naturalistic, probing techniques such as non-criterion-based observation, interviews, and examination of extant material. Figure 19.8 summarizes key points in this chapter.

EXTENDED EXAMPLE

In this last contribution to the Extended Example, we describe a formative and summative evaluation of our photography course. To see it, go to the Learning Resources Web site.

READINGS AND REFERENCES

Baker, E. L. (1970). Generalizability of rules for empirical revision. *AV Communication Review, 18*(3), 300–305.

Baker, E. L., & Alkin, M. (1973). Formative evaluation of instructional development. *AV Communication and Review, 21*(4), 389–418.

Borich, G. D. (Ed.). (1974). *Evaluating educational programs and products.* Englewood Cliffs, NJ: Educational Technology Publications.

Boutin, F., & Chinien, C. A. (1992). Synthesis of research on students selection criteria in formative evaluation. *Educational Technology, 32*(8), 28–34.

Cambre, M. A. (1981). Historical overview of formative evaluation of instructional media products. *Educational Communication and Technology Journal, 29*(1), 3–25.

Campbell, D. T., & Stanley, J. C. (1963). *Experimental and quasi-experimental designs for research.* Chicago: Rand McNally.

Cennamo, K. (1986). *Report on a beginning logo lesson.* Unpublished student project, University of Texas at Austin.

Dick, W., & Carey, L. (1990). *The systematic design of instruction* (3rd ed.). Glenview, IL: Scott, Foresman.

Eisner, E. W. (1979). *The educational imagination: On the design and evaluation of school programs.* New York: Macmillan.

Fitz-Gibbon, C., & Morris, L. L. (1975). Theory-based evaluation. *Evaluation Comment, 5*(1), 1–4.

Flagg, B. N. (1990). *Formative evaluation for educational technologies.* Hillsdale, NJ: Erlbaum.

Heck, S., Steigelbauer, S. M., Hall, G. E., & Loucks, S. F. (1981). *Measuring innovation configurations: Procedures and applications.* Austin, TX: Research and Development Center for Teacher Education, University of Texas.

Holloway, R. E. (1981). *A methodology for assessing the implementation of educational innovations: Analysis and revision.* Washington, DC: National Institute of Education, Basic Skills Group. (ERIC Document Reproduction Service No. ED 202 866.)

Hughes, A. S., & Keith, J. J. (1980). Teacher perceptions of an innovation and degree of implementation. *Canadian Journal of Education, 5*(2), 43–51.

Kearsley, G. (April, 1986). Analyzing the costs and benefits of training: Part 2: Identifying the costs and benefits. *Performance and Instruction, 25*(3), 23–25.

Kearsley, G. (1993). Costs and benefits of technology-based instruction. In G. M. Piskurich (Ed.), *The ASTD handbook of instructional technology* (pp. 16.1–16.19). New York: McGraw-Hill.

Kimpston, R. D. (1985). Curriculum fidelity and the implementation tasks employed by teachers: A research study. *Journal of Curriculum Studies, 17*(2), 185–195.

Kirkpatrick, D. L. (1983). Four steps to measuring training effectiveness. *Personnel Administrator*, November, 19–25.

Komoski, P. K. (1974). An imbalance of product quantity and instructional quality: The imperative of empiricism. *AV Communication Review, 22*(4), 357–386.

Loucks, S. F. (April, 1983). *Defining fidelity: A cross-study analysis.* Paper presented at the annual meeting of the American Educational Research Association, Montreal, Quebec, Canada. (ERIC Document Reproduction Service No. ED 249 659.)

Medley-Mark, V., & Weston, C. (1988). A comparison of student feedback obtained from three methods of formative evaluation of instructional materials. *Instructional Science, 17*, 3–27.

Morris, L. L. (1978). *Program evaluation kit.* Beverly Hills, CA: Sage Publications.

Owen, J. M., & Lambert, F. C. (1995). Roles for evaluation in learning organizations. *Evaluation, 1*(2), 237–250.

Parry, S. B. (1996a). Measuring training ROI. *Training and Development, 50*(5), 72–77.

Parry, S. B. (1996b). Was it the training? *Training and Development, 50*(3), 28–44.

Parry, S. B. (1996c). How much is the benefit? *Training and Development, 50*(4), 20–24.

Phillips, J. J. (1991). *Handbook of training evaluation and measurement methods* (2nd ed.). Houston, TX: Gulf Publishing.

Popham, W. J. (1988). *Educational evaluation* (2nd ed.). Upper Saddle River, NJ: Prentice-Hall.

Posavac, E. J., & Carey, R. G. (1997). *Program evaluation: Methods and case studies* (5th ed.). Upper Saddle River, NJ: Prentice-Hall.

Reeves, T. C., & Hedberg, J. G. (2003). *Interactive learning systems evaluation.* Englewood Cliffs, NJ: Educational Technology.

Roitman, D. B., & Mayer, J. P. (August, 1982). *Fidelity and reinvention in the implementation of innovations.* Paper presented at the Annual Convention of the American Psychological Association, Washington, DC. (ERIC Document Reproduction Service No. ED 225 058.)

Rosen, M. J. (1968). *An experimental design for comparing the effects of instructional media programming procedures: Subjective vs. objective revision procedures* (Final Report). Palo Alto, CA: American Institutes for Research. (ERIC Document Reproduction Service No. ED 025 156.)

Rothkopf, E. Z. (1963). Some observations on predicting instructional effectiveness by implementation inspection. *Journal of Programmed Instruction, 2*(2), 19–20.

Saroyan, A. (1993). Differences in expert practice: A case from formative evaluation. *Instructional Science, 21*, 451–472.

Saroyan, A., & Geis, G. L. (1988). An analysis of guidelines for expert reviewers. *Instructional Science, 17*, 101–128.

Scriven, M. (1972). Pros and cons about goal-free evaluation. *Evaluation Comment, 3*(4), 1–4.

Shrock, S. A., & Coscarelli, W. C. C. (1989). *Criterion-referenced test development: Technical and legal guidelines for corporate training.* Reading, MA: Addison-Wesley.

Smith, P. L., & Wedman, J. F. (1988). Read-think-aloud protocols: A new data-source for formative evaluation. *Performance Improvement Quarterly, 1*, 13–22.

Stevens, J. J., & Aleamoni, L. M. (1985). The use of evaluative feedback for instructional improvement: A longitudinal perspective. *Instructional Science, 13*, 285–304.

Tessmer, M. (1993). *Planning and conducting formative evaluations.* London: Kogan Page/Taylor & Francis.

Tessmer, M. (1994). Formative evaluation alternatives. *Performance Improvement Quarterly, 7*(1), 3–18.

Thiagarajan, S. (1978). Instructional product verification: 20 questions and 200 speculations. *Educational Communication and Technology Journal, 26*(2), 133–141.

Wager, J. C. (1983). One-to-one and small group formative evaluation: An examination of two basic formative evaluation procedures. *Performance and Instructional Journal, 22*(5), 5–7.

Weston, C. B. (1986). Formative evaluation of instructional materials: An overview of approaches. *Canadian Journal of Educational Communication, 15*(1), 5–17.

Weston, C. B., McAlpine, L., & Bordonaro, T. (1995). A model for understanding formative evaluation in instructional design. *Educational Technology Research and Theory, 43*(3), 29–48.

White, R. T., & Gagné, R. M. (1978). Formative evaluation applied to a learning hierarchy. *Contemporary Educational Psychology, 3*, 87–94.

Worthen, B. R., & Sanders, J. R. (1987). *Educational evaluation: Alternative approaches and practical guidelines.* New York: Longman.

V

CONCLUSION

Chapter 20, Conclusions and Future Directions," the sole chapter in this section, summarizes where the text has taken us and emphasizes some key points that we do not want you to forget, especially the recommendations and exhortations on taking charge of and adapting the design process yourself. The chapter and text conclude with some speculations about the future of instruction and instructional design.

CONCLUSIONS
AND FUTURE DIRECTIONS

CHAPTER OBJECTIVES

At the conclusion of this chapter, you should be able to do the following:

- Describe and explain the major principles underlying instructional design.
- Describe how instructional design practice may differ from principles and procedures presented in instructional design texts, and explain why it may differ.
- Determine and explain the degree of precision and formality that would be appropriate to apply in a situation.
- Given a situation, select an appropriate fast-track technique for instructional design.
- Discuss future trends in instructional design practice.

OVERVIEW

This chapter has three sections: (1) a summary of the major design principles presented in each chapter of this book, (2) a discussion of the appropriate use of instructional design technology, and (3) a description of what we and others view as future trends in instructional design.

A SUMMARY OF THE MAJOR PRINCIPLES GUIDING INSTRUCTIONAL DESIGN

Following is a set of major principles that underlie instructional design. These principles are abstracted from the chapters of this text and, as such, represent a summary of the text in principle form.

1–2. General principles and assumptions that underlie instructional design (ID) are as follows:
   a. ID is a systematic process (as opposed to a fortuitous, haphazard activity).
   b. ID has a problem-solving orientation (needs assessment leads to activities directed at improvement of instruction, which in turn lead to evaluation).
   c. ID is learning and learner-centered (as opposed to teaching or medium-centered).
   d. ID has as a goal efficient, effective, and appealing instruction.
   e. ID insists on congruence between objectives, instruction, and evaluation.
   f. ID is both theoretic and empirical (as opposed to "intuitive").

3. The design of instruction must be directed by needs and shaped to fit the learning environment.

4. Instructional design must include consideration of the following learner characteristics:
   a. Likenesses and differences.
   b. Changing and stable characteristics.
   c. Specific prior learning.

5. The more precisely learning goal(s) are identified and analyzed to determine necessary components of learning tasks and their prerequisite skills and knowledge, the more effectively and efficiently these goals will be attained.

6. Assessment of learning is guided by goals of the instructional system and should employ particular techniques to ensure adequacy of the assessment. Frequently, assessment design involves trade-offs in validity, reliability, and practicality.

7. Instructional strategies can do the following:
   a. Provide the framework for learning at both micro and macro levels.
   b. Be more generative or more supplantive depending on the task, context, and learners.
   c. Be organized around the expanded instructional events, a framework for instructional strategies.

8– A fundamental element in the design of instruction
15. is the character of the learning task. Effectiveness of instruction can be improved when instructional strategies are based upon supporting the cognitive demands of different types of learning (using the framework provided by the expanded instructional events).

16. At the macro level, such as in units, courses, and programs of study, attention must be given to articulation and a form of curriculum organization should be designed that takes into account setting, learners, and learning goals.

17. Regardless how well instruction has been designed, appropriate implementation is essential to its success in facilitating learning.

18. Instructional designers are involved with management both as managers of design projects and with management strategies which are part of the instruction itself.

19. Evaluation of instruction should be conducted as part of the design/development process (formative) and to estimate the value of completed instruction (summative).

20. Design should reflect appropriate technology (see the next topic).

"APPROPRIATE" INSTRUCTIONAL DESIGN

An issue to which we have alluded throughout the text but have not directly confronted is the level of effort that is required for any particular instructional design project. The issue is illustrated by remarks overheard in the halls after our classes: "This instructional design stuff is completely crazy! Classroom teachers (or training designers) can't possibly do all of this! We don't have enough time!"

A friend in the advertising and marketing field shared with us an expression, sometimes called the *golden triangle*, that reflects some harsh realities of projects in either advertising or instruction: "Given three criteria for doing a job—high quality, low cost, and rapid completion of the job—you may have any *two*." In other words, "I can give it to you fast and inexpensively, but it won't be as good; I can give it to you fast and very well-done, but it won't be inexpensive; or I can give it to you inexpensively and well-done, but it will take a long time." The trade-offs expressed in this wry analysis illustrates the dilemmas often faced by instructional designers who have limited resources and high demands.

In a book called *Small Is Beautiful,* E. F. Schumacher (1973) espoused the concept of "appropriate technology." His concern was predominantly with product (hardware) technology, rather than process technology, such as instructional design. However, the principles he advocated can be wisely applied to ID. His suggestion was that when we recommend the employment of a "technology," it may not be wise to export an example of the "highest tech" thing that we have. For instance, to a farming culture that has been using hand implements, a plow may be a more "appropriate" innovation than a tractor.

Leslie Briggs compared different levels of instructional design sophistication to using automobiles of different costs.* He noted that a Cadillac has many desirable attributes and that in some situations, such as transporting heads of state or participating in funeral processions, it is a clear choice (if not *de rigueur*), particularly when compared to a lower-cost vehicle such as a Chevy. However, it is important to recognize, he pointed out, that both the Cadillac and the Chevy will get you there.

The same concept of appropriate technology can apply to the amount of formality and precision used in applying instructional design. Due in large measure, perhaps, to the prescriptive nature and systematic orientation of instructional design, novice designers typically have the idea that all instructional design projects should undergo the same level of rigorous analysis and design effort. The practicality of instructional design itself has been at times called into question by authors in the field for the amount of time and effort that it takes to employ instructional design principles (e.g., Merrill, Li, & Jones, 1990a, 1990b; Rogoff, 1984; and Rosenberg, 1991). No doubt you have had similar frustrations over the effort required to fully complete some of the design activities that we have suggested. Rather than discard the tools of instructional design when situations make it difficult to use them to their fullest, it is better to learn ways of "tailoring" their application to the situation. This is the basic idea behind appropriate design.

The concept of appropriate design speaks to the problem of feasibility and advisability of instructional design practice in real-world situations. The "appropriate design" concept suggests that it is not only possible but also advisable to perform design functions at varying levels of effort, depending on available resources,

criticality of the task, the level of accountability of the educational or training agency, and expectations/requirements of the client agency. These variances in effort (as enabled by resources) lead to different levels of precision and amount of detail in documentation. The "low road" will include more design tasks "done in your head" but may nonetheless, under certain circumstances, result in completely legitimate, appropriate instructional design. Let's take a closer look at how resources, criticality, accountability, and expectations affect the design process.

RESOURCES

When personnel, physical resources, and time do not allow a full application of the principles described in this text, it is still possible to improve instruction over what would otherwise be used if systematic instructional design were not employed. For example, when resources do not allow for a full learning task analysis, it is better to informally reflect on lesson goals and the kinds of learning that should lead up to them rather than to be totally unconcerned with prerequisites. When time does not allow a full four-phase formative evaluation, it is better to try out materials with a few learners and keep in mind the need for future revision than it is to be unaware of the value of feedback and verification of materials by the learners themselves. In many cases within the text, we have suggested a few of these less-demanding alternatives, as the following examples illustrate.

Needs Assessment

"For teachers or trainers who are designing instruction for their own classrooms, a needs assessment can be rather informal but is nonetheless important. At the most basic level, such needs assessment can be directed at determining what portions of the curriculum involve learning tasks with which, year after year, a large number of students experience difficulty in learning and for which no readily available instructional solution exists" (Chapter 3, p. 43).

Learner Analysis

"How do designers find out about the general characteristics of the target audience? If the designers are developing for their own classrooms, they can observe, talk to, and assess their learners to determine their characteristics. Even then they may wish to conduct some additional research to find out more about the learners" (Chapter 4, p. 70).

*These comments come from classes that Prof. Briggs taught at Florida State University.

Task Analysis

"How can we determine what the information-processing steps are for a particular goal? One of the simplest and most often-used techniques is to simply do a mental review of the steps that one might go through in completing a task. And often, that is exactly what we do if time is short or the task is simple" (Chapter 5, p. 83).

Instructional Strategy

"Although these instructional events have been synthesized from a review of research, if you observe master teachers, you may see them including these events whether they have heard of them or not. Teachers probably follow this pattern because they have discovered that students who experience these events tend to learn better than students who do not" (Chapter 7, p. 131).

Instructional Delivery

"These media are not by any means necessary to learn intellectual skills. For instance, many generations have been educated without the use of computer-driven interactive video systems. However, one of these alternatives will be the medium of choice in instances where its attributes are needed. In other words, many intellectual skills are readily learned by all learners in the target population through books, handouts, or conventional media. Conventional media should be used when they will work as well as more elaborate technologies" (Chapter W-1, p. 6).

Formative Evaluation

"Trying out materials with learners can help instructional developers determine where revisions are necessary. As a matter of fact, materials that have been tried out with only one or two representative students and then revised based on the information gained are substantially more effective than the original instruction" (Chapter 19, p. 327).

"If there were many problems in instruction and the revisions were substantial, the designer may wish to go through another round of one-to-one evaluations before proceeding to the next stage. If money or time is not available for further evaluation, the designer has still obtained information that helps eliminate most severe problems. This allows for a product that is substantially more effective than it was before the revisions" (Chapter 19, p. 331).

CRITICALITY

The extent to which a task may be deemed "critical" should influence the level of instructional design effort. Among the dimensions of criticality is that of hazard. Instruction for potentially hazardous tasks, such as operating nuclear power plants, parachute packing, controlling air traffic, and providing medical assistance, involves learning skills that, if neglected or improperly performed, can lead to life-threatening consequences for the trainee and/or other people. Our technological society has made it increasingly possible for one person's actions to put not only their own safety in jeopardy but also the safety and welfare of thousands of others. Training for such tasks is a serious business, not to be left to serendipity or happenstance.

Another dimension of criticality is the requirement for homogeneity of goals. For some critical tasks, everyone must be able to perform at the same level. For example, aircraft mechanics must be predictable in their assembly of engines after tear-down. One aircraft mechanic's skills must be very much like those of the others, whereas a great deal more variability in achievement level can be tolerated among graduates of a barber school. Frequently, the need for homogeneity of achievement level is based on some hazard-related concern, as would be the case with aircraft mechanics. Sometimes the need for homogeneity of mastery is based on other factors, such as management, product quality, or cost-control. An example is the training of fast-food industry employees: it is important to the success of a chain of hamburger restaurants that each restaurant serve hamburgers that consistently represent that chain's product. Training of employees is a major contributor to ensuring that consistency.

Criticality has been considered previously in this text, particularly in the design of assessments: In life-and-death situations, such as training learners in CPR, training parachute packers, or training employees in safety practices, we should be less willing to make compromises in validity and reliability in order to bow to issues of practicality. Resources should be made available to ensure the most highly reliable and valid instruments possible in such circumstances. In contrast, in cases of informal education, such as a community-center course on embroidery, the consequences of incorrect assessment of competence may not have severe consequences for anyone, in which case more radical compromises might be made for the sake of practicality (Chapter 6).

Another dimension of criticality is the centrality of the goal to be achieved. This aspect appears in K–12 education as well as in training environments. Some skills or knowledge is so central to learning that if it is not acquired, future learning is in jeopardy. An example of such a central feature is acquiring reading comprehension ability in elementary school or being able to apply the concept of "variance" in statistics. These central skills and knowledge may also be difficult to acquire. Such central goals are critical and require careful design.

Instruction for critical tasks must be designed and conducted with the best that our field has to offer. On the other hand, a great deal of education is conducted in which the exact learning task is not critical. Frequently in such situations, those who deliver the educational experiences are not even concerned about defining the learning goal at hand, much less the criticality of that learning goal. Such situations are often found in those educational environments that are as much care-taking as they are instructional. In educational situations that are more activity-centered, many proceed under vague, changing, or pluralistic goals for learning. This results in a situation in which some of the tools of instructional design may not be applied with the same rigor as situations where attainment of particular learning goals is imperative. In some of these situations, achievement of specific learning goals may not be considered as "critical."

ACCOUNTABILITY

Related to criticality, accountability has to do with the degree to which the ID developers and the organization delivering the instruction are held seriously accountable for the effects of training, especially poor performance after instruction. There have been situations in which litigation has been instigated against instructional agencies (school systems and training agencies) because the instruction was deemed inadequate. This can lead to serious implications. Sample (1989) discussed the issue of liability in "failing to train to standard." After summarizing and illustrating the legal theory behind civil suits involving forms of liability applicable to deficiencies in training (under 43 United States Code [USC], Sec. 1983 and 42 USC, Sec. 1983), Sample provides an eight-step set of recommendations for preventing and limiting liability for failure to train to standard. In summary form, these recommendations are as follows: (1) appropriate job-task analysis; (2) development of appropriate job-related performance measures; (3) modification of selection criteria for hiring personnel who would perform high-liability tasks; (4) use of a standard instructional systems design model to inform and guide the instructional design process; (5) development of educational units employing certification procedures to document individual competence in high-liability

tasks; (6) use of field supervisors employing qualification procedures on the job shortly after training and at regular intervals thereafter; (7) maintenance of records of training and written documentation of concerns; and (8) the purchase of individual liability insurance.

For situations in which the possibility of legal or moral responsibility is high, particularly in cases in which criticality is also a factor, instructional design should be applied precisely and formally documented. Although such care may not avoid legal suits and/or personal anguish, it will certainly provide information justifying decisions that were made in the design process.

EXPECTATIONS/REQUIREMENTS OF THE CLIENT AGENCY

The expectations and requirements of the client agency for the scale of the instructional design effort vary. Not all client agencies want or need equal effort (and expense) in their instructional design projects. Within a single agency, not all projects will be given the same priority. And priorities for attention to the various phases and facets of the instructional design process will also vary within an organization. For example, organization *A* may be accustomed to spending a great deal of effort on task analysis but relatively little on formative evaluation, while organization *B* may prefer (and find it natural and inevitable) to spend less time on task analysis and more on formative evaluation. Policy makers within the organization have ideas as to the amount of effort each project should be given. The wise instructional designer will be sensitive to this reality and not expect that all projects will be given unlimited design and development resources. Not only are we talking about the difference in the amount that can be spent on the production of materials, we are also addressing the question of level of effort in the design *process* itself. There are many occasions when a less ambitious approach will yield completely satisfactory results for the problems and priorities at hand.

WHAT INSTRUCTIONAL DESIGNERS DO

Which instructional design activities do practicing instructional designers actually incorporate into their systematic design? Wedman and Tessmer (1992) examined this question by surveying 35 practicing instructional designers. Although their data are potentially biased because the majority of the respondents were from one training agency, the findings identify for this group of designers those aspects of design that are deemed "most appropriate" to the particular situations in which they most commonly operated. The activities that the respondents "always" or "usually" performed are listed in the following table:

ID Activity	Percentage of Respondents
Write learning objectives	94
Select media formats	86
Select instructional strategies	85
Develop test items	82
Summative evaluation	75
Identify types of learning	74
Determine if need requires instruction	70
Conduct task analysis	66
Conduct needs assessment	63
Assess entry skills	54
Formative evaluation	49

It is interesting to note that with the exception of formative evaluation, at least half of the respondents reported doing all of the ID activities about which Wedman and Tessmer asked them in most situations. The three phases of design that we have identified as essential—analysis in the form of objectives (Where are we going?), strategy selection (How will we get there?), and assessment item writing (How will we know when we're there?)—were the most frequently employed aspects of instruction design.

Wedman and Tessmer also asked the respondents for reasons why the ID activities might be eliminated. Surprisingly, the two most frequently cited reasons were not limitations in time and money, but "decision already made" and "considered unnecessary." These reasons for omitting ID processes were most frequently cited for the following activities: needs assessment, determine if need can be resolved by training, conduct task analysis, assess entry skills, and pilot test. "Not enough time" was frequently identified as a reason to omit needs assessment, task analysis, and formative evaluation. Formative evaluation was the only design activity for which "cost constraints" was frequently identified as a reason for omission.

This study was preliminary and descriptive in nature. There is no way to know which factors were considered in determining whether to *include* certain design activity. Also, we do not know to what degree of precision or formality an activity had to be completed for the designers to consider it completed. However, we feel that considering the constraints under which designers frequently operate, it is very encouraging that they are able to include so much design so frequently.

Winer and Vazquez-Abad (1995) conducted a replication of Wedman and Tessmer's study with members of the National Society for Performance and Instruction in Montreal. These respondents answered the same questions as the participants in the Wedman and Tessmer study. There were some significant differences in responses between the two groups: The Montreal designers engaged in entry skills assessment 76 percent of the time, as compared to 54 percent in the original study, and they conducted pilot testing 77 percent of the time, in comparison to 49 percent in the Wedman and Tessmer group. When asked why certain design activities were not done, the Montreal group differed from the Wedman and Tessmer group on two reasons. "Client won't support" was given more often by the Montreal group, and "considered unnecessary" was given less often by the Montreal group. The most significant difference between the two groups was their different attitudes and inclusion rates for pilot testing. The Montreal group considered pilot testing more necessary and engaged in it more often.

How do inexperienced and experienced instructional designers differ? Pieters and Bergman (1995) surveyed graduates of the Educational Technology program at the University of Twente regarding their practice of instructional design activities. Although their responses cannot considered representative, as only about 30 percent of the graduates returned the surveys, some interesting findings suggest further study. For example, the more experienced designers reported a greater emphasis on problem definition and analysis activities than the novices. The novices reported more activities involving contact with clients.

What are the important features of successful ID projects? Greer (1992) asked readers of *Performance and Instruction* who were involved in instructional design activities to respond to a survey regarding the nature of their jobs and what factors led to successful ID projects. Halprin and Greer (1993) reported the results from the twenty-eight readers who responded. During project planning the respondents found the following factors to contribute to project success:

- Adequate support by project sponsors and senior managers.
- Clear definition of project objectives, time frames and roles of team members.
- Close adherence to the needs assessment findings and recommendations.
- Clear communications plans. (p. 17)

During design, development, and production, the following factors were deemed as important to project success:

- Excellent subject matter experts.
- Dedicated and highly motivated instructional designers.

- Talents of the production staff.
- Outcomes of the project were well-defined.
- Systematic ID process was followed.
- Instructional strategy was effective. (p. 17)

Halprin and Greer also discussed factors that inhibit project success. The most commonly mentioned problems were time, cost, and production problems.

In summary, instructional designers in training environments appear to include many instructional design activities in their jobs. They do not include all activities in all situations, but rather appear to adjust their design model to the circumstances of the design task. Unfortunately, we do not have the same types of data from instructional designers who work in K–12-school-related jobs.

Four Ways to Adapt the ID Process

In the introduction to their study of adapting instructional design practice to the requirements of a situation, Wedman and Tessmer (1990) cited their "Practitioner's Lament" with which they represent the practicing instructional designer's quandary:

What do you do
When you have no time
No time to do "model" ID?
Do you skip some steps,
Or water them down,
Combine, or maybe all three? (p. 2)

We have identified four different approaches as techniques for dealing with situations in which full or "traditional" implementation of instructional design practice may not be possible. These approaches involve skipping design tasks, combining design tasks, and "watering down" design tasks in order to meet the requirements and constraints of the situation. Each of these approaches deals in its own way with the question of "appropriate" design (in terms of resources, criticality, and accountability). These approaches are (1) the layers of necessity model, (2) rapid prototyping, (3) windows of opportunity, and (4) use of computer resources to assist the design process.

One model to guide the designer is found in Tessmer and Wedman's **layers of necessity** model (1990; Wedman & Tessmer, 1991), which emphasizes performing the design process in multiple layers, with each layer representing a complete cycle of design activity. (This is a kind of elaboration, similar in concept to the Elaboration Model for organizing instruction.) This model proposes five fundamental phases of design: situational assessment, goal analysis, instructional strategy development, materials development, and evaluation and revision. Each of these phases can have multiple and more formal aspects. For example, "situational analysis" may include a formal needs assessment and learner preassessments.

Design projects requiring a higher degree of sophistication and care will cascade the process to further layers, with each layer more extensive and elaborated than the previous one. Thus projects with minimal requirements from a resources and criticality standpoint may be well served by instructional design that produces "good enough for now" instruction. For instruction that requires it, more sophisticated design work is done over time in subsequent design/development efforts. The researchers provided principles for selecting layers—determining what instructional design activities would be engaged in for a given project—in a subsequent paper (Wedman & Tessmer, 1991). The principles reflect the relationships between the factors of load (or costs), payoff, and pressure. A potential limitation of the layers-of-necessity approach is that it is heuristic, rather than algorithmic: Its successful use depends on the user's ID experience. A further discussion of context-sensitive design is provided in Tessmer and Wedman (1995).

A second approach for an experienced designer to take when money and time are very limited is **rapid prototyping** (Tripp & Bichelmeyer, 1990). A prototype is an "executable version" of the final instructional product (Jones, Li, and Merrill, 1992). It is generally used to effectively and concretely communicate with the client an idea of what the final product will be like. In contrast to noniterative design approaches, the instructional media are selected early in the design process and the prototypes for instruction are rendered in the media of the final product.

Rather than using a layered approach, Tripp and Bichelmeyer recommended an overlapping approach in which the analysis phase overlaps both the development and formative evaluation phases. In other words, the designer actually begins the design work while conducting the front-end analysis. Overlapping functions illustrated in Figure 20.1 represent the idea that "the analysis of needs and content depends in part on the knowledge that is gained by actually building and using a prototype instructional system" (p. 35). For an experienced designer who can anticipate the results of much of the analysis, and in cases in which the instructional medium is mutable (such as a computer program), rapid prototyping may be useful. You might recognize this as an example of "combining steps," a technique Wedman and Tessmer mentioned in their "Practitioner's Lament." Potential limitations of rapid prototyping is that it requires experienced designers, its successful use is strongly dependent on the quality and quantity of information that is available early in the

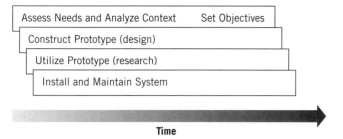

Time

Figure 20.1 Rapid Prototyping ISD Model.
Source: Adapted from Tripp & Bichelmeyer (1990). Used with permission of Macmillan Publishing Company.

project, and it may be more susceptible to the "whims" of the design staff.

A third approach, which Noel (1991) recommended based upon his experience, is a **windows of opportunity** strategy. He was involved in a large-scale development of a middle school curriculum for Botswana. As a result of his experiences, he concluded that in such a mega-project in which any designer may enter at any time, it may not be possible to follow the entire systematic process with all components of the project. Noel recommended looking for "windows of opportunity" in which systematic design procedures are timely and appropriate. He gave the example of a project in which he was only able to use the instructional design phase of formative evaluation. He seized the opportunity to make substantial improvements by using a particular phase of the process as a "tool." Even though Noel's experience was with a rather large-scale project, similar compromises may be made in smaller scale projects in which time and resources are limited. Knowledge of the full instructional design process assists people who need to make such compromises. They are in a good position to predict problems that may occur and develop "work-arounds" for deficiencies resulting from compromises. You might recognize from the "Practitioner's Lament" that this is an example of "skipping steps." The "windows of opportunity" option can be limited in that it requires flexibility and confidence from the designer, its effects are unpredictable, its principles are not yet documented, and it requires experienced designers for its best use.

A fourth approach is the use of **computer resources** to assist in the design process. Gayeski (1991) described many software tools that can be used to assist in the design and development process in various ways. Examples of such systems described by Gayeski include the following: Alberta Research Council and Computer-Based Training Systems, Ltd.'s computer-assisted course and curriculum development environment; U.S. Air Force Subject Outline Curriculum Resource and Tutoring Expert System (SOCRATES); Courseware, Inc., Computer-Aided Analysis (CAA); U.S. Army Automated Systems Approach

to Training (ASAT); Gustafson and Reeves IDioM course development expert system; OmniCom Associates Design Station and Content Expert Interviewer (CAI); Automated Test Development Aid (ATDA); U.S. Army Research Institute Automated Knowledge Acquisition Tool (AKAT); AT&T's Training Delivery Consultant and Training Test Consultant; Sealand & Associates CBT Cost Justification Model; U.S. Navy Authoring Instructional Materials software (AIM); Simulation Design Tool for Training Development (SDTD); Elron Technologies, Inc., Automated Courseware Expert (ACE); and Electronic Vision, Inc., Interactive Video Design Toolkit. As an example, the AIM software created by the Navy has been used in the development of almost 150 courses by 1993 (Wulfeck, Dickieson, Apple, & Vogt, 1993). It supports the following *curriculum development* functions: developing a profile of the learners, creating a training path for each learner, selecting an introduction and objectives, developing a trainer manual, and generating learner handout.

An ambitious project in using expert system computer resources to enhance the instructional design process, which is under way as of this writing, is the Utah State University "Second Generation Instructional Research Project" (Merrill, 1994; Merrill, Li, & Jones, 1990a, 1990b). Insufficient research evidence exists at this time to conclude for which designers and in which situations such automated tools may be appropriate.

Spector, Polson, and Muraida (1993) and Spector and Ohrazda (2004) have presented many of the issues and difficulties in attempting to automate the instructional design process, such as an expert system, and creating a computer-based instructional design tool, such as an advisor. Numerous automated tools that assist designers in one or more design activities have reached completion and are available for instructional designers' use (e.g., *Designer's Edge*™ developed by Allen Communications; *ID Expert* developed by M. David Merrill and associates (Merrill, 1998); and *PlanAnalyst*, a Macintosh application developed by Bernie Dodge (1994). Potential limitations of the automated tools option is that such tools may limit flexibility and adaptability of the design approach, the initial outlay for the system may be expensive, and the quality of the design highly depends on the quality of the system.

The implications of the adaptations of the instructional design process described above are many and not completely understood at present. There is a clear trend toward improving the efficiency of the overall process. The old expression "All solutions bring new problems" certainly applies to instructional design. Instructional designers must answer the following questions: How will the role of designers change? What knowledge will designers need? Since no one can answer these questions with any certainty, it appears likely that genuine expertise and depth of knowledge of instructional design will become more important in the future. Intelligent decision making in selecting from alternatives such as rapid prototyping or different forms of computer assistance will require a better understanding of instructional design than that required of the typical designer in day-to-day work that employs conventional means. Furthermore, making good use of the products of alternative approaches to design will require a high degree of instructional design expertise to avoid mistakes on a grander scale than previously thought possible.

Figure 20.2 presents a fast-track option selection aid (Smith, Ragan, McMichael, & Miles, 1993) to support a designer's decisions regarding which type of fast-track option to use under particular conditions. The three conditions that we have chosen as key to such decisions are amount of development time available (low/high), accountability of the design agency (low/high), and criticality of the learning goal (low/high) (factors that we discussed earlier in this chapter). As accountability and criticality of learning goal tend to co-vary (if one is high, the other tends to be high and vice versa), we have included them together as one decision point. A fourth factor that could be considered in this aid is the level of expertise of the instructional designer.

E X E R C I S E   A

1. Directions: For each of the following three scenarios involving the development of instruction, consider the level of precision and formality that can/should be employed in the instructional design procedures. Be prepared to discuss your answers.

Scenario 1: You are the instructional designer for a $1.5 million project sponsored by the National Science Foundation to develop a predominantly print-based, tenth-grade general science curriculum for students who are not college-bound. Your time lines indicate a distribution date 36 months after project start-up.

Scenario 2: You are the instructional designer for an in-house project to develop training for managers at a long-distance phone company on legal issues involved in interviewing and hiring. Since there has been some recent new legislation, it is imperative that the employees acquire this knowledge as soon as possible. You have decided to make the instruction via stand-up delivery, with the first class five months after project start-up. Your deliverables are an instructor's guide (including lecture notes and overhead transparency masters), a ten-minute introductory video, a student handbook, and all assessment instruments.

Scenario 3: You are a fourth-grade public school teacher. It is Saturday afternoon and you are developing your lesson plans for next week. You must plan for instruction in reading, language arts, math, social studies, science, art, music, and physical education for the week.

2. What features must instructional planning include in order for you to feel right about considering the planning as reflecting instructional design? List them and provide a rationale for your decision.

3. Refer to exercise 4 in Chapter 19. Would you recommend a fast-track option to Ms. Sanders? Why or why not? If you would recommend an option, which would you recommend and why?

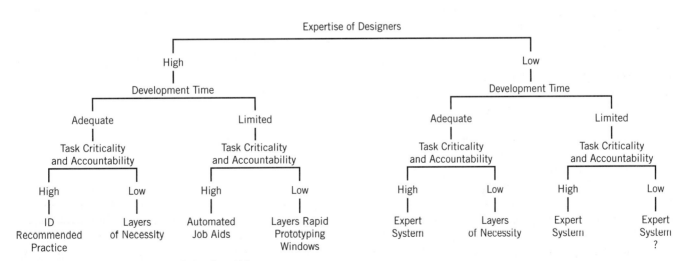

Figure 20.2   Fast-track Options Selection Aid

FUTURE DIRECTIONS FOR INSTRUCTIONAL DESIGN

As a form of technology (a *process* technology), instructional design is one area in which we should be able to anticipate particularly rapid and significant change. Whereas distant future estimates are anybody's guess, some near future predictions have a high probability of becoming reality. Having an idea of what to look out for can help the designer keep up with changes and developments in the field. The following paragraphs reflect the incredibly wide array of technical and scientific work in progress. Among the thousands of candidates, we have selected six areas of work that we have reason to believe will yield significant contributions to instructional design in the near future: microelectronic technologies, ID tools and models, new contexts, and new assumptions.

Microelectronic Technologies

INFORMATION INFRASTRUCTURES. The *World Wide Web,* a global interconnection of computers along with graphical front-end interfaces called "Web browsers," has been hailed as a more significant development than the personal computer. Although characterizing such a complex, capable system in one statement oversimplifies, the single quality that more than any other seems to set the Web apart is the more or less instant and, by some measures, free, distribution of interactive multimedia materials in addition to text and database applications to a potential global audience. The amount of material that is available on the Web and its ability to facilitate searching, both within sites and across them, makes it qualitatively different from any communications technology that has preceded it. Its potential for providing educational resources and experiences on a worldwide basis seems unprecedented. Development of high-quality Web-suited learning resources and educational programs on large and small scales are in use (Kahn, 1997, 2001). Web-assisted and Web-delivered courses and entire degree programs are widely available on the Web.

A potential downside to Web-based learning resources at this time is the lack of "refereeing" for information accuracy and potential bias in information-directed searches, and attrition and effectiveness issues with instructional programs. Metadata projects may become of increasing assistance in the information issue, and accrediting agencies may assist in quality control. Current instructional and educational resource development can benefit from what is state-of-the-art in instructional design and the future evolution of instructional design should be anticipated to support and improve future online education development.

As the Internet's utility and power seems destined to continue to grow, intranets—local networks—are as well becoming increasingly integrated, convenient, and powerful. Information infrastructures are becoming able to serve learning in both individual and collaborative modes, making informal, self-directed learning increasingly fused with intentioned or formal learning and instruction. Many experts anticipate that it will become increasingly difficult to differentiate the kind of information help offered by the electronic information infrastructure and the help offered by a person. What is more ambitious now than information provision is the ability of the information infrastructure to offer events supporting learning such as learning guidance and feedback. A promising development along those lines is the development of online learning communities. Online learning communities use the Web for learning in more ways than just provision of information and can be expected to grow in significance in the future. For an interesting example that fuses the Internet with powerful intranets, explore the Aurora Learning Community Association on the Web by using "ALCA" in a Web search.

EXPERT SYSTEMS AND SMART OBJECTS. In 1984, more than twenty years ago as of this writing, Roger Schank observed that of all the potential applications under consideration, including military, construction, medicine, and transportation, it was education—specifically the delivery of instruction—that appeared to have the greatest potential benefit from *artificial intelligence* (A.I.). The benefit from machine-based mixed-initiative instruction (intelligent tutors) has yet to be felt in any widespread way, despite the fact that many research and development projects have seen successful completion. A primary limitation stems from the amount of time and effort that intelligent tutors and ICAI (intelligent computer-assisted instruction) require. It is likely that developments in A.I. authoring and knowledge bases may make ICAI development a less daunting task. Another application of A.I. techniques that appears to have particularly high promise in instruction is the use of expert systems as instructional designers. It may be more efficient in the short run to employ machine intelligence to help *design* the instruction rather than to *deliver* it. This is because of the wide applicability of an expert system designer, as compared to the more limited utility of an expert system created to teach a particular set of objectives or a subject (Merrill, Li, & Jones, 1990a, 1990b; Spector and Ohrazda, 2004).

Smart objects, a more current development of interest, are micro-level devices integrated within other objects such as toys, tools, and appliances. Smart objects may be less ambitious than older more broadly-targeted A.I. efforts, and consequently may be more feasible. A goal of smart objects as of this writing is "awareness" of environment and consequent ability to anticipate a user's intent for use of that object. The abilities of individual smart objects may be enhanced with partnership in the information infrastructure. Nanotechnology and robotics may contribute as well.

INTERACTIVE TECHNOLOGIES. In the 1980s and 1990s, CD-ROMs became widely employed to deliver instructional and training software. The more recent DVDs provide high-quality motion video in a compact, digital format. CDs continue to be widely used for both storage for textual materials and interactive multimedia training. DVD's add to these capabilities high quality video. These technologies—as well as others that involve the marriage of video, computers, and sometimes other media, such as telecommunications systems and print—have enormous promise in increasing the density and processing of digital information to and from visual and auditory materials. And, as more and more of these technologies become wireless, their impact and integration with people's lives increases.

Although interactive technologies are not required to support artificial intelligence and adaptive instruction, the number of instructional-medium attributes of materials and experiences that they can support should increase dramatically. Highly realistic simulations, up to and including virtual reality, may become available with affordable equipment. If this happens, we may see the emergence of *virtual learning communities*.

Instructional Design Tools and Models

In the future, we can expect the models that we employ to guide instructional design to become increasingly powerful, sophisticated, and efficient. Over twenty-five years ago, Hannum and Hansen (1989) provided a particularly insightful and prescient discussion of changes that could be anticipated in instructional design thinking. Although many of their projections are reflected as reality in this text and other resources in our field, not all of Hannum and Hansen's points are even yet addressed by current practice. Hannum and Hansen noted the following five changes in ID models as ways in which they may be broadened from their original roots in behavioral learning psychology, general systems theory, and audiovisual and communications theory:

1. Front-end analysis shaped by anthropological methods.
2. Design and delivery shaped by the psychology of perception and cognitive sciences.
3. Implementation shaped by market research techniques.

4. Evaluation influenced by anthropology and sociology.
5. Design of training programs shaped by job design.

Other improvements in instructional design models that are described include the following:

1. Development of alterable models.
2. Development of iterative rather than linear models, which can model the movement back and forth between phases to revisit those steps that need it based on subsequent decisions.
3. "Layered" models within models that elaborate on design procedures.
4. Graduated models, from the ideal to the "quick and dirty." (Hannum & Hansen, 1989)

In addition, we expect much more attention to the principles underlying design (from learning, psychology, sociology, communications, human factors, etc.) than the particular model that is followed. We also anticipate seeing a greater appreciation of the influence of society and culture in all decisions that are made.

PERFORMANCE TECHNOLOGY. In the future, business and industry may increasingly use the "performance technology" standpoint rather than "instruction" as the umbrella under which instructional design operates. People who practice in this area are often called *performance technologists*. The performance technologist is interested in instruction as only one tool among many alternatives, which can range all the way from provision of job aids and incentives to delivery of psychological or counseling services. For the performance technologist, the central concern is not learning but performance on the job. Learning may or may not be what is needed in a particular situation. This point of view is entirely consistent with our view of instructional design as evidenced in Chapter 3 (especially the section on determining instructional needs). Although it is a somewhat different standpoint, performance technology is not at all contradictory to instructional design as we have described it. In a business or industry that employs a performance technology approach, instructional design will (or should be) the primary area of expertise held by those who—once instruction is determined to be needed—will be the key agents in its development. Thus far, the relevance of performance technology has been restricted to business and industry, although the role that it could play in public education has not been ignored (Earle, 1994; Shrock, 1990). Gilbert's (1978) and Gery's (1991) texts are good sources of more information on performance technology.

The competencies and knowledge base that performance technologists require have been identified by a number of sources (Brethower, 1995; Dean, 1995a,

1995b; Gayeski, 1995; Stolovitch, Keeps, & Rodrigue, 1995). Numerous authors have recommended the characteristics of a suitable academic preparation for performance technologists (Carr, 1995; Harless, 1995; Medsker, Hunter, Stepich, Rowland, & Basnet, 1995). Traditional instructional design programs have varied in the degree that they have incorporated performance technology courses into their curriculum (Dick & Wager, 1995; Rossett, 1990). Some programs have developed cooperative programs with HRD, business, psychology, and other programs that teach about solutions to performance problems other than training. Some have incorporated one or two courses in their instructional design programs. Other programs have attempted to provide an orientation to performance technology in some of their existing courses. It is critical that instructional design students who plan to work in training settings develop knowledge, if not skills, in interventions that are alternatives to training. Without this orientation designers may have difficulty in recognizing performance problems that are amenable to non-training solutions. With some exposure to issues of incentives, performance support systems, selection, ergonomics, organizational development, and organizational psychology, instructional designers can work cooperatively with specialists that are skilled in designing and implementing these other interventions.

ELECTRONIC PERFORMANCE SUPPORT SYSTEMS. An outgrowth of the performance support concept discussed above, electronic Performance Support Systems (EPSS) are computer-based information systems designed to deliver just-in-time training (Hudspeth, 1992). The purpose of EPSSs is to provide necessary information and cognitive tools at the time and place where they are needed in the work setting (Gery, 1991). Although individuals can learn (i.e., acquire new capability) from such systems, EPSSs are often designed as an alternative to training. That is, they are designed to fill immediate information needs, like the help files in applications software or like the cue cards on a photocopier. Some EPSSs are designed to play an advisory role by anticipating users' information needs or providing hints to help users locate and utilize the information they need. Other EPSSs include conventional computer-based training. Instructional designers in some training environments are developing EPSSs as part of the solutions for performance problems. One of the major issues in designing such systems is to determine what knowledge can be available but not necessarily learned, what information needs made require advisement, and what job skills must be solidly learned.

ADVANCES IN THEORY. Developments in foundational elements will find their way into application through fu-

ture generations of instructional design theories, models, and principles. People who are interested in instructional design will stay abreast of new developments in learning, cognition, human information processing, perception, philosophies, and the role of culture and society in learning that may bear on instruction. Translation of new knowledge about learning, cognition, and other bases into instructional design principles and practice will change what we consider as feasible. Just as we have seen in the past twenty-five years, in the future we can expect to see science and philosophy contributing to instruction by making it more efficient, effective, and appealing than ever before. Issues that continue to be of interest, pointing to future directions in the field are (1) supplantive versus generative instructional strategies, (2) instruction in cognitive or learning strategies, (3) the affective aspects of learning, (4) the role that context and the learning community plays in an individual's and a group's learning. Each of these issues has been discussed at length previously in this text:

1. Increased maturation of instructional theory is leading us to realize that both supplantive and generative instructional strategies have their place in instruction. We have tried to point this out in the chapters of this text that deal with instructional strategies (Chapter 7).

2. A matter of some debate is where to place the emphasis between teaching learners to be better learners on their own—instruction in cognitive strategies or learning strategies—and development of instruction in the areas to be learned (Chapters 2 and 13).

3. The affective aspects of learning is a third area of current and future interest, given our increased recognition of the importance of motivation in learning and our improving tools for designing instruction that is appealing (Chapter 14).

4. The study of learning within social contexts is being forwarded with energy and brilliance by scholars in the area of learning science. We can anticipate substantial help from learning scientists in our understanding of the role of context in learning, the interactions of learners and context, and the design of exploratory and situated learning. (Chapter 3)

In the future, we expect an expansion of the theoretical body of knowledge that instructional designers must investigate. From Performance Technology areas like theories that influence the theories related to artificial intelligence design, organizational theory, and organizational psychology will be more utilized by designers. Many will also expand their knowledge about curriculum theory, research and theory related to teachers' thought processes and planning, and educational reform. In addition, theories related the influence of society on learning and language will have an increasing importance for instructional designers.

New Contexts: Public School Applications of Instructional Design

Leaders in the field of instructional design have developed a commitment to improving the quality of public education through implementation of instructional design practice in the schools. They have proposed two very different approaches to this implementation: preparing teachers and pre-service teachers to apply instructional design principles in their classes or restructuring school to incorporate more systematically designed technology-based instruction.

PREPARING TEACHERS TO DO INSTRUCTIONAL DESIGN.   It is fairly common to find teacher education programs that include instructional design in the curriculum, either as integrated into media design courses (Savenye, Davidson, & Smith, 1991), as a single course Klein (1990), or in more than one course (Reiser & Radford, 1990). Although course assessments indicate that students in these courses do learn to use instructional design principles (Klein, 1990; Reiser & Radford, 1990; Savenye et. al., 1991), a study by Reiser (1994) suggested that the longer teacher education students have been out of the class, the less they use instructional design skills. However, a study by Reiser and Mory (1991) that examined the planning of a former student from a graduate design class found that she continued to use instructional design principles far more thoroughly and consistently that an experienced fellow teacher who had no formal ID instruction. In a comparison of ID-instructed and non-instructed teachers across the United States, Martin (1990) found that both groups of teachers reported using ID principles in their planning. In most of these studies much of the teachers' ID-based planning was done mentally. Very little of the process was recorded in plan books. This approach seems consistent with our "appropriate technology" perspective described earlier in this chapter. To date, we can find no research investigating the effects of ID-based planning on students' classroom performance.

Many educators in the ID field believe that the focus of instructional designers' efforts should be at the point where everyday decisions are made, at the point where the major influence on learning appears to be, with the teachers. A number of educators insist that the impact of ID-instruction on students' performances is too limited, too little, and too late. They suggest that instructional design may have a more important impact at another level, by impacting the instructional materials, particularly the technology-based materials, that are used in schools. We believe that preparing teachers to plan systematically will have little influence without well-designed instructional materials and that well-designed instructional materials will have little impact if teachers do not use and value some fundamental principles of instructional design.

RESTRUCTURING SCHOOLS THROUGH INSTRUCTIONAL DESIGN.   Technology has made implementation of major innovations in curricula feasible but still not widespread in public education in the United States. Computers are fairly widely used in these settings (particularly to teach computer skills), but the curricular reforms that computers and other technology make possible and that have been demonstrated repeatedly (e.g., the Cognition and Technology Group, 1992; and the Peakview School experience reported by Wilson, Hamilton, Teslow, & Cyr, 1994) have not seen widespread, common use. Interestingly, education and training in other settings such as business and military environments has seen a greater influence from technology than American public education. In other words, technology (particularly computer technology) has made possible improvements in school curricula and instructional practices on a large scale that have not yet been implemented on a large scale. Why? In order to fully enjoy the benefits of technology, a restructuring of public education in the United States will be required. Current school system organization is based on independent, virtually autonomous school districts established and maintained at the township level, and reliance on a teacher-in-classroom functional organization for delivery and management of learning experiences. Commendable school restructuring work, which emphasizes empowerment of teachers, is well underway (Peterson, McCarthey, & Elmore, 1996; Reigeluth, Garfinkle, & Carr, 1995). In addition, other structural changes in the system of public education will be required to make nontrivial applications technology on a widespread basis.

The most interesting and powerful uses of technology in both education and training appear to be in those that clearly fit within integrated curriculum designs. The World Wide Web is most widely viewed as an exploratory learning environment; interest in computer-based instruction has been supplanted by interest in computer-based learning environments; informative video is considered passé, while interest is high in interactive multimedia that support exploration and interaction with microworlds and simulations. There is no lack of interest in the design and development of technology-based instruction of a highly generative sort.

If we can recall the plight of the 1930s school teacher in a progressive school (p. 294), teaching the entire third-grade curriculum through projects, we remember that the genius and effort required was beyond the capacities of most mortals. Reconsider the same scenario with inclusion of the best technology can offer. Fitting a project with student interests can be facilitated with information on learners that was not feasible to gather before computer-based testing and recordkeeping. Project descriptions and materials to support projects can be made available on the Web in a variety that would not have been available to all but perhaps an extremely fortunate handful only a few years ago. Assistance in tracking student progress, and even expert system assistance in instructional management, can be delivered by computer. The mechanics of script development, set design, and even set construction can be facilitated by computer. The performance itself might be virtual, with the production being a multimedia presentation accessible by millions in a Web site.

The areas described as the future are both here and on the way. They are not only areas of development for which we can anticipate significant change and contributions to instructional design, but they also are all areas that have a high probability for interconnection and synergy. While we may be somewhat confident that these areas will be key to the future of instructional design, we are less certain as to what will emerge once we mix these elements together.

Instructional design is a "technology" of instruction in the most fundamental sense of the term. Too often we associate *technology* with equipment or with the uses of a class of equipment, such as computer technology. However, a technology consists as much of processes and ideas as it does of things and ways to use them. The history of technology has repeatedly confirmed that as a new and exciting device or system is used and developed, it becomes less and less important compared to the ideas, concepts, models, theories, and new technologies that evolve and emerge as products of its use.

In the past years, instructional design has been the most powerful and influential "technology" of instruction for the improvement of learning in business and industry, and government/military training, surpassing even popular and widely discussed product technologies such as computers and multimedia learning environments. Just as we can expect continuing advances in computer technology, video, telecommunications, and other media, we will also see advances in process technologies—not only those that may accompany various media but also the more comprehensive, integrative, and process-oriented technology of instructional design.

NEW ASSUMPTIONS

Instructional designers will continue to be challenged to consider their assumptions about what knowledge is and how it is acquired and their own value systems re-

garding learning. We will investigate the interplay of our own beliefs about knowledge, values, and ethics with those of our client agencies and prospective learners. When confronted with attributions of what we believe, such as "objectivism," we will be more knowledgeable and articulate about the accuracy of these attributions. We will begin to realize that our decisions are not "value free," that someone's values are being represented in these decisions, and we will more carefully consider the implications of these decisions on affected groups. When asked why we do particular things, we will be able to justify our actions both in theoretical and philosophical terms. Our assumptions may change or they may not, but, we hope, both old and new assumptions will be considered reflectively, not retaining old assumptions because they are comfortable nor accepting new assumptions because they are popular.

E X E R C I S E   B

Beginning with the instructional design model presented in Chapter 1 and using the chapter summaries and summary diagrams, construct your own representation of the content of this text. The process of constructing your own summary by incorporating the content of chapters within the framework of the design model can assist your assimilation of the ideas you have studied in this text. It may also improve your recall of the main points, and it should provide you with a graphic organizer to end all graphic organizers!

S U M M A R Y

This chapter provides four elements to conclude this text: a summary of major principles that guide instructional design, a review of what designers do in actual practice, a discussion of "appropriate" design, and a discussion of future developments.

The discussion of major principles guiding instructional design provided the reader with a summary of this text presented in a different light. The review of what designers do indicated that the "cup is half empty, and it's half full." That is, designers use instructional design skills and principles in their day-to-day jobs. However, one of the things that designers must learn is when and how to adjust design to the demands of the context. The discussion of appropriate design focused upon the proper level of engagement in design activities. The decision points bearing on that level center around questions of available resources for the design project and criticality of the learning task. The discussion of future developments provided areas in which we can anticipate significant changes in the near future. Indeed, there are so many changes in the evolution of instructional design that designers must be more and more grounded in the theories undergirding our field, more reflective in the educational philosophies associated with learning and instruction, more knowledgeable about the history of education and instructional design, more skilled in the application of design, and more experienced in the problem finding and solving that allows us to contribute to the future of others.

READINGS AND REFERENCES

Branch, R. C. (1994, March). Common instructional practices employed by secondary school teachers. *Educational Technology*, 25–34.

Brand, S. (1988). *The media lab: Inventing the future at M.I.T.* New York: Penguin.

Brethower, D. M. (1995). Specifying a human performance technology knowledge base. *Performance Improvement Quarterly, 8*(2), 17–39.

Brown, D. (1988). Twelve middle-school teachers' planning. *The Elementary School Journal, 89,* 69–87.

Carr, A. A. (1995). Performance technologist preparation: The role of leadership theory. *Performance Improvement Quarterly, 8*(4), 59–74.

Carr, C. (1992). PSS!: Help when you need it. *Training and Development,* 31–38.

Cennamo, K. S., & Ertmer, P. A. (1995, February) *Teaching instructional design: An apprenticeship model.* Paper presented at the annual conference of the Association for Educational Communications and Technology, Atlanta, GA.

Clark, C., & Peterson, P. (1986). Teacher's thought process. In M.C. Wittrock (Ed.), *Handbook of research on teaching* (pp. 255–296). New York: Macmillan.

Cognition and Technology Group. (1992). The Jasper experiment: An exploration of issues in learning and instructional design. *Educational Technology Research and Development, 40*(1), 65–80.

Darwazeh, A. N. (1995, February). *The effect of training in instructional designer competencies on teachers' planning routine and their students' academic achievement.* Paper presented at the annual conference of the Association for Educational Communications and Technology, Anaheim, CA.

Dean, P. J. (1995a). Examining the practice of Human Performance training. *Performance Improvement Quarterly, 8*(2), 68–94.

Dean, P. J. (1995b). The performance technologist's library. *Performance Improvement Quarterly, 8*(2) 144–149.

Dick, W. (1993). Enhanced ISD: A response to changing environments for learning and performance. *Educational Technology, 33*(2), 12–15.

Dick, W., & Wager, W. (1995). Preparing performance technologists: the role of a university. *Performance Improvement Quarterly, 8*(4), 34–42.

Dodge, B. J. (1994, February). Design and formative evaluation of PLANalyst: A lesson design tool. Paper presented at the annual meeting of the Association for Educational Communications and Technology, Nashville, TN.

Driscoll, M. P., Klein, J. D., & Sherman, G. P. (1994, March) Perspectives on instructional planning: How do teachers and instructional designers conceive of ISD planning practices. *Educational Technology,* 34–42.

Earle, R. S. (1994, March). Instructional design and the classroom teacher: looking back and moving ahead. *Educational Technology,* 6–10.

Gayeski, D. (1995). Changing roles and professional challenges for human performance technology. *Performance Improvement Quarterly, 8*(2), 6–16.

Gayeski, D. M. (1991). Software tools for empowering instructional developers. *Performance Improvement Quarterly, 4*(4), 21–36.

Gery, G. (1991). *Electronic performance support systems: How and why to remake the workplace through the strategic application of technology.* Boston: Weingarten Publications.

Gilbert, T. (1978). *Human competence: Engineering worthy performance.* New York: McGraw-Hill.

Greer, M. (1992, July). Critical attributes of ID project success: Part I. The survey. *Performance and Instruction,* 12–17.

Gustafson, K. L. (1993). Instructional design fundamentals: Clouds on the horizon. *Educational Technology, 33*(2), 27–35.

Halprin, M., & Greer, M. (1993, July). Critical attributes of ID project success: Part II. The survey results. *Performance and Instruction,* 15–21.

Hannum, W., & Hansen, C. (1989). *Instructional systems development in large organizations.* Englewood Cliffs, NJ: Educational Technology Publications.

Harless, J. (1995). Performance technology skills in business: Implications for preparation. *Performance Improvement Quarterly, 8*(4), 75–88.

Hlynka, D., & Belland, J. (1991). *Paradigms regained.* Englewood Cliffs, NJ: Educational Technology Publications.

Holcomb, C., Wedman, J. F., & Tessmer, M. (1996). ID activities and project success: Perceptions of practitioners. *Performance Improvement Quarterly, 9*(1), 49–61.

Hudspeth, D. (1992, June). Just-in-time education. *Educational Technology,* 7–11.

Hudzine, M., Rowley, K., & Wager, W. (1996). Electronic performance support technology: Defining the domain. *Performance Improvement Quarterly, 9*(1), 36–48.

Jones, M. K., Li, Z., & Merrill, M. D. (1992). Rapid prototyping in automated instructional design. *Educational Technology Research & Development, 40*(4), 95–100.

Kahn, B. (Ed.), (1997). *Web-based instruction.* Englewood Cliffs, NJ: Educational Technology.

Kahn, B. (Ed.), (2001). *Web-based training.* Englewood Cliffs, NJ: Educational Technology.

Kember, D., & Murphy, D. (1990). Alternative new directions for instructional design. *Educational Technology, 30*(8), 42–47.

Klein, J. (1991). Preservice teachers' use of learning and instructional design principles. *Educational Technology Research & Development, 39*(3) 83–89.

Martin, B. (1990). Talk about teaching: Instructional systems design within teacher education. *Educational Technology, 30*(5) 32–33.

McCutcheon, G. (1980). How do elementary school teachers plan? The nature of planning and influences on it. *The Elementary School Journal, 81,* 4–23.

Medsker, K., Hunter, P., Stepich, D., Rowland, G., & Basnet, K. (1995). HPT in academic curricula: survey results. *Performance Improvement Quarterly, 8*(4), 22–33.

Merrill, M. D. (1998). ID Expert: A second generation instructional development system. *Instructional Science, 26*, 243–262.

Merrill, M. D. (1994). *Instructional design theory.* Englewood Cliffs, NJ: Educational Technology Publications.

Merrill, M. D., Li, Z., & Jones, M. K. (1990a). Limitations of first generation instructional design. *Educational Technology, 30*(1), 7–11.

Merrill, M. D., Li, Z., & Jones, M. K. (1990b). Second generation instructional design. *Educational Technology, 30*(2), 7–14.

Muraida, D. J., & Spector, J. M. (1993). The advanced instructional design advisor. *Instructional Science, 21*, 239–253.

Noel, K. (1991, April). *An application of an ISD approach to curriculum development and change in a large-scale educational project: The case of Botswana.* Paper presented at the annual meeting of the American Research Association, Chicago, IL.

Perez, R. S., & Emery, C. (1995). Designer thinking: How novices and experts think about instructional design. *Performance Improvement Quarterly, 8*(3), 80–95.

Pieters, J. M., & Bergman, R. (1995). The empirical basis of designing instruction. *Performance Improvement Quarterly, 8*(3), 118–129.

Quinn, J. (1994). Connecting education and practice in an instructional design graduate program. *Educational Technology Research and Development, 42*(3), 71–82.

Quinn, J. (1995). The education of instructional designers: Reflections on the Tripp paper. *Performance Improvement Quarterly, 8*(3), 111–117.

Ragan, T. J., & Smith, P. L. (2004). "False dichotomies, red herrings, and straw men: Overcoming barriers to facilitating learning. *Educational Technology, 44*(3), 50–52.

Reiser, R. A. (1994). Examining the planning practices of teachers: Reflections on three years of research. *Education Technology, 34*(3), 11–16.

Reiser, R. A., & Mory, E. H. (1991). An examination of the planning practices of two experienced teachers. *Educational Technology Research and Development, 39*(3), 71–82.

Reiser, R. A., & Radford, J. (1990). Preparing pre-service teachers to use the systems approach. *Performance Improvement Quarterly, 3*(4), 40–52.

Richey, R. (1995). Trends in instructional design: Emerging theory-based models. *Performance Improvement Quarterly, 8*(3), 96–110.

Richey, R. C. (1993). Instructional design theory and a changing field. *Educational Technology, 33*(2), 16–20.

Rogoff, R. L. (1984). The training wheel: A simple model for instructional design. *The Magazine of Human Resources Development, 21*(4), 63–64.

Rosenberg, M. (1991, April). *Building bridges to business: Opportunities and challenges for academia.* Address at the annual meeting of the Association for Educational Communications and Technology, Orlando, FL.

Rossett, A. (1990). Performance technology and academic programs in instructional design and technology: Must we change? *Educational Technology, 30*(8), 48–51.

Rowland, G. (1992). What do instructional designers actually do? An initial investigation of expert practice. *Performance Improvement Quarterly, 5*(2), 65–86.

Rowland, G., Fixl, A., & Yung, K. (1992). Educating the reflective designer. *Educational Technology, 32*(12), 36–44.

Sample, J. (1989). Civil liability for failure to train to standard. *Educational Technology, 29*(6), 23–26.

Savenye, W., Davidson, G., & Smith, P. (1991). Teaching pre-service teachers instructional design in a computer literacy course. *Educational Technology, Research, and Development, 39*(3), 49–58.

Schank, R. (1984). *The cognitive computer: On language, learning, and artificial intelligence.* Reading, MA: Addison-Wesley.

Schumacher, E. F. (1973). *Small is beautiful: Economics as if people mattered.* London: Blond & Briggs.

Shrock, S. A. (1990). School reform and restructuring: does performance technology have a role? *Performance Improvement Quarterly, 3*(4), 53–73.

Smith, P. L., Ragan, T. J., McMichael, J., & Miles, K. (1993, February). *Fast track instructional design.* Paper presented to the annual convention of the Association for Communications and Educational Technology, New Orleans, LA.

Spector, J. M., & Ohrazda, C. (2004). Automating instructional design: Approaches and limitations. In D. M. Jonassen (Ed.), *Handbook of research on instructional communications and technology* (pp. 685–699). Mahwah, NJ: Erlbaum.

Spector, J. M., Polson, M. C., & Muraida, D. J. (Eds.). (1993). *Automating instructional design: Concepts and issues.* Englewood Cliffs, NJ: Educational Technology Publications.

Stolovitch, H. D., Keeps, E. J., & Rodrigue, D. (1995). Skill sets for the human performance technologist. *Performance Improvement Quarterly, 8*(2), 40–67.

Tessmer, M., & Wedman, J. F. (1990). A layers of necessity instructional development model. *Educational Technology Research and Development, 38*(2), 77–85.

Tessmer, M., & Wedman, J. (1995). Context-sensitive instructional design models: A response to design research, studies, and criticism. *Performance Improvement Quarterly, 8*(3), 37–53.

Tripp, S. D., & Bichelmeyer, B. (1990). Rapid prototyping: An alternative instructional design strategy. *Educational Technology Research and Development, 38*(1), 31–44.

Wager, W. W. (1993). Instructional system fundamentals: Pressures to change. *Educational Technology, 33*(2), 8–13.

Wedman, J. F., & Tessmer, M. (1990). The "layers of necessity" ID model. *Performance and Instruction, 29*(4), 1–7.

Wedman, J. F., & Tessmer, M. (1991). Adapting instructional design to project circumstance: The layers of necessity model. *Educational Technology, 31*(6), 48–52.

Wedman, J. F., & Tessmer, M. (1992, April). *Instructional designers' decisions and priorities: A layers of necessity study.* Paper presented at the annual conference of the National Society for Performance Improvement, Miami, FL.

Wedman, J., & Tessmer, M. (1993). Instructional designers' decisions and priorities: A survey of design practice. *Performance Improvement Quarterly, 6*(2), 43–57.

Wilson, B. G., Hamilton, R., Teslow, J. L., & Cyr, T. A. (1994). *Technology making a difference: The Peakview Elementary School study.* Syracuse, NY: ERIC Clearinghouse on Information and Technology.

Winer, L., & Vazquez-Abad, J. (1995). The present and future of ID practice. *Performance Improvement Quarterly, 8*(3), 55–67.

Winn, W. (1989). Toward a rational and theoretical basis for educational technology. *Educational Technology Research and Development, 37*(1), 35–46.

Wulfeck, W. H., Dickieson, J. L., Apple, J., & Vogt, J. L. (1993). The automation of curriculum development using the Authoring Instructional Materials (AIM) system. *Instructional Science, 21,* 255–267.

AUTHOR INDEX